LIFE 50

The First Fifty Years

1936-1986

LITTLE, BROWN AND COMPANY

BOSTON   TORONTO

Editor:
Philip B. Kunhardt Jr.

Managing Editor:
David Maness

Design and Production:
Gene Light

Chief Writer:
Frank K. Kappler

Associates:
**Edward Kern; Elsie B. Washington,
Gretchen Wessels, Margaret Williams**

Picture Coordinator:
Gedeon de Margitay

Copy Staff:
Eleanor Van Bellingham (Chief);
**Sharon Kapnick; Nikki Amdur,
Florence Tarlow; Frank L. Gander,
Larry Nesbitt, Frank Perich**

Production Assistant:
John Macellari

Valuable assistance was provided by (in alphabetical order): Susan L. Caughman, Peter J. Christopoulos, Debra A. Cohen, Judith Daniels, Mary N. Davis, Kathleen Doak, Roger Donald, John Downey, Elaine M. Felsher, Paula Glatzer, June O. Goldberg, Andrew Horne, Hanns Kohl, Benjamin Lightman, Laura Ludwig, Mary Jane McGonegal, Lori McGriff, Ann M. Morrell, Gail Ridgwell, Carmin Romanelli, Sarah Rozen, Marie A. Schumann, Maxine H. Shepard, Mary Y. Steinbauer, Richard B. Stolley, Thomas Stone, Cynthia A. Van Roden, Cornelis Verwaal, Christiana Walford, Beth B. Zarcone.

This book is dedicated to LIFE's founder
Henry Robinson Luce

Six publishers and nine managing editors have guided the magazine during its 50 years.

PUBLISHERS:
Roy E. Larsen (1936-45)
Andrew Heiskell (1946-60)
Charles D. Jackson (1960-64)
Jerome S. Hardy (1964-70)
Garry Valk (1970-1977)*
Charles A. Whittingham (1978-   )

MANAGING EDITORS:
John Shaw Billings (1936-44)
Daniel Longwell (1944-46)
Joseph J. Thorndike Jr. (1946-49)
Edward K. Thompson (1949-61)
George P. Hunt (1961-69)
Ralph Graves (1969-72)
Philip B. Kunhardt Jr. (1973-82) *
Richard B. Stolley (1982-85)
Judith Daniels (1985-   )

* 1973-1977: publication ceased except for 2 special issues a year.

FIRST EDITION
Library of Congress Cataloging-in-Publication Data
        LIFE, The First 50 Years 1936-1986
1. LIFE (Chicago, Ill.) 2. Photography, Journalistic. I. LIFE (Chicago, Ill.) II. Title: LIFE, The First 50 Years 1936-1986 TR 820.F49 1986 779'.09'04 86-2842
ISBN 0-316-52613-4

Published simultaneously in Canada by Little, Brown and Company (Canada) Limited

Acknowledgments to photographers and illustrators, including permission to reprint previously copyrighted material, appear on pages 312-319.

PRINTED IN THE UNITED STATES OF AMERICA

Contents

Introduction 4

The First Issue . . 6

The First Decade
Depression and War   15

1936 16

1937 18

1938 22

1939 26

1940 30

1941 34

1942 40

1943 44

1944 50

1945 54

Essay 60

The Second Decade	The Third Decade	The Fourth Decade	The Fifth Decade
Peace and Prosperity 76	*Hope and Despair* 134	*Violence and Change* 198	*Rebirth and Renewal* 252
1946 78	*1956* 136	*1966* 200	*1976* 254
1947 82	*1957* 140	*1967* 204	*1977* 256
1948 86	*1958* 144	*1968* 208	*1978* 258
1949 90	*1959* 150	*1969* 212	*1979* 262
1950 94	*1960* 154	*1970* 216	*1980* 266
1951 98	*1961* 158	*1971* 220	*1981* 270
1952 102	*1962* 162	*1972* 224	*1982* 274
1953 106	*1963* 166	*1973* 228	*1983* 278
1954 110	*1964* 172	*1974* 230	*1984* 282
1955 114	*1965* 176	*1975* 232	*1985* 286
Essay 118	*Essay* 182	*Essay* 234	*Essay* 290

Introduction

LIFE's first issue caused a sensation and gave birth to an American institution. It has remained one, after enduring a humbling period of transformation

There had never been anything like it before. In the first place it was big; you could spot it a block away by its bold black-and-white picture on the cover and the four large white letters that spelled its name leaping out of that bright rectangle of red—LIFE. Inside were the best pictures taken the world over. They showed people and places so strange and unlikely you could hardly believe they existed. They showed celebrities and famous sights, and they showed the commonplace as well: men and women at their daily routines, passing fancies and old diversions, the goodness of the earth and the magnificence of the planets. Using the camera with intelligence and sensitivity and courage, LIFE opened windows, held up mirrors, captured both the dangerous and the lovely, and stirred emotions.

This magazine had many moods. Outrageous it could be on one page, tender on the next. Or dignified and then suddenly irreverent or comic. It admired beautiful women, was fascinated by the rich and famous. It held in awe the soaring structures man built as well as the quiet strength of Main Street and the comfort of the corner store. It could lash out and bark at individuals, but its occasional gruffness came out of its devotion to human dignity. It stood for democracy, free enterprise and hard work. It hated war but reported on dozens of them—often so vividly that hands trembled as they turned the pages. Most of all it worshiped America and was harshly critical when it thought the nation was failing to live up to its great traditions.

For 36 years the weekly LIFE befriended America. During those years the cellars and attics of the U.S. filled up with ever-rising piles of well-fingered keepsake issues. Finally television caught up with it, passed it by. Now news came on glass screens in living rooms, and the pictures moved and talked. So, at the end of 1972, after 1,864 consecutive issues, the country kissed goodbye its weekly institution. But for the next five years two special issues a year, 10 in all, kept people from forgetting.

Then, in 1978, LIFE was back, this time as a monthly. Many of the magazine's most important original ingredients survived. In a different world, one grown satiated with fleeting images, it still had the power to move and excite with the frozen moment.

Its big pages, now mostly in color, still could spellbind. It still could convey that simple but uncanny sorcery that a camera in the right hands can conjure up. To the delight of old fans and a host of new ones, LIFE took wing again. Now, after seven years of growing, the magazine entered its fiftieth year.

On these pages you will find every cover LIFE published through 1985, as well as a reproduction in miniature of the entire first issue. Also in reduced size are many stories and pages as they originally appeared in the magazine. (Even the smallest type on these reductions can be read with magnification.) Crowded with images as this book may be, it does not attempt to be a definitive history of the magazine. It is, rather, a pictorial survey of LIFE's evolution, including points both high and low. Entire aspects of the magazine's fascinating journey are omitted. This book hardly touches at all, for instance, upon the individual photographers, the reporters, the writers or the editors who were, and are, responsible for the magazine's content and personality. It does not retell any of the thousands of wonderful stories—warm or chilling, hilarious or sad—behind LIFE's effervescent, often turbulent half century. It barely brushes on the truly remarkable production side: Who could believe that at one point it took seven million pounds of paper to put out a single issue, 200,000 pounds of ink to print it, 400 miles of wire to bind it and 360 railroad cars to ship it to every far corner!

Sometimes you may feel that this book is arbitrary in its choice of a picture or the reproduction of a page when dozens of other examples could and would have been chosen by editors with different tastes or inclinations. More than 5,000 images are reproduced here, each selected with a specific point in mind. Yet to LIFE-o-philes second-guessing will be the name of the game. Almost everyone will miss a favorite.

Nor has this book been shaped and made for insiders, for students of journalism or for photography buffs, no matter how intriguing it may be to these readers. It is for everyone with eyes, for all who understand how unparalleled the LIFE era was and still is, and who wish to witness its unfolding.

First top team: (from left) Managing Editor
John S. Billings, Editor-in-Chief Henry R.
Luce, Executive Editor Daniel Longwell.

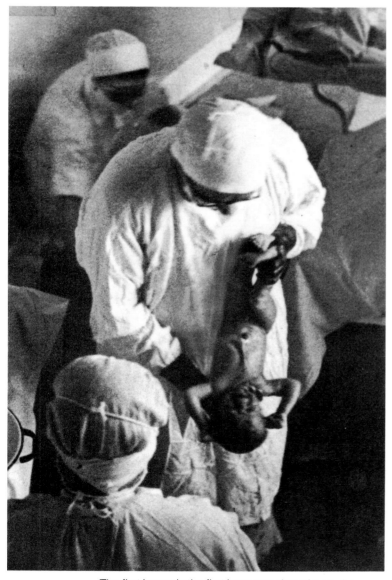

The first image in the first issue was that of a newborn
infant. Of course, the headline read: "Life Begins."

After the pages on which the magazine's entire first issue appears, this book is divided by 10-year periods into five parts, and the treatment of each LIFE decade consists of two sections. First comes a selective display of the magazine's content during each decade. It is followed by a section of large photographs that appeared during the same span, arranged now not by chronology but by a theme for each spread. Often these pictures are less well recalled than many others, but as a result they should be all the more fascinating.

Because they have been reproduced so often, some of the best-remembered LIFE photographs have not been included. A sampling, though, of the magazine's greatest images does appear, in much reduced size as each year is revealed, under the heading Classic Photos. In each case they are presented in combination with a casual list of happenings—both important and trivial—during that particular year. With these annual Currents and Events we have tried to re-create the environment in which LIFE's evolution as an enterprise and its journalistic contributions can be better understood.

In judging LIFE's first 50 years, it is helpful to keep in mind the words that Henry Luce used back in 1936 to describe the mission of this not-quite-born publication. They began:

To see life; to see the world; to eyewitness great events; to watch the faces of the poor and the gestures of the proud; to see strange things—machines, armies, multitudes, shadows in the jungle and on the moon; to see man's work—his paintings, towers and discoveries; to see things thousands of miles away, things hidden behind walls and within rooms, things dangerous to come to; the women that men love and many children; to see and to take pleasure in seeing; to see and be amazed; to see and be instructed....

It is a remarkable editorial vision, simply stated, great in scope yet steadfastly human and enduring. It speaks to the magic of seeing. How well LIFE has worked that magic over the years is ultimately for you to decide.

Philip B. Kunhardt Jr.
Editor

The First Issue

The ambition of the new publishing enterprise was to collect "the cream of all the world's pictures." In doing so, it delivered— if not to the tastes of all—something of interest to everyone

In February 1936, Henry R. Luce, the 36-year-old founder and editor of *Time* and *Fortune,* returned from a two-month honeymoon in Cuba with his new wife, Clare Boothe, and announced that he was going to start a picture magazine. For some time it was not widely known that the bride, herself a successful editor, had pushed the idea. Names for the experimental issues that followed included *Parade, Look, Scene* and *Show-Book of the World.* (*Dime* was rejected when Luce was persuaded that someday the price might have to go up.) In August Luce bought the title of a venerable but fading humor magazine, *Life,* for $92,000. No one particularly liked the trial versions, but Luce barged ahead. "We'll learn how to do this in actual production," he said.

Work on the first issue began in the fall. Circulation was guaranteed at 250,000, and ad rates were set accordingly: $1,500 for a full black-and-white page, $2,250 for color. On Thursday, November 19, the issue hit the newsstands, and all 466,000 copies sold out within four hours.

Today the issue that began it all is not only a collector's item and an entertaining curiosity, it is also worth a close look because—in its simplicity, its wide-eyed wonder, its likes and dislikes, its inspired way of choosing and combining pictures—it exposed the genes that would grow into the most successful publishing yearling in history. Reproduced on the following pages is that entire issue.

The pictures for the cover story on Fort Peck, Mont., did not arrive until a few days before the deadline. They were taken by the distinguished industrial photographer Margaret Bourke-White, who had closed down her studio to sign on as one of LIFE's original staff photographers. Her film recorded a new American frontier, where men lived and loved in shantytowns near the dam they were building. Archibald MacLeish, a *Fortune* writer destined to earn fame as poet and playwright, was drafted to write the captions. Luce personally fixed upon the cover choice. The lead story that resulted has been called the first picture essay.

The contents list *(page 7)* faced a full-page House of Heinz ad that closely mimicked the magazine's design. (The editors weakly signaled their concern by placing the word "Advertisement" at its top.) Twenty-three stories and departments were included. Three consisted of merely one photo: impregnable Fort Knox, which would soon hold half the world's gold *(page 50);* an aerial view of Fort Belvedere, Edward VIII's favorite palace *(page 53);* and a one-legged mountain climber *(page 69).* A Northwestern coed doing an easy cartwheel *(page 47)* needed two.

Luce's instincts told him to include something about everybody's favorite subject: the elements ("Overweather," *pages 22, 23*); an outstanding American woman (Helen Hayes, *pages 32-35*); a lively American business (NBC, *pages 36-39*); a foreign country (Brazil, *pages 40-44*); a dashing male star (Robert Taylor, *pages 60-63*), followed by a cultural postscript on the original *Camille* story; and nature (black widow spiders, *pages 84, 85*).

Hayes was a feature subject because she not only was a great actress but also encompassed many of the old-fashioned virtues that Luce deemed important in women. Taylor was an easy pick: His career was at a high, and his new film, with Garbo in the *Camille* title role, was about to be released. NBC had just turned 10 years old, and radio was every family's passion. The crude drawing for "Overweather" peered into the future and pointed out that at 35,000 feet no weather exists and that once planes were designed to fly at such "placid altitudes," winds blowing from west to east would "whip transport planes across the continent in eight or 10 hours." "Black Widow" showed a wicked female spider succumbing to the amorous advances of a male before she ate him. "Brazil," the issue's "duty story" (the editors knew that anything on South America, though undoubtedly educational, usually put U.S. readers to sleep), was littered with gratuitous slurs: "Brazilians are charming people but are incurably lazy"; and Brazil was a country where "a drop of white blood makes a man 'white.'"

In all, the issue mirrored many of Luce's personal prejudices and passions, including an unwavering pride in the U.S. The introduction *(page 3)* pointed out that the first lady of the theater was American, the No. 1 screen lover was an American, and the subject of Art was "represented not by some artfully promoted Frenchman but by an American"—John Steuart Curry *(pages 28-31).*

Luce's second-favorite country, China, the place of his birth to missionary parents and of his childhood, was attended to twice: by a Chinese cemetery in San Francisco *(page 21)* and by a school where "slant-eyed and shy" students "learn to say *very* instead of *velly*" *(page 24).* His dislike for anything tinged by Communism may have been at the root of the sly poke at Russians having fun and getting clean by personal order of Stalin *(page 76).* The thin item showing Pan Am pilots at Midway Island hitting golf balls among the gooney birds *(pages 86-88)* would have been justified on the basis of its sheer wackiness.

All else aside, for Luce and the staff the four departments collecting "the cream of all the world's pictures" were among the most important sections of the magazine: American Newsfront *(pages 18-21),* President's Album *(pages 26, 27),* The Camera Overseas *(pages 54-59)* and Private Lives *(pages 78-82).* Their broad scope as well as the opportunities they provided to indulge in marketable spice and gossip had obvious appeal.

The issue closed with a feature that was immediately famous and would be long lived: LIFE Goes to a Party. (Many readers would make it a habit to read the magazine back to front in order to visit each new Party right off.) This first shindig *(pages 90-94)* involved a hunt by French blue bloods, who bagged 900 birds and 250 hares during one day's merriment.

That was all of it, and it added up to a spectacular start. Nonetheless, as Luce and his editors had cautiously pointed out in the introduction, "The first issue of a magazine is not the magazine. It is the beginning." And so it was.

6

LIFE

NOVEMBER 23, 1936 10 CENTS

REG. U.S. PAT. OFF.

From the opener, LIFE had its act together

The beginning: These 96 pages plus covers, from monumental Fort Peck Dam to the party in France LIFE decided to go to, were a clear portent of the future magazine. Over the years successive editors added features and their own aesthetics, but the basic elements of the first issue remained at the core of what the staff affectionately referred to as "Big Red."

LIFE

NOVEMBER 23, 1936 10 CENTS

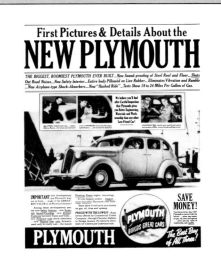

KNOCK··KNOCK! WHO'S THERE?

First Pictures & Details About the
NEW PLYMOUTH

PLYMOUTH

AMATEUR HOUR

LIFE

THIS GIFT SAVES YOUR WIFE
200 HOURS
OF HARD WORK A YEAR

Announcing

THE NEW
FORD V-8 CARS
FOR 1937

LIFE

10,000 MONTANA RELIEF WORKERS MAKE WHOOPEE ON SATURDAY NIGHT

THE TIN CITY RODEOS . . .

. . . RUN ALL NIGHT

NELSON
LAUNDRY

MONTANA SATURDAY NIGHTS: FINIS

"OVERWEATHER"

THE NEW
"OVERWEATHER"
PLANE WILL
TRAVEL UP TO
THE 30,000
FOOT LEVEL

Chinese School

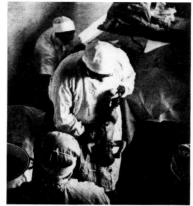

THIS IS WHEELER, MONTANA

ONE OF THE SIX FRONTIER TOWNS AROUND FORT PECK IN MR. ROOSEVELT'S NEW WILD WEST

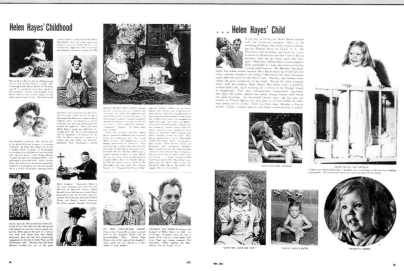

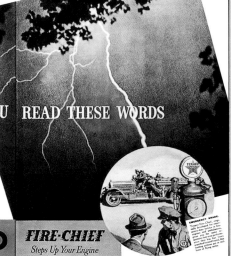

...and don't forget *Chessie*

America's Sleepheart

Wholly distilled to keep your engine clean

ONE-LEGGED MAN ON A MOUNTAIN

Fly the "MAIN LINE"

UNITED'S MID-CONTINENT AIRWAY

UNITED AIR LINES

OLDSMOBILE ANNOUNCES—

A NEW SIX . . . A NEW EIGHT

Each with a Style Distinctly its Own!

TWO BIG NEW CARS . . . TWO FRESH NEW STYLES . . . TWO GREAT NEW VALUES.

WILSON & CO.

RUSSIA RELAXES

Tender Made Ham

The Wilson label protects your table

PRIVATE LIVES (CONTINUED)

THE "JONES SEASON" IS HERE!

JONES DAIRY FARM SAUSAGE

Jones Dairy Farm, Mary P. Jones, President, Ft. Atkinson, Wisconsin

BLACK WIDOW

I. THE WIDOW AND HER MATE

II. THE WIDOW AND HER ENEMY

II. THE WIDOW AND HER CHILDREN

BUT...

Life Goes To a Party

WITH FRENCH ARISTOCRATS AND SIR GEORGE CLERK

A COACHMAN DRIVES YOU OUT

...TO THE BEATERS IN THE FIELD

AND ALL THE GUESTS HAVE FAMOUS NAMES

Enjoy Your Thanksgivings 1940-1950

Seagram's Crown
BLENDED WHISKIES
A MOST WHOLESOME FORM OF WHISKEY

When *Doctors* **"Feel Rotten"**
—This Is What *They* Do!

Life's Party (CONTINUED)

SEND NO MONEY

Price $1.98

The "Old" is Out

So—the "old" is out
The "New" is Here

ZENITH
LONG DISTANCE RADIO

America's Most Copied Radio—Always a Year Ahead

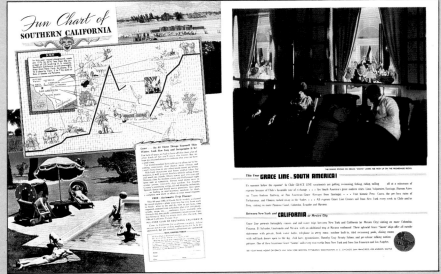

*The newsstand newcomer, whose outsize proportions were
for a time unique, easily stood out from the crowded displays.*

1936-1945
Depression and War

The unanticipated immediate success of the magazine threatened to break the back of 13-year-old Time Inc., its publisher. The low advertising rates, locked in by prepublication commitments, had been based on an estimate that turned out to be a fraction of actual circulation. At the same time, expenditures were staggering. Each copy, with a cover price of 10 cents, cost more than twice that to produce. As a result, the company was losing millions—about $50,000 every week.

Nonetheless, to meet the demand, it was decided to boost print orders to the extent that available presses could accommodate them. Projections indicated that circulation could eventually reach five to six million. The first goal was a run of one million while setting about to renegotiate the long-term advertising contracts.

Not only was there a period of dangerous living financially, but the brash new giant was staggering about editorially too—redefining and refining itself again and again, improving its look, expanding its scope. Along the way it occasionally faltered. There were conspicuous indiscretions. The editors veered into vulgarity by publishing a striptease under the guise of showing how a wife should undress in front of her husband. They ran a cover story about watermelons, which included the stereotypical statement that "nothing makes a Negro's mouth water like a luscious, fresh-picked melon." They dished up tabloid-quality pictures in cookie-cutter shapes and sizes.

The growing pains began to ease, however, as the ink on the bottom line changed from red to black. The instinctive urge toward respectability led to a quieting down, to more thought about subjects and the way they were treated. The esteemed critic Bernard DeVoto summed up the impressive metamorphosis early: "LIFE, whose original formula called for equal parts of the decapitated Chinaman, the flogged Negro, the surgically explored peritoneum, and the rapidly slipping chemise, has decided to appeal to more normal and more intelligent minds. It now spends much more energy on the news and on a kind of visual journalistic investigation, which becomes increasingly interesting as it becomes more expert."

Along with the reconfirmation that news coverage should be a major editorial resource came the discovery that the camera was capable of distilling beauty from the commonplace. The photograph, Luce said, can "dramatize . . . the normal and calm as distinct from that which is disruptive or fantastic. . . . The photograph [is] an extraordinary instrument for correcting that really inherent evil in journalism, which is its unbalance between the good news and the bad."

But in the mid-'30s and at the turn of the '40s the world knew little that was normal and calm. The earliest memorable images LIFE's cameras recorded were of both man and nature at their most disruptive: violence on picket lines, the sullen scenario of the sit-down strike, the ravages of dust storms on the land and on the faces of dispossessed farmers—the bitter harvest of the Great Depression. And when war began to destroy whole countries and peoples, the disruptive became the unimaginable. This growing horror hastened LIFE's maturation. "Though we did not plan LIFE as a war magazine," Luce once commented, "it turned out that way." It was not only *a* war magazine; it was *the* war magazine.

During the charged and ominous years of the first half of the '40s, the magazine threw enormous effort into coverage of the fighting. Its photographers, artists and correspondents were in the thick of battles everywhere, bringing to Americans at home and troops in the field the war's key events. LIFE's pages vividly reported the Allies' progress as they broke the Axis in Africa and Europe, and slogged their way, island by island, to victory in the Pacific.

When the atomic explosions at Hiroshima and Nagasaki finally brought the fighting to a close, LIFE had become an important, responsible magazine—and would remain so. Even as the country had achieved great new status in the world as a consequence of war, LIFE too had arrived at greatness.

1936

By year's end the editors had largely fixed on the shape and tone of their precocious weekly

Armed with the new wonder from Europe, the fast 35mm camera with its revolutionary capacity to deliver candid pictures, the magazine eagerly set about delivering to the world an unprecedented reflection of itself. In doing so, and to stay close to the news, it also was taking advantage of new fast-drying inks and coated paper capable of running on high-speed rotary presses. Furthermore, the four original staff photographers (Margaret Bourke-White, Peter Stackpole, Thomas McAvoy and Alfred Eisenstaedt) were joined, even as the first issue was on the presses, by Carl Mydans. Thereafter the roster of photographers on staff and working on assignment lengthened so swiftly that the editors were dependent less and less on the resources of the news photo agencies, and Publisher Roy E. Larsen would report to Luce, well before the magazine's first anniversary, that LIFE's pages were dominated by pictures of its own origin.

Hollywood newcomer Merle Oberon had what both LIFE and its readers adored: a fascinating face, a divine figure. As Merle's star rose over the years, she was a recurring subject.

A story on jitterbugging met three cravings that became editorial constants: to keep up with the latest fads, to capture fast action and to pay tribute to lasting loves—in this case, the art of dance.

From the first, damsels in bathing suits were to the editors of the new magazine what a controlled substance is to an addict. The occasion for this studied array was a bow to the virtuosity of a now legendary P.R. man, Steve Hannagan, who publicized the potent sun over Miami Beach.

Squeamishness was not a bar to a riveting photo. In a report on China, the caption confessed: "This is an old picture."

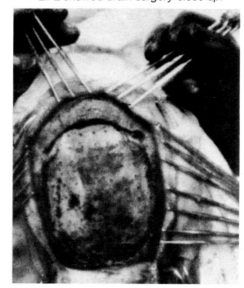

Japanese pearl divers provided lovely lagniappe: bathing beauties legitimately stripped for action.

In its second issue, science-struck LIFE showed brain surgery close up.

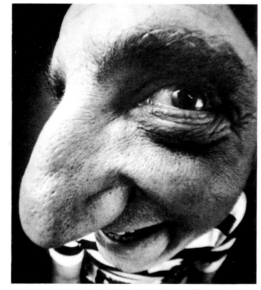

Enchanted by sports heroes, the editors decided Detroit's Dutch Clark had football's "perfect face."

Zeroing in on Jimmy Durante's nose with the then new fish-eye lens resulted in this stopper.

Royalty-watching began early. This frame from a banned-in-Britain newsreel caught Edward VIII, preabdication, lazing on the Mediterranean with divorcée Wallis Simpson.

NOVEMBER 23, 1936

NOVEMBER 30, 1936

DECEMBER 7, 1936

DECEMBER 14, 1936

DECEMBER 21, 1936

DECEMBER 28, 1936

1937

Focus quickly moved to big news events, famous people. But layouts at times were a hodgepodge

Rapidly developing its own personality, the magazine concentrated its growing resources on how America was living. In doing so, it treated pictures with reverence: Prints were rarely retouched (when they were, the caption said so), and the aesthetics of cropping them could cause a crisis. Example: On April 26—for the first, and last, time—a cover appeared without the big red logo, lest it impinge on the rooster's comb. And, still pushing printing technology to meet the demands of a mass-circulation weekly, on December 27 it published its first cover in full color.

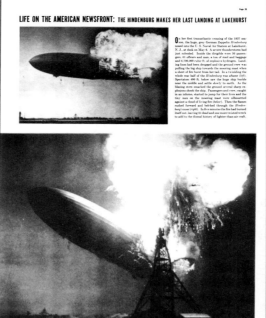

LIFE ON THE AMERICAN NEWSFRONT: THE HINDENBURG MAKES HER LAST LANDING AT LAKEHURST

Photos of the Hindenburg's growing fireball opened the coverage. They were followed . . .

When FDR named Joe Kennedy envoy to Britain, LIFE introduced his family: Patricia, John, Jean, Eunice, Bobby, Kathleen, Ted, Rosemary, Joe Jr., with Rose.

At the start of FDR's second term, a report on his administration included these rather cartoony pages on the NRA and its boss, Hugh Johnson.

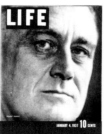 JANUARY 4, 1937

 JANUARY 11, 1937

 JANUARY 18, 1937

 MARCH 22, 1937

 MARCH 29, 1937

 APRIL 5, 1937

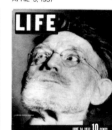 JUNE 7, 1937

JUNE 14, 1937

 AUGUST 16, 1937

 AUGUST 23, 1937

 OCTOBER 25, 1937

NOVEMBER 1, 1937

Japanese pearl divers provided lovely lagniappe: bathing beauties legitimately stripped for action.

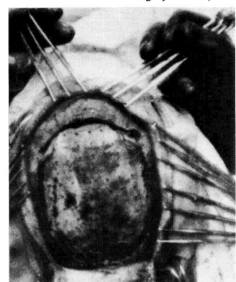

In its second issue, science-struck LIFE showed brain surgery close up.

Nosing out the gossip, the camera caught Edward, Prince of Wales, with Wallis at a nightclub.

Enchanted by sports heroes, the editors decided Detroit's Dutch Clark had football's "perfect face."

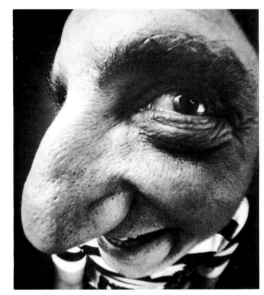

Zeroing in on Jimmy Durante's nose with the then new fish-eye lens resulted in this stopper.

CURRENTS AND EVENTS

WORLD: Spanish Civil War Erupts • Germany Occupies Rhineland • Italy at War with Ethiopia • Britain's Edward VIII Abdicates • British Troops Fight Arab, Jewish Terrorists • Stalin Purges Foes • Berlin-Rome Axis Established • Nazis Press Czechs for Sudetenland • Juntas Take Over in Latin America • Management-Labor Strife Pandemic • Japan Pounds China • 25 Nations Agree to Smash Drug Traffic.

U.S.A.: FDR Wins in Landslide • Social Security Takes Effect • Bruno Hauptmann Executed • Schmeling Kayos Louis • Jesse Owens Wins Four Olympic Golds • National Debt: $34 Billion.

FIRSTS: Use of Polaroid Glass • Bottle Screw Caps • Hydroponicum (soilless plant culture) • Artificial Heart • High-Definition TV • Racially Mixed Band (Goodman).

MOVIES: Modern Times • Mr. Deeds Goes to Town • The Story of Louis Pasteur • A Midsummer Night's Dream • The Great Ziegfeld • Dodsworth • A Tale of Two Cities • The Green Pastures • Anthony Adverse • Rhythm on the Range • Follow the Fleet.

SONGS: The Way You Look Tonight • Let's Face the Music and Dance • I've Got You Under My Skin • It's D'lovely • Is It True What They Say About Dixie? • There's a Small Hotel • Until the Real Thing Comes Along • You're the Top • Stompin' at the Savoy • The Touch of Your Lips.

STAGE: Idiot's Delight • Stage Door • Tovarich • You Can't Take It with You • Brother Rat • The Women • Macbeth (Orson Welles's Negro People's Theatre) • Bury the Dead • Red, Hot and Blue • On Your Toes.

BOOKS: Gone With the Wind (Mitchell) • Not So Deep As a Well (Parker) • The People, Yes (Sandburg) • Drums Along the Mohawk (Edmonds) • In Dubious Battle (Steinbeck) • How to Win Friends and Influence People (Carnegie) • Inside Europe (Gunther) • It Can't Happen Here (Lewis) • The Crack-Up (Fitzgerald) • Eyeless in Gaza (Huxley).

FADS: Jitterbugging • Candid Photography • Auto Trailers.

Royalty-watching began early. This frame from a banned-in-Britain newsreel caught Edward VIII, preabdication, lazing on the Mediterranean with divorcée Wallis Simpson.

NOVEMBER 23, 1936

NOVEMBER 30, 1936

DECEMBER 7, 1936

DECEMBER 14, 1936

DECEMBER 21, 1936

DECEMBER 28, 1936

1937

Focus quickly moved to big news events, famous people. But layouts at times were a hodgepodge

Rapidly developing its own personality, the magazine concentrated its growing resources on how America was living. In doing so, it treated pictures with reverence: Prints were rarely retouched (when they were, the caption said so), and the aesthetics of cropping them could cause a crisis. Example: On April 26—for the first, and last, time—a cover appeared without the big red logo, lest it impinge on the rooster's comb. And, still pushing printing technology to meet the demands of a mass-circulation weekly, on December 27 it published its first cover in full color.

LIFE ON THE AMERICAN NEWSFRONT: THE HINDENBURG MAKES HER LAST LANDING AT LAKEHURST

Photos of the Hindenburg's growing fireball opened the coverage. They were followed . . .

When FDR named Joe Kennedy envoy to Britain, LIFE introduced his family: Patricia, John, Jean, Eunice, Bobby, Kathleen, Ted, Rosemary, Joe Jr., with Rose.

At the start of FDR's second term, a report on his administration included these rather cartoony pages on the NRA and its boss, Hugh Johnson.

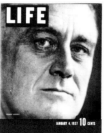 JANUARY 4, 1937

 JANUARY 11, 1937

 JANUARY 18, 1937

 MARCH 22, 1937

 MARCH 29, 1937

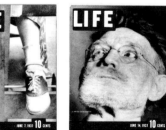 APRIL 5, 1937

 JUNE 7, 1937

 JUNE 14, 1937

 AUGUST 16, 1937

AUGUST 23, 1937

 OCTOBER 25, 1937

 NOVEMBER 1, 1937

. . . by a sequence from ignition to ashes and a page of ground crew and survivors fleeing. Then . . .

. . . juxtaposition: a sea shadow, a final scar.

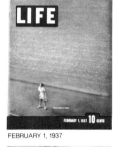
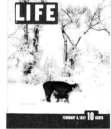

JANUARY 25, 1937

FEBRUARY 1, 1937

FEBRUARY 8, 1937

FEBRUARY 15, 1937

FEBRUARY 22, 1937

MARCH 1, 1937

MARCH 8, 1937

MARCH 15, 1937

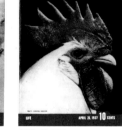

APRIL 12, 1937

APRIL 19, 1937

APRIL 26, 1937

MAY 3, 1937

MAY 10, 1937

MAY 17, 1937

MAY 24, 1937

MAY 31, 1937

JUNE 21, 1937

JUNE 28, 1937

JULY 5, 1937

JULY 12, 1937

JULY 19, 1937

JULY 26, 1937

AUGUST 2, 1937

AUGUST 9, 1937

AUGUST 30, 1937

SEPTEMBER 6, 1937

SEPTEMBER 13, 1937

SEPTEMBER 20, 1937

SEPTEMBER 27, 1937

OCTOBER 4, 1937

OCTOBER 11, 1937

OCTOBER 18, 1937

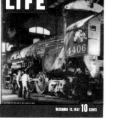

NOVEMBER 8, 1937

NOVEMBER 15, 1937

NOVEMBER 22, 1937

NOVEMBER 29, 1937

DECEMBER 6, 1937

DECEMBER 13, 1937

DECEMBER 20, 1937

DECEMBER 27, 1937

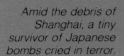

Amid the debris of Shanghai, a tiny survivor of Japanese bombs cried in terror.

A Mississippi mob first tortured, then lynched a young black accused of killing a white man.

The death of a Loyalist soldier, recorded just as an insurgent's bullet hit him, brought home the bloodiness of the civil war in Spain.

CURRENTS AND EVENTS

WORLD: Hitler Repudiates Versailles Treaty • Italy Conquers Ethiopia • Spanish Rightists Surge Forward • Stalin's Purges Escalate • Nazi, Fascist Attacks on Europe's Jews Intensify • Chamberlain Succeeds Baldwin as Britain's P.M. • Japan Expands Hold on China • Britain Ponders Creation of Jewish State • FDR Asks Quarantine of Aggressor Nations • All-India Congress Party Calls for Independence • Nazi Planes Level Guernica • Britain's George VI Ascends Throne • Duke of Windsor Marries Wally Simpson.

U.S.A.: Management-Labor Violence Mounts • FDR Presses for Supreme Court Reorganization • Thousands of Farms Foreclosed • Zeppelin Hindenburg Explodes • Aviatrix Amelia Earhart Disappears • Louis Takes Title from Braddock.

FIRSTS: Supermarket Shopping Carts • Blood Bank • Nylon • Contraceptive Clinic • Automatic Transmissions in Cars.

MOVIES: Snow White and the Seven Dwarfs • The Awful Truth • Dead End • The Good Earth • The Life of Emile Zola • Lost Horizon • Stage Door • A Star Is Born • Winterset • A Day at the Races • On the Avenue.

SONGS: Bei Mir Bist Du Schön • The Lady Is a Tramp • Whistle While You Work • A Foggy Day in London Town • The Dipsy Doodle • I've Got My Love to Keep Me Warm • One O'Clock Jump • Let's Call the Whole Thing Off • In the Still of the Night • The Merry-Go-Round Broke Down • So Rare • That Old Feeling • Thanks for the Memory.

STAGE: High Tor • I'd Rather Be Right • Golden Boy • Room Service • Of Mice and Men • Babes in Arms • Pins and Needles.

BOOKS: U.S.A. (Dos Passos) • The Late George Apley (Marquand) • Of Mice and Men (Steinbeck) • To Have and Have Not (Hemingway) • The Citadel (Cronin) • Northwest Passage (Roberts) • The Hobbit (Tolkien) • Man's Hope (Malraux) • The Devil and Daniel Webster (Bénet).

FADS: Knock-Knock Jokes • Jive Talk • The Lambeth Walk.

This Remington-like scene of a postblizzard Hereford roundup was part of a cover story on winter in Wyoming.

In Palm Springs, Douglas Fairbanks Sr. dived playfully over the head of his inattentive new bride, Lady Ashley.

Coeds and their weekend dates lined a staircase during a supper dance at Smith College.

In a story about Georgia's chain gangs, the caption to this photo archly relayed the claim that officials permitted "this painful discipline for only an hour at a time."

Barbara Flemming, 2½, of Allentown, Pa., deservedly won in a contest for Best Baby Picture of the Year.

Evangelist Aimee Semple McPherson assumed her familiar "angel" pose in Los Angeles on a fund-raiser to fight a slander suit.

Ernest Hemingway, "novelist and amateur of war," wrote captions for four pages of frames excerpted from The Spanish Earth, a documentary film on the fighting in Spain. Hemingway had also written the voice-over for the sound track.

Running for reelection as New York City's mayor, Fiorello LaGuardia importuned the electorate.

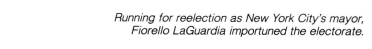

Following the coronation, George VI accepted acclaim with the Queen and Princesses Elizabeth and Margaret.

Visiting Vassar, LIFE snapped a coed engrossed in her hometown newspaper.

1938

As the world teetered at the abyss of war, the magazine created a furor with a celebrated story

Early in its second year, shortly after an ad trumpeted "80,000 subscribers, 1,000,000 newsstand buyers and 14,400,000 other readers," LIFE had lost $5 million. FDR, Luce told colleagues, had inquired wryly if it was true he was making such a success that he was going bust. "I said, 'Well, Mr. President, I've got *my* next year's budget balanced.' " Then, even as rumors flew that the magazine would cease publication, the editors risked a highly controversial feature. New York State censors had banned as obscene a semidocumentary movie about the birth of a baby, though it had been widely praised by medical and social groups. LIFE decided to adapt the material but to warn subscribers a week in advance that it would appear. The five-page article included 33 frames from the movie plus supplementary drawings. Initially the issue was barred in 33 cities, but the magazine fought the censorship, and most bans were lifted amid vast, and valuable, publicity. A Gallup poll, taken soon afterward, showed that 61 percent of all readers believed the landmark story had been pursued in a good cause.

Subscribers had been warned by mail that a controversial story about the educational film would run.

The film had three elements: the "education" of an

JANUARY 3, 1938

JANUARY 10, 1938

JANUARY 17, 1938

JANUARY 24, 1938

JANUARY 31, 1938

FEBRUARY 7, 1938

FEBRUARY 14, 1938

FEBRUARY 21, 1938

APRIL 4, 1938

APRIL 11, 1938

APRIL 18, 1938

APRIL 25, 1938

MAY 2, 1938

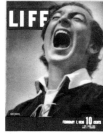

MAY 9, 1938

MAY 16, 1938

MAY 23, 1938

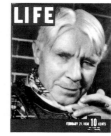

Gloria Vanderbilt, 14, danced at a "Juniors" ball. LIFE was born too late to cover the bitter 1935 battle for custody between her mother and aunt but quickly picked up on the continuing drama of her life.

In a Picture of the Week that surfaced in Paris, an Italian fighting for Franco chuted to safety as his plane burned. "Both pilot and fuselage have been retouched," the editors dutifully warned readers.

A shabbily dressed Hitler, hat in hand, met a resplendent Il Duce.

They starred together for the first time in Love Finds Andy Hardy.

FDR reviewed the fleet from the bridge of the USS Houston.

CURRENTS AND EVENTS

WORLD: Germany Annexes Austria, Sudetenland • Munich Pact Reached, Britain's Chamberlain Announces "Peace for Our Time" • Persecutions of Jews Mount • Stalin's Show Trials, Purges Continue • Spanish Civil War Grows Bloodier • Japan Advances in China • Palestinian Arabs, Jews Clash • "Wrong Way" Corrigan Flies Atlantic.

U.S.A.: Economic Depression Persists • CIO Asks Government to End Goon Tactics vs. Strikers • House Un-American Activities Committee Activated • Louis Kayos Schmeling • Orson Welles's Broadcast "War of the Worlds" Traumatizes Nation.

FIRSTS: Nuclear Fission (Germany) • Synthetic Chlorophyll • Xerography • Ballpoint Pen • Two Successive No-hit Games (Vander Meer) • Tennis Grand Slam (Budge).

MOVIES: The Adventures of Robin Hood • Marie Antoinette • Alexander's Ragtime Band • Test Pilot • Bringing Up Baby • Little Miss Broadway • Love Finds Andy Hardy • Boys Town • The Citadel • The Lady Vanishes • Pygmalion • Jezebel.

SONGS: A-Tisket A-Tasket • This Can't Be Love • Flat Foot Floogie • Get Out of Town • My Heart Belongs to Daddy • I'll Be Seeing You • Jeepers Creepers • My Reverie • September Song • Ti-Pi-Tin • Two Sleepy People • You Go to My Head • Boo Hoo • This Can't Be Love • Tutti Frutti • Small Fry • Love Is Here to Stay • Hooray for Hollywood.

STAGE: Our Town • On Borrowed Time • Abe Lincoln in Illinois • Shadow and Substance • Here Come the Clowns • The Boys from Syracuse • Knickerbocker Holiday • Leave It to Me • The Swing Mikado • I Married an Angel • Hellzapoppin'.

BOOKS: It's Later than You Think (Lerner) • Homage to Catalonia (Orwell) • Brighton Rock (Greene) • Rebecca (Du Maurier) • All This, and Heaven Too (Field) • The Unvanquished (Faulkner) • Uncle Tom's Children (Wright) • Alone (Byrd) • The Prodigal Parents (Lewis) • Listen! the Wind (A. Lindbergh) • The Rains Came (Bromfield) • The Robe (Douglas) • My Son, My Son! (Spring).

FADS: Bingo • Chain Letters • Truckin' (dance) • Slumber Parties • Drive-ins • Bobby Sox and Saddle Shoes • Zoot Suits.

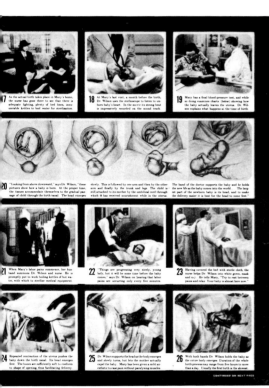

ctress, diagrams and an actual birth.

A box on actress Eleanor King ended the story.

FEBRUARY 28, 1938

MARCH 7, 1938

MARCH 14, 1938

MARCH 21, 1938

MARCH 28, 1938

MAY 30, 1938

JUNE 6, 1938

JUNE 13, 1938

JUNE 20, 1938

JUNE 27, 1938

JULY 4, 1938

JULY 11, 1938

JULY 18, 1938

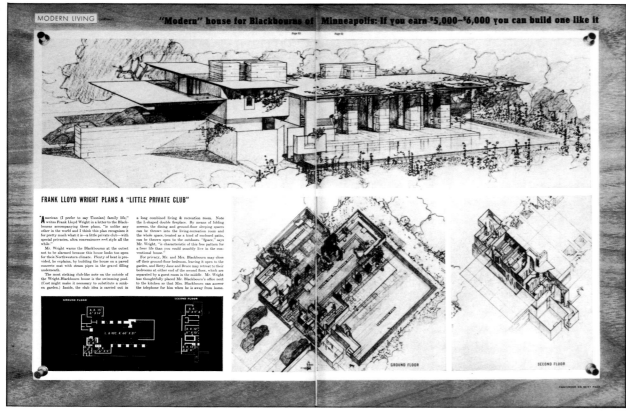

"Modern" house for Blackbourns of Minneapolis: If you earn $5,000–$6,000 you can build one like it

FRANK LLOYD WRIGHT PLANS A "LITTLE PRIVATE CLUB"

GROUND FLOOR   SECOND FLOOR

JULY 25, 1938

AUGUST 1, 1938

AUGUST 15, 1938

AUGUST 22, 1938

This Frank Lloyd Wright house was part of an architectural coup: LIFE had eight architects design real homes for families earning $2,000 to $10,000 a year.

AUGUST 29, 1938

SEPTEMBER 5, 1938

When Anschluss melded Austria into the Reich, the editors ran this 1916 picture of Hitler (right) with Bavarian comrades, saying that 22 years later, because of Germany's resurgence under the Nazis, he had "won the [first] World War single-handed."

SEPTEMBER 12, 1938

SEPTEMBER 19, 1938

SEPTEMBER 26, 1938

OCTOBER 3, 1938

OCTOBER 10, 1938

OCTOBER 17, 1938

The polished curves of José de Rivera's bronze Bust reflected a good part of the Sculptors' Guild exhibition at the Brooklyn Museum. The editors pointed out that while the piece had "a richness and dignity that only a great master could equal in marble," it, along with most modern works, would probably over time prove to be "valueless and silly."

As Hedy Lamarr made her U.S. bow, fully clothed, in the movie Algiers, the editors recalled her sensational film of five years earlier, the Czech-made Ecstasy, in which, at 18, she was praised by critics and cut by censors for nude swimming and orgasmic love scenes.

OCTOBER 24, 1938

OCTOBER 31, 1938

NOVEMBER 28, 1938

DECEMBER 5, 1938

Herded by storm troopers the caption called "uniformed plug-uglies," Jews scrubbed anti–Nazi party emblems off walls and sidewalks in Chemnitz, Saxony. The scene, the editors pointed out, "was re-enacted in Vienna a few days after the Nazis took over Austria."

At New York Auto Show time, head-on portraits of 22 of the new 1939 models made a sexy spread.

NOVEMBER 21, 1938

DECEMBER 12, 1938

DECEMBER 19, 1938

DECEMBER 26, 1938

ON PARADE

AMERICA'S FAVORITE INDUSTRY

Every U.S. business from pea-growing to steel-making and from chiropractic to corset-making holds an annual convention or exposition. The many millions conventioneers who attend their 10,000 meetings are average Americans and their doings and thinkings make the U. S. what it is. But, because their automobile purpose it to sell themselves and their goods to the public, newspaper editors feel they must bury convention news at the bottom of back pages.

The shows which know they will make front-page news are the fancy affairs sponsored annually in major U. S. cities by the automobile industry to introduce new models. They make the front page because this industry is not only America's largest and most typical, it is also the American people's favorite industry. It has emancipated man by putting 85 h.p. in his hands, giving him a feeling of limitless power. And the automobile, though a servant to many, still reigns unconfested as America's No. 1 form of recreation. When the Automobile Show makes its bow in New York on Nov. 11, and similar shows open throughout the nation, millions will flock to see the glitter of enamel on the twenty-two 1939 cars which you see here. Like the couple at left, they will gingerly settle in the back seat of some sedan while the salesman reels off his tempting, polished sales talk.

The 1939 cars present no revolutionary mechanical improvements. But because Americans spend a large part of their lives in autos and are more conscious of the dangers of driving, the new cars are roomier, more comfortable and safer. Gear-shift levers on steering columns, pop-up cigaret lighters, spotlights to indicate ignition-switch keyhole, safety-signal speedometers flashing red at 50 m.p.h., and other gadgets make new cars more livable. To suit Mr. Jones who wants a better looking car than Mr. Smith's, the 1939 auto has new lines which accentuate the big, bold front and tapering body.

These facts coupled with business recovery, dealer enthusiasm and low used-car stocks make auto manufacturers unreservedly optimistic. Hundreds of thousands of new models have already been ordered. And Detroit, after a year in the doldrums, has hired more than 100,000 men, is forcing production schedules closer and closer to 1937 levels, still is unable to fill all its orders.

CONTINUED ON NEXT PAGE

1939

Emphasis was on domestic news as the U.S. leaned to "America First"

The final year of the '30s was pivotal for the magazine, whose goal it was to be the great chronicler of the American scene. It looked out across the U.S. and saw a nation gradually emerging from the Depression—its recuperating economy fueled largely by orders from Britain and France for war matériel—and loath to get mixed up in what many believed should be "Europe's war." Nazi Germany had refused to participate in the New York World's Fair, but Mussolini's Italy was there, with a 200-foot waterfall at its pavilion. LIFE's coverage of the exposition entailed intricate logistical planning, an experience that was to serve the editors well in future years. Then, in September, came the blitzkrieg. Cities lay in ashes, fleets of bombers darkened skies, convoys braved subs and stormy seas. War, sadly, translates into great pictures, and so LIFE joined battle.

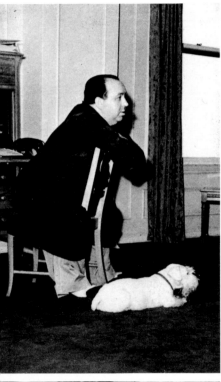

Alfred Hitchcock, "who somewhat resembles his Sealyham, Mr. Jenkins," checked into the Beverly-Wilshire Hotel prior to making his first American movie, Rebecca.

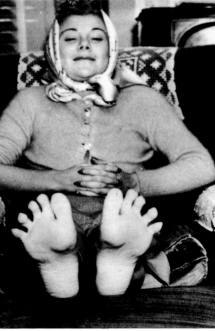

Olympian-turned-pro Sonja Henie, in Boston with her ice carnival, showed how she exercised her "million-dollar-feet."

This aerial view of the New York World's Fair centered on the two theme structures: the Trylon and the Perisphere. The color photo, part of a cover story that previewed the exhibition, was duplicated in black and white on the facing page, with 31 exhibitors' buildings labeled and their prime displays briefly described. Among them were RCA's closed-circuit TV, GE's man-made lightning and General Motors' "Futurama" projecting a highway-laced U.S.A. in 1960—already presaged in the parkway cloverleaf just outside the GM theater.

JANUARY 2, 1939

JANUARY 9, 1939

JANUARY 16, 1939

JANUARY 23, 1939

JANUARY 30, 1939

FEBRUARY 6, 1939

FEBRUARY 13, 1939

FEBRUARY 20, 1939

FEBRUARY 27, 1939

MARCH 6, 1939

MARCH 13, 1939

MARCH 20, 1939

MARCH 27, 1939

APRIL 3, 1939

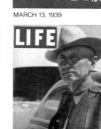
APRIL 10, 1939

APRIL 17, 1939

APRIL 24, 1939

MAY 1, 1939

MAY 8, 1939

MAY 15, 1939

MAY 22, 1939

MAY 29, 1939

JUNE 5, 1939

JUNE 12, 1939

JUNE 19, 1939

JUNE 26, 1939

JULY 3, 1939

JULY 10, 1939

JULY 17, 1939

JULY 24, 1939

JULY 31, 1939

AUGUST 7, 1939

AUGUST 14, 1939

AUGUST 21, 1939

AUGUST 28, 1939

CLASSIC PHOTOS

A misogynist monkey fleeing jungle females opted for the sea.

Contralto Marian Anderson, barred from Constitution Hall, sang on the steps of the Lincoln Memorial.

A French poilu sat guard in the "Phoney War" on the Western Front.

CURRENTS AND EVENTS

WORLD: Spanish Loyalists Capitulate to Dictator Franco • German Storm Troopers Take Over in Czechoslovakia • U.S.S.R. Invades Finland • Britain, France Guarantee Poland's Independence • Italy Overruns Albania • Japan Sweeps Deeper into China's Interior • Germany, U.S.S.R. Sign Nonaggression Pact • Poland Succumbs to Blitzkrieg • Britain, France Declare War on Germany, U.S. Asserts Neutrality • Gandhi Again Endures "Fast unto Death."

U.S.A.: FDR Calls for Strong National Defense • Economy Picks Up as Arms Sales Soar • Einstein Secretly Advises FDR A-bomb Can Be Built • Supreme Court Rules Sit-down Strikes Illegal • Submarine Squalus Sinks • San Francisco, New York World's Fairs Open • Sinatra Joins Harry James Band • After 2,130 Consecutive Games, Ailing Lou Gehrig Benches Himself.

FIRSTS: Helicopter • Jet Plane • DDT • Transatlantic Airmail • Commercial U.S.-Europe Flight (Clipper).

MOVIES: Gone With the Wind • The Wizard of Oz • Wuthering Heights • Dark Victory • Goodbye, Mr. Chips • Intermezzo • Mr. Smith Goes to Washington • The Women • Ninotchka.

SONGS: God Bless America • All the Things You Are • Beer Barrel Polka • Over the Rainbow • Frenesi • I Didn't Know What Time It Was • I'll Never Smile Again • Our Love • Meadowlands (Red Army song) • Three Little Fishies.

STAGE: Life with Father • The Philadelphia Story • The Time of Your Life • The Little Foxes • The Man Who Came to Dinner • Too Many Girls • DuBarry Was a Lady.

BOOKS: The Grapes of Wrath (Steinbeck) • The Yearling (Rawlings) • Kitty Foyle (Morley) • Abraham Lincoln: The War Years (Sandburg) • Wind, Sand and Stars (Saint-Exupéry) • The Web and the Rock (Wolfe) • Wickford Point (Marquand) • Adventures of a Young Man (Dos Passos) • Pale Horse, Pale Rider (Porter) • Finnegans Wake (Joyce) • Tropic of Capricorn (Miller) • The Day of the Locust (West) • Mein Kampf (Hitler, in English).

FADS: Swallowing Goldfish • Sleigh Bells on Socks.

SEPTEMBER 4, 1939

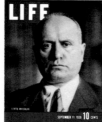
SEPTEMBER 11, 1939

SEPTEMBER 18, 1939

SEPTEMBER 25, 1939

OCTOBER 2, 1939

OCTOBER 9, 1939

OCTOBER 16, 1939

OCTOBER 23, 1939

OCTOBER 30, 1939

NOVEMBER 6, 1939

NOVEMBER 13, 1939

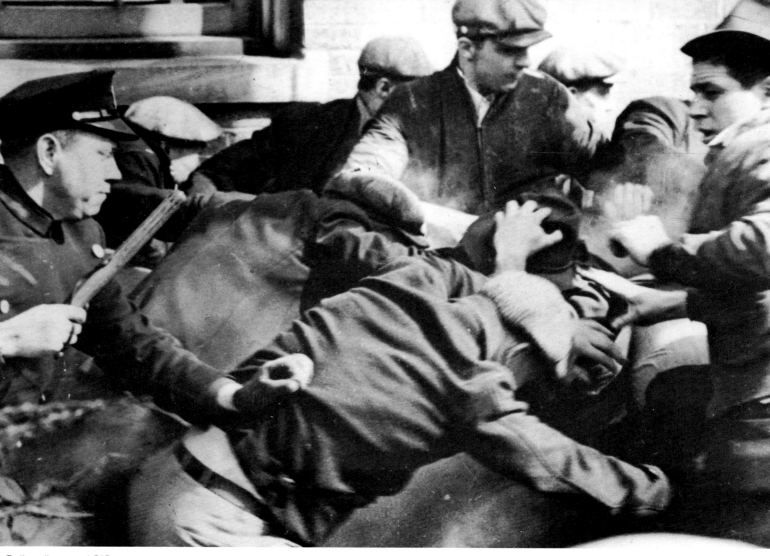

Police dispersed CIO pickets seeking to stop members of an independent union from working at an Erie, Pa., coffin factory. Jurisdictional strikes, sniffed LIFE, just irritate the public.

Scarecrow Ray Bolger watched Judy Garland, as Dorothy, oil Tin Woodsman Jack Haley in The Wizard of Oz—*one of a banner film year's blockbusters.*

Children wielded clubs ("enthusiastically but inaccurately," said the editors) in a western rabbit drive.

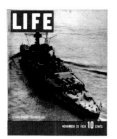

NOVEMBER 20, 1939

NOVEMBER 27, 1939

DECEMBER 4, 1939

DECEMBER 11, 1939

DECEMBER 18, 1939

DECEMBER 25, 1939

In costume and custom derived from the comic strip Li'l Abner, Texas coeds treed a prospective date on Sadie Hawkins Day.

France's luxury liner Paris lay afire at Le Havre, hard by the dry-docked Normandie, herself to burn later at a New York pier.

LIFE *scanned the American scene as Europe went to war. The message was exquisitely ironic.*

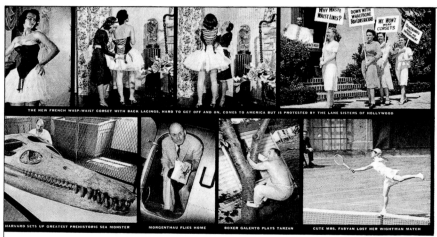

THE NEW FRENCH WASP-WAIST CORSET WITH BACK LACINGS, HARD TO GET OFF AND ON, COMES TO AMERICA BUT IS PROTESTED BY THE LANE SISTERS OF HOLLYWOOD

HARVARD SETS UP GREATEST PREHISTORIC SEA MONSTER — MORGENTHAU FLIES HOME — BOXER GALENTO PLAYS TARZAN — CUTE MRS. FABYAN LOST HER WIGHTMAN MATCH

BILL ROBINSON AT WORLD'S FAIR — CATHOLIC NUNS LEARN TO DANCE AT CHICAGO SCHOOL — NEGROES HOLD MASS BAPTISM AT NEWPORT NEWS, VA. — VETS' DRUM MAJORETTES

SABOTAGE BLAMED ON TRAIN WRECK — LAST RITES FOR DEAD HOLIDAY MOTORIST — J. P. MORGAN EATS AS "QUEEN MARY" DOCKS — SCHOONER IS WRECKED ON MASS. COAST

MOST ALIKE TWINS IN CONTEST — MOST UNALIKE TWINS IN CONTEST — SENATOR'S DAUGHTER SINGS "DIXIE" — QUEEN OF JEWISH WAR VETERANS — QUEEN OF GRAPE FIESTA

INSURANCE & MONOPOLY — CHICAGO COMMUNISTS CELEBRATE 20TH ANNIVERSARY — MRS. HENRY C. PHIPPS AT RACES — SEC. WALLACE AT WORLD COTTON CONFERENCE

A HIT IN GEORGE WHITE'S "SCANDALS" IS ANN MILLER, WHO, WITH NO APPARENT MUSCLES IN HER LEGS, DOES A SLINKY VERSION OF THE MEXICONGA

THE WEEK THE WAR BEGAN

LIFE presents a retrospective close-up of the last days of an American era

by NOEL F. BUSCH

After two weeks of the summer's hottest weather and a long drought, heavy thunderstorms in the northeastern U. S. cooled the air. In the South and the Far West, the sun shone brightly toward the end of a dry and pleasant summer in which the Dakotas reported first-rate wheat crops and Kansas cattle fattened faster than usual. In Chandler, Okla., a 6-year-old invalid named Joe Kalka managed to crawl a quarter of a mile from his house and fall face down into a 6-in. puddle of water, where he drowned.

On the grass tennis courts of the Merion Cricket Club, near Philadelphia, Frank Parker of Beverly Hills, Calif., and John Bromwich of Australia faced each other in the final match of the final series of world-wide competition for the Davis Cup. Bromwich's victory gave Australia its first Cup series in the U. S. since 1914—the year before Anthony Wilding, the star member of its team, was killed in Northern France. At Saratoga, Colonel Edward Bradley, proprietor of Bradley's at Palm Beach, watched his 2-year-old Bimelech win the Hopeful Stakes, feature race of the August meeting which had drawn almost as big crowds, according to reporters, as any "since the War."

Naturally, the "war of nerves" in Europe, hourly bulletins on which kept over 40,800,000 radios, was the country's chief topic of conversation. Whether Franklin Roosevelt would run for a third term was a close runner-up. The old Greek theory that wars happen every 30 years because each generation is curious about the matter was subtly corroborated by the country's mood. John Dos Passos, Scott Fitzgerald, Cyril Hume, Sinclair Lewis and most of the other good writers of the previous decade were either hacking in Hollywood or showing signs of being written out. Newcomers, with the possible exception of John Steinbeck in his *Grapes of Wrath*, did not seem to have much to say. Buckminster Fuller's dymaxion house had not solved the troubles of the building industry any more than New Deal credit schemes.

Meanwhile, vacationists put away their fishing rods or put up their sailboats, examined their summer tans for the last time and began thinking about moving back to the city. Over the long holiday weekend, at thousands of country clubs and roadhouses the last dance music of the summer tinkled into the mild nights. Much of it was "swing" or "boogie woogie" to which "cats" or "alligators" either danced the "shag" or listened in a proud, self-conscious trance.

Peculiar things were going on in the theatrical business which, instead of being excited about the opening of the new season, was vastly disturbed about an intramural labor dispute crystallizing somehow with the re-opening of the musical comedy *Leave It to Me*, featuring Sophie Tucker. Threatened by the Sophie Tucker crisis were the nine shows that had weathered New York's summer—among them *Hellzapoppin*, *The Philadelphia Story*, *Yokel Boy*, *The Little Foxes* and *Tobacco Road*. Meanwhile movies like *The Wizard of Oz*, with Jack Haley and Judy Garland, and *Fifth Avenue Girl*, starring Ginger Rogers, were packing the nation's biggest movie theaters. According to *Variety*, the most popular tune of the week was *Beer Barrel Polka*, replacing *Three Little Fishes*.

Women all over the U. S. were excited by the return not only of the bustle but also of the laced corset. Revealed at the Paris openings five weeks before, these curious garments—which suggested the Middle Ages to some fashion critics and the year 1914 to others—began to make their appearances in U. S. shop windows, establishing the return of the "hourglass" figure. A New York publisher gravely considered publishing the monograph of a Midwestern savant, advancing the hypothesis that the cycles of women's fashions and the cycles of political behavior were connected by laws of behavior both obscure and inflexible.

John Jacob Astor, whose father was drowned on the *Titanic*, and his wife, the former "Tucky" French, were among those who, at Newport, R. I., attended a pageant entitled *Epic of Newport*, with a cast of 1,000, mostly townsfolk. The "little season" started in Connecticut and on Long Island where, at Southampton, the Harry Payne Binghams had James Burden of New York down for the weekend. Ordinary weddings increased but there were none of social brilliance. En route from a vacation at Owosso, Mich.,

74

CONTINUED ON PAGE 78

75

1940

While now reporting war's terrors, there was still room for fun and games—and the presidency

The early stages of the war were dark days of defeat for the democracies—dark days literally because much of the early fighting took place in the north of Europe in fall and winter. LIFE had sent photographer Carl Mydans and his wife, Shelley, a staff reporter, to observe the developing war clouds; and when the U.S.S.R. pounced on Finland, Mydans moved to that snow-shrouded battleground and made memorable pictures of bombarded civilians and white-garbed ski troops heroically resisting the Red Army. On the home front, while plumping for Roosevelt's policy of noncombat aid to the Allies, the magazine supported Wendell Willkie's presidential campaign.

A torpedoed British freighter plunged, bow last, into the Atlantic.

East End fires silhouetted London's Tower Bridge during a night bombing by Germany's Luftwaffe.

Emperor Hirohito reviewed the Japanese fleet from the bridge of his flagship Hiei near Yokohama.

This German newsreel sequence of the Führer, overjoyed at France's imminent surrender, provided an intimate look at Hitler, as the story said, but his "jig" later proved to be not completely authentic. A Canadian film editor had doctored the movie footage to repeat the dictator's onetime raising of his right foot, converting the gesture into a dance.

JANUARY 1, 1940

JANUARY 8, 1940

JANUARY 15, 1940

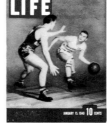
JANUARY 22, 1940

JANUARY 29, 1940

FEBRUARY 5, 1940

FEBRUARY 12, 1940

Finns driven from their farming village by Soviet bombers huddled fearfully in the snow of a birch glade.

FEBRUARY 19, 1940

FEBRUARY 26, 1940

MARCH 4, 1940

MARCH 11, 1940

MARCH 18, 1940

MARCH 25, 1940

APRIL 1, 1940

APRIL 8, 1940

APRIL 15, 1940

APRIL 22, 1940

APRIL 29, 1940

MAY 6, 1940

MAY 13, 1940

May 20, 1940

MAY 27, 1940

JUNE 3, 1940

JUNE 10, 1940

JUNE 17, 1940

JUNE 24, 1940

JULY 1, 1940

JULY 8, 1940

JULY 15, 1940

JULY 22, 1940

JULY 29, 1940

AUGUST 5, 1940

AUGUST 12, 1940

AUGUST 19, 1940

AUGUST 26, 1940

SEPTEMBER 2, 1940

SEPTEMBER 9, 1940

SEPTEMBER 16, 1940

SEPTEMBER 23, 1940

SEPTEMBER 30, 1940

OCTOBER 7, 1940

OCTOBER 14, 1940

OCTOBER 21, 1940

OCTOBER 28, 1940

NOVEMBER 4, 1940

NOVEMBER 11, 1940

NOVEMBER 18, 1940

NOVEMBER 25, 1940

DECEMBER 2, 1940

DECEMBER 9, 1940

DECEMBER 16, 1940

DECEMBER 23, 1940

DECEMBER 30, 1940

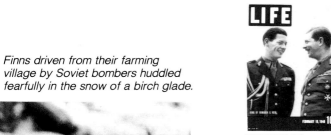

German infantrymen rushed a fortified bunker in Belgium. LIFE called such "agile, cunning" teams the key to the Wehrmacht's victory in Flanders.

In Michigan's 40-0 romp over Ohio State, Heisman winner Tom Harmon scored three TDs and kicked four conversions.

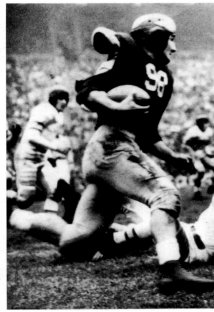

After Vivien Leigh won her Gone With the Wind Oscar, LIFE followed her home from the Awards dinner to see her place it on her mantel.

A model wearing roller skates showed off a $2.98 "Skaterina" outfit in Rockefeller Center.

CLASSIC PHOTOS

Campaigning Wendell Willkie visited hometown Elwood, Ind.

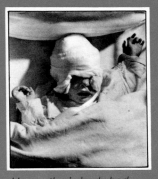

Her mother's body had shielded this Welsh bombing victim, age 2.

Tired British soldiers awaited evacuation at Dunkirk.

CURRENTS AND EVENTS

WORLD: Hitler's Forces Overpower Norway, Denmark • Panzers, Stukas Blitz Low Countries • Finland Surrenders to Red Army Legions • New Prime Minister Churchill Offers Britain "Blood, Toil, Tears, Sweat" • German Armor Knifes into France • British, French Troops Pushed to Dunkirk, Evacuated by Naval, Civilian Vessels • Mussolini Declares War on Britain, France • Japan Demands China's Surrender • Soviets Take Over Lithuania, Estonia, Latvia • Germans March into Paris, Pétain Sets Up Cooperative Government in Vichy • Britons Stiffen for Invasion • Luftwaffe Looses Air Blitz on London, RAF Retaliates with Night Bombing of Germany • Italy Invades Greece • British Tanks Hit Italian Armor in Africa • Exiled Soviet Leader Trotsky Assassinated in Mexico • Batista Takes Over in Cuba.

EFORE US
ROOSEVELT

Taking the stump at last only 13 days before the elections, Candidate Roosevelt combined some defense inspection with campaigning even though trip was paid for by the Democratic Committee. Above: he tells shipyard workers at Camden, N. J. to "keep up the speed."

16,000 people, with thousands more outside, jammed Philadelphia's Convention Hall to hear Roosevelt charge his opponent with falsification, defend his domestic record, and promise to keep the nation at peace. Below: he makes first rear-platform talk, at Wilmington, Del.

THESE ARE THE THINGS THAT PEOPLE THREW AT CANDIDATE FOR PRESIDENT

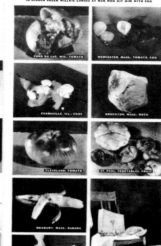

IN SUDDEN ANGER WILLKIE LUNGES AT MAN WHO HIT HIM WITH EGG

The week before the election, the editors, who admired Wendell Willkie and had covered his campaign in depth, summed up the issues in relatively impartial style. The magazine set forth each candidate's positions as it imagined partisans on both sides might describe their beliefs about the two men (at center). To that presentation was added a page (near left) that indignantly illustrated the barrage of things thrown at Willkie while touring the nation.

Cannibals in the New Hebrides broiled a dismembered human for dinner. The photo was taken by renowned explorer Osa Johnson.

Londoners bedded down in an Underground station at the height of the Battle of Britain.

U.S.A.: FDR Sells Britain 50 Over-Age Destroyers • U.S. Orders All Aliens Fingerprinted • Draft Law Passed • Supreme Court Rules Schools May Compel Saluting of Flag • FDR Swamps Willkie for Unprecedented Third Term.

FIRSTS: Synthetic-Rubber Tire • Black U.S. General (B. O. Davis) • Black on Postage Stamp (Booker T. Washington).

MOVIES: Abe Lincoln in Illinois • Boom Town • The Grapes of Wrath • The Great Dictator • Pride and Prejudice • Rebecca • The Long Voyage Home • Our Town • The Philadelphia Story • Kitty Foyle • My Little Chickadee • Dr. Kildare Goes Home • Northwest Passage • Fantasia • Pinocchio • Tin Pan Alley.

SONGS: Ballad for Americans • All or Nothing at All • Fools Rush In • I Hear a Rhapsody • How High the Moon • Cabin in the Sky • The Last Time I Saw Paris • The Nearness of You • Taking a Chance on Love • When You Wish upon a Star • You Are My Sunshine • This Is My Country.

STAGE: There Shall Be No Night • Juno and the Paycock • The Male Animal • Johnny Belinda • The Corn Is Green • Charley's Aunt • My Sister Eileen • Pal Joey • Panama Hattie.

BOOKS: For Whom the Bell Tolls (Hemingway) • How Green Was My Valley (Llewellyn) • Native Son (Wright) • You Can't Go Home Again (Wolfe) • To the Finland Station (Wilson) • My Name Is Aram (Saroyan) • The Power and the Glory (Greene) • Pal Joey (O'Hara) • Journey into Fear (Ambler) • Farewell, My Lovely (Chandler).

TOPS IN RADIO, '30s: Amos 'n' Andy (Premiere, '28) • N.Y. Philharmonic ('30) • Bing Crosby ('31) • Kate Smith ('31) • The Woman in White ('33) • The Romance of Helen Trent ('33) • The Lone Ranger ('33) • André Kostelanetz ('34) • Fibber McGee and Molly ('35) • One Man's Family ('35) • Your Hit Parade ('35) • Lum and Abner ('35) • Metropolitan Opera Auditions ('35) • Vox Pop ('35) • Phil Baker ('35) • Major Bowes' Amateur Hour ('36) • Gang Busters ('36) • Columbia Theater Workshop ('36) • Edgar Bergen and Charlie McCarthy ('37) • Myrt and Marge ('37) • Tony Wons' Scrapbook ('37) • Jack Benny ('32) • Lux Radio Theater ('34) • Bob Hope ('35) • Fred Allen ('34) • The Shadow ('30) • Information Please ('38) • Metropolitan Opera ('31) • Easy Aces ('36) • Lady Esther Serenade ('31) • Dick Tracy ('38).

FADS: Roller-Rink Skating • Calypso Music.

1941

Preoccupation with the domestic scene continued. Then came the traumatic shock of Pearl Harbor

Although the U.S. was technically still at peace, the subject of war dominated every issue. After FDR was sworn in for his third term, the magazine stepped up its support for his pro-Allies policy. It ran stories on West Point, on Fort Bragg, on shipbuilding; it published a special issue on the U.S. armed forces and their materiel. In articles and in occasional editorials, a departure for LIFE, the editors focused on the nation's obligations in a war-torn world, urging that it take a stronger stand and arm adequately for the direct involvement they deemed inevitable. As the President strove to convince Americans that Hitler's goals constituted a threat to all democracies, LIFE charged him with moving too slowly. After the Japanese bombs hit Pearl Harbor, Henry Luce wrote and signed an editorial: "This is the day of wrath. The disaster . . . was an episode. But it was also a sign. It was a sign of all the weakness and wrongness of American life in recent years."

Actress-model Jinx Falkenburg, 22, was LIFE's candidate for the year's "No. 1 Girl."

Bette Davis turned 33 while skiing at home in Littleton, N.H., where she was a deputy sheriff.

Ingrid Bergman, 25, won kudos as "Sweden's most promising export since Garbo."

Dorothy McGuire, 23, looked "little like an actress," but caught fire in Broadway's Claudia.

The coiffure of Veronica Lake, 22, as a "property of world influence," got three pages of attention.

In Go West, Young Lady, Ann Miller, 18, danced using "every inch of her 5 feet 5 to advantage."

SCIENCE

IN CBS TELEVISION STUDIO TWO CAMERAS (CENTER BACKGROUND) GET TWO ANGLES ON PERFORMER. DIRECTORS WATCH IMAGES ON RECEIVER SCREENS, EDIT TRANSMISSION

Large-screen television here reproduces a Brooklyn Dodgers home game on full-sized movie screen. Reproducing tube projects image onto curved reflector, in rear of cylinder (*left*), which transmits much-enlarged image onto movie screen. Operator (*right*) controls quality of image.

TELEVISION
COLOR AND BIG-SCREEN IMAGES OPEN NEW HORIZONS

During this last summer, two years since television made its fanfared studio debut, the biggest television news was made, as before, in the laboratory. In the laboratory, it now appears, television will stay for the duration of the emergency. At the bottom of any priorities list, television's audience will continue to be limited by the insignificant number of sets sold and selling. Television's promoters, however, are satisfied that their Federal Communications Commission commercial franchise, their 22 stations and audience of 6,000 receiver sets are a nucleus on which television will survive and be ready to expand when the war ends. Meanwhile they are cheered by two recent milestones in television's technical progress: large-screen projection of television images (*at left*) and color television (*opposite page*).

Large-screen television, which was developed by NBC engineers and has successfully demonstrated its power to project television programs on a full-sized movie screen, opens up a new horizon for practical application of the television art. Color television is the invention of CBS's engineers, headed by young Dr. Peter C. Goldmark. It employs a simple principle first applied to color movies, explained on the opposite page. As compared with the 30-to-1 contrast range of black-and-white television, CBS's color system has demonstrated an almost unlimited reproduction range for all colors, hues and shades in the spectrum. Though its resolution of detail is weaker than black-and-white television, CBS's color television system transmits much more information, in clear and brilliant images. There is every reason to believe that all television programs in the future will be transmitted in color.

Pale delicate colors of bowl of flowers provide an exacting test for the CBS color television system. All colors will be reproduced at receiver by mixture of the primary colors, red, green and blue, which are represented in the filters of the color drum and disc (*below*).

Flowers televised appear with their colors accurately reproduced. Kodachrome reproduction of color television image does not do entire justice to it. In particular, horizontal lines on image picked up by camera at close range are not apparent to the eye at normal viewing distance.

Inside the television camera inverted image appears on ground glass at left. Color drum at right, with red, green and blue filters, spins at 1,200 r. p. m. Filters pick out own colors in subject, transmit them separately to inside of electronic scanning tube to right of drum.

Color disc, held by inventor Peter C. Goldmark, spins in front of cathode-ray tube. Synchronized with color drum, disc transmits the successive single-color images picked up by camera. Persistence of vision in eyes blends separate color images into integrated full-color picture.

In the television studio, Victor Moore, Vera Zorina and William Gaxton perform for color television camera (*left*). Color television can handle hundreds of thousands of different shades and tones of all colors as against 30 shades of gray for black-and-white television.

Performers televised show program possibilities of color television. Exaggerated in reproduction, loss of image detail is compensated by colors, which convey information lost in black-and-white transmission. Color image resists room illumination much better than black-and-white.

52

The magazine, increasingly making use of full color on its own pages, saw a colorful future for video.

In her syndicated column, Eleanor Roosevelt had expressed dismay at a Bureau of Labor Statistics report that, under wartime pressure, food prices had risen 14 percent in one year. LIFE scoffed that the revelation would come as "no news at all to U.S. housewives." Then, in a typical gambit designed to translate dry information into visual terms, the editors bought a sampling of real food and labeled each item with its old and new prices.

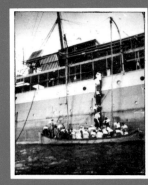

Germans sank Egypt's Zamzam with 138 still neutral Americans aboard, including LIFE's Dave Scherman. From his lifeboat, he caught passengers leaving the ship to be taken aboard the raider.

A Marseillais wept as regimental flags were shipped abroad to safety.

Rita Hayworth, the quintessential pinup, knelt on her bed.

"Playful, mischievous" Triple Crown winner Whirlaway smiled for this portrait.

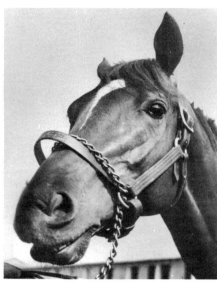

Mud-wallowing Bob Hope in Caught in the Draft reflected the movies' frequently comic approach to the ordeals of "universal service."

A state prosecutor waved a leather lash at Georgia Governor Eugene Talmadge, who favored clemency for Ku Klux Klansmen who had used whips on pro-union mill workers.

CURRENTS AND EVENTS

WORLD: Nazis Overrun Yugoslavia, U-Boat Attacks Punish Allied Shipping • British Sink Battleship Bismarck • Japanese Cut China's Supply Routes at Sea, on Land • U.S.S.R., Japan Sign Neutrality Pact • Italians Surrender Tobruk to British Armor • Afrika Korps Joins Desert War • Rudolf Hess Makes Mystery Solo Flight to England • Germany Invades U.S.S.R., Stalin Calls for Scorched-Earth Policy • FDR, Churchill Meet on Destroyer off Newfoundland • Tito Organizes Yugoslav Resistance • Smolensk, Kiev Fail to Nazi Onslaught, Leningrad Isolated • Mud, Extreme Cold Bog Down Wehrmacht's Thrust Toward Moscow • Japanese Bomb Pearl Harbor • Germany, Italy Declare War on U.S. • Japanese Land on Wake Island, Bataan.

U.S.A.: Nation Digs In for War, Rationing Begins • FDR Enunciates Four Freedoms: of Speech, of Worship, from Want, from Fear • MacArthur Incorporates Philippine Forces into U.S. Army • Mount Rushmore Monument Completed • DiMaggio Hits Safely in 56 Consecutive Games • Ted Williams Bats .406.

FIRSTS: Liberty Ship • Quonset Hut • Penicillin Treatment • Commercial TV License (W2XBS, N.Y.C.), FM Station (W47NV, Nashville) • Woman Test Pilot (Alma Heflin).

MOVIES: Citizen Kane • Kings Row • The Little Foxes • Here Comes Mr. Jordan • How Green Was My Valley • The Man Who Came to Dinner • Meet John Doe • Suspicion • The Maltese Falcon • Sergeant York • Major Barbara • Dumbo • The Road to Zanzibar • You'll Never Get Rich.

SONGS: Bewitched (Bothered and Bewildered) • The White Cliffs of Dover • Waltzing Matilda • Blues in the Night • Deep in the Heart of Texas • How About You? • I Don't Want to Walk Without You • I Don't Want to Set the World on Fire • I'll Remember April • This Love of Mine • There! I've Said It Again • Flamingo • Don't Take Your Love from Me • Tonight We Love • The Hut Sut Song.

STAGE: Watch on the Rhine • Arsenic and Old Lace • Blithe Spirit • Junior Miss • Angel Street • Lady in the Dark • Best Foot Forward • Let's Face It.

BOOKS: Berlin Diary (Shirer) • Darkness at Noon (Koestler) • Out of the Night (Valtin) • The Keys of the Kingdom (Cronin) • Mildred Pierce (Cain) • H. M. Pulham, Esq. (Marquand) • Reveille in Washington (Leach) • The G-String Murders (Lee) • The Last Tycoon (Fitzgerald).

FADS: Color in Women's Cotton, Wool Hosiery • Campus Blanket Parties • Floppy Hats.

JANUARY 6, 1941

JANUARY 13, 1941

JANUARY 20, 1941

JANUARY 27, 1941

FEBRUARY 3, 1941

FEBRUARY 10, 1941

FEBRUARY 17, 1941

FEBRUARY 24, 1941

MARCH 3, 1941

MARCH 10, 1941

MARCH 17, 1941

MARCH 24, 1941

MARCH 31, 1941

APRIL 7, 1941

APRIL 14, 1941

APRIL 21, 1941

APRIL 28, 1941

MAY 5, 1941

MAY 12, 1941

MAY 19, 1941

MAY 26, 1941

JUNE 2, 1941

JUNE 9, 1941

JUNE 16, 1941

JUNE 23, 1941

JUNE 30, 1941

JULY 7, 1941

JULY 14, 1941

JULY 21, 1941

JULY 28, 1941

AUGUST 4, 1941

AUGUST 11, 1941

AUGUST 18, 1941

AUGUST 25, 1941

SEPTEMBER 1, 1941

SEPTEMBER 8, 1941

SEPTEMBER 15, 1941

SEPTEMBER 22, 1941

SEPTEMBER 29, 1941

OCTOBER 6, 1941

OCTOBER 13, 1941

OCTOBER 20, 1941

OCTOBER 27, 1941

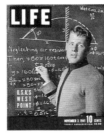
NOVEMBER 3, 1941

NOVEMBER 10, 1941

NOVEMBER 17, 1941

NOVEMBER 24, 1941

DECEMBER 1, 1941

DECEMBER 8, 1941

DECEMBER 15, 1941

DECEMBER 22, 1941

DECEMBER 29, 1941

The issue of December 15, 1941, with this opening page, was on newsstands nationwide on Wednesday, December 10th, three days after bombs rained on Pearl Harbor. The issue just the week before had carried a premonitory lead article under the headline: "The Ancient Imperial Power of Japan Comes to a Showdown with America." Its text ended with these words: "The stage was set for war, a distant, dangerous, hard, amphibious war for which the American nation was not yet fully prepared."

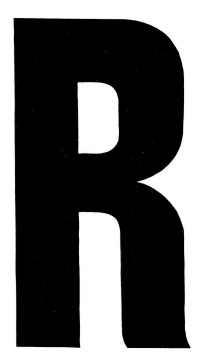

WAR

JAPAN LAUNCHES RECKLESS ATTACK ON U. S.

IN DESPERATE GAMBLE ON VICTORY OR SUICIDE IT STRIKES FIRST BLOW AT HAWAII

Out of the Pacific skies last week World War II came with startling suddenness to America. It was 7:35 a. m. on a Sunday morning—the aggressors' favorite day—when two Japanese planes, wearing on their wings the Rising Sun of Japan, flew out of the western sky over the Hawaiian island of Oahu. Japan had seized the initiative and was making the most of the aggressor's privilege to strike the first blow. With reckless daring Japan aimed this blow at the citadel of American power in the Pacific, the great naval fortress of Pearl Harbor.

Close observers of Japan have said for years that if that country ever found itself in a hopeless corner it was capable of committing national hara-kiri by flinging itself at the throat of its mightiest enemy. Japan has found itself in just such a corner. It could not retreat without losing all and it could not advance another step without war. It took the desperate plunge and told its enemies in effect: "If this be hara-kiri, make the most of it."

Japan's daring was matched only by its barefaced duplicity. There was no warning—not even such an ultimatum as Hitler is wont to send while his legions pour across some new border. At the very moment the first bombs fell on Pearl Harbor Japan's two envoys in Washington were in Secretary Hull's office at the State Department, making their blandest protestations of peaceful intent. Ambassador Nomura and Envoy Kurusu had come with the answer to Hull's note. He read it through and then, for the first time in many long, patient years, the soft-spoken Secretary lost his temper. Into the teeth of the two

Japanese, who for once did not grin, he flung these words: "In all my 50 years of public service I have never seen a document that was more crowded with infamous falsehoods and distortions—on a scale so huge that I never imagined until today that any government on this planet was capable of uttering them."

NOMURA AND KURUSU BEFORE CONFERENCE WITH HULL

The two Japanese scurried out of his office and home to their Embassy.

Even as Hull spoke, America sprang to arms. Wherever it was in the wide ocean, the U. S. Fleet went into action and all over the Pacific U. S. garrisons stood ready. In Washington President Roosevelt dictated his war message to Congress. From Army and Navy headquarters the prearranged orders went out which transformed the U. S. into a nation at war. In the face of an attack so clear that no man could argue it, the nation stood absolutely united. Senator Wheeler, the leader of Isolationists, spoke for all when he said: "The only thing now is to do our best to lick hell out of them."

How much or how long it would take to lick Japan, no man could say. The U. S. Navy has always been supremely confident of its ability to sink the Japanese Fleet in open battle or, if the enemy ships refused battle, to strangle the island empire by blockade. In recent months the vulnerable Philippine station has been strengthened by the addition of squadrons of heavy bombers. With new British warships at Singapore, plus the combined land-air strength of the British, Dutch and Australian forces, America has a long-range superiority over Japan. It may be, indeed, that America's greatest danger is overconfidence. There will surely be more naval losses and more strong attacks on American islands because Japan has a strategic and tactical advantage at the outset of this Pacific war. It will take not only all-out U. S. military might but great persistence and great courage to hurl back attack and to win the final victory.

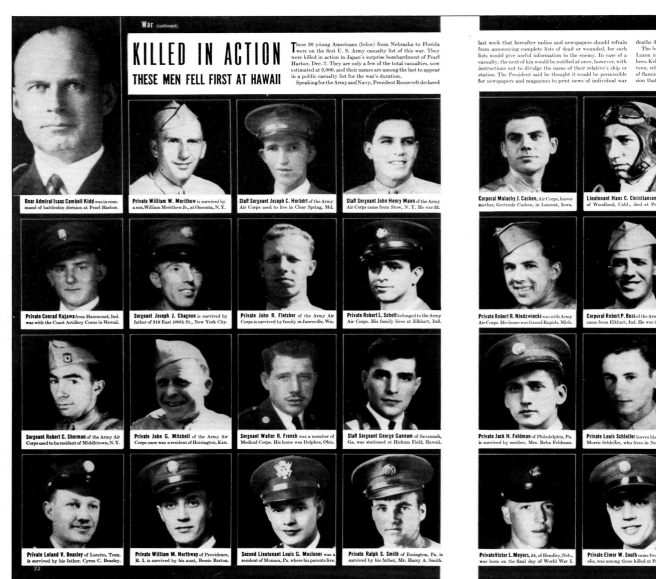

KILLED IN ACTION
THESE MEN FELL FIRST AT HAWAII

These 30 young Americans (below) from Nebraska to Florida were on the first U. S. Army casualty list of this war. They were killed in action in Japan's surprise bombardment of Pearl Harbor, Dec. 7. They are only a few of the total casualties, now estimated at 3,000, and their names are among the last to appear in a public casualty list for the war's duration.

Speaking for the Army and Navy, President Roosevelt declared last week that hereafter radios and newspapers should refrain from announcing complete lists of dead or wounded, for such lists would give useful information to the enemy. In case of a casualty, the next of kin would be notified at once; however, with instructions not to divulge the name of their relative's ship or station. The President said he thought it would be permissible for newspapers and magazines to print news of individual war deaths if military or geographical information was withheld.

The bravery of Captain Colin Kelly Jr. (right) on Dec. 12 off Luzon in the Philippines provided America with its first war hero. Kelly dove his plane straight at the Japanese battleship, Haruna, released a stick of high explosives almost into the mouths of flaming guns, and then vanished himself in the mighty explosion that ushered the 29,000-ton ship to the bottom of the sea.

Rear Admiral Isaac Cambell Kidd was in command of battleship division at Pearl Harbor.

Private William W. Merithew is survived by a son, William Merithew Jr., at Oneonta, N.Y.

Staff Sergeant Joseph C. Herbert of the Army Air Corps used to live in Clear Spring, Md.

Staff Sergeant John Henry Mann of the Army Air Corps came from Stow, N.Y. He was 22.

Corporal Malachy J. Cashen, Air Corps, leaves mother, Gertrude Cashen, in Lamont, Iowa.

Lieutenant Hans C. Christiansen, Air Corps, of Woodland, Calif., died at Pearl Harbor.

Corporal Vincent M. Horan belonged to the Air Corps, used to live in Stamford, Conn.

Captain Colin Kelly Jr. who sank the Haruna is survived by wife and son in Brooklyn, N.Y.

Private Conrad Kujawa from Hammond, Ind. was with the Coast Artillery Corps in Hawaii.

Sergeant Joseph J. Chagnon is survived by father of 319 East 100th St., New York City.

Private John R. Fletcher of the Army Air Corps is survived by family in Janesville, Wis.

Private Robert L. Schott belonged to the Army Air Corps. His family lives at Elkhart, Ind.

Private Robert R. Niedzwiecki was with Army Air Corps. His home was Grand Rapids, Mich.

Corporal Robert P. Buss of the Army Air Corps came from Elkhart, Ind. He was 26 years old.

Private Eugene L. Chambers of Army Air Corps was formerly a resident of Apollo, Pa.

Private Horace A. Messam was from Barberton, Ohio and is survived by his father Ernest.

Sergeant Robert C. Sherman of the Army Air Corps used to be resident of Middletown, N.Y.

Private John G. Mitchell of the Army Air Corps once was a resident of Hoisington, Kan.

Sergeant Walter R. French was a member of Medical Corps. His home was Delphos, Ohio.

Staff Sergeant George Gannam of Savannah, Ga. was stationed at Hickam Field, Hawaii.

Private Jack H. Feldman of Philadelphia, Pa. is survived by mother, Mrs. Reba Feldman.

Private Louis Schleifer leaves his father, Mr. Morris Schleifer, who lives in Newark, N.J.

Second Lieutenant George A. Whiteman of the Army Air Corps was from Sedalia, Mo.

Private William Coyne Jr., who was 20 years old, was Kansas City's first known casualty.

Private Leland V. Beasley of Loretto, Tenn. is survived by his father, Cyrus C. Beasley.

Private William M. Northway of Providence, R.I. is survived by his aunt, Bessie Barton.

Second Lieutenant Louis G. Moslener was a resident of Monaca, Pa. where his parents live.

Private Ralph S. Smith of Essington, Pa. is survived by his father, Mr. Harry A. Smith.

Private Victor L. Meyers, 24, of Hendley, Neb., was born on the final day of World War I.

Private Elmer W. South came from Indianapolis, was among those killed at Pearl Harbor.

Private Theodore F. Byrd Jr. of Army Air Corps is survived by father in Tampa, Fla.

Sergeant James E. Guthrie from Nathalie, Va., is survived by his father, Claude Guthrie.

22

CONTINUED ON NEXT PAGE 23

Pictures of 30 GIs, rounded up on the basis of the Army's first list of more than 3,000 Pearl Harbor dead, graced LIFE's report on U.S. casualties. The editors also singled out Navy battleship chief Rear Adm. Isaac Kidd and Air Corps Capt. Colin Kelly Jr.

A staff sergeant and his wife found each other, unhurt, after Pearl Harbor.

Sandbags piled against windows of San Francisco's Pacific Telephone & Telegraph building illustrated coast-to-coast defense measures.

Smoke from the burning battleship Arizona stained the sky of the Army's Hickam Field in the first pictures of the Pearl Harbor attack.

Reacting to Pearl Harbor, LIFE offered a simplistic service for readers—and for their Chinese allies.

A lead article on U.S. war production caught Lockheed workers speeding P-38 fighters through the assembly lines.

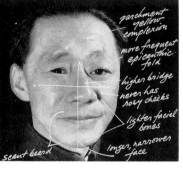

HOW TO TELL JAPS FROM THE CHINESE

ANGRY CITIZENS VICTIMIZE ALLIES WITH EMOTIONAL OUTBURST AT ENEMY

parchment yellow complexion
more frequent epicanthic fold
higher bridge never has rosy cheeks
lighter facial bones
scant beard
longer, narrower face

earthy yellow complexion
less frequent epicanthic fold
flatter nose
sometimes rosy cheeks
heavy beard
massive cheek and jawbone
broader, shorter face

Japanese warrior, General Hideki Tojo, current Premier, is a Samurai, close to type of humble Jap than highbred relatives of Imperial Household. Typical are his heavy beard, massive cheek and jaw bones. Peasant Jap is squat Mongoloid, with flat, blob nose. An often mistaken clue is facial expression, shaped by cultural, not anthropological, factors. Chinese wear rational calm of tolerant realists. Japs, like General Tojo, show humorless intensity of ruthless mystics.

Chinese journalist, Joe Chiang, found it necessary to advertise his nationality to gain admittance to White House press conference. Under Immigration Act of 1924, Japs and Chinese, as members of the "yellow race," are barred from immigration and naturalization.

JCONTINUED ON NEXT PAGE] 81

39

1942

The many moods of the Picture of the Week feature, and other innovations, added scope

Once the nation had been plunged into war, the mix of pictures available from all sources inevitably weighed toward more serious subjects; and even the lighter ones mirroring home-front activities were informed in greater measure with roll-up-the-sleeves determination and morale boosting. The early editorial lark-

PICTURE OF THE WEEK

No one, then or in all the years that followed, was able to spell out the criteria for the one photo that stood out above all others obtainable for a given issue. Whether by consensus or the fiat of the managing editor, it simply was the "Picture of the Week." It was positioned soon after the contents lineup on a right-hand page. The caption to it was placed on the facing left-hand page, usually under the headline-and-arrow device shown above. The four selections at right sample the range of subjects chosen: human interest, beauty, drama, newsworthiness.

Britain's Queen Mother Mary held her grandchild, Harry, the Duke of Gloucester's son, for christening.

Vera Zorina's performance in the "Ballet of the Elephants" at the circus opening was dedicated to armed forces relief funds.

Scale models, constructed for the magazine by designer Norman Bel Geddes, demonstrated how "the most difficult operation in war," an amphibious landing, is executed.

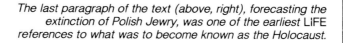

The last paragraph of the text (above, right), forecasting the extinction of Polish Jewry, was one of the earliest LIFE references to what was to become known as the Holocaust.

iness of the magazine was noticeably diminished. But it was not gone: The editors leavened the chronicling of the U.S. military effort with the continuing use of gimmickry, in one instance organizing a feature that made gentle fun of the pain to couples caused by called-to-duty separations (Kisses story, next page).

Churchill posed after addressing the Canadian Parliament.

Her child dead, a Malayan mother and a wounded woman (left) wept after Japanese tank shells struck a Singapore street.

Russians found their guerrilla son, slain by the Germans.

Two Japanese sailors scrambled up the fire-control tower of a destroyer torpedoed by a U.S. submarine.

Postelection, goodwill ambassador Wendell Willkie met Gen. and Mme. Chiang Kai-shek.

CURRENTS AND EVENTS

WORLD: Philippines, Singapore, New Guinea Fall to Japan, 75,000 Allied Prisoners Suffer Bataan Death March • U.S. Pacific Fleet Wiped Out in Java Sea • B-25s Bomb Japan • Coral Sea Victory Blocks Further Japanese Advances • At Midway Japan Loses Four Carriers • U.S. Marines, Army Attack Guadalcanal • Chinese Retake Many Inland Cities, Towns • Nazis Push Toward Volga, Erase Czech Village of Lidice in Reprisal for Resistance • Wehrmacht Grinds to Halt at Stalingrad • Panzers Pushed out of Egyptian Desert • B-17s Hit Rouen in First All-U.S. Bombing of Europe • Eisenhower Leads Invasion of North Africa • French Scuttle Own Fleet • Hitler Adopts "Final Solution": Elimination of All Jews • 26 "United Nations" Sign Anti-Axis Declaration • Mount Etna Erupts • Cyclone Kills 40,000 in Bengal.

OTHER BATTLES: Dieppe Raid • El Alamein • Tobruk • Leningrad Siege • Aleutians.

U.S.A.: Japanese-Americans Forcibly Moved from West Coast Homes to Inland Internment Camps • Unemployment Eases, WPA Ends • Gas Rationing Instituted Nationwide • U-Boats Land Saboteurs on Long Island, Florida Coasts, Six Executed • Alcan Highway Opens • Fire at Boston's Cocoanut Grove Nightclub Kills 493 • Australian-Born Labor Leader Harry Bridges Ordered Deported as Communist Alien • Normandie Burns at N.Y. Pier • Henry Kaiser, Howard Hughes Design Spruce Goose.

FIRSTS: Controlled Nuclear Chain Reaction • V-Mail • V-1 Rocket • Magnetic Recording Tape.

MOVIES: Casablanca • In Which We Serve • Wake Island • Mrs. Miniver • This Above All • Woman of the Year • Random Harvest • The Pride of the Yankees • H. M. Pulham, Esq. • George Washington Slept Here • Bambi • Holiday Inn • Yankee Doodle Dandy • The Road to Morocco.

SONGS: This Is the Army, Mr. Jones • White Christmas • You'd Be So Nice to Come Home To • I Left My Heart at the Stage Door Canteen • Don't Get Around Much Anymore • Paper Doll • I Had the Craziest Dream • Serenade in Blue • That Old Black Magic • Jingle, Jangle, Jingle • Be Careful! It's My Heart • The Lamplighter's Serenade • One Dozen Roses.

STAGE: The Skin of Our Teeth • Porgy and Bess • By Jupiter • This Is the Army • Star and Garter • Rosalinda.

BOOKS: The Moon Is Down (Steinbeck) • See Here, Private Hargrove (Hargrove) • They Were Expendable (W. L. White) • The Last Time I Saw Paris (Paul) • My World and Welcome to It (Thurber) • The Robe (Douglas) • Frenchman's Creek (Du Maurier) • Admiral of the Ocean Sea (Morison) • The Stranger (Camus) • The Company She Keeps (McCarthy).

FADS: Short Hairdos • Clothes Patches • Women's Slacks.

MASS DEATH   ON RED PRISONERS AND POLES

e such murder is shown below. The desperate at left tried to escape and was hung on the ire of the Nazi prison camp as a warning to s inside. On this page are shown corpses of prisoners stripped of their warm clothes by Germans.

terrible prison camps in Poland, notably Biala and the "Uman pit," the wounded are left . At Biala Podlaska, an open field with 150,000 , they die by hundreds daily, making room undreds. Polish civilians who threw bread and or even spoke to the Russians were shot. Pole harbored an escaped Russian, the whole ity was to be exterminated.

ermans give to all this a kind of nightmare on the grounds that "surrounded" Russians vay, already prisoners and ought to stop fight- they emphatically do not stop fighting, they d the sale of the old-fashioned rules for the n of prisoners-of-war.

On Nov. 26 and again on Jan. 7, Soviet Russia formally and violently charged the German Government with a systematic campaign to exterminate Russian prisoners-of-war. The Germans sneered that the Russians were merely trying to boost their soldiers' morale, and the campaign went on. Its effect has been to make the Russian soldier even more reluctant to surrender and it has not improved his attitude toward any German prisoner he may personally take.

Even more atrocious is the German policy toward civilians—Polish, Jewish and Russian. The intent here is to exterminate these "alien" peoples who clutter up *lebensraum* that Germans want. Some 83,000 Poles have been executed by the Nazi conquerors and 1,500,-000 deported to Germany as raw labor, the women as civilian or military prostitutes. Official notices in the *Oßdeutscher Beobachter* required all females between the ages of 14 and 18 in the city of Posen to report to the city employment office. In Poland German Gauleiters Greiser and Frank announced: "Not a single

Pole must remain in the western provinces in ten years' time. . . . Poles can go on living in the Remainder State [of Poland] as second-class people serving the German interests."

The Germans first eliminated potential Polish leaders: doctors, lawyers, professors, intellectuals, the rich and well-born, many of whom had been mildly pro-German before the war. The permissible punishment for violation of any Nazi rule whatever, published or not, was death. The whole population is living on a starvation level, side by side with the well-fed German Army. Some evidences of this are shown on this page.

This methodical massacre takes on an emotional quality of sadism as applied by the Nazis to the Jews. Herded in Polish ghettos, forbidden to walk out or use a railway, machine-gunned in their synagogs, thrown by thousands into the rivers, stripped of clothing and food and possessions, the Jews of Poland are literally dying out. These are the grim statistical facts. The details of human agony are multiplied beyond the telling.

Slow starvation drew tight the skin over this Jewish baby's skull, bloated his belly and finally killed him.

Road of Russian soldier corpses being carted to bur- prisoners have escaped by pretending to be corpses.

Polish dead in Warsaw are checked out methodically by a Polish supervisor. Nazis' idea of posthumous humiliation for Poles is to bury them in Jewish cemeteries after execution.

Advanced hunger is seen on the faces of these Polish children in Warsaw. Notice the yawn of hunger on the boy s, left and the ill-fitting make-shift excuses for clothing on smaller children.

oner was shot by his German guards when he strag- is left face down on the muddy road where he fell.

They died of hunger. Three Polish children and a baby are tumbled together. The bewildered, ceaseless misery of this death is perhaps the most painful way for children to die.

Dead Jews from the Warsaw ghetto are buried in a mass grave. The Jewish ghettos in particular have been swept by terrible epidemics of typhus, cholera and pneumonia, killing thousands.

A kiss was still a kiss, but LIFE demonstrated *definitively the difference* (Vive la . . .) *the girl makes.*

Japanese-Americans who had been removed from the proscribed West Coast "combat zone" carried their luggage, in the teeth of a piercing wind, to their internment barracks in California's Owens Valley. "The Japs," LIFE noted (using the terminology of the day), "commented afterward on the courteous treatment they had received."

SPEAKING OF PICTURES . . .
. . . THESE LIPS SEND KISSES TO U. S. FIGHTING MEN

JANUARY 5, 1942	JANUARY 12, 1942	JANUARY 19, 1942	JANUARY 26, 1942	FEBRUARY 2, 1942	FEBRUARY 9, 1942

FEBRUARY 16, 1942	FEBRUARY 23, 1942	MARCH 2, 1942	MARCH 9, 1942	MARCH 16, 1942	MARCH 23, 1942

MARCH 30, 1942	APRIL 6, 1942	APRIL 13, 1942	APRIL 20, 1942	APRIL 27, 1942	MAY 4, 1942

MAY 11, 1942	MAY 18, 1942	MAY 25, 1942	JUNE 1, 1942	JUNE 8, 1942	JUNE 15, 1942

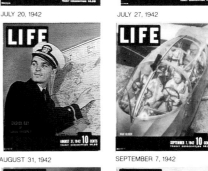

British commandos landed on the crags of Vågsöy, Norway, under fire from "crack German snipers in the hills."

JUNE 22, 1942	JUNE 29, 1942	JULY 6, 1942	JULY 13, 1942	JULY 20, 1942	JULY 27, 1942

AUGUST 3, 1942	AUGUST 10, 1942	AUGUST 17, 1942	AUGUST 24, 1942	AUGUST 31, 1942	SEPTEMBER 7, 1942

SEPTEMBER 14, 1942	SEPTEMBER 21, 1942	SEPTEMBER 28, 1942	OCTOBER 5, 1942	OCTOBER 12, 1942	OCTOBER 19, 1942	OCTOBER 26, 1942	NOVEMBER 2, 1942

NOVEMBER 9, 1942	NOVEMBER 16, 1942	NOVEMBER 23, 1942	NOVEMBER 30, 1942	DECEMBER 7, 1942	DECEMBER 14, 1942	DECEMBER 21, 1942	DECEMBER 28, 1942

1943

Matchless resources produced a landmark story that foreshadowed great sequels—one in granite

With Americans fighting on three continents, and no end in sight, the editors racked their talents to find new ways, photographic and otherwise, to bring the cataclysm home to readers—and to deliver the home theater to the warriors abroad. They dug up childhood photos of new war heroes, commissioned leading artists to paint combat scenes, reported on a typical Sunday in America and on what life was like for women whose husbands were POWs. And 38 years before the national Vietnam Veterans Memorial was designed, LIFE utilized the crushing weight of numbers to measure freedom's cost by printing, unillustrated, an overwhelming casualty list.

A National Guard company at Kasserine Pass lost 23 men from Red Oak, Iowa. LIFE visited the town and showed where every one of them lived. Many of the missing later turned up as POWs.

WAR HITS RED OAK

A small prairie town gets word that 23 of its boys are missing in action after a battle in North Africa

In North Africa in February, the Axis armies turned suddenly and heavily on American soldiers at Fahl, pushed them back past Kasserine. Before they were stopped, Nazis had overwhelmed and engulfed one whole National Guard company.

In Red Oak, Iowa, a few weeks later, the story of what had happened to the company fell suddenly and heavily on the population, which is less than 6,000. Twenty-three of the boys were from Red Oak. The casualty list set them all down as "missing in action."

For the people in Red Oak, it wasn't just a casualty list. Looking at the names they could see a picture of their town. Each name meant a certain person who lived in a specific house. Kenneth Abraham was Ken Abraham who lived over the "Gr..."

26

LOUISIANA ____ CONTINUED

STARKS
Fountain, Earnest Cecil
SULPHUR
O'Quain, John G.
TALLULAH
Jones, Thomas R.
TANGIPAHOA
Davis, John Quitman
THIBODAUX
Vicknair, Andrew W.
TICKFAW
Faller, Clarence
TORO
McNeely, Herman M.
TROUT
Yeager, Richard O.
VARNADO
Beatty, James Alfred
Temples, Houston

VIDALIA
Burke, Glover J., Jr.
VINTON
Arledge, Eston
Stoddard, William E.
VIVIAN
Holland, Thomas J.
WEST MONROE
Beauman, Harlan H.
Grant, Boyd Sutcliff
Hislop, William
Johnson, Thomas M.
WESTWEGO
Fontenot, Elmo
WINNSBORO
Bell, Marion F.
Smith, Victor

MAINE

ALFRED
Gay, Harold
Tibbetts, H. K., Jr.
AUBURN
Hanscom, Bertram A.
AUGUSTA
Cummings, Fred W.
Gagnon, Paul E.
Guerrette, Philip
Mason, Emerson E.
Penton, Thomas J.
BANGOR
Coffin, John L., Jr.
Fernald, Percy E.
Orr, Willard C.
Snodgrass, James A.
BATH
Dobbins, Richard Henry
BETHEL
Allen, Stanley W.

LEWISTON
Dionne, Joseph N. R.
LINCOLN
Savage, Harold O.
LITTLE DEER ISLE
Hutchinson, W. T., Jr.
MADAWASKA
Matthews, William E.
MADISON
Belanger, Maurice A.
Robichaud, Joseph W.
MILLINOCKET
D'Agostino, Joseph A.
Elliott, Francis Ernest
MILO
Hatt, Edward
MONMOUTH
Bonin, Ferdinand R.
MORRILL
Lucas, Donald O.

KENNEDYVILLE
Naundorf, Ralph L.
LANHAM
Bryan, Hugh M.
LINTHICUM
Lowe, Lionel L.
LINWOOD
Black, George W.
LITTLE ORLEANS
Swain, Elmer T.
LUCERNE
Hahn, Walter R.
MARYLANDPARK
Parker, Harry L.
McDANIEL
Scott, Charles B.
MECHANICSVILLE
Hayden, Albert Eugene
MIDDLE RIVER
Phinney, Nelson
MIDLAND
Allen, Joseph Bernard
MONKTON
Hamilton, Leonard
MOUNT AIRY
Poole, Roger W.
MOUNT RAINIER
Dobbins, Lawrence S.
NAYLOR
Richards, James A.
OCEAN CITY
Townsend, Linwood E.
RASPEBURG
Frese, Paul H., Jr.

MASSAC

ADAMS
Marsden, Nelson Adolph
ALLSTON
Taylor, Zenas R.
Walsh, Paul E.
AMESBURY
Landry, James J., Jr.
Zagranis, Lawrence C.
ANDOVER

For Independence Day the editors listed every U.S. serviceman killed in the first 18 months of the war. Magnified (left) is one area of the 24 pages devoted to 12,987 names.

JANUARY 4, 1943

JANUARY 11, 1943

JANUARY 18, 1943

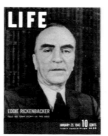
JANUARY 25, 1943

FEBRUARY 1, 1943

FEBRUARY 8, 1943

FEBRUARY 15, 1943

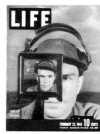
FEBRUARY 22, 1943

APRIL 26, 1943

MAY 3, 1943

MAY 10, 1943

MAY 17, 1943

MAY 24, 1943

MAY 31, 1943

JUNE 7, 1943

JUNE 14, 1943

"..." in the middle of town. John Grove was the one who lived on Fifth Street. ... addresses had a double sadness. Mae Stife on Corning Street lost two sons, ... Frank and Private Dan. Her daughter Marie lost her husband, Darrell ... Gillespies on Second Street counted two sons lost—Charles, 22, and Frank, ... Duane Dodd and his cousins, the Halbert boys, were missing. ... news was a sharp crack on the chin to Red Oak. Everybody knew somebody ... the missing list. But the town rolled with the punch, came back grim and reso... Casualty lists aren't new to Red Oak. In the last war all but a dozen of this ... many were gassed, wounded or killed. The dead are buried in the cemetery, hid... by the trees at the upper left of above picture. This time the company was in the

first U. S. contingent in Northern Ireland and North Africa. On the way to Africa its ship was torpedoed; Some of the boys were in the regimental band and Dennis Smith lost his baton—he was drum major—and Dale Thompson lost his piccolo. So when they got to Africa, they had nothing to do but fight.

Last week, spring wandered into Red Oak. The wrens were bustling about their nesting business. The children were playing hopscotch on the sidewalks. The red oaks, which give the town its name, were covered with their first pale leaves. With spring, came better news. The Red Oak casualty list got more specific. The ominous term "missing in action" was clarified. Instead of having been killed, many of the boys had been taken prisoner. Last week, Red Oak was feeling a little less grim.

27

   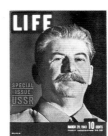  

MARCH 1, 1943   MARCH 8, 1943   MARCH 15, 1943   MARCH 22, 1943   MARCH 29, 1943   APRIL 5, 1943   APRIL 12, 1943   APRIL 19, 1943

JUNE 21, 1943   JUNE 28, 1943   JULY 5, 1943   JULY 12, 1943   JULY 19, 1943   JULY 26, 1943   AUGUST 2, 1943   AUGUST 9, 1943

CLASSIC PHOTOS

A friendly New Guinea native guided a blinded Aussie to an aid station.

All-time favorite pinup Chili Williams drew 100,000 letters.

One of the first pictures of U.S. dead released by censors showed three GIs on Buna.

CURRENTS AND EVENTS

WORLD: Allies Attack Japanese-Held Burma, Pound New Guinea, New Britain, Timor • Guadalcanal Falls to U.S. Forces • Chinese Stem Japanese Offensive, Add Support to Allied Invasion of Burma • Tarawa Retaken After Most Costly Military Operation in U.S. History • Von Paulus Surrenders at Stalingrad • Germans Take Kharkov • Triumph at Kursk, in War's Greatest Tank Battle, Gives Soviets Strategic Edge • Red Forces Recapture Smolensk, Kiev • Aleutians in U.S. Hands Again • Allies Bomb Ruhr Cities Round-the-Clock • Afrika Korps Surrenders Unconditionally • Africa-Based Allied Forces Overrun Sicily • Disgraced Duce Resigns, Placed Under House Arrest • U.S., British Troops Land on Mainland Italy • New Italian Government Declares War on Germany • Nazi Paratroopers Rescue Mussolini • FDR, Churchill Meet in Casablanca, Follow Up with Chiang in Cairo, Stalin in Tehran • Mexico, Brazil, Bolivia Declare War on Axis Powers.

OTHER BATTLES: Salerno • Kasserine Pass • Bizerte • Buna • Bougainville.

U.S.A.: FDR Orders U.S. Share Nuclear Know-how with Britain • Government Seizes Mines Closed by Strikers • 34 Die in Detroit Race Riots • Jefferson Memorial Dedicated.

FIRSTS: Five-Star Generals • Aqua-lung • Air-to-Surface Guided Missile (Luftwaffe, against HMS Egret) • Postal-Zone Numbering • Streptomycin • Income-Tax Withholding.

MOVIES: So Proudly We Hail • This Is the Army • Stage Door Canteen • Watch on the Rhine • For Whom the Bell Tolls • The Human Comedy • The Outlaw • Song of Bernadette • My Friend Flicka • DuBarry Was a Lady.

SONGS: Comin' In on a Wing and a Prayer • Gertie from Bizerte • Pistol-Packin' Mama • Oh What a Beautiful Mornin' • People Will Say We're in Love • The Surrey with the Fringe on Top • Everything's Up to Date in Kansas City • Oklahoma! • Do Nothin' Till You Hear from Me • Bésame Mucho • You'll Never Know • Holiday for Strings • I Couldn't Sleep a Wink Last Night • I'll Be Seeing You • Sunday, Monday or Always • A Lovely Way to Spend an Evening • Speak Low • They're Either Too Young or Too Old • Shoo Shoo Baby • Tico-Tico • Mairzy Doats.

STAGE: Tomorrow the World • The Voice of the Turtle • Kiss and Tell • The Two Mrs. Carrolls • Othello (Robeson) • Oklahoma! • One Touch of Venus • Something for the Boys • Carmen Jones • Winged Victory.

BOOKS: One World (Willkie) • The Fountainhead (Rand) • The Apostle (Asch) • The Human Comedy (Saroyan) • A Tree Grows in Brooklyn (Smith) • Journey in the Dark (Flavin) • Guadalcanal Diary (Tregaskis) • Being and Nothingness (Sartre).

FADS: Women's Sweaters (for all occasions) • Reflective Dim-Out Anklets • His-and-Her Bow Ties.

AUGUST 16, 1943   AUGUST 23, 1943   AUGUST 30, 1943   SEPTEMBER 6, 1943   SEPTEMBER 13, 1943

In 1900 Sarah West, of Salem, Oreg., removed a splinter from a little boy named Tam. LIFE ran the photo as a 1943 Picture of the Week because Tam, full name Thomas Gatch, had become commander of a battleship that sank four Japanese warships and downed 32 planes in the Pacific.

Lest servicemen around the world be deprived of the "Big Red," an ad-less Overseas Service Edition was sent to all theaters of war.

Charlie Chaplin, 54, slipped a wedding ring ("fumblingly," the magazine reported) on his fourth bride, playwright Eugene O'Neill's daughter Oona, 18.

SEPTEMBER 20, 1943

SEPTEMBER 27, 1943

OCTOBER 4, 1943

OCTOBER 11, 1943

OCTOBER 18, 1943

OCTOBER 25, 1943

NOVEMBER 1, 1943

NOVEMBER 8, 1943

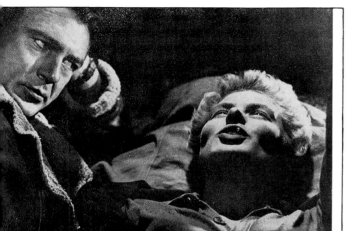

MOVIE OF THE WEEK:
For Whom The Bell Tolls

The stars of the movie are Gary Cooper as Robert Jordan and Ingrid Bergman as Maria. In this sequence which takes place in a sleeping bag outside the guerrillas' cave, Maria speaks of her happiness and pledges her love to Jordan. Love scenes play a predominant part in *For Whom The Bell Tolls*, contain much of the original Hemingway dialogue, have been handled with delicacy.

Last week the premiere of the Technicolor movie version of Ernest Hemingway's best-seller *For Whom The Bell Tolls* took place in New York City. Not since *Gone With The Wind* has there been so much pre-release discussion about a movie. For the three years that it has been in the making there has been talk about: 1) the casting of the film, 2) its political implication and 3) the sleeping-bag scene (*see above*). Now that the movie is released the discussion will not stop. Although it has been publicized as "one of the greatest movies of all time," *For Whom The Bell Tolls* is hardly that. To most it will be a good picture that for various reasons misses being a great one. The chief complaint will be the length of the movie. Running for almost three hours it becomes tiring, lacks a natural humor and more than once becomes self-conscious.

Hemingway's book grew out of his experiences in Spain in 1937-1938 when he was

The guerrilla band rushes out of their cave hide-out as a flight of planes drones overhead. Spotting them as German and Italian planes, they take cover under the overhanging ledges of rock.

Guerrilla Leader Pilar, when in ugly but "much woman," fights as well as the men. Here she uses a pile of logs as a shield while shooting a Nationalist guard during the battle for the bridge.

Not all the weekly movies were blockbusters like this one.

Pitch-in supper achieves degree of formality by use of best linen and candles. After it was over, Doris Hosmer (*lower right*), guest of honor, cheerfully lent a hand with the dishes.

D. A. M. S. E. Ls prepare for the night (*above*) with conscientious cold-creaming and hairbrushing, following an evening of lively jitterbugging and quieter bridge. But wait—they aren't in bed yet.

Life Goes to a Slumber Party

Indianapolis D.A.M.S.E.L. club welcomes a new member with a pillow fight

Pillow fight begins as someone inadvertently mentions bed. Top of the heap in this pile-up is Julie Gerlach. Others (*reading downward*) are Beverly Potts and Phyllis Hobbs.

Patty Rice takes aim on bended knee as she defends herself against frontal attack. She is club president and daughter of Shortridge High's vice-principal. Spotted pajamas belong to Phyllis Hobbs.

The slumber party is an old and honored institution among girls in their teens. It answers the need for gregarious interchange of ideas and gossip in the intimate setting of the boudoir.

In Indianapolis there are more than 25 high-school clubs to keep this interesting custom alive. They bear such names as K.W.A.K., Hi-Jinx, A.L.A.S., T.A.B.U.

LIFE would go to any party that promised lively pictures.

PICTURES TO THE EDITORS

Readers' pictures tended to be oddball, such as this one of a cow that poked into a barrel of apples.

NOVEMBER 15, 1943

NOVEMBER 22, 1943

NOVEMBER 29, 1943

DECEMBER 6, 1943

DECEMBER 13, 1943

DECEMBER 20, 1943

DECEMBER 27, 1943

For centuries painters had used eyewitness accounts to reconstruct, usually well after the fact, historic battle scenes. After the camera's invention, dependence on such art diminished rapidly. However, in addition to the outstanding contributions of their own photographers, the tradition-minded U.S. armed services used the tal-

THESE ARTISTS PAINTED EXPERIENCE BY BATTLE

MITCHELL JAMIESON

The invasion of Sicily was painted by Lieut. Mitchell Jamieson (right). Jamieson himself was one of the first to set foot on Sicilian shore from an LST, like the one shown on page 78, in the early hours of dawn on July 10. He went along on this expedition as official artist-reporter for the U. S. Navy.

In 1939 Jamieson was a struggling artist in Washington, D. C., working as a night watchman at the Corcoran Gallery of Art and painting by day. He was still a night watchman when the Section of Fine Arts discovered him and commissioned him to paint a mural for the Marlboro, Md. Post Office. Later he painted a mural for the Willard, Ohio post office and another for the Department of Interior Building. In turn, the Navy discovered Mitchell Jamieson, in 1942 commissioned him to paint action pictures of the Navy at war.

DWIGHT SHEPLER

Sitting on the deck of the cruiser Santa Cruz (pp. 52, 53) is Navy's official artist Lieut. Dwight Shepler of Everett, Mass. with one of his sketches of the U.S.S. South Dakota. Like all other Navy artists, Shepler is a trained seaman as well as painter. He was serving as deck officer during the heat of the Battle of Santa Cruz when his ship was hit by a Jap bomb which went through the cruiser's fantail and exploded below. Immediately after the fight Shepler went on duty as an artist to record the scenes of the battle. Six weeks later he made his eyewitness records of Guadalcanal (pp. 50, 51). Before the war Dwight Shepler shipped out to sea as a mate and assistant navigator on a schooner that was bound for the Galapagos Islands. Then, too, he painted when not on active duty, just as he is doing today.

FLOYD DAVIS

LIFE readers are already familiar with the work of Floyd Davis who painted the famous canvases of "Bermuda at War" (LIFE, Sept. 21, 1942). Last May LIFE again called upon this artist to report in art on what England looks like during the war. Upon his arrival there Davis visited the American Eighth Air Force Bomber Command and found the fliers in the midst of preparations for a raid on Hamburg. Davis hung around and made sketches. When, on the morning of July 25, a great armada of more than 250 planes flew across the channel in America's first raid on Hamburg, Floyd Davis was on one of the Fortresses. What he saw is reproduced on pages 68 and 69. Returning safely to England he then set to work on his real assignment—the painting of England itself at war. These will appear in a later issue of LIFE.

PAUL SAMPLE

Last March Paul Sample left his wife and child in New Hampshire for his fourth trip as war artist-correspondent for LIFE. He had already done paintings on board an aircraft carrier in the Atlantic and a series of canvases on naval aviation (LIFE, Jan. 4). This time Sample set out for the Pacific to paint an American submarine base. There Sample, like his fellow artist Floyd Davis, embarked on a secret mission—submarine patrol in the Central Pacific. He was the only reporter on board. From quick notes and sketches made in the cramped quarters of the sub during this trip he later developed the paintings on pages 54-59. Upon returning safely to the U. S. in June he completed his current war-reporting jobs for LIFE. Paul Sample asked for leave of absence from his regular peaceful duties as Artist-in-Residence at Dartmouth College in Hanover N.H. where he has been painting since 1938.

AARON BOHROD

The paintings of jungle fighting on Rendova Island in New Georgia were done by Aaron Bohrod last August while the actual battle was still going on. Bohrod was in one of the first boatloads that hit the beaches of Rendova in the face of Jap fire. There, like every other soldier, he had to dig his own foxhole and fight for cover. And there, living in the jap tent shown at right, he painted his stirring pictures of this great campaign.

Bohrod left his home in Chicago to go on this assignment as artist for the War Department, returned as LIFE's correspondent when the War Department's project was ended last June. Recently appointed Artist-in-Residence at Southern Illinois Normal University, he has asked for leave of absence to continue reporting the war for LIFE. He is now preparing to set out on another assignment.

FLETCHER MARTIN

Sitting on the wreckage of a Nazi tank near Mateur in North Africa, Fletcher Martin is shown here making one of his sketches which he later used in developing his paintings of the North African campaign. As war artist-correspondent for LIFE Martin arrived at Casablanca just as the Germans began to fall back before American and British armies. He followed the battle to Algiers, Tunis, Cape Bon and Mateur. At Mateur he was the only correspondent to report the spectacular story of the critical assault on Hill 609 by two platoons of American troops. Returning to the U. S. in June he completed his canvases and painted the picture of the wounded soldier reproduced on the cover. The original painting of this is now on exhibition in New York's Midtown Galleries where Fletcher Martin is having his second one-man show.

Six artists contributed to the year-end collection.

"BOMBARDMENT—GUADALCANAL."

"ACTION ON THE RIVER."

GUADALCANAL: THE JAP

Paintings of the Solomons campaign by Navy Lieut. Dwight Shepler reflect the feelings of our fighters toward their fierce enemy

"TORPEDOED."

Navy Lt. Dwight Shepler was on Guadalcanal six weeks after his cruiser was hit.

NORTH AFRICA: REAR

"ALGIERS DOMINO"

STREAM CROSSING.

LIFE's Fletcher Martin followed as U.S., British troops halted the Afrika Korps.

HILL 609

THIS IS HILL 609 FROM THE SOUTHEAST, A GRAY, INDISPUTABLE OBJECTIVE WHICH PROVED TO BE THE KEY TO BIZERTE.

FIRST LIEUT. MARVIN A. GOOD, 28. SECOND LIEUT. FRANCIS J. KENYON, 26. SECOND LIEUT. FRANK COCKETT, 28. SECOND LIEUT. ALDEN L. HARDY, 21. SECOND LIEUT. ELDON WILSON, 25.

Martin caught the emotional cost of the fight for "the key to Bizerte."

RENDOVA: THE JUNGLE

Aaron Bohrod's paintings of the first landings in New Georgia bring home the darkness, the rot, the confusion and the fears of fighting in a primeval world

"BRINGING IN THE AMMO."

"THE LANDING."

"UNLOADING BARRACKS BAG."

LIFE's Aaron Bohrod landed with the first troops to hit Rendova, New Georgia.

"WOUNDED PRISONER."

"RENDOVA RENDEZVOUS."

"NEW GEORGIA SKY."

Bohrod looked up to a clean and distant war, and close by, to bloody hell.

ents of on-the-scene artists-in-uniform to record, with a subjective and interpretive eye, the panoramas of war. LIFE also recognized the value of such coverage and commissioned some of America's finest painters as its own artist-correspondents. They, too, had official access to combat areas and carried simulated officer rank.

The result, as LIFE correspondent John Hersey wrote in the introduction to a portfolio of their work published in the year's last issue: "Very little war art has had such authenticity as this. . . . What is important in [these] pictures is not their technique, their design or their content, but the careful blend of these things which is mood."

LIFE's Paul Sample was the only reporter aboard a U.S. sub on secret patrol.

Sample's art was painted from notes and sketches made aboard the sub.

LIFE's Floyd Davis boarded a B-17 for the first U.S. raid on Hamburg.

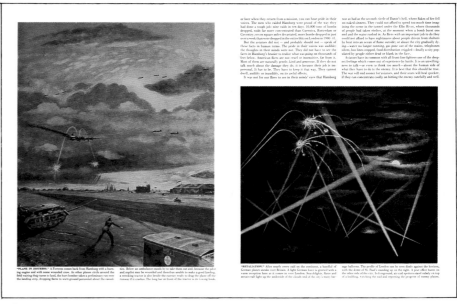

Davis then returned for his real assignment: painting England at war.

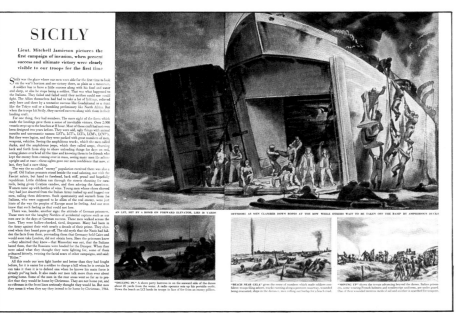

Navy Lt. Mitchell Jamieson boarded an LST to land early on the shore of Sicily.

The editors chose artist Martin's work to show how sketches became final art.

1944

It was the pivotal year of the war, and heroic photographers covered the action magnificently

"The most sobering fore-fact of 1944 is death. This is the last year on earth for a lot of American young men." So went LIFE's first editorial of the new year. (Editorials were now a weekly feature.) And the fact also darkened the magazine's tone. Most of the best photographers had

Amid devastating German fire, while still wading with the first wave through shallow-water obstacles, Robert Capa snapped away. These historic photos were from his initial take.

CURRENTS AND EVENTS

WORLD: U.S. Hits Japan's Home Islands, Wins Decisive Battle in Philippine Sea • Tojo Resigns • Stilwell Leads Joint U.S.-Chinese Force to Victories in Burma • Red Army Lifts 880-Day Siege of Leningrad, Retakes Odessa, Crimea • Allies Land at Anzio en Route to Rome • Huge Allied Invasion Force Lands on Normandy Beaches, Patton Cuts Off Germans in Brittany • V-bombs Fall on London • Allies Invade Southern France • Paris Liberated by Resistance, Free French • Allied Airborne Troops Seize Holland Bridges • Massive German Counterattack Drives "Bulge" in U.S. Lines, Cuts Off Bastogne Garrison • Hitler Escapes Assassination by Reichswehr Officers • U.S., Britain, U.S.S.R., China Convene at Dumbarton Oaks to Set Up UN • El Salvador Quells Army Revolt in 48 Hours.

OTHER BATTLES: Cherbourg • St. Lo • Arnhem • Aachen • Ardennes • Huertgen Forest • Monte Cassino • Eniwetok • Marshalls • Saipan • Guam • Leyte.

U.S.A.: FDR Tours Pacific War Zone • U.S. Repeals Chinese Exclusion Act • Simplified-Tax Bill Enacted • FDR Wins Fourth Term with Truman as V.P.

FIRSTS: Rocket Airplane • Eye Bank • Black State Department Official (Ralph Bunche).

MOVIES: Destination Tokyo • The White Cliffs of Dover • See Here, Private Hargrove • The Purple Heart • Gaslight • Lifeboat • Jane Eyre • Double Indemnity • National Velvet • Since You Went Away • To Have and Have Not • Laura • Dragon Seed • Up in Arms • Lady in the Dark • Going My Way • Meet Me in St. Louis • Cover Girl.

SONGS: Lili Marlene • Long Ago and Far Away • Sentimental Journey • Spring Will Be a Little Late This Year • It Could Happen to You • I'll Walk Alone • Swinging on a Star • Dream • I Should Care • Twilight Time • Don't Fence Me In • Rum and Coca-Cola • Ac-cent-tchu-ate the Positive • Strange Music (Grieg).

STAGE: Harvey • Ten Little Indians • Anna Lucasta • Chicken Every Sunday • Jacobowsky and the Colonel • The Late George Apley • I Remember Mama • Dear Ruth • Seven Lively Arts • Mexican Hayride • Song of Norway • Bloomer Girl • On the Town • Follow the Girls • Catherine Was Great.

BOOKS: A Bell for Adano (Hersey) • The Razor's Edge (Maugham) • Forever Amber (Winsor) • Brave Men (Pyle) • The Lost Weekend (Jackson) • Dangling Man (Bellow) • Freedom Road (Fast) • Yankee from Olympus (Drinker Bowen) • Strange Fruit (Smith) • Immortal Wife (Stone) • The Building of Jalna (de la Roche).

FADS: I.D. Bracelets • Hair Ribbons (to signal love-life status) • Skimpy Bathing Suits (to save material).

CLASSIC PHOTOS

Shamed and shorn in punishment, a Frenchwoman carried her German-sired child amid neighbors' taunts.

Marshal Tito took a phone call at his secret HQ in Yugoslavia.

gone off to war. The light touch was all but eliminated from home-front pictures; even images of pretty girls were few and far between. There were spectacular photographs of cities being bombed, ships sunk, beaches littered with dead. Then came D-Day, and the young men wading to-ward death were pictured from their midst by photographer Robert Capa. Thereafter men armed only with cameras strove to join the first troops on every beachhead. Capa defined their passion for all time: "If your pictures aren't good enough, you aren't close enough."

A week after D-Day, Allied barrage balloons floated protectively over busy Omaha Beach. The photograph was taken by Frank Scherschel.

Our World-Wide War: France (continued)

A week after first landings, the Normandy beachhead had changed from a battlefield to a gigantic port area. Allies had captured small fishing ports like Ouistreham and Isigny, but the beach was still the best place to land reinforcements, equipment and supplies. A great fleet of heavyweight landing craft, forced to remain offshore on first day, came in close to unload. LST's, however, still could not get right up to the beach. Gentle slope of the continental shelf off the Norman shore usually grounded them about 50 yards out. Two LST's which appear under big barrage balloon in the foreground are in this predicament. This busy scene was photographed by LIFE's Frank Scherschel. Barrage balloons which fill sky over supply fleet are moored too low for protection against high-level bombers or dive bombers, but would mean trouble for planes making low-level strafing runs. Balloon in foreground is tethered to windlass on slope. Along the beach are a few landing craft sunk in the first landings. Water, now at high tide, covers obstacles which barred path to the shore on June 6. At left center an amphibious truck winds up road from the beach. In left foreground is casemate which commanded this stretch during landings. The impressive variety of this scene, repeated for 60 miles, was described for United Features last week by Scripps-Howard Correspondent Ernie Pyle: "I walked for a mile and a half along the water's edge of our many-miled invasion beach. . . . You could see trucks tipped half over and swamped. You could see partly sunken barges, and the angled-up corners of jeeps, and small landing craft half submerged. And at low tide you could still see those vicious six-pronged iron snares that helped snag and wreck them. . . . There were boats stacked on top of each other, their sides caved in, their suspension doors knocked off. In this shore-line museum of carnage there were abandoned rolls of barbed wire and smashed bulldozers and big stacks of thrown-away lifebelts and piles of shells still waiting to be moved. In the water floated empty life rafts and soldiers' packs and ration boxes, and mysterious oranges. On the beach lay, expended, sufficient men and mechanism for a small war. . . . And yet we could afford it."

CONTINUED ON NEXT PAGE 27
CONTINUED ON NEXT PAGE 29

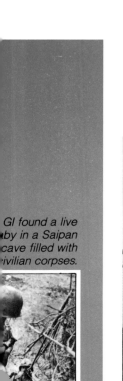

GI found a live baby in a Saipan cave filled with civilian corpses.

After the West Point graduation ceremony, held coincidentally on June 6, D-Day, Mamie Eisenhower and her brand-new 2nd Lt. son John turned to the radio for news of the invasion.

MARK CLARK RIDES PAST ST. PETER'S IN ROME WITH GENERALS GRUENTHER AND KEYES IN THREE-STAR JEEP

THE TAKING OF ROME
ALLIED TROOPS SEE THE SIGHTS OF THE ANCIENT CITY

The fall of Rome on June 4 was almost immediately overshadowed by the events on the western shore of Festung Europa. But the offensive that, beginning May 11, had swept 130 miles up Italy and pulverized the German Tenth and Fourteenth Armies was an achievement and omen too portentous to be overlooked. Slugging toe to toe with the Germans, the Americans with Britons, Canadians, Frenchmen, Italians, Czechs and Poles had thrown the Germans into a rout that an allied spokesman called a "catastrophe." The strange sight of the Americans capturing the city that was once the center of the world, the *Caput Mundi*, is seen on the following pages in the pictures by LIFE Photographers John Phillips, Carl Mydans and George Silk. On June 8 Lieut. General Mark Clark had a 10-minute audience with the Pope who had declared from the balcony of St. Peter's, "Rome has been spared. This day will go down in the annals of Rome." The city was safe, virtually untouched by battle. But the cities south of it had seen hard fighting and the disintegration of the German Army (pages 92-95). Last week the American offensive roared north of Rome, apparently hell-bent for Florence.

CONTINUED ON NEXT PAGE 87

Led by a jeepload of brass, the Fifth Army rolled past St. Peter's. This big story was overshadowed by D-Day.

JANUARY 3, 1944

JANUARY 10, 1944

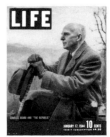

JANUARY 17, 1944

When editor-author Henry Seidel Canby chose the 100 foremost books of 1924-44, LIFE collected them all for a picture.

A GI "liberator" of Chartres got a grateful kiss. Back in the U.S. photos like this infuriated wives and sweethearts.

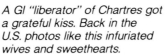

Noticeably thinner, FDR acknowledged cheers for his fourth-term victory from neighbors in Hyde Park, N.Y. Henry Luce was to express regret that LIFE had not, before the election, called attention to the President's failing health.

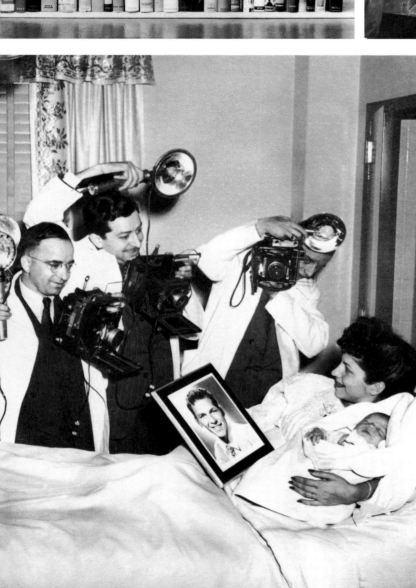

Frank Sinatra Jr., in the arms of mother Nancy, never opened his mouth during his first press conference in Jersey City, N.J., at the age of 18 hours. He weighed in at a hefty 8 lb. 13 oz.

Sensitive to the morale of servicemen and civilians, many advertisers "war-angled" pitches for their products.

The Army Air Force's first jet, the *Bell P-59*, was the frontispiece for a three-page explication of the principles of jet propulsion.

This historic picture, of the first blacks ever commissioned as Navy officers, was headlined *"First Negro Ensigns."* The term *"black,"* considered pejorative, was unacceptable until the 1960s.

JANUARY 24, 1944

JANUARY 31, 1944

FEBRUARY 7, 1944

FEBRUARY 14, 1944

FEBRUARY 21, 1944

FEBRUARY 28, 1944

MARCH 6, 1944

MARCH 13, 1944

MARCH 20, 1944

MARCH 27, 1944

APRIL 3, 1944

APRIL 10, 1944

APRIL 17, 1944

APRIL 24, 1944

MAY 1, 1944

MAY 8, 1944

MAY 15, 1944

MAY 22, 1944

MAY 29, 1944

JUNE 5, 1944

JUNE 12, 1944

JUNE 19, 1944

JUNE 26, 1944

JULY 3, 1944

JULY 10, 1944

JULY 17, 1944

JULY 24, 1944

JULY 31, 1944

AUGUST 7, 1944

AUGUST 14, 1944

AUGUST 21, 1944

AUGUST 28, 1944

SEPTEMBER 4, 1944

SEPTEMBER 11, 1944

SEPTEMBER 18, 1944

SEPTEMBER 25, 1944

OCTOBER 2, 1944

OCTOBER 9, 1944

OCTOBER 16, 1944

OCTOBER 23, 1944

OCTOBER 30, 1944

NOVEMBER 6, 1944

NOVEMBER 13, 1944

NOVEMBER 20, 1944

NOVEMBER 27, 1944

DECEMBER 4, 1944

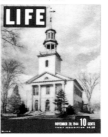
DECEMBER 11, 1944

DECEMBER 18, 1944

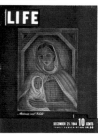
DECEMBER 25, 1944

1945

A chain of historic events challenged the staff to record them well. The challenge was met

The war's final year was a kaleidoscope of great events. The conflict ended—two conflicts, really, the one in Europe in May and Japan's Armageddon in August—and on the way to those epochal victories President Roosevelt died, Hitler committed suicide and the Atomic Age was ushered in with the explosion of the world's first nuclear bomb. Long before V-J Day, Americans began to scent victory, and things began to pop once more on the home front. Along with the images of history LIFE ran more and more of the kinds of stories that made its prewar mix so successful: packages packed with startling pictures and fascinating information. Its photographers came home from the various theaters of war to picture not generals and admirals but favorites old and new: Marlene, Ingrid, Bing, the first black ballplayer in the majors and a movie star not yet known to all the world simply as Liz.

THE END IN NORTH GERMANY came on the heath of Lüneburg where Admiral Hans-Georg von Friedeburg, commander of German navy (*facing camera*), surrendered 600,-000 men in Germany, Holland, Denmark. His face still showing signs of weeping, the admiral heard Field Marshal Montgomery (*in beret*) read acceptance of surrender into a microphone.

THE WAR ENDS IN EUROPE

At 2:41 A.M. on Monday, May 7, the German army surrendered. This was the moment the world had waited for through 2,076 days of war. This was the moment of victory.

It came at the end of an incredible week. Each day the sun, rising over Europe in the east, looked down on the earth below and saw new climaxes. Moving westward, it saw first the people of Russia turbulent with such joy and relief as no great mass of people has ever known so suddenly. It saw the last bitter struggles in the hills of Czechoslovakia, where German rear guards ironically fought off one enemy so that their main force could flee to the less-dreaded mercy of another enemy. When the sun came over Germany it was a wonder that it did not stand still, as it did for Joshua when he battled the Amorites, for it saw events there which blotted out one function of the sun: the marking of time. The age of science, the 20th Century, the present time vanished. Instead there were images from Attila's times—men starved to death in prison enclosures, murdered, burned up in vindictive, final panics. There was an image from Wagner's myths: a blazing room in the Reich Chancellery in Berlin, a pyre for a fake god who may or may not have been consumed in flames. There was a flashback to Shakespeare: a tent on the blustery, rain-swept heath of Lüneburg where Montgomery, a man capable of Shakespearean fustian, said as he prepared to accept a surrender, "This is the moment!"—and then addressed the vanquished emissaries when they approached as if they were annoying intruders on an unknown errand, "What do you want?"

Down in Italy the sun saw a tyrant hanging by his heels beside a woman to whose underclothes a locket was pinned with an inscription from the tyrant, "I am you and you are I"—an upside-down dictator groping for identity with a dead mistress in a crazy world. At the meridian called Zero the sun looked down on a London scarred by most complicated and evil inventions and on a stoic people at last released in victory. Beyond the ocean the sun saw a vast, productive country unsure what "victory" meant but joyous, noisy and hopeful; and on the western rim of the continent a parley of men squabbling over details when the future of humanity should have been in their throats. Out across the waters toward the end of its circling the sun came to a green island named Okinawa, where other men were fighting some more.

27

The glorious news from Europe was tempered with the warning that men still fought on "a green island named Okinawa."

THIS DRAWING SHOWS MORE GRAPHICALLY THAN AERIAL PHOTOGRAPHS (PP. 26-27) EFFECT OF ATOMIC BOMB HIT ON HIROSHIMA. SMOKE BILLOWS 40,000 FEET

WAR'S ENDING

ATOMIC BOMB AND SOVIET ENTRY BRING JAP SURRENDER OFFER

The war against Japan was finally coming to an end last week. On Aug. 5 the first atomic bomb was let loose on Hiroshima (*see pp. 30-31*). On Aug. 8 Russia declared war on and attacked Japan. Same day, the second atomic bomb fell, this one on Nagasaki.

On Friday, Aug. 10, the Tokyo radio broadcast an appeal for peace. Even before the official note had reached Washington through neutral channels, President Truman summoned his top military advisers to discuss the offer. The Japs, who in mid-July had vainly asked the Russians to mediate the Pacific war, now agreed to the Potsdam ultimatum, with one condition. They wanted Emperor Hirohito (*see p. 35D*) to retain his sovereignty and "prerogatives." A day of wild speculation and mild celebration followed while the President communicated by phone with Chungking, Moscow and London. The U. S., which had taken the lead in the negotiations, answered for all the Big Four. On Saturday morning Aug. 11 Secretary of State Byrnes sent a note to Tokyo accepting the Jap offer with the stipulation that the Supreme Allied Military Commander, presumably General of the Army Douglas MacArthur, rule Japan through the authority of the Emperor.

The people of the world, although thrilled by the prospect of peace, were shaken by the new weapon (*see p. 87B*), which had brought it about. Even General Carl Spaatz, whose airmen dropped the bombs, said hopefully, "Wouldn't it be an odd thing if these were the only two atomic bombs ever dropped?"

25

After the A-bombs hit Hiroshima and Nagasaki, but before officials released actual photos of the explosions, the editors stayed abreast of the historic news by employing an artist to illustrate the havoc.

JANUARY 1, 1945

JANUARY 8, 1945

JANUARY 15, 1945

JANUARY 22, 1945

JANUARY 29, 1945

FEBRUARY 5, 1945

FEBRUARY 12, 1945

FEBRUARY 19, 1945

APRIL 23, 1945

APRIL 30, 1945

MAY 7, 1945

MAY 14, 1945

MAY 21, 1945

MAY 28, 1945

JUNE 4, 1945

JUNE 11, 1945

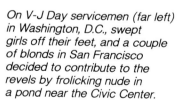

Londoners, less restrained than Americans in celebrating victory over Germany, "went happily mad on V-E Day."

On V-J Day servicemen (far left) in Washington, D.C., swept girls off their feet, and a couple of blonds in San Francisco decided to contribute to the revels by frolicking nude in a pond near the Civic Center.

FEBRUARY 26, 1945

MARCH 5, 1945

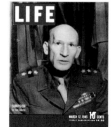

MARCH 12, 1945

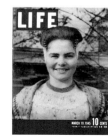

MARCH 19, 1945

MARCH 26, 1945

APRIL 2, 1945

APRIL 9, 1945

APRIL 16, 1945

JUNE 18, 1945

JUNE 25, 1945

JULY 2, 1945

JULY 9, 1945

JULY 16, 1945

JULY 23, 1945

JULY 30, 1945

AUGUST 6, 1945

AUGUST 13, 1945

AUGUST 20, 1945

AUGUST 27, 1945

SEPTEMBER 3, 1945

SEPTEMBER 10, 1945

SEPTEMBER 17, 1945

SEPTEMBER 24, 1945

OCTOBER 1, 1945

"Purse-mouthed" Foreign Minister Shigemitsu and Imperial General Staff Chief Umezu arrived aboard the carrier Missouri *to sign Japan's surrender.*

Debs and their partners waited for the polka to start at New York's Debutante Cotillion, renamed the Allied Flag Ball.

Marlene Dietrich climbed to the dais at the opening of the Paris Stage Door Canteen.

Actress Janet Blair humanely shed a sweater to "keep some destitute European girl warm next winter."

Jackie Robinson surveyed the Brooklyn Dodgers' Ebbets Field, where he would be playing the next year.

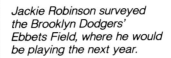

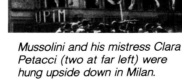

Mussolini and his mistress Clara Petacci (two at far left) were hung upside down in Milan.

Pope Pius XII handed yule gifts to Roman children. "He seemed supremely happy."

"New Movie Moppet" Natalie Wood, 6, played with a pampered pet.

An Allied soldier viewed a cremation furnace at Vught in the Netherlands.

Returning GIs crowded Queen Mary's *decks.*

The wreckage of a B-25 bomber clung, 79 stories up, to the hole it made by crashing into the Empire State Building.

Larry Jim Holm, an Iowa farm boy, and pal walked tracks in a mini-essay on "A Boy and His Dog."

On April 12, following the death of FDR, Vice President Harry Truman took the oath of office from Chief Justice Harlan F. Stone as Mrs. Truman and Cabinet members looked on.

A GI danced with a Montmartre girl in a story on Yanks in "Pig Alley."

OCTOBER 8, 1945

OCTOBER 15, 1945

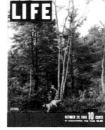
OCTOBER 22, 1945

OCTOBER 29, 1945

NOVEMBER 5, 1945

NOVEMBER 12, 1945

NOVEMBER 19, 1945

NOVEMBER 26, 1945

DECEMBER 3, 1945

DECEMBER 10, 1945

DECEMBER 17, 1945

DECEMBER 24, 1945

A house cut off by snowdrifts was part of "Maine Winter," illustrating the poems of Robert P. Tristram Coffin.

At the Academy Awards ceremony, Ingrid Bergman, Barry Fitzgerald (left) and Bing Crosby clutched their wartime Oscars ("made of plaster this year").

DECEMBER 31, 1945

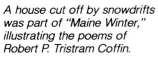

In Santo Tomás, Manila, two liberated Americans were photographed by LIFE's Carl Mydans, who had himself spent nine months there as a POW.

General Eisenhower, in N.Y.C. for victory parade, jovially greeted Mayor Fiorello LaGuardia.

The most-decorated soldier, Lt. Audie Murphy, got a non-GI haircut in hometown Farmersville, Tex.

To explain air-conditioning, LIFE substituted bulbs for the body heat of four bridge players and made the moving cool air visible by adding smoke to it.

Celebrating China's V-J Day, a smiling Chiang Kai-shek toasted Communist chief Mao Tse-tung.

Service exempt, one-armed Pete Gray played center field for the St. Louis Browns. By special rule he could drop his glove to throw.

Famed Balinese dancer Pollok served tea to U.S. officers, one of whom was hiding a stitched eye.

Fresh from National Velvet, *Elizabeth Taylor, "the most romantically appealing of Hollywood's child actresses," posed with favorite mount Peanuts.*

WAR PHOTOGRAPHERS

The war photographer made his name in World War II. In earlier wars the danger and glamour attached itself to the war correspondent, to swashbucklers like Richard Harding Davis and Winston Churchill. But to take a picture it is necessary to get up beside the infantryman, beside the bomber pilot, on the bridge of the fighting warship, in the invasion landing boat. And in doing so, the photographer took risks, hour after hour and year after year.

There were many photographers covering this war—and covering it superbly well. LIFE had 21 of them on its staff. After Pearl Harbor those 20 men and one woman spent a total of 13,000 days outside the U. S., of which half of the days were spent in combat zones. In that time five of them were wounded in action, two were torpedoed, nearly half of them got soaked in amphibious landings and about a dozen of them contracted malaria, sometimes complicated by dysentery and dengue fever. At this price they reported a war as a war had never before been reported. They bobbed up from the Arctic convoys to the beachheads of the South Pacific, from the Burma jungles to the deserts of North Africa, from the plains in the Ukraine to the tundras in the Aleutians, from the Himalayas to the mountains of the Balkans, from Normandy to Berlin, and finally from Manila to Mt. Suribachi in Tokyo.

Though cautious officers often tried to keep photographers in the back waves of invasion landing boats, they were often to be found in the first wave or, on occasion, even a little ahead of the first. Sometimes they got the picture nobody had asked for, the picture looking back at the advancing infantrymen. Nor would it be safe to tell these people that the atomic bomb won the war. They know that the American soldier, sailor and airman won it. W. Eugene Smith wrote of his "wonderful" 7th Division on Okinawa before he was hit. Eyerman became one of the most devoted veterans of Task Force 58. Scherschel and Bourke-White swore by the air forces. Others came to believe that the greatest fighting men alive were the Marines.

To celebrate these 21, who carried the chief burden in LIFE's reporting of that long and hazardous war, LIFE dedicates the following 16 pages of this issue. No photographer would admit that any one picture is necessarily his best, but the portfolio of war photographs that follows makes a remarkable documentation of World War II. Photographer Margaret Bourke-White has said that Capa and Silk are the two greatest war photographers she knows of, blessed by their intelligence, audacity, luck and little 35-mm. cameras. But actually it is almost impossible to choose from among the score of combat photographers on LIFE's staff. They brought back the war, as a home front has never before seen it, and at length, with luck, they brought home themselves.

If the combat artists of World War II were "warriors who carried strange weapons—rolls of canvas, tubes of paint, brushes, pencils and notebooks," as LIFE correspondent John Hersey described them, the magazine's 21 war photographers—who were artists too—carried weapons just as strange and cumbersome. Their equipment included several cameras and lenses of many types, exposure meters and other supplies, including film, film, film. The total pack weight often was equal to that of a beach-hitting infantryman. And to get the riveting pictures selected for this portfolio, they had to be there: in the first wave of an amphibious assault, or with GIs bridging a river under fire. As Carl Mydans put it: "A major difference between a war photographer going into combat and a member of the armed forces is that the soldier or Marine has no choice."

CARL MYDANS

ROBERT CAPA

Mydans had been with MacArthur before the Philippines fell and returned with him. Capa was told by a paratrooper over Sicily: "I don't like your job—it's too dangerous."

J. R. EYERMAN

DAVID SCHERMAN

MARGARET BOURKE-WHITE

Eyerman at Palermo, multitalented Scherman (he was later to be a staff writer and editor) at Berchtesgaden and Bourke-White with troops in the Apennines zeroed in on the fires of war.

CURRENTS AND EVENTS

WORLD: FDR, Churchill, Stalin Meet at Yalta • Red Army Captures Warsaw, Reaches Oder, Races Toward Berlin • Fifth Army Breaks Through in Apennines • FDR Dies, Truman Sworn In • Mussolini, Mistress Shot by Partisans, Hung by Heels in Milan • Air Raids Destroy Dresden • Western Allies Cross Rhine, Meet Soviet Troops at Elbe • Red Army Takes Berlin • Germany Surrenders • Allied Troops Land on Luzon • B-29 Raid Fires Tokyo, Kills 120,000 • Philippines Liberated • Truman, Churchill, Stalin Confer at Potsdam • A-bombs Erase Hiroshima, Nagasaki • U.S.S.R. Declares War on Japan • Japanese Surrender • Chiang-Mao Talks Break Down, Civil War Erupts • Arab League Formed to Block Jewish State in Palestine • Gandhi, Nehru Call for British Withdrawal from India • De Gaulle Elected President of France • War Crimes Trials of 21 Top Nazis Begin at Nuremberg • Argentine Military Government Arrests Dissidents, Peronist-Led Rioters Attack Jews.

OTHER BATTLES: The Bulge • Nijmegen • Iwo Jima • Okinawa.

U.S.A.: B-25 Crashes into Empire State Building • 45 Manufacturers of Artificial Limbs Indicted for Price Gouging • Shirley Temple, 17, Marries Flier John Agar.

FIRSTS: A-bomb Explosion (Alamogordo, N.Mex.) • Fluoridated Water Supply (Grand Rapids, Mich.).

MOVIES: The Story of G.I. Joe • Objective Burma! • A Bell for Adano • The Corn Is Green • The Keys of the Kingdom • Laura • Leave Her to Heaven • The Lost Weekend • Saratoga Trunk • Mildred Pierce • Spellbound • Blithe Spirit • The Bells of St. Mary's • State Fair • A Tree Grows in Brooklyn • Anchors Aweigh • A Song to Remember.

SONGS: It's Been a Long, Long Time • Autumn Serenade • If I Loved You • June Is Bustin' Out All Over • It's a Grand Night for Singing • It Might as Well Be Spring • Laura • For Sentimental Reasons • Give Me the Simple Life • Let It Snow! Let It Snow! Let It Snow! • On the Atchison, Topeka and the Santa Fe • Till the End of Time (Chopin) • Oh! What It Seemed to Be • Dig You Later.

STAGE: The Glass Menagerie • State of the Union • The Hasty Heart • Dream Girl • Deep Are the Roots • Carousel • Up in Central Park • Are You With It? • Billion Dollar Baby.

BOOKS: Animal Farm (Orwell) • Christ Stopped at Eboli (Levi) • Brideshead Revisited (Waugh) • Cannery Row (Steinbeck) • The Thurber Carnival (Thurber) • Stuart Little (White) • The Age of Jackson (Schlesinger) • Captain from Castile (Shellabarger) • Daisy Kenyon (Janeway) • The Black Rose (Costain).

FADS: Surplus GI Equipment (for leisure, sports) • Women's Short-Legged Overalls.

CLASSIC PHOTOS

A weeping Navy musician at Warm Springs, Ga., played "Nearer My God to Thee" when FDR died.

They kissed in Times Square on V-J Day.

MacArthur made good his "I shall return" pledge to the Philippines.

Of Strock's photo of U.S. dead on Burma, LIFE said: "Words are never enough." George Silk, accompanying the Ninth Army in Germany, paused over the body of a GI on a footbridge.

As a live baby was plucked from among Okinawa corpses, Smith again asked himself, "What am I doing here?" Hoffman, in Burma with fever-ravaged GIs, was treated to a meal of dog meat.

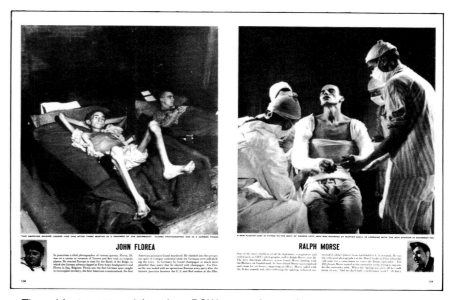

Shrout, Davis and Stackpole covered the Pacific; Elisofon, Africa and Europe; Phillips, the Middle East and Europe. Vandivert left China and Burma to turn his lenses on the push to V-E Day.

The subject, a starved American POW, was a far cry from Florea's career specialty: Hollywood stars. In a classic essay, Morse followed the odyssey of a GI hit by a mortar shell burst.

Picturing sniper-threatened Parisians on Liberation Day was, to Scherschel, "like covering a strike in Milwaukee." The widely traveled Rodger covered the V-1 blitz from London.

Landry, who saw French partisans catch a collaborationist, and Kessel, who covered the Greek civil war, ranged afar; between them they bracketed all the war's theaters.

A Few Favorites 1936-1945...

EARLY CRUSHES THAT LASTED A LIFETIME

In 1938 LIFE photographed Katharine Hepburn, one of its first loves and enduring favorites, against the plane in which her "best beau" Howard Hughes was about to fly around the world—with her aboard, rumor had it. The reclusive billionaire did make the flight—without her.

In its second month LIFE was already on a last-name basis with the performer who, as actor and singer as well as dancer, had a triple hold on the editors' affections. This photo appeared in a 1937 spread titled simply "Astaire," in which "this hard-working professional" drew early plaudits. It was the centerpiece of a 12-page feature on dance.

Royalty-watching with an eye to the future, LIFE in 1937 spotted 11-year-old Princess Elizabeth's "erect, direct manner" and the "mischievous grin" of Margaret, 7.

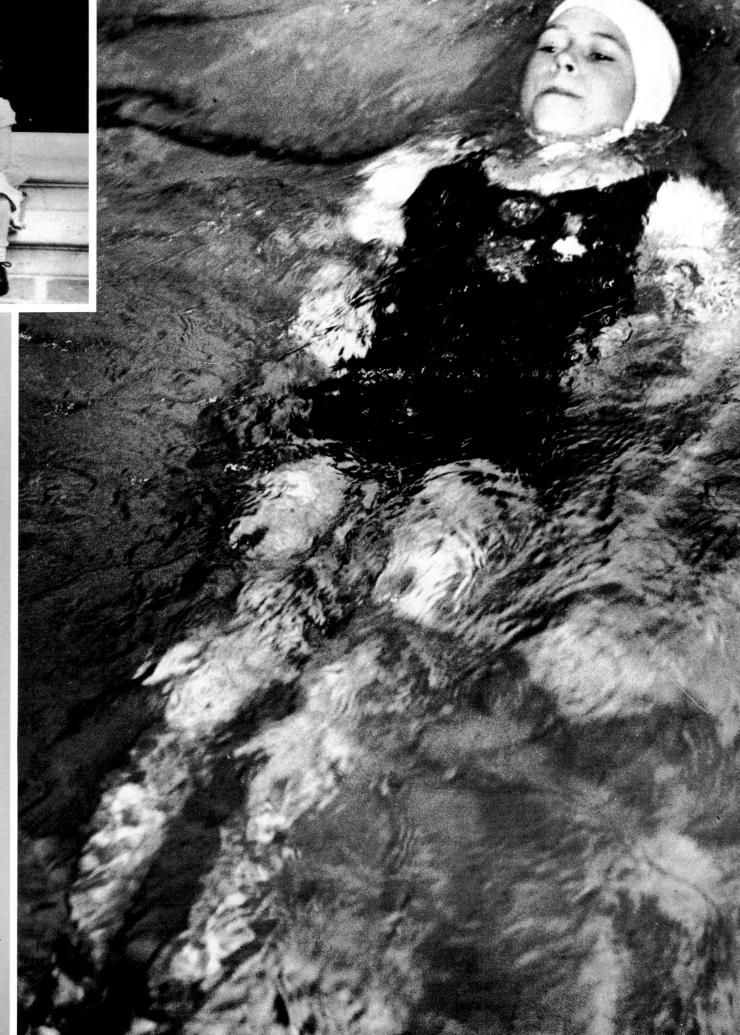

Princess Elizabeth, 13, demonstrated a smooth backstroke at the Mayfair Bath Club in 1939—and won a prize for girls 9 to 14. When Queen Elizabeth handed her the award, the magazine observed, she "curtsied politely and said, 'Thank you, Mummie.' "

Shirley Temple, already the queen of films (she was to be No. 1 at the box office five years in a row), was given additional big play in 1937 when an on-set mishap bruised her near the eye, and the studio hyped the incident. One newspaper enhanced the handout photo by darkening the "shiner," and LIFE, using the retouched print, pointed out the fakery.

By 1942 nature had taken its lovely course and Shirley's studio had to confess that she was 13, two years older than previously peddled (a fact that had been withheld even from her). In publishing her first "glamour" portrait coincident with her birthday, the editors noted that "Shirley has escaped the usual awkwardness of a teen-age kid."

The camera caught the 1942
plunge toward a Buffalo pavement
of a despondent divorcée "in the last
dreadful split second before death."

The week this youth leaped from the 17th
floor of New York's Hotel Gotham, LIFE noted,
some 300 others in the U.S. had "killed
themselves without making any worthwhile
newspictures." A page of dramatic
photos, taken before the young man jumped,
followed this spectacular 1938 shot.

Aussie soldiers, landing in 1942 by a dam during a night maneuver, were blasted skyward by an explosive charge. Their boat disintegrated, but they received only bruises.

AN ADDICTION TO EVERYBODY'S FAVORITE SUBJECT: THE WEATHER

A 1943 tornado cut a swath across Minnesota farmland and created one of the most dramatic pictures ever made of nature as a great destroyer. It was part of a 15-page study of weather, ranging from a primer of the earth's atmosphere to an analysis of weather's effect on warfare. Explaining the power of this tornado, the caption pointed out that its destructiveness was concentrated in a path that was only 50 feet wide at this moment.

A LOVE OF DANCING THAT NEVER TIRED

The editors called this dance style, demonstrated at a 1938 American Legion Jitterbug Jamboree, "catch-as-catch-can."

A bouncy 1938 bobby-soxer at
Greenwich Village's Webster Hall
performed a hard-core Big Apple.

A high-flying Lindy Hopper
from Queens, N.Y., nearly
reached the ceiling in this
1940 Picture to the Editors.

A tireless night-trick
(four p.m. to midnight)
employee whirled at
a 1942 after-work party
of Lockheed toilers.
"Only the kids," sighed
the text, "can take
the Swing Shift."

STARTLING IMAGES AS THE CAMERA PRIED

In a 1939 Versailles dawn, as the guillotine blade fell "with a slight whirring sound" toward the neck of a murderer, the camera clicked—illicitly. The covert photography and the raucousness of the crowd combined to end France's policy of public executions.

The remains of the slain revolutionary Leon Trotsky were cremated in Mexico City in 1940. The photographer was an official witness. The process took an hour and 40 minutes, the editors reported, and the ashes weighed about 6 lbs.

The body of murderer Roscoe "Red" Jackson fell through the trapdoor in Missouri's last public hanging, in 1937. Lethal gas thereafter replaced the noose.

"A crime is being committed here," gloated the caption under this 1937 picture of a nighttime milk snatcher at work. A Portland, Oreg., photographer, fed up with the thefts of his home-delivered milk, had wired decoy bottles to flashbulbs and his prefocused camera, producing an ultimate in candid pictures.

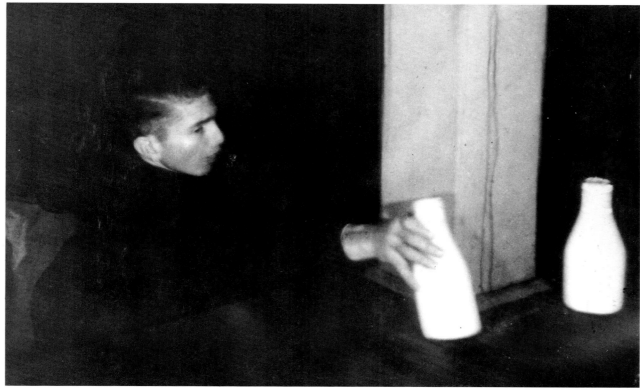

Fueled by longtime artistic jealousy, two distinguished French playwrights, Edouard Bourdet (in homburg) and Henri Bernstein, dueled outside Paris in 1938. Bernstein cut Bourdet's arm; they quit unreconciled.

ACTION-FREEZING MIRACLES

A bullet traveling 2,700 feet a second was stopped cold in 1939 by a millionth-of-a-second flash of stroboscopic light. For editors eager to freeze action in every field, from a hummingbird's wings to the dance, the strobe was a godsend. Photographer

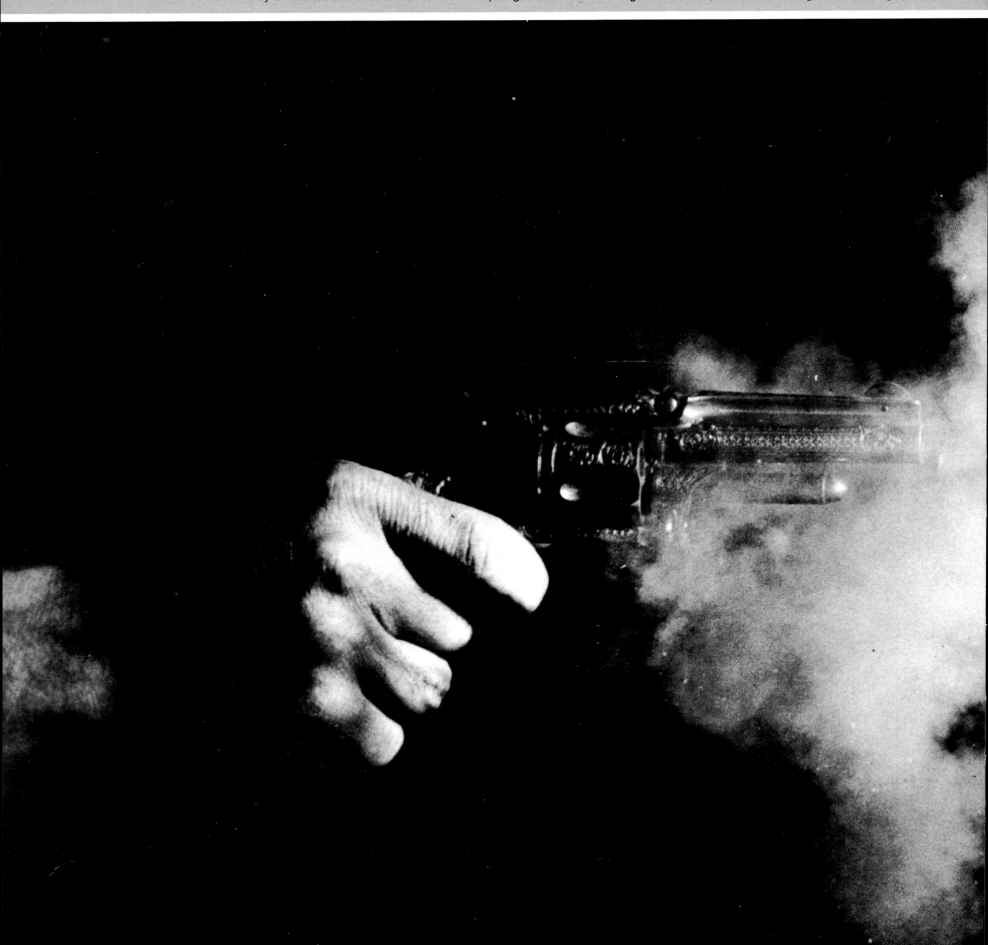

Gjon Mili later was to carry the technique to artistic heights with multiple-exposure studies of ballet dancers and athletes.

A PUNNING DELIGHT IN SHOWING PEOPLE AND THINGS "LIFE-SIZE"

Always proud to use the magazine's outsize pages to dramatic effect, the editors found Paul Del Rio, just 19 inches tall at age 18, made to order as the subject for a 1938 two-page spread. The midget—born in Madrid of normal parents—had two sisters who toured exhibition circuits with him, but at 22 and 33 inches they were too big to fit into the parameters of the story.

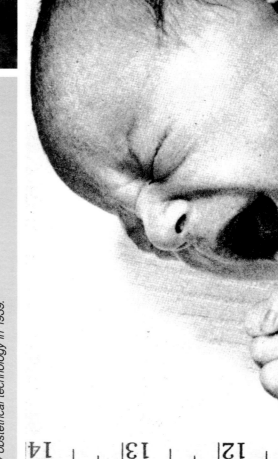

This 4-lb. baby boy in Boston's Lying-In Hospital was photographed beside a tape measure to show how tiny were the premature infants being saved by obstetrical technology in 1939.

LIFE-SIZE PORTRAIT OF WORLD'S SMALLEST MAN

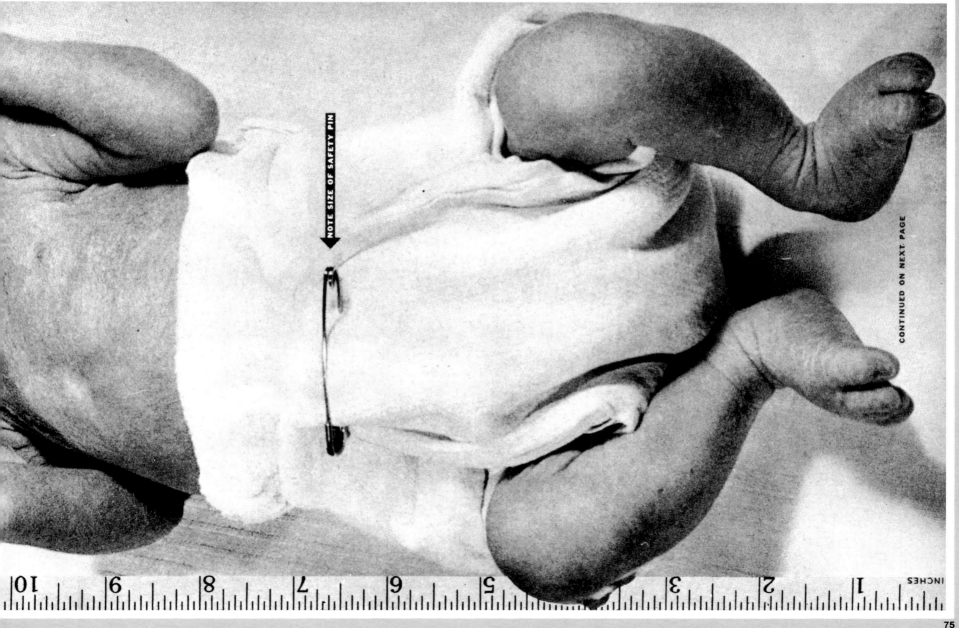

NOTE SIZE OF SAFETY PIN

CONTINUED ON NEXT PAGE

INCHES

1946-1955
Peace and Prosperity

There had been conflicts in the world since LIFE's start-up; hostilities in Spain and the Japanese assaults on China were followed by World War II. Now the fighting was ended, for a time, and the magazine could turn its attention and its talents to reporting on a world at peace but forever altered. The changes were dramatic, and they were coming fast. The staff relished the opportunity and the responsibility of covering them.

Despite emphasis on the widening schism between the West and its former ally, the U.S.S.R., despite brilliant reportage of the bloody, frustrating "police action" in Korea (1950-53), the elements that contributed to peace and prosperity dominated the decade's pages. For overall, this was a period of unprecedented national growth and influence, centering on the essentially happy and carefree eight years of the Eisenhower presidency. The great surge of progress was coupled with a wonderful mood of well-being. By 1955 the editors felt free to write a Fourth of July headline observing lightly that "Nobody Is Mad with Nobody."

The magazine itself was booming. In the early '50s Publisher Andrew Heiskell could boast that the editors looked at half a million pictures to choose the 10,000 or so published annually and that weekly sales were 5.2 million copies, which sometimes had as many as 200 pages. Inside this "incredible package," available "52 times a year for as little as $3.75 a subscription," as Heiskell pointed out, was a matchless editorial mix of fascinating photos and fine prose dealing with news, personalities, entertainment, sports, science, history, fashion and the arts. There was, also, opinion.

Shamelessly patriotic, politically biased, steeped in a hard-line ethic that encompassed a steadfast belief in democracy and free enterprise, the editors took seriously the magazine's capacity to influence opinion and events. On the editorial page, under its longtime chief John K. Jessup, LIFE spoke out sharply against communism and made the case for rearmament, NATO and the rebuilding of Germany. Jessup described the era as a time "when peace-loving Americans gradually faced the fact that peace must be waged as well as loved."

To explore seminal subjects thoroughly, entire issues occasionally were devoted to such themes as schools and U.S. growth. There were also series, sweeping treatments of primal topics, presented in multichapter form—for example, "The World We Live In" and "The Epic of Man." Accompanied by distinguished text, illustrated with elaborately researched and imaginative artwork, the series distilled and energized the gigantic strokes of mankind's past and future.

Such big journalistic acts aside and despite publication during this period of more than 2,500 color photographs annually, fast-closing black-and-white pictures continued to be the special resource that separated LIFE from its direct competition for advertising dollars: *The Saturday Evening Post, Look* and *Collier's*. Delivered at a slower pace were the picture essays, which employed techniques that, in sum, translated to a widely recognized new art form. They were the work of such great camera practitioners as W. Eugene Smith, Leonard McCombe, Gordon Parks and Eliot Elisofon, as well as that of Margaret Bourke-White and Alfred Eisenstaedt. Typically the subjects of the essays were themselves commonplace: a country doctor, a fight trainer, a career girl. It was a rare year in which a staffer was not chosen Photographer of the Year by the National Press Photographers Association, and usually the winning portfolio was assembled around a LIFE essay.

In its second decade the magazine's major architect was its fourth managing editor, Edward K. Thompson. Except for a World War II stint in uniform, in the course of which he served on Eisenhower's staff, EKT (as his colleagues often referred to him, based on the initials he used to approve final copy and layouts) had been with the magazine practically from its launch. He took over in the fall of 1949 at the age of 42 and held the helm for a strenuous 12 years before relinquishing it to spend an additional six years in the policy-setting post of editor. A consummate journalist with a wide range of interests and expertise, and unerring judgment about people and pictures, Thompson had demanded a free hand in running the magazine—and had gotten it. It was Thompson who shaped LIFE during its most successful years.

To illustrate all the stuff "most American families" dreamed of in 1946, the editors shipped the ingredients to one bucolic home site. For "the dream's supreme moment just before waking," the editors (perhaps mindful of the commuting problem) added a helicopter.

1946

In the aftermath of war, the expanding magazine was delighted to resume its attention to old loves

The nation's immediate goal, which LIFE eagerly shared, was to get "back to normalcy." The war just ended and the possibilities for future ones echoed on the magazine's pages. The war-crimes trials at Nuremberg ("Nürnberg" in German), the plight of war orphans and refugees, and the consequences of A-bomb testing demanded the attention of conscientious chroniclers. So, as important new issues evolved, the magazine addressed them by publishing

At Nuremberg, ex-Reichsmarschall Hermann Göring, "a far cry from the obese dandy of the days of Nazi power," talked to his lawyer.

A GI guarded each cell in the prison where the top 20 Nazi defendants were held. "To prevent suicides, guards look into cells every 30 seconds."

NÜRNBERG TRIAL EN...

its first lengthy texts. Meanwhile, the staff photographers, now 29 strong, happily turned their lenses on the pleasures of peace. Like a soldier who had been parted from his beloved for the duration, LIFE again embraced Hollywood, peeked into the lives of people in high places and low, kept its eye peeled for fashions and fads, and for pretty women. And, to guard its well-founded reputation for prescience, it looked ahead to man's landing on the moon.

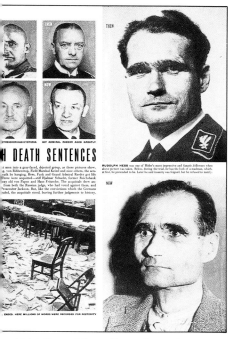

At trial's end the editors showed "then" and "now" pictures of Göring and Hess, plus Ribbentrop, Funk, Streicher, Raeder.

In one of an unprecedented group of informal pictures, Japan's Emperor Hirohito posed while perusing Stars and Stripes "near 'cherished' busts of Lincoln and Darwin."

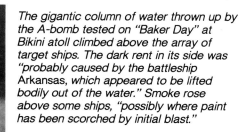

The gigantic column of water thrown up by the A-bomb tested on "Baker Day" at Bikini atoll climbed above the array of target ships. The dark rent in its side was "probably caused by the battleship Arkansas, which appeared to be lifted bodily out of the water." Smoke rose above some ships, "possibly where paint has been scorched by initial blast."

JANUARY 7, 1946

JANUARY 14, 1946

JANUARY 21, 1946

JANUARY 28, 1946

FEBRUARY 4, 1946

FEBRUARY 11, 1946

FEBRUARY 18, 1946

FEBRUARY 25, 1946

MARCH 4, 1946

CLASSIC PHOTOS

Mahatma Gandhi, 76, sat by his spinning wheel and read his correspondence.

Orphaned Polish children awaited deportation from Palestine by Britain.

An Austrian orphan, six, ecstatically held gift shoes from the Red Cross.

CURRENTS AND EVENTS

WORLD: Europe Swept by Food Shortages, Inflation • Communists Take Over in Czechoslovakia, Yugoslavia, Bulgaria, Albania, Romania, Poland • Hungary Proclaimed Republic • Italy's Victor Emmanuel Abdicates • French Socialist Léon Blum Emerges as Premier • Stalin Resumes Purges • Government Nationalizes Bank of England, Coal Mines • Churchill Delivers "Iron Curtain" Warning • Nuremberg Tribunal Condemns 12 Nazis, Göring Commits Suicide • Greek Civil War Erupts • Zionists Blow Up British HQ in Palestine • Perón Elected Argentine President • Nationalist, Communist Truce in China Ends in Full-scale Civil War • Ho Chi Minh Begins Campaign for United Indochina, French Bomb Haiphong.

U.S.A.: Inflation, Housing Shortage, Nuclear Age Dominate Discourse • Strikes Idle 4.6 Million Workers • Troops Seize Railroads, Coal Mines • A-bomb Tested at Bikini Atoll • U.S. Birthrate Soars • Returning Vets, Aided by GI Bill, Crowd Campuses • Admiral Byrd Leads Expedition to South Pole.

FIRSTS: Fulbright Scholars • Dymaxion House (Fuller) • Bikini Swimsuits • Electronic Digital Computer • Electric Blanket • Italian, Japanese Women Gain Suffrage • Bone Bank • Mobile Telephone.

MOVIES: The Best Years of Our Lives • To Each His Own • The Seventh Veil • Anna and the King of Siam • Henry V (Olivier) • Notorious • The Postman Always Rings Twice • The Yearling • It's a Wonderful Life • Duel in the Sun • The Big Sleep • The Razor's Edge • Brief Encounter • Open City • Gilda • The Harvey Girls • Blue Skies • The Jolson Story • The Road to Utopia.

SONGS: Come Rain or Come Shine • Full Moon and Empty Arms (Rachmaninoff) • The Girl That I Marry • Doin' What Comes Natur'lly • All Through the Day • Five Minutes More • It's a Good Day • The Old Lamp-Lighter • Shoofly Pie and Apple Pan Dowdy • There's No Business Like Show Business • I Got the Sun in the Morning • They Say It's Wonderful • Zip-a-Dee-Do-Dah • La Vie en Rose • Chiquita Banana • All I Want for Christmas Is My Two Front Teeth.

STAGE: Born Yesterday • Another Part of the Forest • The Magnificent Yankee • O Mistress Mine • Present Laughter • No Exit • Annie Get Your Gun • Call Me Mister • Lute Song.

BOOKS: Baby and Child Care (Spock) • Hiroshima (Hersey) • The Member of the Wedding (McCullers) • All the King's Men (Warren) • Mr. Blandings Builds His Dream House (Hodgins) • The Snake Pit (Ward) • The Hucksters (Wakeman) • Arch of Triumph (Remarque) • The Berlin Stories (Isherwood) • Zorba the Greek (Kazantzakis).

FADS: Bubble Gum • Tasseled Stocking Caps • The Eskimo Diet.

"THOU SHALT NOT"
1 LAW DEFEATED
2 INSIDE OF THIGH
3 LACE LINGERIE
4 DEAD MAN
5 NARCOTICS
6 DRINKING
7 EXPOSED BOSOM
8 GAMBLING
9 POINTING GUN
10 TOMMY GUN

"THOU SHALT NOT" IS A STAGED PHOTOGRAPH MADE IN 1940 SHOWING VIOLATIONS OF 10 PROMINENT "DON'TS" OF HOLLYWOOD MOTION-PICTURE CENSORSHIP

MOVIE CENSORSHIP

It confuses British movie makers but U.S. producers get around it

American film producers are inured by now to the Hays Office code which regulates movie morals. The code's main rules are set down in the photograph above which shows, in one fell swoop, many things producers must not do. But British producers, trying to distribute their wares widely in the U.S., have suddenly run into trouble over the code. Two British films were found to be objectionable for the U.S.: *The Wicked Lady* because of too much

bare bosom, *The Notorious Gentleman* because of too little gentility (see p. 84).

Puzzled, the British called on Joseph I. Breen of the Johnston (once Hays) Office for advice. Mr. Breen went to England and explained the rules. He probably did not mention that U.S. producers, knowing that things banned by the code help sell tickets, have been subtly getting around the code for years, as pictures on the following pages testify.

CONTINUED ON NEXT PAGE 79

The magazine was happy to illustrate all the "moralistic" taboos inflicted on the film industry by its self-imposed Production Code.

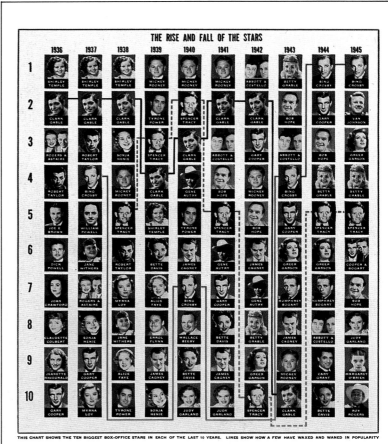

THE RISE AND FALL OF THE STARS

THIS CHART SHOWS THE TEN BIGGEST BOX-OFFICE STARS IN EACH OF THE LAST 10 YEARS. LINES SHOW HOW A FEW HAVE WAXED AND WANED IN POPULARITY

THE MOVIES

1936 STARS HAVE LASTED WELL BUT NEW FACES ARE COMING UP

Each year the *Motion Picture Herald*, a prominent movie trade paper, publishes a list of the 10 stars who have drawn the most paid admissions during the preceding 12 months. The chart above shows who these people have been during the past 10 years. The fact that 100 places are filled by 36 faces is a tribute to the continued popularity of actors like Clark Gable and Bing Crosby; of actresses like Shirley Temple and Greer Garson.

Yet many great Hollywood stars are not represented. Ingrid Bergman, who will undoubtedly be 1946's top female money-maker, does not appear. Neither does the late Carole Lombard, nor Ronald Colman, nor Katharine Hepburn, nor James Stewart. Instead there is a cowboy named Autry, two clowns named Abbott and Costello, an ice-skater named Henie. Whatever their talents, however, the golden 36 were the era's most popular entertainers.

CONTINUED ON NEXT PAGE 65

LIFE traced the ups and downs of a decade's stars: Shirley Temple, Mickey Rooney, Abbott & Costello, Betty Grable, Bing Crosby.

1 STARTING FOR THE MOON, the rocket climbs 200 miles above the U.S. east coast. Inside the earth's shallow atmosphere (*luminous band on the horizon*) it flies like an ordinary airplane at a comparatively low speed. At the lower right is Long Island. At its left end is New York City. In the distance are the Great Lakes.

TRIP TO THE MOON

Artist paints journey by rocket

The idea of a trip to the moon, an irresistible combination of high adventure and escape from this imperfect planet, has always fascinated the people of the earth. Daniel Defoe wanted to make the journey "on the backs of two vast bodies with extended wings." Jules Verne dispatched his travelers in a shell fired out of a colossal cannon. In this century more practical men have seriously thought of getting to the moon by rocket. Shown here is the scientifically realistic rocket journey conceived by Chesley Bonestell, a Hollywood special-effects artist and amateur astronomer whose paintings of Saturn's moons have been published in LIFE (May 29, 1944).

Although radar signals have been sent to the moon, rockets are not likely to get there for some time. Present rocket motors develop only about a sixth of the velocity—seven miles per second—necessary to get out of the earth's gravitational field. But there is a strong chance that atomic energy will provide power for trips to the moon—and beyond

2 OVER EUROPE AT SUNSET, 600 miles up in its climb above the earth, the rocket uses the full power of its atomic-fueled engines. Below is the south coast of England. The boot of Italy stretches toward the horizon.

CONTINUED ON NEXT PAGE

Relying on painstaking research, artist Chesley Bonestell, commissioned by the editors, painted a rocket and views of earth that were astonishingly true to the goals and achievements of the U.S. space program some two decades later.

OCTOBER 21, 1946

OCTOBER 28, 1946

NOVEMBER 4, 1946

Snuggled against his late master's effects, General George S. Patton's devoted companion Willie awaited shipment home from Germany.

In midyear the world saw a new version of LIFE, a slimmed-down fortnightly international edition of the plump domestic weekly, edited for English-speaking readers around the world.

 MARCH 11, 1946
 MARCH 18, 1946
MARCH 25, 1946
APRIL 1, 1946
APRIL 8, 1946
APRIL 15, 1946
APRIL 22, 1946
 APRIL 29, 1946

MAY 6, 1946
 MAY 13, 1946
 MAY 20, 1946
 MAY 27, 1946
 JUNE 3, 1946
JUNE 10, 1946
JUNE 17, 1946
 JUNE 24, 1946

JULY 1, 1946
JULY 8, 1946
 JULY 15, 1946
 JULY 22, 1946
 JULY 29, 1946
 AUGUST 5, 1946
AUGUST 12, 1946
 AUGUST 19, 1946

 AUGUST 26, 1946
 SEPTEMBER 2, 1946
 SEPTEMBER 9, 1946
 SEPTEMBER 16, 1946
 SEPTEMBER 23, 1946
 SEPTEMBER 30, 1946
 OCTOBER 7, 1946
 OCTOBER 14, 1946

 NOVEMBER 11, 1946
 NOVEMBER 18, 1946
 NOVEMBER 25, 1946
 DECEMBER 2, 1946
 DECEMBER 9, 1946
 DECEMBER 16, 1946
 DECEMBER 23, 1946
 DECEMBER 30, 1946

"Left to dry by the seaside," an early bikini offered "an interesting clue to the anatomy of its owner."

Argentine dictator Juan Perón breakfasted with his wife, Evita (Duarte), "a small-time actress who had long been known as his mistress by all Buenos Aires."

This N.Y. newspaper cartoon jab at the "Birth of a Baby" story was part of a decade-spanning collection headlined "Kidding LIFE."

1947

Words of historic weight and lasting value enriched the magazine's pages as the nation dominated the world stage and the editors looked to the future

At age 6 Franklin Roosevelt often wrote to his mother, who was away, keeping her up-to-date on his daily activities.

As the world settled into the postwar era, the U.S. emerged as its greatest power, and Henry Luce foresaw the shape of what he called the American Century. To fix it in the span of time, the editors opened the magazine's pages to the lessons of history, frequently relying on the memoirs of the influential and the strong. The editors also commissioned contributions from some of the finest writers. Early on, in pursuing this course, LIFE covered in depth the rites of passage of Britain's monarchy. Then Luce himself suggested to the Duke of Windsor that he write his boyhood reminiscences, which were published hard on the heels of FDR's childhood letters. They started a literary tradition that eventually was to include the memoirs of Winston Churchill, Harry Truman, Douglas MacArthur, Dwight D. Eisenhower, Tito and Nikita Khrushchev, and Churchill's *History of the English-Speaking Peoples*. There was fiction as well. The first coup: persuading Hemingway to write a novella, *The Old Man and the Sea,* which ran in its entirety in a single issue. The editors also felt constrained to tackle new sociological issues. Significantly, probing the future role of U.S. women was a priority.

LIFE

Presents

BOYHOOD LETTERS OF FRANKLIN D. ROOSEVELT

Because a doting mother saved every letter he wrote, historians inherit a treasury of detailed information

SARA D. ROOSEVELT

When Franklin Roosevelt died in 1945, there was no phrasemaker at his deathbed to remark, as Stanton supposedly said of Lincoln, "Now he belongs to the ages." But as surely as the ages have possessed Lincoln, Roosevelt will also be possessed until at last he may supplant Lincoln as history's most completely biographized American. Unlike Lincoln, Roosevelt left an extremely detailed and voluminous legacy of facts.

Much of this legacy exists in his letters, never before published. Herewith LIFE presents an exclusive selection of these letters, covering the period from Roosevelt's first written communication at the age of 5in 1887 to his graduation from Harvard in 1904. For historians and those who loved Roosevelt this correspondence will prove of great interest and increasing value.

Almost solely responsible for this treasure was Roosevelt's mother, Sara Delano. Married at 26 to a man twice her age, she doted on her only child. Ravenously she collected and preserved every scrap of paper on which her boy wrote or drew, as though she were certain that he was hurrying toward greatness and that, if he stole a bird's egg or caught a cold, posterity had a right to know of it.

Beginning in November with volume one, *Early Years*, Duell, Sloan & Pearce will publish Roosevelt's family letters as *F.D.R.: His Personal Letters.*

FRANKLIN AT 5

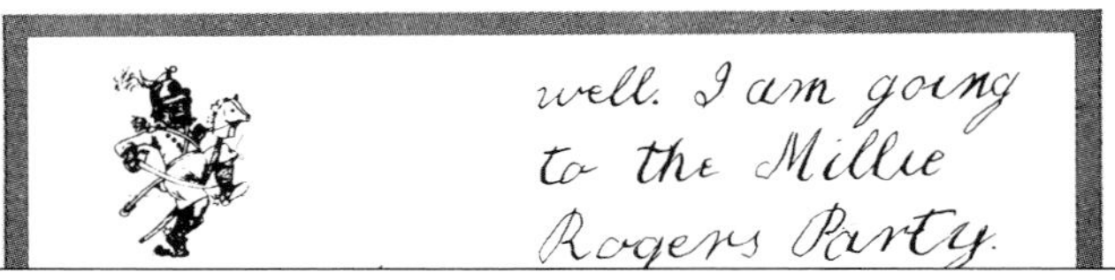

well. I am going
to the Millie
Rogers Party.

THE FOUR GENERATIONS. The great Queen Victoria, who came to my christening, wrote of that event: "The dear fine baby, wearing the Honiton lace robe . . . worn by all our children and my English grandchildren, was brought in . . . and handed to me. I then gave him to the Archbishop and received him back . . . . The child was very good. . . . Had tea with May, and afterwards we were photographed, I, holding the baby on my lap, Bertie and Georgie standing behind me, thus making the four generations."

116

A ROYAL BOYHOOD

by EDWARD, DUKE OF WINDSOR

IN my father's diary for the year 1894, there occurs the following entry: "WHITE LODGE, 23rd June—At 10.0 a sweet little boy was born and weighed 8 lb. . . . Mr. Asquith (Home Secretary) came to see him."

White Lodge in Richmond Park, Surrey, was the home of my maternal grandparents, the Duke and Duchess of Teck, and somehow I imagine that this was the last time my father ever applied to me that precise adjective. But in any case, since Herbert Henry Asquith's star was rising, circumstances favored that my first visitor should be a future Prime Minister of England. It was Ascot Race Week and on the night I was born my grandfather, then Prince of Wales and later Edward VII, was host at a large ball at Virginia Water, in Windsor Great Park, a short distance away. The news of my advent into the world caused a slight stir in that gay concourse. Stopping the orchestra, my grandfather announced, "It is with pleasure that I am able to inform you of the birth of a son to the Duke and Duchess of York. I propose a toast to the young Prince." The dance, I like to think, went on.

THIS IS WHITE LODGE, WHERE I WAS BORN

I was christened Edward Albert Christian George Andrew Patrick David. Edward is a traditional English name and before me had been borne by six English Kings. Albert was in deference to my great grandmother Victoria's express desire that all her descendants bear the name of her beloved husband, Albert, the Prince Consort. I was named Christian for King Christian IX of Denmark, one of my twelve royal sponsors. The last four names are those of the patron saints of England, Scotland, Ireland and Wales, respectively. To my family I was and always have been "David." And I was brought up, in the simple English way, to call my parents "Mama" and "Papa."

It was a wonderful time to be born. Victoria at 75 was in the 57th year of her great reign and had been on the throne as long as all but the oldest Britons could remember. Britain was the most powerful nation on earth. Her seapower, industrial power and financial power were supreme. Her Empire covered a quarter of the earth's surface. Queen Victoria looked out upon a world not riven and shattered, but prosperous and teeming. The Courts of Europe were occupied in no mean measure by her numerous children and grandchildren. The formidable Kaiser Wilhelm II of Germany was her grandson—"William." Another grandson, by marriage, "Nicky," was Czar of All the Russias.

Especially for Britons of the upper and middle classes, this was Britain's golden hour. Income tax was measured in the pence on pound sterling. Socialism was scarcely more than a theory. The first telephone had been installed in a royal residence only four years previously, and eight years would pass before my father acquired his first motor car, a small electric vehicle steered by a horizontal handle bar. It was hard to imagine that anything could shake the structure of the Englishman's world.

The recollections of my early life are very dim. My father, a career officer in the Royal Navy, did not give up his service at sea until 1898, four years after I was born. I passed immediately under the care of nurses and, reflecting Queen Victoria's instinctive attachment for all things Teutonic, one of these nurses was always a German. I learned English and German simultaneously. A nurse appears to have been to blame for an unfavorable first impression that I made upon my parents. It was their custom to have me brought downstairs at tea time. I was, after all, the first-born, and my father, as fathers do, rather looked forward to this interlude at the end of a busy day as an occasion of mutual pleasure and edification. But it seldom turned out that way. Before taking me into the drawing room this dreadful "Nanny" would pinch and twist my arm—why, no one knew, unless it was to demonstrate, according to some perverse reasoning, that her power over me was greater than theirs. The bawling and sobbing which this treatment evoked always ended in my running back to her arms, and in the necessity for my being removed lest I bring further embarrassment to the onlookers of this seemingly pathetic scene. Eventually my mother realized what was wrong, and the nurse left.

My great-grandmother Victoria reigned on for nearly seven years after my birth, long enough to welcome into this world my brother Albert, now King George VI, who was born 18 months after me, my sister Mary, the present Princess Royal, and my brother Henry, Duke of Gloucester.

I can recall being taken by my parents for occasional visits to the great Queen-Empress at the three places where she spent her long life: to Windsor, whose historic Castle dates from Norman times and whence my family and my dukedom take their name; to Balmoral Castle in Aberdeenshire, Scotland; to Osborne, that utterly un-English house in imitation of an Italian villa which she had built for herself on the Isle of Wight.

Although in her journal the great Queen mentions me with affection, the 75 years that separated us naturally prevented her paying me particular attention. In her white tulle cap and black satin dresses she was almost a divinity of whom not only the whole British people but her own family stood in awe. She wore shiny black shoes with elastic sides. But what fascinated me most about her was her habit of taking breakfast in little revolving huts, mounted on turntables so that they could be faced away from the wind. Weather permitting, she would ride over to these shelters in a little carriage drawn by a white pony led by a Highland attendant. Her family would gather around, and later she would call for her secretaries and begin the business of the day.

When Queen Victoria died aged 81 at Osborne, my brother Bertie, my sister Mary, and I were all at our country home, York Cottage, Sandringham in Norfolk, getting over the measles. My father, having caught them from us, broke out with the disease while at Osborne where he had been summoned to her deathbed, and was himself very ill. He was therefore unable to attend her funeral at Windsor and, as my mother remained to nurse him into convalescence, it fell to my grandmother, the new Queen Alexandra, to arrange for us three children to witness the ceremony. As through a haze, I can still see the caisson bearing my great-grandmother's coffin being slowly dragged up the hill by sailors to St. George's Chapel. The day was cold and gloomy, the ceremony mournful and depressing. In the minds of those present there must have been a fleeting sense of the passing of a great era, a foreboding of the political changes that were bound to affect their lives and Britain's destiny.

Victoria stood not only for a reign but a way of life. Diligence and respectability had been the moral pillars of her Court. Yet at the same time her own self-imposed seclusion, which had evoked certain republican rumblings, had imposed upon my grandfather as Prince of Wales more responsibility for public affairs than would normally have been the case. In consequence, his London residence, Marlborough House, and his country estate of Sandringham, in Norfolk, had become the meeting place of diplomats, politicians, industrialists and bankers, artists and their patrons—the new society of Europe and America. With Victoria's passing it was natural that the gay little courts of Marlborough House and Sandringham should move tumultuously to Buckingham Palace, Windsor and Balmoral, where in Victoria's time only bishops, cabinet ministers, aristocrats and courtiers of dry esthetic interests had been admitted. The Edwardian era had arrived in the genial shape of my grandfather; and the effect upon the Victorian was the same as if a Viennese Hussar had suddenly burst into an English vicarage.

The exigencies of parliamentary government required the residence of the sovereign in London at prescribed intervals, a condition much to my grandfather's taste. Buckingham Palace, where Queen Victoria had spent only a few nights a year since her husband's death, needed renovating, and Windsor Castle, also Crown property, was in sore need of modern

COPYRIGHT 1947 BY TIME INC. WORLD COPYRIGHT RESERVED
REPRODUCTION IN PART OR IN FULL IN ALL LANGUAGES STRICTLY PROHIBITED

CONTINUED ON NEXT PAGE 117

Baby Edward lay in the arms of Queen Victoria in 1884. Behind them: her son Albert (Edward VII) and grandson George (George V).

HER WORK

6:30 NURSE BABY
7:15 DRESS SHAWN, RUSTY
7:30 FIX BREAKFAST
7:45 BREAKFAST FOR ALL
8:00 HUSBAND JOHN TO WORK
      WASH DISHES
      CLEAN DOWNSTAIRS
      CALL GROCER'S
9:00 SHAWN, RUSTY IN YARD
      BATHE BABY
      MAKE BEDS
      CLEAN UPSTAIRS
10:30 NURSE BABY
11:00 FIX LUNCH
11:30 LUNCH FOR SHAWN, RUSTY
12:00 JOHN HOME
      LUNCH WITH JOHN
1:00 JOHN TO WORK
      NAPS FOR SHAWN, RUSTY
      WASH DISHES
      NAP FOR MARJORIE
2:30 NURSE BABY
2:45 ROUSE SHAWN, RUSTY
3:00 SHAWN, RUSTY PLAY
      GARDENING OUTDOORS
      OR
      MENDING INDOORS
5:00 FRUIT JUICE FOR BABY
      FIX LUNCH
5:30 SUPPER FOR SHAWN, RUSTY
6:00 JOHN HOME
      BATHS FOR SHAWN, RUSTY
6:30 SHAWN, RUSTY IN BED
      NURSE BABY
7:00 DRESS FOR DINNER
7:15 COCKTAIL WITH JOHN
7:30 FIX DINNER
8:00 DINNER WITH JOHN
9:00 WASH DISHES
10:30 NURSE BABY
10:45 TAKE SHAWN, RUSTY
      TO BATHROOM
11:00 BED

For a 12-page story on the weekly chores of a Rye, N.Y., housewife, LIFE assembled the parts of her burden: 35 beds to make; 750 items of glass and china, and 400 of silverware to wash; food to prepare and laundry to do.

Officials surveyed the carnage after Georgia guards killed prisoners who had refused to work. The editors cited the incident as an example of the domestic travails that persisted despite new U.S. world clout.

Mary Pickford and her husband, Charles "Buddy" Rogers, struck a familial pose on their fabled estate, Pickfair, with their adopted children, Ronald Pickford Rogers, 11, and Roxanne, 6.

A French model who wore a $355 New Look dress into a Paris working-class district for publicity shots had the garment ripped off by impoverished neighborhood housewives.

CLASSIC PHOTOS

A well-heeled matron was very relaxed at the Metropolitan Opera bar.

Albert Einstein and J. Robert Oppenheimer compared notes.

Cancer-ridden Babe Ruth thanked fans at a Yankee Stadium tribute.

CURRENTS AND EVENTS

WORLD: Peace Treaties Signed in Paris • Prussian State Abolished • War Trials Continue in Nuremberg • UN Plans Partition of Palestine • De Gaulle Forms New French Party • Communists Oust Hungary's Premier • Princess Elizabeth Marries Philip Mountbatten • Romania's King Michael Abdicates • Somoza Leads Nicaragua Coup • Trujillo Reelected in Dominican Republic • Philippines Grant U.S. Lease for Military Bases • Communists Gain Control of Manchuria • India Wins Independence, Nation Partitioned into India and Pakistan • Australia Admits 12,000 Displaced Europeans • Thor Heyerdahl Sails Kon-Tiki from Peru to Polynesia • Dead Sea Scrolls Discovered • Tidal Waves Sweep Hawaii • Bullfighter Manolete Fatally Gored.

U.S.A.: Congress Approves Marshall Plan for Europe • CIA Organized Under National Security Council • Ten on Hollywood Black List Imprisoned for Refusing to Testify Before Congress • Coal Mines Returned to Private Owners • Telephone Workers Strike Nationwide • Everglades National Park Founded • Pentagon Rejects Spruce Goose Airplane Design Promoted by Howard Hughes Despite One-Mile Flight.

FIRSTS: Polaroid Camera • Black Major League Baseball Player (Robinson) • Tubeless Auto Tires • Ballistic Missile • Home Tape Recorders • Microwave Ovens.

MOVIES: Great Expectations • Body and Soul • Odd Man Out • Life with Father • Nightmare Alley • The Secret Life of Walter Mitty • Brute Force • Monsieur Verdoux • Shoeshine • The Voice of the Turtle • The Bachelor and the Bobby-Soxer • The Hucksters • Miracle on 34th Street • Fun and Fancy Free.

SONGS: But Beautiful • There! I've Said It Again • Beyond the Sea • Open the Door, Richard • Almost Like Being in Love • Feudin' and Fightin' • Mam'selle • The Gentleman Is a Dope • Heartaches • Chi-Baba Chi-Baba • Come to Me, Bend to Me • The Heather on the Hill • How Are Things in Glocca Morra? • If This Isn't Love • Old Devil Moon • When I'm Not Near the Girl I Love • Too Fat Polka.

STAGE: A Streetcar Named Desire • All My Sons • The Heiress • The Winslow Boy • Command Decision • Medea • John Loves Mary • Brigadoon • Finian's Rainbow • High Button Shoes • Allegro • The Medium and The Telephone.

BOOKS: Gentlemen's Agreement (Hobson) • Tales of the South Pacific (Michener) • The Diary of Anne Frank (Frank) • The Wayward Bus (Steinbeck) • Inside U.S.A. (Gunther) • The Proper Bostonians (Amory) • The Age of Anxiety (Auden) • The Plague (Camus) • Doctor Faustus (Mann) • Across the Wide Missouri (De Voto) • Kingsblood Royal (Lewis) • I, the Jury (Spillane) • Under the Volcano (Lowry) • The Victim (Bellow) • The Woman of Rome (Moravia).

FADS: Bobby Socks as Hair Curlers • Dog Chains on Skirts.

   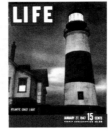    

JANUARY 6, 1947   JANUARY 13, 1947   JANUARY 20, 1947   JANUARY 27, 1947   FEBRUARY 3, 1947   FEBRUARY 10, 1947   FEBRUARY 17, 1947   FEBRUARY 24, 1947

MARCH 3, 1947   MARCH 10, 1947   MARCH 17, 1947   MARCH 24, 1947   MARCH 31, 1947   APRIL 7, 1947   APRIL 14, 1947   APRIL 21, 1947

    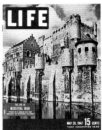   

APRIL 28, 1947   MAY 5, 1947   MAY 12, 1947   MAY 19, 1947   MAY 26, 1947   JUNE 2, 1947   JUNE 9, 1947   JUNE 16, 1947

JUNE 23, 1947   JUNE 30, 1947   JULY 7, 1947   JULY 14, 1947   JULY 21, 1947   JULY 28, 1947   AUGUST 4, 1947   AUGUST 11, 1947

      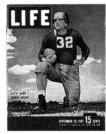 

AUGUST 18, 1947   AUGUST 25, 1947   SEPTEMBER 1, 1947   SEPTEMBER 8, 1947   SEPTEMBER 15, 1947   SEPTEMBER 22, 1947   SEPTEMBER 29, 1947   OCTOBER 6, 1947

OCTOBER 13, 1947   OCTOBER 20, 1947   OCTOBER 27, 1947   NOVEMBER 3, 1947   NOVEMBER 10, 1947   NOVEMBER 17, 1947   NOVEMBER 24, 1947   DECEMBER 1, 1947

DECEMBER 8, 1947   DECEMBER 15, 1947   DECEMBER 22, 1947   DECEMBER 29, 1947

A Madison Square Garden crowd watched in shock as heavily favored champion Joe Louis was sent to the canvas by veteran Joe Walcott in the Bomber's 24th defense of his heavyweight title. Louis came back to win by a decision.

Secret photos, found by the U.S. Army, recorded Hitler's mistress Eva Braun stunting, scantily clad, on a beach.

After a gale Thor Heyerdahl's log-and-rope raft plowed westward across the South Pacific.

Danny Kaye, June Havoc, Humphrey Bogart and (seated) Lauren Bacall listened closely at a House Un-American Activities Committee hearing to unmask communist influence in films.

The editors didn't try to hide their admiration for Albert Schweitzer, calling him (although in quotes) "The Greatest Man in the World."

Allen Funt, creator of radio's Candid Microphone, precursor of his TV Candid Camera, faked picking up a young woman in Central Park as his sound engineer recorded every word they spoke.

Stumping in Florida, G.O.P. presidential hopeful Harold Stassen grinned and gripped.

FRIENDLY ANTELOPE FAWNS NUZZLE AROUND DR. SCHWEITZER AS HE SITS IN AFRICAN JUNGLE WHICH SURROUNDS HIS MISSION

"THE GREATEST MAN IN THE WORLD"

at is what some people call Albert Schweitzer, jungle philosopher

re is a small group of men today, mostly tors, who believe the title of "greatest man world" should go—if it goes to anyone—to ned, shaggy, gray-mustached man above. He rt Schweitzer, Ph.D., Th.D., Mus.D., M.D., ear-old medical missionary who lives among ld cannibals at Lambaréné, deep in the jus-French Equatorial Africa. Two decades ago itzer, who was born in Alsace, made a tre-

mendous impression on European philosophers with his gloomy but scholarly two-volume prophecy of doom, *Philosophy of Civilization*. Before that, in his 20s, he had become recognized throughout the world as the greatest interpreter of the organ music of Bach and as a brilliant theologian and scholar on the life of Jesus. But in 1913, as he approached the height of his fame and as many men looked forward to the further work of one of the

century's most original minds, a Christian shame for the white man's treatment of the Negro drove Schweitzer to go to Africa with his Jewish wife and set up a medical mission for the natives. To be published this fall in the U.S. is *Albert Schweitzer: An Anthology*, a biography and collection of his writings. Next spring Dr. Schweitzer expects to leave the jungles to revisit the civilization he still believes is doomed by man's materialism and false values.

CONTINUED ON NEXT PAGE 95

To open this epochal series, the editors focused on Renaissance man Aeneas Piccolomini, a 15th century poet, politician and pope. In the painting by Pintoricchio at right, he appears as Pius II in the ceremony canonizing Catherine of Siena.

LIFE

ANNOUNCES A SERIES OF ARTICLES ON

The History of Western Culture

On the next 14 pages of this issue of LIFE is a pictorial essay on Renaissance man. It will be followed on April 7 by one on the Middle Ages. These two are the beginning of a series of major LIFE articles on the history and development of Western culture. In approach the spirit of this series will be the spirit which has moved American universities more and more to teach history not in narrow courses but in comprehensive surveys of civilization.

There is today much discussion of saving our civilization but not always enough understanding of what civilization is. There have been many civilizations in the world's history—the historian Toynbee names 21. Our modern Western civilization, which owes much to classical Greece and Rome, had its roots in the Middle Ages and grew most directly out of the Renaissance. In Western eyes today, the ideal kind of man seems to have been the man of the Renaissance. Living in the fresh morning of a new era in history, he was, above all, a rounded man who took all the world for his

opportunity and all knowledge for his province. He was vigorous, creative and enormously confident.

Modern Western man is not so confident. Standing uncertain of his place in history, he does not know where he and his world are going. But if he does not know where he is going, Western man can at least look back and see where he came from. Looking back in this series, LIFE will portray our civilization's history largely through the work of the men who both create and record the culture of their times: the artists. Because the series will show how men lived and what they thought, it will also exhibit the work of the people who built houses and philosophical systems, who fashioned poetry and clothing, who explored the sciences and men's souls. In this way LIFE will try to give Americans a perspective on history. Americans need perspective on their past so that they can determine their future. To an extent they have never had before, they have now the opportunity to preserve and develop the culture which they have inherited and which has in it so much greatness and beauty.

69

1948

In a year of international tensions, a domestic story about a long-shot win stole the show

In this presidential election year, the G.O.P. felt confident of success for the first time since 1932. But the vote produced an upset that upstaged all other big stories, including the Berlin airlift. LIFE had plumped for a Thomas E. Dewey victory, and in the last issue before the polling, a picture of him was captioned: "The next President travels by ferry over the broad waters of San Francisco Bay." The week after Harry Truman pulled off his stunning win, the editors confessed that they had "caught the wrong boat," and in the next issue they made him the cover subject for the first time since the campaign's start. They were proud, however, of developing further what was becoming a journalistic art form: the picture essay (following pages).

THE NEXT PRESIDENT TRAVELS BY FERRY BOAT
OVER THE BROAD WATERS OF SAN FRANCISCO BAY

This full-page editorial goof ran a week before the election. Facing it was an article that said, "Dewey has known all along that he would win."

As Gandhi's body was readied for the pyre, India's Nehru (upper left) and Britain's Earl Mountbatten (top, back to camera) prepared to follow it.

MARCH 1, 1948

MARCH 8, 1948

MARCH 15, 1948

MARCH 22, 1948

MAY 24, 1948

MAY 31, 1948

JUNE 7, 1948

JUNE 14, 1948

JUNE 21, 1948

JUNE 28, 1948

JULY 5, 1948

JULY 12, 1948

SEPTEMBER 13, 1948

SEPTEMBER 20, 1948

SEPTEMBER 27, 1948

OCTOBER 4, 1948

OCTOBER 11, 1948

OCTOBER 18, 1948

OCTOBER 25, 1948

NOVEMBER 1, 1948

Berliners at the edge of Tempelhof Field watched a C-47 bringing food and other supplies from the Western Allies. The city, occupied by the four victorious powers, lay entirely within the Soviet zone of partitioned Germany, and the U.S.S.R. had thrown a land blockade around it as a tactic of the Cold War. At times supply planes were landing every four minutes.

JANUARY 5, 1948

JANUARY 12, 1948

JANUARY 19, 1948

JANUARY 26, 1948

FEBRUARY 2, 1948

FEBRUARY 9, 1948

FEBRUARY 16, 1948

FEBRUARY 23, 1948

MARCH 29, 1948

APRIL 5, 1948

APRIL 12, 1948

APRIL 19, 1948

APRIL 26, 1948

MAY 3, 1948

MAY 10, 1948

MAY 17, 1948

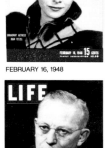

JULY 19, 1948

JULY 26, 1948

AUGUST 2, 1948

AUGUST 9, 1948

AUGUST 16, 1948

AUGUST 23, 1948

AUGUST 30, 1948

SEPTEMBER 6, 1948

NOVEMBER 8, 1948

NOVEMBER 15, 1948

NOVEMBER 22, 1948

NOVEMBER 29, 1948

DECEMBER 6, 1948

DECEMBER 13, 1948

DECEMBER 20, 1948

DECEMBER 27, 1948

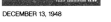

THE BIRTH OF A JOURNALISTIC GENRE

From the start, editors of picture magazines appreciated the value of focusing on people, reporting on their experiences. Stories several pages long and told through photographs were called essays, but never had the camera shared the lives of subjects while they went about their normal routines as if oblivious of the lens. LIFE set about doing exactly that in 1948, and the era of the true photo essay was ushered in by several great exemplars, two of which appear on these pages.

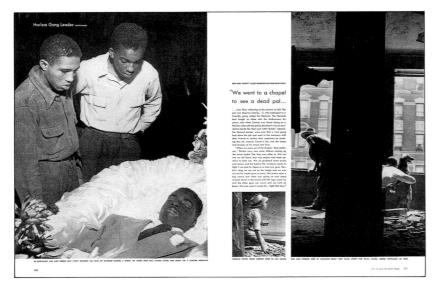

Gordon Parks's "Harlem Gang Leader" pictured Red Jackson's life at society's perimeter. How could Parks have been present in the midst of gang battle? How could he have entered Red's inner life, clicked his shutter without obtruding as Red viewed his dead buddy? The answer: infinite patience, persuasiveness and a humanity that the gang leader and his buddies believed in completely.

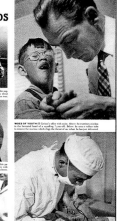

W. Eugene Smith's classic "Country Doctor" recorded, in evocative and intimate pictures, the exhausting, unremitting struggle of a young rural physician against death and disease. This early essay's images are among the pioneering photographer's masterpieces.

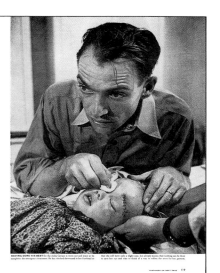

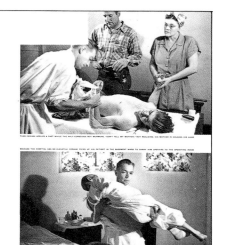

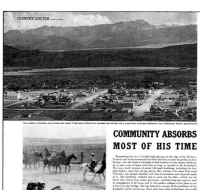

1949

As success followed success, the reach went up to the heavens and down to the underground

Under managing editors John Shaw Billings (1936-44), Daniel Longwell (1944-46) and Joseph Thorndike (1946-49), LIFE had become an institution read by 36 percent of all U.S. families. In this last year of Thorndike's brief tenure the news and do's were dealt with in the magazine's inimitable style (Russia now had The Bomb, Elizabeth Taylor had

MICHELANGELO'S

SISTINE CHAPEL

ITS FRESCOES ARE CONSIDERED THE GREATEST WORK OF ART EVER EXECUTED BY ONE MAN

In 1473 the Renaissance Pope, Sixtus IV, erected a plain brick church in Rome which came to be called the Sistine Chapel in his honor. He commissioned many artists to decorate the walls and to embellish the ceiling with a pattern of stars. But in 1508 Pope Julius II summoned Michelangelo Buonarroti of Florence to repaint the ceiling. Working for four and a half years, Michelangelo covered its 10,000 square feet with 343 colossal figures illustrating the Creation, the Fall of Man and the Flood. On the following 22 pages LIFE reproduces Michelangelo's murals, whose stupendous scope and power have awed the world for centuries.

25

JANUARY 3, 1949

JANUARY 10, 1949

JANUARY 17, 1949

JANUARY 24, 1949

JANUARY 31, 1949

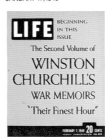

FEBRUARY 7, 1949

FEBRUARY 14, 1949

FEBRUARY 21, 1949

FEBRUARY 28, 1949

Isolating a Michelangelo detail, that of God's hand touching Adam's to give him life, the editors commented: "The hands themselves tell the story. God's is charged with life, while Adam's, an instant before it is touched, still hangs limp and lifeless."

fallen in love), but the year-end issue included a coup. Thorndike had commissioned Frank Lerner to photograph in color Michelangelo's Sistine Chapel ceiling frescoes and the huge mural of *The Last Judgment*. So, for Christmas, readers had an unprecedented close-up view of the "greatest work of art ever executed by one man."

Photographer Frank Lerner worked some 800 hours to get the nine separate, perfect exposures required to cover the ceiling's entire expanse. These "selects" were then integrated to make the single image that appeared in the magazine. To avoid the daytime crowds of St. Peter's Cathedral, Lerner photographed at night, on complicated scaffolding, using 30,000 watts of light to capture the overwhelming power of the 44-by-132-ft. fresco in which Michelangelo envisioned the Creation, Adam and Eve, sin in Eden, and Noah and the Flood.

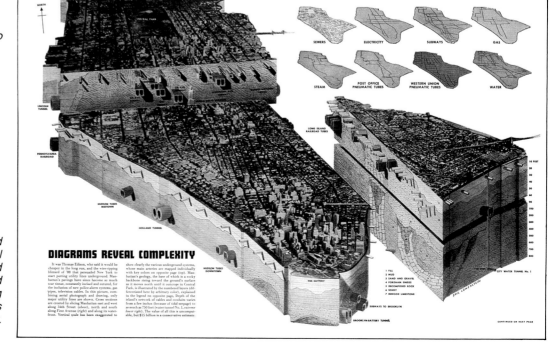

DIAGRAMS REVEAL COMPLEXITY

An 11-page article on the engineering wonders of underground Manhattan included this cutaway illustration combining aerial photography and mechanical drawings. The composite art sliced the island east and west across 34th Street, north and south along First Avenue (segment at right) and vertically along the Hudson River waterfront. Color keys to the main arteries of the various underground systems appeared at upper right.

U.S. DETECTS ATOMIC BLAST IN RUSSIA

EIGHT GIRLS TRY OUT MIXED EMOTIONS

How to illustrate news that the Soviets achieved an atomic explosion in secret? With reaction photos (left to right, top and bottom): Defense Secretary Louis Johnson, pensive; AEC's Sumner Pike, noncommittal; Soviet Foreign Minister Andrei Vishinsky, evasive; French Foreign Minister Robert Schuman, cool; Senate Atomic Energy Committee's Brien McMahon, worried; Army Chief of Staff Gen. Joseph L. Collins, brusque.

Eight bit players were assembled for a story on aspiring actresses. Only one hit stardom.

Billy Graham, during a revival in L.A., wore a newfangled lapel mike that "enables him to move and gesture at will."

"Quickest to latch onto the canasta boom," the editors pointed out, "have been the bridge experts, who are busily teaching canasta, giving lectures and publishing books." The editors then proceeded to do some teaching themselves, taking readers through an entire four-handed game.

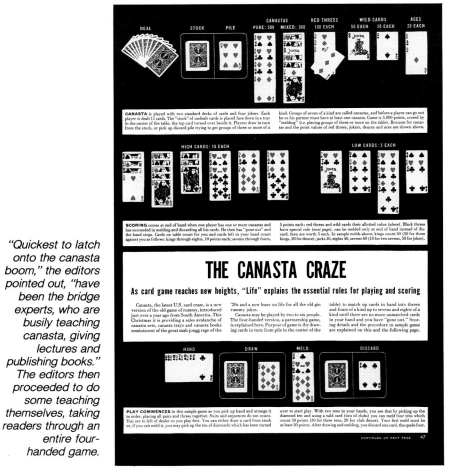

THE CANASTA CRAZE

As card game reaches new heights, "Life" explains the essential rules for playing and scoring

APRIL 25, 1949

MAY 2, 1949

MAY 9, 1949

MAY 16, 1949

JUNE 27, 1949

JULY 4, 1949

JULY 11, 1949

JULY 18, 1949

AUGUST 29, 1949

SEPTEMBER 5, 1949

SEPTEMBER 12, 1949

SEPTEMBER 19, 1949

OCTOBER 31, 1949

NOVEMBER 7, 1949

NOVEMBER 14, 1949

NOVEMBER 21, 1949

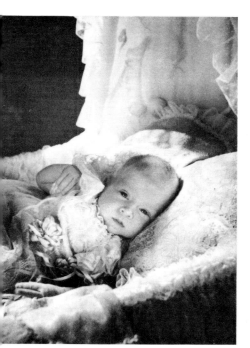

Prince Charles of Edinburgh, just 28 days old, "sat" for his portrait presenting an "absurdly thoughtful face."

Hand in hand, Ingrid Bergman and director Roberto Rossellini explored a ruined castle on Stromboli, where they made a movie and started a fabled romance.

The Turkish cavalry rode out for maneuvers in the snows of its eastern frontier.

Shanghaians formed a crushing queue at a bank selling gold for currency.

A helicopter with lights on its rotor tips traced a night pattern in a timed exposure.

CURRENTS AND EVENTS

WORLD: NATO Established • Adenauer Heads West German Republic • Soviet Bloc Breaks with Yugoslavia • Greek Civil War Ends • Hungary's Cardinal Mindszenty Sentenced to Life for "Treason" • Independent Irish Republic Proclaimed • Israel Moves Capital to Jerusalem from Tel Aviv • Chinese Nationalists Set Up in Formosa • Dutch Grant Independence to Indonesia.

U.S.A.: Truman Inaugurated • 11 Communist Leaders Convicted of Conspiracy • Federal Civil Rights Legislation Enacted • UN Site in N.Y.C. Dedicated • Justice Department Employee Judith Coplon Sentenced for Spying • Framingham, Mass., Heart Study Begins • Record 290 Tornadoes Hit Nation • Minimum Hourly Wage Raised from 40 to 75 Cents.

FIRSTS: Radio Free Europe Broadcast • Prepared Cake Mixes • Cortisone.

MOVIES: All the King's Men • The Champion • The Hasty Heart • The Heiress • I Was a Male War Bride • Letter to Three Wives • Samson and Delilah • The Stratton Story • Twelve O'Clock High • Adam's Rib • Command Decision • Francis • The Barkleys of Broadway • Dancing in the Dark • On the Town.

SONGS: Some Enchanted Evening • A Wonderful Guy • Younger Than Springtime • Honey Bun • Bali Ha'i • This Nearly Was Mine • There Is Nothin' Like a Dame • I'm Gonna Wash That Man Right Out of My Hair • Dear Hearts and Gentle People • Diamonds Are a Girl's Best Friend • Rudolph the Red-Nosed Reindeer • My Foolish Heart • Let's Take an Old-fashioned Walk • Comme Ci, Comme Ca • Mule Train • Crazy He Calls Me • No Moon at All • That Lucky Old Sun • I've Got a Lovely Bunch of Cocoanuts • Maybe It's Because • Mockin' Bird Hill • I Just Don't Like This Kind of Livin' • Rainbow in My Heart • Riders in the Sky.

STAGE: Death of a Salesman • Detective Story • They Knew What They Wanted • Montserrat • The Browning Version • The Big Knife • South Pacific • Regina • Gentlemen Prefer Blondes • Lost in the Stars • Miss Liberty • Touch and Go.

BOOKS: A Rage to Live (O'Hara) • Point of No Return (Marquand) • Dinner at Antoine's (Keyes) • Father of the Bride (Streeter) • Cheaper by the Dozen (Gilbreth, Carey) • The Greatest Story Ever Told (Oursler) • Peace of Soul (Sheen) • The Brave Bulls (Lea) • The Way West (Guthrie) • The Second Sex (De Beauvoir) • The Man with the Golden Arm (Algren) • Nineteen Eighty-Four (Orwell) • The Egyptian (Waltari) • White Collar Zoo (Barnes).

FADS: Canasta • Silly Putty • Shingle Haircuts • Hot-rodding.

MARCH 21, 1949

MARCH 28, 1949

APRIL 4, 1949

APRIL 11, 1949

APRIL 18, 1949

MAY 23, 1949

MAY 30, 1949

JUNE 6, 1949

JUNE 13, 1949

JUNE 20, 1949

JULY 25, 1949

AUGUST 1, 1949

AUGUST 8, 1949

AUGUST 15, 1949

AUGUST 22, 1949

SEPTEMBER 26, 1949

OCTOBER 3, 1949

OCTOBER 10, 1949

OCTOBER 17, 1949

OCTOBER 24, 1949

NOVEMBER 28, 1949

DECEMBER 5, 1949

DECEMBER 12, 1949

DECEMBER 19, 1949

DECEMBER 26, 1949

1950

At mid-century a new editor ordered a look back before the U.S. was rocked by Korea

Even before taking over as managing editor, Edward K. Thompson had sent a memo to correspondents coast to coast that stimulated a torrent of research. The first issue of the new year would be devoted to the half century just completed. The correspondents were instructed to place ads in daily and weekly papers soliciting pictures of family life from 1900 to the present: "Keep your eyes peeled for . . . wall phones,

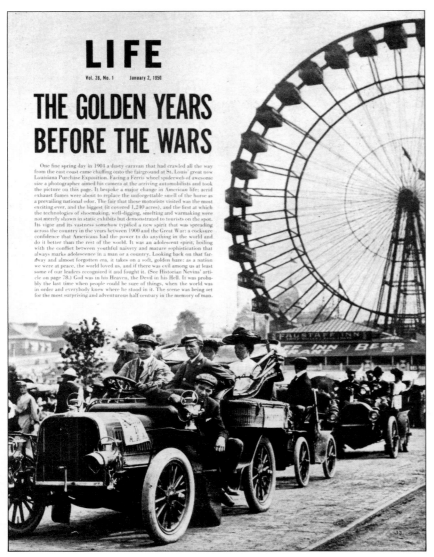

On Broadway Hepburn starred in As You Like It. "Her gams are as good as her iambics."

In the opening image of the "American Life and Times, 1900-1950" issue, cross-country motorists in turn-of-the-century automobiles rolled into St. Louis's Louisiana Purchase Exposition.

LIFE zeroed in on the youngest woman candidate in Britain's election, Margaret Roberts, 23, from Dartford, an "Oxford alumna and chemist." This was one year before she became Mrs. Thatcher and 29 before she became Britain's prime minister.

JANUARY 2, 1950

JANUARY 9, 1950

JANUARY 16, 1950

JANUARY 23, 1950

JANUARY 30, 1950

FEBRUARY 6, 1950

FEBRUARY 13, 1950

FEBRUARY 20, 1950

FEBRUARY 27, 1950

MARCH 6, 1950

MARCH 13, 1950

MARCH 20, 1950

phonograph horns, claw-foot bathtubs, gas lamps converted to electricity, things that have changed and improved the life of the people of this country." The result was "American Life and Times, 1900-1950," an issue crammed with nostalgia and pride—pride that, despite the ups and downs, "no nation could look back on greater achievements." Thompson also embraced and perfected one of the maga-zine's favorite devices, the "setup" picture, for which the editors assembled all there was of some-thing for a single photo: the parts of a complex ma-chine, workers in a large plant, the entire Danish Army, the sitting U.S. governors. Also, the pictures selected were livelier than ever. Tragically, however, images of war soon cast their shadows once again, this time all the way from Korea (next pages).

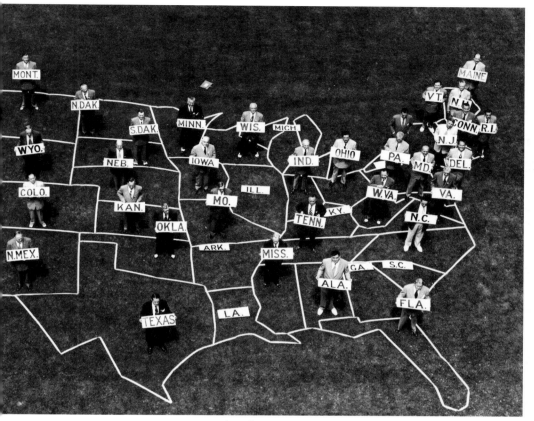

At a Governors' Conference LIFE collected them all. Only New York's Thomas E. Dewey wouldn't hold up his sign.

After Seoul's fall to Communist forces, General MacArthur, "his carefully combed hair resembling a cardinal's skullcap," pondered aboard his private plane the consequences of the Korean campaign.

Spain's Francisco Franco, dewy-eyed in the garb of a Navy captain-general, and his wife attended daughter Carmencita's wedding.

In Eliot Elisofon's wide-ranging picture essay on the Nile River and the areas influenced by it, a Shilluk warrior at Malakal, far upstream in the Sudan, grimaced while performing a fearsome war dance.

Radiant in a satin gown embroidered with beads and seed pearls ("Gift of her studio, it cost $1,200"), Elizabeth Taylor, 18, clasped the hand of her beaming bridegroom, Conrad "Nicky" Hilton Jr., 23, after their Beverly Hills wedding, the first for each.

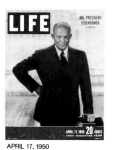

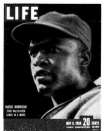

MARCH 27, 1950   APRIL 3, 1950   APRIL 10, 1950   APRIL 17, 1950   APRIL 24, 1950   MAY 1, 1950   MAY 8, 1950   May 15, 1950

Gjon Mili captured a Picasso centaur, outlined with a flashlight.

Black workers sweated in a gold mine in South Africa.

A U. of Michigan drum major inspired a gaggle of kid emulators.

CURRENTS AND EVENTS

WORLD: Britain Convicts German-Born Klaus Fuchs for Giving Soviets Atomic Secrets ● Eisenhower Becomes Europe's Supreme Allied Commander ● North Korea Invades South Korea, UN Responds as Truman Sends U.S. Troops, Appoints MacArthur UN Commander ● U.S.S.R., China Sign 30-Year Alliance, Recognize Vietminh Regime ● U.S., Britain Recognize Vietnam, Cambodia, Laos as Associated States Within French Union ● Czech Government Charges Foreign Diplomats with Espionage ● Spain, U.S. Resume Diplomatic Relations ● Anti-Apartheid Rioting Spreads in South Africa ● Jordan Annexes Arab Palestine.

U.S.A.: Truman Orders H-bomb Development ● Senator McCarthy Charges State Department Infiltrated by Reds ● Alger Hiss Guilty of Perjury ● Puerto Rican Nationalists Attempt to Kill Truman ● Book "Red Channels" Accuses Many in Entertainment, Publishing Industries of Communist Activities.

FIRSTS: Kidney Transplant ● Credit Card (Diners Club) ● Terramycin ● International Passenger Flight by Jet ● Black Woman to Compete at Forest Hills (Althea Gibson).

MOVIES: All About Eve ● Born Yesterday ● King Solomon's Mines ● Stromboli ● Sunset Boulevard ● Harvey ● The Third Man ● Cheaper by the Dozen ● Father of the Bride ● Bitter Rice ● Treasure Island ● The Asphalt Jungle ● Rio Grande ● The Men ● The Sands of Iwo Jima ● The Bicycle Thief ● Young Man with a Horn ● Annie Get Your Gun ● Pagan Love Song ● Cinderella.

SONGS: All My Love ● Rag Mop ● If I Knew You Were Comin' I'd've Baked a Cake ● It's a Lovely Day Today ● Music! Music! Music! ● It's So Nice to Have a Man Around the House ● Frosty the Snowman ● I'm Gonna Live Till I Die ● Luck Be a Lady ● So Long (It's Been Good to Know Yuh) ● Silver Bells ● Be My Love ● Sam's Song ● Mona Lisa ● C'est Si Bon ● A Bushel and a Peck ● If I Were a Bell ● You're Just in Love.

STAGE: The Member of the Wedding ● The Cocktail Party ● Affairs of State ● Come Back, Little Sheba ● The Country Girl ● Bell, Book and Candle ● Guys and Dolls ● Call Me Madam.

BOOKS: Across the River and into the Trees (Hemingway) ● The Wall (Hersey) ● The Disenchanted (Schulberg) ● Kon-Tiki (Heyerdahl) ● The Martian Chronicles (Bradbury) ● The Lonely Crowd (Riesman) ● Live Younger, Live Longer (Hauser) ● The Mature Mind (Overstreet).

TOPS IN RADIO, '40s: Jack Benny (Premiere '32) ● Fred Allen ('34) ● Bob Hope ('35) ● Fibber McGee and Molly ('35) ● Bing Crosby ('31) ● Amos 'n' Andy ('28) ● Red Skelton ('41) ● Edgar Bergen and Charlie McCarthy ('37) ● Kay Kyser's Kollege of Musical Knowledge ('38) ● Walter Winchell ('30) ● Kate Smith ('31) ● Eddie Cantor ('31) ● Dinah Shore ('39) ● Burns and Allen ('32) ● The Romance of Helen Trent ('33) ● Stella Dallas ('37) ● Ma Perkins ('33) ● Portia Faces Life ('40) ● Take It or Leave It ('43) ● Truth or Consequences ('40) ● Your Hit Parade ('35) ● People Are Funny ('42) ● Mr. Keen, Tracer of Lost Persons ('37) ● One Man's Family ('35) ● Jimmy Durante ('43) ● Duffy's Tavern ('41) ● Queen for a Day ('45) ● Abbott & Costello ('42).

FADS: Humanoid Dolls ● Circle Skirts ● Plaid Menswear.

IN ASIA, STALEMATE SNATCHED FROM VICTORY

When North Korea invaded South Korea, the UN called it a "breach of the peace." Under pressure from the U.S. it responded by sending an international force—consisting largely of American troops—commanded by Douglas MacArthur. Photographers Carl Mydans, David Douglas Duncan and Hank Walker hurried to cover the "police action" and soon were sending the magazine searing images of combat that erased the semantic niceties that sought to camouflage a terrible war.

Marines headed for Inchon's beach in an encircling maneuver. The surprise landing triggered China's intervention and abruptly changed the course of the war.

MAY 22, 1950

MAY 29, 1950

JUNE 5, 1950

JUNE 12, 1950

JUNE 19, 1950

JUNE 26, 1950

JULY 3, 1950

JULY 10, 1950

JULY 17, 1950

JULY 24, 1950

JULY 31, 1950

AUGUST 7, 1950

OCTOBER 9, 1950

OCTOBER 16, 1950

OCTOBER 23, 1950

OCTOBER 30, 1950

LIFE

Vol. 29 No. 26   December 25, 1950

Heads bent against the furious cold,
Marines trudge along in the lee of a hill
toward a sea that is always just beyond the horizon.

THERE WAS
A CHRISTMAS

in Korea, although it was all over before the 25th
of December. It was a cold and bitter Christmas, but Americans
can be more thankful for it than for all their parties and presents. It took place
in the valley of the shadow of death, through which Marines
and soldiers fought their way from the Changjin Reservoir to a haven on the
Japan Sea. This is the story of the incredibly gallant
Marines, who fought fantastic odds but brought out their equipment,
their wounded and their dead. This is what it was like
for those who survived unhurt, for those who were wounded and
pulled through and for those whose Christmas is now forever.

◄— This is the face of a man who eats frozen rations
in the snow and who may be interrupted at any moment
to run, to fight or to die.

PHOTOGRAPHED BY DAVID DOUGLAS DUNCAN

*For the Christmas issue
Duncan delivered a martial
masterpiece (left and below)
recording intimately the brutal
yule of Marines cut off from
support and being slaughtered
as they fought their way
from Changjin to the Japan
Sea and safety. In October,
before Chinese troops
charged into the fray, LIFE had
confidently said that the
conflict was winding down
toward North Korea's defeat.*

EYES of men
who have looked at undiluted hell
are not pleasant to meet
soon after. These are the faces
of a general named Lemuel Shepherd
and some other brave men.
There is no fear in their faces
and no great hatred.
They were simply fighting their
way out and hoping to stay alive.

Even at the risk of drawing bullets from snipers,
Marines try to warm themselves at a fire
just before they resume their march at dawn.

Under fire from the nearby hills,
a Marine crouches behind his jeep and waits
for flanking patrols to clean up the Reds.

Wrecked vehicles block the road.
Cobalt, the troops stripped them of their equipment,
shoved them aside and prevailed them.

Across the snowy landscape,
along a single road gashed from the hillside,
the long column makes toward Hamhung.

CONTINUED ON NEXT PAGE

AUGUST 14, 1950

AUGUST 21, 1950

AUGUST 28, 1950

SEPTEMBER 4, 1950

SEPTEMBER 11, 1950

SEPTEMBER 18, 1950

SEPTEMBER 25, 1950

OCTOBER 2, 1950

NOVEMBER 6, 1950

NOVEMBER 13, 1950

NOVEMBER 20, 1950

NOVEMBER 27, 1950

DECEMBER 4, 1950

DECEMBER 11, 1950

DECEMBER 18, 1950

DECEMBER 25, 1950

1951

In further pursuit of the best pictures wherever they might be found, the magazine embarked on its first photo contest

Peace in Korea was thwarted. President Truman relieved General Douglas MacArthur of his Asian commands because he persisted in expressing strong disagreement with policy decisions based on nonmilitary political considerations. As combat continued unabated, battlefield images competed for space with those in a banner year's harvest of picture essays. Edward Clark's "Adoption," Mark Kauffman's "How to Make Marines," and two by W. Eugene Smith, "Spanish Village" and "Nurse Midwife," were but a few of an outstanding crop. Also, to nurture new talent, LIFE announced its first picture competition for young camera artists. The results were amply satisfying. Among the winners were several who became leading professionals (next pages). Similar contests were held in 1966 and 1971.

After his dismissal MacArthur was cheered as a hero in Tokyo, as he entered his headquarters, and later in Manhattan during a ticker-tape parade on Broadway.

CLASSIC PHOTOS

An elder citizen of a Spanish village took leave of his family.

A tiny Korean faced his first meal in a long time.

Winston Churchill surveyed his estate.

CURRENTS AND EVENTS

WORLD: Churchill Returns as Britain's Prime Minister • British Spies Guy Burgess and Donald Maclean, Warned by Double Agent Kim Philby, Flee to U.S.S.R. • European Coal, Steel Community Established • Iran Nationalizes Oil Industry • Egypt Abrogates Alliance with Britain, Bars Israel-Bound Ships from Suez Canal • Jordan's King Assassinated • UN Troops Recapture Seoul from North Korean, Chinese Forces • U.S. Signs Military Pacts with Japan, Philippines • President Juan Perón Reelected in Argentina.

U.S.A.: MacArthur Returns to Triumphant Manhattan Ticker-tape Parade After Truman Fires Him • Constitutional Amendment

Yul Brynner, formerly circus acrobat, TV director and nightclub singer, emerged as the swaggering but likable King of Siam in Rodgers and Hammerstein's smash hit The King and I "as if he had a string of firecrackers under his royal panung."

JANUARY 1, 1951 · JANUARY 8, 1951 · JANUARY 15, 1951 · JANUARY 22, 1951 · JANUARY 29, 1951 · FEBRUARY 5, 1951 · FEBRUARY 12, 1951

FEBRUARY 19, 1951 · FEBRUARY 26, 1951 · MARCH 5, 1951 · MARCH 12, 1951 · MARCH 19, 1951 · MARCH 26, 1951 · APRIL 2, 1951

APRIL 9, 1951 · APRIL 16, 1951 · APRIL 23, 1951 · APRIL 30, 1951 · MAY 7, 1951

May 14, 1951 · MAY 21, 1951 · MAY 28, 1951 · JUNE 4, 1951 · JUNE 11, 1951

AN OLD SOLDIER FADES AWAY INTO NEW GLORY

I am closing my 52 years of military service. When I joined the Army, even before the turn of the century, it was the fulfillment of all of my boyish hopes and dreams. The world has turned over many times since I took the oath on the plain at West Point, and the hopes and dreams have all since vanished, but I still remember the refrain of one of the most popular barracks ballads of that day which proclaimed most proudly that old soldiers never die; they just fade away. And like the old soldier of that ballad, I now close my military career and just fade away, an old soldier who tried to do his duty as God gave him the light to see that duty. Goodby.

The picture above was taken at the moment when General of the Army Douglas MacArthur, 71, completed the never-to-be-forgotten closing words of his speech before last week's historic joint meeting of Congress. His message poured out into the America he had not seen for 14 years, the nation whose sons he had commanded in both defeat and victory. Most Americans listened, and 30 million or more watched by television as he spoke, and they were magnetized by the vibrant voice, the dramatic rhetoric and the Olympian personality of the most controversial military hero of our times.

He had come back "in the fading twilight of life," he said, to speak his considered viewpoint without "rancor or bitterness" as a "fellow American." But he was obliged to come, as all the world knew by now, because his commander-in-chief, the President of the U.S., had stripped him of all of his commands in Asia—because he had been openly critical of the Administration's strategies for war and peace, and he had come back to unprecedented acclaim. An army of Americans seemed to close ranks around the general, like confused back privates hunting in darkness for a confident leader. The homecoming of the almost legendary MacArthur was like nothing else in American history.

It had begun in Tokyo with a tribute from the Japanese people worthy of an emperor—indeed, on the day before the former commander of the occupation forces flew away from the land he had ruled, the emperor himself came in person to pay his farewell respects. Early the next morning 100,000 of Tokyo's citizens lined the streets, a few of them weeping openly, some shouting "Banzai! (May you live a thousand years)." At Honolulu 12 hours later the man who had swept the western Pacific stepped back on American soil and there paid honor to the men who had died in the cause he led in World War II. In San Francisco the next night, when his Constellation landed long after dark, his tumultuous welcome reverberated across the U.S. In Washington 25 hours later he was almost crushed by a mob of admirers, and by the time he spoke to Congress he had the attention not only of all who saw and heard him but of most of the world. He spectacularly challenged the basic assumptions of American policy in the Far East and said that his views "from a military standpoint . . . have been fully shared by practically every military leader concerned with the Korean campaign, including our own Joint Chiefs of Staff." As Congress cheered him, he moved in an ever-growing triumph to New York City (*left*).

▸ TRIUMPHAL RIDE WAS PHOTOGRAPHED BY BILL STAHL OF NEW YORK "MIRROR"

23

JUNE 18, 1951 · JUNE 25, 1951 · JULY 2, 1951 · JULY 9, 1951 · JULY 16, 1951

(22nd) Limits Presidency to Two Terms • Senate (Kefauver) Committee Holds Televised Hearings on Organized Crime • Julius, Ethel Rosenberg, Guilty of Treason, Sentenced to Death • West Point Dismisses 90 Cadets for Cheating • Navy Orders Development of Atomic Sub • Missouri River, Tributaries Flood More than One Million Acres • Joe Walcott Takes Heavyweight Title from Ezzard Charles • Giants' Bobby Thomson Homers to Beat Dodgers for N.L. Pennant • Sugar Ray Robinson Defeats Jake LaMotta for Middleweight Crown.

FIRSTS: Coast-to-Coast Color TV • Thoroughbred Million-Dollar Winner (Citation) • Underground Atomic Explosion • U.S. Space Flight Carrying Live Creatures (Four Monkeys) • Plastic Heart Valve • Pan-American Games (in Argentina).

MOVIES: A Streetcar Named Desire • A Place in the Sun • Quo Vadis • The Red Badge of Courage • The Brave Bulls • David and Bathsheba • The Lavender Hill Mob • Tom Sawyer • Bright Victory • The Thing • Bedtime for Bonzo • Royal Wedding • Alice in Wonderland • Oliver Twist • Rashomon • Show Boat • An American in Paris • Call Me Mister • The Great Caruso.

SONGS: In the Cool, Cool, Cool of the Evening • Kisses Sweeter Than Wine • Unforgettable • Come On-a My House • Cold, Cold Heart • Cry • We Kiss in a Shadow • Whistle a Happy Tune • On Top of Old Smokey • The Little White Cloud That Cried • Because of You.

STAGE: The Rose Tattoo • The Four-poster • I Am a Camera •

The Moon Is Blue • Stalag 17 • Point of No Return • Darkness at Noon • Billy Budd • A Tree Grows in Brooklyn • The King and I • Top Banana • Paint Your Wagon • Two on the Aisle.

BOOKS: From Here to Eternity (Jones) • The Caine Mutiny (Wouk) • The Catcher in the Rye (Salinger) • Lie Down in Darkness (Styron) • The Grass Harp (Capote) • The Cruel Sea (Monserrat) • Return to Paradise (Michener) • The Sea Around Us (Carson) • Requiem for a Nun (Faulkner) • The End of the Affair (Greene) • God and Man at Yale (Buckley) • Moses (Asch) • Pogo (Kelly) • Barbary Coast (Mailer).

FADS: Bomb Shelters • Drive-in Movies • Straw Hats • Narrow Bow Ties • Confederate Emblems on Clothing, Cars.

Of the 10 top winners in the Contest for Young Photographers, seven became famed professionals: Dennis Stock, Elliott Erwitt, Esther Bubley, Alfred Gescheidt, Carroll Seghers II, Robert Frank and Ruth Orkin. Many other noted pros-to-be finished further down among the 1,730 entrants.

Gloucestershire girls basking in sunlit seclusion on a willowed bank were a bonus in William Sumits's photographic navigation of the River Thames from its source at Trewsbury Mead to the sea.

This portrait of a patient new American by Stock, 23, was part of a sensitive picture story about the U.S. arrival of European displaced persons.

Standing "as they might for a curtain call," three stage greats, Helen Hayes, Lynn Fontanne and Katharine Cornell, assembled for a LIFE portrait, part of an 11-page celebration of "200 Years of U.S. Theater."

A "hot cow" injected with irradiated carbon breathed radioactive CO_2 into a gas mask.

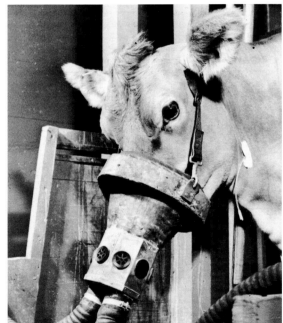

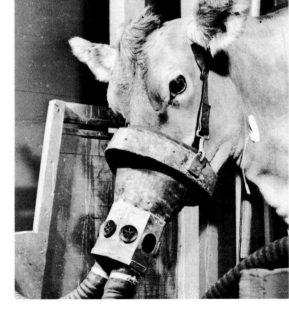

In a gesture of contempt that required no translation, a North Korean soldier saluted LIFE's Joe Scherschel, who accompanied a UN convoy en route to the cease-fire talks.

For a story about Marine recruits at the Parris Island, S.C., boot camp, LIFE followed Platoon 268, under their drill instructor, Sgt. Trope, from the time they picked up their gear and duffels.

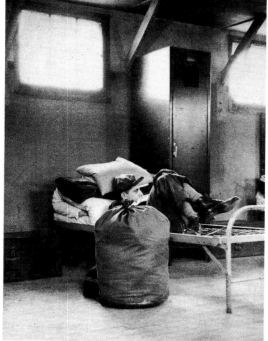

Erwitt, 23, drafted into the Army, recorded the boredom of his buddies on duty with a photographic unit in Germany.

This close-up of an old preacher addressing his congregation was one of four portraits made by Seghers at a worship service.

A handsome movie actor moved from occasional appearances on the edit pages into a holiday ad.

Boys with heads shaved because of widespread scalp infections marched in single file at the Shah of Iran's medical center in Tehran.

I'M SENDING CHESTERFIELDS to all my friends. That's the merriest Christmas any smoker can have — Chesterfield mildness plus no unpleasant after-taste

Ronald Reagan

CHESTERFIELD   Buy the beautiful Christmas-card carton

JULY 23, 1951

JULY 30, 1951

AUGUST 6, 1951

AUGUST 13, 1951

AUGUST 20, 1951

AUGUST 27, 1951

SEPTEMBER 3, 1951

SEPTEMBER 10, 1951

SEPTEMBER 17, 1951

SEPTEMBER 24, 1951

OCTOBER 1, 1951

OCTOBER 8, 1951

OCTOBER 15, 1951

OCTOBER 22, 1951

OCTOBER 29, 1951

NOVEMBER 5, 1951

NOVEMBER 12, 1951

NOVEMBER 19, 1951

NOVEMBER 26, 1951

DECEMBER 3, 1951

DECEMBER 10, 1951

DECEMBER 17, 1951

DECEMBER 24, 1951

DECEMBER 31, 1951

1952

As the Democrats' long hold on the presidency was nearing an end, the battle for the Republican nomination became the roughest in four decades. To win it the supporters of Dwight Eisenhower, the war hero, had to overcome the G.O.P.'s Old Guard, which was totally committed to Senator Robert Taft, Ohio's staunch conservative. The party's choice for Ike's running mate was a 39-year-old California senator, Richard Nixon. To oppose the general, the Democrats nominated Gov-

At a time of great change in American politics, the editors liked Ike and, increasingly, the advantages of long articles

Citizen Ike went on from a visit to his hometown, Abilene, Kans., to win the G.O.P. nomination. V.P. candidate Nixon, accused of having accepted unethical campaign contributions, bared his assets and liabilities on nationwide radio and TV, then wept when Ike called him vindicated.

PICTURE OF THE WEEK

Congressman John F. Kennedy, running for the U.S. Senate, sought the women's vote in Massachusetts with "a new and potent weapon—the political tea."

A Communist bomb made a shambles of the usually placid Place du Théâtre in Saigon and presaged the drawn-out conflict in Vietnam, then under French sway. The bomb, placed in a car trunk by the Vietminh, injured the man in the foreground, killed the driver of the delivery truck as he sat at the wheel and set ablaze vehicles all around the square.

JANUARY 7, 1952

JANUARY 14, 1952

FEBRUARY 25, 1952

MARCH 3, 1952

APRIL 14, 1952

APRIL 21, 1952

JUNE 2, 1952

JUNE 9, 1952

ernor Adlai Stevenson of Illinois. Early on, LIFE donned the "I Like Ike" campaign button. The editors ran six Ike and/or Mamie covers and editorialized, "It is not often that American voters have had a chance to elect a proven great man as their president." Meanwhile, the magazine's fascination with long text pieces deepened and bylined articles, by famed free-lance authors as well as gifted staff writers, became the primary responsibility of a separate department.

Triumphant over Senator Taft and the G.O.P.'s traditional wing, Mamie and Ike and Dick and Pat grinned and waved at the Chicago convention.

Adlai Stevenson at the Democrats' convention, also held in Chicago, was set against running. Convinced a move to draft him was genuine, he said, "I guess I'm stuck."

 JANUARY 21, 1952
 JANUARY 28, 1952
FEBRUARY 4, 1952
FEBRUARY 11, 1952
FEBRUARY 18, 1952

 MARCH 10, 1952
 MARCH 17, 1952
MARCH 24, 1952
MARCH 31, 1952
 APRIL 7, 1952

APRIL 28, 1952
MAY 5, 1952
MAY 12, 1952
May 19, 1952
 MAY 26, 1952

 JUNE 16, 1952
 JUNE 23, 1952
 JUNE 30, 1952
 JULY 7, 1952
 JULY 14, 1952

CLASSIC PHOTOS

Photographer Milton Greene made sure no one challenged Dietrich for title to the world's best legs.

Three British queens—Elizabeth II, her grandmother Mary and mother Elizabeth—paid honor to George VI's coffin.

Moviegoers in Polaroid spectacles watched a movie in three dimensions.

CURRENTS AND EVENTS

WORLD: Britain's George VI Dies, Elizabeth II Mounts Throne • Moscow Ousts U.S. Ambassador Kennan • Egypt's Farouk Abdicates, Republic Formed • Hussein I Crowned in Jordan • Israel, Germany Agree on $822 Million in Restitution for Nazi Atrocities • Anti-French Riots Erupt in Tangier, Tunisia • Mau Maus Rise Up in Kenya • Cuban Army Coup Returns Batista to Power • Puerto Rico Becomes First U.S. Commonwealth • Eva Perón Dies • Korean Armistice Talks Stall, Fulfilling Campaign Promise Eisenhower Inspects UN Troops There • U.S., Japan Sign Mutual Security Pact • Mycenaean Texts (Linear B) Deciphered.

U.S.A.: Eisenhower Defeats Stevenson for Presidency • Churchill Addresses Joint Session of Congress, Urges Arms for Western Europe • Steelworkers End 54-Day Strike • McCarran-Walter Immigration Act Abolishes Racial Restrictions but Retains Nationality Quotas • Railroads Returned to Private Control After 21 Months of Operation by Federal Troops • State Department Restricts Travel to U.S.S.R., Its Satellites • Polio Epidemic Strikes More than 50,000, Salk Vaccine Tested.

FIRSTS: Thermonuclear Bomb • Pocket-size Transistor Radio • Plastic Lenses for Cataracts.

MOVIES: The African Queen • Five Fingers • High Noon • The Big Sky • Hans Christian Andersen • Come Back Little Sheba • Cry, the Beloved Country • Pat and Mike • The Man in the White Suit • Scaramouche • Don't Bother to Knock • The Quiet Man • The Snows of Kilimanjaro • Limelight • Because You're Mine • Where's Charley? • Singin' in the Rain.

SONGS: Botch-a-Me • Do Not Forsake Me • That Doggie in the Window • Feet Up (Pat Him on the Po-Po) • Hi-Lili, Hi-Lo • I Believe • I Saw Mommy Kissing Santa Claus • Jambalaya • Lullaby of Birdland • Out of the Clear Blue Sky • Pretend • Wheel of Fortune • When I Fall in Love • Don't Just Stand There • Goin' Home • Till I Waltz Again with You.

STAGE: The Shrike • The Time of the Cuckoo • The Seven Year Itch • Venus Observed • Dial "M" for Murder • An Evening with Beatrice Lillie • Wish You Were Here • New Faces.

BOOKS: East of Eden (Steinbeck) • Giant (Ferber) • The Old Man and the Sea (Hemingway) • Player Piano (Vonnegut) • Spartacus (Fast) • The Groves of Academe (McCarthy) • The Natural (Malamud) • Charlotte's Web (White) • Invisible Man (Ellison) • Witness (Chambers) • The Saracen Blade (Yerby) • U.S.A. Confidential (Lait, Mortimer) • The Power of Positive Thinking (Peale).

FADS: Scrabble • Panty Raids • Beanies • Poodle, Ponytail Hairdos • Pizzas • Chlorophyll Products.

The Exclusive "HOLLYWOOD" CALENDAR LINE
WESTERN LITHOGRAPH CO.
LOS ANGELES
1952 · FEBRUARY · 1952

While the nation buzzed about the newly come to light nude calendar art for which a broke Marilyn Monroe had posed before making her first film, she lounged barefoot at home listening to favorite records. Her taste in music, LIFE said easily, was "distinctly highbrow, running to composers like the Hungarian modernist Béla Bartók."

As the frontispiece for LIFE's presentation, complete in one issue, of Ernest Hemingway's new novella, The Old Man and the Sea, *the author looked out from a Cuban fishing village much like that of his protagonist's.*

A FUMBLE PLAYER   HAS TROUBLE DISGUISING HIMSELF

Life Goes to a Fumble Party

NEW GUESSING GAME IS PLAYED IN DARK

Photographed in infrared light, a roomful of Denverites pawed one another in a "Fumble Party" that LIFE probably should not have gone to. The messy-looking story drew a torrent of letters from outraged readers.

128   129

PART I

THE EARTH IS BORN

Spawned by a swirl of cosmic dust and forged in elemental fire, the globe on whose familiar face we live spins toward destruction by its parent sun

Text by LINCOLN BARNETT   Paintings by CHESLEY BONESTELL

Earth! Thou mother of numberless children, the nurse and the mother, Sister thou of the stars, and beloved by the Sun, the rejoice! Guardian and friend of the moon, O Earth, whom the comets forget not, Yea, in the measureless distance wheel round and again they behold thee!
SAMUEL TAYLOR COLERIDGE, *Hymn to the Earth*

PRISONED in his paved cities, blindfolded by his impulses and necessities, man tends to disregard the system of nature in which he stands...

CONTINUED ON NEXT PAGE

86

JULY 21, 1952

JULY 28, 1952

AUGUST 4, 1952

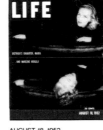
AUGUST 11, 1952

AUGUST 18, 1952

AUGUST 25, 1952

SEPTEMBER 1, 1952

SEPTEMBER 8, 1952

THE *Old Man*
AND THE *Sea*

by Ernest Hemingway

He was an old man who fished alone in a skiff in the Gulf Stream and he had gone eighty-four days now without taking a fish. In the first forty days a boy had been with him. But after forty days without a fish the boy's parents had told him that the old man was now definitely and finally *salao*, which is the worst form of unlucky, and the boy had gone at their orders in another boat which caught three good fish the first week. It made the boy sad to see the old man come in each day with his skiff empty and he always went down to help him carry either the coiled lines or the gaff and harpoon and the sail that was furled around the mast. The sail was patched with flour sacks and, furled, it looked like the flag of permanent defeat.

The old man was thin and gaunt with deep wrinkles in the back of his neck. The brown blotches of the benevolent skin cancer the sun brings from its reflection on the tropic sea were on his cheeks. The blotches ran well down the sides of his face and his hands had the deep-creased scars from handling heavy fish on the cords. But none of these scars were fresh. They were as old as erosions in a fishless desert.

Everything about him was old except his eyes and they were the same color as the sea and were cheerful and undefeated.

"Santiago," the boy said to him as they climbed the bank from where the skiff was hauled up. "I could go with you again. We've made some money."

The old man had taught the boy to fish and the boy loved him.

"No," the old man said. "You're with a lucky boat. Stay with them."

"But remember how you went eighty-seven days and then we caught big ones every day for three weeks."

"I remember," the old man said. "I know you did not leave me because you doubted."

"It was papa made me leave. I am a boy and I must obey him."

"I know," the old man said. "It is quite normal."

"He hasn't much faith."

"No," the old man said. "But we have. Haven't we?"

"Yes," the boy said. "Can I offer you a beer on the Terrace and then we'll take the stuff home."

"Why not?" the old man said. "Between fishermen."

They sat on the Terrace and many of the fishermen made fun of the old man and he was not angry. Others, of the older fishermen, looked at him and were sad. But they did not show it and they spoke politely about the current and the depths they had drifted their lines at and the steady good weather and of what they had seen. The successful fishermen of that day were already in and had butchered their marlin out and carried them laid full length across two planks, with two men staggering at the end of each plank, to the fish house where they waited for the ice truck to carry them to the market in Havana. Those who had caught sharks had taken them to the shark factory on the other side of the cove where they were hoisted on a block and tackle, their livers removed, their fins cut off and their hides skinned out and their flesh cut into strips for salting.

When the wind was in the east a smell came across the harbour from the shark factory; but today there was only the faint edge of the odour because the wind had backed into the north and then dropped off and it was pleasant and sunny on the Terrace.

"Santiago," the boy said.

"Yes," the old man said. He was holding his glass and thinking of many years ago.

"Can I go out to get sardines for you for tomorrow?"

"No. Go and play baseball. I can still row and Rogelio will throw the net."

"I would like to go. If I cannot fish with you, I would like to serve in some way."

"You bought me a beer," the old man said. "You are already a man."

COPYRIGHT 1952 BY ERNEST HEMINGWAY

THE AUTHOR is shown at a Cuban fishing village like the one used by the "old man" of his story.

35

Less than a year after Kang Koo Ri, a starving 5-year-old in a Korean orphanage, had been seen in LIFE as "The Little Boy Who Wouldn't Smile," he reappeared—well fed, well loved and, yes, smiling—in a picture taken by a U.S. jet pilot.

THE LITTLE BOY WHO WOULDN'T SMILE

With histrionic flair, a sixth-grade homeroom teacher in Greak Neck, Long Island, told her class of her mortification over their performance in geography. They had been asked by another teacher what country lay south of Austria, and no one in the class knew the answer.

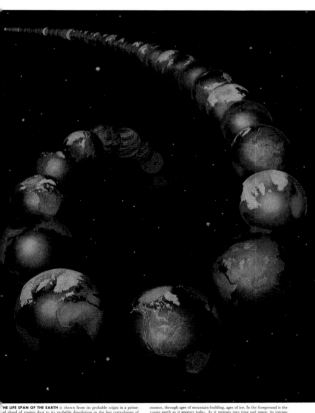

THE LIFE SPAN OF THE EARTH is shown from its probable origin in a primeval cloud of cosmic dust to its probable dissolution in the last convulsions of the dying sun. At center the planet is pictured condensing, cooling, solidifying out of the original solar cloud. For three billion years it rolls through the starry cosmos, through ages of mountain-building, ages of ice. In the foreground is the young earth as it appears today. As it retreats into time and space, its icecap will again advance and recede and continents will change their shape. After a series of solar explosions (yellow intervals) the earth will be destroyed in fire.

Even more ambitious than LIFE's excursion into fiction was its first, and classic, science series, The World We Live In, *of which this was the eloquent opening.*

The knockout punch that made Rocky Marciano the heavyweight champ ("one of the hardest in boxing history") shook a cloud of sweat beads from "Jersey Joe" Walcott's head.

SEPTEMBER 15, 1952

SEPTEMBER 22, 1952

SEPTEMBER 29, 1952

OCTOBER 6, 1952

OCTOBER 13, 1952

OCTOBER 20, 1952

OCTOBER 27, 1952

NOVEMBER 3, 1952

NOVEMBER 10, 1952

NOVEMBER 17, 1952

NOVEMBER 24, 1952

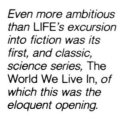
DECEMBER 1, 1952

DECEMBER 8, 1952

DECEMBER 15, 1952

DECEMBER 22, 1952

DECEMBER 29, 1952

1953

The pictorial range was total, from the miracle of conception to the tragedy and drama of death

A pioneering Swedish photographer, Lennart Nilsson, was developing astonishing new techniques for photographing, in microscopic detail, within the human body. LIFE leaped to arrange for publication of his pictures on a continuing basis. The first collaboration contributed to a stunning story on an embryo. At the same time, perversely, the drawn-out conflict in Korea continued to provide the editors with overpowering images of death. Readers often wrote in to ask, "Why does LIFE present such horrible pictures?" An early Editor's Note, a feature Managing Editor Ed Thompson had introduced to the magazine, pointed out that such pictures bore "terrible and vital pertinence to the age in which we live." It also recalled the comment of the editors about a controversial 1938 photo of Spanish Civil War casualties: "Dead men have indeed died in vain if live men refuse to look at them."

JANUARY 5, 1953

JANUARY 12, 1953

JANUARY 19, 1953

MARCH 23, 1953

MARCH 30, 1953

APRIL 6, 1953

JUNE 8, 1953

JUNE 15, 1953

JUNE 22, 1953

AUGUST 24, 1953

AUGUST 31, 1953

SEPTEMBER 7, 1953

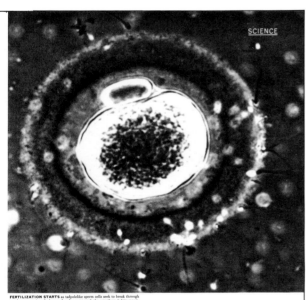

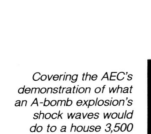

Two brief stories, presented six months apart, fueled conjecture about just when human life begins. The in vitro *views of the fertilization of an ovum (left) were taken by Dr. Landrum Shettles of Columbia University. The picture of a six-week-old embryo (bottom left) was taken by Lennart Nilsson and his associate, Karl Hillgren.*

FERTILIZATION STARTS as tadpolelike sperm cells seek to break through membrane covering of a human female egg to reach the cytoplasm (white mass).

THE START OF LIFE

Fertilization of human egg is shown for first time

The wriggling male sperm in the picture above are about 25 times smaller than this comma, and the female ovum they are trying to penetrate is three and a half times smaller than the period which follows this sentence. When these minute bits of matter are united, they produce a new human life. Last month, a 43-year-old researcher at Columbia University made visible to his colleagues for the first time the very instant of human fertilization. Taking female eggs from hospital patients, Dr. Landrum Shettles exposed them to male sperm and carefully noted the sperm's invasion of the egg's nucleus, which carries the egg's chromosomes and where conception is finally accomplished. The photomicrographs taken by Dr. Shettles in his experiment and reproduced here are remarkable for showing the actual process of life at the earliest stage ever observed.

INSIDE THE EGG the sperm (here magnified 3,000 times) burrows into cytoplasm seeking female nucleus with which male nucleus will fuse in conception.

CONTINUED ON NEXT PAGE   81

ACTUAL SIZE OF
HEAD AT RIGHT

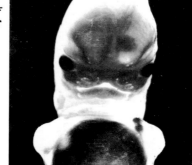
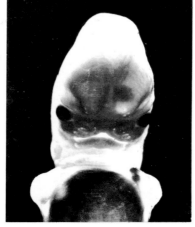

Covering the AEC's demonstration of what an A-bomb explosion's shock waves would do to a house 3,500 feet away, LIFE pictured the detonation and the five stages of destruction, all happening within two seconds. The sequence ended with this eyepopper after 1⅛ seconds.

JANUARY 26, 1953

FEBRUARY 2, 1953

FEBRUARY 9, 1953

FEBRUARY 16, 1953

FEBRUARY 23, 1953

MARCH 2, 1953

MARCH 9, 1953

MARCH 16, 1953

APRIL 13, 1953

APRIL 20, 1953

APRIL 27, 1953

MAY 4, 1953

MAY 11, 1953

MAY 18, 1953

MAY 25, 1953

JUNE 1, 1953

JUNE 29, 1953

JULY 6, 1953

JULY 13, 1953

JULY 20, 1953

JULY 27, 1953

AUGUST 3, 1953

AUGUST 10, 1953

AUGUST 17, 1953

SEPTEMBER 14, 1953

SEPTEMBER 21, 1953

SEPTEMBER 28, 1953

OCTOBER 5, 1953

OCTOBER 12, 1953

OCTOBER 19, 1953

OCTOBER 26, 1953

NOVEMBER 2, 1953

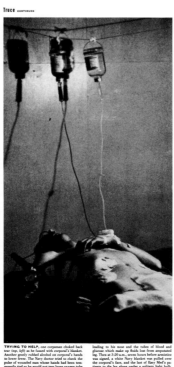

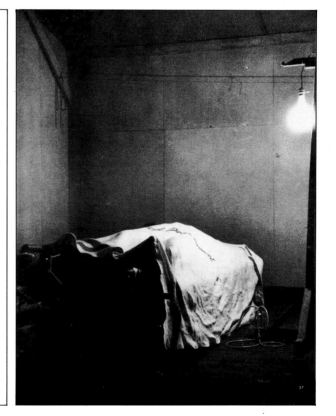

AS ARMY SEARCHLIGHT PROBES RED POSITION (TOP LEFT), FLARES (TOP CENTER) SIGNAL TRUCE AND SOLDIERS (BOTTOM) STAND IN PEACEFUL MOONLIGHT

HOW THE TRUCE CAME TO KOREA

PHOTOGRAPHED FOR LIFE BY MICHAEL ROUGIER AND JUN MIKI

A U.N. searchlight called a "moonbeam" was playing unblinkingly on enemy positions on Old Baldy from Hill 347 on the 7th Division's front, as it had every night for three months. On their left guns of the ROK 1st Division grumbled on. Then from the 1st Marine Division flares burst in the sky. It was 10 o'clock, the hour the truce was to take effect.

The South Korean firing abruptly ended.

Someone switched off "moonbeam" and in the paler light of the real moon, shadowed by scurrying clouds, helmeted, flak-jacketed men stood about. A few muffled shouts went up. From Communist lines loudspeakers blared martial music and occasionally a voice called out in comic-opera English, "Congratulations to the United Nations forces." The GIs chattered a bit. "I'm glad it's over," said one. "I hope I'm not around when the whistle blows again," said another. They told each other that, thanks to the quiet, they would sleep well. But most, keyed up, didn't sleep at all. How the truce came to Korea is shown on this and the next 12 pages. If the deep drama of this event in history was missed for the moment by the world at large, it was frozen in the somber reality by Life's Korean war photographers.

Truce CONTINUED

TRYING TO HELP, one corpsman choked back tear (top, left) as he bathed with corporal's blanket. Another gently rubbed alcohol on corporal's hands to lower fever. The Navy doctor tried to check the pulse of wounded man whose hands had been temporarily tied so he would not tear loose oxygen tube leading to his nose and the tubes of blood and glucose which make up fluids lost from amputated leg. Then at 3:20 a.m., seven hours before armistice was signed, a white Navy blanket was pulled over the corporal's face, and the last of Easy Med's patients to die lay alone under a solitary light bulb.

15

27

The final combat reportage from Korea was an essay, by Michael Rougier and Jun Miki, about corpsmen trying to save a GI who, seven hours before the truce was signed, "lay alone under a solitary light bulb," the last man to die in the war.

Inter-American relations, a longtime concern of Henry Luce's, was served by Time Inc.'s first foreign language magazine, LIFE en Español, circulated throughout Latin America and Spain. Its first issue sold out, and its readership grew steadily, but in only three of its 16 years did it show a profit. Publication was suspended in 1969.

A MATTER OF FORM

For 17 years, from 1952 to 1969, the editors ended every issue with a full-page, single-picture Miscellany—always striking, usually cute. It is not true that it always featured children or animals, but they were way ahead of whatever was in third place.

To add another dimension to their photographic and reportorial coverage of the Korean war, the editors commissioned Michener's short novel and published it in its entirety.

Senator John F. Kennedy of Massachusetts and his bride, Jacqueline Bouvier, a former inquiring photographer, sat down to lunch in Newport, R.I., after two hours of receiving-line handshakes from solons, diplomats, family and friends. "The whole affair, said a guest, was 'just like a coronation.'"

A living relic from prehistoric times, this 5-ft. coelacanth, a close relative to the aquatic forerunners of land animals, lay in the hot African sun after being landed off Mozambique. It sported paddlelike fins on long appendages, vestiges of its own ancestors' means of land locomotion, and "it smelled bad."

NOVEMBER 9, 1953   NOVEMBER 16, 1953

NOVEMBER 23, 1953

John Salling, one of five surviving Civil War veterans, joked with Virginia cronies. The ex-Reb (only one of the five was a Union man) estimated his age at 106.

Sherpa climber Tenzing Norkay, photographed by teammate Edmund P. Hillary, held aloft the flags of Britain, Nepal and the UN on the wind-whipped 29,028-ft. summit of Mt. Everest. They were the first to conquer the mountain.

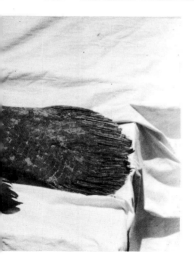

Helen Keller "saw" President Eisenhower's celebrated smile with her left hand as her right received finger signals from her companion, Polly Thomson, that translated Ike's greeting.

NOVEMBER 30, 1953

DECEMBER 7, 1953

DECEMBER 14, 1953

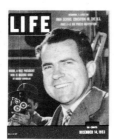

DECEMBER 21, 1953

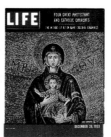

DECEMBER 28, 1953

CLASSIC PHOTOS

East Germans hurled rocks at Soviet tanks putting down a workers' revolt.

Tears welled in the eyes of a GI POW freed by North Korea.

Gene Smith pictured his kids in the woods.

CURRENTS AND EVENTS

World: Stalin Dies, Secret Police Chief Beria Shot as Traitor, Khrushchev Emerges as Party Boss • U.S.S.R. Explodes H-bomb, Key Physicist Sakharov Honored • Soviets Suppress East German Riots • Floods Devastate North Sea Coastal Areas • Russian Jets Shoot Down B-52 over Vladivostok, 16 Airmen Killed • Spain Gets Financial Aid in Exchange for U.S. Bases • Jomo Kenyatta Imprisoned as Mau Mau Terrorist • CIA-backed Coup Ousts Mussadegh, Iran's Shah Returns to Power • Korean Armistice Signed • Vietminh Invade Laos, French Build Fort at Dien Bien Phu.

U.S.A.: Eisenhower, Nixon Inaugurated • California Governor Earl Warren Appointed Chief Justice • Julius and Ethel Rosenberg Executed as Spies • Congress Creates HEW • Financial Aid Granted to France for Fight Against Vietminh • Scientist J. Robert Oppenheimer Barred from Classified Materials • British-born Charlie Chaplin Barred from U.S. as Communist Sympathizer.

FIRSTS: Filter-tip Cigarettes • Transistorized Hearing Aids • Climbers to Reach Mt. Everest's Summit (Hillary, Norkay) • CinemaScope • Woman to Win Tennis Grand Slam (Connolly) • Woman to Fly Faster than Sound (Cochrane).

MOVIES: From Here to Eternity • The Member of the Wedding • Stalag 17 • The Cruel Sea • The Captain's Paradise • Titanic • How to Marry a Millionaire • So Big • My Cousin Rachel • Ruby Gentry • Ohio • The Bad and the Beautiful • House of Wax • The Blue Gardenia • Mogambo • Roman Holiday • The Robe • The Caddy • Forbidden Games • April in Paris • Call Me Madam • Gentlemen Prefer Blondes • Kiss Me Kate • The Band Wagon • Moulin Rouge • Peter Pan • Stars and Stripes Forever.

SONGS: Come What May • Vaya Con Dios • Oh! My Pa-pa • Don't Let the Stars Get in Your Eyes • Cry Me a River • Non Dimenticar • Ruby • Secret Love • Ricochet • Eh, Cumpari! • The Ho Ho Song • Rags to Riches • My One and Only Heart • Crying in the Chapel • Good Lovin' • Downhearted.

STAGE: Tea and Sympathy • The Solid Gold Cadillac • The Fifth Season • Oh, Men! Oh, Women! • My Three Angels • Sabrina Fair • The Crucible • Camino Real • End as a Man • My Sister Eileen • Me and Juliet • Picnic • Wonderful Town.

BOOKS: Too Late the Phalarope (Paton) • **A Stillness at Appomattox** (Catton) • **Battle Cry** (Uris) • **Go Tell It on the Mountain** (Baldwin) • **The Silent World** (Cousteau) • **The High and the Mighty** (Gann) • **A House Is Not a Home** (Adler) • **The Adventures of Augie March** (Bellow) • **Casino Royale** (Fleming) • **Sexual Behavior in the Human Female** (Kinsey et al) • **Science and Human Behavior** (Skinner) • **Life Is Worth Living** (Sheen) • **The Bridges at Toko-Ri** (Michener) • **Come, My Beloved** (Buck) • **Nine Stories** (Salinger).

FADS: Leopard-Print Clothing • Boat-Building Kits • "Li'l Abner" Dolls • Shaggy Hairdos • Fur Dresses, Sweaters.

1954

Milestone events altered for all time perceptions about global defense, racial equality and the need to guard freedom

Just as pictures of the Hiroshima explosion had served to define the Atomic Age, so the picture at right heralded for the public the even more frightening era of the fusion, or hydrogen, bomb. In a test code-named Operation Ivy, an H-bomb blasted one of Eniwetok Atoll's islands, Elugelab, out of the Pacific. Pointing out that one such bomb could incinerate a major metropolis and that two more-powerful devices had been exploded in the 16 months during which the Ivy pictures had remained classified, LIFE set its artist-cartographers to illustrating the monumental problems this threat would pose to cities. The magazine quoted urbanologist-philosopher Lewis Mumford on a question that would preoccupy defense planners from then on: "Is it true, as Lewis Mumford claims, that 'what seems like unlimited power has become impotence'?" Another bomb was metaphorical rather than physical, but its repercussions were almost as wide. In a landmark decision the Supreme Court outlawed racial segregation in U.S. schools. Less sweeping in scope, but similar in its potential to alter society, was the ticking bomb of McCarthyism, exposed but not yet defused, in the nationally televised Army-McCarthy hearings (next page).

The sultan of Morocco wiped blood from a laceration over his eyebrow caused by an assailant's grenade. Despite the evidence of his blood-spattered djellaba, his wounds were superficial.

Georgia's Governor Herman Talmadge (far right) reacted with dismay to the Supreme Court's condemnation of "separate but equal" school facilities. The editors saluted the children named in the five school desegregation cases that had been brought before the court.

5-4-3-2-1 AND THE HYDROGEN AGE   IS UPON US

IT CREATES A NEW MAGNITUDE IN PROBLEMS

ALL PLANS TO EVACUATE CITIES FACE STAGGERING DIFFICULTIES

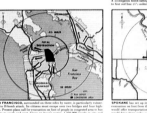

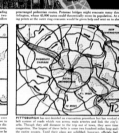

THE FIVE NEGRO CHILDREN MADE FAMOUS BY...

A HISTORIC DECISION FOR EQUALITY

An Army colonel voiced the countdown for the November 1952 explosion of the first H-bomb (left). The AEC-Defense Department photos had been withheld from release for more than a year. In another part of the 10-page story (left, below), some basic principles— and problems—of evacuation were explained in a drawing that showed Washington, D.C., hit by a hypothetical 15-megaton bomb that fell near the White House. Red lines demarked areas of total destruction at 4½ miles and heavy to moderate damage at 10 miles. Maps with similar damage lines illustrated the effect of such a bomb on four other cities: San Francisco, Spokane, St. Louis and Pittsburgh.

JANUARY 4, 1954

JANUARY 11, 1954

JANUARY 18, 1954

JANUARY 25, 1954

FEBRUARY 1, 1954

FEBRUARY 8, 1954

FEBRUARY 15, 1954

FEBRUARY 22, 1954

MARCH 1, 1954

MARCH 8, 1954

MARCH 15, 1954

MARCH 22, 1954

MARCH 29, 1954

APRIL 5, 1954

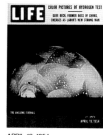
APRIL 12, 1954

APRIL 19, 1954

APRIL 26, 1954

MAY 3, 1954

MAY 10, 1954

MAY 17, 1954

MAY 24, 1954

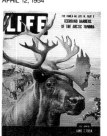
MAY 31, 1954

JUNE 7, 1954

JUNE 14, 1954

JUNE 21, 1954

JUNE 28, 1954

JULY 5, 1954

JULY 12, 1954

JULY 19, 1954

JULY 26, 1954

AUGUST 2, 1954

AUGUST 9, 1954

AUGUST 16, 1954

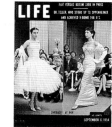
AUGUST 23, 1954

AUGUST 30, 1954

SEPTEMBER 6, 1954

SEPTEMBER 13, 1954

SEPTEMBER 20, 1954

SEPTEMBER 27, 1954

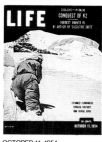
OCTOBER 4, 1954

OCTOBER 11, 1954

OCTOBER 18, 1954

OCTOBER 25, 1954

NOVEMBER 1, 1954

NOVEMBER 8, 1954

NOVEMBER 15, 1954

NOVEMBER 22, 1954

NOVEMBER 29, 1954

DECEMBER 6, 1954

DECEMBER 13, 1954

DECEMBER 20, 1954

DECEMBER 27, 1954

CLASSIC PHOTOS

A subway breeze lifted the skirt of Marilyn Monroe, filming in N.Y. with itchy Tom Ewell.

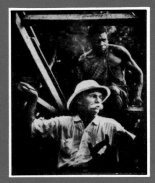

Dr. Albert Schweitzer worked with a carpenter on a hospital building in an African village.

Soil-conserving furrows patterned the parched earth of drought-hit Colorado.

CURRENTS AND EVENTS

WORLD: Moscow Rejects German Reunification, Sovereign West Germany Admitted to NATO • Italy, Yugoslavia Divide Trieste • Nasser Seizes Power in Egypt • Algerian Terrorists Launch Struggle for Independence • Treaty Gives Egypt Suez Canal, Ends British Occupation • U.S., Canada Agree to Build DEW Radar Line, St. Lawrence Seaway • Gibraltar Hit with Anti-British Demonstrations • U.S. Permits Japan to Rearm • Dien Bien Phu, Hanoi Fall to Vietnamese Communists, French Struggle for Indochina Ends • Vietminh Cross into Laos • Cambodia Freed of French Rule • Taiwan, U.S. Sign Defense Pact.

U.S.A.: Racial Segregation in Public Schools Declared Unconstitutional • Senator McCarthy Censured by Colleagues • Puerto Rican Nationalists Shoot Five Congressmen • Secretary of State Dulles Shifts Foreign Policy from Containment to Massive Retaliation in Event of Soviet Attack • Communist Party Outlawed • Monthlong Strike Ties Up Port of N.Y. at Cost of $500 Million.

FIRSTS: Atomic-Powered Sub (U.S.S. Nautilus) • Supersonic Bomber • Solar Battery • Offshore Oil-Drilling Platform • Fuel-Injection Engine • Frozen TV Dinners.

MOVIES: On the Waterfront • Sabrina • The Country Girl • Executive Suite • Désirée • Magnificent Obsession • Bad Day at Black Rock • A Star Is Born • The Barefoot Contessa • Rear Window • Dial M for Murder • Three Coins in the Fountain • Mr. Hulot's Holiday • La Ronde • The High and the Mighty • The Seven Samurai • White Christmas • The Glenn Miller Story • Carmen Jones.

SONGS: Baubles, Bangles and Beads • Fanny • Fly Me to the Moon • Heartbreaker • Hernando's Hideaway • Hey There • The High and the Mighty • I Left My Heart in San Francisco • I Won't Grow Up • I'm Flying • Let Me Go, Lover • The Man That Got Away • Mister Sandman • Papa Loves Mambo • Shake, Rattle and Roll • Sh-Boom • Steam Heat • Teach Me Tonight • That's Amore • Two Hearts • Wanted • Young at Heart • This Ole House • Earth Angel.

STAGE: The Caine Mutiny Court Martial • Bad Seed • Witness for the Prosecution • The Rainmaker • The Tender Trap • Ondine • Teahouse of the August Moon • The Boy Friend • The Pajama Game • Fanny • Peter Pan • The Threepenny Opera • Kismet.

BOOKS: Not As a Stranger (Thompson) • No Time for Sergeants (Hyman) • Live and Let Die (Fleming) • The Blackboard Jungle (Hunter) • The Ponder Heart (Welty) • Tunnel of Love (De Vries) • Bhowani Junction (Masters) • Lord of the Flies (Golding) • Lucky Jim (Amis) • Love Is Eternal (Stone) • McCarthy and His Enemies (Buckley).

FADS: Cuban Mambo • Cha-cha-cha • Short Kilts • Fancy Underpants • Droodles.

An astounded timer at an Oxford University track meet gasped as he clocked medical student Roger Bannister, 25, at 3:59.4 in history's first mile run in less than four minutes.

Vietnamese Buddhist and Roman Catholic refugees fled religious persecution in territory taken over by the Vietminh. Some 40,000 put to sea in anything that would float.

The Highland Park Optimist Club pessimistically donned gas masks at a luncheon to protest civic inaction as a smog blanket hung over L.A. for a third week. The pollution, said the editors, was "enough to take the chromium off a man's Cadillac."

Debbie Reynolds, 22, and Eddie Fisher, 26, exited arm in arm from a Beverly Hills party, given by Eddie Cantor, at which they announced to 500 guests their long-rumored engagement.

After a Dior showing in Paris, rumors abounded that his line favored flat chests (right). A fashion writer reassured a bra maker by demonstrating (below) how boning would lift, not banish, the bust.

Boston lawyer Joseph Welch (left), counsel for the Army, accused by Senator Joseph McCarthy of harboring communists, cross-examined glum-faced Roy Cohn, counsel for McCarthy's subcommittee.

Two minutes after Puerto Rican terrorists shot up the House of Representatives, a photographer in the Ladies Gallery made this time exposure using an illicit camera.

The surviving Dionne quintuplets, Cecile (left), Marie, Yvonne and Annette, bade farewell to their sister Emilie, dead of an epileptic seizure at 20, in their Ontario home.

The board chairman of Remington Rand, Douglas MacArthur, visited President Eisenhower and reminisced about old wars. During the 1952 primary campaign, MacArthur had warned that a military man as Chief Executive "would be a tragic development" for the U.S.

Darryl Zanuck, production boss of 20th Century-Fox, brought a Hollywood party at Ciro's nightclub to a startling climax, doing chin-ups on a trapeze.

1955

An era of good feeling was accented by a suspenseful drama with a happy ending

In the third year of Ike's presidency, the "Eisenhower Era" had settled in and firmly established its character: a time of peace, prosperity and good feeling to its admirers, who definitely included LIFE; of lethargy and blandness to its detractors, whom the editors considered a killjoy minority. Under the magazine's memorable "Nobody Is Mad with Nobody" headline, the editors found the U.S. "a nation up to its ears in domestic tranquillity." Basketball players were not alone in standing tall. Americans, "embroiled in no war, impeded by no major strikes, blessed by almost full employment," enjoyed the world's highest standard of living, bought automobiles at an unprecedented clip, gave the kids amounts of pocket money that would have been considered sinful a decade earlier. Then, from Colorado, where the President was on a hunting vacation, came the shocking news: Ike had suffered a heart attack. LIFE stood watch outside his Denver hospital room until, 49 days after the attack, the President walked out grinning, and America, relieved, went back to living it up.

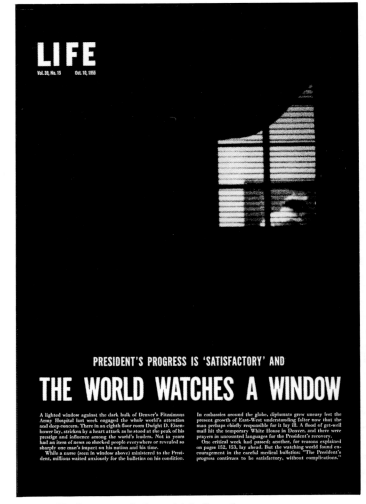

The VIPatient occupied an eighth-floor Army hospital room on which LIFE *kept a telephoto eye. He emerged after seven weeks, and the picture at right was headlined: "Everyone Is Glad to See Ike Up and Around—Include Us In."*

Picasso received French model Bettina Graziani in his Cannes villa for a story on cotton prints utilizing designs by modern artists. LIFE took these fabrics, in resort clothes designed by Claire McCardell, to the studios of Picasso, Léger, Chagall, Miró and Dufy, where models were photographed alongside other creations by the artists.

As allowance-rich teens virtually took over the pop record market, the editors looked, slightly askance, at their music and the controversies emerging about rock's suggestive lyrics and the violence that often erupted at parties where it was played.

JANUARY 3, 1955

JANUARY 10, 1955

JANUARY 17, 1955

JANUARY 24, 1955

JANUARY 31, 1955

FEBRUARY 7, 1955

FEBRUARY 14, 1955

FEBRUARY 21, 1955

Rounding up schoolboy basketball giants, the editors found Wilt "The Stilt" Chamberlain, 18, the 7-ft. center for Philadelphia's Overbrook High.

FEBRUARY 28, 1955

MARCH 7, 1955

MARCH 14, 1955

MARCH 21, 1955

MARCH 28, 1955

CLASSIC PHOTOS

Noel Coward, inevitably, went out in the noonday sun in Las Vegas.

A Tahitian woman preened in a river.

An N.Y. mother and her daughter wordlessly exchanged love.

CURRENTS AND EVENTS

WORLD: Eden Succeeds Churchill as British PM • Algerian Rebels Press Revolt, French Premier Ousted over North African Policy • Tensions Rise Between Greece, Turkey about Cyprus • Israeli, Egyptian Fighting Flares in Gaza Strip • Communist, Nationalist Chinese Forces Clash over Offshore Islands • South Vietnam Proclaimed Republic with Diem as President • Argentina's Perón Forced Out in Coup • Panama's President Assassinated • International Conference on Peaceful Uses of Atomic Energy Held in Geneva.

U.S.A.: Congress Authorizes President to Protect Formosa • Martin Luther King Jr. Leads Black Boycott of Segregated Montgomery, Ala., Bus Lines • Senate Votes Unanimously to Extend Investigations of Domestic Communism, Thousands of Federal Employees Dismissed as Security Risks • AFL, CIO Merge • Presbyterian Church Approves Ordination of Women.

FIRSTS: Oral Contraceptives • Black to Sing at Met (Anderson) • Presidential Press Conference on Film, TV • Speedboat to Exceed 200 MPH • Dripless Paint.

MOVIES: Rebel Without a Cause • To Catch a Thief • The Bridges at Toko-Ri • The Tender Trap • The Rose Tattoo • Battle Cry • Blackboard Jungle • East of Eden • Mister Roberts • The Seven Year Itch • 20,000 Leagues Under the Sea • The Desperate Hours • Marty • Daddy Long Legs • The Seven Little Foys • Guys and Dolls • Lady and the Tramp • Oklahoma!

SONGS: Ain't That a Shame • All at Once You Love Her • Alright, Okay, You Win • Arrivederci, Roma • Band of Gold • C'est la Vie • Cherry Pink and Apple Blossom White • Domani • Dream Along with Me • The Great Pretender • Love Has Joined Us Together • Moments to Remember • Que Será, Será • Smack Dab in the Middle • Something's Gotta Give • The Tender Trap • Unchained Melody • Tutti Frutti • Whatever Lola Wants • The Yellow Rose of Texas • Love Is a Many-Splendored Thing • The Rock and Roll Waltz.

STAGE: Anastasia • The Desperate Hours • Bus Stop • Cat on a Hot Tin Roof • Inherit the Wind • A View from the Bridge • The Diary of Anne Frank • No Time for Sergeants • The Desk Set • Will Success Spoil Rock Hunter? • The Matchmaker • A Hatful of Rain • The Chalk Garden • Silk Stockings • Damn Yankees.

BOOKS: Andersonville (Kantor) • Lolita (Nabokov) • Marjorie Morningstar (Wouk) • The Man in the Gray Flannel Suit (Wilson) • Something of Value (Ruark) • Inside Africa (Gunther) • Bonjour Tristesse (Sagan) • A Night to Remember (Lord) • The Day Lincoln Was Shot (Bishop) • Auntie Mame (Dennis) • The Quiet American (Greene) • Ten North Frederick (O'Hara) • Why Johnny Can't Read (Flesch) • Eloise (Thompson) • Hear Me Talkin' to Ya (Hentoff, Shapiro).

FADS: Coonskin Caps, Frontier Clothing (Davy Crockett) • Happi Coats • Mamie Eisenhower Shirtwaist Dresses.

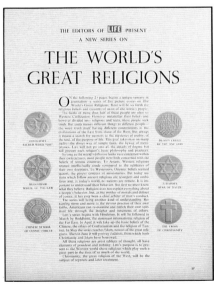

An estate-of-the-art collector of solar heat overwhelmed a house in Tucson, Ariz. It cost $4,000, but the "fuel is free."

A photographer trailed Grace Kelly and actor Jean-Pierre Aumont, her reputed fiancé, to a Cannes restaurant and discreetly photographed the supposedly haughty actress hand-holding and hand-kissing.

This landmark series, on a subject of daunting proportions, was edited by Sam Welles, son of an Episcopal canon. It culminated in a year-end double issue on Christianity and, greatly expanded, became one of the most popular LIFE books.

Kids in their cups and adults of all persuasions flipped for Uncle Walt's new fun park in L.A.

APRIL 4, 1955

APRIL 11, 1955

APRIL 18, 1955

APRIL 25, 1955

May 2, 1955

May 9, 1955

MAY 16, 1955

May 23, 1955

MAY 30, 1955

JUNE 6, 1955

JUNE 13, 1955

JUNE 20, 1955

JUNE 27, 1955

JULY 4, 1955

JULY 11, 1955

JULY 18, 1955

Choreographer Michael Kidd kept Marlon Brando hopping in preparation for his role as gambler Sky Masterson in the film version of Guys and Dolls.

British tourist Christopher Scott, a neophyte snapshooter, scored a scoop by sneaking a photo of Lenin and Stalin embalmed in their Red Square shrine. Picture-taking inside the mausoleum is forbidden.

JULY 25, 1955

AUGUST 1, 1955

AUGUST 8, 1955

AUGUST 15, 1955

AUGUST 22, 1955

AUGUST 29, 1955

SEPTEMBER 5, 1955

SEPTEMBER 12, 1955

SEPTEMBER 19, 1955

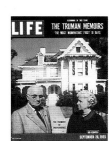

SEPTEMBER 26, 1955

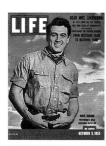

OCTOBER 3, 1955

OCTOBER 10, 1955

OCTOBER 17, 1955

OCTOBER 24, 1955

OCTOBER 31, 1955

NOVEMBER 7, 1955

NOVEMBER 14, 1955

NOVEMBER 21, 1955

NOVEMBER 28, 1955

DECEMBER 5, 1955

DECEMBER 12, 1955

DECEMBER 19, 1955

DECEMBER 26, 1955

Shirley MacLaine, 20, subbed for lame Betty Grable in a 1955 TV show.

A smash in Roman Holiday, Audrey Hepburn, 24, strolled in Beverly Hills in 1953.

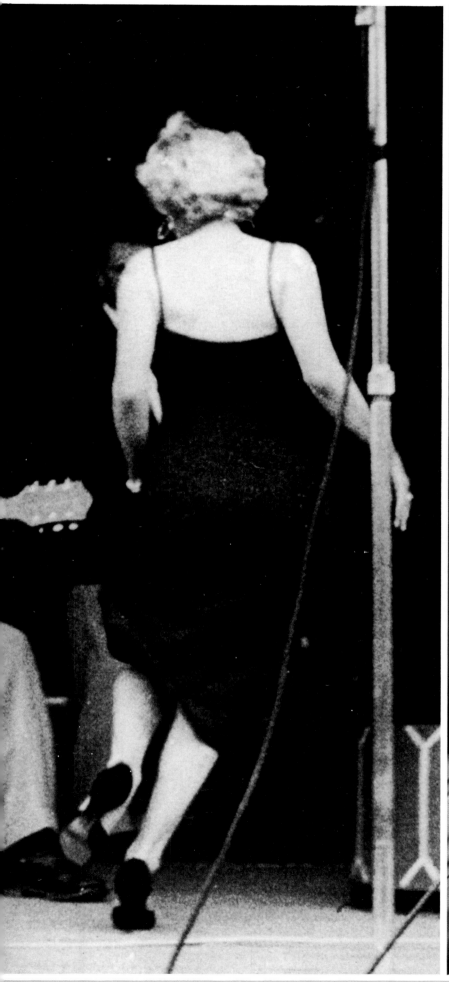

Marilyn Monroe, 28, identifiable even thus, tickled troops in Korea in 1954.

Elizabeth Taylor, 17 in 1949, sat for her first "grown-up" birthday portrait.

THE MARCH OF HISTORY: PLAYFUL PRINCESS TO BURDENED QUEEN

A carefree Princess Elizabeth, 21, played tag with midshipmen on the battleship Vanguard during a 1947 visit by the Royal Family to South Africa. Leaping to avoid a pursuer (top), she was trapped between two more (center) and finally fell into "a historic hug with a brash but happy officer" (bottom).

"Elizabeth Goes as a Princess, Returns as Queen" read the headline on this picture of the black-garbed new monarch as she arrived at London airport in 1952 from Kenya, her visit cut short by the death of her father, George VI. "The times were gray, the Empire had diminished, the future still held all its problems," LIFE commented. "But . . . the queen was on her throne and there was scarcely a man in the wide free world who would not say, God save her."

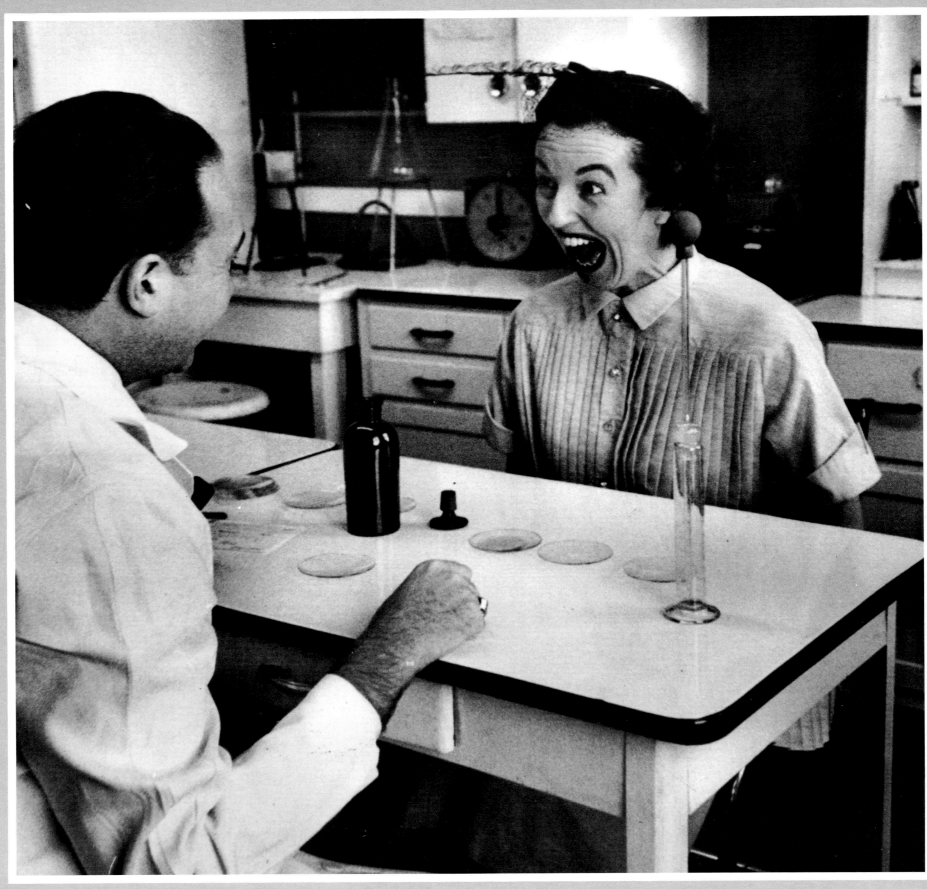

The news transfiguring Mrs. Jane Dill of Northbrook, Ill., as predicted
by a technician in 1954, was that the embryo she carried would be a
girl. The forecasting technique, of which LIFE remarked "most
scientists were profoundly skeptical," had involved a wafer placed on
the tongue. If after chemical processing it remained clear, the baby
would be a girl; if it turned purple, a boy. Mrs. Dill did have a girl.

A New Jersey schoolboy experienced excruciating pain while a doctor tried vainly to free the youth's hand, impaled on a picket of an iron fence. It happened on a January morning in 1948 when Joseph Gondola, 15, slipped on ice while en route to school in Paterson, N.J. Ultimately, the spike had to be sawed off to get the boy to the operating room of a nearby hospital.

KISS, KISS, KISS, KISS, KISS, KISS, KISS, KISS

A surf-sprayed kiss was staged by Robert Wagner and Terry Moore, costars of 1953's Twelve Mile Reef, for a LIFE story titled "A Romp on the Beach."

A military kiss was implanted by a new lieutenant on his bride after West Point's 1946 commencement. Traditionally, the editors warned, "that rock will fall on the girl who refuses to kiss her escort here."

An annual kiss, starting in 1937, was shared by Jack Rodden and Lynn Lee Busby across a Roswell, N.Mex., fence. This was the 1949 record of the rite.

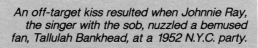

An off-target kiss resulted when Johnnie Ray, the singer with the sob, nuzzled a bemused fan, Tallulah Bankhead, at a 1952 N.Y.C. party.

A "cinematic kiss," LIFE said of the Elizabeth Taylor–Montgomery Clift embrace in 1952's A Place in the Sun, is "that long, tender, graceful swoop and strain which most Americans try to duplicate more or less successfully in their daily lives."

A slow-burning kiss took "somewhat longer" than the five-second exposure the photographer gave it for an in-depth 1950 study of public kissing in Paris.

A calisthenic kiss was best man Jerry Lewis's contribution to the 1951 wedding of Janet Leigh and Tony Curtis.

A hats-on kiss left both hands free for impatient ex-Sergeant Vern Tobias, home in 1946 from Hawaii and discharged, as he embraced his bride-to-be.

With their twin threats of gale and flood, hurricanes pose the kind of reportorial challenge both desk-bound editors and on-the-scene photographers revel in. A flood loosed by Diane, which punished the populous Northeast in August 1955, engulfed this bridge in Putnam, Conn.

ALWAYS AT THE READY FOR THE GAME OF PEEKABOO-BOO

The moment of truth is sometimes the moment of embarrassment, especially in sports. LIFE was on top of the game in 1953 when an Aussie player was depanted down under.

Italy's Lea Pericoli got beaten in her first match at Wimbledon in 1955, but the appreciative crowd loved her while she lasted. With almost every serve, as she whipped her racket down, her frilly skirt went up.

A wrestler at the 1950 Gathering of the Braemar Royal Highland Society exposed a pair of trews that, LIFE observed, would have been less conspicuous had they matched the tartan of his kilt.

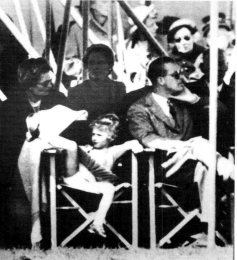

At a 1950 family snapshooting session in Oklahoma City, a possible future Miss America almost wound up posing for nude photos, thanks to a neighbor's playful pup.

Princess Anne of England, 4, her attention span exhausted at the 1955 Royal Windsor Horse Show, indulged in chairborne gymnastics: (from top) tucking her legs up on the braces of her camp chair, straddling its arm, and kicking high in the air. Finally her father, the Duke of Edinburgh, restored propriety by using her blanket for a royal cover-up.

A COMPASSIONATE EYE
FOR THE CONTRARINESS OF FATE

Death that strikes at the moment of supreme happiness or triumph is a recurring theme in life, as in LIFE. That kind of heightened tragedy descended on a Long Island bride in 1946. As Rose De Fabrizio, 21, entered the church on the arm of her father, she fell dead on the steps. She was buried in her wedding gown.

The Very Reverend Claude Willard Sprouse, reelected
president of the Protestant Episcopal Church's House of
Deputies in 1952, accepted the gavel in a ceremony on the
stage of Boston's Symphony Hall. He urged fellow
deputies to "try to push this world a little nearer to the
Kingdom of Our Lord" and then, stepping backward, died.

FREQUENT ATTENTION TO THE SPITTING IMAGE

A U.S. submarine spat forth a torpedo in 1951, and in a historic first, LIFE got its picture underwater, using the latest in photographic equipment.

A British farmer hit a cat flush on the nose with a jet of milk aimed from the udder. Every droplet was halted in its tracks by an exposure of 1/10,000 of a second. The result, the editors exulted in 1948, was a milk-squirting picture to end all milk-squirting pictures.

A spitting archerfish drew a bead on a tweezer-held roach in a 1951 demonstration. "It isn't that the archerfish (Toxotes) dislikes cockroaches; spitting just happens to be the way he hunts his prey."

A spurting youth (or young squirt) created a graceful midair pattern at Washington, D.C.'s Glen Echo Amusement Park in 1953.

1956-1965
Hope and Despair

In the magazine's third decade the editors surveyed the last years of American unity and goodwill and began facing a world increasingly beset by perplexing turns and terrible shocks. Furious challenges to the nation's traditional ideas—of law and order, of right and wrong—came rapidly. The images over the 10-year span reflected the changes: from Ike smiling, Hula-Hoops spinning and the bountiful promise of "new leisure" to the deepening quagmire of Vietnam, a presidential assassination, racial conflict, campus protests, new militancy in the women's movement, a widening generation gap and communist inroads in the Americas.

In 1958, as the five-billionth copy of the magazine rolled off the presses, Henry Luce could still align LIFE's purpose with that of the country's—a straightforward dedication to life, liberty and the pursuit of happiness: to life, because "our job is to observe all we can of life and to give a vivid account of it"; to liberty because "on every issue of the day, using our best fallible judgment, LIFE takes the side that makes for the enlargement and for the deepening of human freedom"; and to the pursuit of happiness because "to be aware of the world you live in, to see it and meet it as reality rather than illusion, this is a condition of sanity and happiness—and to this LIFE makes a contribution." Reflecting this same editorial commitment, the final issue of 1959 was a special titled "The Good Life."

In the course of that year also, the Space Age got under way with the selection of the seven original U.S. astronauts. Determined to be in the vanguard of the new era, the magazine signed exclusive contracts with the new heroes for the rights to their personal stories. It would devote hundreds of pages to their pasts, their families, their training and, finally, to their own accounts of the solo flights.

At the end of 1960 the magazine observed its first 25 years with a look-back issue. A few months later Bob Hope hosted a nationally televised celebration of the anniversary on NBC, in the course of which President Kennedy, while congratulating the magazine, warned the nation of the need for renewed resolution in the years ahead. Were we a people who had already arrived—and who now had no place to go? A LIFE series, titled "The National Purpose," had raised that question earlier in the year.

Just as Ed Thompson had proved himself to be the ideal managing editor of LIFE for the '50s, his successor, George P. Hunt, a longtime associate who took over in the early summer of 1961, was well matched to the '60s. A much decorated Marine officer in World War II, Hunt was not only a born leader but also an accomplished artist. He brought fresh vigor and a bold new look to the magazine's pages. His style was freewheeling and extravagant, characteristics that conveyed the sense that LIFE—circumstances demanding—was as likely to participate in events as to observe them. Whereas the magazine had hitherto spoken with an anonymous collection of voices and restricted its opinions to the editorial page, personal opinion—and conscience—now became an integral part of every issue. Signed reviews of books, movies, music and theater were introduced. The magazine bristled with bylined articles. Investigative reports lashed out at organized crime and at improprieties in government.

In 1964 two of the magazine's finest staff writers, Loudon Wainwright and Shana Alexander, became regular columnists. Wainwright's "The View from Here" and Alexander's "The Feminine Eye" alternated from week to week. They were soon joined by Hugh Sidey's "The Presidency." Based in Washington, D.C., with the Time-Life News Service, Sidey had unique credentials as a White House observer, and in his weekly space he kept close and thoughtful watch on the doings in and around the Oval Office.

In explaining the innovative personal columns to readers, Hunt wrote: "The intent . . . is to say how things feel, not to all of us, but to one of us."

Between appointments early in his presidency, speed-reader JFK turned from his Oval Office desk to a morning paper. Reporting on his love of words, LIFE observed, "He devours printed pages at an enormous rate and retains most of what he reads."

1956

Stirrings of revolt against unfairness and oppression ushered in a time of rising expectations

The period of domestic tranquillity came to an abrupt end. Suddenly, it seemed, lots of people were mad at lots of people. The arrest of Rosa Parks, a Montgomery, Ala., black woman, for refusing to yield her seat to a white, triggered a black boycott of the city's bus line, and that strike's success stirred civil-rights protests throughout the South. Integration of public schools, set for the fall, often met with intense resistance: In some places mobs hanged in effigy officials attempting to enforce or comply with the law, and others overturned the autos of citizens acting in concert with the authorities. Dissent was more fierce abroad. Hungarians rose briefly against their Soviet oppressors, and fell bloodily. The clashes at home and overseas provided a violent visual component to an otherwise typical yield of pictures during a peacetime year. In addition, the editors delivered two single-subject issues devoted to favorite topics: the American woman and the air age.

On the third day of school, in September, National Guardsmen held back white mothers and children seeking to prevent nine black pupils from attending classes in Sturgis, Ky.

PATRIOTS STRIKE
FEROCIOUS BLOWS AT A TYRANNY

Two members of the Soviet-controlled Hungarian secret police force staggered on impact of point-blank fire by Budapest rebels.

At dawn a lifeboat left the Andrea Doria *after her collision with the* Stockholm.

JANUARY 9, 1956

JANUARY 16, 1956

JANUARY 23, 1956

JANUARY 30, 1956

FEBRUARY 6, 1956

FEBRUARY 13, 1956

FEBRUARY 20, 1956

FEBRUARY 27, 1956

MARCH 26, 1956

APRIL 2, 1956

APRIL 9, 1956

APRIL 16, 1956

APRIL 23, 1956

APRIL 30, 1956

MAY 7, 1956

MAY 14, 1956

Marilyn Monroe fed wedding cake to her third bridegroom, playwright Arthur Miller, after their Westchester, N.Y., wedding. They had moved up the date to end wild pursuit by reporters, one of whom died in a car crash.

Rev. Martin Luther King Jr., 27, sat for a mug shot after his arrest as leader of a boycott that virtually halted bus service in Montgomery, Ala.

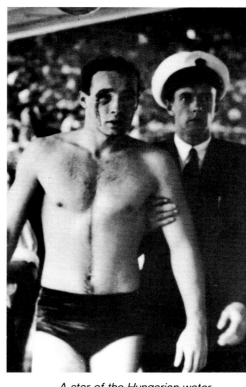

Princess Grace of Monaco, formerly Grace Kelly, honeymooned with Prince Rainier on the yacht Deo Juvante *before it sailed into the Mediterranean "with a nine-man crew and Grace's poodle Oliver."*

A star of the Hungarian water polo team, Ervin Zador, was led, bleeding, from the Olympic pool in Melbourne after being butted by a Soviet defenseman. The Russians insulted and fouled the Hungarians (who won anyway, 4-0). Of the Hungarian squad, 35 defected to the U.S.

MARCH 5, 1956

LIFE — MARCH 12, 1956

LIFE — MARCH 19, 1956

May 21, 1956

MAY 28, 1956

JUNE 4, 1956

JUNE 11, 1956

JUNE 18, 1956

JUNE 25, 1956

JULY 2, 1956

JULY 9, 1956

Girls in Miami clutched at Elvis Presley's clothing.

Estes Kefauver mitted voters.

A Swedish Olympian waited to high-jump.

CURRENTS AND EVENTS

WORLD: Party Boss Khrushchev Denounces Stalin • Polish Workers Demand Bread, Freedom • Soviet Troops Crush Hungarian Revolt • Jordan, Israel Accept UN Truce Proposals, Cease-fire Arranged Among Syria, Lebanon, Jordan • Egypt's Nasser Nationalizes Suez Canal After Britain, France Withdraw Financing for Aswan Dam • Britain, France Attack Egypt, Israel Invades Sinai, UN Orders Cease-fire • Attackers Withdraw, but Israel Holds Gaza Strip • Cyprus's Archbishop Makarios Arrested by British, Deported • British, Mau Mau Fighting in Kenya Ends • South Africa Orders 100,000 Nonwhites to Leave Johannesburg • Castro-Led Guerrillas Land in Cuba to Fight Dictator Batista • Brazil Begins Building New Capital, Brasilia • Nicaragua's President Somoza Assassinated, Son Succeeds Him.

U.S.A.: Uproar in South Follows Supreme Court School Desegregation Ruling • Eisenhower, Nixon Reelected in Landslide • Government Authorizes Construction of 42,500-Mile Highway Network Linking Major Urban Centers • New Law Pays Farmers to Take Croplands out of Production.

FIRSTS: Transatlantic Telephone Cable System (Scotland to Newfoundland) • Atomic Power–Generating Plant (Calder Hall, England) • Ion Microscope • Oral Polio Vaccine • Sub-Carried Nuclear Warhead (Polaris).

MOVIES: Giant • The Man in the Gray Flannel Suit • Moby Dick • War and Peace • Tea and Sympathy • The Rainmaker • Lust for Life • The Ten Commandments • Anastasia • I'll Cry Tomorrow • The Man with the Golden Arm • Trapeze • Around the World in 80 Days • Godzilla • Friendly Persuasion • The Teahouse of the August Moon • High Society • The King and I.

SONGS: Blue Suede Shoes • Heartbreak Hotel • Hound Dog • Love Me Tender • Don't Be Cruel • Blueberry Hill • Hot Diggity • I Could Have Danced All Night • Joey, Joey, Joey • I've Grown Accustomed to Her Face • Just in Time • Long, Tall Sally • Mack the Knife • Memories Are Made of This • The Rain in Spain • Standing on the Corner • You're Sensational • True Love • Bells Are Ringing • Almost Lost My Mind • Mr. Wonderful • Moonglow • Too Close for Comfort • No, Not Much! • On the Street Where You Live • The Party's Over • Picnic • The Poor People of Paris.

STAGE: Waiting for Godot • Separate Tables • Auntie Mame • The Happiest Millionaire • My Fair Lady • Mr. Wonderful • Li'l Abner • Bells Are Ringing • The Most Happy Fella.

BOOKS: The Last Hurrah (O'Connor) • Peyton Place (Metalious) • Don't Go Near the Water (Brinkley) • A Certain Smile (Sagan) • The Search for Bridey Murphy (Bernstein) • Profiles in Courage (Kennedy) • The Organization Man (Whyte) • Love or Perish (Blanton) • Howl (Ginsberg).

FADS: Hypnosis • James Dean (in memoriam) • Bop Jokes.

FIRST LINE PLANES IN REVIEW

Group portrait aloft shows the Air Force's best

Here—flying for the first time ever in a single formation—are planes which make up an almost complete roster of the U.S. Air Force's operational types. These planes, shown over Florida's Gulf Coast, are identified in the drawing at right. Those flying in the lower half of the picture (see key at right for identification) are all jets. Some, with Air Force designations from F-80 through F-94, are older and slower models—which fly at less than sonic speed (about 760 mph at sea level). The newer Century Series, which begins with the F-100, are all supersonic (over 760 mph) and a few of them, including the delta-wing F-102 interceptor, can even climb at supersonic speed. Some of the slower jets, like the F-84, are used as fighter-bombers and also are armed with machine guns, rockets and bombs primarily for tactical use against battlefield targets. The interceptors, including the F-89 and F-94, are armed only with clusters of rockets.

The upper half contains bombers, most of which are powered by jets; support ships like the KC-97 tanker which refuels bombers in flight; and cargo planes like the C-119 and C-124 which carry equipment or men in distant bases and paratroopers in combat. (The C-119 is so slow—250 mph—that by the time it lumbered into place for this picture the F-102 had nearly gotten away.)

It is an axiom in the Air Force that every plane is either so new it is experimental or so old it is obsolescent. The huge B-36 bomber,

FOLD OUT—DO NOT TEAR→

HEAD DOWN over Arizona, Air Force instructor rolls a trainer, leaving the state's highest point, 12,655-foot Humphreys Peak, to hold up the rim of the world.

STEEP BANK tilts lower and a dry creek on the line. To take these rare pictures, Sochurek fixed his camera facing the pilot and sat backward in the front seat.

WORLD UPSET hangs lopsided overhead, tougher unshackles for the pilot. To an aerial acrobat, this is the proper state of things. Right side up is the way he is.

For another story in the issue about the air age, an Air Force instructor rolled a training plane and hung upside down over northern Arizona for the camera of Howard Sochurek.

In the special issue on women this double exposure, in the article "Changing Roles in Modern Marriage," symbolized a basic flaw in troubled pairings: the failure of spouses to accept their emotional responsibilities to each other as males and females.

Julie Andrews, 20, practiced dropping H's in rehearsal with Rex Harrison for a musical named My Fair Lady.

Archers cackled over an errant shot at a Briarcliff, N.Y., party set up by parents. In a series on how elders might do better with their kids, experts urged involvement in planning their offspring's fun. Anyone for archery?

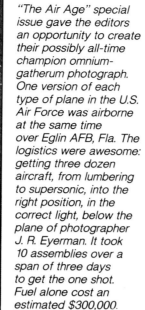

"The Air Age" special issue gave the editors an opportunity to create their possibly all-time champion omnium-gatherum photograph. One version of each type of plane in the U.S. Air Force was airborne at the same time over Eglin AFB, Fla. The logistics were awesome: getting three dozen aircraft, from lumbering to supersonic, into the right position, in the correct light, below the plane of photographer J. R. Eyerman. It took 10 assemblies over a span of three days to get the one shot. Fuel alone cost an estimated $300,000.

IDENTIFICATION of planes shown above can be made by comparing picture with outline drawing at left: 1 B-36 heavy bomber; 2 B-47 medium bomber; 3 KC-97 tanker; 4 RC-121 radar weather plane; 5 B-57 and 6 B-66 light bombers; 7 B-52 heavy bomber; 8 C-131, 9 C-119, 10 C-124 cargo and troop carriers; 11 F-86D all-weather interceptor; 12 F-84G fighter-bomber; 13 RF-84F photo-reconnaissance plane; 14 F-102A, 15 F-94C and 16 F-89H all-weather interceptors; 17 QF-80A target-towing plane; 18 T-33 jet two-seat trainer; 19 F-84F and 20 F-86H fighter-bombers; 21 F-100A fighter.

Althea Gibson, the first black tennis player in the U.S. Lawn Tennis Assn., showed off her range and grace in the French Open Championship. She won.

An acrobatic Minneapolis girl yakked on the phone for an in-depth look at youth titled "Tireless, Talky Teen-agers and Toiling Telephones."

 JULY 16, 1956

 JULY 23, 1956

 JULY 30, 1956

 AUGUST 6, 1956

 AUGUST 13, 1956

 AUGUST 20, 1956

 AUGUST 27, 1956

 SEPTEMBER 3, 1956

 SEPTEMBER 10, 1956

 SEPTEMBER 17, 1956

 SEPTEMBER 24, 1956

 OCTOBER 1, 1956

 OCTOBER 8, 1956

 OCTOBER 15, 1956

 OCTOBER 22, 1956

 OCTOBER 29, 1956

 NOVEMBER 5, 1956

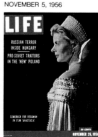 NOVEMBER 12, 1956

 NOVEMBER 19, 1956

 NOVEMBER 26, 1956

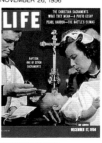 DECEMBER 3, 1956

 DECEMBER 10, 1956

 DECEMBER 17, 1956

DECEMBER 24, 1956

1957

Several crises came together and gave the editors cause to ponder the future

On the very day that Arkansas Governor Orville Faubus used National Guard troops to obstruct the federal order to end segregation in public educational facilities, the Soviet Union launched Sputnik—the first man-made satellite. U.S. education, already in turmoil over the three-year-old Supreme Court decision, suddenly faced the need for agonizing reappraisal. Was the nation's school system too soft in mathematics and science to meet the Soviets' lead in space? Obviously, the free world had badly underestimated the Russians. "It had taken them only four years to break our A-bomb monopoly," LIFE editorialized. "It took them nine months to overtake our H-bomb. Now they are apparently ahead of us in intercontinental ballistic missiles." For the next few months the magazine recorded the series of disastrous tests as would-be U.S. orbiters burst into flames and toppled. Then, along with these worries, the President suffered a mild stroke, and officialdom and the media pondered the complications of transferring power when the occupant of the Oval Office is incapacitated.

In North Carolina and Arkansas, crowds taunted blacks seeking to enter segregated schools. Despite jeers, integration in the Tarheel state proceeded apace. It took federal intervention in Arkansas.

The orbiting rocket section of Sputnik, tumbling end over end above Montreal, appeared (in a time exposure) as a ragged streak in the midst of predawn stars.

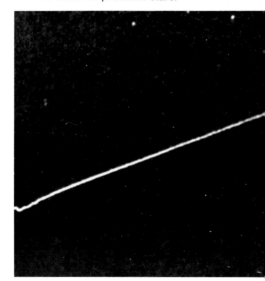

Ecuadoran Indians belonging to a group that had murdered U.S. missionaries picked up gifts dropped by the victims' widows. The wives had returned to carry on the work for which their husbands died. The scene was part of one of the decade's most acclaimed stories, a 10-page picture essay by Cornell Capa.

At Cape Canaveral three seconds after firing, a Navy Vanguard missile carrying a U.S. satellite for orbit fell over in flames and smoke between its gantry and other supporting cranes.

Vice President Nixon, ending a nine-hour White House stint the day after Ike's stroke, rode home to rest before attending a state dinner

JANUARY 7, 1957 JANUARY 14, 1957 JANUARY 21, 1957 JANUARY 28, 1957 FEBRUARY 4, 1957 FEBRUARY 11, 1957

FEBRUARY 18, 1957 FEBRUARY 25, 1957 MARCH 4, 1957 MARCH 11, 1957 MARCH 18, 1957 MARCH 25, 1957

APRIL 1, 1957 APRIL 8, 1957 APRIL 15, 1957 APRIL 22, 1957 APRIL 29, 1957 MAY 6, 1957

MAY 13, 1957 May 20, 1957 MAY 27, 1957 JUNE 3, 1957 JUNE 10, 1957 JUNE 17, 1957

JUNE 24, 1957 JULY 1, 1957 JULY 8, 1957 JULY 15, 1957 JULY 22, 1957 JULY 29, 1957

 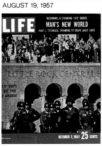   

AUGUST 5, 1957 AUGUST 12, 1957 AUGUST 19, 1957 AUGUST 26, 1957 SEPTEMBER 2, 1957 SEPTEMBER 9, 1957 SEPTEMBER 16, 1957

SEPTEMBER 23, 1957 SEPTEMBER 30, 1957 OCTOBER 7, 1957 OCTOBER 14, 1957 OCTOBER 21, 1957 OCTOBER 28, 1957 NOVEMBER 4, 1957

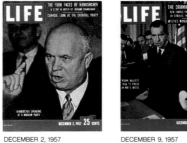

NOVEMBER 11, 1957 NOVEMBER 18, 1957 NOVEMBER 25, 1957 DECEMBER 2, 1957 DECEMBER 9, 1957 DECEMBER 16, 1957 DECEMBER 23, 1957

The Duchess of Kent, representing Queen Elizabeth, danced at Ghana's Independence Ball with Kwame Nkrumah, who led the Gold Coast, a former British colony, to freedom. The tune: Gotta Be This or That.

One Year's Dungaree Debris

20

Actor Grant Williams, as the hero of the year's best special-effects movie, The Incredible Shrinking Man, struggled with a pair of prop scissors 40 times normal size (and weighing 400 lbs.) as he prepared to fight off a spider.

Elizabeth Frances (Liza) Todd, 3 months, with mom Elizabeth, 25, and father Mike Todd made such a happy sight that the editors put the star and baby on the issue's cover.

Saudi Arabian Prince Mashhur peered wide-eyed past royal aides at the ceremonies welcoming his father, King Saud, to Washington, D.C., on his first state visit.

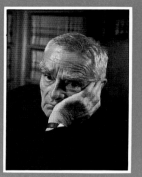

SPEAKING OF PICTURES

THE INVENTORY

The boys' pockets yielded some 476 objects, including pieces of paper, wood and metal. The major, identifiable objects are:

2 coin purses
5 military insignia
3 keys
7 advertising cards
81 picture cards
2 rabbit feet
5 toy guns
10 toy soldiers
2 miniature padlocks
4 Band-Aids
2 Red Cross buttons
4 badges
1 angry note from girl neighbor
4 rolls of caps
3 empty shotgun shells
7 empty .22 shells
13 sea shells
2 small harmonicas
23 stones
1 toy gun rack
6 rubber bands
1 small magnet
2 Valentines
2 wads Kleenex (unused)
2 membership cards
11 school papers
3 school menus
7 Christmas stickers
9 coins, real and play
2 lollipops
2 pieces of chalk
9 crayons
2 birthday candles
2 handkerchiefs
3 theater stubs
11 bubble-gum funnies
2 used flashlights
25 2-inch nails
1 2-inch screw
3 rings
10 charms
2 party tags
7 paper cutouts
1 packet play money
4 small hub caps
1 daily reminder book
9 marbles
1 small screwdriver
1 Halloween mask
1 used TV tube
9 store tags
1 Davy Crockett knife
1 used flashlight battery
1 empty lozenge box
1 plastic measuring spoon
2 plaster animals
1 miniature license plate
1 notebook
6 sandwich bags
4 candy wrappers
1 rubber knife
1 whistle
1 eraser
1 pencil sharpener
1 lump of sugar
1 lariat tie
3 buttons
1 toy guided missile
1 compass
25 acorns

Like all small boys everywhere, Peter Paulding, 9, and his brother Bobby, 7, each day stuff their pockets with priceless boyish treasures and each day forget to remove most of them before their dungarees hit the laundry pile. Fascinated by her findings as she emptied her sons' pockets for laundering, Mrs. George Paulding of Millwood, N.Y. began saving the dungaree debris. Last week Mrs. Paulding put her collection together and LIFE Photographer Ralph Morse hoisted the boys feet-up and pockets turned out over the treasures a whole year's shakedown had produced.

A Millwood, N.Y., mother collected all the artifacts her two young sons left in their jeans when they were to be laundered, and LIFE's Ralph Morse hoisted the kids for a shakedown photograph against one year's harvest.

A model wearing a copy of Givenchy's new "bag" dress was given the eye by a baggy-trousered passerby in Manhattan's Central Park. The editors noted that the fashion was instantly dubbed "the sad sack," and added, "It has the not-to-be-overlooked advantage of covering up minor figure flaws."

Robert Francis Kennedy, 31, counsel of the Senate Committee on Labor and Management, questioned a reluctant witness as Chairman John McClellan followed transcripts of previous testimony.

CLASSIC PHOTOS

Carroll Baker, in the title role of the controversial Baby Doll, sucked sleepily on her thumb.

Judge Learned Hand's portrait was the very picture of ratiocination.

A D.C. cop's friendly warning, for a parade watcher to step back, got a gracious reception.

CURRENTS AND EVENTS

WORLD: European Common Market Established • Macmillan Succeeds Eden as Britain's PM • Molotov, Malenkov Try to Oust Khrushchev, Are Expelled from Central Committee • Israel Withdraws from Gaza Strip and the Sinai • Bourguiba Elected President of Tunisia • Batista Crushes Revolt of Cuban Troops Supporting Castro • Military Junta Declares Duvalier Haiti's President • Mao Launches China's Great Leap Forward Program.

U.S.A.: Federal Law Provides Safeguards for Voting Rights • Senate Committee Opens Hearings on Labor Racketeering • Eisenhower Doctrine Offers Aid to Middle East Countries Opposed to Communist Infiltration • Major John Glenn in F-8 Sets Transcontinental Speed Record (3:23:8.4) • Ford Motor Co. Announces the Edsel.

FIRSTS: Rotary Engine (Wankel) • Atomic-Powered Carrier (U.S.S. Enterprise) • Electric Portable Typewriters (Smith-Corona) • International Geophysical Year.

MOVIES: The Bridge on the River Kwai • Don't Go Near the Water • A Hatful of Rain • Raintree County • The Spirit of St. Louis • 12 Angry Men • Will Success Spoil Rock Hunter? • Operation Mad Ball • The Sad Sack • Peyton Place • The Pride and the Passion • The Prince and the Showgirl • Sayonara • Pal Joey • Funny Face • Silk Stockings • Man of a Thousand Faces • Slaughter on Tenth Avenue • Jailhouse Rock • April Love.

SONGS: Chances Are • Round and Round • Send for Me • Twelfth of Never • All the Way • All Shook Up • April Love • The Banana Boat Song • It's Not for Me to Say • Love Letters in the Sand • Old Cape Cod • Seventy-Six Trombones • Tammy • Maria • Tonight • Wonderful! Wonderful! • Young Love • Jingle-Bell Rock • Whole Lot-ta Shakin' Goin' On • Jailhouse Rock • Wake Up, Little Susie • Fascination • Rang, Tang, Ding Dong • At the Hop.

STAGE: The Waltz of the Toreadors • The Potting Shed • Visit to a Small Planet • The Tunnel of Love • Orpheus Descending • Look Back in Anger • Romanoff and Juliet • Compulsion • Look Homeward, Angel • The Rope Dancers • The Dark at the Top of the Stairs • West Side Story • The Music Man.

BOOKS: Gypsy (Lee) • The Cat in the Hat (Geisel) • The Grinch That Stole Christmas (Geisel) • A Death in the Family (Agee) • Atlas Shrugged (Rand) • By Love Possessed (Cozzens) • The Assistant (Malamud) • The Day Christ Died (Bishop) • The Hidden Persuaders (Packard) • On the Beach (Shute) • On the Road (Kerouac) • Some Came Running (Jones) • Rally Round the Flag, Boys (Shulman) • Memories of a Catholic Girlhood (McCarthy) • Please Don't Eat the Daisies (Kerr) • The Town (Faulkner).

FADS: Elvis Hairdos for Teens • Sword Pins to Signify Dating.

The year produced plenty of "hard" news stories, but "soft" ones often upstaged them

In a Publisher's Preview, readers were informed that news, by definition, is a report of recent events. But the piece hastened to add that "news in a broader sense is anything the reader did not know before." That arguable interpretation opened up a vast new

LIFE
Vol. 44, No. 20 • May 19, 1958

FACING UP TO THE MOB IN LIMA, NIXON AIMS A JUTTING JAW, RIGID FINGER AND SOME STRAIGHT TALK AT HECKLER. MAN IN UNIFORM CAP IS VICE PRESIDENT'S INTERPRETER, LIEUT. COLONEL VERNON WALTERS. BEHIND FINGER IS TYPE OF MATURE, UNSHAVEN "STUDENT" THAT NIXON LATER DESCRIBED AS "REAL PROS"

A VEEP'S ANGER: 'DON'T YOU WANT THE TRUTH?'

A righteously angry man, armed with nothing but a pistol-pointed finger and a stubborn bravery, last week won respect for his nation and himself by standing up to a mob of bullies. It happened in Lima, Peru, where Vice President Nixon was goaded to wrath by denial of the right of free speech.

On his eight-nation tour of South America, the U.S. Vice President had been prepared for a built-in quantity of anti-Yanquism, a body of Latin American resentment of U.S. attitudes currently aggravated by U.S. economic policies which seem to discriminate against South American exports. He had gone through minor flare-ups in Uruguay and Argentina. But in Peru he hit the jackpot of antagonism.

This became a "student" demonstration in Lima's San Marcos university, led by such bewhiskered and antique students that the embarrassed Peruvians themselves were prepared to agree that they were really professional Communists. The Vice President, pursuing a policy of seeking free debate, walked into the clash with eyes open. Despite warnings he went to San Marcos to talk to students. A screeching, spitting, poster-carrying mob of 2,000 barred his way. Nixon got out of his car and strode ahead with a hand outstretched. Instead he got screams of "Viper Nixon, go home!" Then the Vice President got mad. "I'd be glad to go home," he yelled back over an angrily leveled finger. "But first come here and talk." "You are cowards!" "Are you afraid of the truth?" Then

from the mob came rocks. One grazed Nixon's neck and another injured an aide.

Nixon did not get his debate but he came out of the fracas winner and knowing it. "By denying me a chance to speak . . . they exposed themselves to Peru for what they really are," he said. Most Peruvians, some in cheers, others in earnest apologies, seemed to agree. "By his courage and imagination," cabled Correspondent Donald Wilson, "Nixon had turned a sticky situation into a dramatic triumph."

Photographed for LIFE by PAUL SCHUTZER

20 · 21

During a tour of Latin America, Vice President Nixon jabbed a pistollike finger at a "student" heckler in Lima, Peru. The demonstration was, he said, run by professional communists. His challenging question to the harasser drew rocks from the crowd.

LIFE
Vol. 45, No. 16 • October 20, 1958

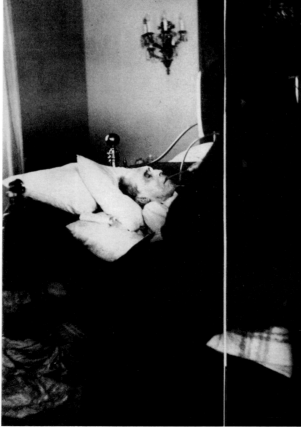

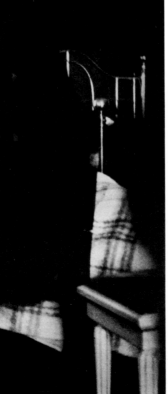

AT CASTEL GANDOLFO prayers are said by villagers and priests who gathered outside the 17th Century residence where the aged Pope lay near death.

DYING, PIUS XII LIES ON COUCH AT FOOT OF HIS BRASS BEDSTEAD AND GASPS OXYGEN THROUGH TUBE

TENDERLY HELD BY MOTHER PASQUALINA, HIS HOUSEKEEPER FOR 41 YEARS

VILLAGE AND WORLD PRAY FOR PIUS XII

A SIMPLE END TO A POPE'S SPLENDID LIFE

One of the greatest men of our age lay dying last week in a simple and ascetic setting. The Supreme Pontiff, Pope Pius XII, born Eugenio Pacelli, was in a plain bedroom at Castel Gandolfo, his summer residence near Rome, tended by the nun who for years had been his housekeeper. In the village square, a few yards away, the faithful, especially the children, knelt in prayer on the cobblestones as village women, stopping to whisper a Hail Mary, filled their water pitchers at the fountain.

Two days before, the frail but indomitable prelate had suffered a stroke that left him blind. Once before in grave illness he had amazed his doctors by swift recovery. This time, though 82, he rallied again. Then came a second and worse stroke, and within hours hope was abandoned.

Just outside the bedroom door a priest described the scene over the Vatican radio and listeners in far lands could sometimes hear the Pope's labored breathing. On Thursday morning the breathing quickened briefly. Then at 3:52 a.m. it stopped. A few moments later, the dean of the College of Cardinals came forward to perform the sad and timeworn ceremony. Leaning over the Pope, he called him by name: "Eugenio, are you dead?" There was no response and he turned to those present and announced, "Pope Pius XII is truly dead." He took from the Pope's hand the Fisherman's ring, symbol of the authority that comes to all Popes from St. Peter.

Here the pomp, pageantry—and piety—of the mighty Church that Pius XII had headed took over and the dramatic rituals of death began. Attendants replaced the Pope's sickbed clothes with rich, velvet vestments. Now Pius lay in state as flags went to half-mast and church bells tolled. Ambassadors from 46 nations paid a last tribute. The next day the body was borne past sorrowing millions through Rome's ancient streets to the mightiest cathedral on earth (following pages). Even in Communist countries millions mourned for the man who had become, partly due to modern communications and his travels, the most famous Pope in history.

Under the towering arches of St. Peter's the Requiem Mass was sung in ancient Gregorian chant and his priest repeated for the Roman Catholic Church's leader the same prayer (below) that is said for the soul of the most humble of his flock: "Eternal rest give unto him, O Lord. . . ."

℣. Requiem ætérnam dona ei. Dómine

BACKGROUND OF A GREAT EVENT

Elsewhere in this issue are other articles on the Papacy. A recent color photo of Pius XII himself is on page 141. The editorial (p. 34) discusses Pius XII as a theologian. On pages 140-148 Emmet Hughes describes the Papacy's enormous burdens and how the Vatican is organized to help carry them. On pages 142-144 is a color portfolio of eight Catholic prelates who are active in administering the Church's affairs and are too high among those considered to be candidates to succeed Pius.

20 · 21

CONTINUED

As Pope Pius XII lay dying in his summer residence at Castel Gandolfo, the camera recorded the tender ministrations of a faithful retainer and the vigil of villagers outside. The magazine's coverage of the pontiff's passing covered 18 pages, including a three-page text piece on the history and responsibilities of the papacy.

Four-month-old Caroline Kennedy, giving her father, Senator John F. Kennedy, a roguish smile, was part of a feature that provided an inside look at the children of political patriarch Joseph P. Kennedy.

range of subjects the editors themselves were interested in, and they proceeded to milk it merrily. In one blockbusting example that resorted to an increasingly favored device, the single-subject special issue, the editors explored "U.S. Entertainment."

Cleveland Browns fullback Jim Brown took a handoff from quarterback Milt Plum (16) and hurtled into the Chicago Cardinals line. He scored three TDs and, in only his second pro year, went on to set a new single-season record for rushing (1,527 yards).

Drinking on all fours, huntsmen of the Bindibu, most primitive of Australian aborigines, knelt in a sheet of rainwater caught in a clay depression.

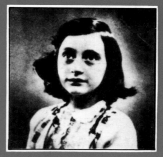

Anne Frank's Amsterdam photomat self-portrait appeared with a story about her last, postdiary days in the death camp of Bergen-Belsen.

High school girls ogled a campaigner.

A woman fainted at the funeral of a Greek Cypriot slain in a riot.

CURRENTS AND EVENTS

WORLD: Khrushchev Assumes Full Control of U.S.S.R. • Algerian Revolt Creates French Political Crisis, De Gaulle Named President • Racial Tensions Erupt in Britain • Egypt, Syria Form United Arab Republic with Nasser as President • U.S.S.R. Agrees to Help Finance Aswan Dam • Iraqi Army Officers Assassinate Pro-Western King, Crown Prince, Proclaim Republic Recognized by Britain, U.S. • Eisenhower Sends Marines to Lebanon, Guarding Against Muslim Rebels • Britain Flies Troops to Support Jordan's Hussein • British Caribbean Isles Join Commonwealth • Chinese Communists Shell Nationalist Outpost Islands off Formosa • Pope John XXIII Succeeds Pius XII.

U.S.A.: Eisenhower Sends Troops into Arkansas to Enforce School Integration • First U.S. Satellite Launched • Presidential Assistant Sherman Adams Resigns, Accepted Gifts from Boston Industrialist • Lana Turner's Daughter, Cheryl, Kills Hoodlum Johnny Stompanato, Mother's Lover • John Birch Society Founded • N.Y. Giants, Brooklyn Dodgers Move to San Francisco, L.A. • Post Office Boosts Letter Postage from Three to Four Cents.

FIRSTS: Presidential Pension Law • American to Win Tchaikovsky Prize (Van Cliburn) • Cadets at Air Force Academy • Stereo LP Records.

MOVIES: Cat on a Hot Tin Roof • The Defiant Ones • A Night to Remember • The Big Country • No Time for Sergeants • The Vikings • The Young Lions • Paths of Glory • Witness for the Prosecution • Run Silent, Run Deep • The Long Hot Summer • Marjorie Morningstar • Ten North Frederick • Vertigo • Indiscreet • The Key • The Naked and the Dead • The Matchmaker • God's Little Acre • The Old Man and the Sea • Houseboat • The Tunnel of Love • South Pacific • Auntie Mame • Gigi • Damn Yankees.

SONGS: Chanson d'Amour • The Chipmunk Song • Gigi • Sugartime • Volare • I Remember It Well • Lollipop • Periwinkle Blue • The Purple People Eater • Thank Heaven for Little Girls • Tom Dooley • Satin Doll • What Do I Care?

STAGE: Two for the Seesaw • Sunrise at Campobello • A Touch of the Poet • Once More with Feeling • The Pleasure of His Company • The Marriage-Go-Round • J.B. • The Gazebo • The Garden District • The Disenchanted • The Entertainer • The Visit • Endgame • The World of Suzie Wong • Flower Drum Song.

BOOKS: Doctor Zhivago (Pasternak) • Ice Palace (Ferber) • Breakfast at Tiffany's (Capote) • Exodus (Uris) • From the Terrace (O'Hara) • The Ugly American (Burdick, Lederer) • The Travels of Jamie McPheeters (Taylor) • Only in America (Golden) • Inside Russia Today (Gunther) • Parkinson's Law (Parkinson) • Anatomy of a Murder (Traver) • Aku Aku (Heyerdahl) • The Affluent Society (Galbraith).

FADS: Hula Hoops • False Eyelashes • Folk Medicine • Sack Dresses • Zorro • Colored Stockings • Fitness Gyms.

 JANUARY 6, 1958

 JANUARY 13, 1958

 JANUARY 20, 1958

 JANUARY 27, 1958

 FEBRUARY 3, 1958

 FEBRUARY 10, 1958

 FEBRUARY 17, 1958

 FEBRUARY 24, 1958

 MARCH 3, 1958

 MARCH 10, 1958

 MARCH 17, 1958

 MARCH 24, 1958

 MARCH 31, 1958

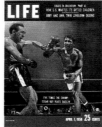 APRIL 7, 1958

 APRIL 14, 1958

 APRIL 21, 1958

 APRIL 28, 1958

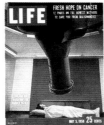 MAY 5, 1958

 MAY 12, 1958

 May 19, 1958

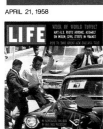 MAY 26, 1958

 JUNE 2, 1958

 JUNE 9, 1958

 JUNE 16, 1958

 JUNE 23, 1958

 JUNE 30, 1958

 JULY 7, 1958

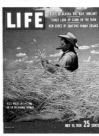 JULY 14, 1958

 JULY 21, 1958

 JULY 28, 1958

 AUGUST 4, 1958

 AUGUST 11, 1958

 AUGUST 18, 1958

 AUGUST 25, 1958

 SEPTEMBER 1, 1958

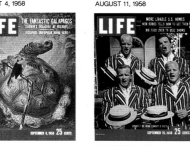 SEPTEMBER 8, 1958

 SEPTEMBER 15, 1958

 SEPTEMBER 22, 1958

SEPTEMBER 29, 1958

OCTOBER 6, 1958

 OCTOBER 13, 1958

 OCTOBER 20, 1958

OCTOBER 27, 1958

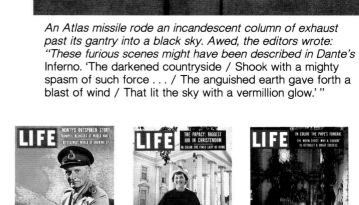

An Atlas missile rode an incandescent column of exhaust past its gantry into a black sky. Awed, the editors wrote: "These furious scenes might have been described in Dante's Inferno. *'The darkened countryside / Shook with a mighty spasm of such force . . . / The anguished earth gave forth a blast of wind / That lit the sky with a vermillion glow.'"*

Jane Fonda, 21, just emerging from the status of being merely "Henry Fonda's daughter," danced the cha-cha at a charity ball in Manhattan's Waldorf-Astoria.

In an essay on "The New-found Joys of Beauty," Bonnie Bea Trompeter, 14, a budding charmer from Westchester, N.Y., listened earnestly, and self-consciously, to a new beach-club acquaintance.

Holding a picture of her hero, Kathy Maloney, 15, emitted a farewell shriek as Elvis Presley sailed from the Brooklyn Army Terminal for a hitch with the Third Armored Division in Germany.

Jason Robards Jr., asked by photographer Eliot Elisofon what "dream role" he'd like to be shown in, chose the hoofer in Robert Sherwood's Idiot's Delight.

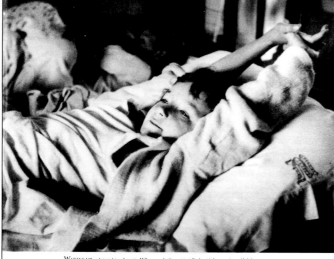

The Awakening Years
When the World Is Young

The young girl, swept from sleep by a sudden flood of light, stretches tremulously awake to another day in her years of awakening, the brief and endlessly varying time of childhood. Her name is Jeanette Miller and on that sunny morning she was 9. Jeanette's father is a fine and sensitive photographer who,

in the four years since he took this picture, has taken many more of Jeanette and of her brothers and sister and all their friends. In them he has by now a unique record of the sorrows and the huge delights, the discoveries and the disappointments that are part of all children's bittersweet experience of growing up.

WAKING UP and stretching, Jeanette Miller elects to stay in bed awhile, caught up in her reveries. "I have a secret world," Jeanette once said, "but I don't want to talk about it because it wouldn't be a secret then." This is one of the first pictures her father took in his record of children growing up.

Photographed by WAYNE MILLER

CONTINUED

Jeanette Miller, of Orinda, Calif., awoke on her ninth birthday to be snapped by her father, photographer Wayne Miller. Five years later he had accumulated 30,000 photos of Jeanette and her three siblings, more than enough on which to build a LIFE story about one family's kids growing up.

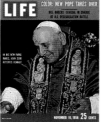

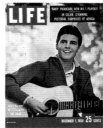

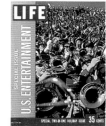

NOVEMBER 3, 1958   NOVEMBER 10, 1958   NOVEMBER 17, 1958   NOVEMBER 24, 1958   DECEMBER 1, 1958   DECEMBER 8, 1958   DECEMBER 15, 1958   DECEMBER 22, 1958

A BEAUTIFUL SHOW-BUSINESS BINGE

"Even as we present these stories," said an Editors' Note that appeared in a fall issue boasting many strong entertainment features, "we are tempted to say, 'You ain't seen nothin' yet.' " The staff was looking ahead excitedly to the special year-end double issue that, between its brassy cover *(right)* and its kiddies' Christmas closing, ranged among Broadway and Hollywood (including, of course, Marilyn), jazz and rock (including, of course, Dick Clark), ballet and the circus, opera, TV, nightclubs, ice shows and cartoons. At the time, many readers weighed in to say it was the most beautiful, spectacular issue of the magazine ever published.

The Radio City Music Hall Rockettes, the chorus line's "last great outpost," cast their symmetrical shadow, "a sight to be seen, like Old Faithful."

The foldout cover featured part of a brass band with 3,000 clarinets, 2,000 trumpets, 1,000 drums, 800 tubas, 1,076 trombones.

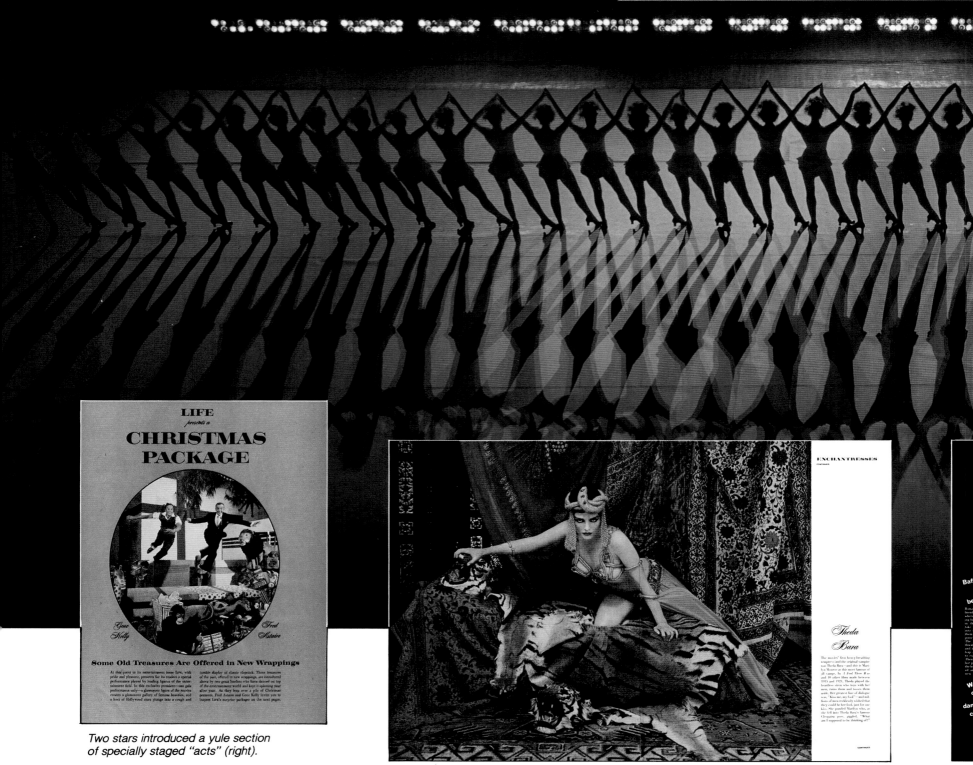

Two stars introduced a yule section of specially staged "acts" (right).

Marilyn Monroe impersonated silent temptress Theda Bara. She also did Clara Bow, Lillian Russell, Marlene Dietrich, Jean Harlow.

The Movies

On the biggest drive-in movie screen the editors could find, Charlton Heston as Moses filled the Utah sky and appeared to be parting the waters of the Great Salt Lake.

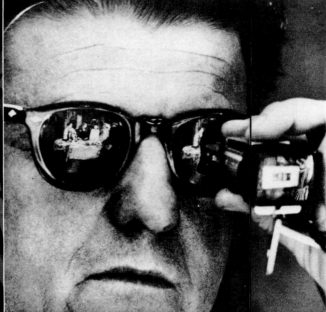

GREAT DIRECTOR, GREAT STORY

With ingenuity, energy and an artist's intuition George Stevens films 'The Diary of Anne Frank'

Photographed for LIFE by RALPH CRANE

The wide-angle view of a complex set and an extreme close-up of George Stevens were part of an eight-page story on the director, "often considered the greatest," as he filmed The Diary of Anne Frank.

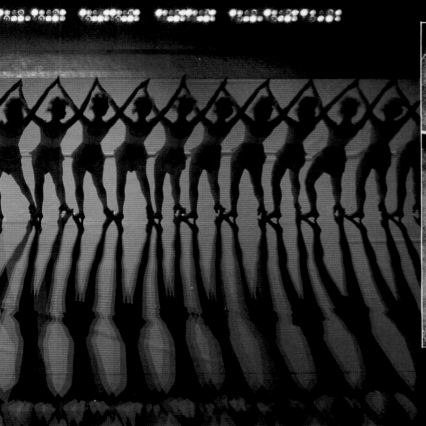

All-star Keystone Kops and bathing beauties followed a LIFE script for a six-page "two-reeler" honoring director Mack Sennett.

HAPPY CHRISTMAS TO ALL, AND TO ALL A GOOD NIGHT!

On the theory that no Christmas is complete without Clement Moore's "A Visit from St. Nicholas," the issue closed with an illustrated version, acted by first graders in Englewood, N.J.

149

1959

At the end of the '50s the living was nice, and easy. But signs of turbulence were starting to mount

Another fat year, and LIFE shared—and celebrated—the general euphoria. *The Good Life* special issue was a paean to such innocent pastimes as boating and the lively arts, which Americans now had the time and money to pursue. There was also a classic Cinderella romance to warm the nation's heart. The big stories, however, were made of sterner stuff and were harbingers of a world at the edge of change. The subject of old age was handled with a broad social concern that anticipated that of the '60s. In the dawning Space Age, the magazine staked out its editorial claim with stories on the monkeys that were the first living passengers to return safely from a ballistic journey through space and on the selection of the first U.S. astronauts. New figures stepped onto the global stage (Fidel Castro, John Kennedy) as old heroes, real and reel (Winston Churchill, Errol Flynn), were moving off.

Fidel Castro's unbuttoned style, in his hotel room and in public, wowed crowds during a U.S. tour five months after overthrowing dictator Batista. Castro had not yet avowed his Marxism, but the wary editors found him evasive about Red influence and were critical of the " 'drumhead' justice in his courts."

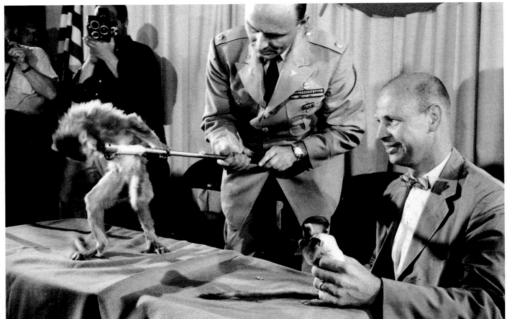

Able, a rhesus, chewed on a handling stick and Baker, a squirrel monkey, nestled in the hands of a Navy doctor at a Washington press conference that dealt with the details of their rocket ride, from launch to splashdown.

It was a case of one artist appraising another's work. While on a visit to a Soviet exhibition in New York, a grandfatherly-looking Ike, himself a Sunday painter, studied the portrait of a factory worker.

JANUARY 5, 1959

JANUARY 12, 1959

JANUARY 19, 1959

JANUARY 26, 1959

FEBRUARY 2, 1959

FEBRUARY 9, 1959

FEBRUARY 16, 1959

FEBRUARY 23, 1959

A debate between Khrushchev and Vice President Nixon began in a Moscow TV studio, where large issues were argued vigorously and spilled over to a U.S. kitchen exhibit, where the Premier jabbed at American gadgetry. The tension didn't break until Khrushchev pointed to an appliance and joked: "This is probably always out of order." Nixon: "Da."

George Silk's cameras were various and famously peripatetic. They usually wound up where no human eye was likely to be. In this instance he placed a swivel-mounted wide-angle lens atop the Churchill Downs starting gate. Silk was a three-time winner of the Magazine Photographer of the Year award.

Asked if they wanted to be the first human in space orbit, six of the original U.S. astronauts raised an affirmative hand. John Glenn, who drew the assignment, lifted two. But Russia's Yuri Gagarin beat him by 10 months.

SPEAKING OF PICTURES

A RARE LOOK AT THE DERBY

MARCH 2, 1959 MARCH 9, 1959 MARCH 16, 1959 MARCH 23, 1959 MARCH 30, 1959 APRIL 6, 1959 APRIL 13, 1959 APRIL 20, 1959

   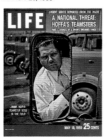     

APRIL 27, 1959 MAY 4, 1959 MAY 11, 1959 May 18, 1959 MAY 25, 1959 JUNE 1, 1959 JUNE 8, 1959 JUNE 15, 1959

FLYNN CONTINUED
THE MEMORIES OF AN IRREVERENT MAN

THE WILD OLD DAYS in Hollywood were the subject of Flynn's favorite stories about prodigious drunks and questionable escapades. Here he tells how John Barrymore's body was spirited from the funeral parlor a few hours after his death by some of Flynn's drunken friends, including a famous movie director. Flynn pantomimed the body (*upper left*), the drunken friends and their difficulties as they carried it to Flynn's house and put it in a chair. Flynn arrived, saw the body and fled screaming (*lower right*). Flynn wound up the story by adding that he did not think it was the correct way to say goodbye to John.

134

CONTINUED

Just days before his death of a heart attack at 50, Errol Flynn was his old ribald, vodka-swilling self. LIFE conceded that he had been a "scamp, bounder, barroom brawler," but pointedly added, "Large numbers of people loved him dearly."

Annie Mahaffey, 80, living in her son's house, poured out her woes to her grandchild, Mary Anne, 7. Annie's story was part of a searching essay on the tribulations of old age and the impact on younger generations when the elderly live with them.

Dancing cheek-to-cheek with Cary Grant in Antibes, Kim Novak was on a romantic high. Of Cary Grant, 55, who had flown over just to see her, she said, "I adore him." Asked about somebody named Mario, a handsome Italian who awaited her in Rome, she was not nonplussed: "I think he is divine."

JUNE 22, 1959

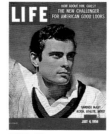

JUNE 29, 1959

JULY 6, 1959

JULY 13, 1959

JULY 20, 1959

JULY 27, 1959

AUGUST 3, 1959

AUGUST 10, 1959

Determined to outshine Ordóñez, his brother-in-law and closest rival, Spain's numero uno matador, Dominguín, fought too close to his bull and was flipped. Not seriously hurt, he was helped to his feet, killed the bull and, amid Olé!s, was awarded an ear.

To the dewy-eyed editors, the motorbike was a "jaunty black charger" and its rider, Steven Rockefeller, 23, a "storybook prince." She was Anne Marie Rasmussen, 21, a grocer's daughter from Norway who had worked on his family's estate. But LIFE was not too stricken to note that the romance might provide an "unexpected fillip" to N.Y. Governor Nelson Rockefeller's chances to win the 1960 GOP presidential nomination.

AUGUST 17, 1959   AUGUST 24, 1959   AUGUST 31, 1959   SEPTEMBER 7, 1959   SEPTEMBER 14, 1959

SEPTEMBER 21, 1959   SEPTEMBER 28, 1959   OCTOBER 5, 1959   OCTOBER 12, 1959   OCTOBER 19, 1959

OCTOBER 26, 1959   NOVEMBER 2, 1959   NOVEMBER 9, 1959   NOVEMBER 16, 1959   NOVEMBER 23, 1959

NOVEMBER 30, 1959   DECEMBER 7, 1959   DECEMBER 14, 1959   DECEMBER 21, 1959   DECEMBER 28, 1959

CLASSIC PHOTOS

A phone booth bulged with 22 students.   Khrushchev visited Lincoln in Washington.

Pianist Arthur Rubinstein's Boston audience overflowed onto the stage.

CURRENTS AND EVENTS

WORLD: Khrushchev Tours U.S., Addresses UN, Calls for Complete Disarmament in Four Years • DeGaulle Offers Independence to Algeria • Pope John XXIII Calls for Ecumenical Council to Unify Christendom • Exiled Archbishop Makarios Returns to Cyprus, Elected President • Anticolonial Protests Spread in Africa • Castro Forces Take Havana • 21 Latin American Nations Censure Dictatorships, but Condemn Outside Efforts to Overthrow Them • China Dissolves Tibetan Government, Dalai Lama Seeks Asylum in India • U.S., U.S.S.R., 10 Other Nations Sign Pact Reserving Antarctica for Scientific, Peaceful Purposes.

U.S.A.: Alaska, Hawaii Achieve Statehood • Eisenhower Signs Landrum-Griffin Bill to Curb Labor Abuses • TV Quiz Show Scandal Escalates, House Subcommittee Investigates • Space Program Accelerates • Oklahoma Repeals Prohibition, Mississippi Remains Only Dry State.

FIRSTS: Satellite to Transmit Photos of Earth (U.S.) • Spacecraft to Land on Moon (Lunik II) • Atomic-Powered Merchant Ship (N.S. Savannah) • Commercial Transcontinental Jet Passenger Service (American Airlines) • Motion Picture with Scent ("Behind the Great Wall").

MOVIES: The Diary of Anne Frank • Room at the Top • Anatomy of a Murder • North by Northwest • Ben-Hur • On the Beach • Anna Lucasta • Some Came Running • Forbidden Fruit • A Night to Remember • Some Like It Hot • Separate Tables • Compulsion • Pillow Talk • The Mouse That Roared • The 400 Blows • Wild Strawberries • Sleeping Beauty • Porgy and Bess.

SONGS: Climb Ev'ry Mountain • My Favorite Things • Dream Lover • Personality • Put Your Head on My Shoulder • The Sound of Music • He's Got the Whole World in His Hands • Take Me Along • High Hopes • Do-Re-Mi • Small World • Lipstick on Your Collar • Sixteen Going on Seventeen • A Teen-Ager in Love • There Goes My Baby.

STAGE: The Miracle Worker • The Tenth Man • Five Finger Exercise • Sweet Bird of Youth • A Raisin in the Sun • Epitaph for George Dillon • A Majority of One • Requiem for a Nun • The Sound of Music • Fiorello! • Destry Rides Again • Gypsy • Once Upon a Mattress.

BOOKS: Advise and Consent (Drury) • For 2¢ Plain (Golden) • Act One (Hart) • The Status Seekers (Packard) • Goodbye, Columbus (Roth) • Advertisements for Myself (Mailer) • The Years with Ross (Thurber) • Hawaii (Michener) • Dear and Glorious Physician (Caldwell) • Henderson the Rain King (Bellow) • The Mansion (Faulkner).

FADS: Garbo Slouch Hats • Loose-Fitting Sweaters • "Hunkerin'" (sociable squatting among undergrads) • Paste-on Costume Jewelry • Barbie Dolls.

1960

The Eisenhower era was ending, and an engaging young presidential candidate came on strong

Eisenhower's presidency had been dedicated, more or less, to hands-off government, with measurably fortunate consequences for the nation. But many, including Henry Luce, fretted that the period had been marred by a faltering sense of mission, a drift born of complacency. While LIFE endorsed Nixon to succeed Ike, Kennedy's call to "get this country moving again" scored points with the editors as well as the voters. In any case, it was indeed time for the U.S. to bestir itself.

An angry Khrushchev was fired up for a confrontation because of a high-flying U.S. spy plane. New racial violence in South Africa lent added force to the civil rights protests at home. During a spirited political year, the magazine made room for a magisterial "Planet Earth" series and for salutes to two royal favorites: It bade farewell to Hollywood's longtime king, Clark Gable, and offered a bouquet to Princess Margaret upon her marriage to commoner Anthony Armstrong-Jones.

LIFE
Vol. 48, No. 21   May 30, 1960

A FIST SHAKEN IN RAG[E] THAT SHOOK THE WORL[D]

In South Africa black mourners buried their dead after the Sharpeville massacre of 72 protesting the imposition of passes.

A WIFE WEEPS FOR HER HUSBAND KILLED BY THE POLICE AT SHARPEVILLE

MARTYRS BURIED AS CRISIS GROWS

SOUTH AFRICA TORN BY FURY

The tragic scene at right was three centuries in the making. These are Africans mourning their own martyrs, slain at Sharpeville by the gunfire of white police as they demonstrated against the Union of South Africa's harsh racial policies (LIFE, April 4). Seventy-two natives died by bullet in one day, but South Africa's travail was only beginning. At least 20 more were killed last week, one of them a babe in arms en route to a hospital. In a village called Country of Hope, 5,000 natives pillaged public buildings and the houses of native constables. Other thousands struck the whole country for one day, and a Johannesburg bus company's patronage dived from 60,000 to 1,200.

The South African white population was dazed and frightened. The Nationalist party government seemed bewildered. The Minister of Bantu (native) Administration said, incredibly, "Race relations are better than ever before," and 12 hours later the Minister of Justice warned the country it was "on the brink of revolution."

Prime Minister Hendrik Verwoerd's government proclaimed a state of emergency under which anyone could be arrested without charge, held without trial for a year. Black resistance had already forced it to go back on its order requiring natives to carry passbooks with them at all times. Finally the tide of African nationalism was pounding at the gates of the Union, a supposedly impregnable citadel of white supremacy. The United Nations took a hand (pp. 38, 39) and white South Africans began to realize how isolated they are at the bar of world opinion. The fury that has beset the country rose out of a racial trouble as old as the nation.

A GRIM CROWD MOURNS THE DEAD AT GRAVE OF 34 SHARPEVILLE VICTIMS →

LIFE
Vol. 48, No. 14   Apr. 11, 1960

Something new in campaigning, a TV debate—the first of four—brought Nixon and Kennedy face-to-face in Chicago.

JANUARY 11, 1960

JANUARY 18, 1960

JANUARY 25, 1960

FEBRUARY 1, 1960

FEBRUARY 8, 1960

FEBRUARY 15, 1960

FEBRUARY 22, 1960

FEBRUARY 29, 1960

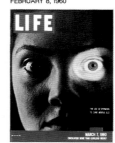

MARCH 7, 1960

"A weak-kneed incompetent!" shouted Khrushchev, referring to Ike. LIFE suggested to Nikita that he "go soak his head."

Days before his fatal heart attack Clark Gable, 59, was at work on Arthur Miller's film The Misfits.

John Kennedy, 43, and brother Bobby, 34, huddled in L.A.

Liam Horey, 8 mos., kept his cool in a pool during a heat wave in Big Spring, Tex.

Socialist leader Inejiro Asanuma was mortally stabbed as he gave a speech in Tokyo.

CURRENTS AND EVENTS

WORLD: Russians Shoot Down U.S. Spy Plane, U-2 Pilot Gary Powers Captured • Khrushchev at UN Denounces U.S. Policies • Israeli Agents Seize Adolf Eichmann in Argentina • Chaos in Congo Republic Leads to UN Intervention • South African Blacks, Marching to Protest New Law Requiring Passes at All Times, Massacred in Sharpeville • Castro Confiscates U.S. Property • Guatemala Joins Nicaragua in Accusing Castro of Fomenting Uprisings, Ike Sends Naval Units to Patrol Region • South Vietnam's Ngo Dinh Diem Regains Power After Coup, Dissidents Organize as Vietcong • South Korea's Syngman Rhee Orders Martial Law as Students Protest Rigged Elections, National Assembly Calls for New Balloting, Rhee Flees to Hawaii.

U.S.A.: Kennedy, Johnson Win Narrow Presidential Victory • Civil Rights Issues Create Turmoil in South • Congress Investigates "Payola" in Recording, Broadcasting Industries, Underworld Influence in Pro Boxing, Teamsters Union.

FIRSTS: Pacemakers • Communications, Weather Satellites • Felt-tip Pen • Laser • Quasars Observed.

MOVIES: Psycho • The Apartment • Elmer Gantry • The Entertainer • Inherit the Wind • Exodus • Tunes of Glory • Hiroshima, Mon Amour • Never on Sunday • Big Deal on Madonna Street • Our Man in Havana • Butterfield Eight • Sunrise at Campobello • Please Don't Eat the Daisies • Spartacus • Suddenly Last Summer • The World of Suzie Wong • The Alamo • The Dark at the Top of the Stairs • G.I. Blues • Can-Can.

SONGS: Are You Lonesome Tonight? • Camelot • Everybody's Somebody's Fool • Hey, Look Me Over • Lollipops and Roses • Green Fields • Itsy Bitsy, Teenie Weenie, Yellow Polka-Dot Bikini • Mr. Lucky • What's the Matter with Kids Today? • The Twist • How to Handle a Woman • If Ever I Would Leave You • Blue Angel • Partin' Time.

STAGE: Toys in the Attic • A Thurber Carnival • A Taste of Honey • Advise and Consent • Becket • Camelot • Irma La Douce • Wildcat • The Unsinkable Mollie Brown • Bye Bye Birdie.

BOOKS: To Kill a Mockingbird (Lee) • Born Free (Adamson) • This Is My God (Wouk) • The Leopard (Di Lampedusa) • The Chapman Report (Wallace) • Rabbit, Run (Updike) • The Sotweed Factor (Barth) • Welcome to Hard Times (Doctorow) • The Rise and Fall of the Third Reich (Shirer).

TOPS IN TV, '50s: Milton Berle (Premiere, '48) • Philco Playhouse ('48) • Show of Shows ('50) • Colgate Comedy Hour ('50) • Arthur Godfrey ('48) • I Love Lucy ('51) • Red Skelton ('53) • Jack Benny ('50) • You Bet Your Life ('50) • Gangbusters ('52) • Dragnet ('52) • Bob Hope ('52) • Jackie Gleason ('52) • Ed Sullivan ('48) • The $64,000 Question ('55) • December Bride ('54) • The Millionaire ('55) • I've Got a Secret ('52) • Alfred Hitchcock Presents ('55) • Gunsmoke ('55) • Perry Como ('50) • Danny Thomas ('53) • Have Gun Will Travel ('57) • The Rifleman ('58) • Maverick ('57) • Real McCoys ('57) • Father Knows Best ('54) • 77 Sunset Strip ('58) • Price Is Right ('56) • Perry Mason ('57) • Kraft Theatre ('47) • Armstrong Circle Theatre ('50) • Big Town ('50) • Life of Riley ('53) • What's My Line? ('50) • Our Miss Brooks ('52) • Bonanza ('59) • The Honeymooners ('55) • Peter Gunn ('58) • Tennessee Ernie Ford ('55) • Rawhide ('59) • The Untouchables ('59) • Omnibus ('52) • Mr. Peepers ('52) • Playhouse 90 ('56).

FADS: The Twist • Trampolines • Outsize Eyeglasses.

The Kennedy clan gathered on victory day. The controversial patriarch had last appeared in public with his candidate son before the convention.

Grandma Moses was congratulated on her 100th birthday by her great-granddaughter Chrissy.

A witch carried off a small captive in this photograph, part of a nine-page portfolio of "spooks to be wary of on Halloween." Photographer George Silk "used family and friends as his models."

THE NATIONAL PURPOSE
DISCUSSION IS RESUMED

'We must climb to the hilltop'

by Senator John F. Kennedy

In his contribution to the series, Kennedy decided the "National Purpose" was the totality of "each one of us . . . at our moral best."

The Dangerous Summer

by ERNEST HEMINGWAY

THE AUTHOR MAKES A DRAMATIC RETURN TO SPAIN AND SEES THE BEGINNING OF A 'DEADLY RIVALRY'

THE SPAIN HEMINGWAY LOVES

This three-part saga proved to be Hemingway's last major writing effort. He was a suicide in 1961. Publication as a book was delayed until 1985.

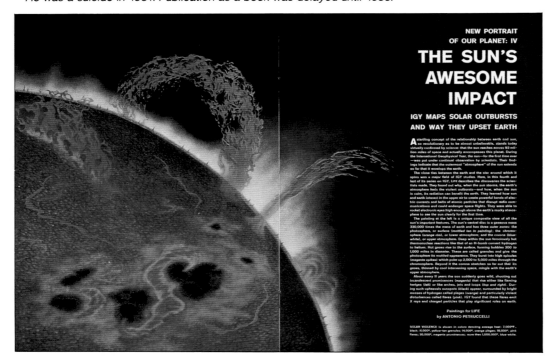

NEW PORTRAIT
OF OUR PLANET: IV

THE SUN'S AWESOME IMPACT

IGY MAPS SOLAR OUTBURSTS AND WAY THEY UPSET EARTH

Paintings for LIFE
by ANTONIO PETRUCCELLI

Vast subjects, parsed with the aid of illuminating graphics and authoritative text, were a LIFE specialty that evolved into Time-Life Books.

MARCH 14, 1960 · MARCH 21, 1960 · MARCH 28, 1960

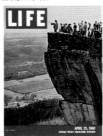  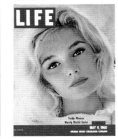

APRIL 25, 1960 · MAY 2, 1960 · MAY 9, 1960

JUNE 6, 1960 · JUNE 13, 1960 · JUNE 20, 1960

  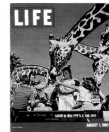

JULY 18, 1960 · JULY 25, 1960 · AUGUST 1, 1960

AUGUST 29, 1960 · SEPTEMBER 5, 1960 · SEPTEMBER 12, 1960

OCTOBER 10, 1960 · OCTOBER 17, 1960 · OCTOBER 24, 1960

  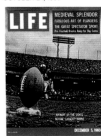

NOVEMBER 21, 1960 · NOVEMBER 28, 1960 · DECEMBER 5, 1960

APRIL 4, 1960

APRIL 11, 1960

APRIL 18, 1960

MAY 16, 1960

MAY 23, 1960

MAY 30, 1960

JUNE 27, 1960

JULY 4, 1960

JULY 11, 1960

AUGUST 8, 1960

AUGUST 15, 1960

AUGUST 22, 1960

SEPTEMBER 19, 1960

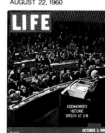
SEPTEMBER 26, 1960

OCTOBER 3, 1960

OCTOBER 31, 1960

NOVEMBER 7, 1960

NOVEMBER 14, 1960

DECEMBER 12, 1960

DECEMBER 19, 1960

DECEMBER 25, 1960

Astronauts' Training in Weightlessness PART II
'The Eerie World of Zero G'
by SCOTT CARPENTER

Scott Carpenter briefed readers on weightlessness as experienced in training
two years before he became, in Aurora 7, America's second man in orbit.

SPEAKING OF PICTURES

Here Is the Whole 'Life'   Photographic Staff

Gathered for a group portrait, this "unique and impressive assemblage"
was acknowledged to be the creator-perfecters of photojournalism.

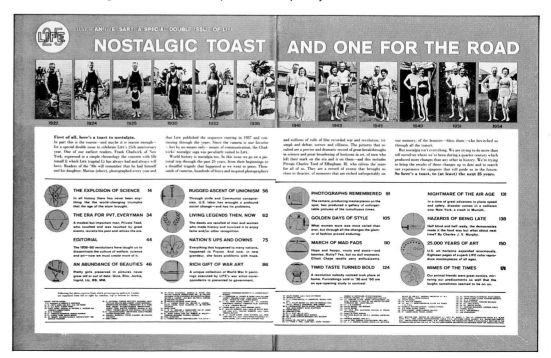

NOSTALGIC TOAST   AND ONE FOR THE ROAD

For its Silver Anniversary issue, LIFE harked back all the way to 1936
but also looked forward over a similar span to its golden milestone.

1961

A new editor and a new art director gave the magazine a bolder, more spacious look

It was the year in which man leapt into space. Around LIFE there was much talk also about space of another kind: white space—blank areas between pictures and around text material. George Hunt, the new managing editor, in collaboration with Bernard Quint, successor to Charles Tudor as art director, changed the look of the magazine suddenly and dramatically. The Hunt-Quint team also blew up otherwise ordinary photographs so they jumped off the page and juxtaposed them to add insight. Frequently they exploited the magazine's generous size still further by "bleeding" pictures—printing them to the very edges of a page. They used type as a design element—surprinting it on pictures. But the most striking change was the removal of the red band that had bordered the bottom of every cover since Vol. I, No. 1, in order to claim every square millimeter of space from each cover negative.

Cosmonaut Yuri Gagarin, returning from "Out of This World," strode along a red carpet in Moscow. The story quoted Gagarin: "I saw for the first time the earth's shape . . . the feelings which filled me I can express with one word—joy."

CURRENTS AND EVENTS

WORLD: U.S. Breaks Diplomatic Ties with Cuba, Bay of Pigs Invasion Fails • East Germany Builds Berlin Wall • UN Secretary General Hammarskjöld Dies in Plane Crash • JFK Increases U.S. Advisers in South Vietnam • Angolans Rebel Against Portuguese Rule • South Africa Leaves British Commonwealth, Incurs UN Censure for Apartheid • Pope John XXIII Issues Encyclical (Mater et Magistra) Condemning Materialism, Birth Control • Chou En-lai Walks Out on Moscow Party Congress, Heralding Sino-Soviet Break.

U.S.A.: In Farewell Address, Ike Warns Nation of Danger in Military-Industrial Complex • JFK Inaugurated • Peace Corps Established • Alabama Mobs Attack Freedom Riders Protesting Bus Segregation • Ernest Hemingway Dies of Self-Inflicted Gunshot • Malcolm X Advocates Black Power, Racial Separation • N.Y. Yankee Roger Maris Hits 61 Homers* • Widespread Point-Shaving in College Basketball.

FIRSTS: Man in Orbit (Gagarin) • Genetic Code Broken • U.S. Suborbital Flight (Shepard) • Televised Presidential News Conference • Nonstop Two-way English Channel Swim (Abertando) • Nondairy Creamer.

MOVIES: The Hustler • A Raisin in the Sun • Splendor in the Grass • El Cid • Judgment at Nuremberg • One, Two, Three • The Misfits • The Absent-Minded Professor • The Guns of Navarone • Misty • Breakfast at Tiffany's • Summer and Smoke • Breath-less • La Dolce Vita • Two Women • West Side Story • Fanny • Babes in Toyland • Flower Drum Song • Wild in the Country.

SONGS: Moon River • Where the Boys Are • Big Bad John • The Bilbao Song • I Believe in You • Michael—Row the Boat Ashore • Travelin' Man • Yellow Bird • Happy Birthday, Sweet Sixteen • I'm a Woman • Baby, You're Right • Kiss Me Quick • Can't Help Falling in Love • The Fly • Hit the Road, Jack • Little Sister • Barbara Ann.

STAGE: Come Blow Your Horn • Rhinoceros • Mary, Mary • Purlie Victorious • The Caretaker • A Shot in the Dark • Take Her, She's Mine • The Night of the Iguana • A Man for All Seasons • Ross • The Blacks • How to Succeed in Business Without Really Trying • Subways Are for Sleeping • Milk and Honey.

BOOKS: The Agony and the Ecstasy (Stone) • Franny and Zooey (Salinger) • The Carpetbaggers (Robbins) • Daughter of Silence (West) • The Making of the President, 1960 (White) • A Nation of Sheep (Lederer) • Ring of Bright Water (Maxwell) • Shadows on the Grass (Dinesen) • Nobody Knows My Name (Baldwin) • The White Nile (Moorehead) • Fate Is the Hunter (Gann) • Catch-22 (Heller) • A Burnt-Out Case (Greene) • The Moviegoer (Percy).

FADS: Yo-Yos • Rocking Chairs • Surfboarding • The Jackie Kennedy Look • Bed-Pushing • Decorated Sneakers.

CLASSIC PHOTOS

In Africa a zebra herd raced across a grassy plain.

Using crayons on a photo, Picasso transformed both himself and a friend into bacchanalian revelers.

As Jackie looked on, JFK responded to the crowd at his inaugural ball.

LIFE

Emotions of the Nation
SHEPARD

Ride in Astronaut's Capsule, So . . .
AND U.S.A. FEEL 'AOK'

When the seven Astronauts were narrowed down to three for the first U.S. ride into space (LIFE, March 3) LIFE characterized Navy Commander Alan Shepard as "a cool customer." Last week Shepard climbed into a Mercury capsule atop a fuming, temperamental Redstone missile at 5:20 a.m. More than three hours later he had the hole in your little problems and light that candle?"

The candle was finally lit and Shepard and the capsule he rode in made U.S. history. While the whole nation watched with a gripping sense of personal and emotional involvement, Shepard soared off into space for the most grueling ride any American has ever taken. The man and the machine

returned safely to earth. Then, apparently unaffected by the extreme forces of his flight, Shepard trotted easily across the carrier deck with the manner of the fighter pilot he used to be rather than that of a national hero.

But Alan Shepard was a heroic figure. He did not fly as far, fast or high as Russia's Yuri Gagarin. However, he controlled the flight of his capsule—which Gagarin did not—and carried out his fantastic mission under the relentless pressure of television and worldwide publicity.

The nation caught Shepard's spirit of confidence. Though the U.S. still has far to go to catch up with the Russians in space, Shepard went a long way toward lifting American heads higher. "Everything AOK [all perfect]. . . . Dye marker out," he said as his capsule hit the water. He was still a cool customer and the U.S. was warmly proud.

ASTRONAUT CONTINUED

STIRRING SIGHT   IN THE SKY; TENSE WATCHERS ON THE GROUND

◄ CURLING CONTRAIL, twisted by the winds aloft, marks path of rocket to point where Redstone shot

off. Capsule and booster, both invisible, are now following their separate trajectories back to earth.

WAITING WIVES, whose Astronaut husbands are at launching, stand transfixed on beach as missile

takes off. In foreground (from left) are Betty Grissom, Jo Schirra, Rene Carpenter, Marge Slayton.

CONTINUED 29

Big Pipe in the Backyard under Three Feet of Earth

[detailed instructional text on building a backyard bomb shelter, including "List of materials you will need" and diagrams labeled END VIEW, SIDE VIEW]

Alan Shepard's rocket ride was lower and slower than Yuri Gagarin's, though it did indeed make Americans "warmly proud." In 15 minutes, from Cape Canaveral lift-off to Atlantic splashdown 302 miles away, it reached an altitude of 115 miles. Other astronauts' wives watched the ascent from nearby sands (center).

JANUARY 6, 1961

JANUARY 13, 1961

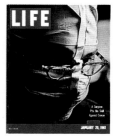

JANUARY 20, 1961

JANUARY 27, 1961

FEBRUARY 3, 1961

FEBRUARY 10, 1961

FEBRUARY 17, 1961

FEBRUARY 24, 1961

MARCH 3, 1961

MARCH 10, 1961

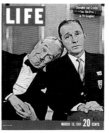

MARCH 17, 1961

MARCH 24, 1961

The hand of an East German reaching over a gray wall in West Berlin surmounted a dreadful symbol, the "all but permanent barrier between the hapless people in both sectors."

A message from President Kennedy urging readers to "consider seriously the contents of this issue of LIFE" preceded a 13-page article on how to build, stock and live in a bomb shelter.

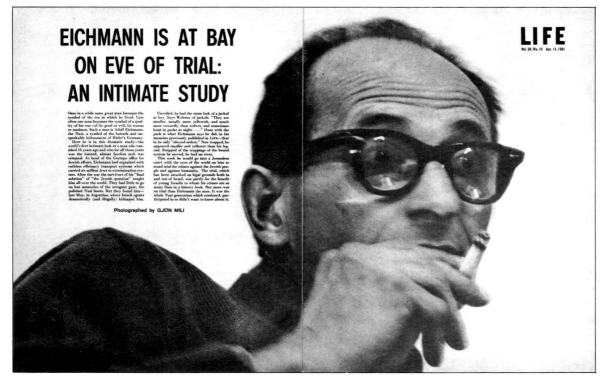

EICHMANN IS AT BAY ON EVE OF TRIAL: AN INTIMATE STUDY

Photographed by GJON MILI

LIFE
Vol. 50, No. 15 · Apr. 14, 1961

BEST IN THE BIG LEAGUE

LIFE *followed the Nazi "jackal" Eichmann through his daily regimen in an Israeli prison. His routine included much reflective smoking and, during Passover, matzos on his breakfast tray.*

Rounding up NFL quarterbacks, the photographer got all 14, and their footballs, in the right place at the right time—for a perfect-pattern play.

MARCH 31, 1961

APRIL 7, 1961

APRIL 14, 1961

APRIL 21, 1961

Delightedly catching up with the Twist (teens did it in 1959), the editors caught a N.Y. café society crowd doing it for a Girl's Town benefit.

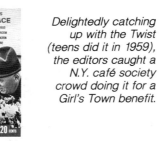

APRIL 28, 1961

MAY 5, 1961

MAY 12, 1961

MAY 19, 1961

Olympian-turned-pro Cassius Clay trained for his ninth win by punching underwater.

MAY 26, 1961

JUNE 2, 1961

JUNE 9, 1961

JUNE 16, 1961

Chiang Kai-shek sat for this portrait on Taiwan, his island fortress.

Marilyn Monroe "appeared to relish" a ball game with ex-husband Joe DiMaggio.

JUNE 23, 1961

JUNE 30, 1961

JULY 7, 1961

JULY 14, 1961

JULY 21, 1961

JULY 28, 1961

AUGUST 4, 1961

AUGUST 11, 1961

AUGUST 18, 1961

AUGUST 25, 1961

SEPTEMBER 1, 1961

SEPTEMBER 8, 1961

PROUD SOLDIERS

THE

CIVIL WAR

A CENTURY-OLD DRAMA STILL STIRS THE NATION

THE nation never faced a crisis more strange and bitter, never rang more loudly with daring nor suffered more with bloodshed and hate. It was never so deeply riven as by this conflict, which strove only to unite it. And no other event has so compellingly kept the nation's interest or left its mark so deeply upon the nation's soul.

This week, by presidential proclamation, marks the beginning of the Civil War Centennial. And in this issue LIFE begins a six-part series on the great conflict. On the following

pages specially commissioned paintings and the words of Bruce Catton, Pulitzer prize-winning historian of the war, describe acts of heroism that the struggle called forth. Continuing at two-week intervals, the series will show the great battles; will tell what a soldier's life was like; will explain, with the help of a famous living general, how this war changed all wars. Two other Pulitzer prize-winners will take part in the series, one to describe life on the home fronts, the other to tell how profoundly the war has shaped our present lives.

These vintage photos opened a six-part pictorial history of the Civil War. In addition to Bruce Catton, two other Pulitzer prizewinners, Margaret Leech and Robert Penn Warren, contributed to the accompanying text.

STORY OF THE WEEK

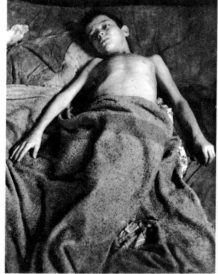

A Brave Boy, Symbol of Impoverished Millions, Is Rescued from a Rio Slum

THE COMPASSION OF AMERICANS   BRINGS A NEW LIFE FOR FLAVIO

This Story of the Week (a new feature) offered a happy sequel to a powerful picture essay published a month before. Gordon Parks (near left) had recorded the plight of Flavio, an emaciated 12-year-old head of a household in a Rio favela, or slum. Money poured in from readers. Parks returned to Rio, rescued the family and took the boy to Colorado for treatment of his near-fatal asthma.

SEPTEMBER 15, 1961

SEPTEMBER 22, 1961

SEPTEMBER 29, 1961

OCTOBER 6, 1961

OCTOBER 13, 1961

OCTOBER 20, 1961

OCTOBER 27, 1961

NOVEMBER 3, 1961

NOVEMBER 10, 1961

NOVEMBER 17, 1961

NOVEMBER 24, 1961

DECEMBER 1, 1961

DECEMBER 8, 1961

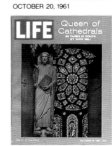
DECEMBER 15, 1961

DECEMBER 22, 1961

161

1962

Along with a new format came a commitment to sort out the good guys from the bad guys

In the first full year under its new managing editor, the magazine moved closer to subjects both photographically and reportorially. Less evident now was LIFE's established posture—at times knowing, frequently bemused, at times wide-eyed but always preserving a certain distance. More common now was a style of openhearted celebration—of humanity, of life, of the

After the frightening suspense of her husband's reentry into the atmosphere, Annie Glenn's face lit up at the news that he had splashed down safely and was aboard a U.S. destroyer.

Suspense for a Nation and a Family—
then Sweet Pride **HE HIT THAT 'KEYHOLE IN THE SKY'**

No man was ever more alone than John H. Glenn Jr., Lieut. Colonel, USMC, at this awesome and historic moment when he rode his upside-down volcano to a long-awaited date with space. And no man at any instant in human history was ever less alone, in the hopes and prayers of the world. People in Perth, Australia, left their lights on for him; Pope John in Rome prayed for him; the Japanese stayed up half the night to hear him safely off. And in the U.S. his fellow Americans swallowed capsule-sized lumps in their throats as he spoke back to earth from the stars. Time, the simple mathematical device by which men measure their days, vanished for Glenn as he hurtled into three sunsets and three dawns, through four Tuesdays and three Wednesdays in only five short hours. His feat was born out of a vast panorama of human and technical effort, of the patience and the skills of tens of thousands, all focused like a burning glass to create that sudden instant of flame—and then orbital flight. As Glenn soared into the nation's history —by "hitting a keyhole in the sky," as he described his own [...] through those mi [...] piness and succe [...] more. Theirs are [...]

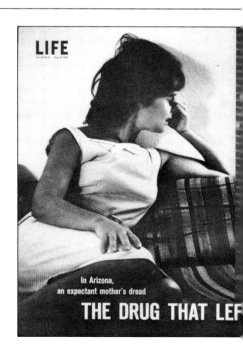

In Arizona, an expectant mother's dread **THE DRUG THAT LEF**

The younger children slumped or fidgeted. But Rene Carpenter and Scotty, her oldest, sat riveted before the TV set in their Cape Canaveral beach house as they awaited the signal that Scott, the second U.S. astronaut to orbit, had successfully made reentry. His landing was 250 miles off the mark.

JANUARY 5, 1962

JANUARY 12, 1962

JANUARY 19, 1962

JANUARY 26, 1962

FEBRUARY 2, 1962

FEBRUARY 9, 1962

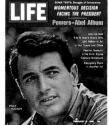
FEBRUARY 16, 1962

FEBRUARY 23, 1962

earth's bounty. A delight in man's fellowship with man and a scorn for those who would denigrate and destroy it—these were feelings unself-consciously expressed in story after story. Even the ongoing saga of the astronauts and the cosmonauts and the conquest of space was transfigured into a paean to the restless, questing human spirit, as well as to the tender ties of family.

A snapshot of Fidel Castro bobbing in the ocean seemed to symbolize his plight after the missile crisis. The Russians pulled their rockets out of Cuba. "The question now," the magazine intoned, "was how long Castro would be able to stay afloat."

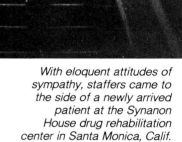

A distant shape against the sky, an Atlas missile blasted off from the gantry-cluttered landscape at Cape Canaveral. Strapped down inside the nose was John Glenn, launched on his historic flight as the first American to orbit the earth. He circled it three times and splashed down on target.

Babies were born without arms as one of the many side effects when thalidomide, a general-purpose tranquilizer, was taken by pregnant women. Already barred in the U.S., the pills were hurriedly withdrawn but not in time to prevent 8,000 defective births worldwide.

With eloquent attitudes of sympathy, staffers came to the side of a newly arrived patient at the Synanon House drug rehabilitation center in Santa Monica, Calif.

Young Tom Whalen of Detroit, a Peace Corps volunteer, was an absorbed witness to a fiesta in Zipacon, Colombia.

At the University of Mississippi, local lawmen waited, chortling, for James Meredith, the first black to challenge the color bar at Ole Miss. They vanished when the rioting started.

In Britain, mless baby's play
TRAIL OF HEARTBREAK

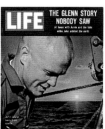

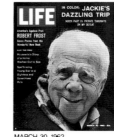

MARCH 2, 1962

MARCH 9, 1962

MARCH 16, 1962

MARCH 23, 1962

MARCH 30, 1962

APRIL 6, 1962

APRIL 13, 1962

APRIL 20, 1962

APRIL 27, 1962

MAY 4, 1962

MAY 11, 1962

MAY 18, 1962

MAY 25, 1962

JUNE 1, 1962

JUNE 8, 1962

JUNE 15, 1962

JUNE 22, 1962

JUNE 29, 1962

JULY 6, 1962

JULY 13, 1962

JULY 20, 1962

JULY 27, 1962

AUGUST 3, 1962

AUGUST 10, 1962

AUGUST 17, 1962

AUGUST 24, 1962

AUGUST 31, 1962

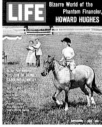

SEPTEMBER 7, 1962

SEPTEMBER 14, 1962

SEPTEMBER 21, 1962

SEPTEMBER 28, 1962

OCTOBER 5, 1962

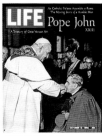

OCTOBER 12, 1962

OCTOBER 19, 1962

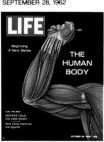

OCTOBER 26, 1962

NOVEMBER 2, 1962

NOVEMBER 9, 1962

NOVEMBER 16, 1962

NOVEMBER 23, 1962

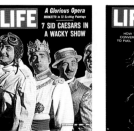

NOVEMBER 30, 1962

DECEMBER 7, 1962

DECEMBER 14, 1962

DECEMBER 21, 1962

A luminous, superrealistic still life of fruit and game, by 17th century Flemish painter Jan Fyt, signaled the editors' intensified attention to the arts. It was part of a story about the Kress Foundation's many gifts to museums over the years, a largesse that was about to end.

Kevin Gorman, 9, of Rye, N.Y., got an archery lesson from experts, Masai warriors, while visiting his stepfather in Kenya. In fair exchange (far right) Kevin then showed a new tribal friend, to whom he gave the nickname Busybody, how to swing a baseball bat properly.

An in-tight look at a young entrepreneur, whose obsessive drive in the end proved counterproductive, provided one of the year's most forceful stories. In it, a major element of the new journalistic approach was represented: examination of human values, magnified by boldness of design.

An artful arrangement of vegetables for a picture essay celebrating the harvest made a still life as sumptuous as any painting. "Food," the text pointed out poetically, "is life, beauty and pleasure wondrously combined."

REMEMBER MARILYN

A picture of Marilyn Monroe at 19 led off a story marking the star's tragic demise. "Her death has diminished the loveliness of the world in which we live."

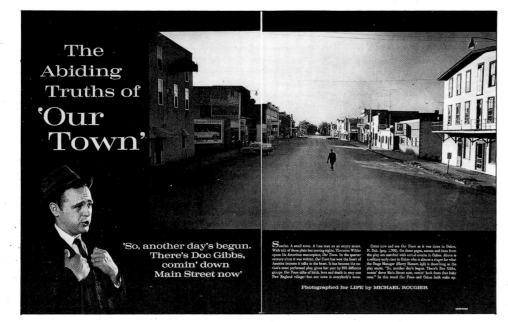

The Abiding Truths of 'Our Town'

'So, another day's begun. There's Doc Gibbs, comin' down Main Street now'

Photographed for LIFE by MICHAEL ROUGIER

When the city's nine dailies were struck, the magazine crashed a special edition. In subsequent weeks, for the strike's duration, a 12-page news section was folded into copies sold in the N.Y.C. area.

When the PTA of tiny Oakes, N.Dak., chose to perform Thornton Wilder's classic celebration of small-town virtues, LIFE covered a performance and juxtaposed pictures from the play with comparable images taken from daily life in Oakes.

CLASSIC PHOTOS

Survivors of an Iran earthquake rushed to a truck bringing food.

President Kennedy took a democratic dip in the surf at Santa Monica, Calif.

A huge spinnaker bellied on would-be America's Cup defender Nefertiti.

CURRENTS AND EVENTS

WORLD: U.S.S.R. Frees Pilot Gary Powers in Exchange for Spy Rudolf Abel • Algeria Wins Independence from France • UN Troops Quell Congo Republic Civil War • Castro Releases 1,113 Bay of Pigs POWs for $53 Million in Food, Medical Supplies • Soviet Missile Bases in Cuba Discovered, U.S. Quarantine Forces Khrushchev to Dismantle Them • U.S. Creates Military Assistance Command in South Vietnam • Pathet Lao Takes Over Northern Laos • Thailand Coalition Under Premier Souvanna Phouma Supported by Britain, Australia, U.S. • Pope John XXIII Opens 21st Ecumenical Council (Vatican II).

U.S.A.: Supreme Court Rules Scheduled Recitation of School Prayers Unconstitutional • Black Student James Meredith Seeks to Enroll at U. of Mississippi, U.S. Troops Move In to Control Campus Riots • Richard Nixon Quits Politics After Defeat in California Gubernatorial Race • Government Bans Segregation in Housing, Military Reserves, Transportation • Freedom Rides Continue • Marilyn Monroe Dies in L.A., Apparent Suicide.

FIRSTS: Nuclear Warhead Fired from Sub (Polaris) • City-Owned TV Station (WNYC, N.Y.) • Synthetic Wigs (Dynel) • Underwater Channel Swim (Baldasare, using Aqua-lung).

MOVIES: Advise and Consent • Long Day's Journey into Night • Billy Budd • Birdman of Alcatraz • The Longest Day • The Children's Hour • Freud • Light in the Piazza • Lawrence of Arabia • Lolita • The Manchurian Candidate • Sergeants Three • Sweet Bird of Youth • To Kill a Mockingbird • Walk on the Wild Side • What Ever Happened to Baby Jane? • The Music Man • Gypsy • Divorce—Italian Style • A Taste of Honey • Sundays and Cybele.

SONGS: I Can't Stop Loving You • Roses Are Red • Blowin' in the Wind • Ramblin' Rose • Days of Wine and Roses • Any Day Now • The Girl from Ipanema • Breaking Up Is Hard to Do • Desafinado • Call Me Mr. In-Between • That Happy Feeling • Quiet Nights of Quiet Stars • Second Hand Love • The Wah-Watusi • Mashed Potato Time • Let Me In • Twistin' the Night Away • He's a Rebel • Lonely Teardrops.

STAGE: A Thousand Clowns • Who's Afraid of Virginia Woolf? • Never Too Late • Oh Dad, Poor Dad, Mama's Hung You in the Closet and I'm Feeling So Sad • Seidman and Son • Beyond the Fringe • I Can Get It for You Wholesale • No Strings • Little Me • A Funny Thing Happened on the Way to the Forum.

BOOKS: Another Country (Baldwin) • Ship of Fools (Porter) • Pale Fire (Nabokov) • A Long and Happy Life (Price) • The Thin Red Line (Jones) • Letting Go (Roth) • The Reivers (Faulkner) • Youngblood Hawke (Wouk) • Tropic of Capricorn (Miller) • Silent Spring (Carson) • One Flew Over the Cuckoo's Nest (Kesey) • Big Sur (Kerouac).

FADS: "Twist" (fringed) Apparel • The Cleopatra Look • *Last Year in Marienbad* Hairdos • Intercollegiate Tiddlywinks.

1963

Three shots in Dallas still reverberate in images that are forever burned in memory

Though the historic issue carried a November 29 dateline, its normal deadline was Saturday, November 23—one day after John Fitzgerald Kennedy was killed. Most of the issue had already closed, with a cover story on Roger Staubach, the Naval Academy's outstanding quarterback. From Friday afternoon deep into Sunday, the editors ripped the issue apart to make room for the rapidly accumulating assassination coverage, which ultimately filled 37

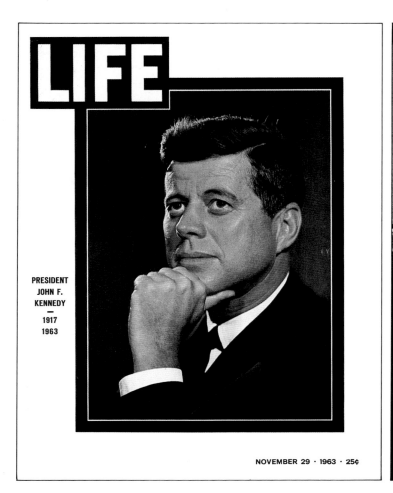

LIFE

PRESIDENT
JOHN F.
KENNEDY
—
1917
1963

NOVEMBER 29 · 1963 · 25¢

THIRD SHOT. Oswald's last bullet, fired at a range of more than 250 feet about two seconds after the shot which hit the governor, struck the President in the rear right part of his head (6). Mrs. Kennedy, only a few inches from being hit herself, shouted, "Oh no! Oh no!" and climbed toward the big rear deck of the Lincoln, desperately seeking help (7).

AID. Secret Service agent Clinton Hill jumped from the following car and rushed to catch the presidential car. As Mrs. Kennedy moved toward him he grabbed a handle and put a foot on the bumper (8). Mrs. Kennedy reached toward him as he climbed aboard (9), and the car sped toward the hospital, bearing the wounded governor—and the dead President.

The big red logo was replaced for the first time by a black one on the cover (above) of the issue that dealt immediately with the assassination. Coverage the next week included the photograph (right) of the sorrowing Kennedy family as it followed the slain President's coffin to St. Matthew's Cathedral in Washington, D.C.

pages. The following week's edition devoted 34 pages to the post-Dallas ceremonies and observances. Though print orders were greatly increased, both issues were quick sellouts, and scarcity was such that the 25-cent copies often were hawked for $5, $10, even $20. In the face of this demand, the two issues were soon combined in a special Memorial Edition priced at 50 cents, the profits from which were contributed to the Kennedy memorial library.

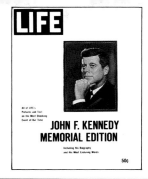

The crucial frames from the movie taken by amateur Abraham Zapruder, acquired exclusively by a quick-thinking staffer, ran in both the November 29 and the Memorial editions. In 1975 the original film was returned to Zapruder's heirs, who donated it to the National Archives.

A drawn Jacqueline Kennedy and a concerned Lady Bird Johnson listened as Lyndon B. Johnson took the oath of office aboard Air Force One before leaving for Washington with the body of the President.

Jack Ruby coolly leveled his gun at JFK's assassin, Lee Harvey Oswald, before pulling the trigger. This picture of the Sunday slaying made 90 percent of the remade magazine's press run.

Based on the only interview Jacqueline Kennedy permitted, this moving afterword was the result of a call she made to Theodore H. White, author of The Making of the President, 1960 and a LIFE contract-writer. Reached in a Manhattan dentist's chair, White hired a limousine to race through a raging storm to Hyannis Port, then dictated his story over the phone. The December 6 issue had already closed, but two pages were opened up to accommodate the editorial prize.

On his third birthday, John Fitzgerald Kennedy Jr. faced his father's coffin and saluted just the way he had seen soldiers salute his dad.

CLASSIC PHOTOS

A Buddhist monk in Saigon immolated himself in protest against Ngo Dinh Diem's government.

Queenly of mien, Dame Edith Sitwell prepared for a reading of her own poetry.

Susan Strasberg, in the new Mona Lisa hairdo, essayed an enigmatic Mona Lisa wink.

CURRENTS AND EVENTS

WORLD: U.S.S.R., Britain, U.S. Ban Nuclear Tests in Atmosphere, Space, Underwater • British War Secretary Profumo Resigns in Sex-Tinged Spy Scandal • Kim Philby of British Intelligence Defects to Russia, Revealed as Third Man in 1951 Burgess-Maclean Spy Case • Major Earthquake Rocks Yugoslavia • Italian Dam Collapses, Wave Drowns 1,800 • Ghanaian Students in Bulgaria, U.S.S.R. Charge Hosts with Racial Bias • Kenya Wins Independence • Hurricane Flora Slams into Haiti, 2,500 Perish • Buddhist Priests, Nuns in South Vietnam Immolate Selves to Protest Policies of Diem Regime, Diem Assassinated After Military Coup • Indonesia's Sukarno Becomes President for Life.

U.S.A.: NAACP's Medgar Evers Shot to Death in Jackson, Miss. • Informer Joseph Valachi Identifies Organized Crime Bosses to Senate Committee • Texas Financier Billie Sol Estes Convicted of Huge Fraud • Dr. Martin Luther King Jr. Leads March on Washington to Push Equal Rights for Blacks • President Kennedy Slain in Dallas, Lyndon Johnson Sworn In, Chief Justice Warren Heads Panel to Investigate Assassination.

FIRSTS: Use of Artificial Heart in Operation (DeBakey) • U.S.-Born Person Beatified (Mother Seton) • Polaroid Color Film • State Lottery (New Hampshire).

MOVIES: Heavens Above! • Hud • Cleopatra • 8½ • Tom Jones • The L-Shaped Room • The Leopard • Lilies of the Field • The Birds • The Ugly American • Dr. No • The Great Escape • Lord of the Flies • Knife in the Water • David and Lisa • Love with the Proper Stranger • Charade • The Cardinal • The Condemned of Altona • Under the Yum-Yum Tree.

SONGS: All My Loving • Call Me Irresponsible • Charade • Dominique • Guantanamera • Hello Muddah, Hello Fadduh • He's So Fine • Blue Velvet • Go Away, Little Girl • Our Day Will Come • If I Had a Hammer • More • Puff the Magic Dragon • Wives and Lovers • Ballad of Hollis Brown • As Long As He Needs Me • Detroit City.

STAGE: Barefoot in the Park • The Milk Train Doesn't Stop Here Anymore • Photo Finish • Enter Laughing • Luther • The Ballad of the Sad Café • Rattle of a Simple Man • Tovarich • 110 in the Shade • Oliver! • She Loves Me.

BOOKS: The Group (McCarthy) • The Centaur (Updike) • Caravans (Michener) • The Sand Pebbles (McKenna) • V. (Pynchon) • Cat's Cradle (Vonnegut) • Powers of Attorney (Auchincloss) • A Singular Man (Donleavy) • The Fire Next Time (Baldwin) • The Feminine Mystique (Friedan) • The American Way of Death (Mitford) • What Is Remembered (Toklas) • Beyond the Melting Pot (Glazer, Moynihan).

FADS: Piano-Wrecking • Teen Party Crashing in Gangs • The Bardot Bowler (hat) • Sweater for Two (two necks, two sleeves).

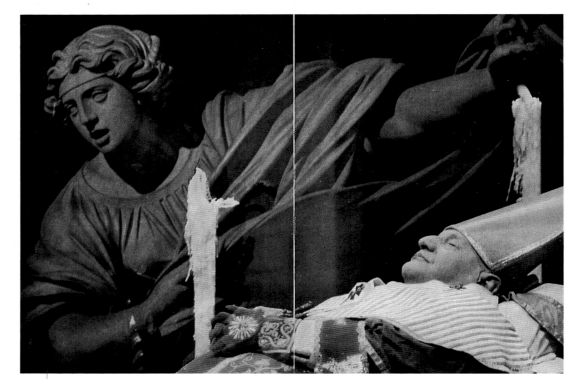

The marble St. Veronica in St. Peter's seemed, in this deliberate double exposure, to hover above the body of Pope John XXIII lying in state.

A 30-ton, 50-ft. humpback whale, "as large as a dinosaur," was caught in an unprecedented camera closeup as it burst from the Atlantic.

The spectacle of racial turbulence in Birmingham

THEY FIGHT A FIRE THAT WON'T GO OUT

Police in Birmingham, Ala., used a water jet "like a battering ram" on demonstrators practicing Martin Luther King Jr.'s "nonviolent direct action" against segregation.

Nelson Rockefeller married "Happy" Murphy, the campaign worker he had danced with four years earlier, before either was divorced.

A door chained from within was the ominous opening image for an article about the fear that stalked Boston while a sex strangler walked abroad.

He would be the subject of many future magazine stories, but Navy football star Roger Staubach was yanked from LIFE's lineup for the November 29 issue.

JANUARY 4, 1963

JANUARY 11, 1963

JANUARY 18, 1963

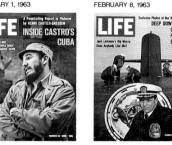
JANUARY 25, 1963

FEBRUARY 1, 1963

FEBRUARY 8, 1963

FEBRUARY 15, 1963

FEBRUARY 22, 1963

MARCH 1, 1963

MARCH 8, 1963

MARCH 15, 1963

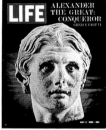
MARCH 22, 1963

MARCH 29, 1963

APRIL 5, 1963

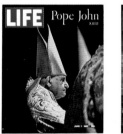
APRIL 12, 1963

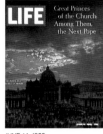
APRIL 19, 1963

APRIL 26, 1963

MAY 3, 1963

MAY 10, 1963

MAY 17, 1963

MAY 24, 1963

MAY 31, 1963

JUNE 7, 1963

JUNE 14, 1963

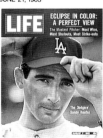
JUNE 21, 1963

JUNE 28, 1963

JULY 5, 1963

JULY 12, 1963

JULY 19, 1963

JULY 26, 1963

AUGUST 2, 1963

AUGUST 9, 1963

AUGUST 16, 1963

AUGUST 23, 1963

AUGUST 30, 1963

SEPTEMBER 6, 1963

SEPTEMBER 13, 1963

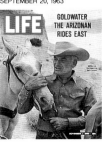
SEPTEMBER 20, 1963

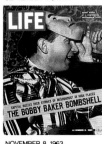
SEPTEMBER 27, 1963

OCTOBER 4, 1963

OCTOBER 11, 1963

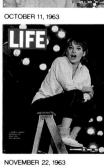
OCTOBER 18, 1963

OCTOBER 25, 1963

NOVEMBER 1, 1963

NOVEMBER 8, 1963

NOVEMBER 15, 1963

NOVEMBER 22, 1963

NOVEMBER 29, 1963

After the emotional drain of reporting the assassination, the year-end double issue devoted to "The Movies" came as a relief. Many months in the making, it was designed to be a stopper of a topper for a year that had been punctuated with several great series and picture essays. It featured as its star turn a major section in which box office favorites re-created great celluloid roles of the past. The concept was largely that of associate editor Mary Leatherbee, who succeeded in getting Hollywood's highest-paid stars to provide the free performances by first persuading a most reluctant Cary Grant to play Charlie Chaplin's tramp. Once she was able to drop his name, all the other luminaries fell in line.

The 190-page issue's triple foldout cover ecumenically featured not a Hollywood production but a crew in Tokyo's Toho studio filming a spectacular starring Toshiro Mifune, Japan's No. 1 motion picture star.

Face Is Familiar, But—

Here he comes, debonairly twirling that bamboo walking stick, shuffling out of the golden age of slapstick comedy, unmistakably, inimitably, the one and only . . . Wait a minute, wait a minute. This is really a fantastic facsimile created by a devilishly debonair, most untrumplike fellow who specializes in man-about-town roles and is the least likely man in the world to get pasted with a custard pie.

Photographed for LIFE by BERT STERN

A bronze Poseidon looming over the sea introduced the first installment of an epochal eight-part series on Greece. "Almost every phase of our lives bears [the Greeks'] indelible stamp," said the preface. "Doctors still recite the Hippocratic Oath. . . . Athletes dream of the Olympics . . . and a third-hand version of the Pygmalion myth, My Fair Lady, *was the world's most successful musical show."*

GREECE: PART I

With its stern features and regal gaze the bronze Greek sea-god Poseidon, shown against a background of his watery realm, personifies divine majesty. The majesty is human, too, for ancient Greeks saw man not as a servant of the gods but as their near-equal. They respected the gods but saved their deepest admiration for man.

"Wonders are many," wrote the tragedian Sophocles, "and none is more wonderful than man." In this wonder lay not only what man is, but what man might aspire to be. In all the Greeks ever did they never ceased trying to grasp and express the essence of what makes a man a man, and the ideals he should strive to fulfill.

THE WORTH OF MAN

– Photographed for LIFE by GJON MILI

Staffer Leatherbee plied Grant with flowers and notes, then cajoled him by phone (running time: one hour, plus; he was too much the gentleman to hang up on her). He finally capitulated, showed up in costume for the photo session and handed her a velvet-bowed package "for the year's most memorable performance." In it was an Oscar.

Gordon Parks: a talented Negro tells in fiction, fact and photograph

How It Feel

Timed for maximum impact during this period of hard-won integration was a report by Gordon Parks—photographer, artist, poet, novelist (and later, filmmaker)—based on his own boyhood in Kansas and on a tour of Harlem, spanning joy and violence.

DECEMBER 6, 1963

DECEMBER 13, 1963

DECEMBER 20, 1963

The 14-page section opened with this two-page spread showing the participants in stills from their most recent films. The rationale for the plugs: the stars were so perfect in their classic-role getups that they might not be recognized.

To Be Black

Gordon Parks, a Negro born in the border state of Kansas—neither north nor Deep South—spent a large part of his life fighting for a place in the white world. He won that place and became a famous photographer, a member of LIFE's staff. Now he has turned to writing and has produced his first novel, a violent and perceptive fictional autobiography.

His novel, The Learning Tree (Harper & Row), tells how it feels to grow up a Negro boy in America. On a recent visit home Parks took the photographs on these pages to evoke the book's mood; the little boy above, running for safety before a line storm, might be Parks himself, age 12. The novel ends while the hero is still a boy, but on the pages following his color pictures, Parks tells some of the things that happened to him in real life afterward and are still happening to him now.

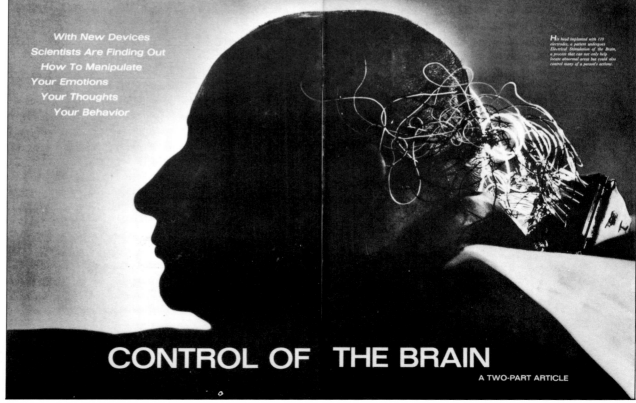

With New Devices
Scientists Are Finding Out
How To Manipulate
Your Emotions
Your Thoughts
Your Behavior

His head implanted with 110 electrodes, a patient undergoes Electrical Stimulation of the Brain, a process that can not only help locate abnormal areas but could also control many of a person's actions.

CONTROL OF THE BRAIN

A TWO-PART ARTICLE

This two-parter by LIFE writer Robert Coughlan exploring the alteration of human behavior by electronic and chemical means was evidence of the editors' increasing interest in the biomedical field. It was to lead to several landmark series on the human body, as organ transplants and synthetic replacements became more ingenious and more common.

1964

After the assassination, a shrinking, changing, ever more ambiguous world quickly emerged

A kaleidoscope of developments tested the magazine's resources. Nikita Khrushchev was forced off the world stage and became an unperson. A devastating earthquake rocked Alaska. Many people simply refused to accept the Warren Commission's painstakingly reasoned conclusion that Lee Harvey Oswald had acted alone in killing President Kennedy. And as if all this were not heavy enough, four Liverpudlian rockers sporting medieval hairdos were bent on subverting the world's youth, fashion designers looked beyond the transparent blouse to the topless bathing suit, and the New York Yankees, along with the House That Ruth Built, were sold to CBS, to the consternation of traditionalists. Amid such upheaval, the nation had to choose its next chief executive, even as the martyred President's successor was emerging as a paradox: a strong son of Texas who picked up his pet beagles by the ears, yet who steadfastly demonstrated uncommon social vision.

General Douglas A. MacArthur lay in repose in a Manhattan armory "after three wars, innumerable honors and 84 years."

Elizabeth Taylor's intimate revelations to staffer Richard Meryman, elicited in long tape-recorded sessions, emerged in his series of studies about fame and what it means to those who have it. Earlier subjects were Marilyn Monroe and Sir Laurence Olivier.

On an epochal pilgrimage Pope Paul VI, the first pontiff to fly and the first in a century and a half to leave Italy, blessed followers, including a flock of half-immersed photographers, beside the Sea of Galilee.

In an augural essay headlined "A Little War, Far Away—and Very Ugly," Americans manned choppers carrying South Vietnamese troops.

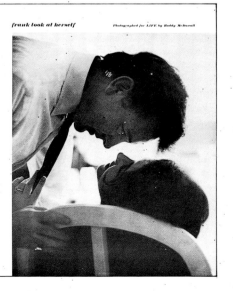

In a rare photograph, Lee Harvey Oswald clowned for a ninth-grade classmate's camera. The picture was part of a detailed clinical study of Oswald based on a national reportorial sweep by the staff.

As southerners forcefully slowed desegregation, Martin Luther King Jr. still preached nonviolence.

172

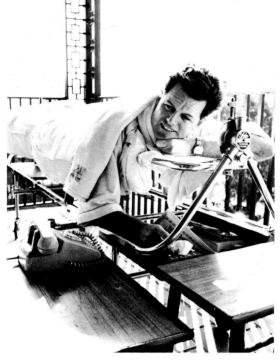

Hard-hitting U.S. Attorney General Robert Kennedy was cited as a possible running mate for President Johnson.

Senator Ted Kennedy, his back broken in a plane crash, lay in an orthopedic bed that could be rotated "like a typewriter roller."

The most powerful earthquake ever to hit North America ripped Anchorage, Alaska, with a force of 200,000 megatons, cleaving the ground and heaving up shattered houses at crazy angles.

THE VIEW FROM HERE
by Loudon Wainwright

The Strange Case of Strangelove

I found myself at the edge of tears as I watched a series of nuclear explosions fill the screen and heard a sweet female voice singing. "We'll meet again, don't know where, don't know when, but I know we'll meet again some sunny day." This happened at the very end of *Dr. Strangelove or: How I Learned To Stop Worrying and Love the Bomb*, and I had been laughing wildly for an hour and a half. The emotional switch surprised me at the time. Was I sad that the movie's world was ending? Was I having an attack of hysteria brought on by the film's repeated and stunning outrages? Or had I suddenly arrived after prolonged laughter — at a glimpse of some awful truth?

This truth had something to do with the sheer ridiculousness of humanity's posture in its terribly complex, life-and-death affair with the bomb. In the blinding light of the explosions that end all life, such virtues as efficiency, patriotism and steadfastness seem somewhat fragile. It struck me at the time and it strikes me now that *Dr. Strangelove* is a brilliant and edifying, even a moral, movie. Many moviegoers, who have been breaking headline records in theaters all over the country, apparently share this opinion.

The verdict is not, however, unanimous. Of course, there is no good reason why such a strong dose of comic medicine should be universally admired. Some will find violent flaws in the picture; others will be offended at the suggestion that man's efforts to control the bomb are futile. Such efforts have been successful, these people might say, for almost 20 years.

But some influential and highly placed critics have attacked the film with extraordinary bitterness, as though it were downright disloyal. Their assault, it seems to me, is right in tune with the rigid and inappropriate behavior that is lampooned on the screen. "Defeatist," "destructive of morale," "malignant," "evil," "sick" are some of the words being used to describe the film, and there is the distinct suggestion throughout most of the adverse criticism that since any damn fool knows we can't ban the bomb, it would be a good thing if we could just ban this dreadful picture. One noted political reporter on a Washington newspaper writes: "As Communists could dream of a more effective anti-American film to spread abroad than this one. United States officials, including the President, had better take a look at this one to see its effect on the national interest."

What is there about *Dr. Strangelove* that's getting these people so upset? To be sure, the plot and the characters are not particularly reassuring when taken straight. As rumor U.S. Air Force general, without the knowledge of the President, who is a sane kook, instructs his airborne nuclear bombers to attack their Russian targets. It turns out that the Russians have a "Doomsday Device" which will go off automatically when the U.S.S.R. is hit, and that this super-super deterrent, whose radioactive ingredients have a killing "half-life" of 93 years, will then wipe out humanity. Suspense builds through a crescendo of nightmare jokes, and the long and short of the plot is that our plane gets through, drops its bombs and the Doomsday Device begins its chain of world-ending explosions.

Stanley Kubrick, the mild, bright 35-year-old who directed, produced and collaborated on the writing of *Dr. Strangelove*, puts a comic spin on the whole ghastly business. And it is just that spin which appears to have undone his angriest critics. Repelled by a comedy which flows in both from top to bottom fully and outright doom, they miss the point of the satire. Instead they deal grimly with the accuracy of specific details, details which the satirist has plainly made up. One important critic, at his third dismented review of the picture, writes: "Kubrick is saying that the top-level scientists . . . the diplomats, the military, the prime ministers and even the President of the United States are all futile dolts or maniac monsters who are completely unable to control the bomb. . . . It passes belief that everybody in command could be as foolish and befuddled as they're shown here." A professional foreign policy expert writes: "Had [Kubrick] set out to make a wild farce about the publicly available facts under the command and control of our nuclear forces. This he has not done — to the detriment of the trust which the American public rightly reposes in the integrity and competence of our political leadership and of the professional leaders of the armed services. . . ."

In their anger these men have failed to realize that Kubrick had no interest in making a picture based on the "publicly available facts," and that he isn't asking people to believe that everybody in command is as foolish as felt as in the movie. As a satirist, he is involved in revealing human folly through burlesque.

"Why should the knock be approached with solemn reverence?" Kubrick asks. "Reverence can be a paralyzing state of mind. For us the comic sense is the most intensely human reaction to the mysteries and the paradoxes of life. I just hope some of them are illuminated by the satire, suggestions and the style of the film. And I don't see why an artist has to do any more than produce an artistic experience that reflects his thinking."

It seems strange, even paradoxical, that Kubrick has to defend the artist's prerogatives in the U.S. About a month ago, shortly after the opening of *Dr. Strangelove* in New York, Marshal Rodion Y. Malinovsky, the Soviet defense minister, delivered a verbal spanking to Russian artists and writers who Mr. Malinovsky thought were creating dangerously picture scenes. Speaking about a particular Russian film, he said: "We all know the bitter failures of the best period of the war and their causes. But in portraying all this the artist cannot confine himself to a position of abstract humanism and forget about the terrible reality of the struggle that we were involved in our interests."

What Malinovsky was really saying is that it's important to make films or books or paintings that don't conform to Soviet political or military ideals. Strangelove's American detractors in their vehement regrets that Kubrick did not employ the literal truth in his savage fiction and that his wild caricatures of U.S. leaders are not at all like the ones who are currently in charge of our destinies sound a lot like the marshal. And their outrage underlines another truth — that the half-life of Not Getting the Point is forever.

LIFE's first columnist's first column dealt with the now-classic black comedy that had stirred sharp controversy.

GOP presidential candidate Barry Goldwater waxed playfully pugnacious with his bulldog.

Arthur Miller's startling play—is it good taste?

MARILYN'S GHOST TAKES THE STAGE

Most of the audience already knew. Before they took their seats at the New York opening of Arthur Miller's new play, *After the Fall*, they had heard that a major character named Maggie bore a more than casual resemblance to Miller's second wife, the late Marilyn Monroe.

But even forewarned, they were not prepared for what they saw. When a gifted new star, Barbara Loden, put on a blond wig and appeared in a succession of diaphanous costumes, she was not merely disporting herself in the Monroe manner. It was frequently a Monroe impersonation—and the effect was uncanny, as if a ghost had been conjured up. On top of that, Miller had written scenes dealing with Maggie's addiction to sleeping pills, her promiscuity, her desperate need for love and reassurance.

Since Miller is a major U.S. playwright, and since his play was sponsored by New York's august new Lincoln Center, it would be wrong to dismiss his work as sensationalism. Miller was writing, with all the honesty he could muster, about a lawyer named Quentin—obviously a Miller spokesman—and how he came to terms with his life, and himself. But charges of bad taste have been thrown at Miller by many who admired him. On page 66 Playwright Miller explains eloquently why he has written this play.

In the play Barbara Loden, wearing pajama top, evokes Marilyn Monroe. Above, in life, Marilyn embraces Author Miller after their 1956 marriage.

CONTINUED 64A

When Arthur Miller wrote the late Marilyn Monroe, his second wife, into his play After the Fall, *it gave the editors a chance to present yet another picture of MM, or at least of her "ghost," in the form of her stage impersonator, Barbara Loden. A 1956 picture of the real Mrs. Miller and her bridegroom ran with it.*

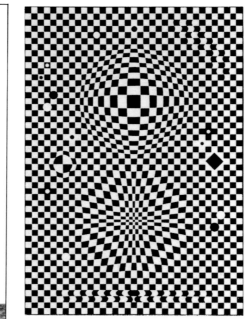

In a nine-page exploration of the new Op Art, Victor Vasarely's "eye-bulging" Metagalaxy competed with other artists' assemblages of lines, dots and assorted shapes to boggle the eye.

In a new series titled "Great Dinners," a perfectly cooked trout leapt from a pool of sliced almonds. For the chef, if not the photographer, the message was: "The less fancy you are, the better the fish will be."

Trout in an Almond Pool

The fish, done in classic amandine style, suits the season

Just as a fisherman's heart beats faster at the sight of a trout splashing in a mountain stream, a food lover happily anticipates a well-cooked trout—which in this photographic fantasy is leaping from a pool of almonds. The flavor of trout is as delicate that as a rule the less fancy you are in cooking it the better the fish will be. The dish shown here is classic trout amandine, which calls for sautéing the fish in butter and garnishing it with sautéed almonds. The almonds add a touch of sweetness—but do not dominate. The trout, in season now in all of the U.S., is part of a menu (next page) full of things that are never better eating than they are right now.

PHOTOGRAPHED BY JOHN DOMINIS

JANUARY 3, 1964

JANUARY 10, 1964

JANUARY 17, 1964

JANUARY 24, 1964

JANUARY 31, 1964

FEBRUARY 7, 1964

FEBRUARY 14, 1964

FEBRUARY 21, 1964

FEBRUARY 28, 1964

MARCH 6, 1964

MARCH 13, 1964

MARCH 20, 1964

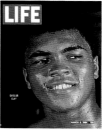

MAY 22, 1964

MAY 29, 1964

JUNE 5, 1964

JUNE 12, 1964

JUNE 19, 1964

JUNE 26, 1964

JULY 3, 1964

JULY 10, 1964

SEPTEMBER 11, 1964

SEPTEMBER 18, 1964

SEPTEMBER 25, 1964

OCTOBER 2, 1964

OCTOBER 9, 1964

OCTOBER 16, 1964

OCTOBER 23, 1964

OCTOBER 30, 1964

Just before their first trip to the U.S., "Mopheads" Paul McCartney, 21, George Harrison, 21, John Lennon, 23, and Ringo Starr, 23, were introduced to readers. The photo (far left) was complemented by an indulgent Editor's Note disserting at length on "Beatlemania" as a passing fad. Three weeks later (near left) The Four had landed and Beatlemania was pandemic.

"The topless bathing suit," commented columnist-to-be Shana Alexander, taking note of the supporting loop in Rudi Gernreich's headline-making design, "is no good for sunning because it leaves disastrous strap marks." The practical appraisal was proffered in a bylined story that followed the spread at left. Her conclusions: "A bare-breasted woman in broad daylight is chiefly unnerving."

Me? In That!

The unwitting ingenuity of a fashion designer sets off an uneasy buzz over toplessness everywhere

  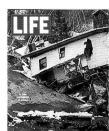     

MARCH 27, 1964   APRIL 3, 1964   APRIL 10, 1964   APRIL 17, 1964   APRIL 24, 1964   MAY 1, 1964   MAY 8, 1964   MAY 15, 1964

    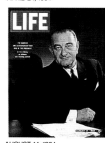   

JULY 17, 1964   JULY 24, 1964   JULY 31, 1964   AUGUST 7, 1964   AUGUST 14, 1964   AUGUST 21, 1964   AUGUST 28, 1964   SEPTEMBER 4, 1964

    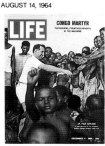 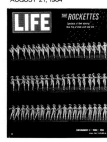  

NOVEMBER 6, 1964   NOVEMBER 13, 1964   NOVEMBER 20, 1964   NOVEMBER 27, 1964   DECEMBER 4, 1964   DECEMBER 11, 1964   DECEMBER 18, 1964   DECEMBER 25, 1964

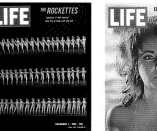

1965

In an eventful year, Churchill's funeral led to an editorial tour de force high in the sky

As LIFE approached its 30th year the editorial staff was in top professional form. No subject seemed too challenging to cover. The world cooperated by producing a bumper crop of momentous happenings, the most colorful of which was the solemn pageantry of Winston Churchill's funeral. The magazine's long relationship with the great man had been

LIFE
Vol. 58, No. 5   February 5, 1965

1874–1965. At 80, Sir Winston put on the medals he had so nobly earned—the Order of Merit on his breast, the Garter Star below his other decorations.

THE LAST HONORS

Enfolded by the stone walls that King William Rufus raised in 1097, draped by the Union Jack he zealously had guarded for 90 years, Sir Winston Churchill lay at the heart of British history. Sovereigns and one commoner (Gladstone) had lain here in state in Westminster Hall. In the filtered twilight of an English winter his guards—these are Royal Navy officers—stood in the formal funerary attitude with heads bowed and their bare swords grounded. The symbol of the most prestigious honor bestowed on him in life, the Order of the Garter, lay enshrined on a black pillow over his head. Now, in death, mightier and more affectionate honors came to him. The queen, peers and notables approached, and the people he had served, walking by patiently and somberly as living testimony that the indomitable spirit has outlived the clay.

27

The 23-page story of Sir Winston's funeral opened with a muffled visual drumroll. Facing a formal portrait was the lying-in-state scene at London's Westminster Hall, with the flag-draped coffin and a four-man honor guard in marmoreal attitudes of mourning.

The funeral came to a climax with the solemn obsequies at St. Paul's, where the casket was borne up the aisle between rows of dignitaries.

LIFE
Vol. 58, No. 15   April 16, 1965

GETTING THE WORD. Marine helicopter squadron is briefed. At right, crew chief Farley carries M-60 machine gun to copter.

Photographer Larry Burrows' report from Da Nang, Vietnam

Larry Burrows

One Ride with Yankee Papa 13

It was another day's work for the U.S. Marines' Helicopter Squadron 163 in Vietnam. In the salty morning the crews huddled at Da Nang for the final briefing on their mission: to airlift a battalion of Vietnamese infantry to an isolated area about 20 miles away. Intelligence reports indicated that the area was a rendezvous point for the Communist Viet-cong, who come down the Ho Chi Minh trail from the north.

Among those listening at the briefing were Lance Cpl. James C. Farley (right), crew chief of the copter Yankee Papa 13, and LIFE Photographer Larry Burrows (left), who had been covering the war in Vietnam since 1962 and had flown on scores of helicopter combat missions. On this day he would be riding in Farley's machine—and both were wondering whether the mission would be a no-contact milk run or whether, as had been increasingly the case in recent weeks, the Vietcong would be ready and waiting with .30-caliber machine guns. In a very few minutes Farley and Burrows had their answer, as shown in his chilling photographic and word report on these pages. And after Yankee Papa 13 had limped back home bullet-riddled and bloodstained, Burrows received a special souvenir from Lt. Colonel Norman Ewers, the squadron skipper. Said Ewers as he handed Burrows a set of air crewman's wings, an emblem given to some few Marines and damned few civilians: "You've earned it."

24

A young Marine helicopter crewman's baptism of blood under Vietcong fire was LIFE's first major story about the toll, in physical and mental suffering, on Americans serving in Vietnam. But, amid growing antiwar sentiment, the magazine declared that U.S. policy, although "supremely difficult," was nevertheless "a right one."

Lance Corporal James Farley opened up on the Vietcong as soon as his chopper landed. The picture was snapped with a remote-control camera rigged to his machine gun.

marked through the years by numerous stories and covers, including 42 installments of his own writings. To do justice to the historic ceremonies, the normal deadline was postponed for three days and a chartered DC-8 was equipped to serve as an airborne photo lab and editorial office. The plane flew to London, picked up film and Europe-based correspondents, turned around immediately with a total of 40 staffers aboard and headed straight for the printing plant in Chicago. In flight thousands of photographs were developed, selected and laid out, and the story—fully written, edited and checked—was ready to roll by the time the plane touched down at O'Hare, to be met by a traffic-busting escort to the printer.

At Waterloo Station Churchill's coffin was placed aboard a special train for burial at Blenheim, his ancestral family seat.

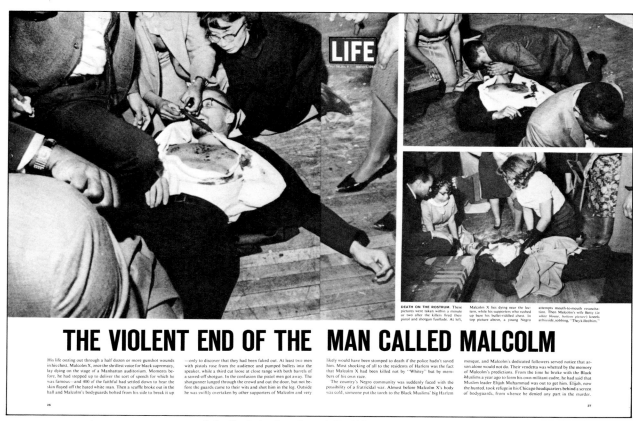

A fusillade to the chest felled Malcolm X, victim of the Black Muslims he had once served. Malcolm had been the most fiery apostle of vengeance against "Whitey" until visits to the Third World broadened his views and turned him to the ideal of brotherhood. In LIFE's sympathetic assessment, he paid the price of his apostasy.

After the skirmish the corporal hovered in shock over wounded buddies rescued from another copter riddled with Vietcong fire.

In the Watts ghetto of Los Angeles, a minor police arrest set off the decade's worst race riot. Mobs set fires, looted and heaved bricks at firemen, screaming "Burn, baby, burn!" The toll, after National Guardsmen restored order: "24 dead, 891 injured, 201 buildings destroyed, property damage approaching $200 million."

JANUARY 8, 1965

JANUARY 15, 1965

JANUARY 22, 1965

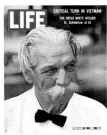
JANUARY 29, 1965

FEBRUARY 5, 1965

FEBRUARY 12, 1965

FEBRUARY 19, 1965

FEBRUARY 26, 1965

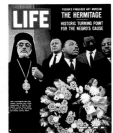
MARCH 5, 1965

MARCH 12, 1965

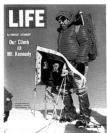
MARCH 19, 1965

MARCH 26, 1965

APRIL 2, 1965

APRIL 9, 1965

APRIL 16, 1965

APRIL 23, 1965

APRIL 30, 1965

MAY 7, 1965

MAY 14, 1965

MAY 21, 1965

MAY 28, 1965

JUNE 4, 1965

JUNE 11, 1965

JUNE 18, 1965

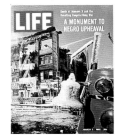

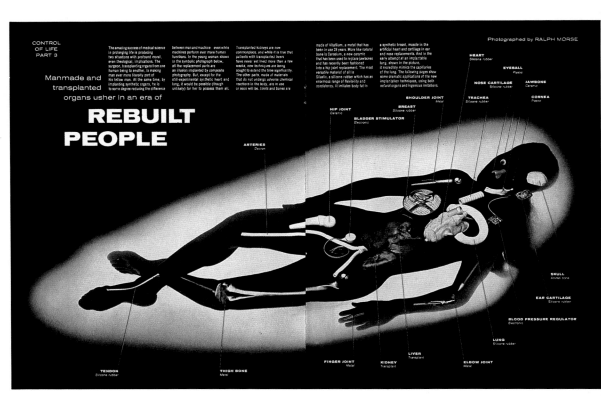

CONTROL OF LIFE PART 3

Manmade and transplanted organs usher in an era of

Photographed by RALPH MORSE

REBUILT PEOPLE

An array of artificial body parts and transplant organs led off a report on the revolutionary new frontiers of medicine. One photograph in the story showed a calf fitted with the then most futuristic device of them all—a mechanical heart.

Congo Premier Tshombe took aim with a Soviet-made sniper's rifle captured from Communist-supported rebels.

At the end of an all-out slide home, giant-in-any-uniform Willie Mays also got his lumps from the ump.

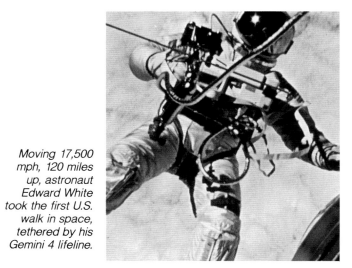

Moving 17,500 mph, 120 miles up, astronaut Edward White took the first U.S. walk in space, tethered by his Gemini 4 lifeline.

New photo methods dramatize surges of the city today

Sweep of Creative Powe

Photographed by HOWARD SOCHUREK

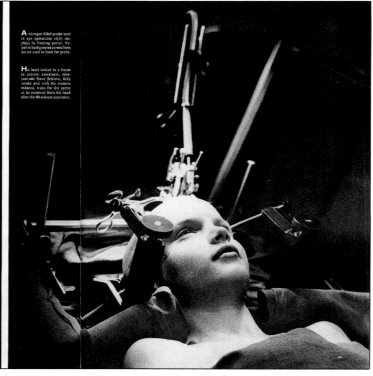

Supercold surgery gives doctors a new weapon
Healing with An Icy Lance

A steel probe driven two and a half inches into his brain, this crippled boy is undergoing a revolutionary operation that can heal in seconds bodies long twisted by disease. For years doctors faced with Parkinson's disease, dystonia and other afflictions involving abnormal muscular movement have had few methods of treatment. But now a New York doctor has pioneered a radical new operating technique—cryosurgery—which freezes and destroys errant brain cells causing the trouble. Other doctors have used cryosurgery to destroy tumors, operate on eyes and even to perform tonsillectomies. This boy's brain operation—for dystonia—is painless and almost bloodless. It is performed while the patient is fully conscious. A hollow probe, insulated save for its silver tip, is delicately guided into the crippling brain cells. Then liquid nitrogen at subzero temperature is pumped into the probe. Tissue surrounding the uninsulated tip freezes—and most of the crippling vanishes instantly. After tests have insured that the freezing is not affecting healthy tissue, the temperature is lowered to −80° C. to kill the abnormal cells and make the treatment permanent.

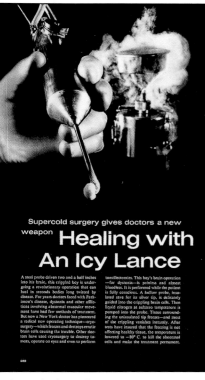

A nitrogen-filled probe used in eye operations (left) displays its freezing power. Vapor in background comes from device used to load the probe.

His head locked in a frame to prevent movement, nine-year-old Steve Schiavo, fully awake and with his tremors reduced, waits for the probe to be removed from his head after the 90-minute operation.

A surgical needle still buried in his brain, Steve Schiavo, 9, rested after cryosurgery to relieve his muscular spasms. The accompanying story pointed out that the technique could cure by spot-freezing brain cells that cause tremors.

Publisher Harry Abrams's maid Cleo Johnson checked out the works of a Rauschenberg painting, as part of a piece on pop art.

Knees already banged up, 'Bama's Joe Namath would sign with the N.Y. Jets for a then staggering $400,000—for three years.

Sochurek spent most of the summer flying over U.S. cities, using new techniques in photography: infrared color film and anamorphic lenses.

Video recording, LIFE predicted, "may blow the whole home entertainment field wide open."

CLASSIC PHOTOS

President Johnson proudly showed off the scar from his gallbladder operation.

A cat with an al dente smile was ladled out of leftover pasta.

A chopper's crew chief wept after a 'Nam mission.

CURRENTS AND EVENTS

WORLD: Winston Churchill, 90, Dies • Crop Failure Forces U.S.S.R. to Buy Wheat from Australia, Canada • Constantine II Dismisses Leftist Greek Premier Papandreou • Rhodesia's Prime Minister Declares Independence from Britain • General Mobutu Emerges as President of Congo Republic • U.S. Sends Troops to Intervene in Dominican Republic Civil War • Guinea Alleges French Plot to Overthrow Head of State • War Rages Between India, Pakistan.

U.S.A.: LBJ's State of the Union Speech Calls for a "Great Society" • Dr. King Leads Alabama "Freedom March" • Medicare Established • Massive Power Failure in Northeast Blacks Out Seven States • FTC Rules Cigarette Packs Must Carry Health Warning • Federal Housing, Higher Education Acts Become Law • Blacks Riot in L.A.'s Watts Ghetto, National Guard Restores Order • Connecticut Birth-Control Ban Declared Unconstitutional • Space Program Accelerates in Series of Gemini, Pioneer Missions.

VIETNAM: U.S. Lands First Combat Contingent, 3,500 Marines, at Da Nang • Bomb Wrecks U.S. Embassy in Saigon • U.S.S.R. Admits Supplying Arms to Hanoi • Planes Bomb North in Reprisal for Vietcong Attacks on U.S. Ground Forces in South • Ho Chi Minh Rejects LBJ Proposal that UN Negotiate Peace • Johnson Doubles Monthly Number of Draftees, to 35,000 • Antiwar Demonstrations Increase.

FIRSTS: Man to Walk in Space (Leonov) • Black U.S. Cabinet Officer (Weaver, HUD) • Round-the-World Flight over Both Poles • All-News Radio Programming (WINS, N.Y.).

MOVIES: The Agony and the Ecstasy • Cat Ballou • The Cincinnati Kid • The Greatest Story Ever Told • Help! • How to Murder Your Wife • The Ipcress File • King Rat • The Pawnbroker • Ship of Fools • The Spy Who Came In from the Cold • A Thousand Clowns • Thunderball • What's New, Pussycat? • Darling • Hush . . . Hush Sweet Charlotte • Juliet of the Spirits • Life at the Top • The Sandpiper • The Yellow Rolls-Royce • Those Magnificent Young Men in Their Flying Machines • The Sound of Music.

SONGS: It's Not Unusual • My Girl • I Got You Babe • Hang On Sloopy • The Shadow of Your Smile • The Impossible Dream • Dulcinea • Do I Hear a Waltz? • Do You Believe in Magic? • Game of Love • Help! • Help Me, Rhonda • I Hear a Symphony • Satisfaction • Stop! In the Name of Love • Turn! Turn! Turn! • Sounds of Silence • What the World Needs Now Is Love • Like a Rolling Stone • Yesterday • Wooly Bully • Mrs. Brown You've Got a Lovely Daughter • Look of Love • You've Lost That Lovin' Feelin'.

STAGE: The Odd Couple • The Right Honourable Gentleman • The Royal Hunt of the Sun • Inadmissible Evidence • Marat/Sade • Do I Hear a Waltz? • The Amen Corner • Half a Sixpence • Flora, the Red Menace • The Roar of the Greasepaint—the Smell of the Crowd • Pickwick • On a Clear Day You Can See Forever • Man of La Mancha.

BOOKS: The Source (Michener) • Hotel (Hailey) • An American Dream (Mailer) • The Looking Glass War (Le Carré) • Unsafe at Any Speed (Nader) • Kennedy (Sorensen) • A Thousand Days (Schlesinger) • The Making of the President, 1964 (White) • The Autobiography of Malcolm X (Haley) • The Kandy-kolored Tangerine-flake Streamline Baby (Wolfe) • Is Paris Burning? (Collins, Lapierre) • Manchild in the Promised Land (Brown).

FADS: The Mod Look • Op Art Fabrics • Being "In."

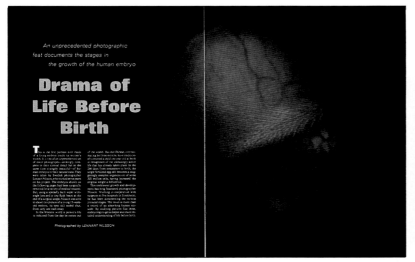

An unprecedented photographic
feat documents the stages in
the growth of the human embryo

Drama of
Life Before
Birth

Photographed by LENNART NILSSON

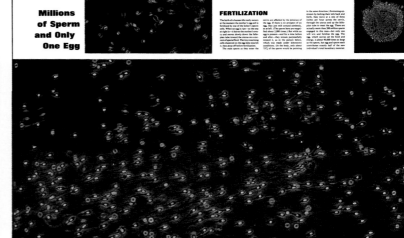

**Millions
of Sperm
and Only
One Egg**

FERTILIZATION

A Primitive Brain, Heart, Eye, Limbs

3½ WEEKS

4 WEEKS

5 WEEKS

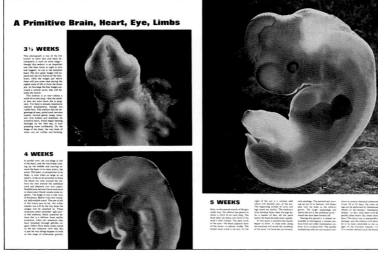

The Change—Embryo to Fetus

6½ WEEKS

8 WEEKS

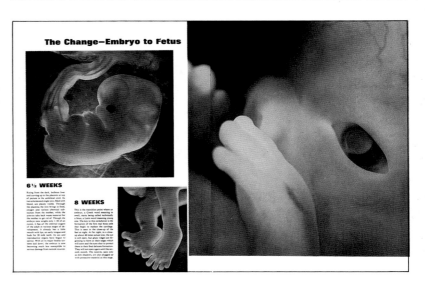

Growing Bones and
Cramped Quarters

12 WEEKS

16 WEEKS

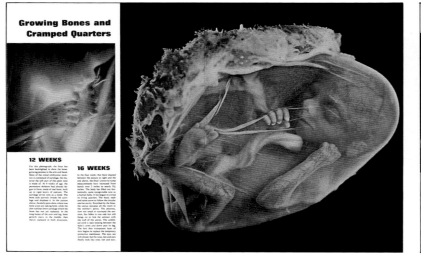

A Thumb to Suck, a Veil to Wear

18 WEEKS

28 WEEKS

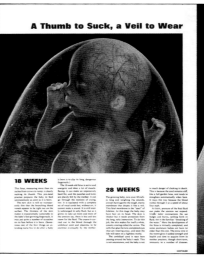

*Among the many extraordinary photographic essays to appear in 1965,
perhaps the two most memorable appear in near entirety on these pages. The
now world-famous photographs by Swedish photographer Lennart Nilsson
traced the stages of human reproduction from fertilization to just before birth.
The images, strangely beautiful and haunting, were a photographic feat
that took Nilsson seven years to accomplish. The opening picture—that
of the head of a live baby taken inside the womb—prompted one
gynecologist to exclaim, "This is like the first look at the back of the moon!"*

JUNE 25, 1965

JULY 2, 1965

JULY 9, 1965

JULY 16, 1965

JULY 23, 1965

JULY 30, 1965

AUGUST 6, 1965

AUGUST 13, 1965

AUGUST 20, 1965

AUGUST 27, 1965

SEPTEMBER 3, 1965

SEPTEMBER 10, 1965

SEPTEMBER 17, 1965

SEPTEMBER 24, 1965

'We are animals in a world no one knows'

A LIFE SERIES IN TWO PARTS

Photographed by BILL EPPRIDGE

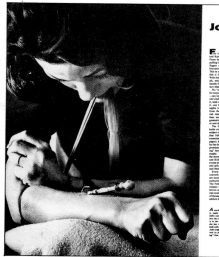

PART I

John and Karen, Two Lives Lost to Heroin

To get money, Karen prostitutes and pushes, John loots cabs

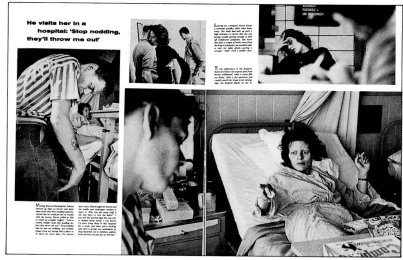

He visits her in a hospital: 'Stop nodding, they'll throw me out'

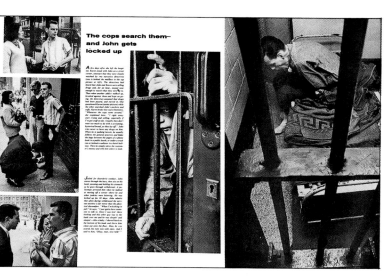

The cops search them—and John gets locked up

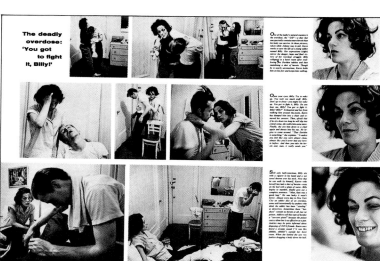

The deadly overdose: 'You got to fight it, Billy!'

They looked like a clean-cut, upwardly mobile young couple. But Karen was a prostitute and John, her live-in boyfriend, was a burglar, and both lived for just one thing—their next shot of heroin. The diary of their lives among the denizens of "Needle Park" on Manhattan's West Side provided an insider's view of the desperate world of drug addiction, exposing it as an emerging social problem on a large scale. Associate editor James Mills and photographer Bill Eppridge became so much a part of the scene while working on the story for months that Eppridge was picked up by a suspicious narcotics detective.

OCTOBER 1, 1965

OCTOBER 8, 1965

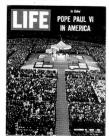

OCTOBER 15, 1965

OCTOBER 22, 1965

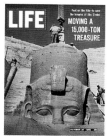

OCTOBER 29, 1965

NOVEMBER 5, 1965

NOVEMBER 12, 1965

NOVEMBER 19, 1965

NOVEMBER 26, 1965

DECEMBER 3, 1965

DECEMBER 10, 1965

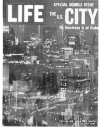

DECEMBER 17, 1965

DECEMBER 24, 1965

A Few Favorites 1956-1965...

NEW STARS BEGAN TO SHINE IN THE GALAXY OF ALL-TIME GREATS

Jackie Gleason, in 1962 "the hottest performer in show business," sank a short putt during a stopover in Denver and exulted in his best I-am-the-greatest Ralph Kramden manner.

"One Sophia per picture is blessing enough," bubbled the editors in 1964, but—mamma mia!—in Yesterday, Today and Tomorrow La Loren, 30, played three roles: a Roman call girl (below), a Milan society woman and a perennially pregnant Neapolitan.

Elvis Presley, 23, in 1958 was measured, weighed and, at 6 ft. ½ in. and 185 lb., not found wanting by the Army. Presley's manager moaned that his hitch would cost the U.S. $500,000 a year in lost taxes.

This was the face with which First Lady Jacqueline Kennedy launched at least one ship, a Polaris submarine, in 1962. Said she through the champagne froth: "Je te baptise Lafayette."

Natalie Wood, caressed by LIFE's cameras since she was 6, rehearsed in 1962 to take it all off for her role as stripper Gypsy Rose Lee in Hollywood's version of the Broadway musical Gypsy.

Looking veddy British with bowler, spats and brolly, Cassius Clay—not yet Muhammad Ali but already in his own mind The Greatest—promenaded in New York's Rockefeller Center in 1963 before going to London for his bout with British heavyweight Henry Cooper.

TAKING GREAT PLEASURE IN GRACE, WHATEVER ITS FORM

Aboard a ship bound for Monaco and the 1956 wedding ceremony that would make her a princess, Grace Kelly failed in a game of charades to communicate to teammates an opaque four-word expression, "Watch the danger line," and collapsed into this ballerinalike posture that expressed her final despair.

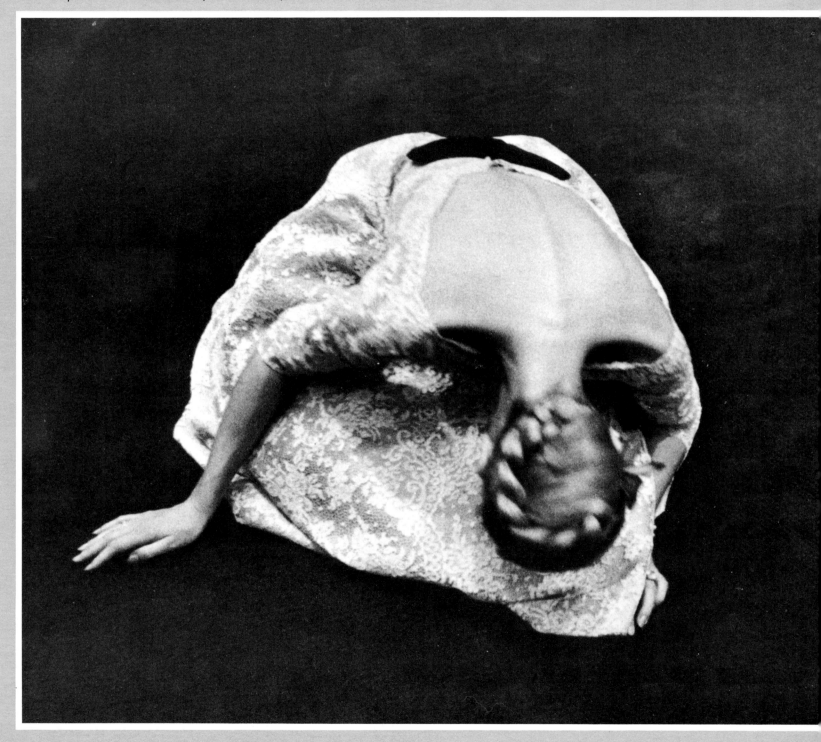

A whippet with the "theatrical presence" necessary to win ribbons sat at elegant ease during the 1964 Westminster Kennel Club show in New York. "The hammiest prima donnas in the U.S.," observed LIFE, *not unadmiringly, "are the country's top-winning show dogs."*

AWE AND ENTHUSIASM FOR THE ASTONISHMENTS OF NATURE

A violent 1965 eruption under Lake Taal in the Philippines, the 26th in a span of 400 years, blasted a huge cove into nine-square-mile Volcano Island and formed a pearl of an isle-within-an-isle. Just behind it lay the water-filled crater created by a 1911 convulsion that killed 1,400. The 700-foot-wide cauldron seething at the center of the new crater (inset, right) rose 15 feet above the inlet's surface. Estimates of the death toll amid this breathtaking setting this time ran as high as 500.

A GENIUS FOR MAKING THE INVISIBLE VISIBLE

To science photographer Fritz Goro fell the "impossible" assignments, such as picturing in 1963 the awesome power of the ultrathin laser beam. He caught it in the act of cutting through a razor blade in a thousandth of a second.

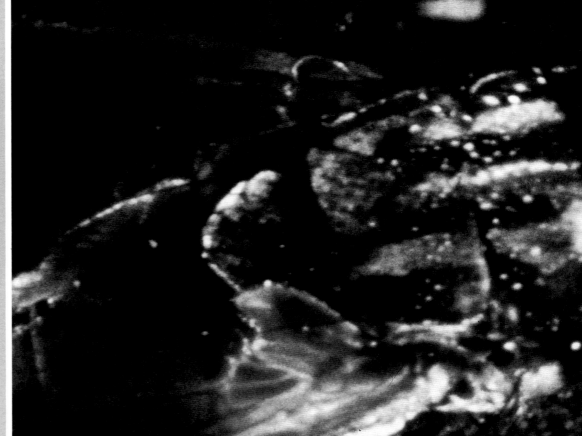

To illustrate the infinitesimal dimensions of microelectronic elements, Goro in 1961 zeroed in on one corner of a 14-transistor microchip placed next to a housefly whose eye was larger than the minuscule light bulb used to test the chip's circuitry.

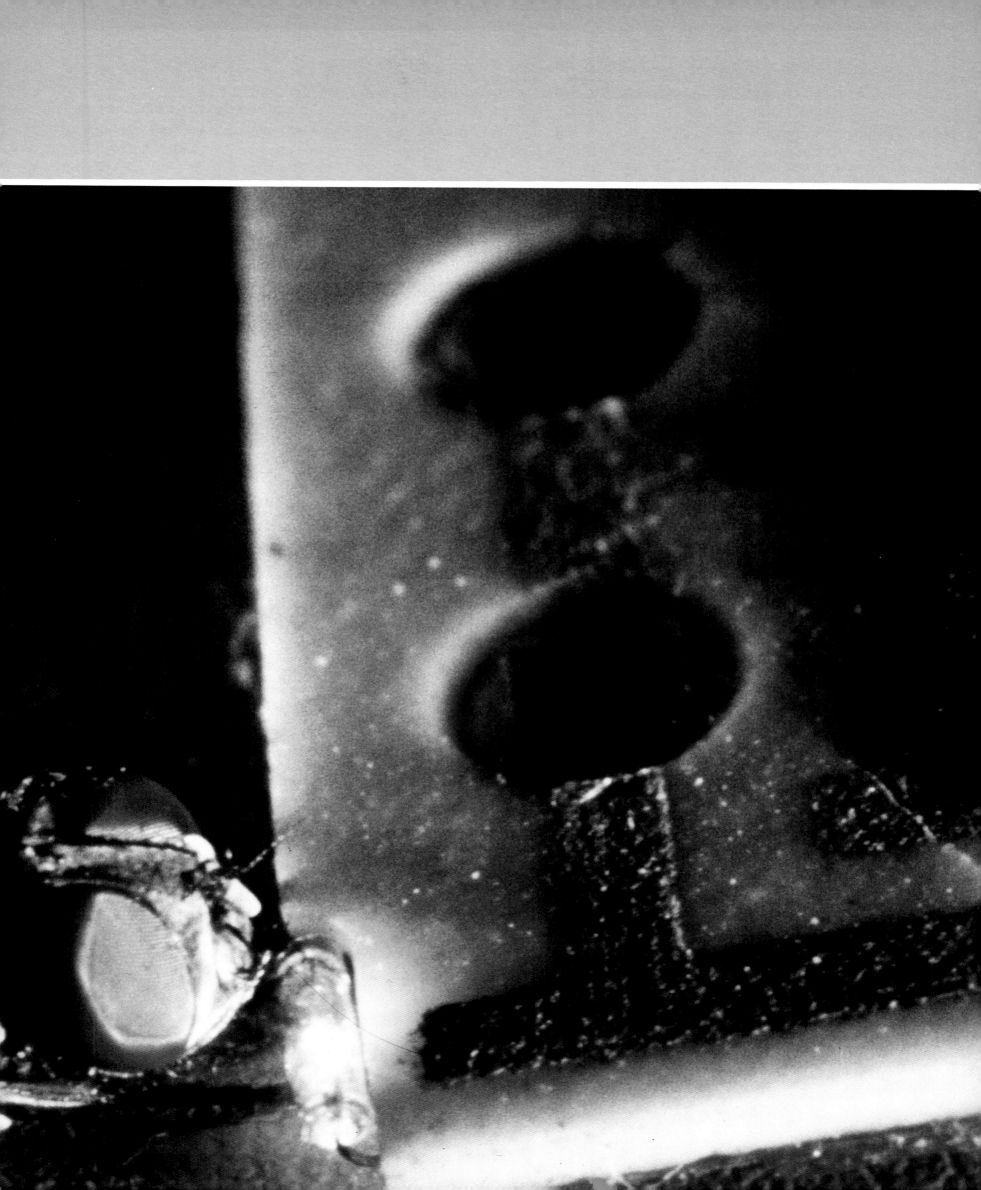

In October 1962 President Kennedy made the grave decision to risk a direct military confrontation with the U.S.S.R. by clamping a blockade—he called it a quarantine—around Cuba. Reconnaissance pictures revealed Soviet-made missiles already in place that could deliver thermonuclear bombs to targets ranging all the way from Lima, Peru, to Hudson Bay in Canada.

The Pictures Tha

President Kennedy decided to stop the shipment of arms to Cuba the basis of the alarming evidence revealed in these extraordinary rec naissance photographs. Taken by high-flying U.S. aircraft, they s with chilling clarity the speed and extent of the Russian efforts on island.

One of the most startling of the thousands of photographs—so 30,000 feet of film in all—analyzed by the President and his adviser this one of a fully operating medium-range missile base, manned Russian technicians and able to shoot its missiles as far into the U as Norfolk or Houston. These are mobile missiles which ride abo

A low-flying Navy patrol plane photographed a Soviet vessel as it neared Cuba. From their shapes the slatted crates seemed to hold planes whose wings were already attached. Beside the crates, inside the ship's rails, fuselages were apparently stowed in sections.

purred Us to Act

ailers. In this photograph eight of the sharp-nosed rockets can be seen
ll cradled aboard their transporters (1). When they are to be fired,
ctors back the trailers up to ingenious launchers which pick the rockets
f the trailers, stand them up and shoot them. Three of these launchers
e visible here (2). Supporting equipment—truckloads of rocket fuel,
r example—can be seen at (3), and the oblongs at (4) are tents to house
e Russian crews that man the missile sites. This base was put up and
operation in less than a week. It was the appalling swiftness with which
went into commission, as well as the other elements of the offensive
ild-up (*see following pages*), which spurred the Administration to act.

The steeple of a classroom building at the Oregon State College of Education in Monmouth lurched and crashed to the ground in a windstorm spun off from a 1962 typhoon in the western Pacific. It battered the West Coast from San Francisco to Puget Sound.

Race car driver Roger McCluskey, held by his seat belt against tremendous centrifugal force, spun toward an infield light pole during a time trial for the 1964 Reading, Pa., Sweepstakes. He wound up right side up and suffered only a broken arm.

The editors sometimes went to great lengths, in time as well as distance, to get an arresting image. This pretty Frenchwoman's spill from a scooter, caught by the pioneering pre–World War I French photographer Jacques Lartigue, appeared in 1963 in a three-part essay titled "1913."

A jerry-built tower at the Indianapolis Speedway toppled when spectators who crammed it, at $5 to $10 a head, all leaned forward at once during a breathless moment at the 1960 Memorial Day races.

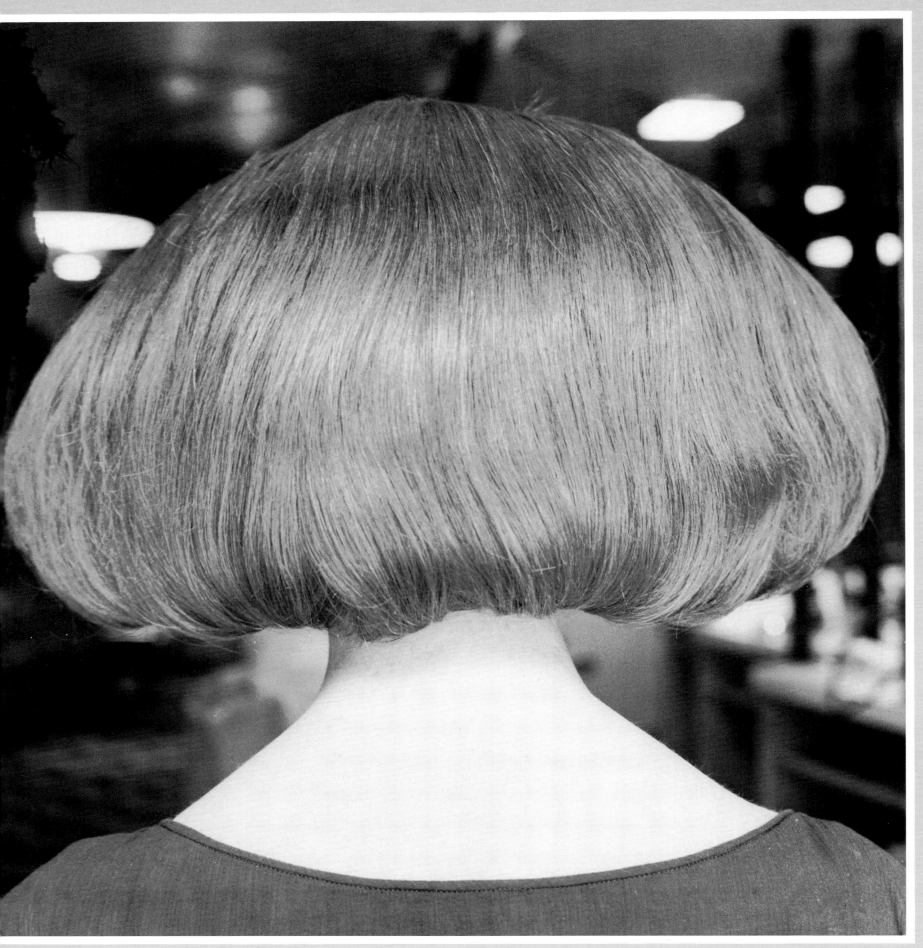

Homing in from the rear on a "mushroom-mopped" woman wearing the bouffant hairdo popular in 1956, the editors found the style "impractical for windy, daylight hours" and suggested it would be "a dismaying sight to find in the theater seat directly ahead."

A woman of Burma's Padaung tribe sported in 1958 the ultimate collection of status-symbol copper neck rings. LIFE was not abashed to caption her *"A Chin-up Girl."*

ANYBODY DUMB ENOUGH TO SAY ANIMALS ARE DUMB?

Two zoo chimps in Chessington, England, in 1959 worked out an efficient way of drinking together. A steady-handed attendant kept an even flow of milk going to top banana Wendy while Toots, second in the dripping order, got the overflow.

Frieda, a sybaritic weimaraner of Costa Mesa, Calif., in 1956 overcame her species' aversion to bathing and reveled in bath-day plunges in her owner's garage. With this sitting she took her place on a long list of tub-soakers, from Marlene Dietrich to Edward G. Robinson, who permitted LIFE to watch their ablutions.

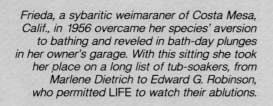

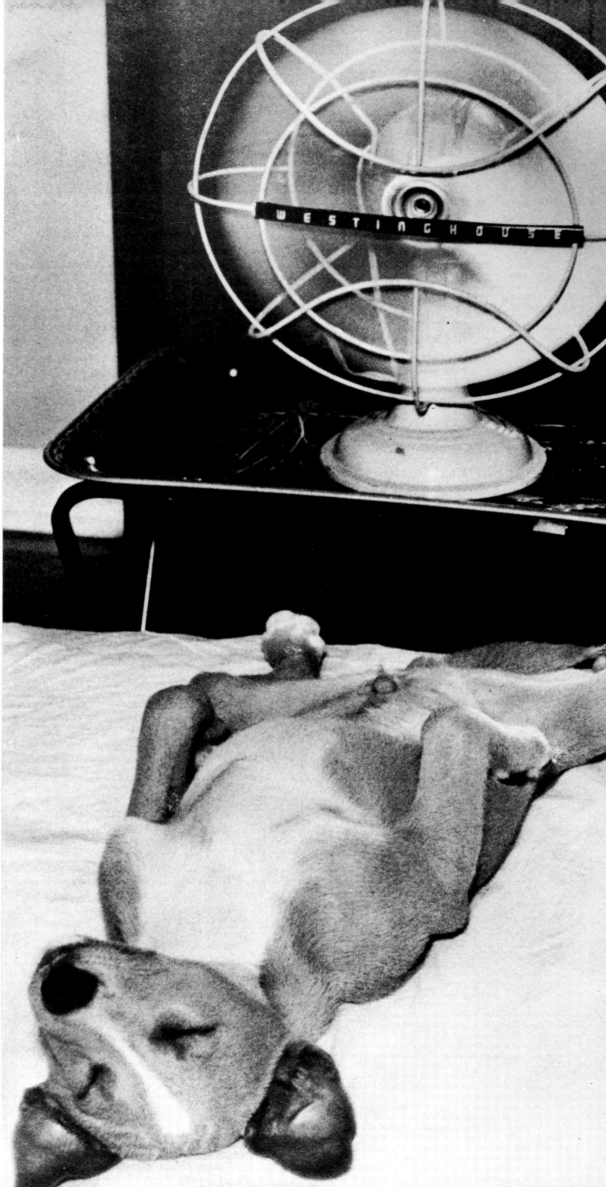

One hot day in the summer of 1960, a mongrel pup owned by a Philadelphia photographer unlawfully climbed onto his master's bed and flaked out in front of a whirring fan. The irate photog, a pro, first got the picture, then spanked Cookie. The caption writer, also a pro, did his job too: he called the pup "a hot dog."

At the Evansville, Ind., zoo in 1962, a monkey developed a symbiotic, or dentist-client, relationship with a hippopotamus, happily a vegetarian. The monk, "an excellent substitute for dental floss," daily probed Hippy's gums for unchewed grain and fruit, to be removed for his own chew-it-yourself project.

Ookie, the New York Aquarium's 2-year-old walrus, ogled her he-walrus neighbor, Olaf, in 1961 across a plank fence that had been repeatedly raised till it was 7½ ft. high. "Aquarium marriage brokers" fondly hoped she'd retain this interest at maturity, three years off.

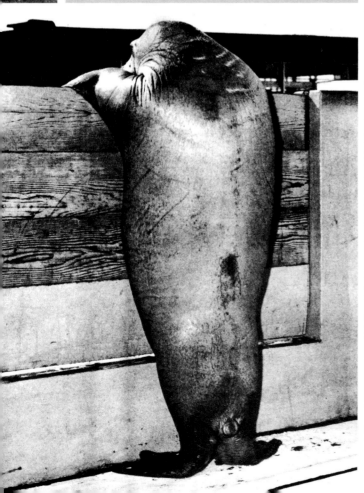

1966-1975
Violence and Change

LIFE's fourth decade got under way in 1966 with no signs of the harsh times that lay ahead. The issues were fat with ads, the stories varied and imaginatively conceived. After an issue that devoted 35 pages to soul-searching the pros and cons of U.S. involvement in Vietnam, the magazine handed down its verdict: The goal of stopping communist expansionism justified the nation's pain. But sentiment against the war was spreading day by day, and that, too, drew the magazine's careful attention.

Meanwhile, the editors were taking on organized crime and corruption in government, and doing so in such a determined and superior way that *Newsweek* would judge LIFE to be "perhaps the most important investigative journal of the day." Concurrently, ambitious special issues and historical series—on the Roman empire, on China, on ancient Egypt—were being produced. So were such current marvels of photography as "The Great Cats of Africa" and "To See America."

Henry Robinson Luce died in 1967. With him went his personal sense of mission and conscience. Not that good, caring people did not remain in charge of the company he had founded and motivated. But all else conceded, the plain truth was that Luce had owned the place. He had invented his magazines, paid to launch them, nurtured them and put his stamp on them. Stockholders notwithstanding, he was the Proprietor. No one else could be quite so fervent as he about keeping people "well informed about the time of man in which they live, and thereby perhaps helping them and ourselves a little to understand where we stand between the mud and the stars."

That same year self-doubt and frustration began to grip the nation. By 1968 a revolutionary process was sweeping the land. The generation gap widened. Long-standing sexual codes were being shattered. Black power raised its fist. American flags went up in flames, as protest against the war flared and protest against the protest turned violent. The ghettos seethed with unrest and hostility. The Democratic convention in Chicago was besieged by the young marching to a new beat. "Wherever we look, something's wrong," LIFE lamented.

But most of all, 1968 would be remembered as the year of the assassin. In April Dr. Martin Luther King Jr. was killed. Two months later Robert F. Kennedy was felled in Los Angeles. No matter that the magazine's coverage of that frightful year was managed with distinction. Economic factors beyond its control provided clear signals that the end was beginning. Advertising pages lost because of a weakened national economy were expected to return—but didn't. By 1969 the issues were thin. LIFE was losing money. Lots of it. In February *The Saturday Evening Post* folded. *Look* was in trouble. Speculation was rife that the big, mass-circulation weekly magazines were destined for extinction.

In May the sixth and last managing editor for the weekly LIFE was appointed. Ralph Graves had been an assistant managing editor under George Hunt for six and a half years, until he was called by Editor-in-Chief Hedley Donovan to assist in overseeing all Time Inc.'s publications. Now he was asked to captain a suddenly sinking editorial ship and told to save it.

Graves set about creating a solid, to-the-point magazine that utilized bold, colorful covers and clean, simple layouts. His long apprenticeships under two predecessors had taught him how to get the most out of talent, how to delegate responsibility, to put good lieutenants in place. He also proved to be an exceptionally efficient and decisive manager. But the deck he was given to play was stacked against him. Not even drastic cutbacks in the staff and in the editorial budget could compensate for the advertising revenue flown to television. Greatly increased postal rates for subscribers' copies made the task even more daunting.

Time Inc. held on through 1972. Going biweekly was considered, and rejected. But the losses were huge and projections for the future dire. On December 8 the entire staff was assembled and informed that the final issue of the month would be the last. In a farewell statement to the magazine's readers, the editor-in-chief wrote: "We still own the name LIFE, of course, and it is not impossible that the familiar red-and-white logotype will reappear someday. . . ."

In fact, only a few months later a special LIFE issue observing the 25th anniversary of Israel was published. A series of one-shot specials followed. They did well financially and also served to keep the magazine alive in the public's mind. By the end of 1975 a small group of former LIFE staffers, under the aegis of Time Inc.'s Magazine Development Group, was hard at work devising a dummy for a monthly version of the magazine.

As elite Army troops, rifles extended, blocked the passage of war protesters
on the steps of the Pentagon in 1967, one young demonstrator stepped
forward and quietly began inserting pink carnations in the gun barrels.

1966

In Vietnam, "escalation" was the word; at home, "black power" and a new meaning for "trip"

The first year of the weekly's fourth, and unhappily truncated, decade was action packed. It was filled with events and images of the kind that the editors themselves had hoped never to see again—of shell bursts, blood and shattered bodies. While the war in Vietnam grew more vicious, at home the diehards' resistance to integration caused black extremists

A village exploded and disappeared in a phosphorous cloud as a lone U.S. bomber headed for home. "Every day in Vietnam," LIFE observed, "U.S. air power executes 700 strikes like this. . . . The air war is the most intense, difficult and hotly controversial engagement in our history—controversial largely because of its inevitably indiscriminate nature that at times kills innocent civilians as well as Vietcong."

Marines on a hillock south of the Demilitarized Zone helped carry a badly wounded comrade to an aid station after a medic, who was on the spot when he was hit, had ministered to him.

to plot urban guerrilla warfare against "whitey" and spawned the coinage "black power." The hideousness of the conflict in Southeast Asia, hammered home by remorseless, up-close reportage, moved more Americans than just confirmed pacifists and the far left to question the U.S. involvement. LIFE's position was made clear by Hedley Donovan, the editor-in-chief, after a tour of South Vietnam. In a five-page editorial he proclaimed that the war *was* worth winning. Unconnected with either conflict, but exacerbating both, was another exploding phenomenon: LSD (lysergic acid diethylamide), the hallucinogen whose sudden pervasiveness caused LIFE to devote a cover story to a pill.

by RUSSELL SACKETT

Plotting
IF NEGRO LEADERSHIP

A War
FAILS, EXTREMISTS

On 'Whitey'
ARE SET AND EAGER FOR VIOLENCE

To probe the movement of hard-core black extremists who differed with Martin Luther King Jr.'s policy of nonviolence, associate editor Russell Sackett investigated for six months, traveling from Harlem to Watts. A veteran of 12 years' coverage of the racial crisis, Sackett won the confidence of a dozen groups dedicated to overthrowing "whitey's oppression."

Although he was not yet a candidate for President, Bobby Kennedy, as a U.S. senator from New York, raised a harvest of hands in Marion, Iowa, while campaigning in midterm congressional elections for the Democratic ticket.

In Manchester, N.H., President Johnson also sought support for Democrats running for Congress. But he made the mistake of grasping one hand too many and grimaced as an overenthusiastic admirer squeezed his hand too hard.

James Meredith fell to the pavement in Mississippi, hit by a shotgun wielder (lower left). He was on a solo walk to the university in Jackson that he had helped integrate in 1962 and left to move north. His intent: to demonstrate no fear of returning to his native state—the same sort of fear that kept Mississippi blacks from voting.

The Family of Levi Smith

A series on an uncommon American family that draws strength from its traditions in a time of change

Encircled by three generations of his family, Levi Smith stands to carve the Thanksgiving turkey. In a time when so much family life in America has splintered, when so much makes the individual from his past, this day and this ceremony bring parents, children and grandchildren back to share the celebration and one another. With this moment, in the spacious old Smith house in Burlington, Vt., LIFE begins a four-part series on the family of Levi Smith. This first chapter focuses on the patriarchal figure of Levi, now in his 82nd year, and his wife Julia. Following chapters will be devoted to their three sons and 15 grandchildren, and to the life that they have all woven together.

The Smiths are a large and close-bound family. Two of the sons, who carry on their father's profession, live in houses that adjoin Levi's, and the third, until this autumn, lived only a few minutes away. The daughters-in-law visit back and forth daily, and the grandchildren are always in and out of one another's houses. The family's roots go four generations deep in Vermont and even deeper into American history. Yet they have had to struggle with the strains of modern life, the searches for identity and independence, the restless questioning of old values that all families experience. No family so large and complex could hold together so closely in this day without the conviction that it is important to do so. The Smiths have achieved it through the wisdom and endurance of Levi Smith, who has made the house he inherited from his father seem to the several generations "a place of permanence, the safest house in the world."

Written and Photographed by BARBARA and GREY VILLET

As America debated changes in values, the editors launched a series on generations-old roots in Vermont.

MASAYA NAKAMURA

This study by Masaya Nakamura was part of an essay on photography's preemption of the artist's "time-honored subject, the nude." It appeared in LIFE's 30th anniversary issue.

HORROR SPAWNS A MASTERPIECE

FOUND DEAD: Herbert W. Clutter, a wealthy Kansas farmer. He, his wife and two children were found bound and shot to death.

WEALTHY FARMER, 3 OF FAMILY SLAIN

H. W. Clutter, Wife and 2 Children Are Found Shot in Kansas Home

Truman Capote's best-seller on a Kansas crime

Photographed by RICHARD AVEDON

Truman Capote posed on a lonely Kansas road near the scene of the mass murder about which he had written his novellike book of nonfiction In Cold Blood.

In a celebration of nonagenarian cellist Pablo Casals, pianist Rudolf Serkin, Casals's old colleague, came offstage after playing a Schubert sonata at the Prades Festival and nervously awaited the Master's verdict. It was: "Beautiful, beautiful." Gjon Mili's camera caught the moment's essence.

Ronald Reagan celebrated his primary victory in the California gubernatorial race, looking as if he had fulfilled his most famous movie line, "Win one for the Gipper."

Jan Armstrong sagged at the TV set as word came that her husband, Neil, and fellow astronaut David Scott had safely ended their Gemini 8 mission with an unscheduled splashdown in the Indian Ocean.

Richard Kiley as the addled knight Don Quixote flourished a crooked sword in Dale Wasserman's adaptation of the Cervantes novel, a surprise Broadway musical hit.

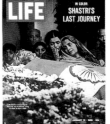
JANUARY 21, 1966

JANUARY 28, 1966

MARCH 11, 1966

APRIL 22, 1966

JUNE 3, 1966

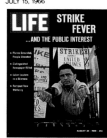
JULY 15, 1966

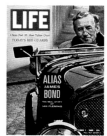
AUGUST 26, 1966

OCTOBER 7, 1966

NOVEMBER 18, 1966

FEBRUARY 4, 1966

FEBRUARY 11, 1966

FEBRUARY 18, 1966

FEBRUARY 25, 1966

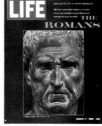
MARCH 4, 1966

MARCH 18, 1966

LSD
MARCH 25, 1966

APRIL 1, 1966

APRIL 8, 1966

APRIL 15, 1966

APRIL 29, 1966

MAY 6, 1966

THE BIG SNOOP
MAY 13, 1966

MAY 20, 1966

MAY 27, 1966

JUNE 10, 1966

THE TRUE COLOR OF THE MOON
JUNE 17, 1966

JUNE 24, 1966

JULY 1, 1966

JULY 8, 1966

JULY 22, 1966

THE NINE NURSES
JULY 29, 1966

HIGHEST PHOTOS OF EARTH TAKEN BY MAN
AUGUST 5, 1966

THE TEXAS SNIPER
AUGUST 12, 1966

Luci's Wedding
AUGUST 19, 1966

SEPTEMBER 2, 1966

LSD ART
SEPTEMBER 9, 1966

ASSASSINATION IN SOUTH AFRICA
SEPTEMBER 16, 1966

CHINA
SEPTEMBER 23, 1966

SEPTEMBER 30, 1966

James Bond Is Born
OCTOBER 14, 1966

A SAFARI BACK TO INNOCENCE
OCTOBER 21, 1966

OCTOBER 28, 1966

THE PRESIDENT'S TRIP
NOVEMBER 4, 1966

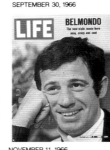
BELMONDO
NOVEMBER 11, 1966

A MATTER OF REASONABLE DOUBT
NOVEMBER 25, 1966

DECEMBER 2, 1966

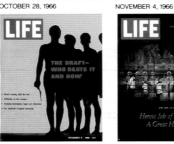
DECEMBER 9, 1966

DECEMBER 16, 1966

PHOTOGRAPHY
DECEMBER 23, 1966

CLASSIC PHOTOS

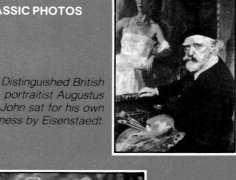

Distinguished British portraitist Augustus John sat for his own likeness by Eisenstaedt.

Four Cleveland Browns defenders resembled muddied gladiators as they waited for Green Bay's huddle to end.

CURRENTS AND EVENTS

WORLD: U.S. Bomber, Tanker Collide over Spain, Lost H-bomb Recovered by Sub • Landslide Engulfs Aberfan, Welsh Mining Community • Raging Flood Destroys Florence's Age-old Treasures • Guerrilla Warfare Persists on Israel's Borders with Syria, Jordan • Upheaval, Change Affect Ghana, Guinea, Congo, South-West Africa, Bechuanaland, Basutoland • Verwoerd, Architect of Apartheid, Assassinated by a White, Vorster Takes Over as PM • Junta Overthrows Argentina's Government • Mao Launches Cultural Revolution • Indira Gandhi Becomes India's PM.

U.S.A.: Supreme Court in Miranda Decision Curbs Police Interrogation Powers • James Meredith, on Lone March to Boost Black Voter Registration, Shot in Mississippi • Madman Mounts Austin, Tex., Tower, Wounds 33, Kills 12 • Chicago Ex-Convict Rounds Up Nine Nurses, Kills Them One by One • Daughter of U.S. Senator-to-Be Charles Percy Victim of Unsolved Murder • Supreme Court Upholds Obscenity Conviction of Ralph Ginzburg, Publisher of Eros, but Rules Material of Redeeming Social Value Uncensorable • Ronald Reagan Elected California Governor.

VIETNAM: U.S. Cost for Year Totals $21 Billion, Troop Count Climbs to 389,000 • Bombings of North Mount • Buddhists in South Rebel, Many Self-Immolate • U.S. Attacks Targets in Cambodia • North Rejects Peace Overtures.

FIRSTS: Soft Moon Landing (Luna IX) • Soft Venus Landing (Venus III) • Docking in Space (Gemini VIII) • Medicare • Black U.S. Senator Elected (Brooke, Mass.).

MOVIES: Dr. Zhivago • The Russians Are Coming . . . • Who's Afraid of Virginia Woolf? • Georgy Girl • A Man for All Seasons • Blow-Up • Alfie • Our Man Flint • Harper • Arabesque • Lady L • The Group • Born Free • This Property Is Condemned • Fantastic Voyage • Hawaii • The Fortune Cookie • Is Paris Burning? • Fahrenheit 451 • The Sand Pebbles • Funeral in Berlin • The Quiller Memorandum • Cul de Sac • Khartoum • Loves of a Blonde • Hotel Paradiso.

SONGS: Born Free • Cabaret • Alfie • Eleanor Rigby • Feelin' Groovy • Georgy Girl • The Ballad of the Green Berets • California Dreamin' • Mame • If He Walked into My Life • Is That All There Is? • A Man and a Woman • Good Vibrations • Monday, Monday • A Groovy Kind of Love • On a Clear Day You Can See Forever • Over and Over • See You in September • Strangers in the Night • Sunny • Scarborough Fair • What Now, My Love? • Winchester Cathedral • Yellow Submarine • We Need a Little Christmas • Willkommen • Yesterday, When I Was Young.

STAGE: A Lion in Winter • The Killing of Sister George • Don't Drink the Water • Wait Until Dark • Sweet Charity • Mame • Cabaret • I Do, I Do!

BOOKS: Valley of the Dolls (Susann) • The Fixer (Malamud) • Tai-Pan (Clavell) • The Last Gentleman (Percy) • Human Sexual Response (Masters, Johnson) • In Cold Blood (Capote) • Rush to Judgment (Lane) • The Last Battle (Ryan) • Everything but Money (Levenson) • With Kennedy (Salinger) • Death of a President (Manchester) • Papa Hemingway (Hotchner) • A Choice of Weapons (Parks) • The Proud Tower (Tuchman) • The Battle of the Little Big Horn (Sandoz) • Inquest (Epstein).

FADS: Miniskirts • Paper Jewelry, Dresses • Transparent Vinyl Dresses • LSD • Batman • Topless Waitresses • Pantsuits • Granny Eyeglasses.

1967

It was another turbulent year, in whose dark course the man who had inspired LIFE died

The year was not far advanced when Henry Robinson Luce died. But his journalistic legacy, born of his driving moral force and the boundless curiosity that had informed and sustained all his undertakings, was reconfirmed in the energy and authority with which LIFE covered the often shocking events of 1967. The crescendo of black rage exploding in Newark and flaming in Detroit was documented in unforgettable images. The mounting anguish and frustrations of the war in Vietnam, conveyed in powerful photographs, were counter-pointed by vivid coverage of Israel's slashing desert victory in the Six-Day War—a conflict that cost the magazine another fine talent. "Human life is tragic and triumphant and also comic, but never absurd," Luce once wrote. Thus, he would have fathomed, and accepted, the contrast between the deep humiliation of the human spirit as manifested in the degradation of U.S. prisoners in Vietnam and that spirit's triumphant affirmation in the death in action of a brave and dedicated combat photographer.

LIFE Vol. 62, No. 24 June 16, 1967

Israeli Thrust — The Astounding 60 Hours

SPECIAL **LIFE** EDITION

ISRAEL'S SWIFT VICTORY

Israeli forces plunged at dawn into the Egyptian Sinai, launching a blitz that led to a brilliant victory. Rushing to report a war that began and ended in a single editorial week, LIFE dispatched 17 reporters and photographers to cover the campaign from both sides. Their words and pictures produced not only the lead story of the year but also a special issue (cover, left) that was crash-closed over a single weekend. All but one of the journalistic team survived the war. Paul Schutzer (right), who had earned a place among LIFE's most esteemed and best-liked young photographers, was killed during the first hours of battle, when the Israeli half-track on which he was riding was knocked out by Egyptian fire.

EDITORS' NOTE

In Memory of Paul Schutzer

Last week, covering the war in the Middle East, Paul Schutzer, LIFE Photographer, was killed in action. He was with a unit of Israelis, riding a half-track personnel carrier, up front with the armored point attacking across the strip toward Gaza. He was shot just as the carrier took a direct hit from an Egyptian antitank shell and burst into flame.

Paul was 36—a young age—but he seemed younger. His brown hair, friendly hazel eyes and handsome boyish face all told so much about his buoyancy and warmth. Indeed, Paul was a man deeply concerned with the human spirit, and it was this—his compassion for people—that made him the brilliant photographer he was.

Remember, for a moment, some of the stories he did and the events he covered—the Berlin Wall, the Iranian earthquake, the Algerian War, Eastern Europe with that memorable portraiture of life there, a delightful characterization of the Italian man, his coverage of Nixon jeered and assaulted in Venezuela, of John F. Kennedy through his campaign, the fury of Hurricane Audrey when it battered Louisiana, the Winter Olympics at Innsbruck, the scaling of the North Wall of the Eiger. He went into Cuba to cover the Castro crisis, into Lebanon with the Marines and again with the Marines in Vietnam, from where he returned with an unforgettable story about them and Doc Lucier, the Navy corpsman. Paul got around. His was a full life, but he made it even fuller by an inner drive to probe with taste and dignity into the effect of events upon people. Many photographers do this, but Paul's special fascination with his fellow man, and his understanding of him, made his work exceptional.

PAUL SCHUTZER

Paul was Jewish, and during his trip through the Eastern countries, he saw Auschwitz and was shocked profoundly. On many occasions he had been to Israel, but Auschwitz brought the larger meaning of that country home to him. I visited Israel three years ago, and Paul insisted on being my guide. Quoting the Torah, quoting Biblical poetry and lore, he took me from place to place exuding his love for the country, for its flowers and hills, for its buildings and communal camps, for its marchers and its progress—and for its struggle. One perhaps can console oneself that Paul died where he wanted to die and gave his life for what he felt most. And that is true. But we have lost an exceptional, first-rate man—in Yiddish this type is called a *mensch*. Paul was a *mensch*.

Paul was also a poet and this was so evident in his approach to the world. Even in his bitterest or tragic pictures there shines through the lyric thought that in suffering comes hope. The lovely things entranced him, too; and then his sense of beauty would take on a distinctive charm. A friend of Paul recalls sitting with him at a cafe in Rome. It was a Roman Sunday—one of those warm cloudless Italian summers. They were on the Appia Antica, and the great old city sprawled in front of them. Paul watched the soft landscape through his glass of white wine, and he caught the sunlight in it. He looked at it for a while and said, "I would like to photograph the world through this topaz."

George P. Hunt

GEORGE P. HUNT,
Managing Editor

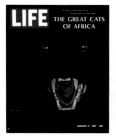

THE GREAT CATS OF AFRICA

JANUARY 6, 1967

JANUARY 13, 1967

JANUARY 20, 1967

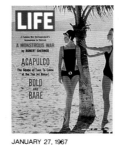

ACAPULCO
BOLD AND BARE

JANUARY 27, 1967

THE THREE ASTRONAUTS

FEBRUARY 3, 1967

At Montreal's Expo 67 a seemingly gargantuan father smiled down at his Brobdingnagian baby in a movie show, which had one vertical screen and one flat on the floor. The multitiered audience was held spellbound by the interplay of images on the two screens.

At a propaganda press conference in North Vietnam, captured Navy pilot Richard A. Stratton kept bowing, slowly and wordlessly, as if he were drugged, following a broadcast of his taped "confession" to war crimes. Safely home after the war, Stratton and other ex-POWs gave harrowing accounts of the savage tortures to which they had been subjected by their captors.

Detroit's ghetto shimmered in the heat of a burning building. President Johnson had to call out federal troops to end the riot that "ranked as the worst in U.S. history."

This scene was the endpiece for the tribute to (from left) Apollo 12's Gus Grissom, Ed White and Roger Chaffee (back to camera). It appeared the week they died in a capsule fire. Their comrades: Rusty Schweickart, Jim McDivitt, Dave Scott.

CLASSIC PHOTOS

A medic in Vietnam realized that the Marine he had ministered to was dead.

The style at Acapulco was bare and bold.

Joe Bass Jr., 12, bled in riot-torn Newark.

CURRENTS AND EVENTS

WORLD: Treaty Among 62 Nations Limits Military Use of Outer Space • Cosmonaut Dies in Reentry Crash • Stalin's Daughter Svetlana Gains U.S. Asylum • Greek Junta Seizes Power, King Flees • Israel Wins Six-Day War, Defeating Egypt, Syria, Jordan • USS Liberty Attacked by Israel in International Waters, 34 Die, 75 Wounded • Congo Premier Tshombe Flees Treason Death Sentence, Hijackers Fly Plane to Algeria, Hold Him Captive There • Cuban Revolutionary Che Guevara Killed by Bolivian Troops • Red China Tests H-bomb Successfully, Engages in Border Clashes with India • Expo 67 Opens in Montreal.

U.S.A.: Race Riots Hit More than 100 Cities During Long, Hot Summer • House Denies Congressional Seat to N.Y.'s Adam Clayton Powell for Misuse of House Funds, He Wins Reelection Overwhelmingly • Teamster Boss Jimmy Hoffa Begins Eight-Year Prison Term • Jack Ruby, Oswald's Killer, Dies in Jail • Astronauts Grissom, White, Chaffee Killed in Apollo Capsule Fire • Time Inc. Founder Henry R. Luce Dies • Muhammad Ali Appeals Five-Year Sentence, Fine for Rejecting Military Service.

VIETNAM: U.S. Launches Biggest Offensive to Date Northwest of Saigon • Bombers Based in Guam Moved to Thailand • Losers Charge Election Fraud as Nguyen Van Thieu, Nguyen Cao Ky Take Office as President, Vice President • Thousands March on Washington in War Protest.

FIRSTS: Black Supreme Court Justice (Marshall) • Human Heart Transplant • Synthetic DNA • 3-D Holograph Movies.

MOVIES: In the Heat of the Night • Cool Hand Luke • In Cold Blood • Barefoot in the Park • Bonnie and Clyde • Casino Royale • A Countess from Hong Kong • The Dirty Dozen • Divorce American Style • Enter Laughing • Thoroughly Modern Millie • To Sir, with Love • The Way West • The Flim-Flam Man • The Night of the Generals • Ulysses • The Battle of Algiers • The Tiger Makes Out • You Only Live Twice • The Taming of the Shrew • La Guerre Est Finie • Elvira Madigan • Closely Watched Trains • Persona • Up the Down Staircase.

SONGS: All You Need Is Love • By the Time I Get to Phoenix • The Beat Goes On • Can't Take My Eyes off You • Daydream Believer • Feelin' Groovy • Gentle on My Mind • Alice's Restaurant • There's a Kind of Hush • Happy Together • It Must Be Him • Light My Fire • Michelle • Ode to Billy Joe • Penny Lane • Release Me • Ruby Tuesday • Somethin' Stupid • Up, Up and Away • Yesterday • Sgt. Pepper's Lonely Hearts Club Band.

STAGE: Rosencrantz and Guildenstern Are Dead • There's a Girl in My Soup • MacBird! • Fortune and Men's Eyes • Scuba Duba • The Homecoming • You Know I Can't Hear You When the Water's Running • Hello Dolly (all-black cast) • Sherry • Hallelujah Baby.

BOOKS: The Confessions of Nat Turner (Styron) • The Arrangement (Kazan) • The Chosen (Potok) • Topaz (Uris) • Rosemary's Baby (Levin) • Go to the Widow-Maker (Jones) • Washington, D.C. (Vidal) • The Manor (Singer) • Incredible Victory (Lord) • Our Crowd (Birmingham) • Nicholas and Alexandra (Massie) • Division Street, America (Terkel) • The New Industrial State (Galbraith) • Why Are We in Vietnam? (Mailer) • Death of a President (Manchester) • The Gabriel Hounds (Stewart).

FADS: The Twiggy Look • Posters • 3-D Tick-tack-toe.

'We want to live our own lives'

Photographed by BILL EPPRIDGE

Looking pretty much like their contemporaries on a Club Med spree or a Fort Lauderdale spring recess, the U.S.S.R.'s self-characterized "Fourth Generation" cavorted, notably more unbuttoned than their forebears.

A classic black-and-white essay dwelt with nostalgia upon the Shakers, a doomed and splintered order living out its days in tranquillity and seclusion amid the austerely beautiful surroundings that made its tradition famous.

Serene in their faith, the aged women sit in silent communion. They are Shakers, stalwarts of an all but extinct sect whose members only a few decades ago were numerous enough to fill their meeting halls (*right*). In 1774 their predecessors fled to America from England, where they had been called, derisively, "Shakers" for their custom of dancing in a frenzy to express religious ecstasy. In time they too adopted the

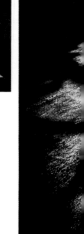

name. To Shakers, work is also a form of prayer, and in America they prayed long and hard. Inventive as they were pious—their many innovations included the flattened-out broom and the circular saw—Shakers became most famous for the beauty locked in the simplicity of design of their furniture and handicrafts. Theirs was the most successful of all communal experiments in the New World and at their peak, during the decade just before the Civil War, they had 6,000 members in 18 communities. Because all Shakers are celibate and rely on conversions to replenish their numbers, their order began to disintegrate. Today just two active communities exist with a total membership of 18, all women: the one at Sabbathday Lake, Maine (*above*) and another at Canterbury, N.H. Said one sister who died last year: "We are not defeated as a people, but intend to be true to our trust, valiant to the end with heads lifted, hearts courageous and colors flying."

A handmade box of gentle grace, bath...

BEGINNING A NEW 'LIFE' SERIES

"The fanged lips drew back and up, the red tongue curled; the lower jaw dropped and dropped till you could see halfway down the hot gullet; and the gigantic dog-teeth stood clear," wrote Rudyard Kipling of a leopard, that majestic animal on the opposite page, "black as the pit and terrible as the Demon."

Images of untethered grace and implacable ferocity, the great cats of Africa are admired as much as feared, and ever since man huddled in caves, they have inspired that awe reserved for unearthly mysteries. Civilization now crowds them toward confinement in the major African game preserves. To record the glory and supremacy of the cats, Photographer John Dominis stalked them for eight months, tracking them by day, camping near them through the night. His pictures will appear in three successive issues of LIFE. This week's essay shows the leopard, a creature of nocturnal stealth who often hunts quarry three times his size, always alone. Next week comes the cheetah, that sculpted, unnaturally elegant greyhound killer of the African savanna. The following week the lion rounds out an extraordinary album of animals in their wild and splendid world.

THE GREAT CATS OF AFRICA

Photographed by JOHN DOMINIS

For months John Dominis stalked with his camera the likes of this night-prowling leopard. The results earned him the Magazine Photographer of the Year award.

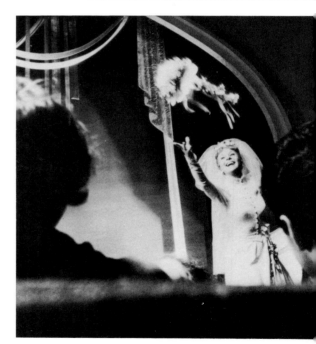

After the wedding scene in I Do, I Do, the Broadway musical based on the play The Four-Poster, Mary Martin tossed her bridal bouquet to the audience, which was made to feel, in the intimately staged production, "like guests at a party."

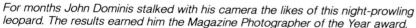

 FEBRUARY 10, 1967

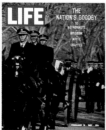 FEBRUARY 17, 1967

 FEBRUARY 24, 1967

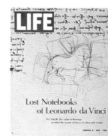 MARCH 3, 1967

 MARCH 10, 1967

 MARCH 17, 1967

 MARCH 24, 1967

 MARCH 31, 1967

 APRIL 7, 1967

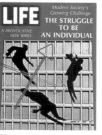 APRIL 14, 1967

 APRIL 21, 1967

 APRIL 28, 1967

 MAY 5, 1967

MAY 12, 1967

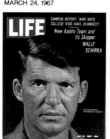 MAY 19, 1967

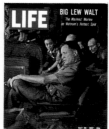 MAY 26, 1967

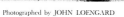

Serene twilight of a once-sturdy sect

The Shakers

Evening sunlight at Shakertown Museum, Pleasant Hill, Ky.

Photographed by JOHN LOENGARD

Jimmy Hoffa shook hands with marshals in the Lewisburg, Pa., prison yard. After 10 years the feds had nailed the Teamster boss for jury tampering. Hoffa was sprung by President Nixon in 1971. He disappeared in 1975, presumably murdered.

When she was 8, Papa Joe Stalin called her "My Little Sparrow." In 1967, at 42, Svetlana defected. Her memoirs appeared in LIFE.

Oblivious of the curves cresting above him, goateed Joe Namath, the Jets' partying quarterback, was snapped in Miami in the rare act of missing a passing opportunity.

JUNE 2, 1967

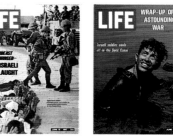

JUNE 9, 1967

JUNE 16, 1967

JUNE 23, 1967

JUNE 30, 1967

JULY 7, 1967

JULY 14, 1967

JULY 21, 1967

JULY 28, 1967

AUGUST 4, 1967

AUGUST 11, 1967

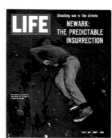

AUGUST 18, 1967

AUGUST 25, 1967

SEPTEMBER 1, 1967

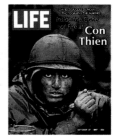

SEPTEMBER 8, 1967

SEPTEMBER 15, 1967

SEPTEMBER 22, 1967

SEPTEMBER 29, 1967

OCTOBER 6, 1967

OCTOBER 13, 1967

OCTOBER 20, 1967

OCTOBER 27, 1967

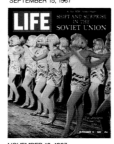

NOVEMBER 3, 1967

NOVEMBER 10, 1967

NOVEMBER 17, 1967

NOVEMBER 24, 1967

DECEMBER 1, 1967

DECEMBER 8, 1967

DECEMBER 15, 1967

DECEMBER 22, 1967

1968

Sanity seemed lost in horror after horror, while protests raged at home and abroad

"How many times must we live through these throat-paralyzing sequences of days of gunplay, grief and muffled drums?" LIFE asked editorially when first Martin Luther King Jr. and then Robert F. Kennedy were shot to death within two months. The gunning down of King, on an April Thursday, sadly caused the magazine to deploy all the skills it had developed in covering the assassination of

The day after Dr. Martin Luther King Jr. told a cheering crowd, "It really doesn't matter with me now because I have been to the mountaintop," the apostle of nonviolence was slain on a Memphis motel balcony with a single rifle bullet in the head. The April 12 issue, on the presses since Wednesday night, was twice remade: on Thursday, the day of the shooting, for a King cover and an essay-length memorial tribute; and then again on Friday, to include a detailed story when spot pictures arrived late from rioting Memphis. They had been taken by Joseph Louw, a young black South African who was working on a King documentary for public TV and staying in the motel.

Eugene McCarthy, campaigning against Robert Kennedy in the Indiana Democratic primary, stirred up young voters by attacking Selective Service chief General Hershey. Although RFK won the state, 42 percent to 27 percent, it was the anti-Vietnam zeal McCarthy aroused that drove LBJ out of the race.

JANUARY 5, 1968

JANUARY 12, 1968

JANUARY 19, 1968

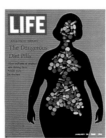

JANUARY 26, 1968

FEBRUARY 2, 1968

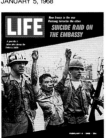

FEBRUARY 9, 1968

FEBRUARY 16, 1968

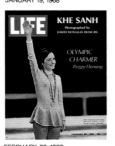

FEBRUARY 23, 1968

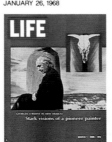

MARCH 1, 1968

MARCH 8, 1968

John F. Kennedy five years before: the speedy tracking down of spot pictures, the halting of the presses, the cover change, the late makeover of the issue. And then in June the same terrible test of journalistic resources was repeated as the campaigning senator was felled in a corridor of L.A.'s Ambassador Hotel, with the difference that this time LIFE's photographer was already on the scene. The news was unsettling in all quarters: Protest against the increasingly ugly Vietnam war led to student takeovers of college administrative offices and to rioting in Chicago, site of the Democratic national convention; Biafrans fought a war of secession while their children starved; Czechs lost what little freedom they had wrested from their Soviet masters. It surely was not the best of times.

MARCH 15, 1968

MARCH 22, 1968

His face an ashen mask, Robert Kennedy lay in a pool of his own blood on a hotel corridor floor in Los Angeles. Busboy Juan Romero tried to comfort him. Staff photographer Bill Eppridge, who had been covering Kennedy's primary campaign, had just snapped Bobby shaking hands with Romero and other kitchen help when assassin Sirhan Sirhan's two .22 pistol shots hit the senator. A 96-page extra edition (below) on the ill-starred brothers was on the stands the following week, along with the regular issue.

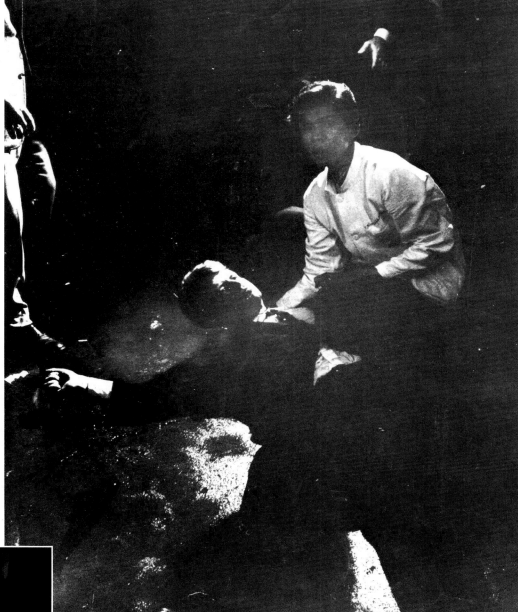

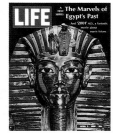
MARCH 29, 1968

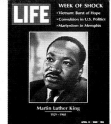
APRIL 5, 1968

APRIL 12, 1968

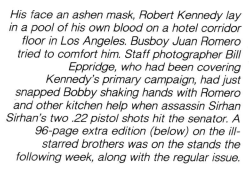

APRIL 19, 1968

APRIL 26, 1968

MAY 3, 1968

MAY 10, 1968

MAY 17, 1968

MAY 24, 1968

MAY 31, 1968

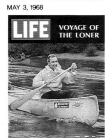
JUNE 7, 1968

JUNE 14, 1968

JUNE 21, 1968

JUNE 28, 1968

CLASSIC PHOTOS

U.S. Olympians raised black-gloved fists in victory.

A Harlem mother and son rested after a bout with the husband.

CURRENTS AND EVENTS

WORLD: Czechs Institute Liberal Reforms, 200,000 Soviet, Warsaw Pact Troops Invade, Force Repeal • UN General Assembly Condemns Apartheid, Portugal's Colonial Policies in Africa • Trudeau Becomes Canada's PM • U.S. Bomber Carrying Unarmed H-bombs Crashes in Greenland • Israeli Commandos Raid Beirut Airport Following Border Clashes with Lebanon • Aswan Dam Completed • Mexico City Hosts Olympic Games • USS Pueblo, Intelligence Ship, Seized by North Korea, Held for Year • Papal Encyclical Bars All Artificial Means of Contraception.

U.S.A: LBJ Announces He Will Not Seek Reelection • Martin Luther King Jr., Robert F. Kennedy Assassinated • Blacks Riot in Many Cities • 10,000 Antiwar Protesters Clash with Police, National Guardsmen at Democrats' Convention in Chicago • Nixon-Agnew Ticket Defeats Humphrey-Muskie • Students Create Campus Turmoil Nationally Demonstrating Against University Investment Policies, Government Involvement in Vietnam • Congress Passes Truth in Lending Act • Poor People's March on Capital Protests Hunger • Kerner Commission Cites White Racism as Major Cause of Civil Disorder by Blacks • Cesar Chavez Organizes Nationwide Grape Boycott to Win Gains for Farm Workers.

VIETNAM: In Tet Offensive Communists Attack 100 Towns, Bases • Siege of Garrison at Khe Sanh Lifted After 76 Days • Preliminary Peace Talks Begin in Paris • Bombardments of North Halted • Opposition to War Mounts.

FIRSTS: Supersonic Airliner • Manned Moon Orbit • Black to Win Men's U.S. Tennis Open (Ashe).

MOVIES: Bullitt • 2001 • Guess Who's Coming to Dinner • The Graduate • The Heart Is a Lonely Hunter • The Lion in Winter • The Odd Couple • Planet of the Apes • The Producers • Rachel, Rachel • Rosemary's Baby • The Subject Was Roses • The Thomas Crown Affair • I Love You, Alice B. Toklas • The Good, the Bad and the Ugly • Finian's Rainbow • Funny Girl • Oliver! • The Yellow Submarine.

SONGS: The Dock of the Bay • Hey, Jude • Little Green Apples • Hair • Good Morning, Starshine • Aquarius • MacArthur Park • Mrs. Robinson • I Say a Little Prayer • This Guy's in Love with You • Wichita Lineman • The Windmills of Your Mind • Harper Valley P.T.A. • Folsom Prison Blues • Those Were the Days • Abraham, Martin and John • Jumpin' Jack Flash • As I Went Out One Morning • Grazin' in the Grass • Lady Madonna.

STAGE: Plaza Suite • The Man in the Glass Booth • The Great White Hope • The Prime of Miss Jean Brodie • I Never Sang for My Father • A Day in the Death of Joe Egg • The Boys in the Band • Lovers and Other Strangers • Hair • Zorba • Jacques Brel Is Alive and Well....

BOOKS: The Day Kennedy Was Shot (Bishop) • Airport (Hailey) • True Grit (Portis) • Myra Breckinridge (Vidal) • Couples (Updike) • Preserve and Protect (Drury) • Welcome to the Monkey House (Vonnegut) • The Armies of the Night (Mailer) • The Electric Kool-Aid Acid Test (Wolfe) • Slouching Towards Bethlehem (Didion) • Soul on Ice (Cleaver) • The Double Helix (Watson) • The Naked Ape (Morris) • The Algiers Motel Incident (Hersey) • Tell Me How Long the Train's Been Gone (Baldwin).

FADS: Unisex Clothing • Gold-Chain Necklaces.

Jeering Czechs threw Molotov cocktails at Soviet tankmen who, joined by other Eastern Bloc forces, invaded their country to stifle the new freedom that flowered briefly during the "Prague Spring."

Ibo tribesmen, volunteers for the army of Biafra, a tiny breakaway nation seeking to secede from Nigeria, gathered at a militia training center to learn the art of guerrilla warfare.

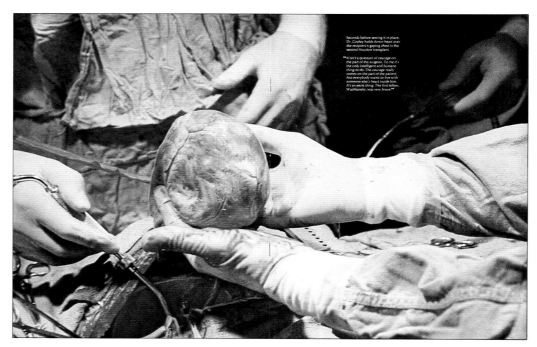

During what was the still-controversial heart transplant procedure, its leading practitioner, Dr. Denton Cooley of Houston's St. Luke's Episcopal Hospital, held an ailing heart from a chest cavity soon to be filled with a donor's healthy substitute.

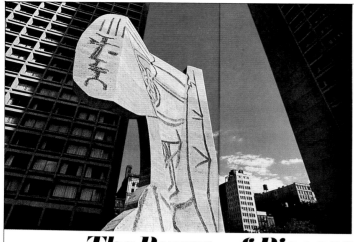

The Power of Picasso

The text introducing the year-end issue on Picasso carried the headline "Here comes a giant, all five feet three of him." This first image was a close-up of his concrete sculpture located near Manhattan's Washington Square. A wide-angle lens was used to create the impression that the environs of the statue were converging upon it.

JULY 5, 1968

JULY 12, 1968

JULY 19, 1968

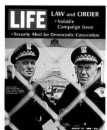

JULY 26, 1968

AUGUST 2, 1968

AUGUST 9, 1968

AUGUST 16, 1968

AUGUST 23, 1968

AUGUST 30, 1968

SEPTEMBER 6, 1968

SEPTEMBER 13, 1968

SEPTEMBER 20, 1968

An activist student at N.Y.'s Columbia University sat in the chair of dispossessed president Grayson Kirk and smoked an expropriated cigar.

Chicago cops charged antiwar demonstrators in Grant Park as the Democrats held their strife-torn convention in the Hilton Hotel.

SEPTEMBER 27, 1968

OCTOBER 4, 1968

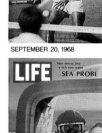

OCTOBER 11, 1968

OCTOBER 18, 1968

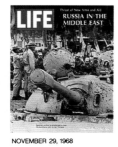

Newlyweds Aristotle and Jacqueline Kennedy Onassis sported celebratory smiles after the nuptials on the Greek island of Skorpiós and so, almost, did Jackie's daughter, Caroline.

In an article on the human potential movement, members of a clothes-shedding encounter group outside Palm Springs, Calif., experienced "the friendly physical closeness that dispels the doubts of even the obese, the underendowed and the inhibited."

OCTOBER 25, 1968

NOVEMBER 1, 1968

NOVEMBER 8, 1968

NOVEMBER 15, 1968

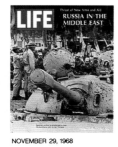

NOVEMBER 22, 1968

NOVEMBER 29, 1968

DECEMBER 6, 1968

DECEMBER 13, 1968

DECEMBER 20, 1968

DECEMBER 27, 1968

1969

The sixth managing editor took charge as U.S. pride soared with Apollo 11 and sagged over the war's toll

Three weeks after Ralph Graves moved into the managing editor's office in early June, LIFE sent to press a story that brought home overwhelmingly the cost of pursuing the nation's policy in Southeast Asia. The story's power lay in its unadorned simplicity: a collection of high school yearbook–type pho-

The roundup of 242 fallen servicemen filled 12 pages. Most of the pictures were provided by their families. For some, either a photograph was not available or their kin would not release one. The names of those men were listed at the end. Reader response to the gallery ranged from the complaint that it was a low journalistic trick, to praise for delivering the most eloquent argument till then for quitting Vietnam.

Photographs of the massacre at Mylai, taken on his own by official Army photographer Ronald Haeberle, documented the most notorious atrocity of the Vietnam war. They had been kept under wraps for 19 months before surfacing. LIFE chose to print, among other pictures of the outrage as it unfolded, the arrival of the GI unit at the hamlet, women and children huddled in terror, and a tangle of corpses in a ditch.

tographs listing every U.S. serviceman who had been killed during a recent, arbitrarily chosen week. Then, culminating years of LIFE's close coverage of the space program, came man's first landing on the moon. That exhilarating human triumph stood in shocking contrast to the abyss of human failure on earth as revealed soon after in the horrifying details of the massacre by U.S. troops of over 100 civilians—women, children and old men—at Mylai. Such dissonance was deeply felt by the nation's youth, whose get-together at Woodstock that summer was recognized by the editors as a landmark event.

Shooting through the window of the lunar module, astronaut Buzz Aldrin recorded its touchdown on the moon (top four frames at bottom left) and then Neil Armstrong climbing down the ladder onto the moon's surface (lower frames). Nineteen minutes later Aldrin, too, descended and aimed his camera at his own boot (below), leaving an imprint on the virgin lunar dust. The editors compiled a full report of Apollo 11's saga in an extra issue (cover, right).

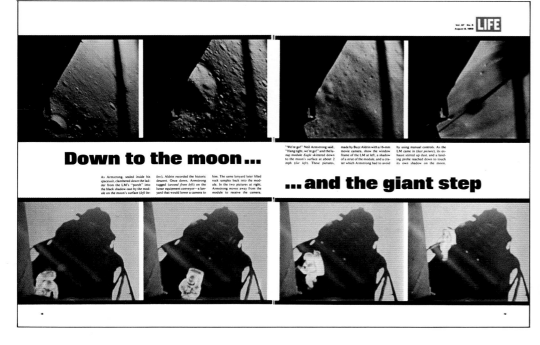

Down to the moon...

...and the giant step

The Big Woodstock Rock Trip

Hundreds of thousands of kids mob a Catskill mountain farm

The original plan was for an outdoor rock festival, "three days of peace and music," in the Catskill village of Woodstock. What the young promoters got was the third largest city in New York State, population 400,000 (give or take 100,000), location Max Yasgur's dairy farm near the town of White Lake. Lured by music, the country and some strange kind of magic ("Woodstock? Doesn't Bob Dylan live in Woodstock?"), young people from all over the U.S. descended on the rented 600-acre farm.

It was a real city, with life and death and babies—two were born during the gathering —and all the urban problems of water supply, food, sanitation and health. Drugs too, certainly, became the young rock festival's mystical communal experience. Farmer Max Yasgur's 35-acre alfalfa field was left a shambles.

A frenzied drummer, a young girl carried away by the music—such vignettes captured the spirit of Woodstock, the New York rock festival that turned out to be a tribal gathering of the disenchanted young.

Three days of heady music (and of sometimes headier marijuana) left the shelterless Woodstock throngs feeling they had shared a mystical communal experience. Farmer Max Yasgur's 35-acre alfalfa field was left a shambles.

A moment before, photographer Mel Finkelstein and Jackie Onassis were both standing outside a Manhattan theater, where she had just seen the film I Am Curious (Yellow). *Mel fell. He claimed she threw him with a judo flip. She insisted he tripped over his own feet. He did not press charges.*

At the University of Chicago's Billings Hospital a young patient, fatally stricken with leukemia, spoke openly about her hope and despair while an unseen audience of chaplains, students, social workers and hospital staffers observed her through one-way glass. The girl was a subject in a seminar aimed at teaching professionals how to help patients cope with approaching death.

As the number of special issues increased, the Woodstock festival offered an obvious editorial opportunity.

One film turns life upside down for the new star named Ali

A star and suddenly much in demand after her first leading role in Goodbye, Columbus, onetime model and bit player Ali McGraw "even at age 30 is very much the New Girl" of the year, the editors decided.

ILLUSIONS ETCHED IN ANGUISH

To produce this haunting image of pity and suffering, photographer Max Waldman restaged a scene from the play Marat/Sade in which nuns in an insane asylum aided an inmate.

JANUARY 10, 1969   JANUARY 17, 1969

JANUARY 24, 1969   JANUARY 31, 1969

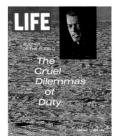
FEBRUARY 7, 1969

FEBRUARY 14, 1969

FEBRUARY 21, 1969

FEBRUARY 28, 1969

MARCH 7, 1969

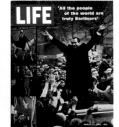
MARCH 14, 1969

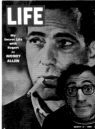
MARCH 21, 1969

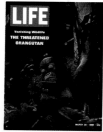
MARCH 28, 1969

APRIL 4, 1969

APRIL 11, 1969

APRIL 18, 1969

APRIL 25, 1969

MAY 2, 1969

MAY 9, 1969

MAY 16, 1969

MAY 23, 1969

MAY 30, 1969

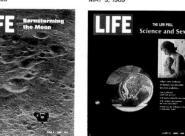
JUNE 6, 1969

JUNE 13, 1969

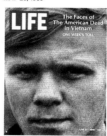
JUNE 20, 1969

JUNE 27, 1969

JULY 4, 1969

JULY 11, 1969

JULY 18, 1969

JULY 25, 1969

AUGUST 1, 1969

AUGUST 8, 1969

AUGUST 15, 1969

AUGUST 22, 1969

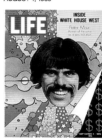
AUGUST 29, 1969

SEPTEMBER 5, 1969

SEPTEMBER 12 1969

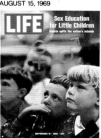
SEPTEMBER 19, 1969

SEPTEMBER 26, 1969

OCTOBER 3, 1969

OCTOBER 10, 1969

OCTOBER 17, 1969

OCTOBER 24, 1969

OCTOBER 31, 1969

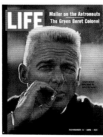
NOVEMBER 7, 1969

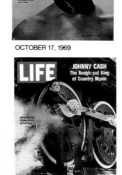
NOVEMBER 14, 1969

NOVEMBER 21, 1969

NOVEMBER 28, 1969

DECEMBER 5, 1969

DECEMBER 12, 1969

DECEMBER 19, 1969

DECEMBER 26, 1969

CLASSIC PHOTOS

A Vietnamese wailed over the body of her husband, victim of a Vietcong massacre.

A rustic commune family gathered in their tepee for bedtime stories.

A Manhattanite paraded the long-haired, miniskirted look.

CURRENTS AND EVENTS

WORLD: SALT Talks Begin in Helsinki • Civil Strife Mounts in Northern Ireland • De Gaulle Resigns, Pompidou Succeeds Him as President • Brandt Heads Socialist Regime in Bonn • Giant Oil Field Discovered in North Sea • Golda Meir Becomes Israel's Premier • Arafat Elected PLO Chairman • Captain Gaddafi, in Military Coup, Assumes Control of Libya • Nationalist Rebels in Angola, Mozambique, Guinea Fight Portuguese • El Salvador, Honduras in Undeclared War • Military Commanders Take Over in Brazil, Bolivia • Antigovernment Riots in Pakistan Lead to Resignation of President Ayub Khan • Ho Chi Minh Dies.

U.S.A.: James Earl Ray Gets 99 Years for Killing Dr. King • Sirhan Sirhan Convicted for RFK Slaying • Eisenhower Dies • Senator Ted Kennedy's Career Blighted Following Auto Accident on Chappaquiddick Island • Rock Festivals at Woodstock, N.Y., Altamont, Calif., Draw 300,000 Each • Supreme Court Justice Abe Fortas, Under Fire for Ties to Stock Manipulator, Resigns • Nixon Appoints Warren Burger Chief Justice • Trial Begins of Chicago Eight, Protest Leaders at '68 Democratic Convention • Campus Demonstrations Spread • Miracle N.Y. Mets Win World Series.

VIETNAM: Vietcong, South Vietnamese Join U.S.-North Representatives in Paris Peace Talks • Nixon Announces Phased Troop Withdrawal • Mylai Massacre Revealed • Mass Moratorium Day Demonstrations Held Nationwide.

FIRSTS: Man on Moon (Armstrong) • Human In Vitro Fertilization • Supersonic Passenger Jet Flight (Concorde) • Implantation of Artificial Heart in Human • Giant Passenger Jet (747).

MOVIES: Midnight Cowboy • True Grit • The Love Bug • Alice's Restaurant • The Wild Bunch • The Secret of Santa Vittoria • Easy Rider • Goodbye, Columbus • Bob & Carol & Ted & Alice • Butch Cassidy and the Sundance Kid • The Sterile Cuckoo • Take the Money and Run • Royal Hunt of the Sun • Stolen Kisses • Tell Them Willie Boy Is Here • I Am Curious (Yellow) • Downhill Racer • The Prime of Miss Jean Brodie • Marlowe • Chitty Chitty Bang Bang.

SONGS: Come Saturday Morning • I'll Never Fall in Love Again • Raindrops Keep Fallin' on My Head • Leaving on a Jet Plane • Lay Lady Lay • My Cherie Amour • A Boy Named Sue • Games People Play • Get Back • Honky Tonk Women • Hurt So Bad • I've Gotta Be Me • Sugar, Sugar • Wedding Bell Blues.

STAGE: Butterflies Are Free • Play It Again, Sam • Ceremonies in Dark Old Men • To Be Young, Gifted and Black • 1776 • Oh Calcutta! • Promises, Promises • Celebration.

BOOKS: The Godfather (Puzo) • The Love Machine (Susann) • Slaughterhouse Five (Vonnegut) • Portnoy's Complaint (Roth) • The Inheritors (Robbins) • The Andromeda Strain (Crichton) • Ada (Nabokov) • Bullet Park (Cheever) • The First Circle (Solzhenitsyn) • Force 10 from Navarone (MacLean) • A Small Town in Germany (Le Carré) • Naked Came the Stranger ("Ashe") • The Making of the President 1968 (White) • The Selling of the President 1968 (McGinniss) • The Valachi Papers (Maas) • An Unfinished Woman (Hellman) • Ernest Hemingway: A Life Story (Baker) • The Collapse of the Third Republic (Shirer) • The 900 Days (Salisbury) • The Kingdom and the Power (Talese) • Grant Takes Command (Catton) • Instant Replay (Kramer) • The Arms of Krupp (Manchester) • The Season (Goldman).

FADS: Bell-bottom Pants • Couples in Unisex Outfits.

1970

As grievances mounted, extremism spread and produced a gap that was more than generational

Although they had been around for quite a while, all the big issues seemed to come to a head as the world turned into the '70s: black power, women's lib, the sexual revolution, the "drop out" youth culture—and the war in Southeast Asia, where the U.S. had been enmeshed for half a decade. Activism exploded on all fronts. The raised fist was everywhere, even at the Miss America contest. And when National Guardsmen, who had been issued live ammunition, fired not warning shots but lethal ones into the crowds of stone-throwing Kent State students protesting the war—killing four—the repercussions were traumatic. The incident served to radicalize Americans who, even after My-lai, had been on the fence about Vietnam.

National Guard troops, called out by Ohio Governor James Rhodes after Kent State students had broken windows in town and set fire to an ROTC headquarters, leveled guns at rampaging antiwar protesters on the campus. LIFE called the killing of four young people—Jeffrey Glenn Miller, Sandra Lee Scheuer, Allison Krause and Bill Schroeder—"senseless and brutal murder at point-blank range."

At their St. Louis foundation for sex research, Dr. William H. Masters and his associate Virginia E. Johnson used jointed wooden artist's models for demonstrations as they conducted a counseling session. Their best-seller Human Sexual Inadequacy had just been published, four years after their pioneering work, Human Sexual Response.

Just waiting for

On cult leader Charles Manson's ranch, north of L.A., a clutch of his followers, faithful even as he was being tried for the grisly murders of actress Sharon Tate and six others, snuggled into a natural environment under a rock.

JANUARY 9, 1970

JANUARY 23, 1970

JANUARY 30, 1970

FEBRUARY 6, 1970

FEBRUARY 13, 1970

FEBRUARY 20, 1970

FEBRUARY 27, 1970

APRIL 10, 1970

APRIL 17, 1970

APRIL 24, 1970

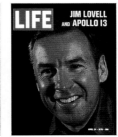
MAY 1, 1970

MAY 8, 1970

MAY 15, 1970

MAY 22, 1970

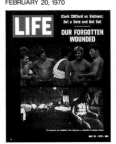
MAY 29, 1970

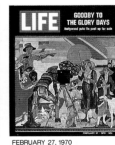

In California's Marin County courthouse a defendant, his trial invaded by a friend who supplied arms, held two guns on the judge as a fellow inmate made a juror hostage also. A shotgun was tied to the judge's neck with a cloth. The desperadoes did get outside, taking only the judge with them. There lawmen shot the inmates to death, but the judge did not survive.

BLOODY BREAKOUT AT SAN RAFAEL

It was a sunny, drowsy Friday morning in San Rafael, Calif., and the courtroom on the second floor of the Marin County Hall of Justice was almost empty. James D. McClain, an inmate of nearby San Quentin, was standing trial for stabbing a prison guard. The witnesses, mostly, were other prisoners. A small scattering of spectators lounged indifferently in their seats.

Among them was a tall, thin young man wearing a baggy car coat. He had been at the trial the day before, the bailiff recalled, with the same baggy coat, but without the small bag that lay at his feet. It was then 11, and the bailiff remembers thinking it was odd to be wearing a heavy coat in August and that perhaps he ought to get a better look at this young man. But by then the youth had pulled a .38-caliber revolver out of the bag and it was too late. One of the boldest, bloodiest judicial attempts in the annals of modern crime was under way.

The young man was Jonathan Jackson, a 17-year-old Pasadena high school student and a self-proclaimed revolutionary. Schoolmates recalled that he occasionally talked about "dying draped over a wall" and "being gunned down in a revolutionary action." He also bragged that he had recently served as a bodyguard for Angela Davis, a controversial black Communist college professor whom the regents had ousted from UCLA. And in fact,

In the courtroom hallway, William Christmas (far left) keeps a firm grip on a woman hostage, while convict James D. McClain points a shotgun and a pistol at Superior Court Judge Harold Haley. The shotgun is tied to the judge's neck with a piece of cloth.

Self-exiled Black Panther Information Minister Eldridge Cleaver and his wife, Kathleen, sat in their Algiers home beneath a picture of Panthers founder Huey Newton.

Nude lovers groped before a group grinding out one of a new flood of small-cost, big-profit porno films—a "cynical business," said the editors.

 arlie

Charlie Manson's faithful—some oldtimers, some newcomers—cluster under a boulder to pose for this portrait. From left are Dennis Rice, Catherine Share, Mary Brunner, Chuck Lovett,

Ginny Gentry, Cathy Gillis, Lyn Fromme, Sandra Good Pugh and Ruth Ann Moorhouse. With them in spirit is Manson—shown above in picture days on the spread—now on trial for murder.

Incredibly, in spite of all the tragedy and horror this place has come to signify, they are still here, on this phony ranch where the only things that seem real are the corral stench and the animals that make it. They are waiting, these empty-eyed waifs with the cracked-doll faces, for Charlie Manson to come back and run his macabre little kingdom and make things here the way they used to be. It is an unlikely hope: 30 miles to the southeast, across the barrens of the ranch and down the dividing freeway to Los Angeles, Charlie, with the rest of an ex-con, grinds out his nights in a floodlighted cell and awaits to stack away his days in a crowded courtroom. There he and three other members of the ranch commune are on trial for the savage murders last year of Actress Sharon Tate and six other people. It has been a happening of a trial. His lawyer, appointed against Manson's will, has maintained a macabre barrage of objections throughout prosecution questioning of Linda Kasabian,

the turncoat disciple who became the state's key witness against Charlie. Two of the lawyers have been jailed for breaching the court's etiquette. Even President Richard M. Nixon asserted a brief mile when he pronounced Manson guilty and Manson flaunted the resulting headlines before the jury in an effort to trigger a mistrial ruling. But little of the melodrama of the court trial of their lives compares to the human drama unfolding in the ranch. Here, the waifs who still cling silent among his followers back at the tawdry ranch where he once lived. Here some dozen young women and men, homeless drifters, carry on their aimless survival. They feed the bees—is brought in by blind, 83-year-old George Spahn, the owner of the place and the man who tried to make the onetime movie set into a kind of day-camp dude ranch before Manson and his people moved in. They make the daily garbage run for food, slop a dinner together, join in guitar-accompanied singing, love each other. Some take drugs. All wait for Charlie, the 35-year-old loser they worship, to return.

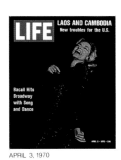
CLASSIC PHOTOS

A Kent State coed confirmed to her horror that a fellow student had been killed.

Women marched down N.Y.C.'s Fifth Ave. demanding equality.

CURRENTS AND EVENTS

WORLD: SALT Talks Resume • Nuclear Weapons Nonproliferation Treaty Ratified • Israeli Troops Clash with Arabs in Lebanon, Jordan, Syria • Egypt's Nasser Dies, Sadat Takes Over • Assad Becomes Syrian Premier Following Coup • Jordan Battles Palestinian Guerrillas • Nigeria's War with Biafra Ends, Death Toll Estimated at Two Million • Allende Elected Chile's President • DeGaulle, Salazar Die.

U.S.A.: Campus Unrest Widespread, 448 Colleges Closed or on Strike at One Point • Chicago Seven (Bobby Seale Tried Separately) Acquitted • Father Daniel Berrigan Convicted of Burning Draft Records • Right to Vote Granted 18-Year-Olds • Millions Observe Earth Day • Cigarette Ads on Radio, TV Banned.

VIETNAM: U.S. Troop Strength Falls Below 400,000 • Drive into Cambodia Launched, Ends After Mass Protests in U.S. • Green Beret Forces Fight North Vietnamese in Laos.

FIRSTS: U.S. Women Generals • Picture Phones.

MOVIES: M*A*S*H • Airport • Diary of a Mad Housewife • The Boys in the Band • Catch-22 • Patton • Zabriskie Point • On Her Majesty's Secret Service • Beyond the Valley of the Dolls • Five Easy Pieces • They Shoot Horses, Don't They? • The Great White Hope • I Never Sang for My Father • A Man Called Horse • Satyricon • Hello, Dolly.

SONGS: Bridge over Troubled Water • The Candy Man • Everything Is Beautiful • For All We Know • I'll Be There • Rubber Duckie • We've Only Just Begun • What Are You Doing the Rest of Your Life? • Side by Side • And I Love You • Band of Gold • Hello Darlin' • If I Were Your Woman • Let It Be.

STAGE: Last of the Red Hot Lovers • Borstal Boy • Conduct Unbecoming • Sleuth • Steambath • The Effect of Gamma Rays on Man-in-the-Moon Marigolds • Applause • Company • Two by Two • Purlie • Coco • Minnie's Boys.

BOOKS: Deliverance (Dickey) • Islands in the Stream (Hemingway) • Mr. Sammler's Planet (Bellow) • The French Lieutenant's Woman (Fowles) • Love Story (Segal) • Jonathan Livingston Seagull (Bach) • Travels with My Aunt (Greene) • Hard Times (Terkel) • The Greening of America (Reich) • Up the Organization (Townsend) • Future Shock (Toffler) • Sexual Politics (Millett) • Everything You Always Wanted to Know About Sex (Reuben) • Play It As It Lays (Didion) • The Sensuous Woman ("J").

TOPS IN TV, '60s: Gunsmoke (Premiere '55) • Have Gun Will Travel ('57) • Wagon Train ('57) • Andy Griffith ('60) • The Real McCoys ('57) • Rawhide ('59) • Candid Camera ('60) • The Untouchables ('59) • The Price Is Right ('56) • Jack Benny ('50) • Bonanza ('59) • Hazel ('61) • Perry Mason ('57) • Red Skelton ('53) • Danny Thomas ('53) • Dr. Kildare ('61) • Dennis the Menace ('59) • My Three Sons ('60) • 77 Sunset Strip ('58) • Ed Sullivan ('48) • Alfred Hitchcock ('55) • Lassie ('54) • What's My Line? ('50) • Jackie Gleason ('52) • Garry Moore ('58) • Dick Van Dyke ('61) • My Favorite Martian ('63) • Donna Reed ('58) • Bewitched ('64) • Gomer Pyle ('64) • The Fugitive ('63) • Peyton Place ('64) • Walt Disney ('54) • Beverly Hillbillies ('62) • The Lucy Show ('61) • Ben Casey ('61) • Father Knows Best ('54) • Petticoat Junction ('63) • The Munsters ('64) • Gilligan's Island ('64) • Get Smart ('65) • The Man from U.N.C.L.E. ('64) • Lawrence Welk ('55) • The FBI ('65) • Mission: Impossible ('66) • Dean Martin ('65) • Smothers Brothers ('67) • Carol Burnett ('67) • Mayberry R.F.D. ('68) • Julia ('68) • Here's Lucy ('68) • Glen Campbell ('68) • Hawaii Five-O ('68) • Family Affair ('66).

FADS: Granny Dresses • Tie-dyed Fabrics • Old Military Apparel.

As the rock culture swiftly metamorphosed into the drug culture, two of its superstars, the multitalented Jimi Hendrix and the soul belter Janis Joplin, both 27, died— Hendrix apparently from suffocation after vomiting while unconscious from sleeping pills, Joplin from a drug overdose.

To show how VIPs would have looked 100 years ago, photographer John Dornés posed Truman Capote as Dickens's Ghost of Christmas Present.

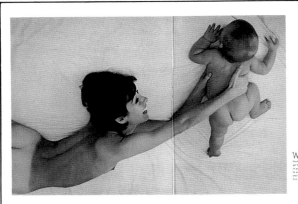

The LIFE Photography Contest found beauty in a New Hampshire pine forest, as seen by Leon Kuzmanoff, and . . .

. . . love in Florida art director Kent Barton's informal portrait of his wife and squirming baby son and . . .

. . . shock in a study by amateur Elliot Gilbert, who saw graffiti on an L.A. tunnel wall and got a chum to pose under it.

JULY 10, 1970

JULY 17, 1970

JULY 24, 1970

JULY 31, 1970

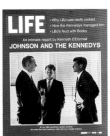
AUGUST 7, 1970

AUGUST 14, 1970

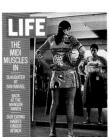
AUGUST 21, 1970

AUGUST 28, 1970

SEPTEMBER 4, 1970

SEPTEMBER 11, 1970

SEPTEMBER 18, 1970

SEPTEMBER 25, 1970

OCTOBER 2, 1970

OCTOBER 9, 1970

OCTOBER 16, 1970

OCTOBER 23, 1970

OCTOBER 30, 1970

NOVEMBER 6, 1970

NOVEMBER 13, 1970

NOVEMBER 20, 1970

NOVEMBER 27, 1970

DECEMBER 4, 1970

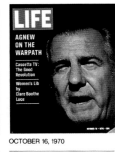
DECEMBER 11, 1970

DECEMBER 18, 1970

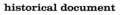
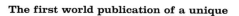

The musical Hair had been a smash hit off Broadway and then a smash hit on Broadway. Now it was a smash hit everywhere (while still being performed on Broadway). Having played in 14 countries, and with six U.S. companies touring simultaneously, it had "gone farther faster than any other show in history."

For more than a year a small LIFE task force had worked in secrecy on the former Soviet premier's manuscript. Security was imposed largely to forestall the expected denial of its authenticity by his successors, who had made Khrushchev a nonperson.

Fashionably long-tressed under his academic cap, Amherst senior David Sanger stood with his "bravely smiling" parents for the traditional commencement photo.

The editors plucked a nostalgic phrase from the lyrics of an innocent old song and used it in the subhead for this parent-stunning story about dorm living at Oberlin.

Rock Hudson was asked, just prior to release of Pretty Maids All in a Row, to take a dim view of the knee-concealing midiskirt. He did manage an unenthusiastic look amid starlets wearing the new fashion, which was replacing the mini. He was also quoted as saying, "Yechh!"

Miss Montana (Kathy Huppe, 18) would not refrain from revealing her stand on Vietnam, so Miss America beauty contest officials barred her from the finals. LIFE awarded her an orchid.

1971

Probing the moon and its own psyche, the U.S. found new values and new superstars

"The old order changeth, yielding place to new." Many stories of this transitional year evoked Tennyson's line. Photographer Larry Burrows died in action, in a helicopter crash, after surviving nine years of the war in Indochina. Margaret Bourke-White, one of the original four LIFE photographers, died also, after a long battle with Parkinson's disease. The Vietnam war was losing its moral edge: Retired Brig. Gen. Telford Taylor, the Nuremberg war trials

LIFE
VOL. 70, NO. 6
FEBRUARY 18, 1971

Larry Burrows came to the magazine in 1942, at 16, as a helper in its London photo lab. Lincolnesque in build, he appeared to lope into battle, "either the bravest man I ever knew or the most nearsighted," said a colleague.

Silhouetted in the stark glare of a burning vehicle, one South Vietnamese soldier runs for cover while others huddle nearby.

A Frantic Night on the Edge of Laos

A great photographer's last news story

by JOHN SAAR

Four days after he took the photographs on these pages, Larry Burrows was reported missing in Laos. He had covered the war in Indochina—and survived it—for nine years (see page 3). When South Vietnamese troops began moving to the Laotian border early this month, Burrows and Correspondent John Saar went with them. They were at Langvei when the terrible incident shown here took place. Saar went back to Saigon to file this report. Burrows stayed on at the border, hoping for a chance to get into Laos. Last Wednesday he got his wish: a ride into Laos with a squadron of five South Vietnamese helicopters. Four of them lost their way in the green-swathed, jagged mountain ranges and wandered north. There they came under heavy North Vietnamese antiaircraft fire. Two of the aircraft, including the one carrying Burrows and four other photographers, were hit. They went down and were seen to burn on impact. An aerial survey of the crash site reported no sign of life.

Late afternoon, 6 February 1971. I first hear the distant whistle of a plane as Larry Burrows and I stand chatting at the roadside headquarters of Task Force 11 just three kilometers from the Laos border. Tomorrow, or maybe the day after, this amalgam of elite South Vietnamese army units will pull its armored track carriers back on to dusty Route 9 and head into Laos. We plan to ride with them.

The U.S. advisers are relaxed and pleasant and Task Force 11's commander, Lt. Colonel Bui The Dung, returns our greeting with a warm smile. Everyone knows that across the border in Laos there will be hard battles, but today the mood is lighthearted, almost festive. Chattering and joking, the paratroops are settling in, gouging out slit trenches, stringing tents. Rice savored with onions and vegetables bubbles over dozens of fires, scalding tea in blue-and-white china bowls passes delicately from one hand to the next.

Like a horn on New York's Fifth Avenue, the rising whine of a jet fighter is simply a background noise in Vietnam. I hear it, think "jet on a strike run" and ignore it. Why not? Every so often someone will say, "Hey, look at that jet roll out," and you watch—detached, safe, vaguely sympathetic to the recipients of the ton of high explosive or tanks of napalm. To the allied armies and the press who travel with them, our air power is as innocuous and reliable as home electricity. Only this time the jet was rolling in on us.

In the fading light the diving plane is hardly visible. But two men, a Vietnamese officer and his American adviser, see it, and the three bombs tumbling toward them. They go headlong into a trench. Alabama-born Staff Sergeant Bob Logan later spoke of it as "high diving without a pool." Burrows is talking about film shipments. Two bangs snatch my attention—close, but safe. Then explosions are on us, in us, among us. The world is one terrible kkrrmsssh of sound and blast—and the brain lurches with the impact. For a frozen microsecond I read incredulity and horror on the faces around me, then we are all down and scrabbling for cover.

A shallow cooking trench. Two big fires, two simmering pots inches away. Christ, I'm going to roast to death. But my head is saying, don't move, mortars, mortars, another salvo any moment. I carry that helmet everywhere, where is it? I look around. One man is moving—fast, decisive—toward the impact area: Larry Burrows. The sunset is still pale gold on the mountaintops. Now there is a stronger, wickeder yellow: flames are licking from the turret of a burning track. We run on and Burrows goes prone to frame the scene. We are the first ones here, and the brain can't accept the visual evidence as real. People bleeding, tattered, broken people strewn everywhere by the steel cyclone. Nightmarishly outlined in the half light, dust-gray apparitions already showing ominously dark, spreading blotches rise to an elbow and extend a pleading arm. From all sides comes the elemental moan of men beseeching help.

Pandemonium. Two officers are already on the radio, calling for Medevac helicopters, but most are momentarily shocked into inactivity. And pandemonium in my head. Again it is Burrows who gives me the lead. "Come and help me bring

CONTINUED

Photographed by LARRY BURROWS

26

27

Tricia Nixon entered the White House Rose Garden on the arm of her father, to become Mrs. Edward Finch Cox.

In a bridal gown she made herself, Margaret Sinclair, 22, headed for church to marry, she said, one "Pierre Mercier." But the lucky Pierre was actually Canada's PM Trudeau, 51.

LIFE The New Shape of America
A Cross-Country Look
The Four-Day Work Week
Our Public Lands Up for Grabs
The Good Life in New Towns
What Makes Us Laugh
The Un-Radical Young
TWO-IN-ONE ISSUE 60 CENTS
JANUARY 8, 1971

LIFE THE ELUSIVE HOWARD HUGHES AS REVEALED IN HIS LETTERS
TRICIA NIXON'S ROMANCE WITH ED COX
JANUARY 22, 1971

LIFE BOB HOPE: On the road with an American institution
WAR-WOUNDED CHILDREN OF VIETNAM
'HOT PANTS' TO WEAR ANYWHERE
JANUARY 29, 1971

LIFE Bill Mauldin's Willie and Joe look at THE NEW ARMY
FEBRUARY 5, 1971

LIFE JACKIE-WATCHING
FEBRUARY 12, 1971

LIFE Everybody's Just Wild About Nostalgia
FEBRUARY 19, 1971

LIFE LARRY BURROWS' VIETNAM A Great Photographer's Portfolio
UPROAR OVER SNOWMOBILES
FEBRUARY 26, 1971

LIFE BACKSTAGE WITH ALI AND FRAZIER
BATTLE OF THE CHAMPS
MARCH 5, 1971

LIFE Saucy Feminist That Even Men Like
Germaine Greer
MAY 7, 1971

LIFE The very happy life of Mrs. Joe Hamilton
alias Carol Burnett
MAY 14, 1971

LIFE How the U.S. muffed a chance to end the Vietnam war
by HAROLD WILSON
L.B.J. Back Home
MAY 21, 1971

LIFE Worldwide Success of 'Jesus Christ Superstar'
A REVERENT ROCK OPERA
MAY 28, 1971

LIFE CRISTINA FORD
Rich, impish and almost Americanized
JUNE 4, 1971

LIFE Gala party at the JFK Center
Washington Super Ball
JUNE 11, 1971

LIFE WHITE HOUSE BRIDE
JUNE 18, 1971

LIFE Sinatra Says Good-by and Amen
A farewell to 30 very good years
JUNE 25, 1971

prosecutor, wrote that the long-delayed trial of Lt. William L. Calley Jr. for the Mylai massacre left unanswered "some dark questions about our conduct of the war in Indochina." But change was not all downbeat. LIFE found that the rock opera *Jesus Christ Superstar,* treating Jesus as a modern man, "bridged the generation gap." And it discovered some budding superstars in the rock world, five of them named Jackson.

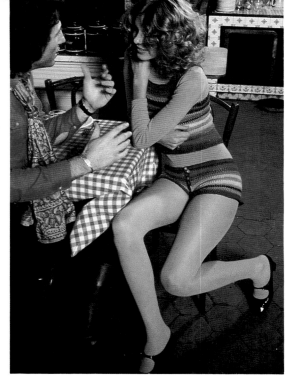

At a Pakistani camp, Senator Ted Kennedy, chairman of the Subcommittee on Refugees, talked with a man who said he had been hungry for four months.

Apollo 15 astronaut Jim Irwin tended to the $13 million moon buggy. It carried him and teammate Dave Scott 18 miles through lunar highlands.

In a delighted look at hot pants—an improbable fad to arrive in midwinter, said the editors—LIFE zeroed in on a warm-blooded Dane in "possibly the shortest shorts in Paris."

Lt. Calley held a press conference from his counsel's window as a Fort Benning court-martial jury pondered his fate.

Chris Brown, as Christ, faced the blood-lusting mob at the climax of the Andrew Lloyd Webber–Tim Rice musical Jesus Christ Superstar.

The wrenching rock opera, 'Jesus Christ Superstar'

'Crucify! Crucify!'

The story is ancient, but the idiom is wrenchingly modern. *Jesus Christ Superstar* is a rock opera based on the suffering and Crucifixion of the Savior. Written by two young Englishmen, Andrew Lloyd Webber and Tim Rice, and first released seven months ago, it has become an international phenomenon. Although an expensive two-record album, it has sold over two million copies in this country alone. It is a hit in such far-flung places as Thailand and Brazil. Because it treats Jesus as a modern man and because the music and lyrics please a variety of tastes, it has bridged the generation gap. Because it is both secular and reverent, it has been embraced by many of the clergy as a way to reach youth. It has even been played on Radio Vatican.

An official full-dress Broadway version is planned for the fall,

but in the meantime churches all over the country have used segments of the opera in their services. An enterprising theater group, the American Rock Opera Company, produced a choral version and booked 177 dates. The members of the company had performed only 22 times, however, when the copyright holders brought suit. They claimed that the opera was being performed without permission, and got an injunction.

One of the canceled dates was in Kansas City, where the Rock Opera Company was to have given two benefit performances on May 15 for the city's Lyric Theater, a serious opera group. In two hectic days, the Kansas City company assembled a cast of its own, went into crash rehearsals and then, with passion and conviction, gave the performance shown on these pages.

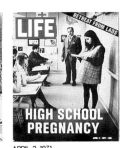
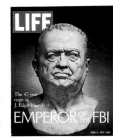
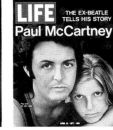

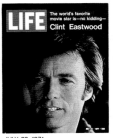

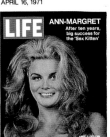

CLASSIC PHOTOS

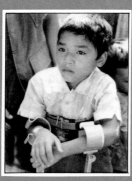

After U.S. treatment, a Vietnam victim, 11, flew back to a land grown strange.

Feminist Germaine Greer, with a pal, giggled watching herself on TV.

CURRENTS AND EVENTS

WORLD: Britain Expels 105 Soviet Reps for Espionage • Three Cosmonauts Aboard Soyuz II Die During Reentry After Docking with Salyut I • Cardinal Mindszenty Accepts Rome Exile after 15-Year Confinement to U.S. Embassy in Budapest • Six Sheikhdoms Form Union of Arab Emirates • Premier of Jordan Assassinated in Cairo • Iran's Shah Celebrates 2,500th Anniversary of Persian Empire • Algeria Nationalizes Oil, Natural Gas Companies • Idi Amin Takes Over in Uganda • Congo Becomes Zaire • Brazilian Guerrillas Free Swiss Ambassador for 70 Political Prisoners • Haiti's Dictator Papa Doc Duvalier Dies, Baby Doc Succeeds Him • U.S. Agrees to Return Okinawa to Japan • Hirohito and Empress Visit U.S. • UN Seats China, Expels Taiwan.

U.S.A.: Nixon Imposes Wage, Price Freeze • Supreme Court Issues Landmark Decisions: Upholds School Busing, Declares Aid to Parochial Schools Unconstitutional, Holds Government Cannot Impose Prior Restraint on Published Materials, Rules Hiring Policies for Men, Women Must Be Same, Imposes Limits on Miranda Decision, Reverses Muhammad Ali's 1967 Conviction for Draft Evasion • Embargo on China Trade Lifted • Rev. Philip Berrigan, Five Others Indicted on Conspiracy to Kidnap Henry Kissinger • Riot in Attica, N.Y., Prison Ends with 43 Dead • Mariner 9 Orbits Mars • L.A. Earthquake Kills 64, Injures Hundreds.

VIETNAM: Attacks Begin on Ho Chi Minh Trail, North's Supply Line from Laos • Lt. Calley Gets Life for Murders at Mylai • Protesters March to Capital Twice for Peace, More than 12,000 Arrested at Second Demonstration • Washington Post, N.Y. Times Publish Pentagon Papers, Secret Defense Department Study of the War • Bombing of North Intensified • U.S. Troop Count Down to 140,000.

FIRSTS: Cancer Virus Isolated • Bone Fractures Knit by Electricity • Legal Off-Track Betting (N.Y.).

MOVIES: The French Connection • Bananas • Klute • The Andromeda Strain • Billy Jack • Dirty Harry • Panic in Needle Park • Shaft • Gimme Shelter • Little Big Man • There's a Girl in My Soup • Husbands • Love Story • Carnal Knowledge • Claire's Knee • The Last Picture Show • Sunday, Bloody Sunday • Harold and Maude • Fiddler on the Roof.

SONGS: Go Away Little Girl • It's Too Late • Joy to the World • Knock Three Times • Never Can Say Goodbye • Put Your Hand in the Hand • She's a Lady • Take Me Home, Country Roads • You've Got a Friend • Rainy Days and Mondays.

STAGE: The Prisoner of Second Avenue • The Trial of the Catonsville Nine • The Gingerbread Lady • The Me Nobody Knows • Happy Birthday, Wanda June • And Miss Reardon Drinks a Little • Abelard and Heloise • The Philanthropist • Old Times • Jesus Christ Superstar • Godspell.

BOOKS: Wheels (Hailey) • The Exorcist (Blatty) • The Day of the Jackal (Forsyth) • The Betsy (Robbins) • The Winds of War (Wouk) • The Other (Tryon) • Rabbit Redux (Updike) • The Book of Daniel (Doctorow) • The Sensuous Man ("M") • Bury My Heart at Wounded Knee (Brown) • Inside the Third Reich (Speer) • Eleanor and Franklin (Lash) • Honor Thy Father (Talese) • Yazoo (Morris) • The Female Eunuch (Greer) • Love in the Ruins (Percy) • The Condor Passes (Grau) • The Onion-Eaters (Donleavy) • The Tenants (Malamud) • The Vertical Smile (Condon).

FADS: Hot Pants • Blue Denim • Conceptual Art.

AUGUST 27, 1971

SEPTEMBER 3, 1971

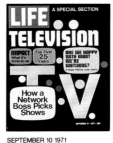

SEPTEMBER 10 1971

SEPTEMBER 17, 1971

Bright Lips of Yesterday

The hat swoops like a piece of jet-age architecture, cartwheeling past the glossiest of red, red lips—the sleek fashion look of the '30s and '40s has resurfaced. Women with plucked brows are slipping into slinky halter-neck dresses, wedgies and chubby jackets, while men are stepping out in two-tone shoes and bow ties.

"Old is in," read the introduction to a LIFE special on nostalgia. The issue concentrated on the craze for the '20s, '30s and '40s, which included this splash of old-time millinery and makeup.

A biracial couple walked across the University of Minnesota campus, "almost lost in the noon spill of students." The picture was part of an essay on interracial dating, "a growing phenomenon with its own set of special problems."

To make this incandescent picture, which won first prize in the magazine's 1971 Photography Contest, Dr. William M. Johannes, a Columbus, Ohio, dentist, shot the sun a half hour before it set on a cloud-filled day. Then, on the same film frame, he took a backlighted close-up of a dandelion puff.

1st Prize

The judges awarded the First Prize to Dr. William M. Johannes, a 60-year-old dentist from Columbus, Ohio, for this incandescent double exposure. First he shot the sun a half hour before it set on a cloudy day. Then, on the same frame of film, he photographed a close-up of a dandelion puff.

SEPTEMBER 24, 1971

OCTOBER 1, 1971

OCTOBER 8, 1971

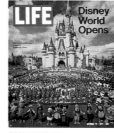

OCTOBER 15, 1971

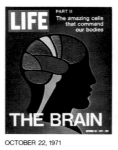

OCTOBER 22, 1971

OCTOBER 29, 1971

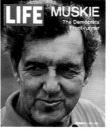

NOVEMBER 5, 1971

NOVEMBER 12, 1971

The Jackson Five had already become big wheels when the editors included them in a 10-page album, "The Rock Family." Lead singer Michael, 13 (out in front, of course), Jackie, 20, Marlon, 14, Tito, 17, and Jermaine, 16, were watched over by their parents, Joseph and Katherine Jackson, in their Encino, Calif., digs.

In an article headlined "An Outrage at Sea," about a British transport on which 21 improperly quartered animals died, the body of a giraffe was shown being ignominiously dumped overboard.

NOVEMBER 19, 1971

NOVEMBER 26, 1971

DECEMBER 3, 1971

DECEMBER 10, 1971

DECEMBER 17, 1971

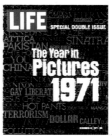

DECEMBER 31, 1971

On the second day of an insurrection in New York's Attica state prison, inmates clustered in the yard or stood atop a wall as they listened to leaders explaining proposed terms for a truce. Some wore football helmets against violence, others identity-concealing hoods. Negotiations proved fruitless. On the fifth day the correction commissioner, supported by Governor Nelson Rockefeller, ended the impasse with guns and gas. In the action 41 men died, nine of them hostages killed by would-be rescuers' bullets.

In an Azusa, Calif., high school an honor student, 16 and pregnant, worked at the blackboard in English class. The school was cited as one of a number in the U.S. that addressed teenage pregnancy not with expulsion but with special programs in regular classes.

1972

The magazine's last year as a weekly featured a long-running hoax and several dramas all too real

Despite a recovering national economy, LIFE's advertising revenues did not revive during the year. The huge circulation actually became a liability, since each copy cost more to produce than it brought in. So the circulation-building, worldwide publicity attending LIFE's cat-and-mouse game with an elusive author named Clifford Irving and the reclusive billionaire Howard Hughes was highly paradoxical, to say the least. Irving had duped book publisher McGraw-Hill, with whom LIFE had subcontracted for first serial rights, into believing that he had Hughes's permission to ghost an autobiography—a surefire best-seller.

It turned out that Irving had used access to Time Inc.'s own rich files on Hughes to lard the manuscript he was concocting, aided by an accomplice, with convincing tidbits, and that he had forged Hughes's signature to a key authenticating document. In the wake of Hughes's personal protest to LIFE and the subsequent efforts of Time Inc. staffers, the hoaxer was exposed, tried and jailed. The flap was embarrassing but also fun. Still, all the attention to the case did nothing to improve the magazine's bottom line, and 36 years after its 1936 debut, the weekly Big Red had to say goodbye *(overleaf).*

A masked Palestinian terrorist stood guard outside the invaded quarters of an Israeli Olympic squad in Munich. Later nine hostages were slain at the airport by the kidnappers, who had sought escape to Cairo.

A boy who just joined up one morning

by DALE WITTNER

In a bitterly ironic story about one American family, the editors produced an in-depth biography of Jerry N. Duffey, whose name constituted the entire casualty list for one week of the winding-down Vietnam war.

The year in pictures The Wallace Shooting

Once again, violence to haunt the political stage

Yet another assassin fired, this time at Alabama Governor George Wallace, paralyzing him. Frames of the shooting as recorded on TV appeared in LIFE's last weekly issue.

Richard Nixon studied a morsel of Chinese cuisine at a Hangchow dinner given to him by his host, Premier Chou En-lai. The President's so-called opening to China helped him clobber George McGovern at the polls.

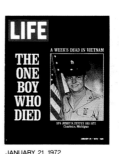

LIFE — SUPER BOWL — SCOUTING REPORT — The Pros rate the two teams — JANUARY 14, 1972

LIFE — THE ONE BOY WHO DIED — A WEEK'S DEAD IN VIETNAM — JANUARY 21, 1972

LIFE — JOHN WAYNE Memoirs of a G-rated cowboy — JANUARY 28, 1972

LIFE — THE HUGHES AFFAIR — Clifford Irving says Howard Hughes looks like this—but did he ever see him? — FEBRUARY 4, 1972

LIFE — DROPOUT WIFE — MARCH 17, 1972

LIFE — HOW THE NIXON ADMINISTRATION BLOCKED JUSTICE — MARCH 24, 1972

LIFE — JACKIE vs. THE JACKIE WATCHER — MARCH 31, 1972

LIFE — WITH THE IRA — APRIL 7, 1972

SHADOW OF DEATH AT MUNICH

The Arab commando, masked figure of doom, keeps watch from the balcony of the Israeli Olympic team's quarters. Inside, two Israelis are already dead, gunned down by the Arabs as they forced their way into the building. Nine other Israelis are being held hostage. Through a long day the hair-trigger negotiations go on. Late in the evening, captors and hostages are lifted by helicopter to an airport 20 miles away. There, the most terrible event in Olympic history ends.

Marlon Brando, "the grandfather of all cool actors," in the title role of the film version of Mario Puzo's novel The Godfather, performed in the garden of his suburban movie compound.

Jill Kinmont's winning battle

A broken life made whole

A follow-up story on Jill Kinmont, who 17 years earlier had been paralyzed from the shoulders down in a fall during an Olympic-trial slalom, revealed that, at 35, she was a certified teacher of Paiute Indian children in California.

FEBRUARY 11, 1972

FEBRUARY 18, 1972

FEBRUARY 25, 1972

MARCH 3, 1972

MARCH 10, 1972

APRIL 14, 1972

APRIL 21, 1972

APRIL 28, 1972

MAY 5, 1972

MAY 12, 1972

CURRENTS AND EVENTS

WORLD: Nixon, Gromyko Sign Agreement to First Phase of SALT Accord • British Troops in Northern Ireland Fire on Catholic Crowd, Kill 13 on Bloody Sunday • European Common Market Accepts Denmark, Britain, Ireland • Japanese Gunmen Kill 30, Wound 76 at Tel Aviv Airport • In Munich PLO Terrorists Murder Israeli Olympic Athletes • Mexico Strikes Huge Oil Reserves • Philippines President Marcos Declares Martial Law.

U.S.A.: At Watergate Apartment Complex in Washington, D.C., Police Arrest Five Men for Breaking into Democratic Party HQ • Nixon Defeats McGovern in Landslide, Visits China, U.S.S.R., Iran, Poland • Alabama Governor Wallace Paralyzed by Assassin's Bullets • Supreme Court Rules Death Penalty Unconstitutional • Equal Rights Amendment Goes to States for Ratification • Hurricane Agnes Inflicts $1.7 Billion Damage in Northeast • Six-Year, $5.5 Billion Program to Build Space Shuttle Authorized • Congress Passes Water Pollution Control Act.

VIETNAM: North Launches Offensive Across DMZ • Bombers Hit Targets Near Hanoi, Mine Haiphong Harbor • Kissinger Negotiates in Paris, Moscow, Saigon.

FIRSTS: American World Chess Champion (Fischer) • Instant Color Camera (Polaroid SX-70) • CAT Scan.

MOVIES: Butterflies Are Free • The Candidate • Deliverance • The Godfather • The King of Marvin Gardens • The Hospital • Last of the Red Hot Lovers • The New Centurions • Play It Again, Sam • Portnoy's Complaint • Slaughterhouse-Five • Sounder • Straw Dogs • What's Up Doc? • Summer of '42 • Diamonds Are Forever • J.W. Coop • Superfly • Minnie and Moskowitz • Nicholas and Alexandra • Chloe in the Afternoon • Cries and Whispers • The Discreet Charm of the Bourgeoisie • The Emigrants • A Clockwork Orange • The Ruling Class • The Garden of the Finzi-Continis • Cabaret • Lady Sings the Blues • 1776.

SONGS: Alone Again (Naturally) • Baby Don't Get Hooked on Me • American Pie • Song Sung Blue • Lean on Me • Papa Was a Rollin' Stone • Everybody Plays the Fool • The First Time Ever I Saw Your Face • I Can See Clearly Now • The Candy Man • I Am Woman • I'll Be Around • I'm Still in Love with You • It Never Rains in Southern California • I'd Like to Teach the World to Sing • I Didn't Get to Sleep at All • Good Time Charlie's Got the Blues • Listen to the Music • Day by Day • Anticipation • Operator • The City of New Orleans • I Believe in Music • Me and Julio Down by the Schoolyard • Help Me Make It Through the Night • Speak Softly Love • Angel • Don't Hide Your Love • Brian's Song • Diamonds Are Forever • Look What They've Done to My Song, Ma • My Guy • If I Were a Carpenter • Love Potion Number Nine.

STAGE: The Sign in Sidney Brustein's Window • 6 Rms Riv Vu • That Championship Season • Sticks and Bones • Grease • Pippin • Sugar • Don't Bother Me, I Can't Cope.

BOOKS: My Name Is Asher Lev (Potok) • The Conspiracy (Hersey) • The Man Who Loved Cat Dancing (Durham) • The Breast (Roth) • Eleanor: The Years Alone (Lash) • Fire in the Lake (Fitzgerald) • August 1914 (Solzhenitsyn) • The Terminal Man (Crichton) • The Stepford Wives (Levin) • The Blue Knight (Wambaugh) • Marriages and Infidelities (Oates) • The Savage God (Alvarez) • Open Marriage (O'Neill, O'Neill).

FADS: Caftans • Mao Jackets • Decorated Blue Jeans.

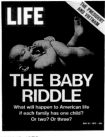

LIFE
THE BABY RIDDLE
What will happen to American life if each family has one child? Or two? Or three?

MAY 19, 1972

LIFE
The Wallace Shooting

MAY 26, 1972

LIFE
RAQUEL On skates as a derby demon
McGOVERN Why his team keeps winning
NIXON in Moscow
The funny disaster of a teacher and his friend

JUNE 2, 1972

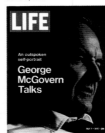

LIFE
Debating the issues of '72
McGOVERN vs. KLEINDIENST ON CRIME
WOMEN IN POLITICS
How are they doing? Where are they going?

JUNE 9, 1972

LIFE
The 50s
WACKY REVIVAL of Hula hoops, Ouimbake, Sock hope, Marilyn Monroe bios, Blacks, Elvis himself —plus a Tele style

JUNE 16, 1972

LIFE
A vivid battle scene from the Nobel Prize winner's new novel of World War I
AUGUST 1914
ALEXANDER SOLZHENITSYN

JUNE 23, 1972

LIFE
KENNEDY vs. CONNALLY They Clash on the Economy
The Great Jesus Rally in Dallas

JUNE 30, 1972

LIFE
An outspoken self-portrait
George McGovern Talks

JULY 7, 1972

LIFE
The Stones Are Rolling Again
The New Role for Fathers Begins at Birth
The Boom in Dome Homes
What is Barbara Walters Trying to Prove?

JULY 14, 1972

LIFE
Five showdown days with the McGoverns
IN THE VICTORY SUITE

JULY 21, 1972

LIFE
Convention Portraits by NORMAN MAILER
The Bare Look

JULY 28, 1972

LIFE
Undercover with a cop who catches crooked cops
ON THE ROAD WITH FLIP WILSON
KILLER

AUGUST 4, 1972

LIFE
The Secret Bobby Fischer
SKYJACKING
The get-tough policy could make it even worse

AUGUST 11, 1972

LIFE
SURGE TO THE OLYMPICS
A 34-page preview of Munich

AUGUST 18, 1972

LIFE
She's at ease in the White House —and seems to like it
PAT NIXON
The young lives of the Reagans and her lonesome walk
STREET GANGS

AUGUST 25, 1972

LIFE
HOW NIXON SEES HIS SECOND TERM by Daniel P. Moynihan
BORED ON THE JOB

SEPTEMBER 1, 1972

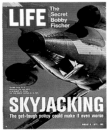

LIFE
WALLA WALLA'S RADICAL REFORMS
Remember Marilyn
SKYJACKING

SEPTEMBER 8, 1972

LIFE
Inside a Tough Prison
OLYMPIC TRAGEDY
From this small Israeli team, 11 would die
Israel

SEPTEMBER 15, 1972

LIFE
The Haywire Olympics
Can they be fixed by 76?

SEPTEMBER 22, 1972

LIFE
As Hanoi releases three fliers, anger over a husband still gone
P.O.W. WIFE
NAM HA
100
MAY DAY

SEPTEMBER 29, 1972

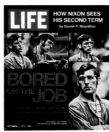

LIFE
A gallery of Sunday heroes without their masks or pads
ROUGH, TOUGH PROS

OCTOBER 6, 1972

LIFE
Shake-up at the FBI
The daring heart surgeon they call 'Ted Terrific'
LUSITANIA
New evidence on the 'unprovoked' sinking that dragged us toward war

OCTOBER 13, 1972

LIFE
FDA—a Consumer looks at the agency that looks after him
The Middle Age Child 6 to 12

OCTOBER 20, 1972

LIFE
A GENIUS AND HIS MAGIC CAMERA

OCTOBER 27, 1972

LIFE
NAMATH
The juicy rewards of a painful life

NOVEMBER 3, 1972

LIFE
QUESTIONS FOR A PEACE
563 POWs: what shape are they in?
1,271 MIAs: how many are alive?
Where does it leave us?
An Ohio town talks of the war

NOVEMBER 10, 1972

LIFE
What will Nixon do with it? by Hugh Sidey

NOVEMBER 17, 1972

LIFE
GEORGE WALLACE FIGHTS BACK
Harry Truman by his loving daughter Margaret
Marine boot camp is still hell

NOVEMBER 24, 1972

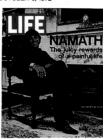

LIFE
With Henry Kissinger in His Paris 'Battle Station'
HARRY TRUMAN by Margaret Truman

DECEMBER 1, 1972

LIFE
DIANA ROSS

DECEMBER 8, 1972

LIFE
Joys of Christmas

DECEMBER 15, 1972

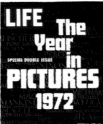

LIFE
SPECIAL DOUBLE ISSUE
The Year in PICTURES 1972

DECEMBER 29, 1972

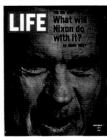

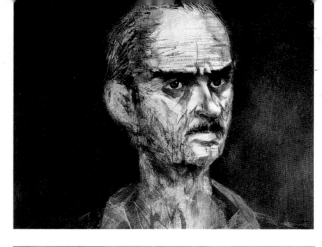

"I've worn jeans in all my movies. Now I have a chance to be glamorous at last," says Liza Minnelli. In the film *Cabaret*, she plays a beautiful, jumping nightclub performer (right) in 1930 Berlin.

Every now and then, in the tilt of a head, the glance of an eye, in the edged poignancy of a lone figure on a spotlighted stage, Liza Minnelli reminds the world of someone it has never forgotten: her late mother, Judy Garland. Through three films and years of nightclub performing (next page), Liza has been pursuing the gleam of her own stardom. Now she has found it, unmistakably. As Sally Bowles, a three-quarters-pretty drifter in prewar Hitler Berlin, she is funny and stirring in the forthcoming movie version of the Broadway hit *Cabaret*. While Germany slips into madness in the background, Liza dances, croons smoky three-in-the-morning melodies and bitter ballads, and acts with the easy authority of someone born to style. At 25, Liza Minnelli is still Judy's daughter, but now she is her own woman.

Artist David Walsh drew Howard Hughes as described to him by Clifford Irving, who said he had interviewed the billionaire in Oaxaca, Mexico. But Danish-born baroness and cabaret singer Nina van Pallandt said she had accompanied Irving there and he had never left her side long enough to have met with Hughes.

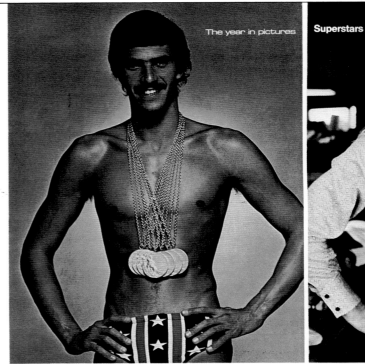

The year in pictures · **Superstars**

The certain smile of champions

Mighty deeds: when he finally got out of the pool in Munich, Mark Spitz was dripping more gold medals—seven—than anyone

Arms akimbo, Mark Spitz, Olympic gold medalist times seven, and Bobby Fischer, the new world chess champion, bestrode the world of competitive games in the corpore sano and mens sana divisions, respectively.

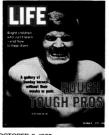

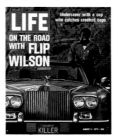

The idea that American women were now standing tall did not thrill the editors, who pronounced clunky shoes, the foundation for all this altitude, unstable and "horrible" looking.

Liza Minnelli, 25, starred on Broadway before winning the lead in the film version of Cabaret. Never thereafter did she need to remind people that she was "Liza, with a Z" or disprove she had succeeded only as the daughter of Judy Garland.

LIZA

'Cabaret' second-generation star finds her own strong voice

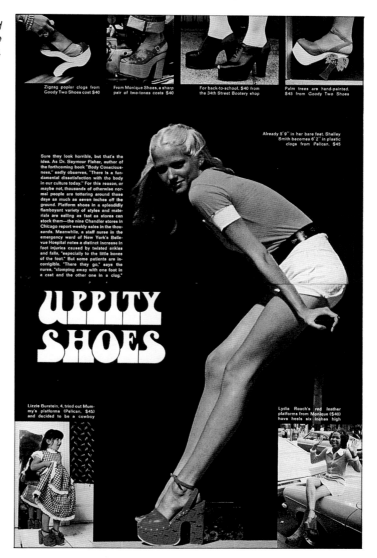

Zigzag poplar clogs from Goody Two Shoes cost $40

From Monique Shoes, a sharp pair of two-tones costs $40

For back-to-school, $40 from the 34th Street Bootery shop

Palm trees are hand-painted. $45 from Goody Two Shoes

Already 5'9" in her bare feet, Shelley Smith becomes 6'2" in plastic clogs from Pelican. $45

UPPITY SHOES

Sure they look horrible, but that's the idea. As Dr. Seymour Fisher, author of the forthcoming book "Body Consciousness," sadly observes, "There is a fundamental dissatisfaction with the body in our culture today." For this reason, or maybe not, thousands of otherwise normal people are tottering around these days as much as seven inches off the ground. Platform shoes in a splendidly flamboyant variety of styles and materials are selling as fast as stores can stock them—the nine Chandler stores in Chicago report weekly sales in the thousands. Meanwhile, a staff nurse in the emergency ward of New York's Bellevue Hospital notes a distinct increase in foot injuries caused by twisted ankles and falls, "especially to the little bones of the foot." But some patients are incorrigible. "There they go," says the nurse, "clomping away with one foot in a cast and the other one in a clog."

Lizzie Burstein, 4, tried out Mummy's platforms (Pelican, $45) and decided to be a cowboy

Lydia Roach's red leather platforms from Monique ($40) have heels six inches high

When the weekly's end came, with the year-end double issue, Managing Editor Ralph Graves ran LIFE's final masthead on the last page, where funny pictures once held sway. The final cover ticked off, in typographical display, the year's stories. The list ended (lower right) with a lump-in-the-throat sign-off.

...gle Olympics. And Bob...decided to sit down and ...rst American to win the

world chess championship. As he demolished Boris Spassky, he went to a Reykjavik tailor and bought himself a three-piece suit.

LIFE

FOUNDER *Henry R. Luce* 1898–1967

EDITOR-IN-CHIEF Hedley Donovan
CHAIRMAN OF THE BOARD Andrew Heiskell
PRESIDENT James R. Shepley
CHAIRMAN, EXECUTIVE COMMITTEE James A. Linen
EDITORIAL DIRECTOR Louis Banks
GROUP VICE PRESIDENT, MAGAZINES Arthur W. Keylor

EDITOR
Thomas Griffith

MANAGING EDITOR
Ralph Graves

ASSISTANT MANAGING EDITORS
Philip Kunhardt   Robert Ajemian   Don Moser   Richard Stolley
David Maness (Administration)

Robert Clive ART DIRECTOR
Charles Elliott, Scott Leavitt COPY EDITORS
Ronald Bailey DIRECTOR OF PHOTOGRAPHY
Mathilde Camacho CHIEF OF REPORTERS
Steve Gelman ARTICLES EDITOR

SENIOR EDITORS
Wilbur Bradbury, Tom Flaherty, Patricia Hunt,
Milton Orshefsky, David Scherman, Dorothy Seiberling,
Josefa Stuart, Hal Wingo

STAFF WRITERS
Loudon Wainwright, Edward Kern,
Richard Meryman, Hugh Sidey, Thomas Thompson

STAFF PHOTOGRAPHERS
John Dominis, Bill Eppridge, Henry Groskinsky,
John Loengard, Michael Mauney, Leonard McCombe,
Ralph Morse, Bill Ray, Co Rentmeester,
John Shearer, George Silk, Grey Villet

ASSOCIATE EDITORS
Sam Angeloff, William Brure, Josephine Burke,
Muriel Hall, Adrian Hope, Tom Hyman, Frank Kappler,
Janet Mason, Alicia Moore, Berry Stainback,
Marian Steinmann, Denny Walsh, Peter Young

ASSISTANT EDITORS
Rosemary Alexander, Audrey Ball, Nelie Blagden,
Kay Bingham, Sean Callahan, Joan Downs, Martha Fay,
Frances Glennon, Richard Gore, Jill Hirschi, Anne Hollister,
Robert Hummerstone, P. F. Kluge, Gilbert Moore, Marion Taylor,
Karen Thorsen, Constance Tubbs, James Watters

REPORTERS
Monica Borrowman, Anne Fitzpatrick, Elizabeth Frappollo,
Judy Gorovitz, Bonne Johnson, Nancy Miller,
Thomas Moore, Ronald Scott, Barrett Seaman, Margarette Tarrant,
Lucy Voulgaris, Elsie Washington, Wilton Woods

BUREAUS
Lucy Lane Kelly (Chief)
WASHINGTON Jack Newcombe, Margery Byers
LOS ANGELES John Frook, Pamela Burke, Judy Fayard, Richard Woodbury
CHICAGO Betty Dunn, Dale Wittner
PARIS Rudolph Chelminski, Robin Espinosa
LONDON Jordan Bonfante, Dorothy Bacon
BONN Gerda Endler

COPY READERS
Dorothy Blunt (Chief), Barbara Fuller, Sydney Dowd,
Nancy Houghtaling, Joan Minors, Chandley Murphy, Mary Orlando,
Joseph Kane

LAYOUT
Eugene Light, John Vogler (Art Directors),
William Shogren (Color), David Young (Production),
George Arthur, John Geist, Medris Ramans,
Lou Valentino, Bernard Weber, Isamé Yamazaki,
Lincoln Abraham, Ernest Loffstad

PHOTOGRAPHIC DEPARTMENT
Barbara Baker, Barbara Brewster, Maureen Chardo, Anne Drayton,
Florence Newsome, Fern Schad, Barbara Ward

EDITORIAL SERVICES
Paul Welch (Director), Frederick Redpath, Norman Airey, Nicholas Costino Jr.,
Peter Draz, George Karas, Doris O'Neil, Herbert Orth, Walter Daran
EDITORIAL BUSINESS MANAGER Richard M. Emerson
SYNDICATION Gideon de Margitay

TIME-LIFE NEWS SERVICE
Murray J. Gart (Chief)

PUBLISHER Garry Valk
GENERAL MANAGER Edward P. Lenahan
ASSISTANT PUBLISHER Robert E. Cowin
ASSISTANT PUBLISHER John U. Crandell

ADVERTISING SALES DIRECTOR Richard J. Durrell
PROMOTION DIRECTOR J. E. Carr Jr.
BUSINESS MANAGER Winston H. Cox
CIRCULATION DIRECTOR Bruce A. Barnet

With pride and affection

This last page of LIFE's last issue is devoted to the people who will miss it most—to the many readers who have told us of their sense of loss, and to the people who worked here. Many of the latter are listed at right on our traditional masthead, but many others, just as professional and dedicated, are not. Last week, 320 people were working for LIFE, half on the editorial side and half on the publishing side. In LIFE's very difficult last years, this was a splendid group of people to be associated with. They thoroughly enjoyed putting out this magazine, and they also enjoyed each other. We will all miss that experience, but we'll remember it with pride and affection.

The response from readers to the closing down of LIFE has been large and generous. But the letter that touches me most was written before the news of LIFE's end. It is from an 11-year-old girl named Marta Flanagan, who lives in Little Neck, N.Y. She was one of 250,000 children whose answers to our questionnaire appear in this issue. Marta Flanagan sent us this letter with her answers:

Dear Sirs: I have adored your magazine for two years. It has always been my favorite magazine. It has articles which interest everybody in the family. Right now I am making a scrapbook of all LIFE Magazine articles which were my favorites. I am making it because then my children will know about my childhood.

P.S. I hope LIFE Magazine is still around until I die.

I had hoped so too, and am sorry it cannot be. As a magazine, we tried to talk to you across all barriers and special interests. We didn't want to reach you as skiers, or teen-agers, or car-owners, or TV-watchers, or single women, or suburbanites, or inhabitants of New York City, or blacks, or whites. Instead, we wanted to talk to you as people, who share the common experience of humanity. I still believe that such talk is important to our country. I am sorry with all my heart that LIFE can no longer make that contribution.

Ralph Graves

RALPH GRAVES, *Managing Editor*

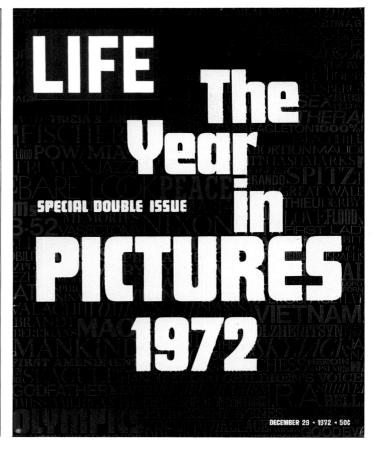

LIFE

The Year in PICTURES 1972

SPECIAL DOUBLE ISSUE

DECEMBER 29 · 1972 · 50¢

1973

A pattern was set, and for the next five years there would be two issues annually

The official phrase had been worded carefully. LIFE would "suspend publication." The expectation, and not merely within Time Inc., was that the magazine would one day be born again. In fact, LIFE was back on newsstands in less than six months, with a one-shot marking Israel's 25th anniversary. Put together by survivors from the shipwrecked

The cover of the first postweekly issue

The Guerrillas Strike Back

In September 1970, Arab guerrillas hijacked three international airliners to a remote area in Jordan, held the passengers captive in the cabins, and demanded the release of terrorists imprisoned in Israel and Europe. Three days later, the Arabs removed the passengers, then dynamited the planes one after the other (above). Several captive guerrillas were finally released in exchange for passengers. The hijacking was only one spectacular incident in a chain of violence (next page) that has gone on ever since the Six-Day War.

The frontispiece for the issue about Israel was an old picture of a young father proudly holding up his infant daughter—born in an early settlement of Italian Jews who had emigrated to the promised land.

A survey of Israel's past included this explosive moment in 1970 when Arab hijackers forced three international airliners to land in Jordan and held the passengers for three days, demanding the release of imprisoned fellow terrorists. When their demands were not met, they released the passengers and blew up the planes.

The year-end cover subjects were President Nixon, Skylab, the latest Arab-Israeli war and Billie Jean King.

Kennedy family members gathered at JFK's grave in Arlington 10 years after his assassination. Sister Pat Lawford was flanked (left to right) by Robert's children: Courtney, Kerry, Michael, David, Maxwell, Christopher and Douglas. Ethel (hidden) knelt behind Pat. At right was Senator Ted Kennedy with wife Joan and son Patrick.

Aboard the plane carrying the body of ex-President Lyndon B. Johnson from Texas to lie in state in the capital, his anguished wife, Lady Bird, was surrounded by comforting friends and family members.

weekly, the issue was laid out in the familiar grand style, with big photographs crisply reproduced on heavy stock. A second special issue, a year-end roundup of news pictures and original stories, was clearly successful enough to warrant making such an editorial package an annual event. Thus a precedent emerged: to publish twice a year.

The sun-loving hedonism of Israel's affluent young people was the subject of an essay, "The Tel Aviv Look."

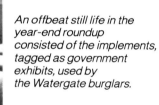

An offbeat still life in the year-end roundup consisted of the implements, tagged as government exhibits, used by the Watergate burglars.

At the Senate Watergate hearings, writer and former CIA agent E. Howard Hunt peered uneasily over his half-glasses as the panel grilled him about the role he had played in the break-in.

CLASSIC PHOTOS

Ex-POW Lt. Col. Robert Stirm came home to a family welcome.

Nixon fox-trotted with a staunch fan at his Inaugural Ball.

CURRENTS AND EVENTS

WORLD: East, West Germanys Establish Diplomatic Relations • Soviet Academy of Sciences Condemns Dissident Physicist Sakharov • Brezhnev, Nixon Sign Pact Limiting Nuclear Warfare • Greek Premier Papadopoulos Abolishes Monarchy, Military Ousts Him • Afghanistan Becomes Republic • Egypt, Syria Attack Israel on Yom Kippur, Cease-fire Ends Conflict After Three Weeks • Arab Nations Limit Oil Production, Precipitating World Energy Crisis • OPEC Formed • Chile Falls in Military Coup, Pinochet Succeeds Allende, an Apparent Suicide • Perón Returns to Argentina After 18-Year Exile, Elected President, Wife Isabel Assumes Vice Presidency • Laos, Pathet Lao Sign Cease-fire.

U.S.A: Senate Holds Hearings as Watergate Scandal Escalates • Vice President Agnew Resigns, Tax Evasion Charges Uncontested, Gerald Ford Succeeds Him • Congress Approves Alaska Pipeline Despite Environmentalists' Protests • Death Penalty Restored in 14 States • Mississippi River Floods 11 Million Acres, Damage Estimated at $322 Million • Supreme Court Rules States May Not Prohibit Abortion in First Six Months of Pregnancy.

VIETNAM: U.S., South Sign Cease-fire with North, Vietcong • U.S. Troops Leave • Bombing of Cambodia Goes On.

FIRSTS: Rabies Vaccine • Push-Through Tabs on Cans • Color Photocopiers • Supermarket Price Scanners.

MOVIES: American Graffiti • Ash Wednesday • The Last American Hero • Live and Let Die • The Life and Times of Judge Roy Bean • Pete 'n' Tillie • The Poseidon Adventure • Last Tango in Paris • Bang the Drum Slowly • Blume in Love • The Day of the Jackal • The Friends of Eddie Coyle • High Plains Drifter • Mean Streets • The Paper Chase • Paper Moon • Save the Tiger • Steelyard Blues • A Touch of Class • Sleuth • Travels with My Aunt • The Way We Were • Up the Sandbox • Day for Night • The Homecoming • State of Siege • The Tall Blond Man with One Black Shoe • Godspell • Jesus Christ Superstar • Man of La Mancha.

SONGS: You're So Vain • Superstition • Killing Me Softly with His Song • The Night the Lights Went Out in Georgia • You Are the Sunshine of My Life • Tie a Yellow Ribbon Round the Old Oak Tree • Bad, Bad Leroy Brown • Midnight Train to Georgia • Touch Me in the Morning • Give Me Love • Live and Let Die • Why Me • Send In the Clowns • Time in a Bottle • Dueling Banjos • Rocky Mountain High • And I Love You So • I Won't Last a Day Without You • Crocodile Rock • My Love • Let's Get It On • Angie • California Saga • Photograph • Till I Get It Right.

STAGE: The Changing Room • The Good Doctor • The Last of Mrs. Lincoln • The Sunshine Boys • The Hot l Baltimore • No Sex Please, We're British • A Little Night Music • Raisin • Seesaw • The Trials of Oz.

BOOKS: Pentimento (Hellman) • The Imperial Presidency (Schlesinger) • The Making of the President 1972 (White) • Fear of Flying (Jong) • Breakfast of Champions (Vonnegut) • The Great American Novel (Roth) • Gravity's Rainbow (Pynchon) • Burr (Vidal) • Ninety-Two in the Shade (McGuane) • Starting Over (Wakefield) • A Crown of Feathers (Singer) • The World of Apples (Cheever) • Rembrandt's Hat (Malamud) • The Summer Before the Dark (Lessing) • The Honorary Consul (Greene) • Evening in Byzantium (Shaw) • Regiment of Women (Berger).

FADS: Wrap Coats • Stacked Bracelets • Kung Fu Movies.

1974

One original issue looked at an ordinary day, the other at an extraordinary year

The first of the two issues created in 1974 was devoted to an intriguing experiment in journalism. It set out to show what people all over America were doing during one arbitrarily chosen day. To produce the 208 pictures that finally were selected for publication, 100 photographers from coast to coast worked around the clock. A few VIPs—including President Gerald Ford breakfasting on his 27th

The cover stated the theme. The preface (below) explained it.

LIFE Special Report

One day in the life of America

LIFE Special Report

The story of a day

Thursday, September 5, 1974 At 6:06 a.m., Eastern Daylight Time, about one minute later than it rose the day before and a minute earlier than it would rise the next, the morning sun of September 5, 1974, first brushes the hulls of lobster boats off Maine's Quoddy Head. Here at the country's most eastern point of land, where America's day begins, the weather is clear and cool, with just a tickle of fall in the brightening air and the northwest breeze. In St. Paul, Minn., occasional showers and thunderstorms are predicted for the evening, and a little rain falls during the day at Denver, where the low temperature is 44 and the high is 83. The skies clear after a foggy start in Wenatchee, Wash., and oppressive "kona" winds from the southwest block the prevailing trades and bring a steamy downpour to Honolulu. Meteorologically, September 5 is just about what a weatherman might look for at this tremulous, equinoctial time of year.

This special edition of LIFE is an effort to show the essence of one day in the enormously complex life of America. It does not purport to be the true and perfect record of a single day. Obviously there can be no such thing, at least not to be gathered and put on pages. One cannot simply collect a day, even though it can be seen, like a shadow, as it passes by in a cycle of light and dark. And although our rigid human schedules make most days seem comfortably the same, they are not the same at all. Days are like fingerprints, no one exactly like another in its whorls and ridges.

America awakes

The issue's opening pages set the poetic tone, with a photograph of the dawn as it arrived in the northern Illinois countryside. It touched with pink the belts of mist lying in the hollows behind a lone automobile. A farmer's wife on her way to work was driving up the dirt road.

In a section of the issue called "After Dark," Rick Surkamer and Lynn Barr, students at the University of Wisconsin, spent part of the evening at a crowded bar in Madison where each seemed "to be in a world of his own."

That same evening, Connie Burtt, 15, of Brooklyn—"who sometimes called himself Ricky Davis"—primped in the mirror of a photomat in a Times Square penny arcade. He then invested 50 cents to take a strip of pictures of himself.

The day's most extraordinary event took place in the White House: a secret meeting among President Ford (left), Alexander Haig (light suit) and two lawyers, which was recorded by Ford's personal photographer. The President and his advisers were discussing the final draft of an official post-Watergate pardon for ex-President Richard M. Nixon, which was to be couriered to him at San Clemente, Calif.

day in office—were among the subjects, but most of the photographs dealt with plain citizens going about their daily lives. The second issue reviewed the departing year in pictures—a year that was overshadowed by the impeachment hearings and Richard Nixon's agonized resignation of the presidency, but one also that was lightened by a fad that was in tempo with the times: streaking.

Foreign-affairs expert Richard Nixon (whose wife Pat and daughter Tricia shared cover space with an oil sheikh, a streaker and Patty Hearst) was in top form while meeting with Anwar Sadat in Cairo. But he nearly died two months after his resignation while undergoing an operation (below, right) for phlebitis.

Patty Hearst was snatched by a group called the Symbionese Liberation Army. Brainwashed, she helped them rob a bank.

Moments

**It's a bird
It's a plane
It's Super-lout**

Bike riders swarmed the heights to watch daredevil Evel Knievel jump Idaho's Snake River Canyon on his Sky Cycle X-2. Although X-2 pooped out in midair, Evel floated safely to earth.

Down for the count of 10 in far-off Zaire was heavyweight champ George Foreman, floored in the eighth by Muhammad Ali.

The String, as a bathing suit, was termed "a barely discreet compromise between discomfort and vulgarity."

Michael O'Brien was led away after he ran naked past 50,000 rugby fans and Princess Alexandra.

At the Kremlin, Sen. Ted Kennedy hugged Teddy Jr., recovering from bone cancer.

CURRENTS AND EVENTS

WORLD: Britain Cracks Down on IRA • France's Pompidou Dies, Giscard Becomes President • Schmidt Succeeds Brandt as West German Chancellor in Wake of Spy Scandal • Israel Reaches Accords with Egypt, Syria • Rabin Takes Over from Meir as Israel's Premier • PLO Granted UN Observer Status • Turks Invade Cyprus • Greece Reverts to Republic • Military Deposes Ethiopia's Haile Selassie • Argentina's Perón Dies, Wife Isabel Leads Nation • President Park of South Korea Survives Assassination Attempt, Wife Shot to Death • India Explodes Nuclear Device • Floods, Cholera, Smallpox Cause 100,000 Deaths in Bangladesh.

U.S.A.: In Wake of Watergate Nixon Resigns, Ford Assumes Presidency, Names Rockefeller Vice President • Economic Recession Hits • Gasoline Shortages Persist, States Limit Highway Speeds to 55 MPH • National Guard Mobilized to Stem Racial Violence in Boston Public Schools.

VIETNAM: Communist Buildup of Troops, Supplies in South Proceeds • Defenders Anticipate Major Offensives.

FIRSTS: TV Subtitles for the Hearing-Impaired • Holographic Electron Microscope • Elected Woman Governor (Grasso, Conn.).

MOVIES: The Exorcist • Lenny • The Day of the Dolphin • Airport 1975 • The Apprenticeship of Duddy Kravitz • Attica • Badlands • Blazing Saddles • Chinatown • Claudine • The Conversation • Daisy Miller • Death Wish • Earthquake • The Gambler • The Great Gatsby • Harry and Tonto • The Trial of Billy Jack • The Last Detail • Murder on the Orient Express • The Odessa File • Sugarland Express • The Three Musketeers • A Woman Under the Influence • Amarcord • Lacombe, Lucien • Love and Anarchy • The Night Porter • The Seduction of Mimi • Scenes from a Marriage • That's Entertainment • The Pedestrian • Cinderella Liberty.

SONGS: Sunshine on My Shoulders • Then Came You • The Way We Were • Having My Baby • We May Never Love Like This Again • Ain't No Way to Treat a Lady • Cat's in the Cradle • Hooked on a Feeling • Feel Like Making Love • Stop and Smell the Roses • You Make Me Feel Brand New • Don't Let the Sun Go Down on Me • Rikki Don't Lose That Number • Please Come to Boston • On and On • Midnight at the Oasis • Sha-La-La • You and Me Against the World • I'll Have to Say I Love You in a Song • One Hell of a Woman • I Won't Last a Day Without You • Haven't Got Time for the Pain • It's Only Rock 'n' Roll • Touch Me • Piano Man • Abra-Ca-Dabra • Devotion • Hangin' Around.

STAGE: Equus • Absurd Person Singular • Clarence Darrow • Thieves • Jumpers • Short Eyes • Will Rogers' U.S.A. • Siswe Banzi Is Dead • Mack and Mabel • Liza • Let My People Come • An Evening with Josephine Baker.

BOOKS: Centennial (Michener) • Watership Down (Adams) • Jaws (Benchley) • Tinker, Tailor, Soldier, Spy (Le Carré) • The Dogs of War (Forsyth) • The Seven-Per-Cent Solution (Meyer) • The Total Woman (Morgan) • All the President's Men (Bernstein, Woodward) • Plain Speaking (Miller) • All Things Bright and Beautiful (Herriot) • More Joy (Comfort) • Something Happened (Heller) • America (Cooke) • Tales of Power (Castaneda) • My Life as a Man (Roth) • The War Between the Tates (Lurie) • Myron (Vidal) • If Beale Street Could Talk (Baldwin) • Cogan's Trade (Higgins) • Winter Kills (Condon) • The Real America (Wattenberg) • The Gulag Archipelago (Solzhenitsyn).

FADS: Streaking • Earth Shoes • The String Bikini.

1975

For the bicentennial a novel approach and rare photos added up to new perspectives

The harvest of stories and pictures for the year-end issue confirmed that 1975 had been an exceptionally dramatic 12-month period. Included were two separate attempts on the life of President Gerald Ford and the nation's chaotic exit from Vietnam. Earlier in the year the

A sampling of the 100 events appeared on the cover (left): a Model T, an original illustration from Huckleberry Finn, the first A-bomb explosion and demonstrating suffragettes. The historic landmarks were culled from a list prepared by prominent scholars and were arranged in five categories. Among the finds was a photograph of a Revolutionary War veteran, Samuel Downing, whose picture (below, left) had been taken in 1864, when he was 102.

LIFE SPECIAL REPORT
THE 100 EVENTS THAT SHAPED AMERICA

GROWTH OF THE NATION

1 Battle of Saratoga 1777
The Revolution's turning point

A ragtag rebel force fired from behind every tree, beat the proud British, and won France as an ally

DEVELOPMENT OF DEMOCRACY

On the year-end cover were (clockwise, from upper left): President Ford, ducking a pistol aimed at him by Lynette "Squeaky" Fromme, a member of Charles Manson's "family" of mass murderers; Patty Hearst; Cincinnati ball players, triumphant over Boston in the World Series; a Khmer Rouge soldier.

A startled President Ford flinched behind his limousine in San Francisco and stared in the direction of the shot fired at him by loner Sara Jane Moore.

The end in Vietnam

It came with astounding swiftness. After 30 years of conflict, in which millions lost their lives and millions more were maimed, the war in Indochina hurtled to its conclusion. Within weeks, Communist forces stormed over South Vietnam, smashed its army, forced the resignation of President Thieu and drove out the last Americans. The lifelong dream of Ho Chi Minh was achieved.

In Saigon demoralized ARVN soldiers drove through corpse-littered streets as the Communists closed in. General "Big" Minh (top left) took over the presidency. An American official (right) fought off panic-stricken South Vietnamese trying to force their way onto an overloaded evacuation plane. President Ford (far right) advertised his "babylift" of Vietnamese orphans.

magazine had again explored new journalistic terrain in an issue devoted to the history of the U.S., as highlighted by 100 great events. The result was a delightful compendium, enriched by unexpected insights, for readers preparing to celebrate the nation's 200th anniversary.

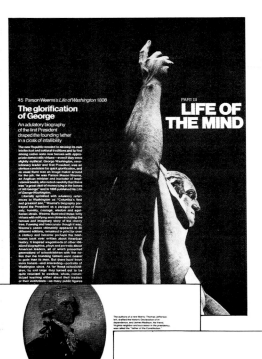

PART III
LIFE OF THE MIND

45 Parson Weems's *Life of Washington* 1808

The glorification of George

An adulatory biography of the first President draped the founding father in a cloak of infallibility

PART IV
THE INVENTORS

62 Early mass production 1798

10,000 muskets

Eli Whitney's bold new way of manufacturing parts for guns foreshadowed the 'American System'

PART V
THE SHAPING OF EVERYDAY LIFE

31 Framing the Constitution 1787

A house united

74 The Croton Aqueduct 1842

Water from a distant river

By reaching 41 miles into the country to get a pure supply, New York was refreshed and brought about a renaissance in bathing.

75 Borden's condensed milk 1856

Preserving food

Seasick cows led to canned milk, and a winter fishing trip to fresh-frozen foods

Off Martha's Vineyard, Mass., a monstrous mechanical shark rose from the deep to "gobble" a hapless bather during the filming of *Jaws*, one of the year's most successful movies. This scene was so scary it was cut.

Thieu's army panicked under the Communists' spring offensive — and a final, frenzied exodus began

Flanked by her children, John and Caroline Kennedy, Jacqueline Onassis stood in a chapel on the Greek island of Skorpiós while attending the funeral of her second husband, Aristotle Onassis. The shipping tycoon, dead at 69, left behind a $500 million fortune and "a legend for opulent living almost unmatched in this century."

CURRENTS AND EVENTS

WORLD: Soviet Bloc, Western Nations Sign Helsinki Accord • Thatcher Succeeds Heath as Leader of Britain's Conservative Party • Ireland's De Valera, Spain's Franco Die • Portugal's Military Prevails Under New Constitution, Grants Independence to African Colonies • West German Terrorists Blow Up Stockholm Embassy • Faisal of Saudi Arabia Assassinated • Egypt Reopens Suez Canal • Muslims Battle Christians in Lebanon • Israel Withdraws from Sinai Oil Fields • Palestinian Terrorists Raid Vienna OPEC Meeting, Kill Three, Take 81 Hostages, Surrender After Flight to Algeria • Conservatives Win in Australia • Chiang Kai-shek Dies • Prince Sihanouk Returns to Cambodia After Five-Year Exile • U.S. Lifts Trade Embargo Against Cuba.

U.S.A: Top White House Aides Involved in Watergate Convicted • Rockefeller Commission Finds CIA Conducted Illegal Operations • Ford Escapes Two Assassination Attempts • FBI Captures Patty Hearst • Teamsters' Jimmy Hoffa Disappears • UMW's Tony Boyle Sentenced to Life for Ordering Execution of Union's Joseph Yablonski • Administration Agrees to Sell Soviets Six to Eight Million Tons of Grain Annually for Five Years.

VIETNAM: Cambodia's Khmer Rouge Seizes Control, Launches Genocide Campaign • Communist Forces Sweep Toward Saigon, South Surrenders Unconditionally • Communist Takeover of Laos Completed • More than 200 Die as Air Force Plane Carrying Orphans Crashes • Clemency Program for U.S. Deserters, Draft Evaders Ends.

FIRSTS: American Saint (Mother Seton) • International Space Project (Apollo 18-Soyuz 19) • Venus Landing (Venera 9).

MOVIES: Alice Doesn't Live Here Anymore • Shampoo • One Flew Over the Cuckoo's Nest • Dog Day Afternoon • Day of the Locust • The Man Who Would Be King • Conduct Unbecoming • Three Days of the Condor • Nashville • The Story of Adele H. • The Great Waldo Pepper • Jaws • Monty Python and the Holy Grail • The Return of the Pink Panther • The Stepford Wives • The Sunshine Boys • Swept Away • At Long Last Love • Funny Lady.

SONGS: At Seventeen • Do You Know Where You're Going To • Fame • Have You Never Been Mellow • Another Somebody Done Somebody Wrong Song • I'm Sorry • Laughter in the Rain • Love Will Keep Us Together • Lucy in the Sky with Diamonds • My Eyes Adored You • My Little Town • Rhinestone Cowboy • Thank God I'm a Country Boy • The Way I Want to Touch You • What I Did for Love • Wildfire • Please Mr. Postman • Mandy • Listen to What the Man Said • Chevy Van • Lonely People • Feelings • Midnight Blue • Operator • Rainy Day People • Disco Queen • The Entertainer • Don't Take Your Love.

STAGE: Same Time Next Year • The Rocky Horror Show • Travesties • A Chorus Line • The Wiz • Shenandoah.

BOOKS: Ragtime (Doctorow) • Looking for Mr. Goodbar (Rossner) • The Eagle Has Landed (Higgins) • Humboldt's Gift (Bellow) • The Great Train Robbery (Crichton) • Shogun (Clavell) • Terms of Endearment (McMurtry) • The Ascent of Man (Bronowski) • Breach of Faith (White) • A Time to Die (Wicker) • Thurber (Bernstein) • Against Our Will (Brownmiller) • Before the Fall (Safire) • JR (Gaddis) • Cockpit (Kosinski) • Winning Through Intimidation (Ringer) • Inside the Company (Agee) • The Ebony Tower (Fowles) • Helter-Skelter (Bugliosi, Gentry).

FADS: Skateboarding • Turtle Racing • Pet Rocks.

A Few Favorites 1966-1975

TRACKING NOTABLES IN AN UNREMITTING STAR WATCH

Jane Fonda, newly assertive at 31, basked nearly nude on an Italian beach after filming Barbarella, an unbuttoned 1968 space fantasy directed by her first husband, Roger Vadim.

A Hollywood star, a professional-class photographer and activist on many fronts, Candice Bergen wore a preferred Sunday outfit during a moment of repose in 1970.

Stand-up comic Woody Allen, 31, the most introverted extrovert in show business, relaxed by leaning over a billiard table and playing alone between Las Vegas performances in 1967.

Angela Lansbury, 42, escapee from Hollywood supporting roles, limbered up backstage in 1967 in preparation for her show-stopping high kicks a year into Broadway stardom as Mame.

Barbra Streisand, named by the editors as "the brightest star of the '60s," dressed down for her role as a prostitute in the 1969 hit The Owl and the Pussycat.

Bob Hope, a longtime LIFE buddy, was on the road as usual in 1971. But as the headline for the cover piece about him pointed out, "The Road Gets Rougher." His staunch support of U.S. troops in Vietnam sparked protests from some among his live audiences at home.

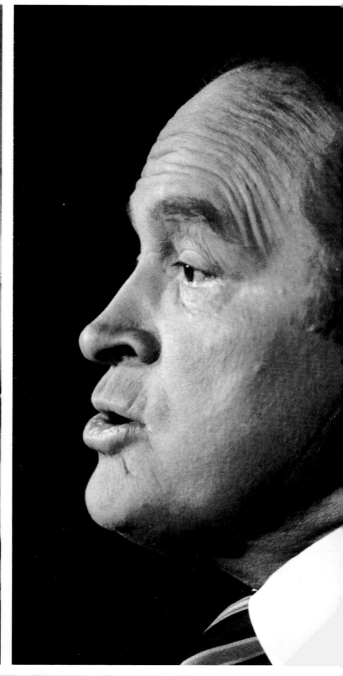

LEAPS OF FAITH AND A TRAGIC TUMBLE

The surf was up off Oahu, and an amateur photographer caught a "wipe-out." He also won third prize in the Amateur Action division of LIFE's 1970 Photography Contest.

As a Tokyo-bound plane took off from Sydney, a man testing his new telephoto lens caught the 1970 death plunge of an Australian who had stowed away in the plane's wheel housing.

Making a movie, Snow Job, in 1972, triple-gold Olympian-turned-pro Jean-Claude Killy performed a gelaendesprung (field jump) off a Matterhorn cornice that was more formidable than any he had encountered in Olympic downhills.

Happily tearing up the Mojave, 650 dust-masked motorcycle enthusiasts raced 75 miles across the desert at speeds up to 85 mph. The 1971 scene was recorded in yet another special issue, this one on the American outdoors. It was inspired by the increasing number of long weekends, due both to labor-contract entitlements and to the shifting of traditional holiday dates. The upshot, LIFE observed, is that "our urge and aim is to go as fast and as far as our legs and wheels and wits can carry us."

As the photographer's helicopter swooped low over the savanna, browsing elephants were startled into a milling herd. The picture, part of an essay on the African species, appeared in a 1967 special issue planned by LIFE's esteemed nature editor Patricia Hunt. Along with the essay ran a fan letter to all wild elephants written by Romain Gary, author of Roots of Heaven. A pertinent excerpt from the text: "The echo of your irrepressible thundering march through the open spaces of Africa keeps reaching me, awakening a confused longing. It sounds triumphantly like the end of acceptance and servitude, an echo of limitless freedom that has haunted our soul since the beginning of time."

**AN EYE FOR
THE PATTERN
THAT DWELLS
WITHIN
THE IMAGE**

*The editors of the magazine,
as well as its art directors,
were always conscious of
the abstract patterns
that reside in every
photograph and every
painting. Those perceptions
influenced the design of
layouts. Even lifted from
their contexts, two
such dissimilar images as
Matisse's Blue Nude, from a
1970 article on the 100th
anniversary of the artist's
birth, and Co Rentmeester's
1972 study of Olympic
sculler Jim Dietz reveal a
striking commonality in their
creative approaches.*

LETTING THE CAMERA SAY A MOUTHFUL

The Joffrey Ballet's Dermot Burke and Trinette Singleton performed to hard rock in 1969's Astarte, "the first 'trip' ballet." It mixed media (a film on a huge screen interpreted their actions) and ended with Burke exiting through a series of doors at stage rear—into the street.

A leopard, "the shrewdest, the loneliest, the most patient and the most vicious of the great cats," dined on a springbok he had dragged up a tree. This invasion of the leopard's privacy was recorded in a memorable 1967 series, "The Great Cats of Africa," the result of eight months of stalking by photographer John Dominis.

Lion tamer Pablo Noël carried togetherness to extremes with his enormous lioness, Pyx, in a 1972 demonstration of calmness and trust. "But," the caption noted, "the first time he loses his head, Noël will be out of a job with the circus."

Deep in the era of the mini and microskirt, Saks Fifth Avenue salespeople eyed a model wearing a longer length designed to push 1970 hemlines profitably below the knee once again. "The mini is dead as a doornail," proclaimed the store's president. His sales staff, obviously, was not so sure.

Mostly female spectators in the county-fair outskirts of Baltimore reacted with everything from not quite delight to a little short of dismay as an "ecdysiast"—the word Baltimore's H.L. Mencken coined as a synonym for stripteaser—performed in Ann Corio's 1966 traveling production of This Was Burlesque.

AN INCURABLE CURIOSITY ABOUT CIRCLES OF ACQUAINTANCE

Plunging at some 125 mph above Perris, Calif., in 1972, a clique of sky divers awaited three latecomers to help set a world record for a group jump. They made it by staying hand-in-hand for the required three seconds before pulling their rip cords.

Pulled up just like an Old West wagon train, a New West–style caravan of motor homes that had gathered in 1970 at Great Falls, Mont., settled in for the night before starting on a 61-day, 5,100-mile trek through British Columbia and western Alaska.

FORMIDABLY FLEXIBLE, FETCHING FEMALES

Cathy Rigby, 19, America's hope for a gymnastics gold medal in the 1972 Olympics, did a perfect split practicing on a balance beam at the beach near her home in Los Alamitos, Calif. At Munich, plagued by injuries, she won many hearts but no medals, placing 10th overall. She retired the next year.

Judith Jamison, at 29 the rising star of Alvin Ailey's rising American Dance Theater, distributed her 5 ft. 10 in. across the stage in 1972, her hypnotic eyes but a foot above the floor.

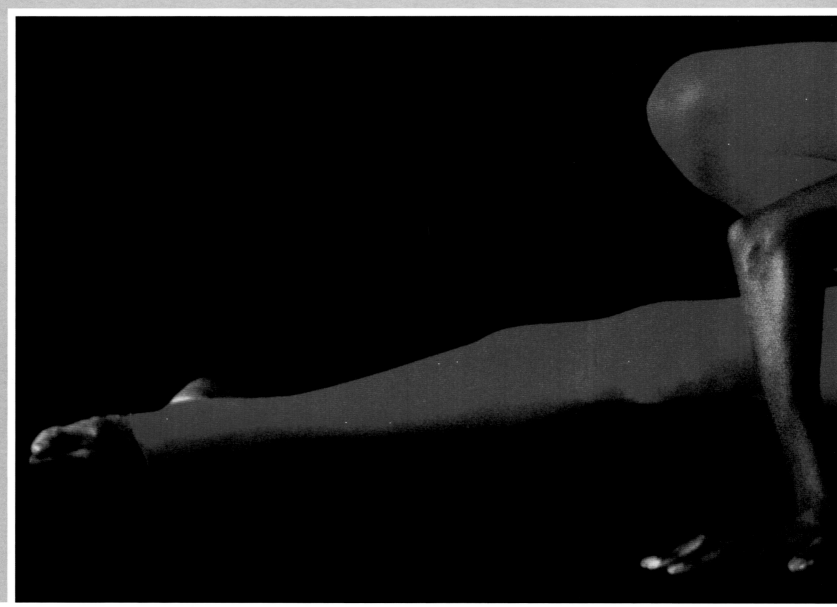

Gelsey Kirkland, 17, George Balanchine's new 1970 Firebird, limbered up before rehearsing for her debut in the Stravinsky classic.

RAPID TURNOVER AS A PHOTOGRAPHIC ASSET

As a raftload of vacationers hurtled the rapids of the Colorado River, some camera-happy soon-to-be dunkees calmly sought to memorialize their misadventure. But Kenneth Klementis of Canoga Park, Calif., had a better, and safer, picture opportunity from his angle on shore. His shot won the $5,000 first prize in the Amateur Action category of LIFE's 1970 Photography Contest, which attracted some 500,000 submissions from more than 40,000 entrants.

How do you say "head over hoofs" in Spanish? After tossing the matador, this bull celebrated by turning a spectacular, if inadvertent, cartwheel. Neither of the 1972 opponents was injured.

1976-1985
Rebirth and Renewal

Less than a year after the weekly was shut down, a 10-page prospectus for a monthly, written by former assistant managing editor Philip Kunhardt, was circulating among the company's higher echelons. In it he urged that a revived LIFE "approach pictures with the conviction that the still photograph provides intense satisfaction in itself." Color capability for every page, gravure reproduction on heavy, high-gloss paper, expectation of a much smaller audience and the need for a much higher price per copy were also emphasized.

Meanwhile, the semiannual issues were proving useful for experiments in design. But the initial dummy for a monthly had to be shelved because of the negative business climate. The time for a launch, it was decided, had not yet arrived.

However, three years and seven special reports later, the projections were more encouraging. Research indicated that TV viewing was down and advertisers were moving back to print. Magazines in general were thriving. A second dummy, readied in early 1978, was an intramural hit, and by spring the corporate decision was "go." Kunhardt was named managing editor. *Fortune*'s assistant publisher Charles Whittingham was chosen publisher. The start-up was scheduled for fall. In late April, to appropriate fanfare and amid considerable excitement, the announcement went out: "LIFE is back!"

The most conspicuous change in the revived magazine was its bolder look, which was signaled on the first monthly cover by a jumbo-size logotype and reinforced by lively graphics throughout. Achieving a new look had from the first been a primary concern of Kunhardt and the art director, Robert Ciano.

Inside, readers could find a great deal

that was comfortably familiar. The magazine opened with Windows, a short section devoted to pure photography, which owed its heritage to Speaking of Pictures. It ended on Just One More, typically a funny one-pager that was, actually, the Miscellany feature under a new name but now in color. Instead of running a news-based Picture of the Week up front, the editors selected the best news photographs of the month and grouped them at the back under the heading LIFE Around the World.

The core of the magazine consisted of photo essays, short as well as long, mostly in color. But most issues also carried a strong human interest story in black and white, of the kind that had been a hallmark of the weekly. The subjects were those that had always sustained the magazine: personalities, art, medicine, nature, sports, science, food, entertainment (now with attention to the rock scene) and sheer spectacle. To complement this pictorial bounty, the monthly again set aside space for a major article, often the work of a well-known author. Also, a substantial personality profile became a regular department; and, beginning in 1980, Loudon Wainwright resumed his column, The View from Here.

There was, however, one important difference. The weekly LIFE had derived much of its energy from the breaking news. Each issue had benefited from a powerful lift-off: a lead story hung on a sturdy news peg. Many of the editorial acts that followed the lead story also had drawn strength from recent headlines, big and small. Now some critics who remembered the weekly were at first concerned by the monthly's lack of immediacy and confused by its more reflective pace. But as the editors gave a keener edge to their stories by digging more deeply behind the

news and anticipating developments, a sharper focus emerged. With it, the magazine extended its appeal and welcomed back not only many who had grown up with it but also a youthful new audience.

The editorial staff was much smaller now—three dozen compared with the 300 or so during the brassiest days. Fortunately, many alumni of the weekly, writers as well as photographers, were available to contribute on a free-lance basis. John Loengard, himself a former staff photographer, was now the picture editor, and in that capacity he also reached out for and encouraged the work of a new generation of camera prodigies.

In mid-1982 Phil Kunhardt, faced with problems of health, resigned. He was succeeded by Richard B. Stolley, a colleague on the weekly and an old friend, who had been the first managing editor of Time Inc.'s highly successful *People* magazine. In the spring of 1985 Stolley was commandeered by Editor-in-Chief Henry Grunwald for a corporate assignment to develop a new magazine, and Judith Daniels was asked to take on the top LIFE editorial position. Among other credits, Daniels had been managing editor of *New York* magazine and *The Village Voice,* as well as the founding editor of *Savvy.* She then distinguished herself in stints with Time Inc.'s Magazine Development Group and other company publications.

In its seven years as a monthly, before its fiftieth anniversary, LIFE devoted itself increasingly to the interests of a bright, energetic, mobile and trendy readership. There was, however, one constant: devotion to the potency of great photography —"images compelling and beautiful," as the charter for the monthly had promised, images "to hold and to keep."

253

1976

An overdue tribute to noteworthy U.S. women provided a grace note to an upbeat year

Nowadays the idea of an issue devoted to remarkable American women would raise few, if any, eyebrows. In 1976 it did. There was some apprehension that the issue might wind up as a soufflé of show-biz types and socialites, decorated with a few great achievers. But the roster of 166 women, past and present, demonstrated the

Cassie Chadwick (below left) swindled a bank out of millions in 1902. Calamity Jane stood beside the grave of husband Wild Bill Hickok, who died in 1876.

On the cover were: Harriet Beecher Stowe (top, circa 1852), author of Uncle Tom's Cabin; *actress Ethel Barrymore, as she appeared in her first hit,* Captain Jinks of the Horse Marines, *in 1901; Lucille Ball, pretelevision, in 1943; and Billie Jean King in 1974, the year she won the U.S. women's open singles for the fourth time.*

Amelia Earhart, at 29, was paired with Julia Ward Howe, a beloved symbol of patriotism, who died in 1901 at 91.

The cover showed gymnast Nadia Comaneci, a tall ship, Jimmy Carter listening to election returns, a July 4 wedding.

A lighter-than-air spectacle in the year-end issue was this flip by Romania's Comaneci, 14, during the Montreal Summer Olympics.

The splendid quest for Olympic perfection

Photographed by Co Rentmeester

After a long vigil Jimmy and Rosalynn Carter hugged on hearing he had the last three electoral votes needed to win.

How proudly we hailed a most glorious 4th

First-prize winner in the photo contest was this parade down Main Street in Plainfield, Vt., led by a very long-legged Uncle Sam.

stunning diversity of their accomplishments and the élan they brought to every field of endeavor—including crime. A similar upbeat mood prevailed in the year's second issue. With the rest of the country, LIFE lauded the 200th anniversary of the Glorious Fourth, whose celebration was climaxed by a visit from the tall ships.

Years before she became the reigning queen of TV sitcoms, Lucille Ball, 32, was a Hollywood trouper with 50 films behind her.

Eyes went to the lissome model, but the remarkable woman here was photographer Imogen Cunningham, 93.

The landscape of Mars, videoed back to Earth with amazing clarity by Viking 2, proved to be a barren, boulder-strewn desert beneath a salmon-colored sky.

New York Harbor, illuminated by rockets' red glare, and a snapshot of a minuteman disarmed of his camera took honorable mentions in the July 4 photo contest.

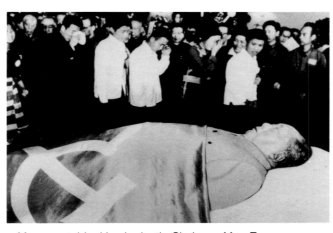

Monumental-looking in death, Chairman Mao Zedong, draped with China's flag, lay in state in Beijing's Great Hall of the People as mourners filed by.

CLASSIC PHOTOS

Youths in Boston attacked blacks on "a sad day for Old Glory."

Citizens Pat and Richard Nixon sat with new friends near the Li River during a second visit to China.

CURRENTS AND EVENTS

WORLD: Soviets, U.S. Sign Pact Limiting Size of Underground Nuclear Tests • Callaghan Succeeds Wilson as British PM • Irish Republic Cracks Down on IRA • British Ambassador to Ireland Killed by Land Mine • East Germany Clamps Down on Dissidents, Puts New Limits on Emigration • Portugal Holds First Free Election in Half Century • Netherlands' Prince Bernhard, Accused of Financial Aggrandizement, Resigns Military, Business Posts • Swedish Socialists Defeated at Polls for First Time in 44 Years • Protests Force Polish Government to Cancel Increases in Food Prices • Marxists Take Over Angola as Civil War Ends • U.S. Ambassador Gunned Down in Beirut • Israel Commando Raid Frees 100 Hostages at Uganda's Entebbe Airport • More than 100 South African Blacks Slain in Riots Stemming from Apartheid • Venezuela Nationalizes Oil Industry • Argentine Junta Overthrows Isabel Perón • Military Coups in Ecuador, Uruguay • China's Mao, Chou En-lai Die • India, Pakistan Resume Diplomatic Relations.

U.S.A: Bicentennial of Independence Celebrated • Carter-Mondale Ticket Narrowly Defeats Ford-Dole • Patty Hearst Found Guilty of Armed Robbery While Kidnapped by Symbionese Liberation Army • Supreme Court Rules Death Penalty Does Not Constitute Cruel and Unusual Punishment • Agriculture Secretary Butz Resigns After Racist Remark • Legionnaire's Disease Kills 29, Affects 182 at Philadelphia Convention • Swine Flu Vaccination Program Discontinued After 51 Cases of Paralysis.

VIETNAM: Hanoi Becomes Capital of North, South • Saigon Renamed Ho Chi Minh City, U.S. Vetoes UN Admission.

FIRSTS: Anglican Women Priests • Women Admitted to Air Force Academy • Women Rhodes Scholars.

MOVIES: All the President's Men • The Bad News Bears • Car Wash • The Front • The Last Tycoon • Marathon Man • Murder by Death • Network • The Omen • Rocky • The Seven-Per-Cent Solution • Taxi Driver • Silent Movie • Harlan County U.S.A. • Leadbelly • The Marquise of O • Missouri Breaks • Robin and Marian • The Shootist • The Tenant.

SONGS: Tonight's the Night • Silly Love Songs • 50 Ways to Leave Your Lover • Afternoon Delight • I Write the Songs • Dream Weaver • All by Myself • Let 'Em In • Muskrat Love • Still the One • Don't Go Breaking My Heart • Tryin' to Get the Feeling Again • Fool to Cry • Rock and Roll All Nite • There's A Kind of Hush • Hello Old Friend • Good Hearted Woman • Don't Pull Your Love • It's O.K. • This One's for You • Inseparable • It's Over • Still Crazy After All These Years • Ob-La-Di, Ob-La-Da.

STAGE: The Norman Conquests • California Suite • Streamers • For Colored Girls Who Have Considered Suicide . . . • The Belle of Amherst • Knock Knock • Pacific Overtures • Bubbling Brown Sugar • Vanities.

BOOKS: Trinity (Uris) • The Gemini Contenders (Ludlum) • The Boys from Brazil (Levin) • Slapstick (Vonnegut) • Ordinary People (Guest) • Kinflicks (Adler) • The Deep (Benchley) • 1876 (Vidal) • Saving the Queen (Buckley) • The Company (Ehrlichman) • Family Feeling (Yglesias) • The World of Our Fathers (Howe) • Roots (Haley) • The Final Days (Woodward, Bernstein) • Scoundrel Time (Hellman) • How It Was (M. Hemingway) • Friendly Fire (Bryan) • The Rockefellers (Collier, Horowitz).

FADS: Reggae • Video Games • Dungeons and Dragons.

1977

For the fourth time an issue was given over to a favored subject: ah, youth!

With all their photogenic bounce, America's young people had always engrossed LIFE's editors. Over the years no less than three issues had been devoted wholly to them. And since the passions of the '60s appeared finally to have spent themselves, 1977 seemed a good time to examine the new youth. "A rather low-key and cautious

The cover featured Rochelle Law of UCLA's women's rugby team. She was part of a story about sports formerly played only by men that were being taken up by the fair sex.

Asked to name the fads, fashions and trivia that they expected to look back on 20 years hence as typical of the year, Illinois high school seniors listed the objects illustrated.

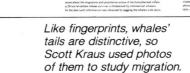

Telltale whale tails

Like fingerprints, whales' tails are distinctive, so Scott Kraus used photos of them to study migration.

On the cover: C3PO and R2D2; President Carter; Farrah; Sadat with Meir; King Tut; Elvis; Queen Elizabeth and Philip; Bert Lance

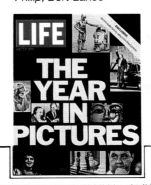

Lovely lift to windward

Sweet trip on the tubes

Alex Haley, author of Roots, visited the Gambian home of his ancestor Kunta Kinte. Leading off the issue, the picture sounded the theme that 1977 was a year of "roots—and new hopes springing from them."

LIFE
SPECIAL REPORT

The year in pictures

The smiling and gentle-faced black man at left has surely done more than any American, living or dead, to make his fellow countrymen wonder about where they come from. In 1977, Alex Haley's book *Roots* sold an astounding five and a half million copies in hardcover and paperback. More spectacularly, in eight consecutive days last January, 130 million of us tuned in for at least part of the television serialization of the story about Kunta Kinte, Haley's African ancestor, who came to these shores as a slave in 1776. It was the greatest popular response in TV history, and whatever the show's shortcomings as either history or drama, it contributed much to racial pride and understanding. Roots—and new hopes springing from them—are evident in many stories in this issue of LIFE. In Jerusalem, Egypt's Sadat took bold initiatives where the past is tangled in bitterness. New treaties giving ultimate sovereignty to Panama have been cast to replace old and outmoded agreements about the Canal. Renewed calls for liberty are finding expression in the work of Amnesty International. The people of Great Britain celebrated a jubilee for a monarch whose predecessors have had no political power for some 150 years. In Houston last November, American women had their most important convention in more than a century of struggle for equal rights. And also at home, a President and his family were photographed in situations so familiar and timeless that we can all find traces of our own roots in the pictures.

CONTENTS

The courage of Sadat: 4
The sweep of 1977 10
An intimate Carter album 28
Jubilee for a queen 40
A flight into terror 44
Uproar over the Big Ditch 52
New style in scholars at Oxford 58
Limelight 64
The fight for human rights 73
The lives and styles of Elvis and Bing 80
Moments preserved 89

The sweep of 1977

Bert Lance sweated hard at questioners during the Senate hearings into his past as a Georgia banker that led to his departure as director of the budget.

The Lance affair

Bert Lance, President Carter's friend and director of the Office of Management and Budget, stared back as senators grilled him about his past practices as a Georgia banker. Aware of the headlines' political impact, Lance resigned.

bunch" was the sum impression, more interested in discovering themselves as individuals than in changing the world. Yet, however laid back they might have seemed compared with their predecessors, their every pursuit—from wind surfing to whale-tail chasing—still vibrated with the exuberance that comes from being, well, just young.

The editors took a look at a high school class of 1984 (whose numerals had "an ominous ring"), and what they saw was most heartening.

Wind surfing was a big new sport and inner-tube rafting a faddish summer pastime.

The year the world's attention focused on
The fight for human rights

A report on Amnesty International opened with this grim carving of a police torture table, made by a prisoner in Chile.

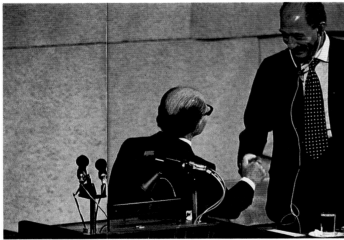

The courage of Sadat

the story of the year

On his pilgrimage of reconciliation Sadat shook hands with Begin in Jerusalem.

A freshly baptized born-again won a hug and a smile from her preacher.

Soccer players winced while awaiting a free kick's shock.

CURRENTS AND EVENTS

WORLD: Queen Elizabeth II Has Silver Jubilee • Spain Holds First Free Elections Since 1936 • Cyprus's Makarios Dies • Begin Becomes Israel's Premier, Approves Settlement of West Bank • Egypt's Sadat Visits Israel • Clash Occurs at Egypt-Libya Border • Egypt Severs Relations with Syria, Iraq, Libya, Algeria • Lebanon's Muslim Leader Jumblatt Slain • Rhodesia's PM Ian Smith Agrees to Plan for Black Majority Rule • U.S., Britain, France Veto UN's Sanctions Against South Africa • U.S., Panama Frame Accord to Transfer Control of Canal Zone by Year 2000 • Military Arrests Pakistan's PM Bhutto • China's Teng Hsiao-Ping, Purged in '76, Made Deputy PM • Cambodia, under Pol Pot, Breaks with Vietnam • Junta Takes Over in Thailand.

U.S.A.: Most Vietnam Draft Evaders Pardoned • Neutron Bomb Tested • Carter Stops Development of B-1 Bomber • Justice Officials Investigate South Koreans for Influence Buying in Congress • Former CIA Director Helms Pleads No Contest to Charges of Giving Senate Misleading Testimony • N.Y.C. Endures Massive Power Blackout, 3,700 Arrested for Looting, Vandalism, Arson • Trans-Alaska Pipeline Begins Operation • Death Penalty Reinstituted After 10 Years • Elvis Presley, Bing Crosby Die.

FIRSTS: Space Shuttle Flight • U.S. Male Saint (Neumann) • Exploration of Outer Solar System (Voyagers 1, 2).

MOVIES: Nickelodeon • Airport 1977 • Annie Hall • A Bridge Too Far • Close Encounters of the Third Kind • The Deep • Equus • Looking for Mr. Goodbar • Oh, God! • Star Wars • Slap Shot • The Spy Who Loved Me • Semi-Tough • Pumping Iron • The Late Show • The Man Who Loved Women • Cousin Angelica • Exorcist II • Fun with Dick and Jane • The Goodbye Girl • Greased Lightning • I Never Promised You a Rose Garden • The Other Side of Midnight • Rollercoaster • Aguirre, the Wrath of God.

SONGS: I Just Want to Be Your Everything • How Deep Is Your Love • Evergreen • Torn Between Two Lovers • You Don't Have to Be a Star • Undercover Angel • Dancing Queen • Da Doo Ron Ron • Southern Nights • You Make Me Feel Like Dancing • Gonna Fly Now • Hotel California • Looks Like We Made It • Don't It Make My Brown Eyes Blue • Nobody Does It Better • Higher and Higher • Blue Bayou • Handy Man • Lucille • The Things We Do for Love • Right Time of Night • So In to You • Margaritaville • Year of the Cat • After the Lovin' • I Wanna Get Next to You • Star Wars • Heard It in a Love Song • Knowing Me, Knowing You • Signed, Sealed, Delivered • Sam • Gloria • Hard Rock Cafe.

STAGE: American Buffalo • Otherwise Engaged • The Gin Game • Dracula • Your Arms Too Short to Box with God • Golda • Side by Side by Sondheim • Annie • Beatlemania.

BOOKS: The Thorn Birds (McCullough) • The Honorable School Boy (Le Carré) • Oliver's Story (Segal) • Beggarman, Thief (Shaw) • Delta of Venus (Nin) • Falconer (Cheever) • The Professor of Desire (Roth) • A Book of Common Prayer (Didion) • Roots (Haley) • All Things Wise and Wonderful (Herriot) • The Grass Is Always Greener . . . (Bombeck) • The Amityville Horror (Anson) • A Rumor of War (Caputo) • The Silmarillion (Tolkien) • How to Save Your Own Life (Jong) • Lancelot (Percy) • Song of Solomon (Morrison) • Your Erroneous Zones (Dyer) • The Second Ring of Power (Castaneda) • Talking to Myself (Terkel).

FADS: Computer Games.

1978

With a splashy new look that emphasized the Art in photography, LIFE was back 12 times a year

The first issue of the monthly, dated October, clearly established that the reincarnated magazine had been designed for the '80s. Just as clearly, however, its roots harked back to LIFE's genesis. Up front the initial issue reaffirmed that the editors were commit-

The curtain raiser for the first monthly issue brought readers up-to-date on the newborn who had appeared in the first picture in the first issue.

THE POWER of THE PICTURE

LIFE is back.

This first issue of the magazine in its new monthly format renews a famous publishing tradition. We are happy to offer LIFE once more to readers who remember it with affection—and to new readers who may not remember it at all.

It has been almost six years now since the management of Time Inc. decided to suspend publication of the weekly LIFE. That decision was made with deep regret: over a period of 36 years, in 1,864 issues, LIFE had made dramatic and significant contributions to the journalism of our time. Although it was not published regularly after 1972, the familiar red and white logotype did appear from time to time —on 10 special issues in the past five years. The good reception of these issues was one of the factors that encouraged us to bring back LIFE as a monthly.

The editors who produced the first issue of LIFE in 1936 had a fascination for photographs that approached awe. "Picture-magic." Editor-in-Chief Henry R. Luce called it, this marvelous power of the photograph to reach out, to reveal, to illuminate, to

catch an instant of action or a blink of high emotion. Luce and his colleagues were putting out a kind of journal that was entirely new to American readers in those days, and they felt, quite rightly, like pioneers. They weren't at all sure where they were going, but they knew that the pictures would have to get them there. "To see life; to see the world; to eyewitness great events," Luce wrote in a prospectus for LIFE, "to see and to take pleasure in seeing; to see and be amazed; to see and be instructed...." From the moment that Margaret Bourke-White took the first cover picture (below, left) of the dam in Fort Peck, Mont., until the magazine closed down, that was what LIFE was all about.

Still, we feel the flutter of butterflies as we start up. The world has taken a lot of turns since 1936, and the consciousness of readers and editors alike has changed tremendously. Issues of LIFE from those early days have an almost antique charm, like

vintage automobiles. The needs of an energetic, well-educated, curious, mobile, modern readership of the late 1970s are surely different even from the needs of audiences of the 1960s and early '70s. Bombarded daily by television pictures bounced off satellites and transmitted in color, it is a sophisticated audience, up on events and trends, hard to surprise, with readers used to looking at images and finding new worlds in them. How do we make a successful claim for their time?

This is a different magazine, but there is still just one answer for us: "picture-magic" again, the very best we can create every month. The power of the picture—to astonish, to teach, to delight, to touch—remains strong. The readers' increased awareness and knowledge sharpen the editors' need to select with care. Our choices, not just of the pictures themselves but of what to cover and how to do it, have to be refined in ways that were not always necessary or even possible then. We must offer more than images to see; they must be images, compelling and beautiful, to hold and to keep.

It is our intention that LIFE should look wonderful every time it appears. The great majority of our pictures will be in color, and all will be printed on high-quality paper by the most advanced techniques and, of course, on the big page size that does greatest justice to the photograph. Within this handsome package, our pictures and our stories will have to convey the continuing sense that this new LIFE, like the old one, is deeply involved with the world it covers, that its capacity for wonder, conviction and caring is as big as ever.

Back in 1936, George Story was born in Portland, Oreg. A photograph taken at his birth (below, left) was the first picture printed inside the first issue of LIFE. In 1961, when he and LIFE were both 25, his picture appeared again, this time with him holding his own daughter. Today Story is 42 and lives in San Diego, where he was photographed on the beach. He is pleased about our decision to come back. We're pleased, too, to have him along as we start out on this renewed adventure. We hope you'll join us.

Here was Speaking of Pictures under a new heading. Placed after the table of contents, it was a bow to "photographic ingenuity and accomplishment"—plus, in this case, humor.

WINDOWS

FOREIGN ENTANGLEMENTS, FAR EASTERN DIVISION

Inside a Royal Retreat

Exclusive Pictures of the Shah's Hideaway by the Caspian

Royalty-watching, a favorite activity of the weekly, was reintroduced in the monthly. This photograph of Iran's shah with his dog was part of a six-page story devoted to the king's opulent lifestyle. It barely touched on the clear signs that his reign was in trouble.

Oh, what a Lovely Way to Fly!

NOVEMBER 1978

DECEMBER 1978

ting themselves to "The Power of the Picture." And as the visual tour on these pages verifies, the members of the 1978 staff were hooked on many of the same addictions that had made the weekly precursor America's biggest magazine.

OCTOBER 1978

Faced with the loss of news stories as a primary journalistic resource, the editors deliberately made the lead story a timeless one, choosing as the subject six clans enjoying a warm, traditional ritual.

Family Reunions

Surely the family is man's best natural defense against the hunch that he doesn't matter at all. In the family's past we find reason for being; in its future we hope to be remembered. No wonder then that thousands of Americans band together every year for one of the most joyful of all rituals, the family reunion. Members of the Rinehart clan, 118 in all, recently convened at a campsite by Lackamas Lake, Wash., for a noisy three-day celebration, and a lot of them paused to pore over an old photograph of their ancestors *(below)*, who first came West in 1854. The Giannini *(right)* gathered 90 strong in San Francisco to show off their children and tell stories about earlier days in Lucca, Italy, the city the first U.S.-bound Giannini left in 1906. Some of the families celebrating across the country had traditions that stretched back 75 years or more. Others, possibly stimulated by the book *Roots* or the television special that grew out of it, were meeting for the first time. The six families shown on these and the following pages had prepared for the events as much as a year in advance—organizing accommodations, mailing invitations and maps, and ordering food for hundreds. But their efforts were rewarded in the glow set off by picnics and dances, hymn sings and horseshoe pitchings—and in endless reminiscences. Reunions—and the familial feelings they occasion—are clearly habit forming. "All we can think about," said one Rinehart at the end of that meeting, "is how to get back together next year."

Long-dead Rineharts loom up at a Washington reunion, and at right an assemblage of Gianninis jams a San Francisco street.

Hands of Hope for a New Life

It was nothing short of a miracle that Clinton Preston survived the accident at all. In one of those common moments of confusion when both parents lose track of an adventurous child, he had vanished in the California sunlight and fallen into less than two feet of water in his uncle's garden fountain. Minutes later, when the terrified Cynthia Preston found her son, he was floating face up in the pool, apparently without life. Frantic resuscitation came too late to prevent great damage to his brain. The case was hopeless, doctors told the Prestons in the months that followed. If he lived, Clinton would never recover, never develop beyond the mute, rigid, staring and helpless creature he had become.

In the more than two years since the accident, Cynthia Preston has flatly refused to accept this prognosis and Clintie has become the focus of a truly extraordinary volunteer effort. On each of six days a week, 30 people—drawn from a total roster of 300—travel to the Prestons' suburban Seattle home to put the boy, now four, through a complex and strenuous form of therapy called patterning. By this method a child is taken over and over through the movements of birth and infancy in the hope that the exercises will set up new and healthy patterns of function in the undamaged parts of his brain. Working now in six hourly shifts a day, Clinton Preston's volunteers have been touching him with patience and love since last March. He may not, of course, ever get much better. But there have been real changes. His body is far less rigid than it used to be, and now and then he smiles.

Photography: Brian Lanker
Reporting: John Frook

A staple of the magazine was to be a strong black-and-white picture essay that focused on ordinary people. Research turned up a community effort to bring one stricken child back into the world through a controversial therapy called patterning. In Seattle a panel of 300 citizens—30 of them daily, six times a week—led a 4-year-old boy, brain-damaged in a drowning accident, repeatedly through the movements of birth and infancy in a program to restore functioning in his healthy brain cells.

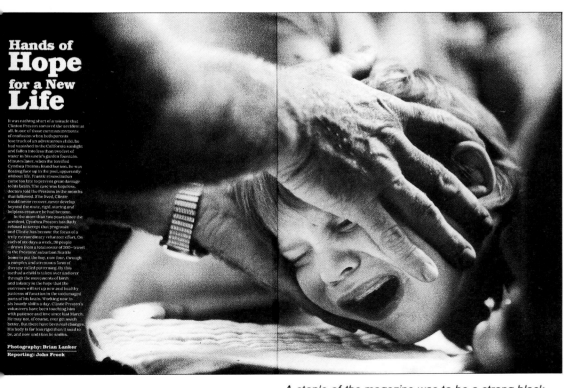

The search for a light and colorful cover story appropriate to the magazine's relaunch resulted in a happy pick: the Atlantic crossing, from the U.S. to France, of Double Eagle II.

CLASSIC PHOTOS

Norman Rockwell, painter of American classics, looked like one himself in his last portrait.

Edgar Bergen, retiring at 75, put Charlie McCarthy into his traveling case for the last time.

CURRENTS AND EVENTS

WORLD: Human Rights Activists Shcharansky, Orlov, Ginzburg Convicted of Anti-Soviet Agitation ● Red Brigade Terrorists Murder Former Italian Premier Moro ● John Paul II Becomes First Non-Italian Pope in More than Four Centuries ● Charlie Chaplin's Body Stolen from Swiss Grave ● Israel Invades Southern Lebanon ● Iran's Shah Imposes Martial Law as Exiled Ayatullah Khomeini Calls for Revolt ● Botha Succeeds Vorster as South Africa's PM ● Kenyatta of Kenya Dies ● Leftist Sandinistas Attack Nicaragua's Somoza Regime ● China Releases 110,000 Political Prisoners, Establishes Diplomatic Relations with U.S. ● Jordan's King Hussein Marries American Elizabeth Halaby.

U.S.A.: Law Extends Mandatory Retirement Age to 70 ● Supreme Court O.K.s Drilling off Mid-Atlantic Coast ● San Francisco Mayor, City Supervisor Assassinated in City Hall ● Congressman, Four Others Shot to Death in Guyana by Members of Religious Cult, 917 Including Leader Jim Jones Die in Aftermath of Murders, Suicides ● Hubert Humphrey Dies ● Alaska Pipeline Bombed.

FIRSTS: Geothermal Generator ● Automatic-focus Camera.

MOVIES: Saturday Night Fever ● Telefon ● The Goodbye Girl ● The Turning Point ● The Choirboys ● High Anxiety ● The Boys from Brazil ● The Buddy Holly Story ● The Cheap Detective ● Coming Home ● The End ● F.I.S.T. ● Foul Play ● Heaven Can Wait ● Interiors ● Midnight Express ● Animal House ● Revenge of the Pink Panther ● An Unmarried Woman ● Who'll Stop the Rain ● Madame Rosa ● Bread and Chocolate ● Sgt. Pepper's Lonely Hearts Club Band ● Grease ● The Wiz ● A Little Night Music.

SONGS: Stayin' Alive ● MacArthur Park ● Three Times a Lady ● You Don't Bring Me Flowers ● You Needed Me ● Too Much, Too Little, Too Late ● Short People ● The Closer I Get to You ● Lay Down Sally ● Just the Way You Are ● Feels So Good ● Still the Same ● Summer Nights ● Slip Slidin' Away ● Love Will Find a Way ● I Go Crazy ● Time Passages ● At the Copa ● Count on Me ● We'll Never Have to Say Goodbye Again ● Ready to Take a Chance Again ● Running on Empty ● The Name of the Game ● Bluer Than Blue ● Fool, if You Think It's Over ● Close Encounters ● Goodbye Girl ● Desiree ● Sweet Talkin' Woman ● She's Always a Woman ● A Wonderful World ● Movin' Out ● Even Now ● The Way You Do the Things You Do ● Native New Yorker ● Lady Love ● Only the Good Die Young ● Thank You for Being a Friend ● Macho Man ● Gettin' Ready for Love ● More than a Woman ● Devoted to You ● Heartbreaker ● Ease on Down the Road ● Mammas, Don't Let Your Babies Grow Up to Be Cowboys ● Blame It on the Boogie ● With a Little Help from My Friends.

STAGE: Chapter Two ● Deathtrap ● On Golden Pond ● The Best Little Whorehouse in Texas ● Da ● Dancin' ● Ain't Misbehavin'.

BOOKS: Chesapeake (Michener) ● War and Remembrance (Wouk) ● Fools Die (Puzo) ● Scruples (Krantz) ● Eye of the Needle (Follett) ● The Far Pavilions (Kaye) ● The World According to Garp (Irving) ● The Last Convertible (Myrer) ● Going After Cacciato (O'Brien) ● If Life Is a Bowl of Cherries . . . (Bombeck) ● The Complete Book of Running (Fixx) ● Mommie Dearest (Crawford) ● A Distant Mirror (Tuchman) ● In Search of History (White) ● The Ends of Power (Haldeman) ● My Mother/My Self (Friday) ● American Caesar (Manchester) ● The Snow Leopard (Matthiessen).

FADS: Hot Tubs.

The Golden Road to a Grand New OZ

In a scene from the new movie version of the classic story, Dorothy and the Scarecrow pass spectacular and strangely familiar landmarks on their way to the Emerald City.

(continued on page)

66

The filming, by director Sidney Lumet and designer Tony Walton, of Broadway's 1975 all-black version of The Wizard of Oz provided an opportunity to do a color "act" on a current movie. This one was right up the editors' alley: the creation of a film fantasyland, using Walton's own original transparencies.

Nicaraguan Rebels at the Barricades

This teenage guerrilla is one of los muchachos who took over the Nicaraguan mountain town of Matagalpa for five days recently. Crouching behind a barricade thrown up against President Anastasio Somoza's National Guard, he symbolized his country's almost total rejection of the dictator. Bankers and businessmen demanded the president's resignation, too, after leftist revolutionaries had occupied the National Palace for 68 hours a few days earlier—imperiling Somoza's grip on a people his family had ruled with an iron hand for 41 years.

Lest great black-and-white news photos be totally lost to the monthly magazine by default, the editors created a section, LIFE Around the World, that collected pictures like this close-up look at a teenage guerrilla in Nicaragua's mountains.

This ethological masterpiece—Adélie penguins, safe on thick pack ice, watching a killer whale break through the summer melt in McMurdo Sound—was part of an 11-page essay excerpted from the book Antarctica by expert nature photographer Eliot Porter.

LIFE not only printed an entire chapter of Fools Die, Mario Puzo's novel about high-stakes Las Vegas gamblers, which had just brought a record $2.2 million for paperback rights, but it also commissioned David Palladini to illustrate it.

Photographer Harry Benson entered the world of Roy Halston Frowick, who had come out of Evansville, Ind., to become, as "just plain Halston," the "most successful American fashion entrepreneur in history."

White-surpliced priests offered Communion to throngs in St. Peter's Square after the investiture of Pope John Paul I. The photographer, David Lees, had for decades been LIFE's highly respected special connection with the Vatican.

The closing-page feature for the monthly was newly titled Just One More. It replaced in color the old Miscellany, which relied each week on an arresting full-page, black-and-white photo. This initial offering was somewhat sexier than the first Miscellany image: a roller-skating horse.

JUST ONE MORE

Assembling for one picture all 28 head coaches of the NFL was a coup reminiscent of LIFE's 1961 roundup of starting quarterbacks. The coaches, though, were not up to the QBs' precision.

1979

To assert its claim as chronicler of the era, LIFE dug deep and circled the earth

In the monthly's first full year, cities whose economies had languished offered evidence of rebounding. The editors welcomed the comebacks, in particular since they could, in reporting the progress, publish evocative archival photographs juxtaposed with coverage of the rebuilding that was apace. Also, new social phenomena had appeared and drew the attention of LIFE staffers

The album of a resurgent Boston, offering before-and-after views of the city's downtown and the waterfront area with its revitalized marketplaces, was followed by overviews of other restoration projects—in New York, Baltimore, Savannah, San Francisco, Seattle.

Lest readers conclude that hot-tubbers were all yuppie Manhattanites or laid-back Californians, LIFE found the average owner to be "positively middle-American, usually a married homeowner in his 40s."

In this pre-Olympiad year the camera zeroed in on the "Lickety-Split Siblings," Eric, 21, and Beth Heiden, 19, of Madison, Wis., as they worked out determinedly on wheeled blades in preparation for the speed-skating competitions on ice. Eric went on to win five gold medals.

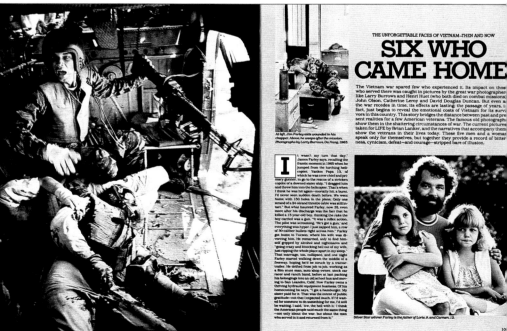

The picture essay on Vietnam and its aftermath, by Brian Lanker, opened with his updating of Larry Burrows's classic photo story on the traumatic 1965 chopper mission of Yankee Papa 13.

who had inherited the old Modern Living franchise. There were, as well, stories with a harder edge. The magazine dug behind the news to visit a PLO training camp for young recruits. And the end of the war in Vietnam, because it had come about in a drawn-out and ambiguous way, prompted a picture essay on the long-term effects of the conflict on six American veterans.

JANUARY 1979

FEBRUARY 1979

American Indians in the state penitentiary at Walla Walla, Wash., enjoyed the privilege of a ritual sweat under canvas. The editors reported it was just one example of the new freedom granted to inmates in the wave of penal reforms that swept the U.S. after the 1971 prison uprising at Attica, N.Y. Riots had led to the deaths of 28 convicts and nine hostages.

's a Hot Tub

dults comfortably and have elaborate lumbing and heating systems. Californtans, naturally, are tops in tubs; they wn an estimated 48,000 of these usuly round receptacles in which to plash, dream, gossip and philander. But

discriminating residents of almost all the other states can buy them, too, for prices ranging from about $1,000 to $3,500 for more sybaritic teak versions. For more on tubs, their uses, inhabitants and history, turn the page.

Photography: Douglas Kirkland

25

82

Sweat Lodge for Braves

Christian worship has long been encouraged in U.S. prisons: the doctrine of sin and redemption might help persuade convicts to mend their ways. In recent years the courts have recognized the right of prisoners to practice other religions as well. After American Indians in Nebraska's state penitentiary went to court and won the right to perform their tribal religions man at public expense —Walla Walla's 80 Indian prisoners easily obtained similar privileges. Accordingly, on a grassy strip beneath the prison wall, there stands a low canvas-covered shelter. Called a sweat lodge, it is a sacred place where Indians purify themselves physically by sweating and spiritually by praying. Periodically, a group of Indians, who sometimes wear ceremonial bells (below), gather at the lodge. They strip, then huddle inside around a fire pit of heated rocks, chanting prayers to the Great Spirit, whom they address as "O Grandfather."

83

This was the opening spread for an exclusive essay with reporting from inside a PLO training camp. The editors concluded that, with the signing by Egypt's Anwar Sadat of a separate peace with Israel, "the Palestinians feel more alone than ever. . . . Bleakly for the world, their only recourse, as they see it, is even more terrorism."

THE EQUATOR
Along Latitude Zero, a Rich Variety of Life and Terrain

LIFE's traversal of earth's most famous imaginary line showed its amazing diversity. Coverage ranged from a parched Kenyan plain to a waterlogged former rain forest at the mouth of the Amazon, from an algae-rich, fish-filled Ugandan lake to a snowstorm at the equator's highest elevation, 16,000 feet up in the Andes.

June 1979

Swinging along as smartly as their raging appearance permits, these boys wear the grim look of children pretending to be adults. But they are not pretending. The guns they carry are real, and loaded. The drills they are about to practice may only be preparing them for an early death. They are young Palestinians training to become fighters in the guerrilla war against Israel, a war whose violence has increased since the signing of the Egypt-Israel peace. Known as *ashbals* (lion cubs) and ranging in age from eight to 14, they are future instruments in a struggle their leaders say may last for generations. About 800 *ashbals* are currently being trained in special terrorist schools operated by the Palestine Liberation Organization amid the refugee camps in Lebanon, where the exclusive photographs on these pages were taken. Since they come mostly from families with members already serving with the guerrillas, the recruiting of *ashbals* is no problem; enlistment, for them, is a natural step to manhood. Once enrolled, they spend virtually every waking moment out of regular school in a harsh training program that makes no concession to age or weakness. Under the eyes of seasoned terrorists they learn to handle all kinds of weapons likely to come into their hands and to strip and reassemble them blindfolded. They become expert at planting and removing land mines, at karate, at concealment and all the other skills needed to kill by stealth and survive in a country where they risk being shot on sight. Despite the danger, live ammunition is always used in their schooling. After three years the boys graduate but may continue training as apprentice guerrillas. At 16 they become full-fledged commandos and are then ready to cross the border to catch a quick and violent glimpse of the land they are taught has always been theirs.

School for Terror

A new generation of Palestinians sees its only hope in a desperate guerrilla war.

Photography: René Burri

Shouldering weapons probably made in China, a squad of young Palestinian terrorists-in-the-making marches out (at left). The boy in the cap is eight.

24

CLASSIC PHOTOS

President Carter collapsed in the heat of a punishing road race near Camp David.

Rubbed out, mob leader Carmine Galante (left) and an aide lay in the garden of a favored Brooklyn restaurant.

CURRENTS AND EVENTS

WORLD: Margaret Thatcher Becomes Britain's First Woman PM • Lord Mountbatten Dies in Explosion Aboard Booby-Trapped Boat in Ireland • Soviet Troops Invade Afghanistan • U.S., U.S.S.R. Sign SALT II Pact • Pope John Paul II Addresses UN • Shah Flees Iran, Khomeini Proclaims Islamic Republic, Muslim Students Storm U.S. Embassy, Take 62 Americans Hostage • Sadat, Begin Sign Peace Treaty • Arab League, PLO Sever Relations with Egypt • Uganda Overthrows Dictator Idi Amin • Sandinista Guerrillas Capture Nicaragua's Capital, Somoza Escapes to Miami • Castro Denounces U.S. at UN • Canada's Trudeau Ousted as PM • Cambodian Capital Falls to Vietnam, Thousands Flee to Thailand • Pakistani Junta Hangs ex-PM Ali Bhutto • U.S. Airlifts Food, Supplies to Thailand Refugee Camps.

U.S.A.: Energy Plant at Three Mile Island, Pa., Shuts Down After Nuclear Accident • Many States Limit Gasoline Sales to Odd-Even Days • FAA Grounds DC-10s After Chicago Crash Kills 272 • Congress Bails Out Chrysler Corp. with $1.5 Billion Loan • U.S. Suspends Iranian Oil Imports, Freezes Assets in Retaliation for Taking of Tehran Embassy Hostages • Estate of Karen Silkwood, Contaminated Employee of Kerr-McGee Plutonium Plant, Wins $10 Million Judgment • UN Ambassador Andrew Young Resigns After Uproar Following Meeting with PLO.

FIRSTS: Unmanned Exploration of Jupiter (Voyager I) • Dating of Viking Artifact in North America, 1065-1080 A.D.

MOVIES: Kramer vs. Kramer • Moonraker • Norma Rae • The Amityville Horror • The In-laws • The Jerk • The Main Event • The Brink's Job • The Deer Hunter • Oliver's Story • Superman • California Suite • Invasion of the Body Snatchers • Apocalypse Now • 10 • Breaking Away • The China Syndrome • Manhattan • Monty Python's Life of Brian • The Muppet Movie • Alien • Hardcore • Star Trek • Yanks • The Rose • All That Jazz • Hair.

SONGS: I Will Survive • Hot Stuff • The Piña Colada Song • Enough Is Enough • Love You Inside Out • Heartache Tonight • Y.M.C.A. • We Are Family • My Life • A Little More Love • In the Navy • Stumblin' In • Chuck E.'s in Love • I'll Never Love This Way Again • She Believes in Me • When You're in Love with a Beautiful Woman • Sharing the Night Together • I Want You to Want Me • You Decorated My Life • Ooh Baby Baby • Lotta Love • Mama Can't Buy You Love • You Can't Change That • Love Is the Answer • Soul Man • Big Shot • The Gambler • I Know a Heartache When I See One • Forever in Blue Jeans • Honesty • Shadows in the Moonlight • I Will Be in Love with You • Happiness • It Hurts So Bad • This Moment in Time • Must Have Been Crazy.

STAGE: The Elephant Man • Whose Life Is it Anyway? • They're Playing Our Song • Sugar Babies • Evita • Sweeney Todd.

BOOKS: Sophie's Choice (Styron) • The Executioner's Song (Mailer) • White House Years (Kissinger) • The Powers that Be (Halberstam) • The Right Stuff (Wolfe) • Aunt Erma's Cope Book (Bombeck) • The Complete Scarsdale Medical Diet (Tarnower) • The Pritikin Program (Pritikin, McGrady) • The Matarese Circle (Ludlum) • Jailbird (Vonnegut) • The Dead Zone (King) • The Last Enchantment (Stewart) • Smiley's People (Le Carré) • Good as Gold (Heller) • Hanta Yo (Hill) • The Ghost Writer (Roth) • Dubin's Lives (Malamud) • Unholy Lives (Oates).

FADS: Superman Regalia • Anti-Iranian Dartboards, Posters.

MARCH 1979

APRIL 1979

MAY 1979

JUNE 1979

DOGS SO RARE

Even if these dogs look familiar to you, they probably aren't. They are, in fact, a pair of Shar-Pei pups, so rare a breed that the American Kennel Club doesn't include it among the 122 officially recognized breeds and won't allow the Shar-Pei—or any of the other dogs pictured on these pages—in their shows. For the masters of these rare dogs, however, their purity is unquestioned; the owners show and breed them and have established their own exclusive kennel clubs. Nevertheless, most of these rare dogs—whose numbers add up to only a small fraction of the total U.S. dog population of 40 million —eventually will win AKC approval and be qualified to appear at such prestigious events as New York's Westminster show. In that case the breeds are likely to become much more popular, perhaps as common as cocker spaniels or at least the flat-faced Shih Tzu, which used to be a rare breed itself.

Shar-Pei

Once used for hunting wild boars and fighting other dogs, this extra-fleshy Chinese breed can still turn easily in its own skin when bitten and bite an aggressor back. (There are about 160 of these in the U.S.)

42

A portfolio of canines so few in number that the AKC would not recognize them as a breed opened with this clearly class-conscious pair. They were outdone in exclusiveness, however, by the Little Lion Dogs, of which there were only 79 in the U.S.

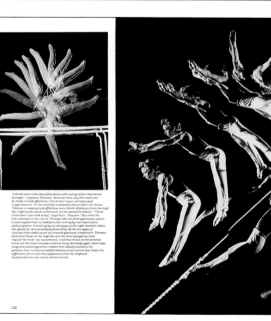

Virtuosic workouts by Olympic hopeful Kurt Thomas, 22, were frozen in kinetic patterns by John Zimmerman's multiple exposures. The U.S. withdrew from the 1980 Moscow Summer Games.

NOVEMBER 1979

DECEMBER 1979

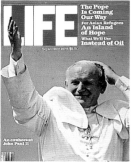

Documenting for roller coaster freaks "The Scariest Rides" in the U.S., a trainload of thrill-seekers did their various things as the notorious Cyclone, at Coney Island in Brooklyn, made its "stomach-wrenching plunge into the abyss" after its slow, clacking climb to the 85-foot peak.

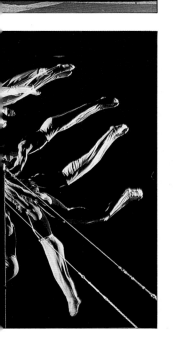

Blondie was one of seven new wave groups the editors said were bent on keeping rock young although it was "approaching the august age of 25."

Choosing the figures who had turned on the most people in the 1970s, the editors paired a couple of golden boys.

In the big splashy worlds of sports and entertainment, here are the people we liked most

FAVORITES

1980

As the decade began, for the first time in a long while the world returned to a more normal disorder.

In addition to war, famine, pestilence and death, the world at the outset of the '80s was rife with folly, beauty, longing, even saintliness. In other words, the world approached normality—with the added fillip that the U.S. was not at war or in the grip of depression or generational revolt. Photographers could turn their state-of-the-art lenses on everything from brutal death in Liberia to tranquillity in Monet's garden, from cancer to burlesque, from Mother Teresa to Muammar Gaddafi.

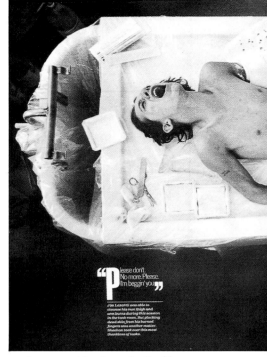

A memorable story dealt with treatment in a N.Y. burn center.

Supermodel Cheryl Tiegs's boyfriend, Peter Beard, photographed her in a variety of swimsuits in outlandish situations for a five-page takeoff on the tried and true bathing-suit act.

These pages opened an eight-page story on a would-be Shangri-la in the Appalachians. It was built by the rapidly growing Hare Krishna movement.

Separately, the four news items had made little impact on the public. But the editors added them up and, in so doing, established that the sum of the near-miss glitches was considerably greater than the parts.

The hand of a malnourished child lay in the compassionate clasp of a priest in the LIFE Around the World section.

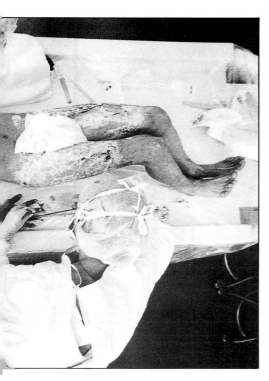

The camera zoomed in as the blood lust of Liberia's new regime was sated.

The Deadly Justice of Revolt

Extraordinary Photographs of Liberia's Brutal Coup d'Etat

The dying man at left, one of four publicly executed for looting and murder, was a horrifying symbol of revolt in the West African republic of Liberia. Five days earlier, on April 12, a posse of soldiers had seized 66-year-old President William R. Tolbert in his wife's bedroom in the executive mansion in Monrovia and then shot and disemboweled him in the opening move of a singularly bloody coup d'etat. The predawn assassination touched off a weekend of jubilant mayhem, during which drunken revelers shook down hapless foreign visitors for cash, cigarettes and sexual favors, and roaring rioters ransacked houses and cruised Monrovia's boulevards in stolen Mercedes-Benzes. At the head of the revolution was a cocky 28-year-old master sergeant named Samuel Kanyon Doe, a member of the indigenous Liberian majority who call themselves "country people." The target of their rage was the ruling elite, those Liberians, a mere 3 percent of the population, descended from American slaves who settled there in 1822. The passion for liberation rose to an even more murderous pitch as Doe and his cohorts initiated quasi-legal steps that resulted in the execution of men who had served in the Tolbert administration.

On an Atlantic beach in Monrovia, life drains from a young Liberian. His public execution was intended as a warning to rioters during the tumultuous first days following the government's overthrow.

51

Drought's Harvest in Uganda

The scenes are heartrendingly poignant, but do not be misled—it is mere succor that is being offered here, not sure rescue. The white priest's hand is indeed extended in compassion, yet only a miracle could save the famished child, now frail and wasted by the ravages of kwashiorkor, chronic malnutrition. Likewise, the hospital bed possesses no magic for the patient collapsed after months of starvation.

This is Uganda, nightmare land where drought has plagued 13 million people still adrift in the chaos left by the mad tyrant Idi Amin, who fled last year. Uganda is not generous in a continent where the macabre remains common enough. Life in a place once described by Winston Churchill as "the pearl of Africa" is often just a kind of semideath. In the Karamoja region, where the drought is most severe, more than 20,000 people

have starved this year alone. Here the Karamojong tribesmen, brigands who have made stealing a way of life for centuries, have traded spears for tommy guns and use them to raid vehicles bringing relief supplies. When the government sends in militia, the soldiers often join the pillaging, and international charities have lost trucks and drivers.

No one's life is safe in Uganda. Ironically, one of the most hazardous places is Mulago Hospital in Kampala, with no working plumbing and no sure supply of medicines. Drugs are known as nurses' gold, and they vanish quickly into "magendo"—the black market. "When you walk into this hospital, you walk into an open sewer," said one grim surgeon, despondent at the lack of anesthetics, syringes, gowns, gloves, blood. "I haven't operated in four weeks."

127

JANUARY 1980

FEBRUARY 1980

MARCH 1980

APRIL 1980

MAY 1980

JUNE 1980

JULY 1980

AUGUST 1980

SEPTEMBER 1980

OCTOBER 1980

NOVEMBER 1980

DECEMBER 1980

CLASSIC PHOTOS

An exile in his own land, dissident Soviet scientist Andrei Sakharov sat with his wife, Yelena Bonner, in Gorky.

The underdog U.S. Olympic hockey team beat the world champion Russians for the gold.

CURRENTS AND EVENTS

WORLD: U.S. Boycotts Summer Olympics, Halts Grain Shipments to U.S.S.R. • Nationwide Strikes in Poland, Workers Establish Independent Trade Union • Tito, Soviet PM Kosygin Die • Saudi Arabia Beheads 63 Extremists Who Raided Mosque at Mecca • U.S. Attempt to Rescue Hostages in Tehran Embassy Aborted • Iran's Shah Dies in Egypt • Iraq, Iran at War • British Commandos Storm Iranian Embassy in London, Free 19 Hostages • Trudeau Returns to Power in Canada • Nicaragua's Exiled President Somoza Assassinated in Paraguay • U.S. Suspends Aid to El Salvador After Murder of Four American Women, Duarte Named President • More than 150,000 Refugees from Cuba, Haiti Arrive by Boat in Florida • Gang of Four on Trial in Peking.

U.S.A.: Mount St. Helens Erupts • Civil Rights Leader Vernon Jordan Wounded by Assailant in Fort Wayne • Miami Blacks Riot After Acquittal of Four Cops Accused of Beating Man to Death • Reagan Wins Presidency • Fire Sweeps Through Las Vegas's Grand Hotel, 84 Die • Beatle John Lennon Shot to Death.

FIRSTS: Nonstop Balloon Crossing of U.S. • Interferon.

MOVIES: Airplane • Ordinary People • Raging Bull • Urban Cowboy • The Tin Drum • Private Benjamin • Coal Miner's Daughter • American Gigolo • Cruising • The Return of the Secaucus Seven • The Empire Strikes Back • The Shining • The Great Santini • Raise the Titanic • Caddyshack • The Elephant Man • Hopscotch • My Bodyguard • The Longest Yard • Being There • The Electric Horseman • Stardust Memories • The Last Metro • Fame.

SONGS: Lady • Upside Down • It's Still Rock and Roll to Me • Do That to Me One More Time • Sailing • Coward of the County • Don't Fall in Love with a Dreamer • Fame • On the Radio • Never Knew Love Like This Before • Steal Away • Him • Hurt So Bad • Hit Me with Your Best Shot • Déjà Vu • September Morn' • Don't Ask Me Why • All Night Long • And the Beat Goes On • On the Road Again • New York, New York • Answering Machine • Don't Say Goodnight.

STAGE: Children of a Lesser God • Talley's Folly • I Ought to Be in Pictures • The Fifth of July • 42nd Street • Barnum.

BOOKS: The Covenant (Michener) • The Bourne Identity (Ludlum) • Princess Daisy (Krantz) • Firestarter (King) • The Key to Rebecca (Follett) • The Fifth Horseman (Collins, Lapierre) • Loon Lake (Doctorow) • Rage of Angels (Sheldon) • A Confederacy of Dunces (Reilly) • Cosmos (Sagan) • Thy Neighbor's Wife (Talese) • The Third Wave (Toffler) • The Brethren (Woodward, Armstrong).

TOPS IN TV, '70s: Marcus Welby (Premiere, '69) • Here's Lucy ('68) • Ironside ('67) • Gunsmoke ('55) • Hawaii Five-O ('68) • Bonanza ('59) • The FBI ('65) • The Mod Squad ('68) • Adam-12 ('68) • Laugh-In ('68) • World of Disney ('69) • Mayberry RFD ('68) • Hee Haw ('69) • Mannix ('67) • All in the Family ('71) • Sanford and Son ('72) • Mary Tyler Moore ('70) • The Partridge Family ('70) • Maude ('72) • Bridget Loves Bernie ('72) • Bob Newhart ('72) • The Waltons ('72) • M*A*S*H ('72) • Kojak ('73) • Sonny and Cher ('71) • The Six Million Dollar Man ('73) • Happy Days ('74) • Barnaby Jones ('73) • Chico and the Man ('74) • The Jeffersons ('75) • Rhoda ('74) • The Rockford Files ('74) • Little House on the Prairie ('74) • Police Woman ('74) • Laverne and Shirley ('76) • The Bionic Woman ('76) • Phyllis ('75) • Starsky and Hutch ('75) • Welcome Back, Kotter ('75) • Baretta ('75) • Barney Miller ('75) • 60 Minutes ('68) • Soap ('77) • Eight Is Enough ('77) • Fantasy Island ('76) • Mork and Mindy ('78) • Taxi ('78) • The Ropers ('79) • Dallas ('78) • The Dukes of Hazzard ('79) • Archie Bunker's Place ('79) • Real People ('79).

FADS: Sony's Walkman • Sensory Deprivation Float Tanks.

This graphic opening to the four-part series showed a patient's hands, positioned as though in prayer, while passing under a CT (computerized tomography) scanner.

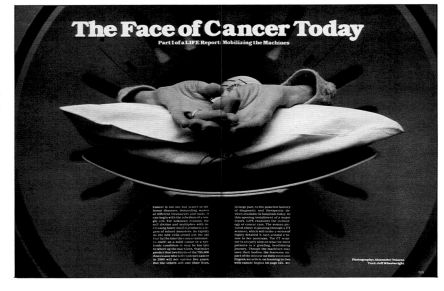

The Face of Cancer Today
Part I of a LIFE Report: Mobilizing the Machines

At this nexus of death and hedonism, said the editors, "virtually every dispute in Middle Eastern politics is played out in microcosm on the streets."

Photography: Alexander Tsiaras
Text: Jeff Wheelwright

LIVING IT UP
among the
RUINS
For torn Beirut's privileged few, pleasure is still the main pursuit

In a haunting essay titled "Teresa of the Slums," camera virtuoso Mary Ellen Mark documented the daily rounds among India's poor of the saintly Mother Teresa.

Death, even in the laundry

The life-and-death battle of Shocktrauma patient Warren Howard

Long after love first found Andy Hardy, The Mick starred with inimitable zest in the Broadway musical Sugar Babies.

Doctors stood in a pool of blood as they fought against time to rescue an emergency patient. The story focused on a trauma center in Baltimore, one of the new services set up to combat lethal shock.

A PAINTER'S PRIVATE EDEN
Monet's Normandy Gardens Bloom Again

Photography: Dmitri Kessel

THE MIGHTY MICKEY
A GREAT OLD PRO BURLESQUES IT UP ON BROADWAY

Photographer Dmitri Kessel replicated four oils by Monet of scenes in his Normandy gardens.

When the Mountain Blew

Camper Gary Rosenquist was parked eight miles away when Mount St. Helens erupted on May 18. He shot the sequence shown in insets, roused the motor home's occupants, then fled, but not before taking this picture of the onrushing ash cloud through his car window.

Following LIFE's tradition of fond simian-watching, Co Rentmeester collected a "Gallery of Gibbons," including this mother and child on their lunch break.

In an interview accompanying this portrait, Gaddafi insisted, "We want nuclear power for peaceful reasons."

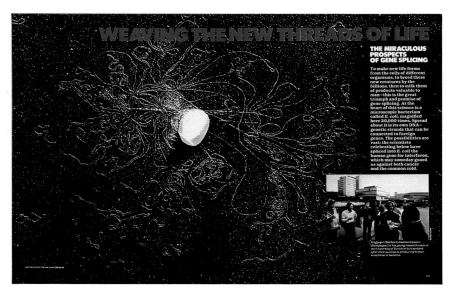

WEAVING THE NEW THREADS OF LIFE

THE MIRACULOUS PROSPECTS OF GENE SPLICING

To make new life forms from the cells of different organisms, to breed these new creatures by the billions, then to milk them of products valuable to man—this is the great triumph and promise of gene splicing. At the heart of this science is a microscopic bacterium called E. coli, magnified here 20,000 times. Spread about it is its own DNA—genetic strands that can be connected to foreign genes. The possibilities are vast: the scientists celebrating below have spliced into E. coli the human gene for interferon, which may someday guard us against both cancer and the common cold.

How to explain gene splicing? Start with five pages of photomicrographs, then add lucid text blocks and captions that describe how scientists are learning to create new forms of life.

The Last Picture of the Shah
Exile's End

This controversial last view of Iran's exiled shah, dead of cancer, offered sharp contrast with the examination of his regime's opulence that appeared just two years before.

A DANCER'S ARCH OF TRIUMPH

Natalia Makarova, on the eve of her 40th birthday, bent over backward to disclaim credit for her two decades of balletic achievement. "God gave me a good instrument," she told a LIFE reporter.

1981

An early spell of national euphoria lasted barely into springtime

A onetime movie actor turned politician swept out of the West into the White House. Home from Iran at long last came 52 embassy hostages. For the first time in five years, NASA launched Americans into space, using a wondrous hybrid machine that orbited as a spaceship and landed as a glider. Then, in the midst of the nation's general feeling of well-being, yet another "kook" with a handgun at-

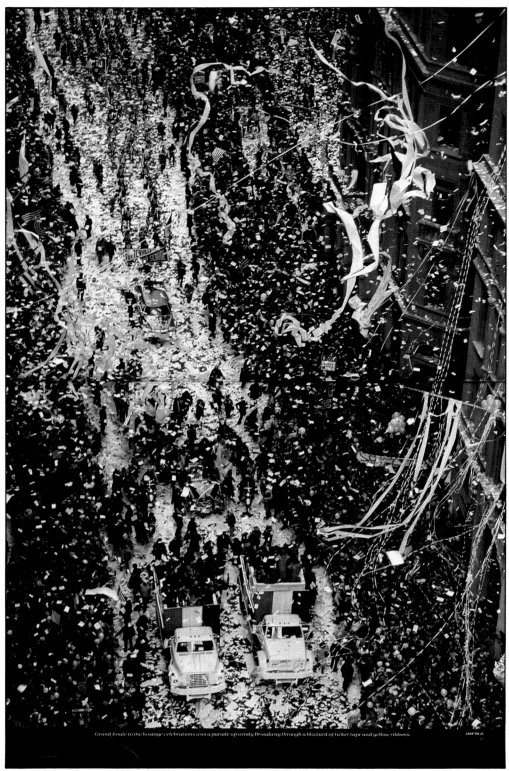

Grand finale to the hostage celebrations was a parade up windy Broadway through a blizzard of ticker tape and yellow ribbons.
JAKE RAJS

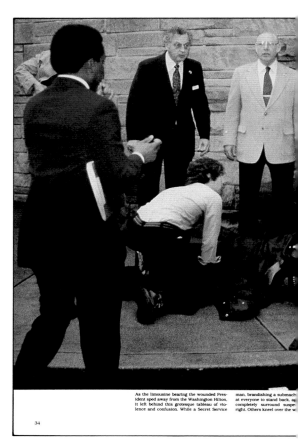

As the limousine bearing the wounded President sped away from the Washington Hilton, it left behind this grotesque tableau of violence and confusion. While a Secret Service man, brandishing a submach... at everyone to stand back, ag... completely surround suspe... right. Others kneel over the w...

34

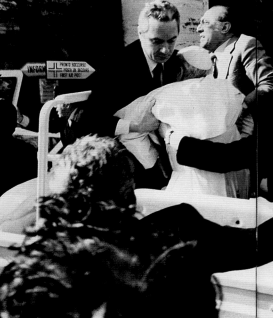

The negotiations that ended 444 days of humiliation for the hostages had been conducted over many months, but the triumphant homecoming, to a Broadway ticker-tape parade, took place on the watch of the newly sworn President. Their return, said LIFE, "turned into a national festival."

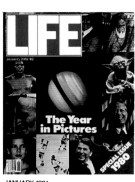

JANUARY 1981

FEBRUARY 1981

MARCH 1981

tempted a presidential assassination. This time the victim's remarkable state of health served him well, and he triumphed over the bullet. The distress caused throughout the land by that early-spring incident was renewed six weeks later when a political assassin shot and wounded Pope John Paul II, and mankind was reminded once again that life and death walk hand in hand.

where they fell—White House Press Secretary James Brady (right) and Patrolman Thomas Delahanty (left) who was shot in the neck, in the midst of the mayhem, in postures of stunned immobility, stand the hotel's manager, William L. Smith (light jacket), and its security chief, Al Fury (dark suit), who had come outside to watch the President leave.

DIRCK HALSTEAD/TIME

35

LIFE AROUND THE WORLD

Protecting the People's Pope

As Pope John Paul II—shown in these photographs taken seconds after he was shot last May—recovers from the attempt on his life, his future security is a matter of utmost concern to Vatican officials. Although most plans are being kept secret, one known change is that the Swiss Guards and police will now be allowed to turn their backs on the Pontiff in order to scan the crowd for would-be assailants. By tradition, turning one's back is deemed disrespectful. On papal visits outside the Vatican, however, security will always be a major problem. Although surrounded by his protective escort, John Paul is committed to mingling with his followers, and this recent brush with death apparently has done little to dissuade him. In the past when church officials have warned him of potential dangers on certain trips, he has shrugged, smiled and proceeded with his plans. A close friend who accompanies the Pope on his travels has begged him to wear a bulletproof shield under his snow-white cassock, but he has declined. In the aftermath of the shooting, prelates have gathered information on all the latest in American bulletproof clothing, yet they are doubtful he will change his mind on the subject. His attitude seems to be that the violence in the world is something from which 'we cannot be wholly sheltered.'

103

A Secret Serviceman brandished a submachine gun beside a knot of agents and cops encircling presidential assailant John Hinckley, as a limousine carried the wounded Ronald Reagan from the Washington Hilton. Others knelt over patrolman Thomas Delahanty and White House Press Secretary James Brady, also hit.

Aides and security guards rushed to support Pope John Paul II just seconds after he was hit by the bullets of Mehmet Ali Agca in Vatican City.

APRIL 1981

MAY 1981

JUNE 1981

JULY 1981

AUGUST 1981

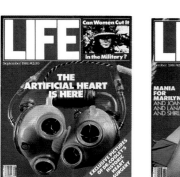

SEPTEMBER 1981

OCTOBER 1981

NOVEMBER 1981

DECEMBER 1981

CLASSIC PHOTOS

A glowing (pregnant) Princess of Wales enchanted Welshmen on her first visit.

President Sadat's assassins fired into the Cairo reviewing stand where he fell under upturned chairs.

CURRENTS AND EVENTS

WORLD: Riots Spurred by Unemployment Sweep Britain • Prince Charles Weds Lady Diana Spencer • Ten IRA Hunger Strikers Die of Starvation in Belfast Prison • U.S. Lifts Soviet Grain Embargo • West German Consortium Signs Deal to Bring Soviet Gas by Pipeline to Western Europe • Polish General Jaruzelski Becomes Premier in Move to Counter Widespread Unrest, Thousands Arrested • Socialist Mitterrand Defeats Giscard for French Presidency • Basque Terrorists Strike in Spain • John Paul II Shot • Italy's Red Brigade Kidnaps U.S. NATO General • Greek Socialist Papandreou Elected PM • Soviet Nuclear Sub Runs Aground in Swedish Waters • Iran Frees U.S. Embassy Hostages After 444 Days • Violence in Lebanon Escalates • Israeli Planes Destroy Iraqi Nuclear Reactor • Egypt's Sadat Assassinated, Mubarak Takes Over • Israel Annexes the Golan Heights • U.S. Sends Aid to El Salvador Government, Mexico and France Ask UN to Recognize Guerrillas • Japan Limits Auto Exports to U.S. • China's Gang of Four, Including Mao's Widow, Convicted of Political Crimes.

U.S.A.: Congress Approves $37 Billion Tax Cut • President, Three Others Seriously Wounded by Assailant • Photographer Arrested for Atlanta Child Murders • Major League Baseball Players Strike • Fruit Flies Threaten California Crops • Government Decertifies Air Controllers Union, Fires Strikers • Skywalks in Kansas City Hotel Collapse, 113 Die, Hundreds Injured.

FIRSTS: Pocket-size TVs • Surgical Treatment of Embryo.

MOVIES: The Competition • Every Which Way You Can • Nine to Five • Breaker Morant • Absence of Malice • Arthur • Atlantic City • Body Heat • Chariots of Fire • Endless Love • Excalibur • Eyewitness • Fort Apache, the Bronx • The Four Seasons • The French Lieutenant's Woman • History of the World, Part I • Mommie Dearest • My Dinner with Andre • Prince of the City • Raiders of the Lost Ark • S.O.B. • Superman II • Stripes • Rich and Famous • Ragtime • Raggedy Man • Wolfen • La Cage aux Folles.

SONGS: Physical • Endless Love • Bette Davis Eyes • Jessie's Girl • I Love a Rainy Night • 9 to 5 • Rapture • The Tide Is High • Slow Hand • Just the Two of Us • Love on the Rocks • Woman • All Those Years Ago • Queen of Hearts • Guilty • I Don't Need You • For Your Eyes Only • Elvira • America • The Winner Takes It All • Hill Street Blues • I Made It Through the Rain • How 'Bout Us • Somebody's Knockin' • Time • The Old Songs • Really Wanna Know You • Touch Me When We're Dancing • Fire and Ice • Say Goodbye to Hollywood • Modern Girl • Fade Away • Who Do You Think You're Foolin' • Fool That I Am • On and On and On.

STAGE: The Dresser • Mass Appeal • Entertaining Mr. Sloane • Key Exchange • A Soldier's Play • Piaf • Woman of the Year • Sophisticated Ladies • Merrily We Roll Along.

BOOKS: Noble House (Clavell) • The Hotel New Hampshire (Irving) • Cujo (King) • Gorky Park (Smith) • The Third Deadly Sin (Sanders) • The Glitter Dome (Wambaugh) • The Cardinal Sins (Greeley) • Tar Baby (Morrison) • Rabbit Is Rich (Updike) • Zuckerman Unbound (Roth) • God Emperor of Dune (Herbert) • A Light in the Attic (Silverstein) • The Sage of Monticello (Malone) • The Soul of a New Machine (Kidder) • Mornings on Horseback (McCullough) • In the Belly of the Beast (Abbott) • The Second Stage (Friedan).

FADS: Punk Fashions • Rubik's Cubes • Jelly Beans.

"Billions of dollars over budget and fully three years behind schedule," the space shuttle Columbia emerged from a Florida hangar for its first flight. Ill-fated Challenger was launched two years later.

This disembodied trio appeared in an album of ancestors titled "Battle of the Bones." The story concerned the dispute between paleoanthropologists Richard Leakey and Donald Johanson over the origins of Homo sapiens.

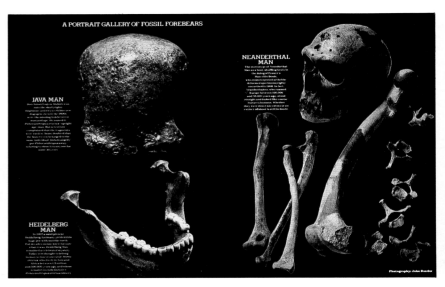

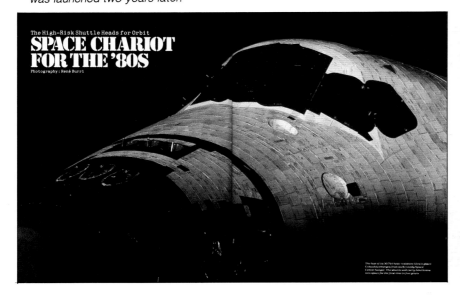

When Argentina's military junta ended leftist terrorism in 1976, it instituted its own. "No fewer than 100 children under seven were listed as disappeared," this seven-page report observed, "an indication that the junta's aim was to intimidate an entire society."

It was to be four more years before Mengele hunters would discover that Auschwitz's "Angel of Death" had drowned in 1979 in Brazil.

The album of exclusive full-page pictures that followed this double portrait—of the Lennons enjoying son Sean and their haven from celebrity in Manhattan's Dakota co-op—ended with this afterline: "All That's Left Are the Songs."

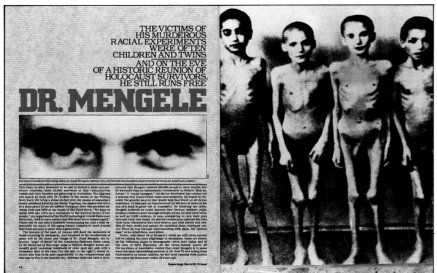

Fear and horror gripped Atlanta. In a year and a half, 19 black children had been kidnapped and slain. Soon after this article was published, chronicling the anguish of their mothers, one of history's greatest manhunts ended with the arrest of Wayne Williams, 23, a black photographer. He received two life sentences for the killings.

Beeched on the Dorset coast in her costume for the filming of John Fowles's best-seller, Meryl Streep looked out over the period story's locale.

MARVELOUS MERYL
SHE IS AMERICA'S FINEST ACTRESS

No other actress her age can match her astounding range. None can match her stage performances in Shakespeare, Chekhov or Brecht; and she can sing and dance too. In *The Deer Hunter* and in *Kramer vs. Kramer*, Streep created complex women on the screen. She is not pretty, perhaps, but many find in her a singular beauty—fragile, feminine, absolutely compelling. In little more than two years, she has become one of the most sought-after actresses in the world. Her next role is that of the enigmatic heroine in the long-anticipated film version of John Fowles's novel, *The French Lieutenant's Woman*. Her name alone will be billed above the title—proof that at 31 she is at the top of her profession.

A Moment Alone at Last

Another exclusive place LIFE visited was "The Private World of Katharine Hepburn." While catching Kate sailing with her brother, the photo also showed her Connecticut house for the first time.

This portrait of the Prince of Wales and his new princess was an intimate installment in the long line of "LIFE Goes to" stories—in this instance "LIFE Goes to the Private Doings After the Royal Wedding." The photographer was Lord Lichfield, a cousin to the queen.

Zeno, a world-class collector of M.M. material, was part of LIFE's own collection—of Foofs ("for anyone who doesn't know, a Friend of Old Film, a fanatical collector of artifacts from the movie past").

SPECIAL PROJECT AMERICAN RENEWAL

TO REVITALIZE THE NATION

On these pages LIFE presents a selection of stories addressed to the need for a national revitalization. It is part of a more comprehensive special project being carried out and published simultaneously by Time Inc.'s seven magazines. Following an introductory essay by Editor-in-Chief Henry Anatole Grunwald, LIFE's stories focus on our system of education. The first is an article by Chester E. Finn Jr. on the need for more rigor and higher standards in the teaching of our children. Then, in picture stories, we show innovative approaches at three very different high schools around the country that have uplifted both the quality of education and the spirit of the school. Finally, through the portraits of five enterprising individuals, we examine the present state of one of our most cherished national ideals —the American pioneer in a raw and beautiful land.

Troubled classroom 82   Young and old together 122
Inner city success 102   Kids who teach kids 116
A new pioneer with a better idea 130

This in-depth poll uncovered all the expected shades of opinion. The bottom line: While 56% of women felt abortion was morally wrong, 67% agreed a woman who wants one should be allowed to get it legally. The statistical results were combined with a story titled "One Woman Makes Her Difficult Choice."

In an unprecedented editorial project, conceived by Editor-in-Chief Henry Grunwald, all Time Inc. publications drew attention to the need for national revitalization. LIFE's contribution was 41 pages calling for better education and use of natural resources. This was the opening page.

Do you personally know anyone who has had an abortion?
Yes.......................... 55%
No............................ 45%

Thinking about the woman or women you know who have had abortions, would you say that, generally speaking, it was the right thing for them to do or not the right thing to do?
Right thing................. 66%
Not the right thing......... 28%

Should a girl who is under 18 years of age have to notify her parents before she can have an abortion?
Yes.......................... 78%
No........................... 18%

If an unmarried high school girl becomes pregnant, do you think her mother should suggest to her that she have the baby or have an abortion?
Have the baby.............. 44%
Have an abortion........... 20%
Not sure................... 36%

Have you yourself ever had an abortion?
Yes........................... 9%
No........................... 90%

Would you say that having an abortion was the right thing for you or not the right thing?
Right thing................. 90%
Not the right thing......... 8%

Would you say you feel very strongly about the abortion issue, somewhat strongly or not that strongly?
Very strongly............... 48%
Somewhat strongly.......... 27%
Not that strongly.......... 21%

Do you feel it would be morally wrong or not morally wrong for an unmarried teenager to have an abortion?
Morally wrong.............. 41%
Not morally wrong.......... 48%
Not sure................... 11%

1982

Even as the magazine published "Trouble in the Family," part of a series on the effects of emotional stress on interpersonal relationships, there was the potential for a wrench within its own editorial tribe. Philip Kunhardt stepped down from the managing editor's post.

LIFE Visits Solzhenitsyn
In Exile in America

"He could breathe fresh air only at certain fixed hours permitted by the prison administration," Aleksandr Solzhenitsyn wrote of a prisoner in his 1968 novel, *The First Circle*, adding, "Yet there was inviolable peace in his soul." Today Solzhenitsyn breathes the fresh air of America anytime he chooses, but he claims he is not at peace. After 11 years in Soviet prisons and Siberia the Nobel prizewinning author was declared a nonperson and banished from Russia by Soviet secret police. Ironically, he still lives in relative isolation. "No Trespassing" signs warn would-be intruders away from his 50 acres of woodland in the hamlet of Cavendish, Vt. His family has been pursued by the press and has received threatening letters. But for the first time in their eight years of exile, Solzhenitsyn, 63, and his wife, Natalya, 42, opened their gate to a photographer and reporter team (Harry Benson and LIFE's David Friend) to share reflections on their primary goal: unmasking the bitter history of the Soviet state. The Solzhenitsyns have created a little Russia in New England, but "separation from our native land becomes more difficult with each passing year," says Natalya. She and her husband hope to see a free Russia in their lifetime—and to return. "If that possibility becomes real," she says, "we will not lose a single day."

The author, in a Kazakhstan beaver hat, and his wife stroll outside the Vermont home they bought six years ago. With additions, it now looks like a ski lodge.

44

Beginning in November 1978 and continuing for the next three years, reporter David Friend exchanged 10 letters with Solzhenitsyn to make this Visit possible.

JANUARY 1982

FEBRUARY 1982

MARCH 1982

APRIL 1982

MAY 1982

JUNE 1982

JULY 1982

AUGUST 1982

SEPTEMBER 1982

OCTOBER 1982

NOVEMBER 1982

DECEMBER 1982

Issues published that winter and spring were smoothly guided in his absence by Eleanor Graves, the executive editor. Then Richard Stolley, the ex-LIFEr who had from its inception pushed the weekly *People* to the top of its class, was asked by the editor-in-chief to take over.

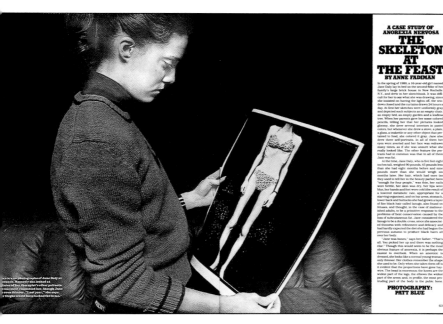

A CASE STUDY OF ANOREXIA NERVOSA
THE SKELETON AT THE FEAST
BY ANNE FADIMAN

PHOTOGRAPHY: PATT BLUE

"Every era has its peculiar disorders," read the introduction to this article. Reminding readers that Freud had treated female hysteria, it went on to observe, "If there is an equivalent today, it is anorexia."

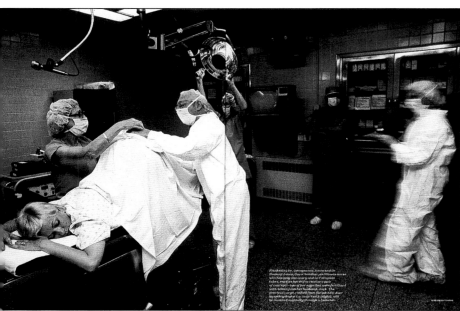

Portraits of 23 of the more than 120 babies conceived in lab dishes since 1978 opened this essay on in-vitro fertilization titled "Small Miracles of Love & Science."

TREATING THE EMOTIONS: Part II
TROUBLE IN THE FAMILY

Photography: Michael O'Brien   Reporting: Janet Mason   Text: Jeff Wheelwright

According to this installment of the popular series, to a therapist "the interactions of household members can be likened to the emotional expressions of a single patient."

CLASSIC PHOTOS

Ailing Henry Fonda and his On Golden Pond *Oscar were fussed over by his wife Shirlee, daughter Amy (right) and granddaughter Vanessa.*

This self-portrait became evidence in the trial of John Hinckley, the would-be presidential assassin.

CURRENTS AND EVENTS

WORLD: Argentina Surrenders Falklands to Britain After 10-Week War • IRA Bombs Kill Nine British Soldiers, Injure 50 in London • Andropov Heads U.S.S.R. After Brezhnev's Death • U.S., Soviet Strategic Arms Reduction Talks Begin in Geneva • Italian Police Rescue U.S. NATO General Held by Red Brigade Terrorists • Kohl Succeeds Schmidt as West Germany's Chancellor • Social Democrats Under Palme Regain Control in Sweden • Israel Invades Lebanon, PLO Dispersed • Israel Draws Ire for Massacre in Refugee Camps Under Its Sway • President-Elect Gemayel Assassinated in Beirut • Israel Returns Sinai Peninsula to Egypt • Iran's Premier Ghotbzadeh Executed • Right Wing Wins Control in El Salvador • China Reorganizes Bureaucracy, Adopts New Constitution • Monaco's Princess Grace Dies in Auto Crash • Britain's Prince William Born.

U.S.A.: ERA Falls Short of Ratification by Three States • AT&T Settles Antitrust Suit, Reorganization of Ma Bell Gets Under Way • Unification Church's Reverend Moon Convicted of Tax Evasion • Shultz Succeeds Haig as Secretary of State • House Committee Investigating Toxic Waste Cleanup Finds Environmental Agency Head Gorsuch in Contempt • NFL Players Strike for Eight Weeks • Carmaker John De Lorean Busted for Cocaine Conspiracy • Marked Increases in Herpes, AIDS, Toxic Shock Syndrome Raise Widespread Concern • Socialite Claus von Bülow Found Guilty of Attempted Wife Murder • N.J. Senator Williams Resigns in Wake of Abscam Probe • Henry Fonda, Ingrid Bergman, John Belushi Die • Capsules Laced with Cyanide Kill Seven in Chicago.

FIRSTS: Disk Camera • Permanent Artificial Heart in Human.

MOVIES: Reds • On Golden Pond • Neighbors • Sharkey's Machine • Whose Life Is It Anyway? • Taps • Buddy Buddy • Rollover • Pennies from Heaven • Ghost Story • E.T. • Missing • An Officer and a Gentleman • Victor/Victoria • Author! Author! • Blade Runner • Conan the Barbarian • Das Boot • Deathtrap • Diner • My Favorite Year • One from the Heart • Porky's • Quest for Fire • Rocky III • The World According to Garp • Tron.

SONGS: Eye of the Tiger • Ebony and Ivory • Chariots of Fire • Rosanna • Key Largo • You Should Hear How She Talks About You • Making Love • Love's Been a Little Bit Hard on Me • Love Is in Control • Always on My Mind • Turn Your Love Around • Even the Nights Are Better • I've Never Been to Me • One Hundred Ways • You Can Do Magic • Take It Away • Love Will Turn You Around • Yesterday's Songs • Oh Pretty Woman • What's Forever For.

STAGE: Amadeus • Agnes of God • Come Back to the Five and Dime Jimmy Dean, Jimmy Dean • Master Harold and the Boys • Torch Song Trilogy • Twice Around the Park • Dream Girls • Pump Boys and Dinettes • Nine • Cats • Joseph and the Amazing Technicolor Dreamcoat • Little Shop of Horrors.

BOOKS: Space (Michener) • The Parsifal Mosaic (Ludlum) • Mistral's Daughter (Krantz) • North and South (Jakes) • The Color Purple (Walker) • Pinball (Kosinski) • Deadeye Dick (Vonnegut) • 2010 (Clarke) • The Man from Petersburg (Follett) • Workout Book (Fonda) • Living, Loving and Learning (Buscaglia) • Megatrends (Naisbitt) • Growing Up (Baker) • Keeping Faith (Carter) • Years of Upheaval (Kissinger) • Edie (Stein, Plimpton) • America in Search of Itself (White) • American Journey (Reeves).

FADS: Brooke Shields Dolls • Personal Computers • Deely Bobbers • Tuxedos for Women.

When a recurrence of
Liz-ophilia smote the editors
of the monthly, they decided
to make a clean breast of
their longtime affair.

Theoni Aldredge's costumes for this "glitzy, glamorous
Broadway musical," about a Supremes-like trio, "telescope a
decade of outlandish show-biz fashion, with dresses layered
like artichokes and sheaths resembling sequined snakeskins."

At President Reagan's 70th birthday
party in the White House East Room,
he graciously cut in on Frank Sinatra
dancing with First Lady Nancy.

Reggie and Elsa, her Lhasa Apsos, aren't in the least dazzled by their mistress's fabled 33.19 carat diamond that Burton gave her.

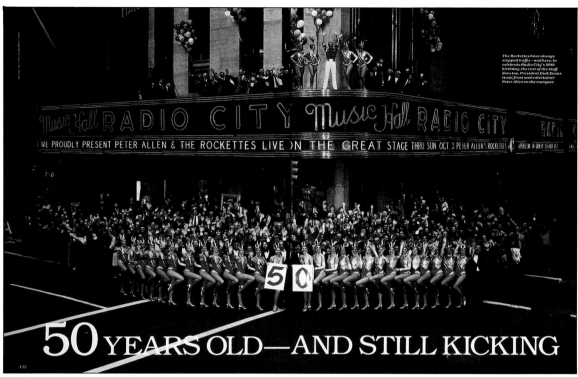

The Rockettes have always stopped traffic—and here, to celebrate Radio City's 50th birthday, the rest of the staff does too. President Dick Evans is out front and entertainer Peter Allen on the marquee.

50 YEARS OLD—AND STILL KICKING

The magazine's salute to an entertainment institution referred to the famously disciplined Rockettes as "the world's most beautiful centipede."

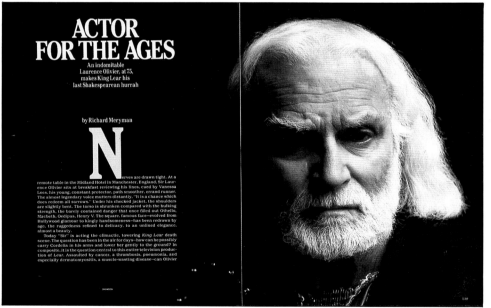

ACTOR FOR THE AGES

An indomitable Laurence Olivier, at 75, makes King Lear his last Shakespearean hurrah

by Richard Meryman

N remote table in the Midland Hotel in Manchester, England, Sir Laurence Olivier sits at breakfast reviewing his lines, cued by Vanessa Lees, his young, constant protector, path smoother, errand runner. The almost legendary voice mutters distantly. "It is a chance which does redeem all sorrows." Under his checked jacket, the shoulders are slightly bent. The torso is shrunken compared with the bulking strength, the barely contained danger that once filed out Othello, Macbeth, Oedipus, Henry V. The square, famous face—evolved from Hollywood glamour to kingly handsomeness—has been redrawn by age, the ruggedness refined to delicacy, to an unlined elegance, almost a beauty.

Today "Sir" is acting the climactic, towering King Lear death scene. The question has been in the air for days—how can he possibly carry Cordelia in his arms and lower her gently to the ground? In composite, it is the question central to this entire television production of Lear. Assaulted by cancer, a thrombosis, pneumonia, and especially dermatomyositis, a muscle-wasting disease—can Olivier

Could Olivier (to complete the unfinished question at the end of the text as shown) carry, at 75, the crushing weight of a Shakespearean tragedy? The answer was a resounding yes. LIFE quoted King Lear: "No, I will weep no more. In such a night/ To shut me out? Pour on; I will endure."

nk Sinatra waltzed the First Lady around the East Room. Ronnie cut in.

149

An actress the weekly LIFE had helped to stardom— way back when she had a last name, Olsson—was still a favorite subject of the magazine "a thousand adolescent fantasies" later.

ANN-MARGRET

GETS HER ACT TOGETHER AND TAKES IT ON THE ROAD

The face—et cetera—that launched a thousand adolescent fantasies salutes her fans in Dallas (above) and her entourage in Atlanta (right).

In 1959, in the annual student variety show at New Trier High School, she squeezed into a chartreuse sheath slit beyond teenage propriety and wiggled her way through an old Irving Berlin number, graphically illustrating such lyrics as "She started this heat wave / By letting her seat wave." Winnetka, Ill., had never seen anything like her; fathers (as one confessed later) "were melting in their chairs." Twenty-three years later, the heat wave is still sizzling, having survived two decades of sometimes snuffy reviews and a near fatal accident. Ann-Margret, 41, is currently undulating cross-country in her first U.S. road show. The ultraslick production—which includes lasers, a 20-piece orchestra, seven dancers and three backup singers—has broken box-office records in Atlantic City, Atlanta and Dallas, and may be headed for Broadway. Dripping with perspiration and black-and-blue from being upended in a torrid dance, the star leaped offstage after a recent ovation into the arms of her husband-manager, Roger Smith. "I feel like I've been shot out of a cannon!" she squealed, as breathless and aroused as if she were still melting those Winnetka fathers instead of 4,000 screaming Atlantans at $15 per. "Yahoo!"

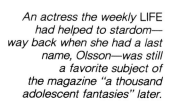

1983

Old hands were joined by new, predominantly women, in probing the big issues of the '80s

New social issues had been shouldering their way to the forefront among the sempiternal ones— among them, the scary spread of herpes, the rush of runaway teenagers and the climb in teenage pregnancies. So, the challenge—as ever it had been—was to hire or assign writers and reporters

A substantial excerpt from Shana Alexander's book on Jean Harris and the death of the Scarsdale Diet doctor was published a decade after Alexander wrote her last Feminine Eye column for LIFE.

JEAN HARRIS'S DEFENSE WAS BUNGLED, THE AUTHOR SAYS, AND HER 15-YEAR SENTENCE WAS A MISCARRIAGE OF

JUSTICE
BY SHANA ALEXANDER

THE KENNEDY ASSASSINATION, 20 YEARS LATER

Of the 135 million Americans now living who recall the events that began on November 22, most know exactly what they were doing when heard about the shooting of John F. Kennedy. It that kind of moment—terrifying, deeply painful yond rationality—and one could struggle back bearable reality only by framing the huge unacc able truth, a vital young President gone, within

4 DAYS THA

IT WAS AN UTTERLY ORDINARY NOVEMBER MORNING

Kids make Thanksgiving pies in Virginia.

Philadelphia bus gets holiday wreath.

Cops win degrees in Louisville.

Reporting: Doris G. Kinney, with Marcia Smith (Dallas) and Penny Ward Moser (Washington, D.C.)

The focus of this in-depth report was an 86-year-old home named for Edna Gladney, a crusader for "nobody's children," whom Greer Garson had portrayed in the 1941 film Blossoms in the Dust.

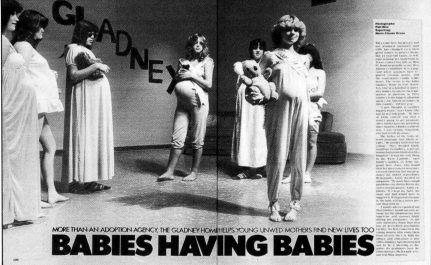

GLADNEY

Photography: Patti Dietz
Reporting: Marie-Claude Wrenn

MORE THAN AN ADOPTION AGENCY, THE GLADNEY HOME HELPS YOUNG UNWED MOTHERS FIND NEW LIVES TOO

BABIES HAVING BABIES

HEALING HERPES
The Heartache Is Worse than the Virus

"We're not curing herpes," said Dr. Michael Truppin, the subject in this story on the newest form of one of the oldest afflictions, "we're making the misery easier to live with."

March 1983

PRINCE RAINIER TALKS CANDIDLY ABOUT HIS FAMILY, THE ACCIDENT AND THE FUTURE OF MONACO

The Legacy of Princess Grace

Photography: Eric Feinblatt and Richard McLeod

Prince Rainier finally acceded to a request from LIFE for cooperation in reporting the impact on Monaco's royal family of Princess Grace's death. When the word came, Managing Editor Stolley flew to Monte Carlo to interview the monarch personally.

in tune with the changing times. In LIFE's fifth decade that meant, and not as a matter of equal rights, the journalistic need for more of the talents of women to provide insights that could add special distinction to both text and photographs. Their work gave a new dimension to the magazine.

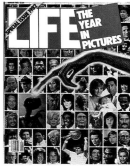
JANUARY 1983

FEBRUARY 1983

MARCH 1983

To mark the anniversary of JFK's assassination, the editors mounted a 24-page section that recapped day by day the traumatic shocks and mournful events that had occurred two decades earlier.

nal margins of one's own life. That tragic event and the four days that followed it ew the stunned attention of the world. "... The mind and heart stand still," said British me Minister Alec Douglas-Home. "Her gallant boy is dead. We mourn here with you, or sad American people," wrote the Irish playwright Sean O'Casey. Watching that cking and mournful weekend of history unfold on television, the whole country was wn together with extraordinary unanimity. On the 20th anniversary of the assassation of President Kennedy, LIFE offers on these pages an album of refreshed recection and new perspectives on four days that still burn in the national memory.

FRIDAY

STOPPED AMERICA

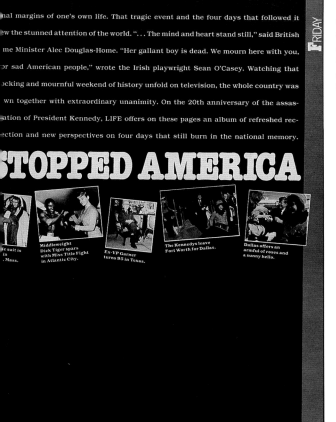

e suit is in Mass.

Middleweight Dick Tiger spars with Miss Title Fight in Atlantic City.

Ex-VP Garner turns 95 in Texas.

The Kennedys leave Fort Worth for Dallas.

Dallas offers an armful of roses and a sunny hello.

APRIL 1983

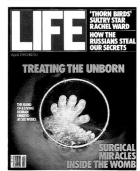
TREATING THE UNBORN

MAY 1983

JUNE 1983

Streets of the Lost
RUNAWAY KIDS EKE OUT A MEAN LIFE IN SEATTLE

After working with photographer Mark for three months on Seattle's streets, writer McCall became so involved in the lives of her subjects that she took a leave to develop this report into a documentary film. It won an Academy Award nomination.

JULY 1983

AUGUST 1983

An Editor's Note recalled the LIFE-long fascination with the human heart. It ranged from a 1937 story on cardiologists to Lennart Nilsson's 1968 peek inside the arteries to Tommy Thompson's 1970s pieces about surgeons Cooley and DeBakey.

The family gather in the living room of Chateau de Marchais, Petit hunting lodge in France. From left: Stephanie, Al

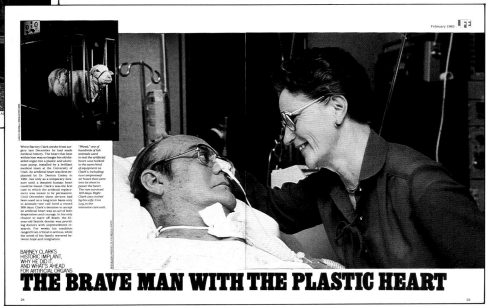

February 1983 LIFE

THE BRAVE MAN WITH THE PLASTIC HEART

BARNEY CLARK'S HISTORIC IMPLANT, WHY HE DID IT, AND WHAT'S AHEAD FOR ARTIFICIAL ORGANS

SEPTEMBER 1983

OCTOBER 1983

NOVEMBER 1983

DECEMBER 1983

CLASSIC PHOTOS

Plugging physical fitness, Ronald Reagan threw his weight around a little.

British frigate Antelope, *hit off the Falklands, exploded in San Carlos Bay.*

CURRENTS AND EVENTS

WORLD: Conservatives Triumph in British Elections • Millions Demonstrate Against U.S. Missile Deployments in Western Europe • IRA Bomb Explodes in London's Harrods • Former Nazi Klaus Barbie Extradited from Bolivia to France • Poles Continue Pro-Solidarity Demonstrations, Lech Walesa Wins Nobel Peace Prize • Adolf Hitler Diaries Prove to Be Forgeries • Armenian Terrorists Bomb Paris Airport • Israeli Commission Investigates Massacre by Christian Phalangists of Palestinian Refugees in Beirut • Shamir Succeeds Begin, Heads Coalition Israeli Government • Terrorists Destroy U.S. Embassy, Marine HQ in Beirut • U.S. Troops in Granada Overthrow Communist Regime • Philippines Opposition Leader Aquino Slain at Manila Airport • Sikh Separatists Escalate Violence in Punjab.

U.S.A.: EPA Head Anne Gorsuch Burford Resigns, Agency's Rita Lavelle Convicted of Perjury • Teamsters Boss Roy Williams Sentenced for Fraud, Conspiracy • Government Buys Out Contaminated Times Beach, Mo. • Surviving Japanese-Americans, Detained During WWII, Get Cash Compensation • Dr. Martin Luther King Jr.'s Birthday Becomes Federal Holiday • Interior Secretary James Watt Quits Amid Controversy over Racial Remark • Supreme Court Strikes Down State Laws Limiting Free-Choice Abortions • Two U.S. Representatives Censured for Sexual Relations with Congressional Pages • Washington State Public Power Company Defaults on $2.25 Billion Debt • Milwaukee Youths Use Home Computers to Invade Records of N.Y.C. Cancer Center, New Mexico Nuclear Weapons Research Installation.

FIRSTS: Black Miss America (Williams) • American Woman in Space (Ride) • Compact Discs.

MOVIES: Gandhi • Sophie's Choice • Tootsie • The Verdict • That Championship Season • Airplane II • Honkytonk Man • Best Friends • Six Weeks • The Big Chill • Blue Thunder • Educating Rita • Flashdance • The King of Comedy • Lovesick • The Man with Two Brains • Max Dugan Returns • National Lampoon's Vacation • Never Say Never Again • Psycho II • Return of the Jedi • The Right Stuff • Risky Business • Star 80 • Staying Alive • Superman III • Tender Mercies • Terms of Endearment • The Star Chamber • The Year of Living Dangerously • Zelig • Yentl • Berlin Alexanderplatz • Cross Creek • Fanny and Alexander.

SONGS: Billie Jean • What a Feeling • Down Under • Beat It • Maneater • Maniac • She Works Hard for the Money • Let's Dance • Never Gonna Let You Go • Up Where We Belong • Puttin' On the Ritz • You Can't Hurry Love • Allentown • Tell Her About It • The Girl Is Mine • All Right • Stand Back • Don't Let It End • I've Got a Rock 'n' Roll Heart.

STAGE: Brighton Beach Memoirs • 'Night Mother • My One and Only • Extremities • Fool for Love • Merlin • La Cage aux Folles.

BOOKS: Ironweed (Kennedy) • Heartburn (Ephron) • Poland (Michener) • Pet Sematary (King) • The Little Drummer Girl (Le Carré) • Christine (King) • The Name of the Rose (Eco) • Hollywood Wives (Collins) • Ancient Evenings (Mailer) • The Anatomy Lesson (Roth) • Days of Vengeance (Petrakis) • In Search of Excellence (Peters, Waterman) • While Reagan Slept (Buchwald) • Lost in the Cosmos (Percy) • Salvador (Didion) • Blue Highways (Moon) • The Price of Power (Hersh) • Dashiell Hammett (Johnson) • In the Spirit of Crazy Horse (Matthiessen).

FADS: Cabbage Patch Dolls • Break Dancing.

This gardenful of brides and grooms was brought together by the Unification Church and the telephoto lens.

Visiting the master sculptor was a natural for LIFE—still art crazy after all these years. Work-obsessed, a fretful Moore noted, "We have so little time and so much left to do."

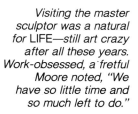

Under the headline "Putting Miami in the Pink," the magazine pictured the results of the latest wrap session by the artist Christo: edging 11 islands off Miami with six million sq. ft. of punk-pink plastic.

Twenty-one years after Miss Marmelstein, Streisand, now a superstar, essayed a boy-girl role in her own filming of an Isaac Bashevis Singer story.

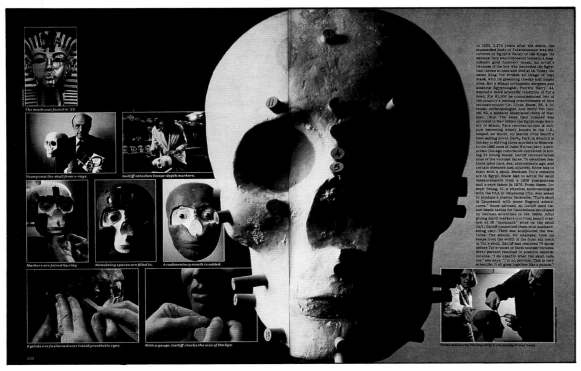

Face completed, Tut stares verily from his pedestal. "Put some hair on him," Snow says, "and he'd get lost in downtown Cairo."

As the King Tut exhibition traveled to popular acclaim, facial reconstruction experts performed their magic step-by-step to re-create the monarch's features. Result: the oldest known new face ever to appear in the magazine's pages.

Butz, with six-month-old friend, was one of seven NFL stars the editors looked at close up to show that "there is elegance amid the mayhem," that there is more to these outsize athletes than just beef.

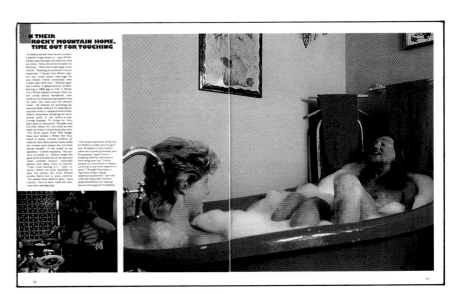

Superstar Willie Nelson and his wife, Connie, became the latest in the magazine's long line of celebrity tubbers when LIFE visited their Colorado retreat: four houses on a 122-acre spread.

A SERIES ON REGIONAL COOKING
NORMANDY

Both the magazine and former executive editor Eleanor Graves, under contract, returned to old predilections with a series on regional cuisines. Graves had produced the classic series Great Dinners for the weekly.

These old baseballs were among the items uncovered in "the nation's attic," the Smithsonian Institution. The story pointed out that 98% of the hoard stored there is never seen by the public.

1984

As patriotism surged, the presses used lots of red, white and blue ink

Orwell's year turned out to be not at all Orwellian, in the dire, alienated sense of his novel *1984*. It was an Olympic year, a presidential election year and the 40th anniversary of D-Day, all of which conspired to make it a time of national pride. The President urged Americans to "stand tall," and not only the U.S. athletes (four years after missing the Moscow Summer

CARL LEWIS: SPRINTS AND LONG JUMP
Whether he is exploding out of the starting blocks or lounging around his Houston house, Lewis, 22, throws off bolts of energy. "I want to get every inch out of life," says the speedster, who hopes to replicate Jesse Owens's 1936 quadruple gold medal performance. Lewis already has one record: a yet-to-be-released vocal, *Going for the Gold.*

AMERICAN EXCELLENCE

A year ago 9,700 of the country's premier athletes began vying for 589 berths in the XXIII Olympiad. On July 28 the American team—ranging from a 447-pound North Carolina wrestler to an 86-pound Texas gymnast, from a 46-year-old Georgia marksman to a Virginia swimmer who just turned 15—will join the march into the Los Angeles Coliseum, and the Games will be on. Photographer Co Rentmeester logged 30,000 miles to create this portfolio of those who represent our nation's best.

Photography: Co Rentmeester   Reporting: Victoria Kohn

Quadruple threat (not counting pop vocals) Carl Lewis, off and running before a backdrop of the Stars and Stripes, was the frontispiece of a 22-page essay on U.S. hopefuls in the Olympics Special Issue.

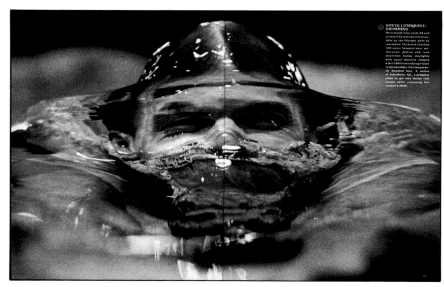

Photographer Co Rentmeester let gold-medal candidate Lundquist's bow wave serve as a distorting lens, converting the breaststroker into some sort of sea monster.

This 120-page extra issue was on the stands two months, bracketing the games.

The New Jersey *fired a dry-run broadside into Lebanese waters. She had broken in her 16-inchers at the Truk islands in World War II and had got off 5,688 shells aimed at North Vietnam.*

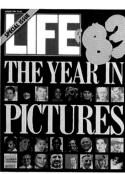

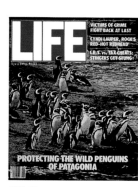

Games) but the city of Los Angeles as well strove to make the August games the most spectacular Olympiad ever. With the help of the Soviet Union and its Eastern Bloc, which retaliated for 1980 by refusing to participate, they succeeded: 174 medals and show-biz-orchestrated fireworks gave the sports carnival a red-white-and-blue finish.

GRIM WORK FOR STUNNERS AND STICKERS

In a story on Aleut seal harvesters, two longtime LIFE concerns—ecology and man's inhumanity to lesser orders—conflicted slightly. The piece quoted an Aleutian view that the slaughter helped an endangered species: the Aleut people.

Four decades after history's greatest invasion, LIFE joined other veterans and multitudes of their fellow countrymen in a D-Day pilgrimage to Normandy. They visited the storied beaches and the resting place of 9,386 who never left.

ON THE BLUFFS THEY CAPTURED, A FINAL RESTING PLACE

The 20th anniversary of the beloved mop-heads' conquest of America was the occasion for the editors to break out dozens of archival photographs of the singers and their fans.

THE BEATLES

MAY 1984

JUNE 1984

JULY 1984

AUGUST 1984

CURRENTS AND EVENTS

WORLD: Allies Mark D-Day Observances • Pact Reached for Hong Kong to Pass from British to Chinese Control in 1997 • PM Thatcher Escapes IRA Bomb in Brighton, England, Hotel • Chernenko Succeeds Andropov as Soviet Chief • Cosmonauts Spend Record 237 Days in Space • Pro-Solidarity Polish Priest Slain by Police, Massive Demonstrations Follow • U.S. Embassy Annex in Beirut Bombed, 14 Die • Peres Takes Office as Israel's PM • World Court Settles U.S.-Canada Dispute over Georges Bank Fishing Rights • Oil Tanker Runs Aground, Huge Oil Slick Fouls Texas Coast • Soviet Oil Tanker Strikes Mine Off Nicaraguan Coast, Incident Exposes U.S. Responsibility • Duarte Wins Salvadoran Presidential Runoff • Cuba Accepts Return by U.S. of 2,746 Undesirable Refugees • Indira Gandhi Assassinated by Sikh Extremists • Poison-Gas Leak in Bhopal, India, Kills More than 2,500 • U.S.S.R., 13 Other Nations Boycott Summer Olympic Games.

U.S.A.: Reagan-Bush Ticket Wins in Landslide • Reagan, Bypassing Congress, Sends $32 Million in Emergency Aid to El Salvador • Supreme Court Rules Home Use of TV Videotapes Legal, Bars Sex Discrimination Only in School Programs Receiving Federal Funds, Allows Some Evidence Obtained Illegally to Be Used in Criminal Trials • Labor Secretary Donovan Indicted for Fraud • Vietnam Veterans Win Class Action Suit Against Manufacturers of Agent Orange, Get $180 Million Settlement • Automaker John De Lorean Acquitted of Cocaine-Trafficking Charges.

FIRSTS: Woman Vice-Presidential Candidate (Ferraro) • Woman to Walk in Space (Savitskaya) • Solo Trans-Atlantic Balloon Flight (Kittinger).

MOVIES: Places in the Heart • The River • Ghostbusters • Gremlins • Indiana Jones • Romancing the Stone • The Karate Kid • The Little Drummer Girl • A Soldier's Story • Under the Volcano • The Natural • The Killing Fields • Starman • Beverly Hills Cop • 2010 • Purple Rain • A Passage to India • Moscow on the Hudson • Racing with the Moon • Broadway Danny Rose • Splash • Police Academy • Red Dawn • Star Trek III • The Flamingo Kid • All of Me • Amadeus • All the Right Moves • Garbo Talks • Conan the Destroyer • Hotel New Hampshire • Silkwood • The Dresser • Scarface • Gorky Park • The Pope of Greenwich Village • The Goodbye People • The Terminator • The Muppets Take Manhattan • This Is Spinal Tap • Nightmare on Elm Street • The Bostonians • Greystoke: The Legend of Tarzan • Swann in Love.

SONGS: What's Love Got to Do with It • Say Say Say • Jump • All Night Long • Let's Hear It for the Boy • Girls Just Want to Have Fun • Time After Time • Joanna • I Just Called to Say I Love You • I Guess That's Why They Call It the Blues • Uptown Girl • To All the Girls I've Loved Before • Sad Songs • Islands in the Stream • Love Somebody • An Innocent Man • I'm So Excited • When Doves Cry.

STAGE: Noises Off • Glengarry Glen Ross • Hurlyburly • Ma Rainey's Black Bottom • The Tap Dance Kid • The Rink • Sunday in the Park with George • Baby.

BOOKS: Lincoln (Vidal) • Tough Guys Don't Dance (Mailer) • God Knows (Heller) • The Aquitaine Progression (Ludlum) • The Fourth Protocol (Forsyth) • The Haj (Uris) • The Life and Hard Times of Heidi Abromowitz (Rivers) • The Sicilian (Puzo) • Iacocca: An Autobiography • Loving Each Other (Buscaglia) • ". . . And Ladies of the Club" (Santmyer) • Home Before Dark (Cheever) • Him with His Foot in His Mouth (Bellow) • Machine Dreams (Phillips) • Love and War (Jakes) • Women Coming of Age (Fonda, McCarthy).

FADS: Light Foods, Beverages • Men's Underwear for Women • Trivial Pursuit • Cazal Eyeglasses • Designer Bandages.

RICH AND RECLUSIVE

On the beach below his Carmel, Calif., retreat, Jackson studies the sunset from his restored 1932 Ford—one of the 64 cars in his $2.5 million collection.

The Prince and Princess of Wales and Prince William, 2, showed off Prince Harry, 20 days old.

"I don't want people to know me completely," the slugger told LIFE. But he let the magazine visit him in his six-room Carmel, Calif., hideaway and his Oakland town house.

EISENHOWER / KENNEDY

"Writing is how I live my own life," says John Eisenhower.

John and Caroline Kennedy share a light moment on the lawn behind theJohn F. KennedyLibrary in Boston, where in June she introduced a computer exhibit that explains electoral college voting.

Photographer Harry Benson and reporter Doris G. Kinney sought out and met with all 23 of the surviving children of families that had resided in the White House. In addition to the three shown here, the scions were of the Carter, Ford, Nixon, Johnson, Truman, Roosevelt, Hoover, Coolidge, Taft and Cleveland families.

The editors included several action pictures of Splash mermaid Daryl Hannah, thus supporting the refreshing rationale: "To match every move, a bathing suit must be as close to nothing at all as possible."

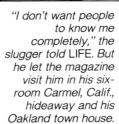

BEAUTY AND THE BEACH

A MOVIE MERMAID SHOWS OFF THE MOST MINIMAL MAILLOTS EVER

SEPTEMBER 1984

OCTOBER 1984

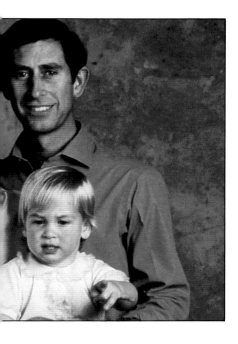

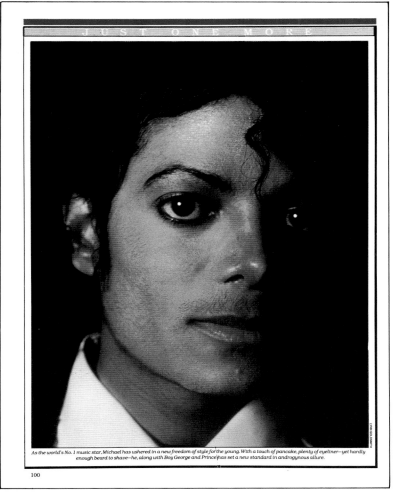

JUST ONE MORE

As the world's No. 1 music star, Michael has ushered in a new freedom of style for the young. With a touch of pancake, plenty of eyeliner—yet hardly enough beard to shave—he, along with Boy George and Prince, has set a new standard in androgynous allure.

100

NOVEMBER 1984   DECEMBER 1984

The world's reigning music star, Michael Jackson, looked out from the Just One More page. "With a touch of pancake, plenty of eyeliner—yet hardly enough beard to shave—he, along with Boy George and Prince, has set a new standard in androgynous allure."

A surfside ecdysiast got down to basics in a six-page essay, "Stolen Underwear," on women's adaptation of men's undergarments—"even jockstraps."

Married 34 years, Ferraro and husband John Zaccaro have lived since 1963 in a Tudor-style house in Forest Hills Gardens, a wealthy Queens enclave. If Ferraro becomes Vice President, Zaccaro says he will remain behind in Queens to attend to his real estate business.

"The Embattled Queen of Queens," Geraldine Ferraro, stood by her husband, John Zaccaro, for their portrait as she had stood by him when his finances were questioned during her campaign as Walter Mondale's running mate.

To accent the resemblance to an action comic strip of the Lucas-Spielberg-Ford team's second outing, LIFE executed its coverage broadly, right down to printing the text panels on comic-book yellow.

STEP-INS STEP OUT

Calvin Klein made two experimental pairs of boxer shorts—with fly and without. "One was sexy, the other looked like an old pair of bloomers," he says. The flies have it in white, black and four pastels ($12).

In the huddle are (from left) men's boxers from Fruit of the Loom (three for $6.19), shorts and tops from Fiorucci ($24, $15) and Swipes by Ithaca ($7, $6).

Now that all of fashion seems to be an androgynous zone, designers are confusing the issue further by predicting that man-tailored underwear for women will also be worn as bathing suits. If so, the styles will have gone back to their aquatic origins. In the 1930s men gave up one-piece union suits for boxer shorts and tank-top undershirts adapted from turn-of-the-century swimsuits. Jockey briefs—copied from a French swimsuit—did not outsell boxers until the 1960s. The Army and Navy made T-shirts popular for men; the jogging craze put them on girls, thus paving the way for today's unisex underwear. "It's athletic, healthy, sexy—a different type of sensuality than lace," says Calvin Klein. "There's a little bit of man in every woman."

For instant beachwear, peel down to a cotton string bikini ($3) and tank top ($6) in basic black, white and seven shades from Swipes by Ithaca.

285

A normal quota of calamitous news was balanced by a run of upbeat stories

War and famine still walked abroad. Terrorist criminals and devastating acts of nature again struck at the innocent. But it was a year with a few telling differences. In Italy, its home country, the Mafia was faced with all-out war waged by an outraged citizenry. In the Middle East, Israel consented to the first prisoner exchange ever with its organized Palestinian enemy. When an earthquake shattered Mexico's capital and lethal mud slides

THE NEW VICTIMS

AIDS IS AN EPIDEMIC THAT MAY CHANGE THE WAY AMERICA LIVES

In a mobile home in the Pennsylvania countryside a father and son are sick and languishing—27-year-old Patrick Burk unable to work, his one-year-old son, Dwight, hardly able to move. Both suffer from AIDS, a wasting of the immune system that has laid their bodies open to lethal infections. When first diagnosed in the U.S. four years ago, AIDS was seen mainly as a homosexual affliction, with intravenous-drug users also vulnerable. Of the 11,000 victims reported to date, three quarters are gay or bisexual. But infectious diseases have a way of breaking out of their pockets. Epidemic polio, for example, began strictly as a child's disease with 132 cases in Vermont and gradually spread to adults all across the country. Patrick Burk fits the original profile of the AIDS patient because he is a hemophiliac who received the virus in a contaminated blood product. Unknowingly, he transmitted it to his wife, Lauren, who in turn passed it to their son in the womb or through her milk. Similarly, the AIDS minorities are beginning to infect the heterosexual, drug-free majority. These new cases are not numerous, but they show the same relentless growth as the earlier risk groups: a doubling every year.

AIDS struck the Burk family all at once. Only after Dwight was diagnosed last August did the parents' symptoms—the unexplained rashes, diarrhea, swollen lymph nodes—make sense to doctors. In December Patrick was hospitalized for a month with a type of pneumonia that defines AIDS; Lauren has the condition called pre-AIDS. A registered nurse, she still drags herself to work at an institution for the retarded in Ebensburg, Pa., where Patrick also was employed. The future is dark, yet Lauren stays cheerful and Patrick has a quiet confidence that he'll beat the disease. "Apart, we'd probably be two of the weakest people," says Lauren. "But together we're strong."

Only the daughter is not infected.

Photography: Lynn Johnson   Reporting: Edward Barnes, Anne Hollister

The prospect of their both dying makes Patrick Burk's

This black-and-white report on the potentially terminal disease went on to study the population center with the highest per capita incidence of AIDS in the U.S., Belle Glade, Fla., an agricultural town of 17,000 in the center of the state.

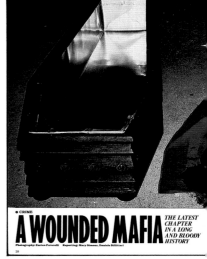

"For the first time," said LIFE in this social history—cum-travelogue set in Sicily, "the war against the Mafia has wide public support in Italy." A three-year-old law had made Mafia membership a crime.

A WOUNDED MAFIA

THE LATEST CHAPTER IN A LONG AND BLOODY HISTORY

CIVIL WAR DESCENDANTS

Six score years ago this month, the surrender papers were signed, bringing to a close the bloodiest, most divisive chapter in American history. Recently LIFE visited the direct descendants of the major heroes. They are a living legacy of the War Between the States

Lincoln

A handspring into the record books

Olympic glory blazed again in The Year in Pictures issue, published in January. Twinkling gymnast Mary Lou Retton stole the show as the games' most popular star.

INSIDE THE IRA

How Ireland's Outlaws Fight Their Endless War

Photography: Harry Benson
Text: S. Edward Barnes

The editors pictured, besides Lincoln, descendants of Jefferson Davis and Generals Grant, Lee, Sherman, Jackson.

During a serious rehearsal for an act of terror, an IRA chief mockingly donned a mask with the royal heir's features.

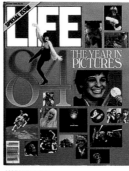

JANUARY 1985

FEBRUARY 1985

MARCH 1985

APRIL 1985

engulfed parts of Colombia and Puerto Rico, massive outpourings of medical and economic aid flowed there in relief. And the newest class of multimillionaires, the superstars of song, twice pooled their immensely lucrative talents to provide food for the world's hungry. Four decades after the first supporters of the United Nations were called starry-eyed "one-worlders," mankind's theme song had become *We Are the World*.

This glimpse of Israel's controversial move appeared in Newsbeat, a 24-page section of black-and-white photos the editors ran, temporarily, to deal with spot news.

Another Newsbeat spread dealt with the quintessential spot-news story, a local fire, and was a virtual classic of its genre.

During LIFE's Visit to South Africa's Bishop Desmond M. Tutu in Johannesburg, the Nobel laureate enjoyed a postnap snack and read the papers in bed.

Juan Carlos and Queen Sofía smiled sonrisas of welcome in Madrid. "Today at 47," said the editors, the king "is hailed as a modern monarch who has led Spain into the world community."

This picture of Mexico brought home the quake's fury even as Americans raised funds and shipped food and clothes.

In a panoramic scene a phalanx of Aussies made it into the pages of the Guinness Book of World Records.

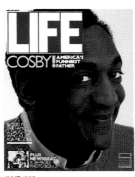

MAY 1985

JUNE 1985

JULY 1985

AUGUST 1985

SEPTEMBER 1985

An Ethiopian orphan, 10, starved as bureaucratic aid dispensers, on a technicality, refused to give him relief-program food.

CURRENTS AND EVENTS

WORLD: Gorbachev Named Soviet Party Chief • Reagan, Gorbachev Hold Geneva Summit • French Government Admits Involvement in Sinking of Greenpeace Vessel off New Zealand • Reagan Visits West German Military Cemetery in Bitburg • Violence Provoked by Apartheid Mounts in South Africa • Israel Completes Troop Withdrawal from Lebanon • Terrorists Hijack TWA Plane en Route from Athens to Rome, Kill U.S. Sailor, Hostages Released Gradually over 17 Days • Egyptian Commandos Storm Hijacked Jet in Malta, 57 Die • Palestinians Seize Italian Cruise Ship, Murder American Passenger Before Surrendering to PLO • Airports in Rome, Vienna Attacked by Terrorists, Casualties Heavy • Ortega Sworn In as Nicaragua's President • El Salvador Rebels Kidnap President Duarte's Daughter, Exchange Her for Political Prisoners • Eruption of Colombian Volcano Kills 25,000 • Earthquake in Mexico Takes 20,000 Lives • Defendants in Aquino Murder Trial Acquitted, Wife Corazon to Oppose Marcos in Philippines Election • Japan Air Lines Jet Crashes with Record Toll of 520 Lives.

U.S.A.: Reagan Undergoes Surgery for Cancer • Chartered Plane Carrying 248 GIs Returning from Sinai Duty Crashes in Newfoundland • New Zealand Bars Visit of All U.S. Naval Vessels Carrying Nuclear Devices • Congressional Disagreements Stall Efforts to Overhaul Income Taxes • Retired Navy Warrant Officer John Walker Arrested with Brother, Son for Espionage.

FIRSTS: Space Probe to Meet Comet Giacobini-Zinner • Diesel Fuel from Vegetable Oil.

MOVIES: Back to the Future • Agnes of God • Blood Simple • Brazil • Jagged Edge • The Breakfast Club • Clue • Cocoon • The Color Purple • Crossover Dreams • Desperately Seeking Susan • The Falcon and the Snowman • Murphy's Romance • National Lampoon's European Vacation • Rambo: First Blood Part II • Jewel of the Nile • Kiss of the Spider Woman • Mask • Out of Africa • Perfect • Prizzi's Honor • Pumping Iron II • The Purple Rose of Cairo • Johnny Dangerously • Mass Appeal • Rocky IV • Runaway Train • A View to a Kill • The Trip to Bountiful • White Nights • Witness • Compromising Positions • The Goonies • Ran • Pale Rider • Sweet Dreams • The Official Story • Eleni • Shoah • Micki & Maude • Twice in a Lifetime • Mishima • When Father Was Away on Business • The Cotton Club • A Chorus Line.

SONGS: Like a Virgin • We Are the World • Careless Whisper • Wake Me Up Before You Go-Go • I Want to Know What Love Is • Every Time You Go Away • Easy Lover • Can't Fight This Feeling • The Power of Love • St. Elmo's Fire • The Heat Is On • Shout • Part-time Lover • Saving All My Love for You • One More Night • You're the Inspiration • Freeway of Love • Sussudio • You Give Good Love • Missing You • Raspberry Beret • If You Love Somebody Set Them Free • We Don't Need Another Hero • Material Girl • Better Be Good to Me • Smooth Operator • Don't Lose My Number • All Through the Night • Glory Days • Too Late for Goodbyes • Angel • Do What You Do • Born in the U.S.A. • Private Dancer • Who's Zoomin' Who • Sugar Walls.

STAGE: Biloxi Blues • As Is • I'm Not Rappaport • Benefactors • A Lie of the Mind • The Search for Signs of Intelligent Life . . . • Grind • Big River • Singin' in the Rain • Song and Dance • Tango Argentino • Tracers • The Mystery of Edwin Drood • Jerry's Girls.

BOOKS: Texas (Michener) • Lake Wobegon Days (Keillor) • Contact (Sagan) • Skeleton Crew (King) • Lucky (Collins) • Cider House Rules (Irving) • The Fourth Deadly Sin (Sanders) • Inside, Outside (Wouk) • Lonesome Dove (McMurty) • World's Fair (Doctorow) • House (Kidder) • Yeager: An Autobiography • I Never Played the Game (Cosell) • A Passion for Excellence (Peters, Austin).

FADS: The Madonna Look • Brooches • Reebok Footwear.

Inspired by a similar gesture in Europe, 43 of America's top singers of pop, rock and country music decided to record a megastar LP that would raise funds to feed famine-struck Africans. Though the recording session was to be kept secret, Willie Nelson tipped off good buddy LIFE writer Cheryl McCall, and the editors arranged for exclusive coverage.

As the magazine showed, there was an underworld of difference between Miami Vice, the prime-time TV hit, and the cast's real-life counterparts on the Miami PD vice squad.

ITS ALL AN ACT FOR PHILIP MICHAEL THOMAS AND DON JOHNSON, BUT WHEN THE DRUG DEALS GO DOWN, THESE COPS PLAY FOR KEEPS

ISABELLA

Signorina Rossellini told editor Watters that although she and her twin, Ingrid Jr., worshiped both parents, she herself adored her father so much she thought she had "what is called an Electra complex."

OCTOBER 1985   NOVEMBER 1985

WE HEED A CERTAIN CALL'

● MUSIC

S RAISE THEIR VOICES TO HELP AFRICA'S HUNGRY

LIFE hung out with the lucky 81 models who competed for the $200,000 first prize awarded for The Look of the Year. The contest producers observed that the best bets to win were those under 20 and characterized the ilk as "baby animals that become the monsters who draw the clients."

THERE'S HIGH STYLE, AND THEN THERE'S

DI'S STYLE

● LIFESTYLE

WHO'S GOT THE LOOK?

'ME!' SAY 35,000 FLEDGLING MODELS

For the rest of Diana's latest outing in the magazine, the editors dropped rhyme for headlines in favor of alliteration: "Bashful in Blue," "Jazzy in Jeans," "Sassy in a Sweater," "Ritzy in a Robe."

● FANTASY

THE MANY FACES OF

JOAN

ALMOST ALL ABOUT EVE

Photography: Reid Miles

As had Marilyn Monroe before her in 1958, Collins portrayed a series of temptresses. Joan went way back for this opener.

LIFE

The Real Cops of Miami Vice
How Your Social Security Works
Countering Terrorism Abroad

SEEING BEYOND THE STARS

A PREVIEW OF AMERICA'S BIGGEST YEAR IN SPACE

DECEMBER 1985

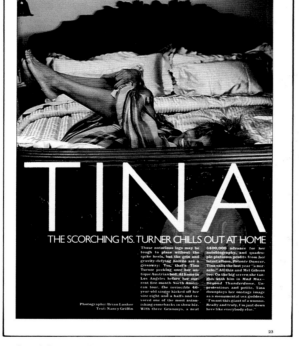

LIFE August 1985

TINA

THE SCORCHING MS. TURNER CHILLS OUT AT HOME

Photography: Brian Lanker
Text: Nancy Griffin

A quick tour of La Turner's L.A. digs—including her pool, her Buddhist altar, her thicket of gold and platinum records—indicated that she was not, despite her insistence, "like everybody else."

AMONG THEIR

SOUVENIRS

INTIMATE HISTORIES FROM DIARIES, PHOTOGRAPHS AND MEMENTOS

Reporting: Naomi Cutner

One section of the World War II extra issue (cover at right) constituted a rare collection of souvenirs, snapshots, and diaries of GIs and nurses.

SPECIAL ISSUE
LIFE 40 YEARS LATER
THE HEROES
THE BATTLES
THE HOME FRONT
WORLD WAR II

A Few Favorites 1975-1986...

CONTINUING THE TRADITION OF EDITORIAL "CRUSHES," A NEW FIRMAMENT

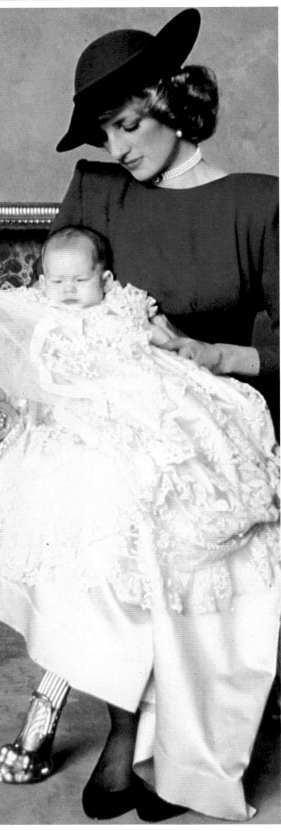

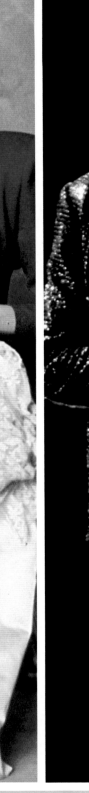

Everyone's favorite 1982 swimsuit model, Christie Brinkley, could leap broad beaches in a bound.

HRH Diana, Princess of Wales, held Prince Henry, 3 months, after his 1985 christening in the lace gown first worn in 1841 by Queen Victoria's eldest daughter.

Michael Jackson, 26, riding high during his 15-city 1984 "Musical Tour of the Decade," paused between numbers to recharge.

Physiologically ready for the mature role of bathing-suit model, erstwhile Pretty Baby Brooke Shields, 17, tooled along a Baja California byway behind a friend in 1983.

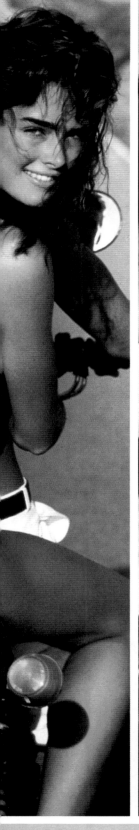

On the set of the hugely successful sitcom The Cosby Show, superstar Bill cracked them up during a 1985 rehearsal.

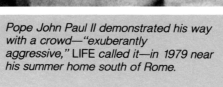

Pope John Paul II demonstrated his way with a crowd—"exuberantly aggressive," LIFE called it—in 1979 near his summer home south of Rome.

From a 1979 story about rock stars' bus tours, Dolly Parton was the one picked to beam on the cover.

**THE PASSAGE OF YEARS HAS CHANGED HOW WE VIEW
OURSELVES, OUR WORLD, OUR UNIVERSE. BUT THE EDITORS
HAVE RESPONDED CONSISTENTLY TO THE TIMELESS
CHALLENGE OF THE MAGAZINE'S ORIGINAL PROSPECTUS:**

"To see life;   *to see the world;*

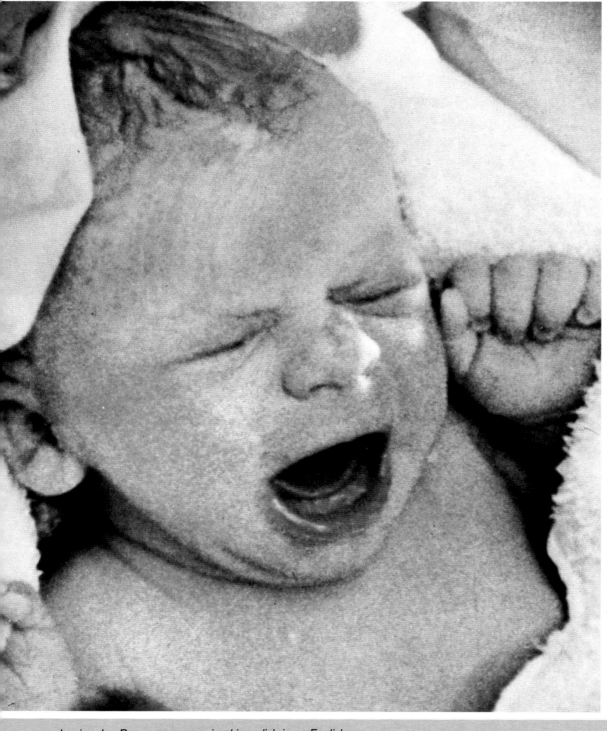

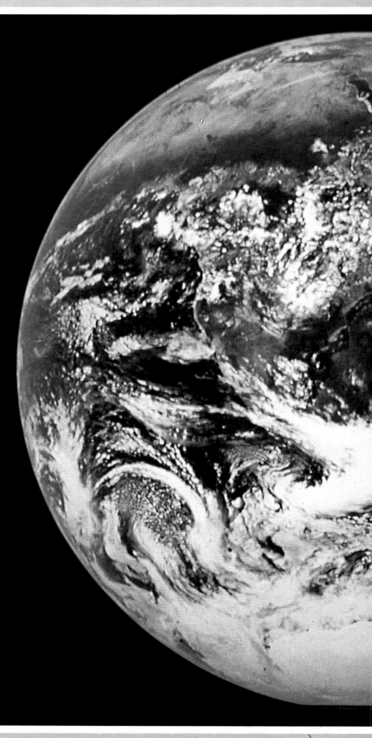

*Louise Joy Brown was conceived in a dish in an English
laboratory and two days later was implanted in her mother's womb.
She was born on July 25, 1978, the world's first test-tube baby.*

*This indelible image was just one in a LIFE collection of
magnificent space photographs assembled for a 1984 issue.
A 1972 view of "Spaceship Earth," glowing sapphirelike
in the blackness of the cosmos, it was recorded
8,000 miles away by Apollo 17 astronaut Ronald E. Evans.*

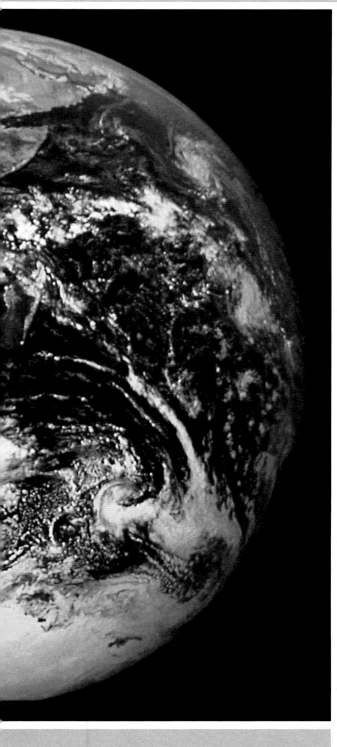

WELCOME BACK TO FREEDOM

OPEN

Released from hostage in Iran in 1981 after 444 days, Lt. Col. David Roeder whooped for joy as he left the plane, in Wiesbaden, Germany, that brought him and 51 other Americans to freedom.

to watch the faces of the poor

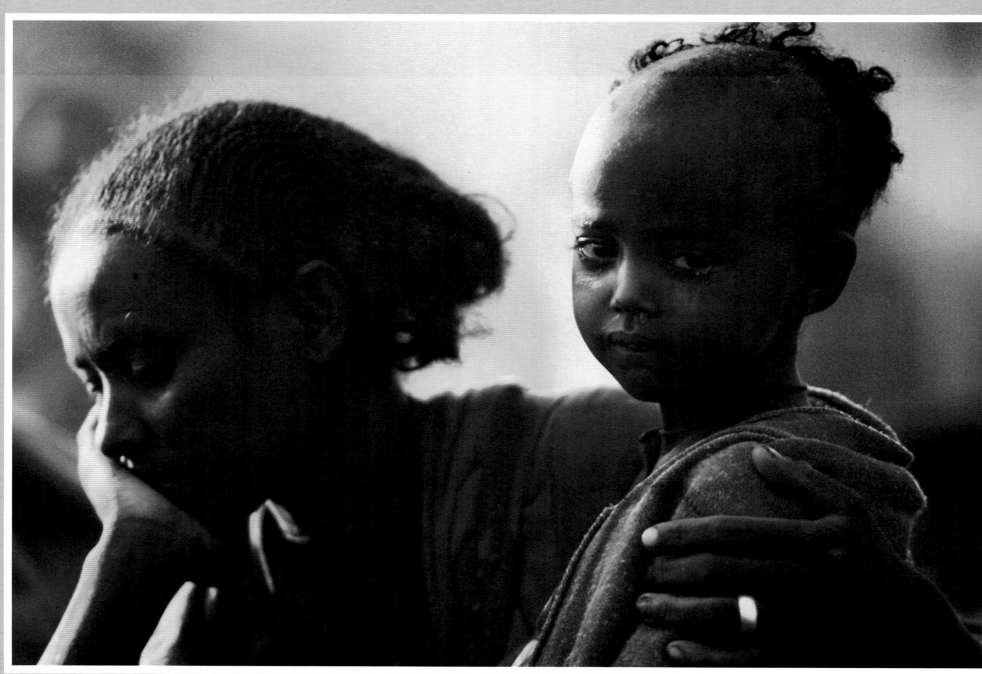

At a camp in Ethiopia's Wollo province, a mother and child, victims of a
decade of drought and civil war, waited in 1984 for food to arrive from the
U.S. and Europe. Despite the shipments, one million died that year.

**and
the
gestures
of
the
proud;**

*Six days after undergoing
a major operation for
cancer in 1985, a ruddy-
cheeked Ronald Reagan
communicated with
photographers from his
window at the Bethesda
Naval Hospital.*

A pair of pygmy marmosets, newborn in 1979, had the Stockholm zoo's monkey-house keeper wrapped around their fingers. And, of course, vice versa.

The prototype of the $200 million swept-wing B-1 bomber stood, in 1982, as "a glowering symbol of the nation's apparent willingness to spend whatever it takes" to counter the U.S.S.R.'s weapons deployments of the previous 15 years. A full system for 100 B-1s was included in a five-year, $200 billion buildup, the largest in peacetime history, planned by the Reagan administration.

armies,

Americans went to Washington by the tens of thousands in 1982 to see the new Vietnam wall, on which the names of every one of the U.S. fallen had been carved in the polished granite. Some pointed. Some trailed a finger "wistfully over the letters, as though trying to coax a dim memory to life." All were deeply moved by the memorial's quiet eloquence.

multitudes,

Thousands of determined competitors jammed Chicago's North Michigan Avenue shortly after the start of the 1978 Mayor Daley Marathon.

shadows
in the jungle

*A chillingly neat 1979
arrangement of skulls and
bones near Suong, Cambodia,
was a grim legacy of the
Communist Khmer Rouge, which
under Pol Pot massacred
half the Cambodian population.*

*The shaded face of earth's sole natural satellite, seen in a multiple
exposure, slid across the sun's flaming orb on February 6, 1979, producing
the last total solar eclipse to be seen in North America until 2017.*

and on the moon;

to see man's work—

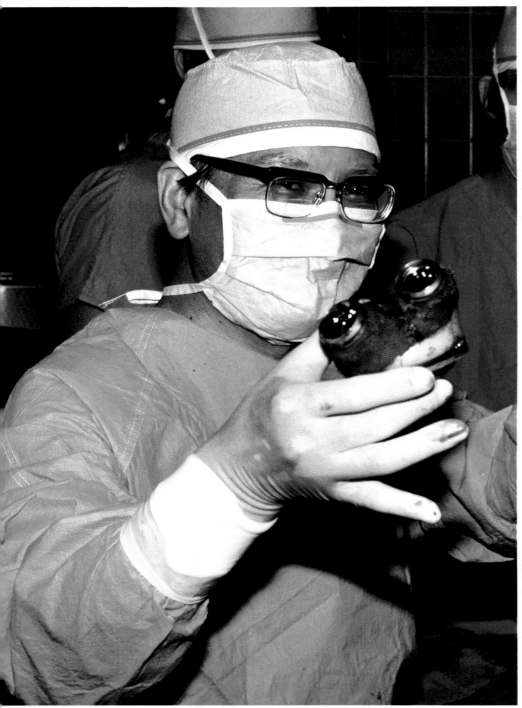

Dr. Tetsuzo Akutsu, designer of an artificial heart, held up a "ventricle" of his artifact after it had been removed in 1981 from a patient at the Texas Heart Institute. The heart had kept the patient alive during a two-day wait for a donor's organ.

Manhattan skyscrapers lined both sides of 42nd Street. The view in 1980 looked west, past the UN Secretariat Building on East River Drive to the Chrysler Building's Art Deco spire, the Hudson River and the New Jersey shore.

In a narrow loft in Manhattan's downtown warehouse district, James Rosenquist, a onetime billboard painter, worked on one section of a 17-by-46-ft. 1981 work, *Star Thief*. *The idea behind it, he said, was "the hope inherent in man's quest for new worlds."*

his paintings,

towers

and discoveries;

Life-size bronze horses pulling bronze chariots driven by bronze generals came to light in 1981 in China's Shaanxi Province. They had been buried for 22 centuries, since the reign of Emperor Qin Shi Huang.

His face smeared with white ceremonial ash, a young hunter belonging to the Murle tribe of the southern Sudan wrestled a wounded kob to the ground in 1979. In Murle legend the kob, a species of antelope, was earth's first animal, pulled from a well hole by a Murle ancestor.

to see things thousands of miles away,

things hidden behind walls

As it had for 20 years, a "death strip" ran along the Communist side of the Berlin Wall dividing East and West Germany. By 1981 a floodlighted barrier of raked sand, lined with fortified fencing and guarded from watchtowers, had been seeded with trip flares.

and within rooms,

The body of Steven Biko, 30, the moderate, nonviolent leader of the black consciousness movement in South Africa, awaited burial in a Pretoria funeral home in 1978. He had been jailed without being charged. The cause of death: brain damage.

things
dangerous
to come to;

As with many perils, the perception of menace in the mildly poisonous green vine snake is greater than the reality—especially, as LIFE said in a 1982 essay on the denizens of the Costa Rican rain forest, when it is shown four times normal size.

the women that men love

In a symbolic bicentennial gesture, Seattle cop Barry Schlecht and Liz Bailey surrendered their independence on Independence Day 1976, at Bainbridge Island, Wash. (It turned out the judge was outside his jurisdiction, and the Schlechts went through another ceremony six months later.)

and many children;

The most famous Liverpudlians since the Beatles, the Walton sextuplets—Jenny (raised hemline), Hannah, Lucy, Sarah, Ruth and Kate—age 2, sat in 1985 for a group portrait during their first formal outing.

to see and to take pleasure in seeing;

Daryl Koehn, 21, jumped for joy on a road outside Concordia, Kans., upon learning in 1977 that she had been chosen as one of the first female Rhodes scholars. Parliament had passed a bill altering the original requirement that recipients embody, among other things, "qualities of manhood."

to see and be amazed;

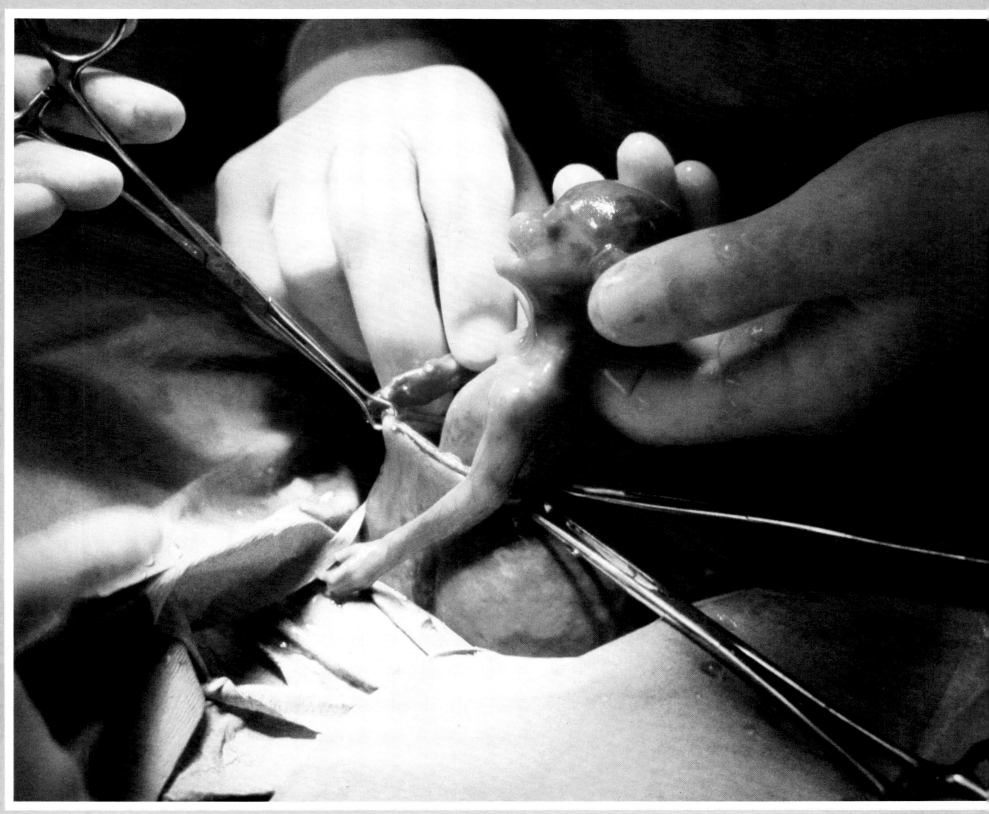

In a 1983 demonstration of new methods for treating the unborn, doctors performed brain surgery on a 96-day-old monkey fetus (equivalent to a 5-month-old human one) lifted from the uterus. The experiment suggested that hydrocephalic human fetuses might be similarly treated.

In 1980, as the cameras aboard Voyager 1 probed within "a cosmic hairbreadth" (77,174 miles) of Saturn, man learned that the planet's rings—the most gorgeous array of sunlit dust in the universe—were not just six in number, as previously thought, but myriad.

thus to see, and to be shown, is now the will and new expectancy of half mankind."

Covers

Attributions of credit to photographers and artists are given as originally published in the magazine. All photographs and artwork are protected by copyright, except those credited to agencies of the U.S. government. Time Inc. owns the copyright to all images credited to LIFE.

1936

11/23, Fort Peck Dam—Margaret Bourke-White, LIFE; 11/30, West Point cadet—Alfred Eisenstaedt; 12/7, Skiing—Paul Wolff; 12/14, Archbishop of Canterbury—Time Inc.; 12/21, Lord Beaverbrook's granddaughter—Time Inc.; 12/28, Metropolitan Opera Ballet—Alfred Eisenstaedt.

1937

1/4, Franklin D. Roosevelt—Harris & Ewing; 1/11, Japanese soldiers—Black Star; 1/18, Henry and Edsel Ford—Russell Aikins; 1/25, England's royal lion—Time Inc.; 2/1, Tennis at Vassar—Alfred Eisenstaedt; 2/8, Winter in Wyoming—Charles J. Belden; 2/15, Japanese Gen. Senjuro Hayashi—Leon Daniel; 2/22, St. Louis fountain triton—Alfred Eisenstaedt; 3/1, Laboratory mice—Henry M. Lester; 3/8, Sun Valley ski lift—Alfred Eisenstaedt; 3/15, Britain's coronation throne—Time Inc.; 3/22, Parachute test—Margaret Bourke-White, LIFE; 3/29, Easter choristers—INS; 4/5, Terrier—Helen T. Farrell; 4/12, English centenarian—Time Inc.; 4/19, S.S. *Queen Mary*—Aerial Explorations, Inc.; 4/26, Leghorn rooster—Torekel Korling; 5/3, Jean Harlow—Martin Munkacsi; 5/10, Boy playing marbles—Time Inc.; 5/17, Dionne quintuplets—NEA Service, Inc.; 5/24, Spring lambs—Hansel Mieth, LIFE; 5/31, Golden Gate Bridge—Standard Oil of California; 6/7, Saddle shoes—Alfred Eisenstaedt; 6/14, Sen. James Lewis—Margaret Bourke-White, LIFE; 6/21, Reno divorcée—Alfred Eisenstaedt; 6/28, Beach scene—Herbert Matter; 7/5, July corn—Dorothea Lange; 7/12, Mannequin—Alfred Eisenstaedt; 7/19, Harlem street shower—Fenno Jacobs; 7/26, Polo pony—Alfred Eisenstaedt; 8/2, Franciscan nun—Wallace Kirkland; 8/9, Watermelon wagon—Al Burgert; 8/16, Camper on a boat—George Karger; 8/23, Transoceanic plane—Clyde H. Sunderland; 8/30, Frog hunt—Horace Bristol; 9/6, Harpo Marx—Rex Hardy Jr.; 9/13, Steel master—Margaret Bourke-White, LIFE; 9/20, Yehudi Menuhin's hands—Horace Bristol; 9/27, Nelson Eddy—Laszlo Willinger; 10/4, Legionnaire's living room—Torekel Korling; 10/11, USC football captain Chuck Williams—George Strock; 10/18, Veils in fashion—Alfred Eisenstaedt; 10/25, Hunting spaniel—Alfred Eisenstaedt; 11/1, Alfred Lunt and Richard Whorf—Vandamm Studios; 11/8, Greta Garbo—Clarence Bull; 11/15, Lightship engineer—Arthur Griffin; 11/22, LIFE birthday baby—H. Armstrong Roberts; 11/29, U.S. capitol—Margaret Bourke-White, LIFE; 12/6, Japanese soldier—Yonosuke Natori; 12/13, Locomotive under repair—James N. Doolittle; 12/20, Chorus girl—Peter Stackpole, LIFE; 12/27, *Comtesse d'Haussonville* (Ingres)—Fernand Bourges.

1938

1/3, Swedish skater—Herbert Matter; 1/10, Koalas—Lane Flinders; 1/17, Oil tanks—Robert Yarnall Richie; 1/24, Alpine skiers—World Graphic Press; 1/31, Student nurses—Alfred Eisenstaedt; 2/7, Gary Cooper—Bob Coburn; 2/14, Egypt's Queen Farida—Alban; 2/21, Carl Sandburg—Bernard Hoffman; 2/28, Monte Carlo fireworks—Time Inc.; 3/7, High school girls—Fritz Henle; 3/14, Jane Froman—Alfred Eisenstaedt; 3/21, Couple at marriage clinic—William Vandivert, LIFE; 3/28, German bugler—Wolfgang Weber; 4/4, Anthony Eden—Time Inc.; 4/11, Fashions—Alfred Eisenstaedt; 4/18, Paulette Goddard—Martin Munkacsi; 4/25, Brooklyn Dodger Tom Winsett—Wide World Photos; 5/2, John N. Garner—Margaret Bourke-White, LIFE; 5/9, Summer fashions—Alfred Eisenstaedt; 5/16, Chinese soldier—Robert Capa; 5/23, Erroll Flynn—Scotty Wilbourne; 5/30, Czech Gen. Jan Sirovy—John Phillips, LIFE; 6/6, Youth problem—Alfred Eisenstaedt; 6/13, Gertrude Lawrence—Peter Stackpole, LIFE; 6/20, Rudolph Valentino—Culver Service; 6/27, Franklin D. Roosevelt—Associated Press; 7/4, West Point wedding—Frank Scherschel, LIFE; 7/11, Shirley Temple—Wide World Photos; 7/18, Camisoles in fashion—Dmitri Kessel, LIFE; 7/25, Queen Elizabeth—Time Inc.; 8/1, Garment workers at play—Hansel Mieth, LIFE; 8/8, Divers in quarry—Arthur Griffin, LIFE; 8/15, Sumerian high priest—University of Pennsylvania; 8/22, Fred Astaire and Ginger Rogers—Rex Hardy Jr., LIFE; 8/29, Goodbye to summer—Knopf; 9/5, Fall fashions—Herbert Gehr (Edmund B. Gerard); 9/12, Hungarian police guard—Margaret Bourke-White, LIFE; 9/19, James A. Farley—Wallace W. Kirkland; 9/26, County fair barker—Alfred Eisenstaedt; 10/3, Czech soldier—Margaret Bourke-White, LIFE; 10/10, Legion drum majorettes—George Strock; 10/17, Carole Lombard—Alfred Eisenstaedt; 10/24, Columbia College's Sid Luckman—Otto Hagel; 10/31, Raymond Massey—George Karger; 11/7, California gubernatorial candidate Culbert Olson—George Strock; 11/14, Brenda Duff Frazier—Acme; 11/21, Japanese boy—Paul Dorsey, LIFE; 11/28, LIFE birthday baby—Ellen Auerbach; 12/5, Ballerina Yvette Chauviré—No Credit; 12/12, Champion Labrador retriever—George Karger; 12/19, Mary Martin—Alfred Eisenstaedt; 12/26, Lutist Mrs. Otto Baldauf—Ansel Adams.

1939

1/2, Wimples in fashion—Alfred Eisenstaedt; 1/9, Romanian boy—John Phillips, LIFE; 1/16, Lucius Beebe—Rex Hardy Jr., LIFE; 1/23, Bette Davis—Alfred Eisenstaedt; 1/30, Air cadet—Carl Mydans, LIFE; 2/6, Peruke hairstyle—Herbert Gehr (Edmund B. Gerard); 2/13, Norma Shearer—MGM; 2/20, France's Chief of Staff M. G. Gamelin—Margaret Bourke-White, LIFE; 2/27, On a Nassau beach—Fritz Henle; 3/6, Tallulah Bankhead—Vandamm Studios; 3/13, World's Fair sculpture—Alfred Eisenstaedt; 3/20, Rep. Joseph Martin—Arthur Griffin, LIFE; 3/27, Spring shower—Alfred Eisenstaedt; 4/3, Realistic dolls—Werner Wolff; 4/10, Texas Ranger—Carl Mydans, LIFE; 4/17, Hildegarde—Avery Slack; 4/24, Neville Chamberlain—Wide World Photos; 5/1, Joe DiMaggio—Carl Mydans, LIFE; 5/8, Cottons in fashion—De Palma; 5/15, Anne Morrow Lindbergh—Paul Cordes; 5/22, World's Fair guide—David E. Scherman, LIFE; 5/29, Eleanor Roosevelt—Mark Kauffman; 6/5, Statue of Liberty—Herbert Gehr (Edmund B. Gerard); 6/12, June Week at Annapolis—Peter Stackpole, LIFE; 6/19, USC sprinter Payton Jordan—Gjon Mili; 6/26, Fads in fashion—Walter Sanders; 7/3, Swimsuits in fashion—George Strock; 7/10, Japanese Home Guard—Paul Dorsey; 7/17, Lord Halifax—Margaret Bourke-White, LIFE; 7/24, Ann Sheridan— Donald Biddle Keyes; 7/31, Diana Barrymore—Fritz Henle; 8/7, U.S. official Paul McNutt—Horace Bristol; 8/14, Young movie actress Sandra Lee Henville—Peter Stackpole, LIFE; 8/21, Boy meets girl—Peter Stackpole, LIFE; 8/28, Alice Marble—Alfred Eisenstaedt; 9/4, Rosalind Russell—MGM; 9/11, Benito Mussolini—Ferdinand Vogel; 9/18, British soldier—AP; 9/25, Britain's General Edmund Ironside—Time Inc.; 10/2, Cordell Hull—Margaret Bourke-White, LIFE; 10/9, Kids' football—Alfred Eisenstaedt; 10/16, German U-boat—Pictorial Press; 10/23, War and fashion—Fritz Henle; 10/30, Veloz and Yolanda—Gjon Mili; 11/6, Planes over England—Charles E. Brown; 11/13, Claudette Colbert—Alfred Eisenstaedt; 11/20, German warship—Combine; 11/27, Arturo Toscanini and granddaughter Sonia Horowitz—Herbert Gehr (Edmund B. Gerard); 12/4, UCLA coed with date—Peter Stackpole, LIFE; 12/11, Betty Grable—© W. Eugene Smith; 12/18, Canadian Gen. Andrew McNaughton—John Phillips, LIFE; 12/25, Merry Christmas—Peter Stackpole, LIFE.

1940

1/1, Queen Elizabeth—Cecil Beaton; 1/8, Bowdoin House party—Alfred Eisenstaedt; 1/15, USC's basketball star Ralph Vaughn—David E. Scherman, LIFE; 1/22, Dutch East Indians—Horace Bristol; 1/29, Starlet Lana Turner—Peter Stackpole, LIFE; 2/5, Swedish aviators—Karl Sandels; 2/12, Valentine's Day hat—Walter Sanders; 2/19, Romania's King Carol and son Mihai—John Phillips, LIFE; 2/26, Carhop—Francis Miller; 3/4, Springtime hats—George Karger; 3/11, French soldier—Stedman Jones; 3/18, Chorus girl—Walter Sanders; 3/25, Sir Neville Henderson—Combine; 4/1, N.Y. Giants baseball rookie John Rucker—AP; 4/8, Actress Anna Neagle—Peter Stackpole, LIFE; 4/15, Government and youth—Knopf; 4/22, Dude outfit—Peter Stackpole, LIFE; 4/29, Winston Churchill—Margaret Bourke-White, LIFE; 5/6, British aerial gunner—Combine; 5/13, Silk shawls in fashion—Alfred Eisenstaedt; 5/20, French Gen. Maxime Weygand—Margaret Bourke-White, LIFE; 5/27, German soldier—Underwood & Underwood; 6/3, Statue of Liberty—Herbert Gehr (Edmund B. Gerard); 6/10, Emperor Hirohito—Underwood & Underwood; 6/17, General Motors' William Knudson—Acme; 6/24, Italy's Marshall Rodolfo Graziani—AP; 7/1, Red Cross girl—Herbert Gehr (Edmund B. Gerard); 7/8, Adm. Harold Stark—Harris & Ewing; 7/15, Rita Hayworth—Peter Stackpole, LIFE; 7/22, Tank commander—John Phillips, LIFE; 7/29, Girl lifeguard—George Karger; 8/5, U.S. vacations—George Karger; 8/12, Republican vice presidential nominee Charles McNary—Acme; 8/19, Parachute trainee—© W. Eugene Smith; 8/26, Couple at Jasper National Park—Horace Bristol; 9/2, Dionne quintuplets—Hansel Mieth, LIFE; 9/9, Singer Carol Bruce—Eliot Elisofon; 9/16, Flight across America—David E. Scherman, LIFE; 9/23, Air-raid victim—Cecil Beaton; 9/30, Wendell Willkie—John Phillips, LIFE; 10/7, Gary Cooper—Peter Stackpole, LIFE; 10/14, Jinx Falkenburg—Walter Sanders; 10/21, Sweaters in fashion—Gjon Mili; 10/28, U.S. sailor—© W. Eugene Smith; 11/4, San Diego campaign rally—William C. Shrout; 11/11, Michigan's Tom Harmon—Carl Bigelow; 11/18, Franklin D. Roosevelt—Otto Hagel; 11/25, Fur coats in fashion—Andreas Feininger; 12/2, Balloonist—John Phillips, LIFE; 12/9, Ginger Rogers—RKO Radio Pictures; 12/16, Greek soldier—Nelly's Photo; 12/23, Couple dressed for a party—John Phillips, LIFE; 12/30, Britain's desert fighters—Wide World.

1941

1/6, Katharine Hepburn—MGM; 1/13, Bathing suits in fashion—George Karger; 1/20, U.S. ski trooper—Horace Bristol; 1/27, Winston Churchill II and mother Pamela—Cecil Beaton; 2/3, Joseph Goebbels and Herman Goering—Eliot Elisofon; 2/10, Lord Halifax—Time Inc.; 2/17, Actress Cobina Wright Jr.—Robert Landry; 2/24, New Zealanders—Margaret Bourke-White, LIFE; 3/3, Fashion—Walter Sanders; 3/10, Washington worker—Eliot Elisofon; 3/17, Panama Canal defense—Robert Yarnall Richie; 3/24, Veils in fashion—Herbert Gehr (Edmund B. Gerard); 3/31, U.S. Navy's new dive-bomber—Robert Yarnall Richie; 4/7, Spring showers—Gjon Mili; 4/14, New York harbor—Walter Sanders; 4/21, U.S. cavalryman—Robert Landry; 4/28, Red in fashion—George Karger; 5/5, *John Harvard* (French)—Otto Hagel; 5/12, Army parachutist—Gabriel Benczur; 5/19, Floppy hats in fashion—Herbert Gehr (Edmund B. Gerard); 5/26, Army nurse—Myron H. Davis; 6/2, Sunday school—Alfred Eisenstaedt; 6/9, Duke and Duchess of Windsor—David E. Scherman, LIFE; 6/16, British soldier with his first U.S. soda—© W. Eugene Smith; 6/23, Lazy fishing—Walter Sanders; 6/30, Mme. Chiang Kai-shek—Margaret Bourke-White, LIFE; 7/7, Gen. George Patton—Eliot Elisofon; 7/14, Sand sailing—Alfred Eisenstaedt; 7/21, British Air Chief Marshal Sir Robert Brooke—Carl Mydans, LIFE; 7/28, Circus family—George Karger; 8/4, British woman auxiliary—Time Inc.; 8/11, Rita Hayworth—Robert Landry; 8/18, U.S. Marine—George Strock; 8/25, Fred Astaire and son—Robert Landry; 9/1, Ted Williams—Gjon Mili; 9/8, Smith college girl—Alfred Eisenstaedt; 9/15, British Capt. Lord Louis Mountbatten—Walter B. Lane; 9/22, Brazilian dancer Eros Volusia—Preston Hart; 9/29, Radio's Quiz Kid Gerald Darrow—Wallace W. Kirkland; 10/6, Farmer's daughter—Eliot Elisofon; 10/13, Lana Turner and Clark Gable—Clarence Bull for MGM; 10/20, Pan American Clipper—George Strock; 10/27, Air-raid spotter—Eliot Elisofon; 11/3, West Point cadet—Alfred Eisenstaedt; 11/10, Gene Tierney—Robert Landry; 11/17, Texas football—George Strock; 11/24, How to knit—Gjon Mili; 12/1, B-17 bomber—Hans Groenhof; 12/8, Gen. Douglas MacArthur—Charles W. Miller Studio; 12/15, Junior Miss—Herbert Gehr (Edmund B. Gerard); 12/22, American flag—George A. Douglas; 12/29, U.S. aerial gunner—Eliot Elisofon.

1942

1/5, Wanted: 50,000 nurses—Eliot Elisofon; 1/12, Pacific Coast defense—Peter Stackpole, LIFE; 1/19, North Atlantic patrol—Eliot Elisofon; 1/26, Air Force women's auxiliary—David E. Scherman, LIFE; 2/2, Thunderbolt fighter—Dmitri Kessel; 2/9, Versailles nightclub chorus in New York—Charles Steinheimer; 2/16, Singer and soldier—William C. Shrout; 2/23, Guns for merchantmen—George Strock; 3/2, Ginger Rogers—Robert Landry; 3/9, Barrage balloon—J. R. Eyerman; 3/16, Infantryman—George Strock; 3/23, Making plane models—Charles E. Steinheimer; 3/30, Shirley Temple—George Hurrell; 4/6, Tail gunner—Frank Scherschel, LIFE; 4/13, Gen. Brehon Somervell—Myron H. Davis; 4/20, Slacks in fashion—Nina Leen; 4/27, Nelson Rockefeller—Myron H. Davis; 5/4, Chinese air cadet—Peter Stackpole, LIFE; 5/11, Ruffles in fashion—Nina Leen; 5/18, Cadet bombardier—William C. Shrout; 5/25, Spring planting—Eric Schaal; 6/1, Hedy Lamarr—Robert Landry; 6/8, Nurse's aide—J. R. Eyerman, LIFE; 6/15, Gen. Joseph Stilwell—George Rodger; 6/22, War bride—Nina Leen; 6/29, USO belle—Johnny Florea; 7/6, American flag—Dmitri Kessel; 7/13, Air Corps gunnery school—Eliot Elisofon; 7/20, Short coat in fashion—Walter Sanders; 7/27, Atlantic convoy—Frank Scherschel; 8/3, General MacArthur's son Arthur—Athol Smith; 8/10, Gen. Claire Chennault—Thomas Kwang; 8/17, Guerrilla warfare expert—Dmitri Kessel; 8/24, "Johnny Jeep" hats in fashion—Nina Leen; 8/31, Torpedo boat ensign—Jack Wilkes; 9/7, Cargo glider—Dmitri Kessel; 9/14, U.S. official Leon Henderson—Thomas D. McAvoy, LIFE; 9/21, Iran's Queen Fawzia—Cecil Beaton; 9/28, Adm. William Leahy—Myron H. Davis; 10/5, Hats in fashion—Philippe Halsman; 10/12, California assembly-line worker—J. R. Eyerman, LIFE; 10/19, Sandbagged Sphinx—Robert Landry; 10/26, Actress Joan Leslie—Robert Landry; 11/2, "Praise the Lord and Pass the Ammunition" phrasemaker Capt. (Chaplain) William Maguire—Jack Wilkes; 11/9, Infantry mountain trooper—J. R. Eyerman, LIFE; 11/16, Vests in fashion—Walter Sanders; 11/23, New England church—Fritz Goro; 11/30, Eighteen-year-old awaiting draft—Walter Sanders; 12/7, Marine ace Maj. John L. Smith—Nelson Morris; 12/14, Coast Guard skipper—William C. Shrout; 12/21, Lonely wife—John Phillips, LIFE; 12/28, *Madonna* (Raphael)—courtesy Beck Engraving Co.

1943

1/4, "Assistant president" Jimmy Byrnes—Myron H. Davis, LIFE; 1/11, Kids' uniforms—Walter Sanders; 1/18, Rita Hayworth—Philippe Halsman; 1/25, Eddie Rickenbacker—Dmitri Kessel, LIFE; 2/1, Dating in Casablanca—Eliot Elisofon, LIFE; 2/8, Plane spotter—Eric Schaal; 2/15, Princess Elizabeth—Cecil Beaton; 2/22, Army air observer—Dmitri Kessel, LIFE; 3/1, Bow ties in fashion—Philippe Halsman; 3/8, Gen. Brehon Somervell—Myron H. Davis, LIFE; 3/15, WAVES—Martin Munkacsi; 3/22, Gen. George Kenney—INP; 3/29, Joseph Stalin—Margaret Bourke-White, LIFE; 4/5, Montgomery berets in fashion—Philippe Halsman; 4/12, Jefferson Memorial—Alfred Eisenstaedt; 4/19, Soldier's farewell—Alfred Eisenstaedt; 4/26, Junior Army-Navy Organization—Alfred Eisenstaedt; 5/3, Matching dress and parasol in fashion—Philippe Halsman; 5/10, PT boat skippers—Dmitri Kessel, LIFE; 5/17, Boy welder—Charles Steinheimer; 5/24, Actress Peggy Lloyd—John Florea; 5/31, Saudi Arabian King Ibn Saud—Robert Landry, LIFE; 6/7, Capt. Joe Foss—Myron H. Davis, LIFE; 6/14, High school graduation—Fritz Goro, LIFE; 6/21, Igor Sikorsky with helicopter—Frank Scherschel, LIFE; 6/28, War souvenir—Nina Leen; 7/5, America's combat dead—Hart Preston, LIFE; 7/12, Roy Rogers and Trigger—Walter Sanders; 7/19, Air Force auxiliary pilot—Peter Stackpole, LIFE; 7/26, 8th Air Force B-24 squadron—David E. Scherman, LIFE; 8/2, British Adm. Sir Max Kennedy Horton—No Credit; 8/9, Steelworker—Margaret Bourke-White, LIFE; 8/16, Japanese soldiers—Paul Dorsey; 8/23, Lindy Hoppers—Gjon Mili; 8/30, Anthony Eden with his dog Nipper—David E. Scherman, LIFE; 9/6, American soldiers hunting Japanese—William Shrout, LIFE; 9/13, Leotards in fashion—Nina Leen; 9/20, Cambridge don Charles Seltman—Hans Wild, LIFE; 9/27, Harvester—Gordon Coster; 10/4, U.S. Ambassador to governments-in-exile Anthony Biddle—Hans Wild, LIFE; 10/11, Half hats in fashion—Philippe Halsman; 10/18, Wartime romance—Sam Levitz; 10/25, Mary Martin—George Karger; 11/1, Thunderbolt fighter—Frank Scherschel, LIFE; 11/8, British Field Marshal Jan Smuts—AP; 11/15, Fur-lined coats in fashion—Walter Sanders; 11/22,

Foot soldiers—Eliot Elisofon, LIFE; 11/29, Gen. Ira Eaker—Margaret Bourke-White, LIFE; 12/6, Earmuffs in fashion—Walter Sanders; 12/13, Chinese Muslim—William Vandivert, LIFE; 12/20, U.S. pilot's wife—Frank Scherschel, LIFE; 12/27, Wounded Soldier with Nurse—illustration by Fletcher Martin.

1944

1/3, Alaska holiday—Dmitri Kessel, LIFE; 1/10, Bob Hope—Peter Stackpole, LIFE; 1/17, Historian Charles Beard—Walter Sanders; 1/24, Margaret Sullavan—Nina Leen; 1/31, British Air Chief Marshal Sir Arthur Tedder—Eliot Elisofon, LIFE; 2/7, George Bernard Shaw—Yousuf Karsh; 2/14, "Wall of Fame" facade of Earl Carroll theater—Ralph Crane; 2/21, Patrice Munsel—Philippe Halsman; 2/28, Actress Ella Raines—Walter Sanders; 3/6, Adm. Chester Nimitz—Robert Landry, LIFE; 3/13, Junior school dance—Alfred Eisenstaedt; 3/20, Ballerina Nana Gollner—Ralph Crane; 3/27, Landing craft, Infantry—George Rodger, LIFE; 4/3, Pooch—Nina Leen; 4/10, British Air Marshal Arthur T. Harris—Combine; 4/17, Esther Williams—Ralph Crane; 4/24, Princess Elizabeth—Yousuf Karsh; 5/1, Homecoming—Kosti Ruohomaa; 5/8, Hattie Carnegie suit in fashion—Philippe Halsman; 5/15, British Gen. Sir Bernard Montgomery—George Rodger, LIFE; 5/22, Model mother and son—Nina Leen; 5/29, Gen. Carl Spaatz—Graphic Photo Union; 6/5, U.S. infantrymen—U.S. Army Signal Corps; 6/12, Bombs falling on Italy—U.S. Army Air Force; 6/19, Gen. Dwight D. Eisenhower—U.S. Army; 6/26, Statue of Liberty—Dmitri Kessel, LIFE; 7/3, Back from the front—U.S. Army Signal Corps; 7/10, Adm. Chester Nimitz—Dmitri Kessel, LIFE; 7/17, Peasant clothes in fashion—Nina Leen; 7/24, Jennifer Jones—Philippe Halsman; 7/31, Soviet Marshal Georgi Zhukov—Gregory Weil; 8/7, Geraldine Fitzgerald—Philippe Halsman; 8/14, Airborne infantry officer in Normandy—Robert Landry, LIFE; 8/21, Amphibious tractors—John Florea, LIFE; 8/28, Pedal pushers in fashion—Zoltan S. Farkas; 9/4, Cordell Hull—Yousuf Karsh; 9/11, Nazi prisoners—INP; 9/18, Thomas E. Dewey—Walter Sanders, LIFE; 9/25, A letter to GIs—Howe Sadler; 10/2, Gen. Lucian Truscott—George Silk, LIFE; 10/9, Helena Rubenstein's Dali room—George Karger; 10/16, Lauren Bacall—Philippe Halsman; 10/23, Soviet scientist Alexei Krylov—G. Vehl; 10/30, U.S.S. *Iowa*—U.S. Navy; 11/6, Celeste Holm—Eileen Darby; 11/13, Gen. Charles de Gaulle—Yousuf Karsh; 11/20, Thanksgiving—Bernard Hoffman, LIFE; 11/27, Gertrude Lawrence—Philippe Halsman; 12/4, B-29s over Formosa—Alexanderson; 12/11, Judy Garland—Philippe Halsman; 12/18, Fredric March—Eileen Darby; 12/25, *Madonna and Child* (Lauren Ford).

1945

1/1, Soldier cleaning gun—David E. Scherman, LIFE; 1/8, Scarves in fashion—Nina Leen; 1/15, Gen. George Patton—Ralph Morse; 1/22, St. John's University basketball—Gjon Mili; 1/29, Wounded soldier—Ralph Morse, LIFE; 2/5, Florida fashions—Nina Leen; 2/12, Soviet soldier—Time Inc.; 2/19, Ski clothes in fashion—Alfred Eisenstaedt; 2/26, Winter soldiers—George Silk, LIFE; 3/5, Flying over San Francisco's Presidio—William C. Shrout, LIFE; 3/12, Gen. William Simpson—William Vandivert, LIFE; 3/19, Dutch girl—George Rodger, LIFE; 3/26, Carol Lynne—Gjon Mili; 4/2, Subdeb clubs—Nina Leen; 4/9, Iwo Jima—© W. Eugene Smith, LIFE; 4/16, Gen. Dwight D. Eisenhower—David E. Scherman; 4/23, Harry S. Truman—Yousuf Karsh; 4/30, War artists—Myron H. Davis, LIFE; 5/7, The German people—William Vandivert, LIFE; 5/14, Victorious Yank—Robert Capa, LIFE; 5/21, Winston Churchill—Yousuf Karsh; 5/28, Starlet Barbara Bates—Phil Stern; 6/4, War loan drive—design by Charles Tudor and Bernard Quint; 6/11, Teenage boys—Nina Leen; 6/18, Girl Scouts in Washington, D.C.—Alfred Eisenstaedt; 6/25, Kindergarten graduation—Nina Leen; 7/2, Pacific fleet destroyers—Eliot Elisofon, LIFE; 7/9, Bathing suits in fashion—Ewing Krainin; 7/16, Audie Murphy—James Longhead; 7/23, Actress Peggy Ann Garner—Eileen Darby; 7/30, Playing on the beach—Harriet Arnold; 8/6, Junior sailors—Allan Grant; 8/13, Jet plane—Erik Miller; 8/20, Gen. Carl Spaatz—Thomas D. McAvoy, LIFE; 8/27, Ballet swimmer—Walter Sanders, LIFE; 9/3, House party—Jerry Cooke; 9/10, Autoworker—William C. Shrout, LIFE; 9/17, Gen. Douglas MacArthur—Andrew Lopez; 9/24, Col. Jimmy Stewart—Peter Stackpole, LIFE; 10/1, June Allyson—Harold Trudeau; 10/8, Gen. Robert Eichelberger—U.S. Navy; 10/15, Fall jewelry in fashion—Ewing Krainin; 10/22, Ohio State's Paul Sarringhaus—Myron H. Davis, LIFE; 10/29, Autumn—Kosti Ruohomaa; 11/5, Fleet's in—Eileen Darby; 11/12, Ingrid Bergman—Philippe Halsman; 11/19, Big belts in fashion—Nina Leen; 11/26, Champion Afghan—Nina Leen; 12/3, Spencer Tracy—Eileen Darby; 12/10, Party dresses in fashion—Philippe Halsman; 12/17, Paulette Goddard—Whitey Schaefer; 12/24, *Procession to Bethlehem* (fresco in Medici Palace)—Fernand Bourges; 12/31, Mountain climbing—Jerry Cooke.

1946

1/7, Winston Churchill's paintings—Hans Wild, LIFE; 1/14, Southern resort fashions—Philippe Halsman; 1/21, Cardinal Spellman—Lisa Larsen; 1/28, Actress Jan Clayton—Philippe Halsman; 2/4, Bob Hope and Bing Crosby—Jack Koffman; 2/11, Lincoln Memorial—George Skadding, LIFE; 2/18, Dorothy McGuire—Ralph Crane; 2/25, Pointer—William C. Shrout, LIFE; 3/4, Figure skater—Ralph Crane; 3/11, Sen. Arthur Vandenberg—Yousuf Karsh; 3/18, Eiffel Tower—Edward Clark, LIFE; 3/25, Actress Lucille Bremer—Philippe Halsman; 4/1, St. Louis Cardinals Red Barrett—Frank Scherschel, LIFE; 4/8, Clown Lou Jacobs—Loomis Dean; 4/15, Spring fashions—Ralph Crane; 4/22, Denver high school—Jerry Cooke; 4/29, Marble Pagoda in Peiping—Dmitri Kessel, LIFE; 5/6, Margaret Leighton—Eileen Darby; 5/13, Northwest vacation—Jerry Cooke; 5/20, *Ice Capades*—Bradley Smith; 5/27, Ozark farmer—Kosti Ruohomaa; 6/3, Children in church—Loomis Dean; 6/10, Donna Reed—Robert Landry, LIFE; 6/17, Play dresses—Lisa Larsen; 6/24, Chief Justice Fred Vinson—Yousuf Karsh; 7/1, Sailing season—Morris Rosenfeld; 7/8, Basque shirts in fashion—Loomis Dean; 7/15, Water gadgets—Roger Coster; 7/22, Mrs. Cornelius Vanderbilt Whitney with coachman—Nina Leen; 7/29, Vivien Leigh—Philippe Halsman; 8/5, Radio's *Juvenile Jury* participant—Jerry Cooke; 8/12, Loretta Young—Robert Landry, LIFE; 8/19, Old Faithful—Alfred Eisenstaedt; 8/26, College fashions—Lisa Larsen; 9/2, Vacation's end—Cornell Capa, LIFE; 9/9, Jane Powell—Martha Holmes, LIFE; 9/16, West Point's Glenn Davis and Felix Blanchard—Alfred Eisenstaedt; 9/23, Dachshund—Frank Scherschel, LIFE; 9/30, Jeanne Crain—Peter Stackpole, LIFE; 10/7, Bing Crosby and Joan Caulfield—Nina Leen; 10/14, Fall fashions—Ralph Crane; 10/21, Gloria Grahame—George Strock; 10/28, One-room school—Bernard Hoffman, LIFE; 11/4, Arab policeman with camel in Palestine—David Douglas Duncan, LIFE; 11/11, High school model Shirley Arnow—Peter Stackpole, LIFE; 11/18, Party raincoats in fashion—Loomis Dean; 11/25, LIFE's 10th anniversary—Herbert Gehr (Edmund B. Gerard); 12/2, Ingrid Bergman—Gjon Mili; 12/9, Jet pilot—Charles Steinheimer; 12/16, Teresa Wright—Philippe Halsman; 12/23, *The Flight into Egypt* (Fra Angelico); 12/30, Dorothy Kirsten—Nina Leen.

1947

1/6, Annapolis "Drag"—Lisa Larsen; 1/13, Resort fashions—Philippe Halsman; 1/20, Homesteading veteran—Jon Brenneis; 1/27, Nantucket lighthouse—Eliot Elisofon; 2/3, Actresses Susan Douglas, Patricia Kirkland and Patricia Neal—Nina Leen; 2/10, Occupation of Germany—Walter Sanders, LIFE; 2/17, Water-skier—Robert Wheeler; 2/24, Texas coed—Loomis Dean; 3/3, Renaissance man in armor—Walter Sanders, LIFE; 3/10, Father's Day bath—Cornell Capa, LIFE; 3/17, Youth center director—Allan Grant, LIFE; 3/24, Eskimo baby—Harmon Helmericks; 3/31, Spring hats in fashion—Philippe Halsman; 4/7, Sunday school pupils—Leonard McCombe; 4/14, Pretty girls and flowering dogwood—Ralph Royle; 4/21, Student veteran—Margaret Bourke-White, LIFE; 4/28, Actress Bambi Linn—Philippe Halsman; 5/5, Riding clothes in fashion—Andre De Dienes; 5/12, Bulgarian PM Georgi Dimitrov—David Douglas Duncan, LIFE; 5/19, Teenager's sundae—Jack Birns; 5/26, Medieval castle—Hans Wild, LIFE; 6/2, Jane Greer—Sharland; 6/9, Ballerina Ricky Soma—Philippe Halsman; 6/16, Cape Hatteras Bay—Kosti Ruohomaa; 6/23, Bathing suits in fashion—Philippe Halsman; 6/30, Ancient and modern Mayan sculpture (from Chichén Itzá)—Dmitri Kessel, LIFE; 7/7, Little girl on merry-go-round—William Sumits, LIFE; 7/14, Elizabeth Taylor—Robert Landry; 7/21, Americans in Heidelberg—Walter Sanders, LIFE; 7/28, Princess Elizabeth—Cecil Beaton; 8/4, *Portrait of a Man in a Red Cap* (Titian)—courtesy The Frick Collection; 8/11, Actress Ella Raines—Arnold Newman; 8/18, Lord Louis Mountbatten—David Douglas Duncan; 8/25, Model Gail Sullivan in college fashions—Arnold Newman; 9/1, Auto racer John Cobb—Jon Brenneis; 9/8, Lady Sarah Fitzalan-Howard—Pat English; 9/15, *Madame Du Barry* (François Drouais); 9/22, Fall fashions—Nina Leen; 9/29, Notre Dame's Johnny Lujack—Hy Peskin; 10/6, Franklin D. Roosevelt at 13—courtesy Franklin D. Roosevelt Library; 10/13, Katina von Oss in *Allegro* opening on Broadway—Arnold Newman; 10/20, Child listening to folk songs—© W. Eugene Smith, LIFE; 10/27, Amb. Lewis Douglas—Arnold Newman; 11/3, Ballerinas Ruth Koesun and Melissa Hayden—Philippe Halsman; 11/10, Rita Hayworth—Johnny Florea, LIFE; 11/17, Boxers—Ylla; 11/24, Subdeb Pamela Helene Dudley Curran—Peter Stackpole, LIFE; 12/1, Gregory Peck—Nina Leen; 12/8, Boyhood portrait of Duke of Windsor—Press Portrait Bureau; 12/15, Nightclub girls—Gjon Mili; 12/22, *Christmas Carols* (Gladys R. Davis); 12/29, Pretty girl in Miami—Ralph Crane.

1948

1/5, Pakistan's Muhammad Ali Jinnah—Margaret Bourke-White, LIFE; 1/12, Midwinter accessories in fashion—Philippe Halsman; 1/19, Violinist Marcia Van Dyke—Johnny Florea, LIFE; 1/26, Resort fashions—Richard Avedon; 2/2, Maine schoolboy—Kosti Ruohomaa; 2/9, Robert A. Taft—Nina Leen; 2/16, Actress Joan Tetzel—Arnold Newman; 2/23, Skiing—Ralph Crane; 3/1, Harold E. Stassen—Philippe Halsman; 3/8, Model Gaby Bouché—John Raymond; 3/15, Sir Laurence Olivier—N. R. Farbman, LIFE; 3/22, Thomas E. Dewey—Philippe Halsman; 3/29, Basket handbags in fashion—Sharland; 4/5, Baseball rookies—George Silk, LIFE; 4/12, Barbara Bel Geddes—Loomis Dean, LIFE; 4/19, *Winston Churchill* (Chandor); 4/26, Collegians in Bermuda—Lisa Larsen; 5/3, Career girl—Leonard McCombe; 5/10, Gov. Earl Warren—Will Connell; 5/17, Mrs. David Niven—Louise Dahl-Wolfe; 5/24, Sen. Arthur Vandenberg—Nina Leen; 5/31, Television ingenue Kyle MacDonnell—Sharland; 6/7, Hooded T-shirts in fashion—Lisa Larsen; 6/14, Actress Phyllis Calvert—Loomis Dean, LIFE; 6/21, Cape Cod weekend—Lisa Larsen; 6/28, Member of Kent School crew—George Silk, LIFE; 7/5, F-84 Thunderjets—Ralph Morse, LIFE; 7/12, Small-town girl—Sharland; 7/19, Fun on the beach—Michael Lavelle; 7/26, Children's ballet school—Peter Stackpole, LIFE; 8/2, Olympic sprinter Mel Patton—Robert Landry; 8/9, Marlene Dietrich—Arnold Newman; 8/16, Little fisherman—Rue Faris Drew; 8/23, Young hunter with pet deer—Jon Brenneis; 8/30, Actress Colleen Townsend—Loomis Dean, LIFE; 9/6, The good life in Madison, Wis.—Alfred Eisenstaedt; 9/13, Marshal Tito—John Phillips, LIFE; 9/20, Actress Joan Diener—© W. Eugene Smith, LIFE; 9/27, SMU's Doak Walker—Michael Lavelle; 10/4, Big industry in America—J. R. Eyerman, LIFE; 10/11, Actress Rita Colton—Sharland; 10/18, Fur jackets in fashion—Gordon Parks; 10/25, University of California football fans—Ralph Crane; 11/1, Gen. Lauris Norstadt—Philippe Halsman; 11/8, Actress Helena Carter—Loomis Dean, LIFE; 11/15, Ingrid Bergman as Joan of Arc—Loomis Dean; 11/22, Harry S. Truman—© W. Eugene Smith, LIFE; 11/29, Dinner hats in fashion—Nina Leen; 12/6, Montgomery Clift—Robert Landry; 12/13, Dwight D. Eisenhower—Harris & Ewing; 12/20, Teenage fun—Alfred Eisenstaedt; 12/27, *The Story of Christ* (Giotto).

1949

1/3, Famous baby Dwight D. Eisenhower II—Nina Leen; 1/10, Debutante Joanne Connelley—Hal Phyfe; 1/17, Resort fashions—Leonard McCombe; 1/24, Skier Emile Allais—Pierre de Boucher; 1/31, Champion cocker spaniel—George Karger; 2/7, Churchill's memoirs—No Credit; 2/14, Viveca Lindfors—Philippe Halsman; 2/21, Dean Acheson—Arnold Newman; 2/28, Children's costume clothes—Nina Leen; 3/7, Marge and Gower Champion—Nina Leen; 3/14, Dorothy McGuire's baby—John Swope; 3/21, Fashion wardrobe—Nina Leen; 3/28, Actress Joy Lansing—Johnny Florea, LIFE; 4/4, U.S. official Paul Hoffman—Yousuf Karsh; 4/11, Boy on fence during spring along the Mississippi—Loomis Dean, LIFE; 4/18, Mary Martin—Philippe Halsman; 4/25, Paris fashion—Gordon Parks, LIFE; 5/2, West Point's Arnold Galiffa—Arnold Newman; 5/9, Missouri coed Jane Stone—Peter Stackpole, LIFE; 5/16, Little boxer—Rue Faris Drew; 5/23, Sarah Churchill—Anthony Beauchamps; 5/30, Baby Franklin D. Roosevelt—Stefan Lorant Collection/Franklin D. Roosevelt Library; 6/6, Summer play clothes in fashion—Lisa Larsen; 6/13, Actress Marta Toren—Philippe Halsman; 6/20, High school graduate—Leonard McCombe; 6/27, Inland sailing—George Silk, LIFE; 7/4, Beach holiday—Ida Wayman; 7/11, Olympian Bob Mathias—Michael Rougier, LIFE; 7/18, Hollywood child Sharon Harmon—Lisa Larsen; 7/25, Girl in plastic beach boat—George Silk, LIFE; 8/1, Joe DiMaggio—Hy Peskin; 8/8, Straw hats in fashion—Nina Leen; 8/15, Actress Brynn Noring—Philippe Halsman; 8/22, Cowboy—Leonard McCombe; 8/29, College fashions—Philippe Halsman; 9/5, Ben Turpin—AP; 9/12, Marshal Tito—John Phillips, LIFE; 9/19, Arlene Dahl—Jon Brenneis; 9/26, Fashion secret—Arnold Newman; 10/3, North Carolina's Charlie Justice—Eliot Elisofon, LIFE; 10/10, J. Robert Oppenheimer—Arnold Newman; 10/17, Actress Jeanne Crain—Arnold Newman; 10/24, Sweden's ideal pretty girl: Haide Goranson—Karl G. Kristoffersson; 10/31, Princess Margaret—Dorothy Wilding; 11/7, Alfred Lunt and Lynn Fontanne—Philippe Halsman; 11/14, Pearls in fashion—Arnold Newman; 11/21, Actor Ricardo Montalban—Alfred Eisenstaedt; 11/28, Dancer Nita Bieber—Ralph Crane; 12/5, Gen. Hoyt Vandenberg—Toni Frissel; 12/12, Beauty on Fifth Avenue: Joan Appleton—Leonard McCombe; 12/19, Little girl clothes in fashion—Nina Leen; 12/26, *God the Creator* from the Sistine Chapel ceiling (Michelangelo).

1950

1/2, Gibson girl look—Arnold Newman; 1/9, Actress Norma de Landa—Leonard McCombe; 1/16, Young skater—George Silk, LIFE; 1/23, Man-tailored shirts in fashion—Gordon Parks, LIFE; 1/30, Childbirth without fear—David Linton; 2/6, Eva Gabor—Philippe Halsman; 2/13, Indonesian woman—Henri Cartier-Bresson; 2/20, Gregory Peck—© W. Eugene Smith, LIFE; 2/27, Atomic explosion—Joint Task Force One; 3/6, Actress Marsha Hunt—Philippe Halsman; 3/13, Spring fashions—Gjon Mili; 3/20, Artist Edward John Stevens Jr.—Arnold Newman; 3/27, Model Anne Bromley—Alfred Eisenstaedt; 4/3, Iris Mann and David Cole on Broadway—Philippe Halsman; 4/10, Young horsewoman—John Dominis, LIFE; 4/17, Dwight D. Eisenhower—Arnold Newman; 4/24, Inexpensive blouses in fashion—Milton H. Greene; 5/1, Actress Ruth Roman—Edward Clark, LIFE; 5/8, Jackie Robinson—J. R. Eyerman, LIFE; 5/15, Beach fashions—Nina Leen; 5/22, Duke and Duchess of Windsor—Philippe Halsman; 5/29, Mrs. William O'Dwyer—Alfred Eisenstaedt; 6/5, Actress Stasia Kos—John Raymond; 6/12, William Boyd (Hopalong Cassidy)—Robert W. Kelley, LIFE; 6/19, Children's beach fashions—Nina Leen; 6/26, Actress Cecile Aubry—Philippe Halsman; 7/3, *Washington at Trenton* (Sully); 7/10, Actress Miroslava Stern—Philippe Halsman; 7/17, Jet pilot—David Douglas Duncan, LIFE; 7/24, Boy Scout—Robert W. Kelley, LIFE; 7/31, 24th Division soldiers—Carl Mydans, LIFE; 8/7, Actress Peggy Dow—Ralph Crane; 8/14, Adm. John Hoskins—David Douglas Duncan, LIFE; 8/21, Broadway chorines—Philippe Halsman; 8/28, *General Douglas MacArthur* (Stephens); 9/4, Two Marines on reconnaissance—David Douglas Duncan; 9/11, American elegance in fashion—Nina Leen; 9/18, Ezio Pinza—Ralph Crane; 9/25, Swedish Red Cross girl—Nina Leen; 10/2, U.S. official Stuart Symington—Philippe Halsman; 10/9, Jean Simmons—Philippe Halsman; 10/16, Winnetka high school girl—Alfred Eisenstaedt; 10/23, Ed Wynn—Philippe

Halsman; 10/30, Faye Emerson—Martha Holmes; 11/6, Horse-show rider—Milton H. Greene; 11/13, SMU's Kyle Rote—Joe Scherschel, LIFE; 11/20, Girl of Shilluk tribe—Eliot Elisofon, LIFE; 11/27, UCLA homecoming queen—Richard Hartt; 12/4, Berlin girl—Nina Leen; 12/11, Lilli Palmer and Rex Harrison—Leonard McCombe; 12/18, Gen. George Marshall—Yale Joel, LIFE; 12/25, Girls Painting—illustrated by John Koch.

1951

1/1, U.S. official Charles E. Wilson—Arnold Newman; 1/8, Starlet Janice Rule—Anthony Beauchamps; 1/15, Rose Parade grand marshal—Edward Clark, LIFE; 1/22, Air-warning supervisor—Mark Kauffman, LIFE; 1/29, Actress Betsy Von Furstenberg—Slim Aarons; 2/5, N.Y.C. Police Commissioner Thomas F. Murphy—Arnold Newman; 2/12, Veiled hats in fashion—Milton H. Greene; 2/19, Adoption of Linda Joy—Edward Clark; 2/26, Debbie Reynolds—Philippe Halsman; 3/5, Dior fashions—Gordon Parks, LIFE; 3/12, Actor Paul Douglas—J. R. Eyerman, LIFE; 3/19, Navy couple—Slim Aarons; 3/26, Child choir singer—Esther Bubley; 4/2, Jet-setter Mercedes Spradling—Leonard McCombe; 4/9, Gen. Omar Bradley—Arnold Newman; 4/16, Esther Williams—Peter Stackpole, LIFE; 4/23, Dalai Lama—Heinrich Harrer; 4/30, Gen. Matthew Ridgway—John Dominis, LIFE; 5/7, Actress Phyllis Kirk—John Raymond; 5/14, Michigan's Sen. Blair Moody and sons—Mark Kauffman, LIFE; 5/21, Beach fashions—Milton H. Greene; 5/28, Falling paratrooper—Hank Walker, LIFE; 6/4, Model Ursula Theiss—Relang; 6/11, Actress Vivian Blaine—Milton H. Greene; 6/18, Iran's royal crown—Dmitri Kessel, LIFE; 6/25, Actress Janet Leigh—Philippe Halsman; 7/2, Sgt. John Pittman with Medal of Honor—Arnold Newman; 7/9, Summer party in Charlotte, N.C.—Lisa Larsen; 7/16, TV actress Dagmar—Alfred Eisenstaedt, LIFE; 7/23, Swimmer Mary Freeman—Hank Walker, LIFE; 7/30, Singer Gary Crosby—John Engstead; 8/6, Vacationing high school girl—Howard Staples; 8/13, Dean Martin and Jerry Lewis—Philippe Halsman; 8/20, Swimmer Barbara Hobelmann—Leonard McCombe; 8/27, Model Rosemary Coover—Milton H. Greene; 9/3, Gina Lollobrigida—Philippe Halsman; 9/10, Japanese PM Shigeru Yoshida—Jun Miki; 9/17, Chorus girl—Peter Stackpole, LIFE; 9/24, Gene Tierney—Philippe Halsman; 10/1, Princess Elizabeth—A. Petrocelli; 10/8, Baby Malayan snow loris—Burt Glinn; 10/15, Zsa Zsa Gabor—Philippe Halsman; 10/22, Bronc rider Casey Tibbs—Hy Peskin; 10/29, TV prop girl—Lisa Larsen; 11/5, Ginger Rogers—Arnold Newman; 11/12, Anthony Eden—Alfred Eisenstaedt, LIFE; 11/19, Lynn Fontanne, Katherine Cornell and Helen Hayes—Philippe Halsman; 11/26, Photography contest winner Regina Fisher—John Raymond; 12/3, Christmas lingerie in fashion—Sharland; 12/10, Harry S. Truman—George Skadding, LIFE; 12/17, Vivien Leigh and Laurence Olivier—Philippe Halsman; 12/24, *Nativity* (Tintoretto); 12/31, Asia special issue—David Douglas Duncan, LIFE.

1952

1/7, Hairstyles—Nina Leen; 1/14, Augustus John—Alfred Eisenstaedt, LIFE; 1/21, Dwight D. Eisenhower—Arnold Newman; 1/28, Model, pianist and painter Phyllis Newell—John Raymond; 2/4, Skater Barbara Ann Scott—Milton H. Greene; 2/11, Olympic skier Henri Oreiller—Mark Kauffman, LIFE; 2/18, Queen Elizabeth II—INP; 2/25, Gloves in fashion—Nina Leen; 3/3, Patrice Munsel—Milton H. Greene; 3/10, Actor Brandon de Wilde—Nina Leen; 3/17, Broadway chorus girl—Sharland; 3/24, Composite: Democratic presidential candidates—Philippe Halsman, Mark Kauffman, LIFE, Arnold Newman; 3/31, Li'l Abner characters—drawing by Al Capp; 4/7, Marilyn Monroe—Philippe Halsman; 4/14, Italian fashions—Mark Shaw; 4/22, Marshal Tito—John Phillips; 4/28, Ike and Mamie Eisenhower's wedding picture—No Credit; 5/5, Actress Diana Lynn—Louis Faurer; 5/12, Gen. Matthew Ridgway—John Dominis, LIFE; 5/19, Actress Miriam "Kerima" Charrière—Lopert Films; 5/26, Stewart Granger—George Silk, LIFE; 6/2, Children's party outfits—Mark Shaw; 6/9, Bridal model Martha Boss—Leonard McCombe; 6/16, Dwight D. Eisenhower—Hank Walker, LIFE; 6/23, Mail order fashions—Christa; 6/30, Nancy Kefauver—Alfred Eisenstaedt, LIFE; 7/7, Arlene Dahl—Milton H. Greene; 7/14, Hangover victim—illustration by Robert C. Osborn; 7/21, Dwight D. Eisenhower—Arnold Newman; 7/28, British starlets Joan Elan, Dorothy Bromiley and Audrey Dalton—John Engstead; 8/4, Adlai Stevenson—Arnold Newman; 8/11, Actress Joan Rice—Philippe Halsman; 8/18, Marlene Dietrich and daughter Maria Riva—Milton H. Greene; 8/25, College fashions—John Raymond; 9/1, Ernest Hemingway—Alfred Eisenstaedt, LIFE; 9/8, Fall fashions—Milton H. Greene; 9/15, Actress Rita Gam—Philippe Halsman; 9/22, LST at polar base—U.S. Army; 9/29, Jackie Gleason TV chorus girls—Leonard McCombe; 10/6, Mrs. Peter Thieriot at San Francisco Opera opening—John Engstead; 10/13, Mamie Eisenhower—Joe Scherschel, LIFE; 10/20, Actress Lucia Bosé—Milton H. Greene; 10/27, Jon Lindbergh—Howard Schutz; 11/3, New UN assembly building—Philippe Halsman; 11/10, Duck hunter Jean Huston—Howard Sochurek, LIFE; 11/17, Dwight D. and Mamie Eisenhower—Hank Walker, LIFE; 11/24, Jewelry in fashion—Milton H. Greene; 12/1, Actress Suzanne Cloutier—Philippe Halsman; 12/8, *The Earth Is Born* (Bonestell); 12/15, Refugee homecoming queen—Robert W. Kelley, LIFE; 12/22, Midget horse—Edward Clark, LIFE; 12/29, Salzburg marionettes—Walter Sanders, LIFE.

1953

1/5, Houses for $15,000—Nina Leen; 1/12, Resort fashions in Majorca—Milton H. Greene; 1/19, U.S. officials Charles E. Wilson and George M. Humphrey—Leonard McCombe; 1/26, Fashion stylist Sigrid Soelter—Lisa Larsen; 2/2, Dwight D. Eisenhower inauguration—Frank Scherschel, LIFE; 2/9, *Miracles of the Sea* (Lewicki); 2/16, Coldstream Guard—Cornell Capa, LIFE; 2/23, Prettiest teacher Nell Owen—John Dominis, LIFE; 3/2, Formosan soldiers—Horace Bristol; 3/9, Stoles in fashion—Philippe Halsman; 3/16, Joseph Stalin and Georgi Malenkov—Sovfoto; 3/23, Starlet Elaine Stewart—Philippe Halsman; 3/30, Coronation fashions—Milton H. Greene; 4/6, Lucille Ball, Desi Arnaz, Desi IV and Lucy Desirée—Edward Clark, LIFE; 4/13, Delicate Arch in Utah mountains—Joseph Muench; 4/20, Marlon Brando—John Swope; 4/27, Queen Elizabeth II—Baron; 5/4, Masai warrior—Weldon King; 5/11, Denim in fashion—Milton H. Greene; 5/18, Indiana coed—Walter Sanders, LIFE; 5/25, Marilyn Monroe and Jane Russell—Edward Clark, LIFE; 6/1, Brooke Hayward—John Engstead; 6/8, Roy Campanella—Ralph Morse, LIFE; 6/15, Coronation of Elizabeth II—James Jarche; 6/22, Mills College graduate—Jon Brenneis; 6/29, Cyd Charisse—Eliot Elisofon; 7/6, Actress Terry Moore—Philippe Halsman; 7/13, Sir Edmund Hillary and Tenzing Norgay—*London Times;* 7/20, Sen. John F. Kennedy and Jacqueline Bouvier—Hy Peskin; 7/27, Can-can lingerie in fashion—William Helburn; 8/3, Actress Nicole Maurey—Francesco Scavullo; 8/10, Irish fashions—Milton H. Greene; 8/17, Actresses Barbara, Madelyn and Alice Wittlinger—Christa; 8/24, Mormon ballerinas on Connecticut beach—Lisa Larsen; 8/31, Donna Reed—Sharland; 9/7, Stegosaurus and Brontosaurus—illustration by R. F. Zallinger; 9/14, Casey Stengel—Mark Kauffman, LIFE; 9/21, Photographer's daughter—© W. Eugene Smith; 9/28, De Cuevas ball—Frank Scherschel, LIFE; 10/5, New citizens—Ralph Morse, LIFE; 10/12, Bare backs in fashion—Sharland; 10/19, Prehistoric Mammals—illustration by R. F. Zallinger; 10/26, Actress Vikki Dougan—Lisa Larsen; 11/2, Sir Winston Churchill—Philippe Halsman; 11/9, Singer Jill Corey—Gordon Parks, LIFE; 11/16, Greece's Queen Frederica—Frank Scherschel, LIFE; 11/23, College art student—Philippe Halsman; 11/30, Queen triggerfish—Fritz Goro, LIFE; 12/7, Audrey Hepburn—Mark Shaw; 12/14, Richard M. Nixon—Walter Bennett; 12/21, Pajamas in fashion—Sharland; 12/28, *Madonna and Child* in St. Mark's, Venice—Dmitri Kessel, LIFE.

1954

1/4, Regulus missile—Hank Walker, LIFE; 1/11, Debutante wardrobe—Philippe Halsman; 1/18, U.S. officials Leverett Saltonstall, William Knowland and Richard M. Nixon with President Eisenhower—Mark Kauffman, LIFE; 1/25, Dancer Diane Sinclair—Gordon Parks, LIFE; 2/1, Tropical wardrobe—William Helburn; 2/8, Sea turtle—Fritz Goro, LIFE; 2/15, Italian hairdo—Mark Shaw; 2/22, Disney undersea moviemaking—Peter Stackpole, LIFE; 3/1, Actress Rita Moreno—Loomis Dean; 3/8, Churchill's granddaughter Arabella—Carl Mydans, LIFE; 3/15, Mrs. Winthrop Rockefeller—Mark Shaw; 3/22, Emperor penguin—Roger Kirschner; 3/29, Actress Pat Crowley—John Engstead; 4/5, The Desert—O. Roach; 4/12, Subteen fashions—Mark Shaw; 4/19, H-bomb test—U.S. Air Force; 4/26, Grace Kelly—Philippe Halsman; 5/3, Rarest stamps—Alex West; 5/10, Bavaria's Neuschwanstein Castle—Duncan Edwards; 5/17, Starlet Dawn Addams—Philippe Halsman; 5/24, Actress Kaye Ballard—Richard Avedon; 5/31, William Holden—Mark Shaw; 6/7, Arctic Tundra—illustration by Rudolph Freund; 6/14, California fashions—Christa; 6/21, Las Vegas chorus girl—Loomis Dean, LIFE; 6/28, Bathing suits in fashion—Paul Himmel; 7/5, Fourth of July—illustration by Rowland Emett; 7/12, Actress Pier Angeli—Allan Grant, LIFE; 7/19, Eva Marie Saint—Philippe Halsman; 7/26, Army counsel Joseph Welch—Gordon Parks, LIFE; 8/2, *Arabian Nights* at Jones Beach theater—Gordon Parks, LIFE; 8/9, Boy cowpuncher with father—Allan Grant, LIFE; 8/16, Africa's spirited children—Ernst Haas; 8/23, Philip, Duke of Edinburgh, in the Yukon—Alfred Eisenstaedt, LIFE; 8/30, Singer Anna Maria Alberghetti—Loomis Dean, LIFE; 9/6, Dior fashions—Mark Shaw; 9/13, Judy Garland—Bob Willoughby; 9/20, Tropical rain forest—illustration by R. F. Zallinger; 9/27, Hydrofoil—Peter Stackpole, LIFE; 10/4, Wellesley girl and UN guide—Philippe Halsman; 10/11, Mountain climber—Mondadori Press; 10/18, Tacoma congressional campaigner—Burt Glinn; 10/25, The Big Ten Look for coeds—Nina Leen; 11/1, Actress Dorothy Dandridge—Nina Leen; 11/8, New Jersey deer—Gjon Mili; 11/15, Gina Lollobrigida—Philippe Halsman; 11/22, Actress Judy Holliday—Mark Shaw; 11/29, Broadway twins Tani and Dran Seitz—Gene Cook; 12/6, Jet-age man—Ralph Morse, LIFE; 12/13, Pius XII—Yousuf Karsh; 12/20, *Measureless Space* (Bonestell); 12/27, *Joseph and Mary* (Breughel)—Dmitri Kessel, LIFE.

1955

1/3, Food shopping—Arnold Newman; 1/10, Greta Garbo—Edward Steichen; 1/17, Soviet soldiers eye the girls—Henri Cartier-Bresson; 1/24, Tahitian girl bathing—Eliot Elisofon, LIFE; 1/31, Spencer Tracy—J. R. Eyerman, LIFE; 2/7, Vigil of Indian girl in Hindu festival—Leonard McCombe; 2/14, Photographer's family—Wayne Miller; 2/21, Princess Margaret—Leonard McCombe; 2/28, Actress Shelley Winters—Sharland; 3/7, Golden Buddha—Howard Sochurek, LIFE; 3/14, Convoy "Shepherd"—Edward A. Wilson; 3/21, Actress Sheree North—Loomis Dean, LIFE; 3/28, Kilauea volcano—Robert Wenkam; 4/4, Confucianism: festival boats—Howard Sochurek, LIFE; 4/11, Grace Kelly—Philippe Halsman; 4/18, Frigate figurehead—Eliot Elisofon, LIFE; 4/25, Sir Anthony Eden and Lady Clarissa—Philippe Halsman; 5/2, *Oklahoma!* movie dancers—J. R. Eyerman, LIFE; 5/9, Pakistani Muslim girl—David Douglas Duncan, LIFE; 5/16, Happi coats in fashion—Mark Shaw; 5/23, Actress Leslie Caron—Emmett Schoenbaum; 5/30, Rare playing cards—Arnold Newman; 6/6, Henry Fonda—Slim Aarons; 6/13, Scranton mother and Sabbath candles—Cornell Capa; 6/20, Las Vegas dancers—Loomis Dean, LIFE; 6/27, The *Constitution* and crew—Yale Joel, LIFE; 7/4, Fourth of July—Allan Grant, LIFE; 7/11, Actress Susan Strasberg—Philippe Halsman; 7/18, Actress Audrey Hepburn—Philippe Halsman; 7/25, Singer Cathy Crosby—Robert Landry; 8/1, Nikolai Bulganin, Dwight D. Eisenhower, Edgar Faure and Anthony Eden at summit meeting—Frank Scherschel, LIFE; 8/8, Golfer Ben Hogan—Yale Joel, LIFE; 8/15, Gen. Douglas MacArthur—H. Foster Ensminger; 8/22, Sophia Loren—James Whitmore; 8/29, Grandson with grandfather—Leonard McCombe; 9/5, Dior fashions—Mark Shaw; 9/12, Joan Collins—J. R. Eyerman, LIFE; 9/19, *Guys and Dolls*—Gjon Mili; 9/26, Harry S. and Bess Truman—Eliot Elisofon, LIFE; 10/3, Rock Hudson—Sanford H. Roth; 10/10, Princess Margaret—Cecil Beaton; 10/17, Princess Ira Furstenberg and gondolier—James Whitmore; 10/24, Director Cecil B. deMille—G. E. Richardson; 10/31, Partygoer Mrs. Averell Clark Jr.—Fred Lyon; 11/7, Europe's first true human Swanscombe Man—illustration by Carrol Jones; 11/14, Dwight D. Eisenhower convalescing—Carl Iwasaki; 11/21, Actresses Judy Tyler, Jayne Mansfield, Diane Cilento, Lois Smith and Susan Strasberg—Philippe Halsman; 11/28, Carol Channing—Mark Shaw; 12/5, Man-made mink in fashion—Mark Shaw; 12/12, Neanderthal bear cult—illustration by R. F. Zallinger; 12/19, Suits of armor for children—Ralph Morse, LIFE; 12/26, Christianity special issue, Werden crucifix—Dmitri Kessel, LIFE.

1956

1/9, Riviera fashions—Mark Shaw; 1/16, Anita Ekberg—James Whitmore; 1/23, Harry S. Truman—John Dominis, LIFE; 1/30, Henry Ford II—Alfred Eisenstaedt, LIFE; 2/6, Shirley Jones—William Helburn; 2/13, Harry S. Truman and Gen. Douglas MacArthur—U.S. Dept. of Defense; 2/20, Actress Claire Bloom—Philippe Halsman; 2/27, Eskimo family—Fritz Goro, LIFE; 3/5, Kim Novak—Leonard McCombe; 3/12, Dwight D. Eisenhower—Hank Walker, LIFE; 3/19, Sir Winston Churchill—Yousuf Karsh; 3/26, Julie Andrews—Leonard McCombe; 4/2, Teenage telephone tie-up—Grey Villet, LIFE; 4/9, Grace Kelly—Peter Stackpole, LIFE; 4/16, Berber girls—David Douglas Duncan, LIFE; 4/23, Jayne Mansfield—Peter Stackpole, LIFE; 4/30, Margaret Truman and husband Clifton Daniel—Arnold Newman; 5/7, Lazy Susan sunbathers—Loomis Dean, LIFE; 5/14, Gainsborough look in fashion—Mark Shaw; 5/21, Beach towels—Philippe Halsman; 5/28, Deborah Kerr and Yul Brynner—James Mitchell; 6/4, Primping in ancient Sumer—illustration by Frederico Castellon; 6/11, Actress Carroll Baker—Peter Stackpole, LIFE; 6/18, Air Age special issue, Air Force Captain at start of roll—Howard Sochurek, LIFE; 6/25, Mickey Mantle—Ralph Morse, LIFE; 7/2, Actress Stephanie Griffin—Milton H. Greene; 7/9, Debutante Beatrice Lodge—Nina Leen; 7/16, Gary Cooper and Tony Perkins—Don Ornitz; 7/23, *Battle of Buena Vista* (Chamberlain); 7/30, Actress Pier Angeli—Philippe Halsman; 8/6, Stricken S.S. *Andrea Doria* and lifeboat—Loomis Dean, LIFE; 8/13, Dirndls in fashion—Mark Shaw; 8/20, Audrey Hepburn—Ettore Naldoni; 8/27, Adlai Stevenson and Eleanor Roosevelt—Cornell Capa; 9/3, *Slave Auction* (Robert Riggs); 9/10, Actress Siobhan McKenna—Philippe Halsman; 9/17, S.S. *Andrea Doria* salvage—Peter Gimbel, Robert Dill, Earl Murray and Ramsey Parks; 9/24, Actress Janet Blair—Ormond Gigli; 10/1, *Egyptian Artist* (Xavier Gonzales); 10/8, Masonic grand masters—Arnold Newman; 10/15, Elizabeth Taylor—Mark Shaw; 10/22, *Bather of Valpincon* (Ingres); 11/29, Plane crash rescue—Dr. Marcel Touze; 11/5, Dwight D. Eisenhower in Minneapolis crowd—Hank Walker, LIFE; 11/12, Rosalind Russell—Mark Shaw; 11/19, Wounded Egyptian soldier—Burt Glinn; 11/26, Ingrid Bergman—Robert Landry; 12/3, Flag on sunken U.S.S. *Arizona*—N. R. Farbman, LIFE; 12/10, Olympic sprinter Bobby Morrow—Richard Meek; 12/17, Baptism—Gordon Parks, LIFE; 12/24, American Women special issue, mother and daughter—Grey Villet, LIFE.

1957

1/7, Richard M. Nixon and Hungarian refugee children—Loomis Dean, LIFE; 1/14, *Li'l Abner* chorus—Gjon Mili; 1/21, Harold Macmillan—Yousuf Karsh; 1/28, B-52—Maj. Harvey Yorke; 2/4, Audrey Hepburn and Mel Ferrer—Philippe Halsman; 2/11, Vacationing swimmer—Milton H. Greene; 2/18, Singer Julie London—Leonard McCombe, LIFE; 2/25, Masked dancer—Eliot Elisofon, LIFE; 3/4, Queen Elizabeth II and the Duke of Edinburgh—Mark Kauffman, LIFE; 3/11, John F. Kennedy—Hank Walker, LIFE; 3/18, Beatrice Lillie and Ziegfeld Follies chorus—Philippe Halsman; 3/25, Princess Caroline of Monaco at her christening—Howell Conant; 4/1, Model Marie-Helene Arnaud—Loomis Dean, LIFE; 4/8, Flying Blue brothers—Yale Joel, LIFE; 4/15, Comedian Ernie Kovacs—Ralph Morse, LIFE; 4/22, Actress Carol Lynley—Mark

Shaw; 4/29, Drag race start—A. Y. Owen; 5/6, Sophia Loren—Leonard McCombe, LIFE; 5/13, Actor Bert Lahr—Mark Shaw; 5/20, Air Force Vertijet—John Bryson; 5/27, Knights of Columbus—Walter Sanders, LIFE; 6/3, Making of a satellite—Hank Walker, LIFE; 6/10, Helicopter safari—Howard Sochurek, LIFE; 6/17, *Mayflower II* voyage—Gordon Tenney; 6/24, Prince Juan Carlos of Spain—Nina Leen; 7/1, Billy Graham—Gjon Mili; 7/8, King Ranch roundup—Eliot Elisofon, LIFE; 7/15, Actress Maria Schell—Leonard McCombe, LIFE; 7/22, Dr. Hannes Lindemann in transatlantic canoe—Peter Stackpole, LIFE; 7/29, Baby-sitter—Leonard McCombe, LIFE; 8/5, Debutante Julia Williamson—Mark Kauffman, LIFE; 8/12, Actress Mai Britt—Don Ornitz; 8/19, Four Du Ponts—Cornell Capa; 8/26, San Simeon's pool—Gjon Mili; 9/2, Balloonist—Maj. David G. Simons; 9/9, *N.Y. Street Gang* (Robert Weaver); 9/16, Cincinnati police chief—Francis Miller, LIFE; 9/23, Model turned actress Suzy Parker—Milton H. Greene; 9/30, Actress Kay Kendall and husband Rex Harrison—Ormond Gigli; 10/7, U.S. troops at Little Rock, Ark.—John Bryson; 10/14, Milwaukee parade for Braves and Manager Fred Honey—Frank Scherschel, LIFE; 10/21, U.S. scientists plot Sputnik orbit—Dmitri Kessel, LIFE; 10/28, Queen Elizabeth II opens Canada's Parliament—Frank Scherschel, LIFE; 11/4, Elizabeth Taylor and daughter Liza Todd—Toni Frissel; 11/11, Air-supported dome for swimming—Bradley Smith; 11/18, Rocket designer Wernher von Braun—Ralph Crane, LIFE; 11/25, Actress Elsa Martinelli—Mark Shaw; 12/2, Nikita Khrushchev—David Douglas Duncan, LIFE; 12/9, Richard M. Nixon and Press Secretary James C. Hagerty—Hank Walker, LIFE; 12/16, *Mary and Jesus* (Michelangelo)—Gjon Mili; 12/23, America's World Abroad special issue, U.S. information officer in Laos—John Dominis, LIFE.

1958

1/6, Space pilot Scott Crossfield—Ralph Morse, LIFE; 1/13, Revolution in Petrograd—illustration by Altron S. Tobey; 1/20, Texas Sen. Lyndon B. Johnson—Hank Walker, LIFE; 1/27, Ski fashions—Loomis Dean, LIFE; 2/3, Shirley Temple and 3-year-old daughter Lori—Leonard McCombe, LIFE; 2/10, Actor Ralph Bellamy—Alfred Eisenstaedt, LIFE; 2/17, Tracking a U.S. satellite—N. R. Farbman, LIFE; 2/24, *Fasching* in Germany—Loomis Dean, LIFE; 3/3, Actress Sally Ann Howes—Milton H. Greene; 3/10, Yul Brynner—Eric Carpenter; 3/17, The McGuire Sisters—William Helbrun; 3/24, Soviet and U.S. high schoolers—Howard Sochurek, LIFE, and Stan Wayman, LIFE; 3/31, Science teachers—N. R. Farbman, LIFE; 4/7, Middleweights Sugar Ray Robinson and Carmen Basilio—George Silk, LIFE; 4/14, Actress Gwen Verdon—Eliot Elisofon, LIFE; 4/21, Jacqueline, Caroline and John F. Kennedy—Nina Leen; 4/28, Willie Mays in San Francisco—Leonard McCombe, LIFE; 5/5, Cancer patient and radiation machine—Esther Bubley; 5/12, Former Iranian Queen Soraya—Gordon Parks, LIFE; 5/19, Actress Margaret O'Brien—Bob Willoughby; 5/26, Venezuelan rioters attack Richard M. Nixon's car—Paul Schutzer, LIFE; 6/2, Charles de Gaulle—Eugene Kammerman; 6/9, French veteran demonstrates—Jean Marquis; 6/16, Children in swings—Yale Joel, LIFE; 6/23, Seniors with yearbook—Gordon Parks, LIFE; 6/30, Federal official Sherman Adams and Dwight D. Eisenhower—Paul Schutzer, LIFE, and Hank Walker, LIFE; 7/7, Lebanese rebels—James Whitmore, LIFE; 7/14, Oklahoma wheat—A. Y. Owen; 7/21, Roy Campanella—Alfred Eisenstaedt, LIFE; 7/28, Marines in Lebanon—Larry Burrows; 8/4, Gen. James M. Gavin—Alfred Eisenstaedt, LIFE; 8/11, Couple sailing—Paul Schutzer, LIFE; 8/18, Anne Frank snapshot and diary—Loomis Dean, LIFE; 8/25, Two airline stewardesses—Peter Stackpole, LIFE; 9/1, Commander William Anderson of submarine *Nautilus*—Gordon Tenney; 9/8, Galapagos Tortoise and Flycatcher—illustration by Rudolph Freund; 9/15, Bing Crosby's four boys—Bill Bridges; 9/22, George Burns and Gracie Allen—Allan Grant, LIFE; 9/29, Gun draw—Ernst Haas; 10/6, Actress France Nuyen—Milton H. Greene; 10/13, British Field Marshal Bernard Montgomery—Mark Kauffman, LIFE; 10/20, Mamie Eisenhower—Edward Clark, LIFE; 10/27, College of Cardinals—Dmitri Kessel, LIFE; 11/3, Aga Khan IV—Hank Walker, LIFE; 11/10, Pope John XXIII—Bruno del Priore; 11/17, Nelson and Happy Rockefeller—Ralph Morse, LIFE; 11/24, Kim Novak—Ralph Crane, LIFE; 12/1, Singer Ricky Nelson—Ralph Crane, LIFE; 12/8, New York society women—Howell Conant; 12/15, Prehistoric Explosion—illustration by Chesley Bonestell; 12/22, U.S. Entertainment special issue, 1,076 trombone players—Hank Walker, LIFE.

1959

1/5, New generation in Shanghai—Henri Cartier-Bresson; 1/12, Sen. Hubert Humphrey—Alfred Eisenstaedt, LIFE; 1/19, Fidel Castro—Andrew St. George; 1/26, Saber-toothed Cat—illustration by R. F. Zallinger; 2/2, Singer Pat Boone—Ralph Morse, LIFE; 2/9, Shirley MacLaine with daughter Sachie—Allan Grant, LIFE; 2/16, Miami chorus girls—Philippe Halsman; 2/23, Gwen Verdon—Philippe Halsman; 3/2, Princess Luciana Pignatelli—Milton H. Greene; 3/9, Jack Paar—Cornell Capa; 3/16, Brazilian jaguar—Dmitri Kessel, LIFE; 3/23, I.D. cards of a Soviet agent—Herbert Orth, LIFE; 3/30, Debbie Reynolds in Spain—Loomis Dean, LIFE; 4/6, *Wagons on the Oregon Trail* (Bierstadt); 4/13, Weightless in space test—Albert Fenn, LIFE; 4/20, Marilyn Monroe—Richard Avedon; 4/27, *Early California Bear Hunt* (James Walker); 5/4, Dalai Lama—Brian Brake; 5/11, Old West silver queen Baby Doe Tabor—De Venny-Wood Studio; 5/18, Jimmy Hoffa—Hank Walker, LIFE; 5/25, Mr. and Mrs. Sherman Adams—Gordon Parks, LIFE; 6/1, Boating in Kansas—A. Y. Owen; 6/8, Audrey Hepburn—Sanford H. Roth; 6/15, Space monkeys Able and Baker—Hank Walker, LIFE; 6/22, First Air Force Academy graduates—Leonard McCombe, LIFE; 6/29, Zsa Zsa Gabor and her ghostwriter—Philippe Halsman; 7/6, Actor Gardner McKay—Allan Grant, LIFE; 7/13, Old age—Carl Mydans, LIFE; 7/20, Heavyweight champion Ingmar Johansson with fiancée Birgit Lundgren—George Silk, LIFE; 7/27, Peace Ships—illustration by Noel Sickles; 8/3, Kingston Trio—Alfred Eisenstaedt, LIFE; 8/10, Wives of Mikoyan, Nixon, Khrushchev and Kozlov—UPI; 8/17, Actress Mai Britt—Leonard McCombe, LIFE; 8/24, Sen. and Mrs. John F. Kennedy—Mark Shaw; 8/31, Rip Van Winkle—illustration by James Lewicki; 9/7, Actors Bill Lundigan and Gene Barry—John Bryson; 9/14, Seven astronauts—Ralph Morse, LIFE; 9/21, Astronauts' wives—Ralph Morse, LIFE; 9/28, Migrating ducks—J. R. Eyerman, LIFE; 10/5, Nikita Khrushchev with Iowa farmer—Hank Walker, LIFE; 10/12, Family doctor—Leonard McCombe, LIFE; 10/19, Mums and missiles in Peking—Brian Brake; 10/26, Quiz star Charles Van Doren faces the press—Ted Russell; 11/2, Jackie Gleason—Mark Shaw; 11/9, Marilyn Monroe—Philippe Halsman; 11/16, Jewelry in fashion—Jack Robinson; 11/23, Mary Martin—Gjon Mili; 11/30, Pretty postage stamps—Otto Hagel; 12/7, Shah's fiancée Farah Diba—Loomis Dean, LIFE; 12/14, Hawaiian volcano erupts—Robert Wenkam; 12/21, Dwight D. Eisenhower in Pakistan—Paul Schutzer, LIFE; 12/28, Composite: The Good Life special issue—Mark Kauffman, LIFE, Nina Leen, George Silk, LIFE, Walter Sanders, LIFE, Hank Walker, LIFE.

1960

1/11, Actress Dina Merrill—Milton H. Greene; 1/18, Ghanaian Speaker of the House—Mark Kauffman, LIFE; 1/25, Father Marquette Conquers Manitou—illustration by James Levicki; 2/1, Dinah Shore—William Helburn; 2/8, U.S. Olympic skiers—A. Y. Owen; 2/15, Navy bathyscaphe—John Launois; 2/22, Henry Fonda and daughter Jane—Leonard McCombe, LIFE; 2/29, Olympic ski jumper—George Silk, LIFE; 3/7, Hypnosis—Jerry Cooke; 3/14, Princess Margaret and Anthony Armstrong-Jones—*London Times;* 3/21, Billy Graham in Africa—James Burke, LIFE; 3/28, Hubert Humphrey and John F. Kennedy—Stan Wayman, LIFE; 4/4, Marlon Brando—Sam Shaw; 4/11, Actress Silvana Mangano—A. Di Giovanni; 4/18, Elopers Gamble Benedict and Andrei Porumbeanu—Philippe Halsman; 4/25, Tourists on lovers' leap—Alfred Eisenstaedt, LIFE; 5/2, Trampoliners—J. R. Eyerman, LIFE; 5/9, Yvette Mimieux—Don Ornitz; 5/16, Princess Margaret and Anthony Armstrong-Jones—No Credit; 5/23, *Minuteman* statue, Lexington, Mass.—Eliot Elisofon, LIFE; 5/30, Nikita Khrushchev with Soviet Defense Minister Rodion Malinovsky—Carl Mydans, LIFE; 6/6, Lee Remick—Sam Shaw; 6/13, Hayley Mills—Loomis Dean, LIFE; 6/20, L.A. freeway—Ralph Crane, LIFE; 6/27, Alaskan walrus—Fritz Goro, LIFE; 7/4, U.S. Politics special issue, convention demonstration—Cornell Capa; 7/11, Nelson Rockefeller and grandchildren—Alfred Eisenstaedt; 7/18, Actress Ina Balin—Sam Shaw; 7/25, Kennedy demonstration at Democratic convention—Howard Sochurek, LIFE; 8/1, Giraffes and children in new-style amusement park—Lynn Pelham; 8/8, Patricia and Richard M. Nixon at Republican convention—Stan Wayman, LIFE; 8/15, Marilyn Monroe and Yves Montand—John Bryson; 8/22, U.S. Olympic swimmers—Howell Conant; 8/29, Record free-fall—U.S. Air Force; 9/5, Ernest Hemingway—Loomis Dean, LIFE; 9/12, U.S. Olympic gymnasts—George Silk, LIFE; 9/19, Grandma Moses—Cornell Capa; 9/26, Norell fashions—Milton H. Greene; 10/3, President Eisenhower at the UN—Ralph Crane, LIFE; 10/10, Doris Day—Bob Willoughby; 10/17, Henry Cabot Lodge and wife Emily—John Bryson; 10/24, Actress Nancy Kwan—Bert Stern; 10/31, Halloween—George Silk, LIFE; 11/7, Earth in Its Magnetic Field—illustration by Antonio Petrucelli; 11/14, Sophia Loren—Emil Schultheiss; 11/21, Victorious John F. Kennedy with mother Rose, wife Jacqueline and sister Eunice—Paul Schutzer, LIFE; 11/28, Actress Carroll Baker—Sam Shaw; 12/5, Baltimore Colts kickoff—George Silk, LIFE; 12/12, Jill Haworth and Sal Mineo—Gjon Mili; 12/19, President and Mrs. Kennedy at John-John's christening—Stanley Tretick; 12/26, Composite: 25th Anniversary issue—Dmitri Kessel.

1961

1/6, Civil War Cavalry Charge—illustration by C. E. Moore; 1/13, Clark Gable—Cornell Capa; 1/20, Cancer surgeon—Elliott Erwitt; 1/27, Kennedys with Sen. John Sparkman at inauguration—Leonard McCombe, LIFE; 2/3, Queen Elizabeth II in India—Hank Walker, LIFE; 2/10, Astrochimp "Ham"—Henry Burroughs; 2/17, Shirley MacLaine—John Launois; 2/24, UN's Dag Hammarskjöld—Elliott Erwitt; 3/3, Astronauts John Glenn, Virgil Grissom and Alan Shepard—Ralph Morse, LIFE; 3/10, Maurice Chevalier and Bing Crosby—Allan Grant, LIFE; 3/17, Model Sheila Finn—Howell Conant; 3/24, Puppets of Jack Paar vs. Ed Sullivan—Yale Joel, LIFE; 3/31, Cherub—Dmitri Kessel, LIFE; 4/7, Ocean fishing—George Silk, LIFE; 4/14, Mrs. Clark Gable and son John—Virgil Apger; 4/21, Cosmonaut Yuri Gagarin greets Khrushchev—Tass Photo; 4/28, Elizabeth Taylor—Allan Grant, LIFE; 5/5, Singer Anna Maria Alberghetti with puppets—Philippe Halsman; 5/12, Astronaut Alan Shepard picked up at sea—Dean Conger; 5/19, Alan Shepard—Ralph Morse, LIFE; 5/26, Jackie Kennedy in Canada—Leonard McCombe, LIFE; 6/2, Fidel Castro—Philippe Letellier; 6/9, John F. Kennedy with De Gaulle—Paul Schutzer, LIFE; 6/16, Princess Hohenlohe—Loomis Dean, LIFE; 6/23, Princess Grace—Chris Kindahl; 6/30, Leslie Caron—Zinn Arthur; 7/7, Dwight D. Eisenhower—Edward Clark, LIFE; 7/14, Ernest Hemingway—Yousuf Karsh; 7/21, Rio slum child Flavio—Carl Iwasaki, LIFE; 7/28, Brigitte Bardot—Walter Carone; 8/4, John F. Kennedy—Yousuf Karsh; 8/11, Sophia Loren—Alfred Eisenstaedt, LIFE; 8/18, Mickey Mantle and Roger Maris—Philippe Halsman; 8/25, West Berliners—Hank Walker, LIFE; 9/1, Jacqueline Kennedy—Mark Shaw; 9/8, U.S. tank soldier—Hank Walker, LIFE; 9/15, Civilian fallout suits—Ralph Morse, LIFE; 9/22, Hurricane Carla—Flip Schulke; 9/29, Dag Hammarskjöld's coffin—Dennis Royle; 10/6, Elizabeth Taylor—Howell Conant; 10/13, African warrior—Eliot Elisofon, LIFE; 10/20, Communist leaders: Marx, Engels, Lenin, Stalin, Khrushchev, Ulbricht, Mao Tse-tung and Castro—Brown Brothers, Sovfoto, Margaret Bourke-White, LIFE, Albert Fenn, LIFE, Brian Brake, Edward Clark, LIFE; 10/27, GI in training for guerrilla war in Vietnam—Ralph Morse, LIFE; 11/3, A daughter's goodbye to National Guardsman called to duty—Larry Burrows, LIFE; 11/10, Nikita Khrushchev—No Credit; 11/17, Minnesota Viking huddle—Eliot Elisofon, LIFE; 11/24, Year-old John F. Kennedy Jr.—Mark Shaw; 12/1, Italian fashions—Mark Kauffman; 12/8, Plum pudding flambé—Ben Rose; 12/15, Chartres cathedral—Gjon Mili; 12/22, Our Splendid Outdoors special issue, campers in the Tetons—Ralph Crane, LIFE.

1962

1/5, Lucille Ball—Ralph Crane, LIFE; 1/12, Community Fallout Shelter—illustration by Ron Kiley; 1/19, Iceboating—George Silk, LIFE; 1/26, Robert Kennedy—Philippe Halsman; 2/2, John Glenn—Ralph Morse, LIFE; 2/9, Seattle World's Fair—Ralph Crane, LIFE; 2/16, Rock Hudson—Leo Fuchs; 2/23, Shirley MacLaine—Allan Grant, LIFE; 3/2, John Glenn back from space—NASA photo by Dean Conger; 3/9, Motorcade for John Glenn with wife and Lyndon Johnson—Ralph Morse, LIFE; 3/16, Richard M. Nixon—Ralph Crane, LIFE; 3/23, Desert housing development—Ralph Crane, LIFE; 3/30, Robert Frost—Dmitri Kessel, LIFE; 4/6, Stretching the Dollar—illustration by Robert Osborn; 4/13, Richard Burton and Elizabeth Taylor—Paul Schutzer, LIFE; 4/20, Audrey Hepburn—Howell Conant; 4/27, Moonsuit test—Fritz Goro, LIFE; 5/4, Seattle World's Fair monorail—Ralph Crane, LIFE; 5/11, Bob Hope—Allan Grant, LIFE; 5/18, Astronaut Scott Carpenter and wife Rene—Ralph Morse, LIFE; 5/25, Prince Juan Carlos weds his princess—Hank Walker, LIFE; 6/1, Rene Carpenter watching Scott go up—Ralph Morse, LIFE; 6/8, Ticker-tape spectators—John Dominis, LIFE; 6/15, Natalie Wood—Paul Schutzer, LIFE; 6/22, Marilyn Monroe—Lawrence Schiller; 6/29, Massachusetts senatorial candidates Eddie McCormack, Teddy Kennedy and George Lodge—Philippe Halsman; 7/6, Balloon—Robert Halmi; 7/13, John F. Kennedy in Mexico—John Dominis, LIFE; 7/20, H-bomb fireball—*Oakland Tribune;* 7/27, Elsa Martinelli models nighties in fashion—Mark Shaw; 8/3, Astronaut Bob White with son—Lawrence Schiller; 8/10, Janet Leigh—Philippe Halsman; 8/17, Marilyn Monroe—Lawrence Schiller; 8/24, Soviet Space Capsules—illustration by Robert McCall; 8/31, Reenactment of the Great Mail Robbery—John Dominis, LIFE; 9/7, Caroline Kennedy on her pony—Marshall Hawkins; 9/14, Composite: The Takeover Generation special issue—Howard Sochurek, LIFE—Robert W. Kelley, LIFE; 9/21, Iran quake victims—Paul Schutzer, LIFE; 9/28, Don Drysdale—Lawrence Schiller; 10/5, Jackie Gleason with TV wife Sue Ann Langdon—Philippe Halsman; 10/12, Pope John XXIII—Yousuf Karsh; 10/19, California special issue, Yosemite at dusk—Ralph Crane, LIFE; 10/26, The Human Body (arm)—illustration by Dr. Paul Peck; 11/2, U.S. Navy off Cuba—Robert W. Kelley, LIFE; 11/9, U Thant and British ambassador consult—Bill Eppridge, LIFE; 11/16, Indian soldier—John Launois; 11/23, Bounty of Food special issue—Dmitri Kessel, LIFE; 11/30, Sid Caesar—Gjon Mili; 12/7, The Human Body (food to fuel)—Ralph Morse, LIFE and illustration by Arthur Lidov; 12/14, Marlon Brando—Eric Carpenter; 12/21, The Sea special issue—Ray Atkeson.

1963

1/4, Greek statue—Gjon Mili; 1/11, Ann-Margret—Philippe Halsman; 1/18, The Trojan Horse—illustration by Eugene Berman; 1/25, Vietcong prisoners—Larry Burrows, LIFE; 2/1, Alfred Hitchcock—Philippe Halsman; 2/8, Greek statue—Gjon Mili; 2/15, Moving Lincoln's body—Illinois State Historical Library; 2/22, Entertainers Alice and Ellen Kessler—Leigh Wiener; 3/1, Snakes—Nina Leen; 3/8, Actress Jean Seberg—Carlo Bavagnoli; 3/15, Fidel Castro—Henri Cartier-Bresson; 3/22, Polaris sub commander John L. From Jr.—Paul Schutzer, LIFE; 3/29, Costa Ricans—John Dominis, LIFE; 4/5, Spartans Stand at Thermopylae—illustration by Stanley Meltzoff; 4/12, Helen Klaben lost in the Yukon—UPI; 4/19, Richard Burton and Elizabeth Taylor—Bert Stern; 4/26, Young Jackie Kennedy—Bert & Richard Morgan Studio; 5/3, Alexander the Great—Dmitri Kessel, LIFE; 5/10, Bay of Pigs—illustration by Sanford Kossin; 5/17, Governor Nelson and Happy Rockefeller—Ralph Morse, LIFE; 5/24, Gordon Cooper—No Credit; 5/31, Gordon and Trudy Cooper—Ralph Morse, LIFE; 6/7, Pope John XXIII—Hank Walker, LIFE; 6/14, St. Peter's—Carlo Bavagnoli;

6/21, Shirley MacLaine—Gjon Mili; 6/28, Medgar Evers's widow, Myrlie, with son—John Loengard, LIFE; 7/5, Paul VI and cardinals in Sistine Chapel—Dmitri Kessel, LIFE; 7/12, Steve McQueen with wife Neile—John Dominis, LIFE; 7/19, Greek sculpture—David Lees; 7/26, Tuesday Weld—Lawrence Schiller; 8/2, Sandy Koufax—Mark Kauffman; 8/9, Averell Harriman and Nikita Khrushchev—Stan Wayman, LIFE; 8/16, Hospital vigil over Kennedy infant—Dan Bernstein; 8/23, Frank Sinatra and Frank Jr.—Philippe Halsman; 8/30, Paris fashions—Carlo Bavagnoli; 9/6, Washington march leaders A. Philip Randolph and Bayard Rustin—Leonard McCombe, LIFE; 9/13, Russia special issue, Soviet schoolgirl—Stan Wayman, LIFE; 9/20, U.S. team on Mt. Everest—William F. Unsoeld; 9/27, New astronauts Frank Borman, Thomas Stafford and James Lovell—Ralph Morse, LIFE; 10/4, DNA molecule—Fritz Goro, LIFE; 10/11, Vietnam's Madame Nhu with daughter Le Thuy—John Loengard, LIFE; 10/18, Grand Duchess Anastasia and family—Culver Pictures; 10/25, Yvette Mimieux—Allan Grant, LIFE; 11/1, Sen. Barry Goldwater—Leonard McCombe, LIFE; 11/8, President Johnson's former aide Bobby Baker—City News Bureau, Washington, D.C.; 11/15, South Vietnam soldiers after overthrow of Diem—James Pickerell; 11/22, Elizabeth Ashley—John Dominis, LIFE; 11/29, John F. Kennedy—Yousuf Karsh; 12/6, JFK's family waiting to join funeral procession—Fred Ward; 12/13, Lyndon B. Johnson—Yousuf Karsh; 12/20, The Movies special double issue, Japanese movie set—Brian Brake.

1964

1/3, S.S. *Lakonia* fire at sea—No Credit; 1/10, Gen. Douglas MacArthur—Yousuf Karsh; 1/17, Pope Paul VI—Sharokh Hatami; 1/24, Canal Zone rioters—Bill Eppridge, LIFE; 1/31, Actress Geraldine Chaplin—Denis Cameron; 2/7, British commando with Tanganyikan mutineers—Jack Garofalo; 2/14, Olympic ski jumper—Ralph Crane, LIFE; 2/21, Lee Harvey Oswald—Mrs. Lee Harvey Oswald; 2/28, Armed Turks on Cyprus—Brian Seed; 3/6, Cassius Clay—Bob Gomel; 3/13, World War I British wounded—Imperial War Museum, London; 3/20, Ambassador Henry Cabot Lodge in Saigon—Larry Burrows, LIFE; 3/27, Charles de Gaulle with Mexico's President Lopez Mateos—Pierre Boulat; 4/3, Carol Channing—Mark Kauffman; 4/10, Alaskan earthquake—Stan Wayman, LIFE; 4/17, Gen. Douglas MacArthur's hat—Arthur Penn; 4/24, Richard Burton—George Silk, LIFE; 5/1, The World's Fair opens—George Silk, LIFE; 5/8, Composite: Campaign buttons for LBJ running mate hopefuls—J. Alex Langley, Walter Bennett, Flip Schulke, Bob Petterson, Ralph Crane, LIFE; 5/15, Luci Baines Johnson—Howell Conant; 5/22, Barbra Streisand—Milton H. Greene; 5/29, Jacqueline Kennedy—George Silk, LIFE; 6/5, Cremation of Nehru—Larry Burrows, LIFE; 6/12, U.S. officer on patrol in Vietnam—Larry Burrows, LIFE; 6/19, LBJ's beagles—Francis Miller, LIFE; 6/26, Pennsylvania Gov. William Scranton with wife and son—John Loengard, LIFE; 7/3, Robert Kennedy with Kennedy family children—George Silk, LIFE; 7/10, Lee Harvey Oswald with wife Marina—No Credit; 7/17, Actress Carroll Baker with Masai warriors—Terence Spencer; 7/24, Sen. Barry Goldwater with wife Peggy—Bill Ray, LIFE; 7/31, Olympic diver—Don Ornitz; 8/7, Marilyn Monroe—Milton H. Greene; 8/14, Lyndon B. Johnson—Yousuf Karsh; 8/21, South Vietnam's Gen. Khanh—Harry Redl; 8/28, The Beatles—John Dominis, LIFE; 9/4, LBJ and daughter Lynda—Howard Sochurek; 9/11, Japan special issue, geisha bowling—Larry Burrows, LIFE; 9/18, Sophia Loren—Alfred Eisenstaedt, LIFE; 9/25, Saturn V Rocket—illustration by Robert McCall; 10/2, JFK's assassination—No Credit; 10/9, Olympic swimmer Donna de Verona—Bob Gomel; 10/16, Berlin escape—Michael de Voss, Michael Werner, Rene Reichenbach; 10/23, Leonid Brezhnev—Yousuf Karsh; 10/30, Four-time Olympic gold medalist Don Schollander—No Credit; 11/6, Actress Shirley Eaton—Loomis Dean; 11/13, LBJ and Hubert H. Humphrey—John Dominis, LIFE; 11/20, Soviet Marshal Rodion Malinovsky and Gen. A. P. Beloborodov—No Credit; 11/27, Vietnam GIs—Larry Burrows, LIFE; 12/4, Congo missionary Dr. Paul Carlson—Smith Kline; 12/11, The Rockettes—Arthur Rickerby, LIFE; 12/18, Elizabeth Taylor—Roddy McDowall; 12/25, The Bible special double issue, *Moses* (Rembrandt)—Stiftung Preussischer Kulturbesitz, Berlin.

1965

1/8, California floods—N. R. Farbman; 1/15, Ted Kennedy—Leonard McCombe, LIFE; 1/22, Peter O'Toole—Ken Danvers; 1/29, LBJ inauguration—John Dominis, LIFE; 2/5, Churchill's casket carried by Grenadier Guards—No Credit; 2/12, Mercenaries mop up in the Congo—Donald McCullin; 2/19, Albert Schweitzer—George Silk, LIFE; 2/26, North Vietnamese postage stamp—Bernard Quint and Herbert Orth, LIFE; 3/5, Aftermath of Malcolm X's death—Nat Fein; 3/12, Actress Julie Andrews—Howell Conant; 3/19, Civil rights face-off at Selma, Ala.—Charles Moore; 3/26, Dr. Martin Luther King Jr. with Archbishop Iakovos and Walter Reuther—Flip Schulke; 4/2, Gemini's splashdown—NASA; 4/9, Robert Kennedy on mountain summit—No Credit; 4/16, Aboard U.S. copter *Yankee Papa 13*—Larry Burrows, LIFE; 4/23, Frank Sinatra—John Dominis, LIFE; 4/30, Fetus—Lennart Nilsson; 5/7, John Wayne—John R. Hamilton; 5/14, Skateboarding—Bill Eppridge; 5/21, Ku Klux Klan defense lawyer—Robert W. Kelley, LIFE; 5/28, N.Y. Congressman John Lindsay—Henri Dauman; 6/4, German measles blood test—Co Rentmeester; 6/11, Waterloo—illustration by Lady Butler; 6/18, Astronaut Ed White during space walk—James A. McDivitt for NASA; 6/25, Indian tiger—Stan Wayman, LIFE; 7/2, Wounded Marine evacuated in Vietnam—Bill Eppridge, LIFE; 7/9, Yachting on the Riviera—Howell Conant; 7/16, John F. Kennedy—Mark Shaw; 7/23, Adlai Stevenson—Joseph Nettis; 7/30, Mickey Mantle—John Dominis, LIFE; 8/6, U.S.S. *Oklahoma City* shells Vietcong—Bill Ray, LIFE; 8/13, Lady Bird Johnson—Stan Wayman, LIFE; 8/20, Draft inductees—Mark Kauffman; 8/27, Riot in Watts section of Los Angeles—Co Rentmeester; 9/3, Astronaut Charles Conrad at lift-off—Bill Taub; 9/10, Expectant mother and video image of her baby's head—Fritz Goro, LIFE; 9/17, Indian soldier wields bazooka in Kashmir—Marvin Lichtner; 9/24, Baja California from spaceship—NASA; 10/1, Eskimo game—Ralph Crane, LIFE; 10/8, Hawaiian beauty Elizabeth Logue—Mark Kauffman; 10/15, Pope Paul VI in Yankee Stadium—Michael Rougier, LIFE, Bill Eppridge, LIFE; 10/22, Mary Martin in Vietnam—Charles Moore; 10/29, Temples of Abu Simbel—Pierre Boulat; 11/5, *John F. Kennedy* (James Fosburgh); 11/12, N.Y.C. Mayor-elect John Lindsay with son—Henri Dauman; 11/19, Manhattan power blackout—Henry Grossman; 11/26, Vietcong prisoner—Paul Schutzer, LIFE; 12/3, Lyndon B. Johnson dancing with Princess Margaret—Mark Kauffman; 12/10, Texas linebacker Tommy Nobis—Mark Kauffman; 12/17, View of Vatican Council from St. Peter's dome—Ralph Crane, LIFE; 12/24, The City special double issue, downtown Chicago—Howard Sochurek.

1966

1/7, Sean Connery—Loomis Dean; 1/14, North Vietnam's Ho Chi Minh and PM Pham Van Dong—Romano Cagnoni; 1/21, Indian PM Shastri lies in state as widow mourns—Larry Burrows, LIFE; 1/28, Actress Catherine Spaak—Howell Conant; 2/4, Sammy Davis, Harry Belafonte and Sidney Poitier—Philippe Halsman; 2/11, Wounded GIs in Vietnam—Henri Huet; 2/18, Model of flu germ—Yale Joel, LIFE; 2/25, Dawn mission over South Vietnam—Larry Burrows, LIFE; 3/4, Bust of a Roman citizen—Gjon Mili; 3/11, Batman—Yale Joel, LIFE; 3/18, Barbra Streisand—Bill Eppridge, LIFE; 3/25, LSD capsule—Lawrence Schiller and Bernard Quint, LIFE; 4/1, Charlie Chaplin and Sophia Loren—Alfred Eisenstaedt, LIFE; 4/8, Capt. Pete Dawkins—Charles Bonnay; 4/15, Louis Armstrong—Philippe Halsman; 4/22, Injured monk in Saigon—Charles Bonnay; 4/29, Actress Julie Christie—Sharok Hatami; 5/6, Jacqueline Kennedy in Spain—Blanco Y Negro; 5/13, Mod male fashions—Henry Grossman; 5/20, Bugging device on model's back—Arthur Schatz; 5/27, Discotheque—John Zimmerman; 6/3, Bust of Marcus Aurelius—Gjon Mili; 6/10, Elizabeth Taylor—Bob Willoughby; 6/17, Angela Lansbury—Mark Kauffman; 6/24, Prescription pills—Ralph Morse, LIFE; 7/1, Moonscape—NASA; 7/8, Actress Claudia Cardinale—Howell Conant; 7/15, Young black militants—Bill Ray, LIFE; 7/22, Birth—Lennart Nilsson; 7/29, Murderer's fingerprints—Art Shay; 8/5, Gemini 10 docking with Agena 10—NASA; 8/12, Texas store window shattered by sniper—Shel Hershorn; 8/19, Luci Johnson and Pat Nugent kneel at their wedding—James E. Blair; 8/26, Strike fever—I. C. Rapoport; 9/2, Paris fashions—Jean-Claude Sauer; 9/9, Psychedelic artist—Yale Joel, LIFE; 9/16, Sophia Loren—Alfred Eisenstaedt; 9/23, Chinese Imperial Magistrate and guards—Rev. Leone Nani; 9/30, Rex Harrison—Eliot Elisofon; 10/7, Author Ian Fleming—Loomis Dean; 10/14, Pro football mayhem: Green Bay Packers and Cleveland Browns—Arthur Rickerby, LIFE; 10/21, Zebra—Eliot Elisofon; 10/28, Wounded Marine—Larry Burrows, LIFE; 11/4, Lyndon B. Johnson in Vietnam—George Silk; 11/11, Jean-Paul Belmondo—Yves Debraine; 11/18, Robert Kennedy—Bill Eppridge, LIFE; 11/25, Frame 230 of JFK assassination film—Abraham Zapruder; 12/2, Actress Melina Mercouri—Henry Groskinsky, LIFE; 12/9, Draftees—Yale Joel, LIFE; 12/16, Restoring the *Last Supper* (Gaddi)—David Lees; 12/23, Photography special double issue, human eye—Lennart Nilsson.

1967

1/6, Black leopard—John Dominis, LIFE; 1/13, Navy patrol in Mekong River—Larry Burrows, LIFE; 1/20, China's Red Guards—Harry Redl; 1/27, Bathing suits in fashion at Acapulco—Howell Conant; 2/3, Astronauts Roger Chaffee, Ed White and Gus Grissom—Ralph Morse, LIFE; 2/10, Gus Grissom's caisson at Arlington—Rowland Scherman; 2/17, Underground-culture leader—John Loengard, LIFE, Bernard Quint, LIFE, Herbert Orth, LIFE; 2/24, Elizabeth Taylor—Robert Penn; 3/3, Leonardo da Vinci sketch—Augusto Meneses; 3/10, U.S. paratroopers over Vietnam—Co Rentmeester, LIFE; 3/17, Charlie Brown and Snoopy—Charles Schultz; 3/24, Composite: Easter in Jerusalem—Herbert Orth, LIFE, Enrico Sarsini; 3/31, Infant-learning experiment—Leonard McCombe, LIFE, illustration by Arthur Lidov; 4/7, Hanoi air-raid alert—Lee Lockwood; 4/14, Sharon Percy weds John D. Rockefeller IV—Stan Wayman, LIFE; 4/21, Composite: The individual—Henri Dauman; 4/28, U.S. pavilion at Expo 67—Mark Kauffman; 5/5, Actress Mia Farrow—Alfred Eisenstaedt, LIFE; 5/12, Truman Capote and actors Scott Wilson and Robert Blake—Steve Schapiro; 5/19, Astronaut Wally Schirra—Ralph Morse, LIFE; 5/26, Gen. Lew Walt—Enrico Sarsini; 6/2, China's cultural Red Guards—Takayuki Senzaki; 6/9, Sir Francis Chichester aboard *Gipsy Moth IV*—Francis Chichester; 6/16, Israeli troops take prisoners in Gaza—David Rubinger; 6/23, Israeli soldier cools off in the Suez Canal—Denis Cameron; 6/30, Aleksei Kosygin and Lyndon Johnson at Glassboro—Ben Martin; 7/7, LBJ, daughter Luci Nugent and grandson Patrick—No Credit; 7/14, Princess Lee Radziwill—Pierre Boulat; 7/21, Kidnapped U.S. official in Vietnam—courtesy Mrs. Gustav Hertz; 7/28, Newark riot victim—Bud Lee; 8/4, Troops patrol Detroit afire—Michael O'Sullivan; 8/11, U.S.S. *Forrestal* disaster—William K. Mason; 8/18, Model Veruschka—Franco Rubartelli; 8/25, Marine and young Vietnamese friend—Co Rentmeester, LIFE; 9/1, Composite: posters—Henry Groskinsky, LIFE; 9/8, Carl Yastrzemski—Jerry Brimacombe; 9/15, Svetlana Alliluyeva—John Dominis, LIFE; 9/22, Svetlana Alliluyeva with son Iosif—No Credit; 9/29, Antiballistic missile test—Clayton J. Price; 10/6, S.S. *Queen Mary* and Arab riflemen—Arthur Schatz, Anna Brick; 10/13, Ingrid Bergman—Bill Ray, LIFE; 10/20, U.S. POW in North Vietnam—DEFA; 10/27, GI at Con Thien—David Douglas Duncan; 11/3, Composite: runaway kids—Fred Kaplan; 11/10, Leningrad music hall girls—Bill Eppridge, LIFE; 11/17, Jacqueline Kennedy in Cambodia—Larry Burrows, LIFE; 11/24, Composite: Gov. John Connally, and Kennedys and Connallys in San Antonio—John Dominis, LIFE, and Zintgraff; 12/1, Composite: American Indian—illustration by Milton Glaser; 12/8, Pearl Bailey—John Dominis, LIFE; 12/15, Human heart recipient Louis Washkansky—Cloete Breytenbach; 12/22, The Wild World special double issue, bull elephant—Peter Beard.

1968

1/5, Katharine Hepburn—Terence Spencer; 1/12, Actress Faye Dunaway—Greene-Eula; 1/19, Human heart and surgeons—Lennart Nilsson; 1/26, Diet pills—Richard Erdoes, Bernard Quint, LIFE; 2/2, Aleksei Kosygin—No Credit; 2/9, Captured Vietcong guerrilla—AP; 2/16, North Vietnamese soldiers—Catherine Leroy; 2/23, Olympic gold medal figure skater Peggy Fleming—Arthur Rickerby, LIFE; 3/1, Painter Georgia O'Keeffe—John Loengard, LIFE, David Lees; 3/8, Black child—Gordon Parks; 3/15, Boris Karloff—Dmitri Kessel, LIFE; 3/22, Ho Chi Minh—Charles Bonnay; 3/29, Jane Fonda—Carlo Bavagnoli, LIFE; 4/5, King Tut's mask—Brian Brake; 4/12, Dr. Martin Luther King Jr.—Fred Ward; 4/19, Mrs. Martin Luther King Jr.—Flip Schulke; 4/26, Former French intelligence chief Philippe Thyraud de Vosjoli—Alfred Eisenstaedt, LIFE; 5/3, Assassin James Earl Ray in third grade—No Credit; 5/10, Paul Newman—Michael Mauney; 5/17, The Generation Gap—illustration by Seymour Chwast, Richard M. Meek; 5/24, N.Y.C. Mayor John V. Lindsay—John Dominis, LIFE; 5/31, Egyptian goddess Serket—Brian Brake; 6/7, Eugene McCarthy—Michael Rougier, LIFE; 6/14, Robert F. Kennedy—Bill Eppridge; 6/21, James Earl Ray and Sirhan Sirhan—left: AP, right: UP; 6/28, Jefferson Airplane—Art Kane; 7/5, The Presidency special issue, presidential seal—Bernard Quint, LIFE; 7/12, Starving children of Biafra—David Robison; 7/19, Young American nomads on Crete—Denis Cameron; 7/26, American and Soviet flight attendants—Arthur Schatz; 8/2, George Wallace, Richard M. Nixon and Ronald Reagan—illustration by Ranan Lurie; 8/9, Air traffic jam—Bob Gomel; 8/16, Mr. and Mrs. Richard M. Nixon, Mr. and Mrs. Spiro Agnew—Arthur Schatz; 8/23, Security chiefs at Chicago convention—Gerald Brimacombe; 8/30, Czech freedom fighters—Hilmar Pabel; 9/6, Hubert Humphrey and Edmund Muskie—Lee Balterman; 9/13, The Beatles—Ronald Fitzgibbon; 9/20, Arthur Ashe—Richard Meek; 9/27, Swedish fashions—Norman Parkinson; 10/4, Machine to probe the sea—Ralph Crane, LIFE; 10/11, *Pope John XXIII* (Manzu)—Sabine Weiss, David Lees; 10/18, Paul Newman and Joanne Woodward—Mark Kauffman; 10/25, Apollo 7 at take-off—U.S. Air Force—NASA and Ralph Morse, LIFE; 11/1, Jacqueline and Aristotle Onassis at their wedding—Bill Ray, LIFE; 11/8, Vietnam war victim—Larry Burrows, LIFE; 11/15, Richard M. Nixon—Charles Bonnay; 11/22, Abolitionist Frederick Douglass—J. R. Eyerman; 11/29, Egyptian soldier tests Soviet tank—Raphael Tarnowski; 12/6, Police violence at the Chicago convention—*Chicago Sun-Times;* 12/13, Baltimore Colts—Arthur Rickerby, LIFE; 12/20, *Mark Twain* (Flagg), and illustration by James McMullan; 12/27, Picasso special double issue, Pablo Picasso at window—Robert Doisneau.

1969

1/10, 1968, The Incredible Year special issue, Earth from Apollo 8—NASA; 1/17, Sirhan Sirhan and lawyers—Robert B. Kaiser; 1/24, Catherine Deneuve—Alex Youssoupoff; 1/31, Washington Monument and plane—George Silk, LIFE; 2/7, Cmdr. Lloyd Bucher of the U.S.S. *Pueblo*—Bob Gomel, T. Tanuma; 2/14, Barbra Streisand—Gordon Parks; 2/21, Richard M. Nixon—George Silk, LIFE; 2/28, Herons—George Silk, LIFE; 3/7, Richard M. Nixon—John Olson, LIFE, except top left, Tom Picton, bottom left, Charles Bonnay; 3/14, Lunar module on Apollo 9—Ralph Morse, LIFE; 3/21, Woody Allen—Philippe Halsman; 3/28, Orangutan—Co Rentmeester, LIFE; 4/4, Sensuality in the arts—Herbert Migdoll; 4/11, Dwight D. Eisenhower's bier in the Capitol—Bob Gomel; 4/18, Mae West—Philippe Halsman; 4/25, Harvard protester—Leonard McCombe, LIFE; 5/2, Singer Judy Collins—Rowland Scherman; 5/9, Peter Falk, Ben Gazzara and John Cassavetes—Marvin Lichtner; 5/16, Composite: high school—Leonard McCombe, LIFE; 5/23, Dan Rowan and Dick Martin—Mark Kauffman; 5/30, Ambulance—Ralph Crane, LIFE; 6/6, Moon surface—NASA; 6/13, Human embryo and mother and infant—Fritz Goro, LIFE, Doris Pinney; 6/20, Joe Namath—Walter Ioos; 6/27, American dead in Vietnam—No Credit; 7/4, Astronaut Neil Armstrong sets out for the moon—Henry Groskinsky, LIFE, Ralph Morse, LIFE; 7/11, Dustin Hoffman and John Wayne—illustration by Milton Glaser; 7/18, Youth communes—John Olson, LIFE; 7/25, Neil Armstrong—Leonard McCombe, LIFE; 8/1, Ted Kennedy—John Loengard, LIFE; 8/8, Flag and footsteps on the moon—NASA; 8/15, Dollar Squeeze—illustration by Dennis Wheeler, Al Freni; 8/22, New York fashions—Vernon Merritt III, LIFE; 8/29, Norman Mailer—Bob Peterson; 9/5, Artist Peter Max—Henry Groskinsky, LIFE; 9/12, Coretta King—Vernon Merritt III, LIFE; 9/19, Children—Michael Mauney; 9/26, N.Y. Mets Jerry Koosman—Herb Scharfman; 10/3, Ballet dancer—Gjon Mili; 10/10, Composite: Revolution—Richard Meek; 10/17, Model Naomi Sims—Yale Joel, LIFE; 10/24, Composite: Dissent—No Credit; 10/31, Marijuana—Co Rentmeester, LIFE; 11/7, Paul McCartney and family—Robert Graham; 11/14, Green Beret colonel—Henry Groskinsky, LIFE; 11/21, Johnny Cash—Michael Rougier, LIFE; 11/28, U.S. mail mess—John Olson, LIFE; 12/5, African antelope—John Dominis, LIFE; 12/12, Apollo 12 moon walk—NASA; 12/19, Cult leader Charles Manson—UPI; 12/26, Composite: '60s special double issue—Charles Bonnay, Larry Burrows, LIFE, Harry Coughenour, John Dominis, LIFE, Bill Eppridge, LIFE, Bob Gomel, Milton H. Greene, Henry Grossman, Yale Joel, LIFE, Leonard McCombe, LIFE, Charles Moore, Lennart Nilsson, John Olson, LIFE, Ken Regan, Percy C. Piddle, Steve Schapiro, Paul Schutzer, LIFE, Hank Walker, LIFE.

1970

1/9, Into the '70s special double issue, human egg—Lennart Nilsson; 1/23, Johnny Carson—Philippe Halsman; 1/30, Snow monkey—Co Rentmeester, LIFE; 2/6, Robert Redford—John Dominis, LIFE; 2/13, Dollar bill—No Credit; 2/20, Architect turned clown—Leonard McCombe, LIFE; 2/27, *The Spirit of Cinema America* (Daugherty)—Henry Groskinsky, LIFE; 3/6, Gold medalist skier Billy Kidd—George Silk, LIFE; 3/13, Hemlines in fashion—Milton H. Greene; 3/20, Former nun—John Olson, LIFE; 3/27, Credit cards—cartoon by Ranan Lurie; 4/3, Lauren Bacall—John Dominis, LIFE; 4/10, Drs. Denton Cooley and Michael DeBakey—Ralph Morse, LIFE; 4/17, Zero Population Growth campaign button—Michael Rougier, LIFE; 4/24, Astronaut Jim Lovell—Ralph Morse, LIFE; 5/1, Chapel Hill coed—Michael Mauney; 5/8, Spiro Agnew—Alfred Eisenstaedt, LIFE; 5/15, Wounded Kent State student—Howard Ruffner; 5/22, Composite: Our Forgotten Wounded—Frank Fischbeck, Co Rentmeester, LIFE; 5/29, Actress Brenda Vaccaro—John Loengard, LIFE; 6/5, Bear Market—illustration by Irwin Glusker; 6/12, Palestinian training camp for kids—Pierre Boulat; 6/19, Actor Dennis Hopper—Henry Grossman; 6/26, Americans in Spanish prison—Pierre Boulat; 7/3, Iowa Boy Scouts with flag—Tim Kantor; 7/10, California girls in the surf—Co Rentmeester, LIFE; 7/17, Rose Kennedy with Ted and Joan—Leonard McCombe, LIFE; 7/24, Candice Bergen—Michael Mauney; 7/31, Nixon's friend Bebe Rebozo—No Credit; 8/7, Lyndon B. Johnson, Robert F. and John F. Kennedy—Jacques Lowe; 8/14, Summer Nomads—illustration by Leonard Kalish; 8/21, Midiskirts in fashion—John Dominis, LIFE; 8/28, Composite: pornography—Al Freni; 9/4, *Liberty Congratulates Woman Voter*—artwork from Culver Pictures; 9/11, Fugitive activist Angela Davis—Tom Burgers; 9/18, Engelbert Humperdinck and Tom Jones—Mark Kauffman; 9/25, Male plumage in fashion—Enrico Sarsini; 10/2, Attorney General's wife Martha Mitchell—Harry Benson; 10/9, Egypt's Gamal Abdel Nasser—Yousuf Karsh; 10/16, Spiro Agnew—Charles Harbutt; 10/23, Muhammad Ali—Gordon Parks; 10/30, Dick Cavett—Michael Mauney; 11/6, Richard M. Nixon at 14—Cummings-Prentiss Studio; 11/13, Richard M. Nixon—Co Rentmeester, LIFE; 11/20, Oberlin students in coed dorm—Bill Ray, LIFE; 11/27, Nikita Khrushchev—Albert Fenn; 12/4, Nikita Khrushchev—Yousuf Karsh; 12/11, Model with health food—Philippe Halsman; 12/18, William, James and Reid Buckley and their families—Alfred Eisenstaedt, LIFE; 12/25, Prizewinning Pictures special double issue—Kent H. Barton.

1971

1/8, Composite: The New Shape of America special double issue—Ralph Morse, LIFE, Co Rentmeester, LIFE, John Dominis, LIFE, Bill Eppridge, LIFE, Suzanne Szasz; 1/22, Tricia Nixon—Ron Galella; 1/29, Bob Hope—Ralph Crane, LIFE; 2/5, Composite: The New Army—Bill Eppridge, LIFE, illustration by Bill Mauldin; 2/12, Jacqueline Kennedy Onassis—Ron Galella; 2/19, Rita Hayworth, Ruby Keeler, Paulette Goddard, Myrna Loy, Joan Blondell and Betty Hutton—Philippe Halsman, Dion McGregor; 2/26, Snowmobiles—Harry Benson; 3/5, Joe Frazier and Muhammad Ali—John Shearer, LIFE; 3/12, Explosion among South Vietnamese soldiers in Laos—Akihiko Okamura; 3/19, Frazier pounds Ali—Frank Sinatra; 3/26, Walter Cronkite—Leonard McCombe, LIFE; 4/2, Pregnant high schooler—Ralph Crane, LIFE; 4/9, J. Edgar Hoover—illustration by Neil Estern; 4/16, Paul McCartney and wife Linda—Henry Diltz; 4/23, Jane Fonda—Bill Ray, LIFE; 4/30, Chinese children marching—Frank Fishbeck; 5/7, Feminist Germaine Greer—Vernon Merritt III, LIFE; 5/14, Carol Burnett—Henry Grossman; 5/21, LBJ with grandson Lyn Nugent—Frank Wolfe; 5/28, Rock-opera star Chris Brown—David Douglas Duncan; 6/4, Christina Ford—Alfred Eisenstaedt, LIFE; 6/11, Ted and Joan Kennedy—Henry Grossman; 6/18, Tricia Nixon—Dick Winburn; 6/25, Frank Sinatra—Michael Rougier, LIFE; 7/2, American Indians—left, courtesy Indiana University, right, Ernst Haas; 7/9, Photography contest winning picture—Larry C. Moon; 7/16, Bess Myerson—Leonard McCombe, LIFE; 7/23, Clint Eastwood—Bob Peterson; 7/30, Chou En-lai—Audrey Topping; 8/6, Ann-Margret—Bill Ray, LIFE; 8/13, Composite: The Woman Problem—Nina Leen, Lee Boltin; 8/20, Princess Anne—Norman Parkinson; 8/27, Composite: Game Plan for the Dollar—illustration by Dennis Wheeler; 9/3, Americans Outdoors special issue, shooting the rapids in inner tubes—Michael Mauney, LIFE; 9/10, Composite: TV's 25th Anniversary—Bernard Waber; 9/17, Heart transplant patients—Lennart Nilsson, Manfred Gygli; 9/24, Jackson Five with parents—John Olson, LIFE; 10/1, Human brain—Lennart Nilsson; 10/8, Americans shop for new cars—Dick Swanson; 10/15, Opening of Disney World—Yale Joel, LIFE; 10/22, The Brain—illustration by Frank Armitage; 10/29, Singer David Cassidy—Bob Peterson; 11/5, Sen. Edmund Muskie—Stan Wayman, LIFE; 11/12, Chess champion Bobby Fischer—Harry Benson; 11/19, Window barred to keep out crime—John Loengard, LIFE; 11/26, Chemistry of Madness—illustration by Vin Giuliani; 12/3, Los Angeles Rams and Baltimore Colts—Arthur Rickerby, LIFE; 12/10, Cybill Shepherd—Berry Berenson; 12/17, Children special double issue, baby—Douglas Faulkner; 12/31, Composite: The Year in Pictures 1971 special double issue—Eugene Light.

1972

1/14, Dallas Cowboys Roger Staubach and Tom Landry—Harry Benson; 1/21, Single U.S. Vietnam casualty in a week—Lee Balterman; 1/28, John Wayne—Bob Willoughby; 2/4, Howard Hughes—illustration by David Walsh; 2/11, Singer Nina van Pallandt—Terry O'Neill; 2/18, Japanese Olympic ski-jump winner—John Dominis, LIFE; 2/25, Elizabeth Taylor—Norman Parkinson; 3/3, Mao Tse-tung—official Chinese source; 3/10, Marlon Brando—Steve Schapiro; 3/17, Dropout wife—Michael Mauney, LIFE; 3/24, Wilt Chamberlain and Kareem Abdul-Jabbar—Marvin E. Newman; 3/31, Jacqueline Onassis—Art Zelin; 4/7, Composite: The Oscars—Bill Ray, LIFE, Mary Ellen Mark, Harry Benson, Eugene Light, LIFE; 4/14, Broiling steak—Co Rentmeester, LIFE; 4/21, Charlie Chaplin with wife Oona—Candice Bergen; 4/28, Composite: The Marriage Experiment—D'Asaro, Mary Ellen Mark, Laurent Corbel, Arthur Schatz, John Dominis, LIFE; 5/5, Olympic gymnast Cathy Rigby—John Dominis, LIFE; 5/12, Vietnam soldier carries wounded buddy—Kichiro Morita; 5/19, The Population Riddle: baby—Michael Mauney, LIFE; 5/26, Cornelia Wallace with wounded husband George—Dr. Frederick Stires; 6/2, Raquel Welch—Bill Eppridge, LIFE; 6/9, Congresswoman Bella Abzug—Leonard McCombe, LIFE; 6/16, Girl with Hula Hoop—Bill Ray, LIFE; 6/23, Alexander Solzhenitsyn—Stern from Black Star; 6/30, Young crusaders for Jesus—Jack and Betty Cheetham; 7/7, Sen. George McGovern—Stanley Tretick; 7/14, Mick Jagger—Jim Marshall; 7/21, George McGovern and grandson Matthew—Stanley Tretick; 7/28, The bare look in fashion—Douglas Kirkland; 8/4, Flip Wilson—John Dominis, LIFE; 8/11, Escape hatch for skyjackers—Co Rentmeester, LIFE; 8/18, Olympic swimmer Mark Spitz—Co Rentmeester, LIFE; 8/25, Patricia Nixon—Harry Benson; 9/1, Autoworker—Michael Mauney, LIFE; 9/8, Marilyn Monroe—Eve Arnold; 9/15, Israeli Olympic team before terrorist attack—UPI; 9/22, Olympic marathon winner Frank Shorter—John Zimmerman; 9/29, Composite: POW wife—Leonard McCombe, LIFE, Marc Riboud; 10/6, Dallas Cowboys tackle Bob Lilly—Max Waldman; 10/13, S.S. *Lusitania*—Topix, George Arthur; 10/20, Youngster—Leonard McCombe, LIFE; 10/27, Dr. Edwin Land with camera—Co Rentmeester, LIFE; 11/3, Joe Namath—Harry Benson; 11/10, Navy POW—Joris Ivens; 11/17, Richard M. Nixon—Harry Benson; 11/24, Gov. George Wallace—Bill Eppridge, LIFE; 12/1, *Harry S. Truman* (Tom Allen); 12/8, Diana Ross—James B. Wood; 12/15, Christmas special double issue, *Christ Child* (Georges de la Tour)—Musée des Beaux Arts, Rennes, France; 12/29, Composite: The Year in Pictures 1972 special double issue—Eugene Light, LIFE.

SPECIAL ISSUES 1973-1977

The Spirit of Israel, smiling Israeli—Thomas Hoepker.
Composite: The Year in Pictures—Harry Benson, NASA, Jacques Burlot, Stephen Green-Armytage.
One Day in The Life of America—Henry Groskinsky, Harald Sund.
Composite: The Year in Pictures—David Burnett, Rene Burri, Syndication International, No Credit.
The 100 Events That Shaped America—Culver Pictures, Bradley Smith, U.S. Army, Underwood & Underwood.
Composite: The Year in Pictures—Elizabeth Sunflower, Steven Weed, John Iacono, Christopher Froehder.
Remarkable American Women—Radcliffe College, Library of Congress, Walter Sanders, Nancy Moran.
Composite: The Year in Pictures—Co Rentmeester, Stanley Tretick, Bruce Bailey, George Silk.
Composite: The New Youth, UCLA woman rugby player—John Zimmerman.
Composite: The Year in Pictures—20th Century-Fox, David Burnett, Fred Maroon, Stanley Tretick, Fox Photos, John Reggero, Wide World Photos, Phil Roach.

MONTHLY LIFE

1978

10, Balloon rising—David Dahl; 11, Mickey Mouse—illustration by Walt Disney Productions; 12, Prince Charles—Serge LeMoine.

1979

1, Shar-Pei dog—Stephen Green-Armytage; 2, Lingerie fashions—Arthur Elgort; 3, Actress Lesley-Anne Down—David McCabe; 4, Eclipse—Robert T. Little, George T. Keene; 5, Three-Mile Island towers—Gregory Heisler; 6, Marlon Brando—Mary Ellen Mark; 7, Tail of a diving whale—William Curtsinger; 8, Microsurgeon—David McCabe; 9, Pope John Paul II—Chuck Fishman; 10, Dolly Parton—Raeanne Rubenstein; 11, Ted Kennedy—Co Rentmeester; 12, Composite: The Decade in Pictures special issue, faces of the '70s.

1980

1, Ayatullah Khomeini—Gianfranco Gorgoni; 2, Actress Mary Astor in 1920—Douglas Whitney Collection; 3, Mickey Rooney—Gregory Heisler; 4, Hare Krishna children—Ethan Hoffman; 5, Man-made gene—Huntington Potter and David Dressler; 6, *Sunday Cat* (Mattie Lou O'Kelley)—courtesy Jay Johnson's America's Folk Heritage Gallery; 7, Cape Hatteras Lighthouse—Mitchell Funk; 8, Miss Piggy—Nancy Moran, Donal Holway; 9, Summer Sun—Frank Oberle; 10, Chinese child—Eve Arnold; 11, Walter Cronkite—Jill Krementz; 12, Child cancer patient—Tom Tracy.

1981

1, Composite: The Year in Pictures special issue, 1980 photographs; 2, Wind surfers in swimsuit fashions, John and Yoko Lennon—Co Rentmeester, Kiashin Shinoyama; 3, Hostage Jimmy Lopez—J. Ross Baughman; 4, Meryl Streep, Atlanta children—Annie Leibovitz, No Credit; 5, Rancher Ronald Reagan, Reagan assassination attempt—Michael Evans, Ron Edmonds; 6, Planets, Beatle wedding—NASA, Terry O'Neill; 7, Dying lake—Harald Sund; 8, Girl in waterfall—Co Rentmeester; 9, Artificial heart, woman soldier—Enrico Ferorelli, Dennis Brack; 10, Marilyn Monroe, Lana Turner, Joan Crawford and Shirley Temple—George Zeno Collection, Lou Valentino Collection, Museum of Modern Art, No Credit; 11, Fetus, Mick Jagger—Lennart Nilsson, Annie Leibovitz; 12, Brooke Shields—Co Rentmeester.

1982

1, Composite: The Year in Pictures special issue, 1981 photographs—Henri Bureau, Tom Zimberoff, John Hanlon, Terry Arthur; 2, Model Christie Brinkley—Patrick Demarchelier; 3, Elizabeth Taylor—Norman Parkinson; 4, Handgun—Co Rentmeester; 5, Laser surgeon—Alexander Tsiaris; 6, Polar bear and cub—Dennis De Mello, Jonathan Becker; 7, Raquel Welch—Andre Weinfeld; 8, Marilyn Monroe—Bert Stern; 9, Liver transplant—Ergun Catagay; 10, Arnold Schwarzenegger and Actress Sandahl Bergman—Tony Costa; 11, Test-tube baby—Frank Cowan; 12, Princess Diana—Don White.

1983

1, Composite: The Year in Pictures special issue, 1982 photographs; 2, Brooke Shields—Bruce Weber; 3, Prince Rainier and children—Eric Feinblatt; 4, Embryo hand—Alexander Tsiaras; 5, Debra Winger—Theo Westenberger; 6, Composite: *Star Wars*—Lucasfilm; 7, Glacier National Park—David Muench; 8, Willie Nelson and family—Harry Benson; 9, Composite: Best and worst cars ever—Michael Melford; 10, Nancy Reagan—Harry Benson; 11, Composite: John F. Kennedy—Alfred Eisenstaedt, LIFE, Arthur Rickerby, LIFE, No Credit, Cecil W. Stoughton, Fred Ward, Jack Beers, Henri Dauman, AP; 12, Barbra Streisand—Greg Gorman.

1984

1, Composite: The Year in Pictures special issue, 1983 photographs; 2, The Beatles—John Loengard; 3, Daryl Hannah in bathing suit fashions—Dustin Pittman; 4, Penguins—Harald Sund; 5, Composite: History of cocaine—Tobey Sanford, Al Freni, FPG, Toni Kasser, various museum collections; 6, Harrison Ford and Kate Capshaw—Eva Serenyi; Previewing the Olympics special extra issue, runner Mary Decker and pole vaulter Bob Richards—Jerry Wachter, AP; 7, Dan Pisner with his quintuplets—Lynn Johnson; 8, Grizzly bear—John Dominis; 9, Michael Jackson—Lynn Goldsmith, Enrico Ferorelli; 10, *Doonesbury* Wedding—illustration by Garry Trudeau; 11, John Jr. and Caroline Kennedy, Julie Nixon, Amy Carter, Margaret Truman and John Eisenhower—Harry Benson; 12, Princess Diana and Prince Henry—Snowdon.

1985

1, Composite: The Year in Pictures special issue, 1984 photographs; 2, Brooke Shields—Bruce Weber; 3, Composite: The Mafia—Nicola Scalfi, Enrico Ferorelli, Publifoto; 4, Songfest for Africa: Willie Nelson, Lionel Ritchie, Tina Turner, Bob Dylan, Bruce Springsteen, Michael Jackson and Cyndi Lauper—Harry Benson; 5, Artificial heart patient Bill Schroeder and surgeon William DeVries—William Strode; 6, Bill Cosby—Lynn Johnson; 7, Composite: AIDS—Michael O'Brien; Composite: World War II special extra issue—AP, insets top to bottom Lou Valentino Collection, U.S. Signal Corps, National Archives, Hugo Jaeger, Joe Rosenthal, AP; 8, Hula Hoopster, Tina Turner—Dustin Pittman, Deborah Feingold; 9, Live Aid: Tina Turner and Mick Jagger, Paul McCartney, Madonna, Mount St. Helens—Gregory Heisler, Duncan Raba, Anthony Suau, Roger Werth; 10, Joan Collins, Halley's Comet—Reid Miles, National Optical Astronomy Observations; 11, Princess Diana—Snowdon; 12, Composite: Space preview—U.S. Naval Observatory, Palomar Observatory Caltech, NASA.

Page 5
Peter Stackpole, LIFE—Andre Da Miano.
Page 14
Time Inc. Archives.
Page 16
Keystone—Miami News Service; No Credit.
Page 17
European; No Credit; James Jarsche—*Detroit News;* Ralph Steiner—Bettmann/UPI.
Page 18
Bachrach Studio.
Page 20
H. S. Wong—Charles J. Belden—Robert Capa; No Credit—Bettmann/UPI; Alfred Eisenstaedt—No Credit.
Page 21
No Credit; Margaret Bourke-White, LIFE—Wide World Photos—Pepita Prann; UK Royal Rota Pool.
Page 22
New York Daily Mirror.
Page 23
Alfred Eisenstaedt; Bettmann/UPI; MGM—Wide World Photos.
Page 24
Time Inc.—Edmund B. Gerard; Jewel Productions (2).
Page 25
Bettmann/UPI.
Page 26
Selznick International Pictures—Frank G. Jason; Fairchild Aerial Surveys.
Page 27
Hansel Mieth, LIFE—*Paris Match;* Thomas D. McAvoy, LIFE.
Page 28
Wide World Photos—C. B. Fortner; MGM.
Page 29
Wide World Photos; Davis Wilburn, *Fort Worth Press.*
Page 30
Bettmann/UPI; Interphoto; Carl Mydans, LIFE—William Vandivert, LIFE.
Page 32
Interphoto; Bob Doty, *Dayton Journal-Herald*—© W. Eugene Smith; Peter Stackpole, LIFE—Wide World Photos; William Vandivert, LIFE; John Topham.
Page 33
Osa Johnson; Hans Wild, LIFE.
Page 34
Charles Thill; Walter Sanders; Robert Landry; George Karger; Robert Landry; Peter Stackpole, LIFE.
Page 35
Alfred Eisenstaedt; David Scherman, LIFE—No Credit; Robert Landry—Paramount Pictures; Ralph Morse—Guy Hayes.
Page 38
Bettmann/UPI; Wide World Photos.
Page 39
U.S. Army Signal Corps—Robert Landry.
Page 40
Wide World Photos; Edmund B. Gerard.
Page 41
© Yousuf Karsh; Bettmann/UPI—U.S. Navy; Thomas Kwang; Bettmann/UPI.
Page 42
Time Inc.—Eliot Elisofon, LIFE.
Page 46
George Silk, LIFE—Ewing Krainin—George Strock, LIFE; *Portland Oregonian*—Bettmann/UPI.
Page 47
No Credit.
Page 50
Robert Capa, LIFE—John Phillips, LIFE—© W. Eugene Smith, LIFE.
Page 51
Sam Shere.
Page 52
Eric Schaal; Ralph Morse, LIFE; Wide World Photos—Bettmann/UPI.
Page 53
Bell Aircraft Corporation—Vories Fisher.
Page 55
News Chronicle, London—Bettmann/UPI; Bettmann/UPI.
Page 56
Carl Mydans, LIFE; Alfred Eisenstaedt; Harold Carter; Margaret Bourke-White, LIFE; George Silk, LIFE—Martha Holmes, LIFE; Peter Urban; Mediterranean Allied Air Force; Martha Holmes, LIFE; U.S. Coast Guard—Wide World Photos; Ed Clark, LIFE; Wide World Photos; Myron H. Davis, LIFE.
Page 57
Kosti Ruohomaa/Black Star; Carl Mydans, LIFE; Walter Sanders, LIFE—Sam Shere, LIFE; James Longhead; Bernard Hoffman, LIFE—Jack Wilkes, LIFE; Wide World Photos; Johnny Florea, LIFE; Peter Stackpole, LIFE.

Page 58
Ed Clark, LIFE; Alfred Eisenstaedt—Carl Mydans, LIFE.
Page 60
Martin Munkacsi.
Page 61
Martin Munkacsi.
Page 62
Courtesy Hutchinson & Co., Ltd.; Combine.
Page 63
New York World Telegram—George Hurrell.
Page 64
Buffalo Courier Express; Roland Harvey.
Page 65
Bettmann/UPI.
Pages 66-67
Lucille Handberg.
Page 68
Bettmann/UPI.
Page 69
Peter Stackpole, LIFE; No Credit—Peter Stackpole, LIFE.
Page 70
Wide World Photos; AFP Photos—AFP Photos.
Page 71
Portland Oregonian—Wide World Photos.
Pages 72-73
Professor Harold Edgerton, MIT.
Pages 74-75
Anette and Basil Zarow—Hansel Mieth, LIFE.
Page 77
Bernard Hoffman, LIFE.
Page 78
Ralph Morse, LIFE; U.S. Army Signal Corps—U.S. Army-Navy Task Force One.
Page 79
Cornelius Ryan; Margaret Bourke-White, LIFE—*Tokyo Sun*/LIFE; American Red Cross (Gerald Walker).
Page 80
Bettmann/UPI.
Page 81
Nina Leen; Thomas D. McAvoy, LIFE; cartoon from *New York Journal-American.*
Page 82
Brown Brothers.
Page 83
Bettmann/UPI—Alfred Eisenstaedt; Ralph Morse, LIFE—Wide World Photos—Sharland; Walter Carone.
Page 84
Gjon Mili.
Page 85
U.S. Army; Kon-tiki Expedition; Martha Holmes, LIFE—Francis Reiss; Leonard McCombe.
Page 86
Margaret Bourke-White, LIFE.
Page 87
Walter Sanders.
Page 88
Wide World Photos; Carl Mydans, LIFE; © Philippe Halsman.
Pages 90-91
Frank Lerner.
Page 92
Loomis Dean, LIFE.
Page 93
Cecil Beaton, courtesy Sotheby's, London; Ivo Meldolesi, Black Star; David Douglas Duncan, LIFE—Henri Cartier-Bresson, Magnum—Andreas Feininger, LIFE.
Page 94
Vandamm Studio—Keystone.
Page 95
Hank Walker, LIFE; Carl Mydans, LIFE—Eliot Elisofon, LIFE; Piero Saporiti; Ed Clark, LIFE.
Page 96
Gjon Mili; Hank Walker, LIFE—Margaret Bourke-White, LIFE—Alfred Eisenstaedt.
Page 98
© W. Eugene Smith, LIFE—John Dominis, LIFE—© W. Eugene Smith, LIFE; Michael Rougier, LIFE; © Philippe Halsman.
Page 100
William Sumits, LIFE; Dennis Stock, Magnum—Joe Scherschel, LIFE; Al Fenn, LIFE; © Philippe Halsman—Mark Kauffman, LIFE.
Page 101
Elliott Erwitt, Magnum; Carrol Seghers II—Dmitri Kessel, LIFE.
Page 102
Hank Walker, LIFE; Wide World Photos; George Skadding, LIFE—Yale Joel, LIFE.

Page 103
George Silk, LIFE; Keystone; Milton Greene—J. R. Eyerman, LIFE.
Page 104
Courtesy Western Lithograph Company; Andre de Dienes.
Page 105
Kenneth C. Cooley; Allan Grant, LIFE—Bettmann/UPI.
Page 106
U.S. Atomic Energy Commission—Karl E. Hillgren, Black Star.
Page 108
Ralph Crane, LIFE; Cecil Beaton, courtesy Sotheby's, London—Lisa Larsen; Terence Spencer.
Page 109
Wide World Photos—Allan Grant, LIFE; Times Newspapers Ltd., London; Michael Rougier, LIFE; © W. Eugene Smith—Wide World Photos.
Page 110
© Coordination.
Page 112
Sam Shaw; © W. Eugene Smith—Margaret Bourke-White, LIFE; *Oxford Mail* (England); Mark Shaw—French Government News Service—Allan Grant, LIFE.
Page 113
Mark Shaw; Robert Phillips (2)—No Credit; Bettmann/UPI—Allan Grant, LIFE; Wide World Photos; Sam Shaw.
Page 115
Bettmann/UPI; Grey Villet; Eliot Elisofon—Loomis Dean, LIFE—Elliott Erwitt, Magnum—Mark Shaw.
Page 116
Paris Match/Garofalo (5); Bill Sears, Black Star—Bettmann/UPI; *Chicago Herald American* from Bettmann/UPI.
Page 117
Christopher Scott—Bob Willoughby.
Page 118
Loomis Dean, LIFE; Mark Shaw.
Page 119
Bettmann/INP; © Philippe Halsman.
Page 120
Bettmann/UPI (3).
Page 121
Keystone.
Page 122
Wallace Kirkland, LIFE.
Page 123
Paterson Evening News.
Page 124
No Credit (left vertical 4); Loomis Dean, LIFE; George Silk, LIFE—Peter Perri.
Page 125
Paramount Pictures (3); Robert Doisneau/Rapho—*New York Journal-American;* No Credit.
Pages 126-127
Providence Journal-Bulletin.
Page 128
Sydney Sunday Sun—Bettmann/UPI; Graphic Photo Union.
Page 129
No Credit; Reflex (4).
Page 130
New York Daily News (2).
Page 131
Boston Record-American.
Page 132
J. R. Eyerman, LIFE—Coe, Norwich, England.
Page 133
Lilo Hess; Mark Kauffman, LIFE.
Page 135
Alfred Eisenstaedt, LIFE.
Pages 136-137
Myron H. Davis; Don Cravens—Loomis Dean, LIFE; Milton H. Greene; *Paris Match*—Bettmann/UPI.
Pages 138-139
Don Wright, *Miami News*—Grey Villet, LIFE; George Silk, LIFE—Leonard McCombe; Thomas D. McAvoy, LIFE—© Philippe Halsman; Yale Joel, LIFE; Grey Villet, LIFE.
Page 140
Hank Walker, LIFE—Robert W. Kelley, LIFE—Cornell Capa, Magnum; Hank Walker, LIFE.
Page 142
Mark Kauffman—Universal International Pictures—Toni Frissel; Hank Walker, LIFE; Hank Walker, LIFE.
Page 143
Walter Daran—© Philippe Halsman; Bill Beal, *Washington Daily News*—Yale Joel, LIFE.
Page 144
Donald Thomson.
Page 145
No Credit—*Cleveland Plain Dealer*/Ray Matjasic; Carl Mydans, LIFE; Larry Burrows—Ed Clark, LIFE.

Page 146
U.S. Air Force.
Page 147
Yale Joel, LIFE; Paul Schutzer, LIFE—William Ray; Eliot Elisofon, LIFE.
Pages 148-149
Yale Joel, LIFE.
Page 150
Andrew St. George; Ed Clark, LIFE—Larry Burrows.
Page 151
Ralph Morse, LIFE—Elliott Erwitt, Magnum.
Page 152
Cornell Capa—Paris Match (2).
Page 153
James Burke, LIFE; Joe Munroe; Burt Glinn, Magnum—Jan Johansson, New York Post; Dmitri Kessel, LIFE.
Page 154
Paul Schutzer, LIFE—George Silk, LIFE.
Page 155
Eve Arnold, Magnum; Hank Walker, LIFE; John J. Horey—Mainichi Shinbun—Paul Schutzer, LIFE—Cornell Capa, Magnum.
Page 158
James Whitmore, LIFE—Eliot Elisofon, LIFE—David Douglas Duncan, LIFE—Paul Schutzer, LIFE.
Page 159
Paul Schutzer, LIFE.
Page 160
Ken Heyman—Flip Schulke, Black Star; John Dominis, LIFE—Lee Lockwood, Black Star.
Page 161
Paulo Muniz.
Page 162
Michael Rougier—Ralph Morse, LIFE.
Page 163
Grey Villet—Wide World Photos—Don Uhrbrock—Charles Moore, Black Star.
Page 164
Courtesy The Kress Foundation—Robert Halmi.
Page 165
Bert Stern; Paul Schutzer, LIFE—Los Angeles Times; George Silk, LIFE—Robert Halmi; Andre de Dienes.
Page 166
© Henri Dauman.
Page 167
Col. Cecil Stoughton; Jim MacCannon, Dallas Morning News—Bettmann/UPI.
Page 168
Wide World Photos; Carlo Bavagnoli—Loomis Dean; Milton H. Greene—John Dominis, LIFE.
Page 169
Alfred Eisenstaedt, LIFE—Arthur Rickerby, LIFE.
Page 172
Paris Match; Larry Burrows, LIFE—courtesy WDSU-TV; Flip Schulke, Black Star.
Page 173
Arthur Rickerby, LIFE; Donal Holloway; Wide World Photos—Bill Reed—Morris Berman/Pittsburgh Post Gazette—Bill Ray, LIFE—Bill Ray, LIFE.
Page 174
Painting by Vasarely, courtesy Sidney Janis Gallery, New York; Terence Spencer—John Dominis, LIFE.
Page 175
William Claxton.
Page 176
Dmitri Kessel, LIFE—Larry Burrows, LIFE (2).
Page 177
Jean Marquis—Larry Burrows, LIFE.
Page 178
Terence Spencer; Herb Scharfman; © Henri Dauman—NASA.
Page 179
Wide World Photos—Rex Features, London; Larry Burrows, LIFE—Birmingham News—Henry Groskinsky, LIFE.
Pages 182-183
Allan Grant, LIFE; Zinn Arthur; Don Cravens; Bill Eppridge, LIFE; Don Ornitz, Globe; Daily Express, London.
Page 184
Howell Conant.
Page 185
Nina Leen.
Pages 186-187
Robert Wenkam (3).
Pages 188-189
Fritz Goro (2), LIFE.
Pages 190-191
U.S. Department of Defense (2).

Page 192
Wes Luchau for O.C.E.—Donald Barrow.
Page 193
Jacques-Henri Lartigue—Indianapolis News.
Page 194
Sharland.
Page 195
Vitold de Golish.
Page 196
Bettmann/UPI; Sonny Brown—Carolyn Parrish.
Page 197
Samuel Dunton, N.Y. Zoological Society; Jack Tinney, Philadelphia Bulletin.
Page 199
Bernie Boston, Washington Star.
Page 200
Larry Burrows, LIFE—Larry Burrows, LIFE.
Page 201
Bill Eppridge, LIFE (2)—Wide World Photos.
Page 202
Gjon Mili—John Loengard, LIFE—Ralph Morse, LIFE—Henry Groskinsky, LIFE.
Page 203
Alfred Eisenstaedt, LIFE—Arthur Rickerby, LIFE.
Page 204
Lee Lockwood, Black Star.
Page 205
Yale Joel, LIFE; Catherine Leroy, Wide World Photos—Howell Conant; Bud Lee.
Page 206
Mark Kauffman, LIFE.
Page 207
Ted Russell—Joe Lippincott; Emmanuel d'Astier.
Pages 208-209
Joseph Louw; Bill Eppridge, LIFE—Grey Villet, LIFE.
Page 210
John Dominis, LIFE; Hilmar Pabel, Stern—Gordon Parks—Romano Cagnoni.
Page 211
Gerald S. Upham; Chicago Daily News—Paris Match, Garofalo; Ralph Crane, LIFE.
Page 212
Ronald Haeberle.
Page 213
NASA.
Page 214
Bill Eppridge, LIFE—Wide World Photos; Leonard McCombe, LIFE—Max Waldman.
Page 215
Larry Burrows, LIFE—John Olson, LIFE; Vernon Merritt III, LIFE.
Page 216
John A. Darnell—Leonard McCombe, LIFE.
Page 217
Gordon Parks; Howard Ruffner—John Olson, LIFE—George Silk, LIFE—Arthur Schatz.
Page 218
Jim Cummins, Camera 5; Turner Ranson, Pictorial; John Dornes—Leon Kuzmanoff; Elliot Gilbert.
Page 219
Grey Villet, LIFE—Vernon Merritt III, LIFE; John Dominis, LIFE.
Page 220
Co Rentmeester, LIFE; Fred Schiffer.
Page 221
Dick Swanson; Enrico Sarsini; Wide World Photos—NASA.
Page 222
Larry Burrows, LIFE; Harry Benson—Michael Mauney, LIFE.
Page 223
John Olson, LIFE; James Cassidy—No Credit; Ralph Crane, LIFE.
Page 224
Ollie Atkins, White House Photo.
Page 225
Steve Schapiro; Wide World Photos—© W. Eugene Smith.
Page 226
Terry O'Neill, Woodfin Camp Agency.
Page 228
David Seymour, Magnum; Bettmann/UPI—Frank Teti; Frank Wolfe, courtesy Lyndon B. Johnson Library.
Page 229
Wide World Photos—Co Rentmeester; Bettmann/UPI—Evelyn Hofer—Gjon Mili.
Page 230
Heinz Kluetmeier; Nancy Moran—David Hume Kennerly.
Page 231
Harry Benson; Tony Korody, Sygma; Syndication International; Ken Regan, Camera 5—Bettmann/UPI; Neil Leifer—James Andanson, Sygma; Neil Leifer.

Page 232
Gary Fong, San Francisco Chronicle.
Page 233
Stanley Forman, Boston Herald-American—Hugh Van Ess, Bettmann/UPI—Edith Blake—J. Garofalo, Paris Match.
Pages 234-235
Lagarde, Camera Press; Michael Mauney; Arthur Schatz; Mark Kauffman; Steve Schapiro; Ralph Crane, LIFE.
Pages 236-237
Leroy F. Grannis; Wide World Photos; John Bryson.
Pages 238-239
Peter Beard—Bill Eppridge, LIFE.
Pages 240-241
Dmitri Kessel, LIFE; Co Rentmeester, LIFE.
Pages 242-243
Herbert Migdoll; John Dominis, LIFE; Henry Groskinsky, LIFE.
Pages 244-245
John Dominis, LIFE; George Silk, LIFE.
Pages 246-247
Carl R. Boenisch; Co Rentmeester, LIFE—Ralph Crane, LIFE.
Pages 248-249
John Dominis, LIFE—Herbert Migdoll—Farrell Grehan, LIFE.
Pages 250-251
Kenneth Klementis; Fernando Botan.
Page 253
David Deahl.
Page 254
Stan Tretick.
Page 255
Stanley Forman, Boston Herald-American; Ollie Atkins—NASA—New China Pictures.
Page 257
Steve Fenn—© Werek.
Page 259
Leon Kuzmanoff—Mary Ellen Mark, Archive.
Page 264
Phil Stewart, Running Times—New York Daily News.
Page 267
Heinz Kluetmeier, Sports Illustrated—Bettmann/UPI.
Page 271
Anwar Hussein—Al Akbar, Gamma-Liaison—Dirck Halstead.
Page 275
John Bryson—Wayne Sorce.
Page 280
Mary Ann Fackelman, The White House—Martin Cleaver, Press Association.
Page 283
Brian Moody, Wheeler Pictures—Prof. Owen Beattie, University of Alberta, Canada.
Page 287
David Townley, Black Star.
Page 288
Mary Ellen Mark, Archive.
Pages 290-291
Patrick Demarchelier; Snowdon; Ken Regan, Camera 5; Bruce Weber; Michael O'Brien; Master Photo; Raeanne Rubenstein.
Pages 292-293
Keystone; NASA; Daniel Simon, Gamma-Liaison.
Page 294
David Burnett, Contact.
Page 295
Dennis Cook, Wide World Photos.
Pages 296-297
Jan Du Singh, Pressensbild/Photoreporters; Co Rentmeester; Susan Meiselas, Magnum.
Page 298
Jay Ullal, Stern—Enrico Ferorelli.
Page 299
Henry Groskinsky.
Pages 300-301
Robert Adelman—Enrico Ferorelli; Henry Groskinsky; New China Pictures.
Pages 302-303
Robert Caputo—Harald Sund—Majofra, Contact.
Pages 304-305
Michael Melford.
Page 306
Bruce Bailey.
Page 307
Patrick Lichfield, Camera Press.
Page 308
Co Rentmeester.
Page 309
Alexander Tsiaras.
Pages 310-311
NASA-JPL.